REGIS ST. LOUIS
SIMONA RABINOVITCH

MONTRÉAL & QUÉBEC CITY

CITY GUIDE

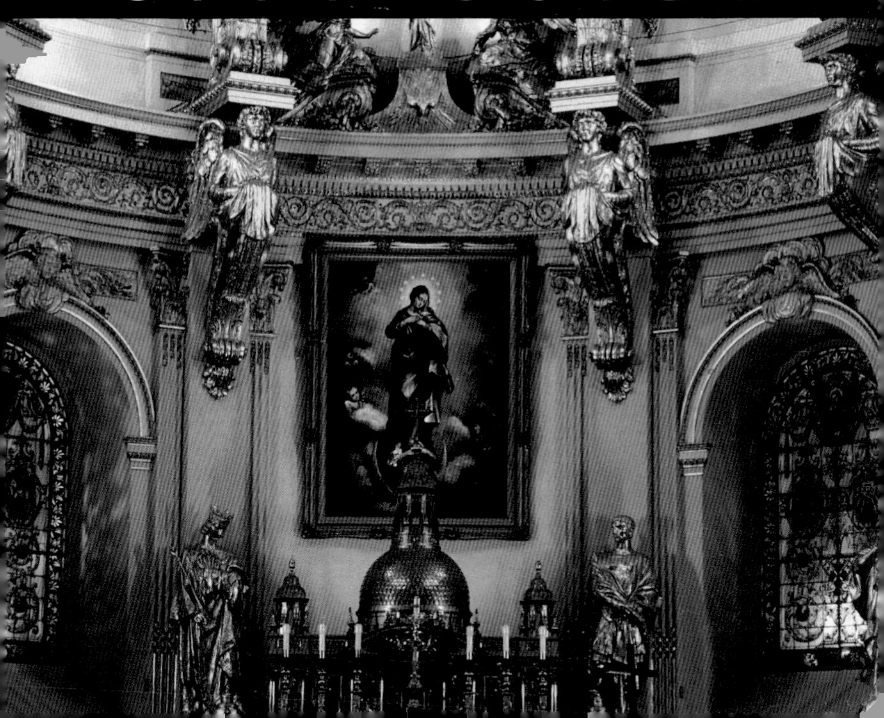

INTRODUCING MONTRÉAL

Pull up a stool at Schwartz's deli (p134) for the best smoked meat in town

GUYLAIN DOY

A captivating blend of old-world beauty and new-world innovation, this bohemian, culture-loving city has many virtues, not least of which is its uncanny ability to astonish.

Montréal is many things to many people, but it is never predictable. Where else in the world will you find French-speaking artists eating gravy- and cheese-curd-covered fries while eagerly following the ice hockey game playing overhead? Amid irresistible patisseries, English pubs, 80-year-old Jewish delis and magnificent food markets reminiscent of Paris, you'll come face-to-face with Montréal in all its surprising diversity. This city is home to over 80 different ethnic groups, with one in three Montrealers an immigrant.

The urban landscape presents an equally strange and wondrous twist on the traditional city. A day's wander might take in the photogenic 18th-century facades of Old Montréal, before moving on to the glittering shops and restaurants of ultramodern downtown and ending at the inviting terraced cafés of Plateau Mont-Royal, perhaps allowing for a cycle along the lovely Canal de Lachine or a stroll through verdant Parc du Mont-Royal. If the weather is cold, there's ice-skating on frozen lakes and endless amusement in the underground city (with its 32km of pedestrian walkways).

Toronto may be Canada's economic capital, but Montréal remains the country's cultural juggernaut, with some 250 theater and dance companies, over 90 festivals and a fascinating medley of neighborhoods where artists, writers and musicians have helped cement the city's reputation as a great arts center.

For the lowdown on Québec City's burgeoning civic scene see p194.

MONTRÉAL LIFE

Overshadowed by bigger, better-known cities like New York and Paris, Montréal quietly revels in its underdog status. Perhaps it's those infamously cold winters or the issue of separatism that once dominated the headlines, but Montréal doesn't have much recognition on the world stage. For locals – and travelers in the know – that's just fine. There are many facts about the city they'd just as soon keep to themselves, like the incredible dining scene: after New York, Montréal has more restaurants per capita than any other city in North America, with scores of different ethnic and regional cuisines on offer. Montréal is also a remarkably green city, where 70% of residents get around without a car. Locals enjoy 2000 hectares of green space and over 450km of bike lanes, with another 400km in the works. In 2009, it also became the first North American city to sponsor a public bike-sharing system – a network to be emulated in London and Boston.

Although residents complain about ongoing gentrification and rising housing costs, Montréal still remains one of the cheapest cities in Canada to rent an apartment ($670 a month for a two-bedroom in 2009, compared with $1100 in Toronto and Vancouver). In business and industry, Montréal does well for itself, boasting the highest number of research centers in Canada, an impressive high-tech sector and the third-largest fashion industry in North America (after New York and Los Angeles). The global economic downturn, however, has contributed to rising unemployment. Other pressing issues are the city's aging infrastructure and its bloated bureaucracy. Montrealers also complain about paying the highest taxes of any province in Canada. In spite of the city's shortcomings, Montrealers remain proud, citing the city's burgeoning film and music industries, its vibrant multiculturalism and its rich intellectual life. Not surprisingly, Montréal does quite well in quality-of-life surveys (often ranking well ahead of Paris, Barcelona and San Francisco for instance), a secret not all locals are eager to share.

'Montréal is a remarkably green city, where 70% of residents get around without a car'

BRIAN CRUICKSHANK

When the temperature drops, take to the ice at the Parc du Bassin Bonsecours (p170)

HIGHLIGHTS

NEIL SETCHFIELD

JEFF GREENBERG / A

OLD MONTRÉAL

In the cobblestone streets of Old Montréal, history lurks around every corner, from the photogenic stone buildings along the waterfront to the archaeological crypts under the old Customs House. The city's birthplace is also the setting for some of Montréal's newest restaurants and boutique hotels.

1 Basilique Notre-Dame
Gaze upon the hallowed interior of this magnificent cathedral (p47)

2 Musée d'Archéologie Pointe-à-Callière
Peer back in time at this fascinating history museum (p50)

3 Rue St-Paul
Stroll the galleries and boutiques along Montréal's oldest street (p54)

4 Garde-Manger
Join trendsetters over market-fresh fare in this stylish little haunt (p120)

5 Old Port
Catch the sunset during a scenic walk along the riverfront (p55)

GUYLAIN DOYL

1

GUYLAIN DOYLE

1. **Musée des Beaux-Arts**
Admire the architecturally stunning home of Canada's oldest museum (p60)

2. **Place des Arts**
Savor performances at this major nexus for the arts, and centerpiece for the Jazz Festival (p65)

3. **Holt Renfrew**
This glittering department store spells trouble for weak-willed label hunters (p107)

4. **Toqué!**
Book early to dine at one of Montréal's most celebrated restaurants (p120)

5. **Le Social**
Join the bohemian party scene in this converted 1899 mansion (p155)

DOWNTOWN

Much more than a mere landscape of skyscrapers, downtown is home to some of Montréal's icons: outstanding museums, venerated concert halls and a world-class university. Shopping, dining and nightlife play key roles in this neighborhood's remarkable vitality.

RICK GERHARTER

2

GUYLAIN DOYLE

2

GUYLAIN DO

GREEN MONTRÉAL

Bonsai-filled botanical gardens, river islands just across from Old Montréal and the glorious Mont-Royal are all essential parts of the (un)urban landscape. Going green for Montrealers also means utilizing the many bike lanes and shopping at local farmers markets.

GUYLAIN DOYLE

1 Parc du Mont-Royal
Head to 'the Mountain' for great views and lush scenery (p79)

2 Parc Jean-Drapeau
Explore the intriguing islands in the middle of the St Lawrence (p57)

3 Marché Jean-Talon
Sample the culinary riches of Québec province at this magnificent market (p82)

4 Canal de Lachine
Join cyclists along this former industrial canal, today lined with parks (p86)

GUYLAIN DO

QUÉBEC CITY: OLD TOWN

Despite turning 400 back in 2008, Canada's oldest city shows no signs of succumbing to senility. Its walled historic center, perched high above the St Lawrence River, shelters fine restaurants and atmospheric hotels, along with excellent museums, lavish cathedrals and a striking citadel.

JEFF GREENBERG / ALAMY

GUYLAIN DOYLE

GUYLAIN DOYLE

1 Panache
Words fail when dining at this culinary heavyweight (p221)

2 Château Frontenac
Book a room inside the world's most photographed hotel (p205)

3 Vieux-Québec
Lose yourself in the narrow streets of this captivating old quarter (p202)

4 Musée de la Civilisation
Get inside the Québécois experience at this thought-provoking museum (p208)

HEMIS / ALA

QUÉBEC CITY: OUTSIDE THE WALLS

Beyond its picturesque Old Town, the surprisingly low-key capital of Québec province has a wealth of green spaces and cultural gems nestled amid bohemian neighborhoods. Further afield, an idyllic island, thundering waterfalls and an aboriginal reserve offer vastly different versions of the Québécois experience.

FRANCIS VACHON / ALAMY

DAVID R. FRAZIER PHOTOLIBRARY, INC. / ALA

❶ Parc des Champs de Bataille
The battlefield that spelled the end of French rule in Canada (p209)

❷ Le Drague
See another side of the city at its most famous drag show (p226)

❸ Musée National des Beaux-Arts du Québec
Discover the little-known masters of the art world (p211)

CONTENTS

THE AUTHORS

Regis St. Louis

A longtime admirer of the free-spirited ethos that rules Québec, Regis has fallen hard for Montréal and Québec City. During research on this book, he mounted his bike and logged hundreds of kilometers along Montréal's (generally) bike-friendly streets, in search of the latest restaurants, galleries and bars around town. He has written over two dozen guides for Lonely Planet, and his articles have appeared in the *Los Angeles Times* and the *Chicago Tribune* among other publications. He lives in New York City, but often daydreams of pulling up stakes and moving to the Plateau. Regis wrote all chapters in this book except Shopping, Drinking, Nightlife and The Arts, and shared duties in Québec City.

REGIS' TOP MONTRÉAL DAY

Like a growing number in Montréal, my favorite way of getting around town is by bicycle. After rising early, I pedal along the Canal de Lachine (p98) for a bit of fresh air before stopping at Marché Atwater (p61) for *chocolatines* (chocolate croissants), café au lait and fresh fruit. After that I head along Rue Notre-Dame (aka Antique Alley), stopping for a peek in some of Montréal's best antique stores. Afterwards, I'll head downtown to take in the latest exhibit at either the Musée McCord (p60) or the Musée des Beaux-Arts (p60). For lunch, I'll go to Old Montréal, stopping at either Le Local (p121) for something decadent, or more likely Olive + Gourmando (p123) for a sure-to-be-fantastic sandwich (plus dessert). In the afternoon, I'll head up to Parc du Mont-Royal (p79) for more cycling action, stopping to take in the fine view over the city from the Chalet du Mont-Royal (p80). After a nice ride, I'll head down toward the Plateau, stopping for a coffee and perhaps a snack at Café Santropol (p133). Afterwards I'll take a stroll along the lovely tree-lined streets, starting at Carré St-Louis (p75) and working my way north along Rue St-Denis, stopping in at book and record stores along the way. As the evening nears, I'll phone a friend for a rendezvous at Bily Kun (p145), followed by tapas at Pintxo (p131). If I still have any energy, I might try to catch a show at Casa del Popolo (p153) or perhaps just have a final nightcap at Le Cagibi Café (p148).

Contributing Author

SIMONA RABINOVITCH

Simona is a Montreal-based writer and journalist specializing in travel, entertainment and the arts. She's lived in California, Israel and New York and is now the editor of *Zink Canada* and contributes to the *Globe & Mail*, *Nuvo*, Spin.com, *Dazed Digital* and others. She also acts and is working on her first book. Simona wrote the Shopping, Drinking, Nightlife and The Arts chapters, as well as sections of the Québec City chapter.

LONELY PLANET AUTHORS

Why is our travel information the best in the world? It's simple: our authors are passionate, dedicated travelers. They don't take freebies in exchange for positive coverage so you can be sure the advice you're given is impartial. They travel widely to all the popular spots, and off the beaten track. They don't research using just the internet or phone. They discover new places not included in any other guidebook. They personally visit thousands of hotels, restaurants, palaces, trails, galleries, temples and more. They speak with dozens of locals every day to make sure you get the kind of insider knowledge only a local could tell you. They take pride in getting all the details right, and in telling it how it is. Think you can do it? Find out how at **lonelyplanet.com**.

GETTING STARTED

Preparing for a trip to Montréal can be as easy as buying a ticket and setting off. While spontaneous adventurers will feel right at home in this bohemian-loving city, it never hurts to do a bit of prep work – particularly if you're going in the height of summer when lodging tends to fill up fast. A well-planned itinerary will also help you to maximize your time, though try to include time for just wandering through some of the city's endearing tree-lined neighborhoods.

No matter your budget, Montréal will welcome you with open arms. Backpackers, first-class travelers and everyone in between will find plenty of places to hang their hat, whether at a European-loving hostel, a boutique hotel, the celebrated five-star restaurant (that you booked well in advance) or the old-school diner on the corner.

WHEN TO GO

Montréal stays open all year round, though few travelers brave the city's darkest days of winter. Most people arrive in summer, when temperatures are pleasant and much of the action moves outdoors. While June through August is undoubtedly the busiest time to visit, it's also the most festive time. This is when the city throws its biggest fêtes, sidewalk tables pack the restaurant-lined streets of Plateau Mont-Royal, and the parks fill with joggers, cyclists and strollers as everyone celebrates the return of warm weather after too many months spent indoors.

While Canadian winters aren't for the delicate, Montréal has plenty of appeal for those who aren't afraid of a little (or a lot of) cold weather. Prices dip noticeably in the off-season (October to April), and people still find ways to get out, from ice-skating on frozen lakes in neighborhood parks to cross-country skiing in Mont-Royal, followed by a meal or a cocktail served fireside at one of the city's cozy dining rooms. You can also head off to the mountains for a ski-getaway less than an hour from town. Those with an aversion to snow can stay indoors, drink beer and watch ice hockey on TV. All are fine ways to get through Montréal's impressively long cold season.

top picks

ONLY IN MONTRÉAL

- La Fête des Neiges (right) Dogsledding, ice sculptures and, best of all, body-warming drinks.
- Festival TransAmériques (opposite) Watch cutting-edge performances (like a man dancing with a back-hoe as we witnessed in 2009).
- Montréal Beer Festival (opposite) Drink beer, speak French.
- Fantasia (p14) Dress up as your favorite anime character and meet people who won't laugh at you for doing so.
- Montréal International Dragon Boat Race (p14) Everyone loves a dragon boat race.
- Nuit Blanche sur Tableau Noir (opposite) See dozens of artists slapping down masterworks in a major street.

FESTIVALS & EVENTS

Described by some as the city of festivals, Montréal has a packed calendar of lively events when entire blocks close to traffic, and stages appear across town for free concerts, improv and cinema. Public holidays are also usually marked with massive downtown parades and raucous concerts. Winter events tend to have fewer out-of-town visitors but Montrealers themselves come out in droves. See p259 for public holiday listings.

January

LA FÊTE DES NEIGES

☎ 514-872514-6120; www.fetedesneiges.com; Île Ste-Hélène, Parc Jean-Drapeau

Montréal's Snow Festival features some ice-sculpting contests, dog-sled races, snow games and costumed characters like mascot polar bear Boule de Neige. It's held over three consecutive weekends in late January and early February.

February

MONTRÉAL EN LUMIÈRE

☎ 514-288-9955, 888-477-9955; www.montrealhighlights.com

Created to help locals shake off the late-winter doldrums, the Montréal Highlights Festival is a kind of wintry Mardi Gras with most events taking place downtown. There are classical music and dance performances, exhibitions, fireworks, celebrity chefs and weirdly wonderful events like a 5km race through the underground city (see the boxed text, p68).

March

ST PATRICK'S DAY PARADE

☎ 514-932-0512; www.montrealirishparade.com

Rue Ste-Catherine turns shamrock-green during this monster event. Hundreds of thousands of Montrealers turn out annually for the 40-plus marching bands and floats on the second Sunday in March.

MONTRÉAL FASHION WEEK

☎ 514-876-1499; www.montrealfashionweek.ca

This twice-yearly fashion event (March for the winter/fall collections and October for the spring/summer collections) is closed to the general public, but is worth noting for the excitement it generates around local fashion and the festivities that spill over into local bars afterwards. Venues change regularly.

April

BLUE METROPOLIS – MONTRÉAL INTERNATIONAL LITERARY FESTIVAL

☎ 514-932-1112; www.blue-met-bleu.com

This festival brings together 200-plus writers from all over the globe for five days of literary events in English, French, Spanish and other languages in the first week of April.

May

BIENNALE DE MONTRÉAL

www.biennalemontreal.org

One of Montréal's most creative events showcases the best and the brashest on the Canadian art scene, including conferences and seminars on contemporary art. Expect interactive, cutting-edge multimedia pieces, often with opportunities for viewer participation. Upcoming dates are May 2011 and May 2013.

FESTIVAL TRANSAMÉRIQUES

☎ 514-842-0704; www.fta.qc.ca

The grande dame of Montréal's dance and theater world, the ever-expanding Festival TransAmériques features some 450 artists representing over a dozen countries. It's held over 18 days from late May to mid-June and includes free shows at outdoor venues as well as paid performances at theaters all across town. The repertoire leans heavily toward the avant-garde. Many shows sell out, so check the website and plan well in advance.

MONTRÉAL BEER FESTIVAL

☎ 514-722-9640; www.festivalmondialbiere.qc.ca

Quaff brews from around the globe inside the old Windsor Station. The five-day event starts late May/early June.

June

TOUR DE L'ÎLE

☎ 514-521-8356; www.velo.qc.ca; Île Ste-Hélène & Downtown

Also known as the Montréal Bikefest, the Tour draws 30,000 enthusiasts for a 50km spin around the Island of Montréal and a big party in the city afterwards. It's staged on the first Saturday in June, with pre-registration.

NUIT BLANCHE SUR TABLEAU NOIR

☎ 514-522-3797; www.tableaunoir.com

Ave du Mont-Royal becomes an artist's canvas on the second weekend in June when the street comes alive with music, various workshops and children's activities.

MONTRÉAL FASHION & DESIGN FESTIVAL

www.festivalmodedesign.com; Ave McGill College

Unlike Fashion Week (left), this colorful couture-loving event is free and open to the public. In mid-June style-hounds descend on Ave McGill College for four days of open-air fashion shows along with performances by live bands and DJs.

FORMULA ONE GRAND PRIX

In 2009, Montréal was dropped from the Formula One race calendar for the first time in 20 years. As this book went to press, negotiations were under way to bring the famously speedy race back to the city. If it does happen, it will take place in mid- to late June on the Circuit Gilles-Villeneuve and undoubtedly bring flashy drivers, crew, entourages and Formula One lovers from all corners of the globe. Don't forget your earplugs.

ST-AMBROISE MONTRÉAL FRINGE FESTIVAL

☎ 514-849-3378; www.montrealfringe.ca

An off-Broadway-style theater and repertory festival of new local and international talent, with dancing, music and the ever-popular drag races (as in drag *queen* races). Held over 10 days from mid-June.

LOTO-QUÉBEC INTERNATIONAL FIREWORKS COMPETITION

☎ 514-397-2000; www.internationaldesfeuxloto-quebec.com

Thousands camp out on rooftops and on the Pont Jacques-Cartier for the planet's hottest pyrotechnics contest accompanied by dramatic musical scores. The 10 shows last 30 minutes each and are held on Saturday nights and a few Wednesday nights from late June to the end of July.

OFF-FESTIVAL DE JAZZ

☎ 514-570-0722; www.lofffestivaldejazz.com

The alternative jazz fest presents around 50 shows in several downtown venues to showcase young new talent. It's held over 10 days in late June and early July.

July

SHAKESPEARE IN THE PARK

☎ 514-931-2644; www.shakespeareinthepark.ca

Families spread out on blankets for performances of the bard's best plays at park stages around town on weekends, usually throughout July and August.

MONTRÉAL INTERNATIONAL JAZZ FESTIVAL

☎ 514-523-3378, 888-515-0515; www.montrealjazzfest.com

With over 400 concerts and nearly two million visitors every year, North America's hippest music fest just gets bigger and better with world music, rock and even pop music sharing the program with jazz legends and upstarts. Hundreds of brand-name musicians hit the halls and outdoor stages, and dozens of concerts are given for free over 13 days from late June to mid-July (see the boxed text, p23).

FESTIVAL INTERNATIONAL NUITS D'AFRIQUE

☎ 514-499-9239; www.festivalnuitsdafrique.com

Celebrates the cultures of Africa and the Caribbean with more than 500 artists from 20-plus countries, with workshops, exotic cuisine and an African market. Held at Pl Émilie-Gamelin and several clubs and halls for 10 days in mid-July.

JUST FOR LAUGHS

☎ 514-845-3155, 888-244-3155; www.hahaha.com; Quartier Latin

More than 650 artists perform in over 1000 shows at this comedy festival which runs for two weeks in mid-July. Past events have featured Jason Alexander of *Seinfeld* fame, Craig Ferguson, John Cleese and Margaret Cho.

FANTASIA

www.fantasiafestival.com

An unabashed love-fest for devotees of international fantasy, action and horror films; Japanese anime geeks are drawn out in droves. Local genre films are also screened during this 18-day festival held in mid-July.

DIVERS/CITÉ

☎ 514-285-4011; www.diverscite.org

Montréal's Gay Pride is *the* event on the Village calendar, drawing more than a million people, even in slow years. The streets around Pl Émilie-Gamelin pulse with dancing, art exhibits, concerts and parades. It's held over one week starting in late July.

MONTRÉAL INTERNATIONAL DRAGON BOAT RACE

☎ 514-866-7001; www.montrealdragonboat.com

Rowing teams from all over the world compete in Chinese dragon boats on Île Notre-Dame, punctuated by entertainment and gastronomic events. Held over one weekend in late July.

August

OSHEAGA FESTIVAL MUSIQUE ET ARTS

www.osheaga.com; Île Ste-Hélène in Parc Jean-Drapeau

On one weekend in early August, Parc Jean-Drapeau becomes a giant stage (actually four of them) for one of the city's grand rock festivals. Some 70,000 fans typically turn up to the powerhouse lineup of performers, which in recent years has included Coldplay, Rufus Wainwright, the Yeah Yeah Yeahs, Gotan Project, Feist and many more. Catch live bands playing each day from 2pm to 11pm. One-day/two-day tickets cost around $75/$130.

LES FRANCOFOLIES

☎ 514-876-8989; www.francofolies.com
The annual musical showcase of international French-language music and theater spotlights today's biggest stars, and those on the rise. There are 200-plus shows and free outdoor presentations over 10 days around mid-August.

MONTRÉAL WORLD FILM FESTIVAL

☎ 514-848-3883; www.ffm-montreal.org
One of the most prestigious film events in Canada, attracting 400,000 visitors to screenings from 70 countries. The stars come out, as well as the directors, producers and writers of the big screen. It's held over 10 days in late August and early September.

NASCAR: NATIONWIDE SERIES

www.circuitgillesvilleneuve.ca; Île Notre-Dame, Parc Jean-Drapeau
Held in late August, this big two-day event brings race lovers from all over North America and beyond to catch the roaring action. Race days are often sweltering – and there's no shade at the track – so plan accordingly.

September

MAGIC OF LANTERNS

☎ 514-872-1400; www.ville.montreal.qc.ca/jardin/en/propos/lanternes.htm; Jardin Botanique
The Jardin Botanique extends its hours into the night and lights up hundreds of Chinese lanterns all over the park. Locals swamp this popular event, running from mid-September to early November.

MANIFESTATION INTERNATIONALE DE CHAMP LIBRE

☎ 514-393-3937; www.champlibre.com
Every two years, this event provides a stage for the fusion of art, architecture and technology in creative – often highly conceptual – exhibits. This fantastic niche event, held at different venues each year, draws everyone from families with small children to retirees. Upcoming editions take place in late September in 2010 and 2012.

October

FESTIVAL DU NOUVEAU CINÉMA DE MONTRÉAL

☎ 514-282-0004; www.nouveaucinema.ca
This festival highlights who is up-and-coming in feature films, documentaries, experimental shorts, videos, narrative features and electronic art forms during 10 days in early October.

BLACK & BLUE FESTIVAL

☎ 514-875-7026; www.bbcm.org
One of the biggest gay events in the Village, with major dance parties, cultural and art shows as well as a killer mega-party in the Olympic Stadium, all in the second week of October.

MONTRÉAL FASHION WEEK

Spring/summer collections are shown in the second session of this twice-yearly event. See the listing under March (p13) for more information.

December

CHRISTMAS AT THE JARDIN BOTANIQUE

☎ 514-872-1400; www2.ville.montreal.qc.ca/jardin
'Tis the season at the Jardin Botanique. The main greenhouse becomes a fairyland of poinsettia Christmas trees and fanciful chandeliers made of plants. Activities in past years have included storytelling for kids, or choirs. It's open the entire month of December.

COSTS & MONEY

The Canadian dollar (the loonie as some call it) has enjoyed a strong showing against the (currently weak) US dollar in the last few years. Against the British pound and the euro, the Canadian dollar hasn't shifted much.

While Montréal isn't the world's cheapest destination, it compares quite favorably with other major American and European cities, and is even a touch less expensive than

Toronto and Vancouver. As elsewhere in the world, accommodations will likely be your biggest expense.

On average, single travelers who stay in a B&B or midrange hotel, eat at least one meal a day out and take in a bit of museum-going and nightlife can expect to spend $175 or so per day. Couples can anticipate paying a bit more – something in the daily range of $250. For those on tight budgets, there are plenty of ways to cut costs, such as sleeping in a hostel, self-catering from local markets and limiting entertainment options.

Breaking things down a bit: midrange accommodations average around $75 to $90 per night for a room in a European-style B&B with a shared bathroom. A room with a private bathroom will cost around $120 to $150 on average for a comfortable midrange option in a good location. Going up a notch, starting at $200 per day, you can stay in a boutique hotel or in a guesthouse with obvious style and charm. At $300 per day and up, the city's best accommodations are at your disposal.

At the low end of the scale, it's possible to bunk in a hostel dorm bed for around $23 per day. Most hostels also have a few private rooms, for around $60 single or double, but these are highly coveted so book early if that's what you're after. In summer, the universities also open their dorms to nonstudents at prices that are hard to beat.

Keep in mind that you'll have to pay tax also, which will add another 16% or so to the bill. Some places include the tax in their prices. Inquire if you're not sure.

Do browse online for accommodation specials – tripadvisor, orbitz, expedia and their ilk often have competitive rates that you won't receive just walking in off the street (or even calling).

When it comes to eating, prices vary widely. A midrange restaurant meal with a glass of wine or beer will cost around $15 at lunchtime and $25 for dinner per person, plus tax and tip (adding another 30% to the bill). If you're dining at one of the city's trendier places, count on spending at least twice that amount.

At the budget end, there are marvelous smoked-meat restaurants where a sandwich still costs just under $5. You can also eat (but not very often) *poutine*, that marvelous mess of fries, gravy and cheese available at fast-food joints (and some specialty restaurants) for around $5 as well. The city's captivating markets are another way to eat less expensively, and make for a fun, free outing in themselves.

Going to museums on free days is another way to save money. Walking around Parc du Mont-Royal (or catching the hippie-loving action of the Sunday tam-tam jams held there in the summertime), outings and picnics along the Canal de Lachine, and strolling the waterfront are all free. In fact, this city is made for walking. Those with stamina can walk from Old Montréal to downtown, over to the Plateau and back to the Quartier Latin, stopping for coffee, ice cream and bistro fare en route. When you tire of walking (or if you're going to Little Italy), hop on the metro, which is generally fast and frequent.

HOW MUCH?

1L of mineral water in supermarket $1.50

Pint of Cheval Blanc $5

Plate of *poutine* $4

One-way metro ticket $2.75

Cappuccino in Little Italy $3

Hockey game ticket $30-100

Dinner for two at Au Pied de Cochon $110

Montreal Gazette newspaper $1

Chocolatine (chocolate croissant) $2.50

Souvenir T-shirt $15

INTERNET RESOURCES

Eat Well Montréal (www.eatwellmontreal.com) Restaurant reviews, with photos, plus comments from other readers.

Fagstein (blog.fagstein.com) Funny, irreverent look at what's happening around the city.

Midnight Poutine (www.midnightpoutine.ca) A highly readable blog covering music, art, film, restaurants and events in Montréal.

Montréal Clubs (www.montreal-clubs.com) Keeps a finger on the pulse of Montréal's latest and greatest dance and party spots.

Podcast Alley (www.podcastalley.com) Type in 'Montreal' or 'Quebec' and hear podcasts covering a whole range of wondrous and obscure topics from food and galleries to hockey and indie rock.

Quebec City Tourism (www.quebecregion.com) Useful tourism website for Québec City and surrounding regions.

Tourisme Montreal (www.tourisme-montreal.org) Helpful state-run site with info on neighborhoods, events and more.

ADVANCE PLANNING

- **Three to six months before you go** If you're going to the International Jazz Festival or another big event, book tickets for shows. Scan www.admission.com for upcoming sports and entertainment events.
- **Two to three weeks before you go** Book a table at one of Montréal's top-notch restaurants like Toqué! (p120). Take a browse through local websites like Midnight Poutine (www.midnight poutine.com) and epicurean Eat Well Montréal (www.eatwellmontreal.com).
- **One week before you go** Check the tourist office website (www.tourisme-montreal.org) to see what art exhibitions are on when you're in town, and take a peek at Montreal Clubs (www .montreal-clubs.com) for parties and nightclub openings.

SUSTAINABLE MONTRÉAL

Going green in Montréal has become easier in recent years thanks to the addition of numerous new bike lanes coupled with the Bixi network (see the boxed text, p169). For a small daily or monthly fee, you can grab a bike from one of 300 stands, take it to your destination and check it in, getting a bit of exercise and sparing the atmosphere a few extra hydrocarbons in the process.

Other ways to travel sustainably: skip the bottled water and drink from the tap. The water is safe here. Shop locally: avoid the big chains and support the small café or grocer on the corner. Do visit at least one market while you're here (the Atwater market near the Canal de Lachine is particularly well placed for a picnic); buying fruit and veggies directly from the vendors cuts out the middlemen and puts more money in the hands of farmers.

Unless you're heading off to explore the Laurentians or the Eastern Townships, there's no reason to rent a car in Montréal. The hassle (and expense) of parking, the one-way streets and the slightly touchy drivers all contribute to the less than pleasurable sensation one has slipping behind the wheel here. The no-driving-necessary rule also applies to Québec City. There are plenty of buses shuttling between the two cities, and you can also take the scenic train. Once in Québec City, places of interest are splendidly close to one another – rather like a medieval village (and parking costs even more there).

HISTORY

THE EARLY SETTLEMENT

The Island of Montréal was long inhabited by the St Lawrence Iroquois, one of the tribes who formed the Five Nations Confederacy of Iroquois. In 1535 French explorer Jacques Cartier visited the Iroquois village of Hochelaga (Place of the Beaver Dam) on the slopes of Mont-Royal, but by the time Samuel de Champlain founded Québec City in 1608, the settlement had vanished. In 1642 Paul de Chomedey de Maisonneuve founded the first permanent mission despite fierce resistance by the Iroquois. Intended as a base for converting Aboriginal people to Christianity, this settlement quickly became a major hub of the fur trade. Québec City became the capital of the French colony Nouvelle-France (New France), while Montréal's *voyageurs* (trappers) established a network of trading posts into the hinterland. After the British conquest of Montréal in 1760, Scottish fur traders consolidated their power by founding the North West Company.

The American army seized Montréal during the American Revolution (1763–83) and set up headquarters at Château Ramezay (p50). But even the formidable negotiating skills of Benjamin Franklin failed to convince French Quebecers to join their cause, and seven months later the revolutionaries decided they'd had enough and fled empty-handed.

INDUSTRY & IMMIGRATION

In the early 19th century Montréal's fortunes dimmed as the fur trade shifted north to the Hudson Bay. However, a new class of international merchants and financiers soon emerged, founding the Bank of Montréal (p54) and investing in shipping as well as a new railway network. Tens of thousands of Irish immigrants came to work on the railways and in the factories,

IRISH IN MONTRÉAL

The Irish have been streaming into Montréal since the founding of New France, but they came in floods between 1815 and 1860, driven from Ireland by the Potato Famine. Catholic like the French settlers, the Irish easily assimilated into Québécois society. Today a phenomenal 45% of Quebecers have Irish ancestry somewhere in their family tree, though many of them don't even know it. Several Québécois family names are a legacy of this era of immigration, when French Catholic priests in Québec City registered settlers' names phonetically upon arrival. So, an 'O'Reilly' in Ireland ended up living as a 'Riel' in the colony. Other names from this period still encountered today include 'Aubrey' or 'Aubry,' from 'O'Brinnan' or 'O'Brennan,' and 'Mainguy' from 'McGee.' In Montréal, most of these immigrants settled in Griffintown, then an industrial hub near the Canal de Lachine. The first St Patrick's Day parade in the city was held in 1824 and has run every year since; it's now one of the city's biggest events. For some terrific reads on the Irish community, check out *The Shamrock and the Shield: An Oral History of the Irish in Montreal* by Patricia Burns and *The Untold Story: The Irish in Canada* (1988), edited by Robert O'Driscoll and Lorna Reynolds.

1500

Semi-sedentary tribes of the Iroquois frequent the island later known as Montréal; they fish, grow corn, squash and other crops and settle one permanent village, Hochelaga (Place of the Beaver Dam), near present-day McGill University.

1535

French explorer and gold-seeker Jacques Cartier sets foot on the island. He encounters natives, returning home with 'gold' and 'diamonds' later revealed as iron pyrite and quartz crystal. Fur pelts, however, catch the merchant's eye.

1642

Under the behest of Louis XIII, Maisonneuve and a group of 50 found the colony of 'Ville-Marie.' Two peerless Frenchwomen, Jeanne Mance and Marguerite Bourgeoys, establish New France's first hospital and school.

mills and breweries that sprang up along the Canal de Lachine (p86). Canada's industrial revolution was born, with the English clearly in control.

The Canadian Confederation of 1867 gave Quebecers a degree of control over their social and economic affairs and acknowledged French as an official language. French Canadians living in the rural areas flowed into the city to seek work and regained the majority. At this time, Montréal was Canada's premier railway center, financial hub and manufacturing powerhouse. The Canadian Pacific Railway opened its head office there in the 1880s, and Canadian grain bound for Europe was shipped through the port.

In the latter half of the century, a wave of immigrants from Italy, Spain, Germany, Eastern Europe and Russia gave Montréal a cosmopolitan flair that would remain unique in the province. By 1914 the metropolitan population exceeded half-a-million residents, of whom more than 10% were neither British nor French.

top picks

HISTORY BOOKS

- *A Short History of Quebec* (1993, revised 2002) by John A Dickinson and Brian Young. Social and economic portrait of Québec from the pre-European period to modern constitutional struggles.
- *City Unique: Montreal Days and Nights in the 1940s and '50s* (1996) by William Weintraub. Engaging tales of Montréal's twilight period as Sin City and an exploration of its historic districts.
- *The Road to Now: A History of Blacks in Montreal* (1997) by Dorothy Williams. A terrific and rare look at a little-known aspect of the city's history and the black experience in New France.
- *Canadiens Legends: Montreal's Hockey Heroes* (2004) by Mike Leonetti. Wonderful profiles and pics on some of the key players that made this team an NHL legend. Whether you're a sports fan or not, Les Canadiens and the mythology around them is an important part of the city's 20th-century cultural history.
- *The Illustrated History of Canada* (2002) edited by Craig Brown. Several historians contributed to this well-crafted work with fascinating prints, maps and sketches.

WAR, DEPRESSION & NATIONALISM

The peace that existed between the French and English ran aground after the outbreak of WWI. Many thousands of French Quebecers signed up for military service until Ontario passed a law in 1915 restricting the use of French in its schools. When Ottawa introduced the draft in 1917, French-Canadian nationalists condemned it as a plot to reduce the francophone population. The conscription issue resurfaced in WWII, with 80% of Francophones rejecting the draft and nearly as many English-speaking Canadians voting for it.

During the Prohibition era Montréal found a new calling as 'Sin City,' as hordes of free-spending, pleasure-seeking Americans flooded over the border in search of booze, brothels and betting houses. But with the Great Depression the economic inferiority of French Canadians became clearer than ever.

Québec's nationalists turned inward with proposals to create co-operatives, nationalize the anglophone power companies and promote French-Canadian goods. Led by the right-wing, ruralist, ultraconservative Maurice Duplessis, the new Union Nationale party took advantage of the nationalist awakening to win provincial power in the 1936 elections. The party's influence would retard Québec's industrial and social progress until Duplessis died in 1959.

1721

After years of on-and-off fighting with the Iroquois, the town erects a stone citadel. The colony continues to grow, fueled by the burgeoning riches of the fur trade.

1760

One year after a resounding victory outside of Québec City, the British seize Montréal. Three years later, France officially cedes its territories to Britain, bringing an end to French rule in Canada.

1832

Montréal is incorporated as a city following the prosperous 1820s. The Canal de Lachine dramatically improves commerce and transport, and gas lamps burn on the city streets. Montréal's first mayor is elected the following year.

GRAND PROJECTS

By the early 1950s the infrastructure of Montréal, by now with a million-plus inhabitants, badly needed an overhaul. Mayor Jean Drapeau drew up a grand blueprint that would radically alter the face of the city, including the metro, a skyscraper-filled downtown and an underground city (see the boxed text, p68). The harbor was extended for the opening of the St Lawrence Seaway.

Along the way Drapeau set about ridding Montréal of its 'Sin City' image by cleaning up the shadier districts. His most colorful nemesis was Lili St-Cyr, the Minnesota-born stripper whose affairs with high-ranking politicians, sports stars and thugs were as legendary in the postwar era as her bathtub performances.

The face of Montréal changed dramatically during the 1960s as a forest of skyscrapers shot up. Private developers replaced Victorian-era structures with landmark buildings such as Place Bonaventure, a modern hotel-shopping complex, and the Place des Arts (p65) performing-arts center. The focus of the city shifted from Old Montréal to Ville-Marie, where commerce flourished.

In 1960 the nationalist Liberal Party won control of the Québec assembly and passed sweeping measures that would shake Canada to its very foundations. In the first stage of this so-called Quiet Revolution, the assembly vastly expanded Québec's public sector and nationalized the provincial hydroelectric companies.

Suddenly Francophones – who had long been denied equal rights in the private sector – were able to work in French and develop their skills in white-collar positions. Still, progress wasn't

THE QUIET REVOLUTION

In 1960 the Rassemblement pour l'Indépendance Nationale (Rally for National Independence, or RIN) was founded in Montréal with the aim of Québec separation from Canada. This was the beginning of the so-called Quiet Revolution that eventually gave French Quebecers more sway in industry and politics and ultimately established the primacy of the French language.

The Front de Libération du Québec (FLQ), a radical nationalist group committed to overthrowing 'medieval Catholicism and capitalist oppression' through revolution, was founded in 1963. Initially the FLQ attacked military targets and other symbols of federal power but soon became involved in labor disputes. In the mid-1960s the FLQ claimed responsibility for a spate of bombings.

In October 1970 the FLQ kidnapped Québec's labor minister Pierre Laporte and a British trade official in an attempt to force the independence issue. Prime Minister Pierre Trudeau declared a state of emergency and called in the army to protect government officials. The next day Laporte's body was found in the trunk of a car. The murder discredited the FLQ in the eyes of many erstwhile supporters. By December the crisis had passed. In the years that followed, the FLQ effectively ceased to exist as a political movement.

While support for Québec independence still hovers around 30% to 45% in the polls, there's little appetite at the moment for another referendum on separation from Canada – the economy is on the upswing these days and real-estate prices surged across the province after Jean Charest of the federalist Liberal Party was elected Québec premier in the spring of 2003.

The separatist movement – much like Lévesque's old Parti Québécois itself – has lost much of its appeal for the majority of citizens. The impassioned separatists who came of age during the heady days of the Quiet Revolution are older now, and a critical mass of rah-rah separatists from the younger generation hasn't emerged to take their place. In the 2007 Québec general election, the Parti Québécois earned its smallest share of the popular vote since 1973, leading some to speculate that the demographic opportunity for separatism may have ended for good.

1847

Bad times arrive. The 1840s see violent protest over colonial reform. A typhus epidemic kills thousands in 1847; then in 1852 comes the Great Fire, which burns much of the city to the ground.

1865

Lured by big industry, immigrants (from Ireland, Italy, Greece, Portugal, China) arrive by the thousands; soon Francophones outnumber Anglophones for the first time since the 1820s. Over the next 40 years, the population will quadruple.

1867

Railways and an active harbor bring wealth to Montréal; tired of foreign rule, representatives of colonies on the Atlantic coast meet and form a Confederation; modern Canada is born.

swift enough for radical nationalists (see the boxed text, opposite), and by the mid-1960s they were claiming that Québec independence was the only way to ensure francophone rights.

As the Francophones seized power, some of the old established anglophone networks became spooked and resettled outside the province. By 1965 Montréal had lost its status as Canada's economic capital to Toronto. But new expressways were laid out and the metro was finished in time for Expo '67 (the 1967 World's Fair), a runaway success that attracted 50 million visitors. It was the defining moment of Montréal as a metropolis, and would lay the foundations for its successful bid to host the 1976 Olympics – an event that would land the city in serious debt.

Meanwhile, things continued heating up in the Quiet Revolution. To head off clashes with Québec's increasingly separatist leaders, Prime Minister Pierre Trudeau proposed two key measures in 1969: Canada was to be made fully bilingual to give Francophones equal access to national institutions; and the constitution was to be amended to guarantee francophone rights. Ottawa then pumped cash into French-English projects which, nonetheless, failed to convince Francophones that French would become the primary language of work in Québec.

In 1976 this lingering discontent spurred the election of René Lévesque and his Parti Québécois, committed to the goal of independence for the province. The following year the Québec assembly passed Bill 101, which not only made French the sole official language of Québec, but also stipulated that all immigrants enroll their children in French-language schools. The trickle of anglophone refugees from the province turned into a flood. Alliance Québec, an English rights group, estimates that between 300,000 and 400,000 Anglos left Québec during this period.

THE NOT-QUITE NATION OF QUÉBEC

The Quiet Revolution heightened tensions not only in Québec but across Canada. After their re-election in 1980, federal Liberals, led by Pierre Trudeau, sold most Quebecers on the idea of greater rights through constitutional change, helping to defeat a referendum on Québec sovereignty the same year by a comfortable margin. Québec premier Robert Bourassa then agreed to a constitution-led solution – but only if Québec was recognized as a 'distinct society' with special rights.

In 1987 the federal Conservative Party was in power and Prime Minister Brian Mulroney unveiled an accord that met most of Québec's demands. To take effect, the Meech Lake Accord needed ratification by all 10 provinces and both houses of parliament by 1990. Dissenting premiers in three provinces eventually pledged their support, but incredibly the accord collapsed when a single member of Manitoba's legislature refused to sign.

The failure of the Meech Lake Accord triggered a major political crisis in Québec. The separatists blamed English-speaking Canada for its demise, and Mulroney and Bourassa subsequently drafted the Charlottetown Accord, a new, expanded accord. But the separatists picked it apart, and in October 1992 the second version was trounced in Québec and five other provinces. The rejection sealed the fate of Mulroney, who stepped down as prime minister the following year, and of Bourassa, who left political life a broken man.

REFERENDUM & REBIRTH

In the early 1990s Montréal was wracked by political uncertainty and economic decline. No one disputed that the city was ailing. The symptoms were everywhere: corporate offices

1917

As war rages in Europe, Quebecers feel no loyalty to France or Britain and resent being conscripted to fight. Tensions seethe between Anglos and French Canadians, who increasingly see themselves as second-class citizens.

1959

St Lawrence Seaway opens, permitting freighters to bypass Montréal. Toronto slowly overtakes Montréal as Canada's commercial engine. The strong-arm, anti-labor Duplessis regime ends. Francophone unions and co-operatives are on the rise.

1970

The separatist-minded Front de Libération du Québec kidnaps a British trade official and labor minister Pierre Laporte (later killing him). Armed soldiers are summoned to Montréal. Although the FLQ was discredited and disbanded, separatism gains support.

had closed and moved their headquarters to other parts of Canada, shuttered shops lined downtown streets, and derelict factories and refineries rusted on the perimeter. Relations between Anglophones and Francophones, meanwhile, plumbed new depths after Québec was denied a special status in Canada.

The victory of the separatist Parti Québécois in the 1994 provincial elections signaled the arrival of another crisis. Support for an independent Québec rekindled, and a referendum on sovereignty was called the following year. While it first appeared the referendum would fail by a significant margin, the outcome was a real cliff-hanger: Quebecers decided by 52,000 votes – a razor-thin majority of less than 1% – to stay part of Canada. In Montréal, where the bulk of Québec's Anglophones and immigrants live, more than two-thirds voted against sovereignty, causing Parti Québécois leader Jacques Parizeau to infamously declare that 'money and the ethnic vote' had robbed Québec of its independence.

In the aftermath of the vote, the locomotives of the Quiet Revolution – economic inferiority and linguistic insecurity among Francophones – ran out of steam. Exhausted by decades of separatist wrangling, most Montrealers put aside their differences and went back to work.

Oddly enough, a natural disaster played a key role in bringing the communities together. In 1998 a freak ice storm – some blame extra-moist El Niño winds, others cited global warming – broke power masts like matchsticks across the province, leaving over three million people without power and key services in the middle of a Montréal winter. Some people endured weeks without electricity and heat but regional and political differences were forgotten as money, clothing and offers of personal help poured into the stricken areas. Montrealers recount memories of those dark days with a touch of mutual respect.

As the political climate brightened, Montréal began to emerge from a fundamental reshaping of the local economy. The city experienced a burst of activity as sectors like software, aerospace, telecommunications and pharmaceuticals replaced rust-belt industries like textiles and refining. Québec's moderate wages became an asset to manufacturers seeking qualified, affordable labor, and foreign investment began to flow more freely. Tax dollars were used to recast Montréal as a new-media hub, encouraging dozens of multimedia firms to settle in the Old Port area.

The upshot is a city transformed and brimming with self-confidence. Rue Ste-Catherine teems with fashionable boutiques and department stores; Old Montréal buzzes with designer hotels and trendy restaurants; once-empty warehouses around town have been converted to lofts and offices.

Montréal's renewed vigor has lured back some of the Anglophones who'd left in the 1980s and '90s. Language conflicts have slipped into the background because most young Montrealers are at least bilingual, and for the first time there are more homeowners than renters, and property prices have soared. Like most other flourishing cities in the world, real estate remains one of the hot topics *du jour*.

Though less divisive than in times past, contemporary Québec faces thorny issues in areas like civil rights of minorities, administration and the welfare state: English-language education is denied to many families and Montréal's new island-wide administration is under severe strain. Jean Charest's Liberals successfully knocked the separatist Parti Québécois out of office in 2003 but the federalist party has had a rocky ride since then and has been the target of dozens of demonstrations by workers for wanting to cut public-sector jobs, hiking day-care prices and pruning Québec's bloated bureaucracy.

1976

The Parti Québécois gains power and passes Bill 101, declaring French the official language. Many businesses leave Montréal, taking 15,000 jobs with them. Montréal stages the Summer Olympics and goes deeply into debt.

1994

Following the defeat of the first referendum on independence in 1980, voters go to the polls again, narrowly defeating Québec gaining sovereignty. Over the next decade the separatist movement slowly fizzles.

2005

Canada becomes the fourth country in the world to legalize same-sex marriage nationwide. Montrealer Michaëlle Jean is installed as 27th governor general of Canada, the Queen's representative in Canada.

ARTS

Montréal is the undisputed center of the French-language entertainment universe in North America and the cultural mecca of Québec. It is ground zero for everything from Québec's sizable film and music industries to visual and dramatic arts and publishing. Actors, directors and writers flock to this cultural capital from all over the province with dreams of making it big. Québec artists don't typically look for recognition from France, English Canada or the US. Though they may want it at some point, they don't need it to survive – the market for them here is insatiable and they have a whole industry behind them.

Québec films reign at the box office, Québec bands dominate the music charts. There are countless TV shows and glossy entertainment and gossip magazines chronicling the careers of French-speaking musicians and movie stars from Québec. The Jutras, named after pioneer filmmaker Claude Jutra, are the province's equivalent to the Oscars, and the Félix awards, named for singer-songwriter Félix Leclerc, are equivalent to the Grammys. There are also awards for theater, comedy and TV – all of which are followed more closely by Quebecers than their English counterparts.

The flourishing arts scene is one of the big draws of Montréal. The city provides a wealth of options for those seeking to tap into first-rate dance and theater, its burgeoning music industry and its eclectic gallery scene.

SOUNDS OF MONTRÉAL: THE WORLD-RENOWNED JAZZ FESTIVAL

In a city that loves festivals, the Montréal International Jazz Festival is the mother of them all – erupting in late June each year, and turning the city into a enormous stage. No longer just about jazz, this is one of the world's biggies, with hundreds of top-name performers bringing reggae, rock, blues, world music – and even jazz – to audiophiles from across the globe.

It started as the pipe dream of a young local music producer, Alain Simard, who tried to sell his idea to the government and corporate sponsors, with little success. 'I was saying that one day this festival would bring thousands of American tourists to Montréal,' Simard says. 'They really made fun of me.'

The first event in 1979 drew 12,000 visitors. Simard had to finance three years of festivals with his own money, but from the beginning there were quality headliners like Ray Charles, Ella Fitzgerald and Pat Metheny. The festival was judged as hip thanks to its laid-back atmosphere, quality acts and free street concerts, and in 1989 it moved from the Quartier Latin to its current home at the Place des Arts.

Now it's the single biggest tourist event in Québec, attracting nearly two million visitors to 400 concerts – and many say it's the best jazz festival on the planet. Miles Davis, Herbie Hancock, Al Jarreau, Sonny Rollins, Wayne Shorter, Al Dimeola, John Scofield and Jack DeJohnette are but a few giants who have graced the podiums over the years. In 2009, Stevie Wonder played a free concert. More and more though, you'll find music of every style under the sun: blues, Latin, reggae, Cajun, Dixieland, world and even pop. Some people lament this change, but festival-goers are voting with their feet and the number of visitors just keeps going up each year.

The magic of the festival's success is its inclusiveness. Attend any of the free outdoor shows on any given night and you may see punks next to seniors next to an immigrant couple from China next to a Sikh family all grooving together at the same gig.

Practicalities

Info Jazz Bell (☎ 514-871-1881, 888-515-0515; www.montrealjazzfest.com) provides events details, free festival programs and maps at kiosks around the **Place des Arts** (Map pp62–3). Most concerts are held in the halls or on outdoor stages; several downtown blocks are closed to traffic. The music starts around noon and lasts until late evening when the clubs take over.

Tickets go on sale in mid-May and are available from the **Places des Arts box office** (☎ 514-842-2112; www.pdarts.com) and **Admission** (☎ 514-790-1245; www.admission.com). The biggest acts cost $100 and up but some very good concerts may be on offer for just a few dollars. Free concerts are held daily from noon to 8pm.

Pay parking garages at the Complexe Desjardins and Place des Arts fill up quickly; take the metro to avoid hassle and traffic. Hotels raise their prices by as much as 50% and early booking is essential. Lawn chairs, bicycles, dogs and your own alcohol aren't allowed – but there's plenty of seating on the steps of the Place des Arts and plenty of beer and food sold from the concession tents that dot the festival grounds.

MUSIC

Sometimes it seems Montréal is all about the music. A friend to experimentation of all genres and styles, the city is home to more than 250 active bands, embracing anything and everything from electropop, hip-hop and glam rock to Celtic folk, indie punk and *yéyé* (exuberant 1960s-style French rock) – not to mention roots, ambient, grunge and rockabilly. No matter what your weakness, you could spend all summer exploring Montréal's great soundtrack, and still end up just scratching the surface.

There are dozens of large and medium-sized venues and theaters that regularly host concerts. The best concert venue of all is downtown Montréal during the celebrated International Jazz Festival (see the boxed text, p23) when the city core is sealed off to traffic and becomes a kind of giant open-air concert venue where the whole city comes to party. The event draws two million people to Montréal each year.

These days there's also another kind of musical tourism going on due to the commercial and critical success of independent bands like Arcade Fire and the Dears as well as the mass punk-pop of Simple Plan in the US and beyond. It's put a spotlight on the city's musical scene and talented bands are making everyone wonder, 'Why didn't we notice this before?' With Québec's huge music industry behind them, Québec's French-language singers, bands and other musicians regularly sell hundreds of thousands of albums a year, although they don't garner much attention among the anglocentric media.

Rock & Pop

For better or worse, Québec's best-known recording artist is Céline Dion. Born in Charlemagne some 30km east of downtown Montréal, Dion was a megastar in Québec and France long before she went on to win five Grammys. In 1983 she became the first Canadian to get a gold record in France.

Genius management from husband/music svengali René Angélil spared Dion much criticism of 'selling out' when she started to work on an English-language career. By alternating English- and French-language releases, she's kept both her English and Québec fan bases happy for decades.

On the rock scene, Arcade Fire remains one of Montréal's top indie rock bands. Their eclectic folk/rock/indie sound and manic ensemble of instruments have made them critics' darlings since their first CD *Funeral* was released in 2004 and hit the top 10 lists all over the US and UK. The group earned a cult following early on, selling over 500,000 copies of *Funeral* around the world without the backing of a major label – buzz being generated mainly through the internet. Their follow-up album *Neon Bible*, released in 2007, received both critical and commercial success, vaulting to number 1 on the Canadian Albums Chart and number 2 on the US Billboard Top 200 charts.

The Stills is another band that has carved a name for itself. Blending garage rock, new wave and alt sounds, they sprinkle their albums with catchy guitar riffs and lush chords (and a few anguished moans thrown in for good measure). Their first album, *Logic Will Break Your Heart* (2003), is generally regarded as superior to later releases.

Rufus Wainwright is another anglophone artist of note who grew up in Montréal. The talented and famously eccentric Grammy-nominated singer and songwriter travels all over the musical map – performing songs of Judy Garland, cutting albums described as 'popera' (pop opera) and recording tracks for big Hollywood films. *Release The Stars* (2007), with elements of pop, melodrama and camp, is a good introduction to his eccentric sound.

In the francophone music industry, the market is crowded with talented artists. The hot name of the moment is the Lost Fingers, who had one of the top-selling albums in Québec in 2009. Their gypsy-jazz-pop sound (and the group's name) owes much to gypsy guitarist Django Reinhardt. They play old Django-style tunes, but brilliantly overlay them with pop songs from the past, singing catchy versions of Michael Jackson's 'Billie Jean' and AC/DC's 'You Shook Me All Night Long' among other surprising offerings. Check out their 2008 debut *Lost in the '80s*.

Other groups of note include DobaCaracol, a talented female duo (Doriane Fabreg and Carole Facal) who bring together African rhythms, reggae and Latin sounds along with lush vocals to create well-crafted songs. Though the two split in 2008 to pursue solo careers, their 2004 album *Soley* is well worth seeking out.

One of the big names of the past is Jean Leloup. Born in Québec City in 1961, Leloup (The Wolf) grew up in Africa, mainly in Algeria, before coming back to Québec with his parents at age 15. Fans say his second album *L'amour est sans Pitié* (1990) is his best, with the mega hit single '1990' still receiving airtime in bars and clubs. In 2003 Jean Leloup retired his name and his old songs and began anew under 'Jean Leclerc,' his legal name – though he has not attained the success of his earlier efforts.

Les Colocs is another household name among Québécois rockers. They were known for outrageous and energetic live shows and evocative lyrics, and are still remembered fondly despite the 10-plus years since the band's breakup (following the suicide of lead singer Dédé Fortin).

On the pop front, singer-songwriter Daniel Bélanger's moody, atmospheric albums and mesmerizing lyrics have been seducing the province's music fans since the 1990s.

Up-and-coming bands and singers to keep an eye out for when you're in town are indie-rock band Malajube, eclectic singer Ariane Moffatt, and Les Breastfeeders, whose infectious mix of '60s rock-styled pop punk have made them one of the best live shows in all of Montréal.

To find out more, MusiquePlus is Québec's all-music-video channel. To find out what's up and coming in indie francophone music, the Université de Montréal's radio station CISM 89.3FM is excellent and the frequency is available in most parts of Montréal.

Jazz

Outside the frenetic weeks of the International Jazz Festival, the contemporary scene in Montréal bubbles away in a few designated clubs and cafés. During the day musicians might teach at McGill University's music school – or play for sidewalk donations.

In the 1940s and '50s, Montréal was one of the most important venues for jazz music in North America. It produced a number of major jazz musicians, like pianist Oscar Peterson and trumpeter Maynard Ferguson. The scene went into decline in the late 1950s but revived after the premiere of the jazz festival in 1979.

Peterson, who grew up in a poor family in a southwestern Montréal suburb, dazzled audiences with his keyboard pyrotechnics for over 60 years until his death in 2007. He was never particularly concerned about fame or commercial success. 'I don't do something because I think it will sell 30 million albums,' Peterson told one reporter. 'I couldn't care less. If it sells one, it sells one.'

The city's other celebrated jazz pianist, Oliver Jones, was already in his fifties when he was discovered by the music world. He had studied with Oscar Peterson's sister Daisy and the influence can be heard in his sound. Since the 1980s he has established himself as a major mainstream player with impressive technique and a hard-swinging style.

Singer and pianist Diana Krall has enjoyed mass appeal without sacrificing her bop and swing roots. In 1993 she launched her career on Montréal's Justin Time record label, and has since gone on to become the top-selling jazz vocalist. Her 1998 album *When I Look Into Your Eyes* earned a Grammy and spent a full year at the top of the Billboard jazz chart.

Originally from New York City, singer Ranee Lee is known for her virtuosity that spans silky ballads, swing standards and raw blues tunes. She has performed with many jazz notables and is a respected teacher on the McGill University music faculty.

The Vic Vogel Big Band, directed by pianist and arranger Vogel, performs razor-sharp arrangements in the Duke Ellington mold. Hard bop drummer and band leader Bernard Primeau was one of Canada's most famous band leaders and was known for promoting young, talented players from obscurity. He died in 2006.

Classical

The backbone of Montréal's classical music scene is the Orchestre Symphonique de Montréal (OSM). The OSM was the first Canadian orchestra to achieve platinum (500,000 records sold) on its 1984 recording of Ravel's *Bolero*. Since then it has won a host of awards including two Grammys and 12 Junos, and has made 88 recordings with leading record labels like Decca and CBS.

The smaller Orchestre Métropolitain du Grand Montréal is a showcase of young Québec talent and as such is staffed by graduates from the province's conservatories. The director is Yannick Nézet-Séguin, a Montrealer and among the youngest to lead a major orchestra in Canada. Its regular cycle of Mahler symphonies is a particular treat for classical-music buffs.

Opera

Over the past 25 years the Opéra de Montréal has become a giant on the North American landscape. It has staged over 600 performances of 76 operas and collaborated with numerous international companies. Many great names have graced its stages including Québec's own Leila Chalfoun, Lyne Fortin, Suzie LeBlanc and André Turp, alongside a considerable array of Canadian and international talent. The company stages six new operas every season including classics like *Le Nozze di Figaro* and *The Magic Flute*.

Locally, new operas are not created, but in 1989 the Opéra de Montréal won a Félix (Québec music award) for the most popular production of the season for *Nelligan,* an opera created in Québec about the life of poet Émile Nelligan by André Gagnon; Michel Tremblay wrote the libretto (see the boxed text, p53).

Folk

English-language folk singers are few and far between in Québec – apart from Leonard Cohen. Best known as a pop icon and novelist of the 1960s, Cohen remains one of the world's most eclectic folk artists. The romantic despair in his compositions recalls the style of Jacques Brel. A second burst of major creativity occurred in the 1980s when Cohen's dry, gravelly baritone could be heard on albums such as *Various Positions* (1984), a treatise on lovers' relationships, and the sleek *I'm Your Man* (1988), which suddenly made him hip again to younger audiences. The aging bard can be heard at the annual Leonard Cohen Event every spring in Montréal.

Chanson

It's hard to understand music in Québec without understanding what they call chanson, no matter how difficult it may seem to penetrate for non-French speakers at the beginning. While France has a long tradition of this type of French folk music, where a focus on lyric and poetry takes precedence over the music itself, in Québec the chanson has historically been tied in with politics and identity in a profound way. With the Duplessis-era Québec stifling any real creative production, Quebecers were tuned into only what was coming out of France, like Edith Piaf or Charles Aznavour.

The social upheaval of the Quiet Revolution (see the boxed text, p20) changed all that, when a generation of musicians took up their guitars, sung in Québécois and penned deeply personal lyrics about life in Québec and, often, independence.

Gilles Vigneault is synonymous with the chanson *Gens du pays* (People of the Country), a favorite on nationalist occasions. Vigneault has painted a portrait of the province in over 100 chanson recordings. Other leading chansonniers include Félix Leclerc, Raymond Lévesque, Claude Léveillé, Richard Desjardins and veteran Jean-Pierre Ferland.

As for new artists, chansonnier Pierre Lapointe is *the* musical sensation in Québec and one of the most exciting and original musicians to emerge this decade. Born in Lac St-Jean, Québec, he's been showered with prizes and adulation for his music from Montréal to France and back again.

You can hear chanson in *boîtes á chanson,* clubs where this type of music is played. Try not to leave Montréal or Québec City without taking in at least one show. Because the songs are so much a part of Québécois culture every Francophone knows the lyrics by heart. Once the shows start the place erupts like a punk concert with everyone singing along at the top of their lungs. Dancing on tabletops is not uncommon.

FILM & TELEVISION

Montréal has a booming film industry, with Québec films regularly steamrolling their foreign (including Hollywood) competition. Homegrown francophone cinema continues to smash box-office records – an event that would have been unimaginable even a few years ago.

Quebecers' appetite for stories about their lives and the people around them is insatiable. It's an enthusiasm some outsiders have difficulty understanding. Québécois films are often full of odd pacing, silences and cultural references that newcomers to the province can have trouble understanding. The Québec cinematic experience is often more about ideas than whether a film is visually exciting.

The foundations of Québec cinema were laid in the 1930s when Maurice Proulx, a pioneer documentary filmmaker, charted the colonization of the gold-rich Abitibi region in northwestern Québec. It was only in the 1960s that directors were inspired to experiment by the likes of Federico Fellini or Jean-Luc Godard, though the subject of most films remained the countryside and rural life. The 1970s were another watershed moment when erotically charged movies sent the province a-twitter. The most representative works of this era were Claude Jutra's *Mon Oncle Antoine* and *La Vraie Nature de Bernadette* by Gilles Carle.

Montréal finally burst onto the international scene in the 1980s with a new generation of directors like Denys Arcand (see the boxed text, below), Louis Archambault, Michel Brault and Charles Binamé. Films are produced in French but dubbing and subtitling have made them accessible to a wider audience.

Animation and multimedia technologies became a Montréal specialty following the success of Softimage, a company founded by special-effects guru Daniel Langlois. Creator of some of the first 3-D animation software, Softimage masterminded the special effects used in Hollywood blockbusters like *Jurassic Park, The Mask, Godzilla* and *Titanic.*

Montréal is also a massive draw for foreign film shoots. The Old Town with its European-style streetscapes and the modern glimmer of downtown makes it a versatile location for film crews. The recent strength of the Canadian dollar, however, has made shooting in Montréal less attractive, and the industry has been down since 2006.

In the world of TV, Québec is no less self-interested. On any given night, as English Canada tunes into imported shows from the US, Québec's airwaves are devoted almost entirely to homegrown content with the odd program or movie from France, or dubbed-American offering, thrown into the mix.

The most enduring genre is the *téléroman,* a cross between a soap opera and prime-time drama. But runaway hit of the day is *Tout le Monde en Parle* (Everybody is Talking About It), a rollicking current affairs show hosted by comedian Guy A Lepage. It's controversial, snappy and the first stop for anyone doing anything in Québec's public arena, from politicians and actors to war heroes and wacko psychiatrists. The province literally grinds to a halt on Sunday nights, as two million Quebecers (almost one-third of the entire population of the province) tune in to find out what people will be talking about for the rest of the week.

QUÉBEC'S MASTER FILMMAKER

No director portrays modern Québec with a sharper eye than Montréal's own Denys Arcand. His themes are universal enough to strike a chord with international audiences: modern sex in *The Decline of the American Empire* (1986), religion in *Jésus of Montréal* (1989), and death in the brilliant tragicomedy *The Barbarian Invasions* (2003). *Invasions* casts a satirical light on Québec's creaking health-care system, the demise of the sexual revolution and the failed ideologies of the 1960s. Many of its misfit-intellectual characters are based on Arcand's own professorial friends.

Born in 1941 near Québec City, Arcand studied history in Montréal and landed a job at the National Film Board making movies for Expo '67. The young director was a keen supporter of francophone rights and the Quiet Revolution, but became deeply disillusioned with Québec politics in the 1970s. He then trained his lens on the establishment in documentaries like *Le Confort et l'Indifférence,* a scathing critique of Québec's first referendum on sovereignty in 1980. *Réjeanne Padovani,* a political thriller, ends with a body being entombed in the fresh concrete of a Montréal freeway.

So far Arcand has been able to resist Hollywood's siren calls. After scoring a big hit with *Decline* (winner of eight 'Genies,' the Canadian Oscars, in 1986), a big US studio asked for a remake of the film in English. Arcand politely refused, and a few years later actor Meg Ryan lobbied for him to direct *Sleepless in Seattle.* But the Quebecer didn't like the script – and rejected a million-dollar offer.

Arcand's best films are inextricably tied to French Canada. This may explain why his only English-language films to date – *Love and Human Remains* (1993) and *Stardom* (2000) – failed to ignite audiences. Arcand himself admits his characters may be too Gallic to work in any language but French.

His latest film is *L'Âge des Ténèbres* (2007), about a government bureaucrat who escapes into a fantasy world; it was the closing film of the Cannes Film Festival.

QUÉBEC ON FILM

- *L'Âge des Ténèbres* (The Age of Darkness, directed by Denys Arcand, 2007) The final installment of his trilogy mines similar territory – taking aim at bureaucratic institutions and the foibles of modern life, while injecting touches of comedy to lighten the darkness.
- *Bon Cop, Bad Cop* (Directed by Érik Canuel, 2006) When a dead body shows up on the Ontario–Québec border, a corrupt Montréal cop and an uptight Toronto cop are assigned together to find the killer. This film crushed every box-office record in the province from biggest opening weekend to highest grossing Québec film ever.
- *C.R.A.Z.Y.* (Directed by Jean-Marc Vallée, 2005) This popular film of a young Montrealer growing up gay swept the 2006 Genie Awards.
- *Maurice Richard* (The Rocket, directed by Charles Binamé, 2005) A fascinating biopic on one of the great legends of sport, Québécois hockey star Maurice Richard.
- *L'Audition* (Directed by Luc Picard, 2005) Directed by and starring one of Québec's most respected actors, this well-told film follows a hit man in Montréal who wants to leave it all behind. Daniel Bélanger, one of the province's most respected singer-songwriters, wrote the score.
- *Les Invasions Barbares* (The Barbarian Invasions, directed by Denys Arcand, 2003) In the sequel to *The Decline of the American Empire* (1986) an estranged family is brought together by the hedonistic, ex-radical father's losing battle with cancer. In 2004 it won the Oscar for best foreign film, Canada's first ever in this category.
- *L'Ange de Goudron* (Tar Angel, directed by Denis Chouinard, 2001) One of the few films about the immigrant experience in Québec, it resonated strongly in multicultural Montréal. The story revolves around an immigrant Algerian family in Montréal, and the conflict between a father who dreams of Canadian citizenship, and his son who wants no part of the country.
- *Les Boys* (Directed by Louis Saia, 1997) Despite the rather formulaic plot, *Les Boys,* along with its three sequels, became the province's most successful movie franchise ever. The story follows the misadventures of an amateur hockey team.
- *Eldorado* (Directed by Charles Binamé, 1995) No other film has captured the spirit of urban life in Montréal quite the way this one has, as it delves into the lives of struggling 20-somethings. The nightclub Foufounes Électriques (p153) plays a starring role.
- *Octobre* (Directed by Pierre Falardeau, 1994) Falardeau's separatist politics are well known and this film, the dramatization of the FLQ crisis based on the book by FLQ cell member Francis Simard, was embroiled in controversy for the director's sympathetic portrayal of the terrorists.
- *Leolo* (Directed by Jean Claude Lazon, 1992) Yet another look – albeit a twisted one – at the life of a working-class Montréal family, Leolo delves into the mind of a slightly mad child convinced he's Italian despite being born into a francophone household.
- *Mon Oncle Antoine* (Directed by Claude Jutra, 1971) One of the all-time classics of Québécois cinema, this poignant coming-of-age story is set in an asbestos mining town and powerfully captures the social and economic life of 1940s Québec.

THEATER

Canada was a desert for playwrights in the early 1960s when a group of disgruntled writers formed the Playwrights' Workshop Montréal, which revolutionized the way in which plays were staged. An important drama center, the workshop has been the key to developing contemporary work and new writers for the Canadian stage. Its pioneers included playwrights such as Dan Daniels, Aviva Ravel, Walter Massey, Justice Rinfret and Guy Beaulne, many of whom are active on Montréal's theater scene today.

Founded in 1968, the Centaur Theatre (p164) is Québec's premier English-language stage for drama. Initially its programming was contemporary-international, eg Miller, Brecht and Pinter. When a second stage for experimental theater was added in the 1970s, the Centaur set about developing English-speaking playwrights such as David Fennario, whose satirical *On the Job* was considered a breakthrough production for the company. Fennario's award-winning *Balconville* paints a compelling portrait of life among Montréal's working class across the language divide. Though originally performed in 1979, it's remained a classic, and is still revived from time to time.

Today the Centaur is considered one of Canada's leading theaters. Works by its playwrights appear in collaborations with other theaters in Canada as well as the USA and Ireland.

Modern theatrical dance in Canada developed in tandem with the drama scene. Les Grands Ballets Canadiens' modern staging of *Carmina Burana* for Expo '67, followed by the 1970 rock ballet adaptation of The Who's *Tommy*, gave the company two of its greatest hits. Together with ballet companies in Winnipeg and Toronto, and the professional schools they spawned, the LGBC helped to form the bedrock of Canadian professional dance and drama.

Québec's fabulously successful Cirque du Soleil set new artistic boundaries by combining dance, theater and circus in a single power-packed show (see the boxed text, above).

One of the most famous playwrights in Québec is Michel Tremblay, whose plays about people speaking in their own dialects changed the way Quebecers felt about their language.

DANCE

Montréal's dance scene crackles with innovation. Virtually every year a new miniseries, dance festival or performing arts troupe emerges to wow audiences in wild and unpredictable ways. Hundreds of performers and dozens of companies are based in the city and there's an excellent choice of venues for interpreters to strut their stuff.

Several major companies established the city's reputation in the 1980s as an international dance mecca. Les Grands Ballets Canadiens (p162) attracts the biggest audiences with evergreens such as *Carmen* and *The Nutcracker*. O Vertigo, MC2 Extase, La La La Human Steps, Fondation Jean-Pierre Perraeault and Les Ballets Jazz de Montréal (see the boxed text, p30) are troupes of international standing. Initially they all struggled but operate today with annual budgets running into the millions of dollars.

A new breed of independent dancer-choreographers has emerged over the past few years. These all-round talents tend to work outside the bounds of formal troupes to diversify and explore a broader spectrum of traditions.

Venezuela-born José Navas is one of the most exciting soloists working today and he also works as choreographer of Compagnie Flak. Dance fans who saw his extraordinary *One Night Only* 10 years ago still rave about it.

Montréal-born Margaret Gillis (www.margiegillis.com) is a modern dancer of international renown and combines performing, teaching and choreography all over the world. She has choreographed solo shows for Cirque du Soleil and usually does at least one performance in Montréal per year.

RAGS TO RICHES CIRCUS STYLE: CIRQUE DU SOLEIL

The real-life story of Guy Laliberté is one of the great Canadian entertainment stories and almost as dramatic as one of the performances for which his company is so well known.

Born in Québec City in 1959, Laliberté spent his youth basking in the kind of hobbies other people label as weird – stilts, fire breathing and accordion playing. But that all changed when he got together with a group of like-minded friends that became the first incarnation of Cirque du Soleil (Circus of the Sun). Their big break came with the 450th anniversary of Jacques Cartier's arrival in New France in 1984 and has snowballed ever since. Performances are riots of dance, acrobatics, music and elements that defy categorization but are just mind-blowing to watch.

Though the no-animals, no-speaking rules have remained true to their roots, these days there is no stereotypical Cirque performer who might be hired. Full-time Cirque scouts comb the world including Eastern Europe and remote parts of China, searching for new performers, tricks and skills to add to their shows. Cirque scouts are also regular fixtures at the Olympic Games, where as soon as the competition is over they burn up the phones with offers to gymnasts, swimmers and any other charismatic amateur athlete who catches their eye. Laliberté's productions also regularly include guest performers and artistic contributions.

Montréal dance icon Margie Gillis choreographed two solos for *LOVE*, the Beatles-inspired Cirque production in Las Vegas. Designer Thierry Mugler created the erotically charged costumes for *Zumanity*, which included metal underwear and latex coats chosen as much for their suggestive connotations as for the sounds they made on stage. Even the setting itself can be quite forward-thinking – as in the mega-production *O*, which took place in a 25ft-deep pool filled with 1.5 million gallons of water. An underwater crew was submerged in the pool for the entire 90-minute performance to catch divers, give them hits of oxygen (about 30L a night for each performer) and direct them out of the pool.

Laliberté has also invested heavily in the city and is a big promoter of alternative sources of energy. To learn more on that front, visit the cutting-edge garbage-powered circus city, TOHU (p87).

BALLET YES, BUT DOES IT SWING?

You notice it right away, the sizzling dynamics and awesome precision of the dancers. Though the faces may have changed during the company's three decades, physical exhilaration remains the trademark of Les Ballets Jazz de Montréal (BJM). Its repertoire has switched from finger-snapping, pelvis-twisting routines to hot-cold contemporary reflections, but its dancers still test the limits with inexhaustible energy.

When the BJM was founded in 1972, the company performed only to jazz music. With artistic director Louis Robitaille's arrival in the late 1990s, its repertoire became more eclectic, both in music and choreography. Today, the company goes by the moniker BJM Danse and while the director acknowledges the company's jazz roots he stresses that his dancers – all of whom are classically trained – need to perform in a fusion of styles. 'Dance isn't one thing anymore. To stay in one direction will kill the company,' says Robitaille. BJM Danse showcases its interpreters' talents, while encouraging works of cutting-edge choreographers such as Jiri Kylian and William Forsythe. Success on the international stage has silenced the critics who once griped that the troupe had strayed from its jazz roots. Vancouverite Crystal Pite, who previously worked for the Ballett Frankfurt, has been their resident choreographer since 2001 and the company is garnering some of the best reviews of its career.

Because it performs before audiences all over the world, BJM Danse has learned to tailor its repertoire to varied tastes. Robitaille notes that in the USA, Asia and much of Canada, spectators like to be entertained, while in Montréal the audience is 'very connected and prefers the avant-garde.'

Transatlantique Montréal Manifestation de Danse Comtemporaine (www.transatlantiquemontreal.com) is a popular two-week contemporary dance festival held at the end of September focusing on new creations by Québécois, Canadian and international performers. This is not to be confused with the Festival TransAmériques (www.fta.qc.ca), an even newer dance fest held from late May to early June. It features an astounding lineup of talent with forward-leaning troupes from all over the world.

Notable troupes include Danièle Desnoyers' Le Carré des Lombes, Sylvain Érnard Danse, Benoît Lachambre's Par b.l.eux and MAPS (run by Suzanne Miller and Allan Paivio).

Danse Danse, put on by Productions Loma, packs its season with international talent at high-profile venues. Tangente plays four-night runs nearly every weekend with performances by emerging and established artists. Agora de la Danse (p162) serves local, midsized companies and choreographers. Finally, Studio 303 fills its agenda with experimental artists and choreographers who present short works and improvisation in the Vernissage Danse series.

LITERATURE

Montréal proudly calls itself the world's foremost cradle of French-language writers, after Paris. But the city also boasts intimate links to many English-language writers of repute.

On the English side, Montréal's most famous literary son is Nobel Prize–winner Saul Bellow. Born in the town of Lachine near Montréal in 1915, Bellow moved with his family to Chicago when he was 10 years old, but wrote about the city in his classic novel *Herzog* (1964). Montréal was a recurring nostalgic theme for the book's middle-aged hero, Herzog.

Caustic, quick-witted and prolific, Mordecai Richler was the 'grumpy old man' of Montréal literature in the latter part of the 20th century. Richler grew up in a working-class Jewish district in Mile End and for better or worse remained the most distinctive voice in anglophone Montréal until his passing in 2001. Most of his novels focus on Montréal and its wild and wonderful characters.

Self-imposed exile also fell to Mavis Gallant, an émigré to France whose witty, bittersweet novels wove in her native Montréal. Gallant won many prizes and wrote short stories that graced the pages of the *New Yorker*.

On the French side, Québec writers who are widely read in English include Anne Hébert, Marie-Claire Blais, Hubert Aquin, Christian Mistral and Dany Laferrière, whose first book *Comment Faire l'Amour avec un Nègre sans se Fatiguer* (the book was released in English as *How to Make Love to a Negro*), a wild and witty look at race relations in Canada, was eventually made into a film whose screenplay was nominated for a Genie award. For stories about everyday life on the Plateau, try Michel Tremblay's short stories.

As for literary trends in the province, many of today's buzz-inducing young writers are immigrants from other French-speaking countries writing about conflicts back home. Lebanese-born Rawi Hage moved to Montréal in 1991 and his first novel *De Niro's Game*, about life in Beirut, was nominated for the 2006 Scotiabank Giller Prize, Canada's highest literary award. Elsewhere, Quebecers never seem to get enough of historical novels, and bookshelves are groaning with fiction set in the province's past.

Writers groups can be contacted via spoken-word venues like the Yellow Door (p166). A literary festival, Blue Metropolis (p13), brings together more than 200 writers for five days of literary events in early April.

PAINTING & VISUAL ARTS

Québec's lush forests and icy winter landscapes have been inspiring landscape artists since the 19th century. Horatio Walker was known for his sentimental interpretations of Québec farm life such as *Oxen Drinking* (1899). Marc-Aurèle Fortin (1880–1970) became famous for his watercolors of Québec countryside, notably the treescapes of the Laurentians and Charlevoix. His portraits of majestic elms along Montréal avenues can be viewed in the Musée des Beaux-Arts (p60), which acquired an extensive collection of Fortin's work in 2007.

William Brymner influenced an entire generation of painters as director of the Art Association of Montréal in the early 20th century. His forte was delicate human figures, interiors and landscapes in the glowing colors of romantic classicism. One of his pupils was Clarence

MONTRÉAL IN LITERATURE

- *A Full Moon in Summer* (Michel Tremblay, 2001) Eleven Montrealers recount their stories of love, piecing together the landscape of an affair and tracing the slopes between intoxicating highs and heartbreaking lows.
- *Around the Mountain* (Hugh Hood, 1967) This collection of 12 Montréal narratives is a documentary-fantasy portrait of its people and ambience in the heady days of Expo '67, from the misadventures of a convivial soldier to the fruitless efforts of an angelic messenger.
- *Bonheur d'Occasion* (The Tin Flute, Gabrielle Roy, 1947) The tragic ironies of WWII provide an escape from the claustrophobic poverty of the Great Depression in working-class Montréal. This gritty urban novel became a million-copies-seller and was made into a film.
- *Book of Longing* (Leonard Cohen, 2006) Cohen's most recent collection of poetry and drawings.
- *Briser le Silence* (Nathalie Simard and Michel Vastel, 2005) Superstar producer and musical svengali Guy Cloutier took Nathalie Simard under his wing as a child and made her, along with her brother René, two of Québec's major singing stars of the 1980s. He also sexually abused Nathalie from the time she was 11. When she pressed charges it rocked the province's entertainment industry to its core. This is her autobiography, a heartbreaking and searing portrait of the dark side of Québec's star system.
- *Dance With Desire* (Irving Layton, 2002) Chosen from across the span of this Montréal poet's long career, these poems feed on the excesses, embarrassments and foolishness of unstifled love.
- *Deadly Decisions* (Kathy Reichs, 1999) This celebrated American crime novelist divides her time between Montréal and North Carolina where she's a university professor. Many of her crime stories, like this one, are based in Montréal and full of keen insights into the city.
- *Les Aurores Montréales* (Monique Proulx, 1996) A captivating collection of short stories where Montréal plays a starring role as its inhabitants fumble through life in the city.
- *Oh Canada! Oh Quebec! Requiem for a Divided Country* (Mordecai Richler, 1992) Montréal-born Richler's scathing critique of Québec's independence movement set off a furor among Canadian politicians – one member of parliament even called for the book to be banned.
- *The Apprenticeship of Duddy Kravitz* (Mordecai Richler, 1959) A rough young hustler becomes obsessed with buying land as his ticket out of the Plateau ghetto; the character type has entered Montréal parlance. Richler won an Oscar nomination for the classic 1974 movie made from the book.
- *The Hockey Sweater* (Roch Carrier, 1979) Due to a mail-order mix-up a child is forced to wear a Toronto Maple Leafs sweater in a small Québec town teeming with Montréal Canadiens fans. A wise parable of the friction between Québec's French and English populations of the era.
- *Two Solitudes* (Hugh MacLennan, 1945) Compelling saga of Anglo-French relations, told through two families on either side of the linguistic divide in pre-WWII Québec.

Gagnon, who produced subtle snowscapes and dazzling fall scenes. Other key artists of the period included Adrien Hébert and Robert Pilot, usually identified by their snowy portraits of Montréal and Québec City.

In the 1940s the modern era of Canadian painting was ushered in by three leading figures: Paul-Émile Borduas, John Lyman and Alfred Pellan, who all worked closely together in Montréal. Borduas developed a radical style of surrealism that came to be identified with an alternative group called the 'Automatistes.'

In 1948 Borduas drafted the manifest *Refus Global* (Global Refusal), which rejected the values of traditional landscape painting in favor of abstract art. The highly controversial document endorsed personal freedoms of expression while attacking state repressions and the dominant place of the church in Québec.

The most prolific of the Automatistes was Jean-Paul Riopelle (1923–2002). Though initially a surrealist, Riopelle soon produced softer abstracts called 'grand mosaics' – paintings created with a spatula and colors juxtaposed like a landscape viewed from an airplane. In the 1980s he abandoned conventional painting to work with aerosol sprays. His most renowned paintings are on permanent display at Montréal's Musée d'Art Contemporain (p60) and the Musée National des Beaux-Arts du Québec (p211) in Québec City.

Abstract painting has been an exciting field to follow in the past few years in Montréal. François Lacasse is a master in manipulating acrylic into new depths that evoke a strong sense of virtuality without the aid of computers. And lithograph artists like Elmyna Bouchard and Francine Simonin are attracting attention throughout Canada and abroad.

Photography & New Media

Québec's strong visual traditions owe much to documentary photography. Montréal's first master photographer was William Notman, who rose to international fame for his portraits, landscapes and urban subjects in the late 19th century. Musée McCord (p60) has a permanent collection of his works.

Documentary photography has fed a strong tradition of Québec photo art since the late 1960s. Most recently, Emmanuelle Léonard took a novel approach by having dozens of people from different walks of life photograph their workplaces themselves; the views of each worker's environment were quite different from what the viewer expected.

The work of photographer-artist Alain Paiement, by contrast, redefines space through spectacular images of urban spaces. For one project Paiement shot the floor area of an apartment house and joined the images into one huge composition. Small ruptures in the picture pointed out the image's structural impossibility.

Nicolas Baier uses computers and digital photography to take inventory of the world around him. Baier takes many pictures of a space and, on an abstract collage principle, cuts and reorganizes them so that parts of the surface represent different moments in time. In one work an image of the artist's bedroom was rearranged in this disconcerting fashion.

Montréal's many new media studios testify to the multimedia revolution that has taken place over the past decade. Kooky machines and organic sounds are the trademarks of Jean-Paul Gauthier, whose work has been shown at Montréal's Musée des Beaux-Arts (p60).

top picks

ART SPACES

- **Musée d'Art Contemporain** (p60) Downtown's showpiece, with world-famous contemporary art.
- **Musée des Beaux-Arts** (p60) Magnificent exhibits and temporary shows spread among two stunning buildings.
- **Centre d'Histoire de Montréal** (p50) Creative temporary exhibitions on the city's storied past.
- **Musée McCord** (p60) A great place to delve into Canadian history.
- **Musée d'Archéologie Pointe-à-Callière** (p50) Time capsule of Montréal's humble beginnings.
- **Galeries d'Art Contemporain du Belgo** (p106) Five floors dedicated to exciting contemporary art, design and architecture.
- **Parisian Laundry** (p114) Cutting-edge gallery that hosts big shows.
- **Fonderie Darling** (p50) Youthfully creative space and symbol of the neighborhood's rebirth.
- **Centre Canadien d'Architecture** (p61) Showcase for urban and green design, plus pretty gardens.

His 'instruments' are tubes and pipes, air compressors, radio interference and sheet metal that produce percussive sounds; in one installation, large springs scratch over rotating mirrors to a soundtrack of shrill cries.

ARCHITECTURE

Montréal's split personality is nowhere more obvious than in its architecture, a beguiling mix of European traditionalism and North American modernism. Lovingly preserved Victorian mansions and stately beaux-arts monuments rub shoulders with the sleek lines of modern skyscrapers, lending Montréal's urban landscape a creative, eclectic sophistication all of its own. Sometimes one building even straddles the divide: the Centre Canadien d'Architecture (p61) integrates a graceful historical greystone right into its contemporary facade.

Other important buildings were meant to break with the past. Place Ville-Marie, a multitowered complex built in the late 1950s, revolutionized urban architecture in Montréal and was the starting point for the underground city (see the boxed text, p68). Since then, architects have explored new forms such as Habitat '67 (p59), a controversial apartment building designed by Montréal architect Moshe Safdie when he was only 23. Located on a promontory off the Old Port, the structure resembles a child's scattered building blocks. The Biosphère (p57) once wore a skin made of spherical mesh, while the Casino de Montréal (p59) cleverly merges two of the most far-out pavilions of Expo '67.

Those heady days are back: Montréal's economic revival has sparked a construction boom. Not since the 1976 Olympics has the city seen such an explosion of large-scale projects, some of which are designed to repair defects in the urban fabric. One of the largest redevelopment projects in Canada was Montréal's $200 million convention center Palais des Congrès (p55) and its adjacent squares. Dubbed the Quartier International, this new minidistrict unites Downtown and Old Montréal by concealing an ugly sunken expressway.

For many visitors, the weathered greystones, such as the old stone buildings along Rue St-Paul, offer the strongest images of Old Montréal. The style emerged under the French regime in Québec (1608–1763), based on the Norman and Breton houses with wide, shallow fronts, stuccoed stone and a steep roof punctuated by dormer windows. But the locals soon adapted the blueprint to Montréal's harsh winters, making the roof less steep, adding basements and extending the eaves over the walls for extra snow protection.

From the 19th century, architects tapped any number of retro styles: classical (Bank of Montréal, p54), Gothic (Basilique Notre-Dame, p47) or Italian renaissance (Royal Bank, p54), to name a few. As Montréal boomed in the 1920s, a handful of famous architects like Edward Maxwell, George Ross and Robert MacDonald left their mark on handsome towers in Old Montréal and Downtown. French Second Empire style continued to be favored for comfortable francophone homes and some public buildings like the Hôtel de Ville (City Hall; p51).

Montréal also boasts the largest collection of Victorian row houses in all of North America. Numerous examples can be viewed in the Plateau such as along Rue St-Denis north of Rue Cherrier, or Ave Laval north of Carré St-Louis. Visitors are inevitably charmed by their brightly painted wrought-iron staircases, which wind up the outside of duplexes and triplexes. They evolved for three important reasons: taxes – a staircase outside allowed each floor to count as a separate dwelling, so the city could hike property taxes; fuel costs – an internal staircase

top picks

ARCHITECTURAL MUST-SEES

- **Basilique Notre-Dame** (p47) Enduring symbol of the city's rich Catholic heritage.
- **Hôtel de Ville** (p51) Picturesque city hall steeped in history.
- **Biosphère** (p57) Wondrous symbol of the future, c 1967.
- **Oratoire St-Joseph** (p88) Monolithic Renaissance-style monument to a monk's resolve.
- **Bibliothèque et Archives Nationale du Québec** (p73) Superb example of contemporary architecture made with people in mind.
- **Olympic Stadium** (p90) The costliest stadium never built?

CANADA'S STAR ARCHITECT MOSHE SAFDIE

Born in Haifa, Israel in 1938, Moshe Safdie graduated from McGill University's architecture program in 1961 and became almost an instant star. He was only 23 when asked to design Habitat '67 (p59), which was actually based on his university thesis. Now based in Boston, Safdie has crafted a stellar career gravitating toward high-profile projects where he can unleash innovative buildings with just the right dash of controversy to get people talking about them.

Most notably, Safdie designed the $56 million, 4000-sq-meter Holocaust Memorial in Jerusalem, Israel, which opened in 2005. He also designed Ottawa's National Gallery of Canada, which opened in 1988 with its trademark soaring glass front, and the Roman Colosseum–like Vancouver Library Square.

Most recently, Safdie's design for the Jepson Center for the Arts in Savannah, Georgia has provoked intense debate, with critics lambasting the imposing structure of glass and stone for 'intruding' into the area's historic character while fans praise its vision toward the future.

Safdie was made a companion of the Order of Canada in 2005, Canada's highest civilian honor.

wastes heat as warm air rises through the stairwell; space – the 1st and 2nd floors were roomier without an internal staircase.

ENVIRONMENT & PLANNING

Montréal is a healthy place to live – so salubrious, in fact, that it is routinely among the world's top cities ranked by quality-of-life indexes, according to the UN.

Air quality is generally good and the waters of the St Lawrence have benefited from strict environmental laws. Some practices, however, remain behind the times: salting of icy winter roads fouls the soil and groundwater despite the availability of substitutes; recycled waste is picked up, but unsorted; household water is unmetered; Québec's subsidized electricity is cheap and thus easy to waste.

CLIMATE

Even the earliest European explorers were surprised by Montréal's seasonal extremes. Temperatures of -20°C to -6°C are typical in January and February and snaps down to -40°C can occur. While Montréal winters of the past have enjoyed a notoriously frigid reputation, the truth is in recent years they've been somewhat milder. It's perhaps one of the few places in the world where the idea of global warming doesn't seem all that bad – at least in the middle of winter!

The warm seasons are short but delightful. First buds appear in late April and blossoms appear in mid-May for a couple of weeks. Summer arrives late. Early June can still be chilly; in brutal, steamy July an air conditioner becomes a major asset. Highs of 25°C or 30°C are common from mid-July to late August. Come September the mercury drops sharply in the evenings, but Indian summers are common in early October.

THE LAND

Montréal occupies an island on the north shore of the St Lawrence River. Officially known as the Island of Montréal, it's bordered on all sides by rivers rather than great expanses of lakes or oceans, meaning the barriers are more psychological than physical. The city proper, lying on a disjointed collection of plateaus and hills shaped by glaciers aeons ago, has an area of 158 sq km, but greater Montréal now encompasses the entire island and several towns on the south bank of the St Lawrence.

The north–south streets of Old Montréal and downtown cross several ridges that challenge some pedestrians. Pleasantly green residential areas around the fringes of Mont-Royal can throw up precipitous inclines and sharp curves. Bicyclists will find the riverside paths a breeze but face a series of hurdles as they head north into the Plateau.

Montréal overlooks rich, rolling farmland along the St Lawrence Valley, but the river has shaped the lives of Quebecers more than any other factor: two-thirds of the province's people live along its banks, and almost everyone draws river water for drinking.

The Laurentians (Laurentides in French) to the northeast are part of the Canadian Shield – the world's oldest mountain range formed more than three billion years ago – and provided the rough-hewn granite you see in Montréal buildings today.

GREEN MONTRÉAL

Some 8% of the city's territory is protected green space, and the abundance of leafy parks, bicycle paths and outdoor recreation options keeps the residents in tune with nature.

Every third resident takes the metro, helping to curb auto emissions. New bicycle lanes have been laid downtown and in Old Montréal; the network of trails is constantly expanding, converting erstwhile commuters from four to two wheels. The extensive network of Bixi bikes, released in 2009, has helped more Montrealers to go green, with over 3000 bikes available (and more on the way) at convenient pick-up-and-go stations all over the city. See the boxed text, p169, for more on this program.

City Hall has pledged to reduce greenhouse gas emissions by 20% by 2012, three times more than what's required by the Kyoto Protocol.

For more on local green issues, see also p17.

URBAN PLANNING & DEVELOPMENT

Since the 1960s the government has spent billions in developing tourist attractions and infrastructure in Montréal. Recently, a number of exciting projects have been realized or are in the works. The 33,000-sq-meter Bibliothèque et Archives Nationale du Québec (p73) opened in the Quartier Latin to huge success in 2005, with a record number of Montrealers flocking to the building each day.

The government has invested millions of dollars on the Main (Blvd St-Laurent), with the widening of sidewalks, the planting of trees and the addition of street lights to certain stretches. Rue Notre-Dame, a two-laned nightmare pocked with potholes that's nonetheless an important artery into Old Montréal, is also slated for modernization, including expansion to four lanes.

One of Montréal's most ambitious urban renewal projects in recent years is well under way on the edge of the Quartier Latin and eastern downtown. The project – dubbed the Quartier des Spectacles – aims to bring new life to this culturally rich area (bordered roughly by Rue Berri, Rue Sherbrooke, Blvd René-Lévesque and Rue City Councillors). Currently the 1-sq-km district houses 30 performance halls, numerous galleries and exhibition spaces; it also hosts various big-ticket festivals. The government has pledged $120 million to making the area a more attractive place to live, work and create in hopes of transforming the Quartier into an international destination.

MONTRÉAL'S MEGACITY

The idea as such was simple: one city, one administration, one urban development plan, and lots of saved tax revenues. So in 2001 the Parti Québécois – when it was still in power at the National Assembly, the province's parliament – put into motion a plan to merge towns across the province into megacities. This included the 28 towns and municipalities on the Island of Montréal being turned into a megacity of 1.8 million people.

The thing is, no referendum was held, and many communities, both anglophone and francophone, felt they'd been bushwhacked. The boroughs across the island that replaced the municipalities could no longer decide how local tax dollars were spent, and there were complaints that public services like snow removal, libraries, garbage pickup and the ambulance service had deteriorated. Many felt their small towns had been better-run.

When Jean Charest was campaigning for election in 2003, he promised Quebecers, including Montrealers, that their municipalities could opt out of the megacity. Charest won the election, kicked the PQ out of office and referendums were held. In Montréal 15 of the former municipalities, mostly in the island's west including upper-class Westmount, did opt out. However, they will have fewer powers than they did before the forced mergers and taxes will likely be raised to cover the cost of de-merging.

The new City of Montréal population is 1.58 million.

GOVERNMENT & POLITICS

For decades Québec politics was dominated by the question: are you separatist or federalist? But since Quebecers voted out the Parti Québécois in the 2003 provincial elections, the entire province has been given a reprieve. These days Québec spends its time clashing with the federal government over respecting the Kyoto accord, fiscal imbalance, toughening gun control and protesting the Canadian military's mission in Afghanistan rather than language and separation issues.

Québec's premier is Sherbrooke-born Jean Charest, elected on an ambitious platform of better health care, better education, tax cuts, and a leaner, less-interventionist government. However, he's had a rocky ride – his decision to raise the price of Québec's cornerstone $5-a-day day-care program to $7 unleashed a torrent of demonstrations, and tens of thousands of Montrealers have flooded the streets during his premiership to protest cuts to the public service and contracting out to the private sector. That's a bizarre twist, since those were the very things he ran on.

Montréal's moderate mayor, Gérald Tremblay, is something of a Teflon man. He has enjoyed healthy approval ratings since his 2001 election and was easily re-elected in 2005, obtaining 53% of the vote. Among other feathers in his cap, he is credited with saving the 2005 World Aquatic Championships with a zero-hour flight to Europe after it was withdrawn from Montréal because of a lack of funding guarantees. He is also remembered for stopping a mugging in 2003 when he saw a student being attacked by robbers near McGill University. As this book went to press he was in the midst of negotiations with Formula One to bring the coveted car race back to the city.

MEDIA

Montréal is the seat of Québec's French-language media companies and has four big TV networks. New-media firms like Discreet Logic and Softimage are renowned for their special effects, and the Cité du Multimédia center in Old Montréal is an incubator for start-ups.

The daily *Montreal Gazette* (www.montrealgazette.com) is the major English-language daily newspaper, with coverage of national affairs, politics and the arts. The big French dailies are the federalist *La Presse* (www.cyberpresse.ca) and the separatist-leaning *Le Devoir* (www.ledevoir.com).

Le Journal de Montréal is *the* city's wild and rollicking tabloid, replete with sensational headlines and photos. Though much derided, the *Journal* does the brashest undercover and investigative reporting in town and has the city's biggest daily circulation.

Four free entertainment mags appear every Thursday: *Mirror* (www.montrealmirror.com) and *Hour* (www.hour.ca) in English; *Ici* (www.ici.ca) and *Voir* (www.voir.ca) in French. They focus on entertainment, culture and local events with some great features and columns.

Canada's only truly national papers are the left-leaning Toronto *Globe and Mail* and the right-leaning *National Post*. *The Walrus* is a Canadian *New Yorker/Atlantic Monthly*–style magazine, with in-depth articles and musings from the country's intellectual heavyweights.

Canada's weekly news magazine *Maclean's* is full of high-quality writing and still holds a certain amount of clout with its special issues. *L'actualité* is Québec's monthly news magazine in French. The glossy, illustrated *Canadian Geographic* carries excellent articles and photography like its sister US monthly *National Geographic*. The Canadian Broadcasting Corporation's site (www.cbc.ca) is an excellent source for current affairs.

SACRED PROFANITY

The French spoken in Québec has a character all its own and cursing is no exception. Here, swear words center on the objects used in church services, a legacy of the church's centuries-long dominance. The words are untranslatable, but where a displeased English speaker might yell 'fuck,' a Quebecer will unleash *'tabarnac'* (from tabernacle). Instead of 'oh, shit!,' a Quebecer will cry *'sacrament!'* (from sacrament). And if you've really messed up, just pray you're never on the receiving end of a combo like *'hostie de câlisse de tabarnac!'* (rough translation: 'host in the chalice in the tabernacle!').

Oddly enough, *fucké,* an adaptation of the English, is mild enough for prime time and means 'broken' or 'crazy.'

MONTRÉAL CHIC

Montréal Fashion Week (p13) used to be a purely Canadian affair, but nowadays is filled with as many buyers from around the world as local fashion writers.

Aside from this biannual event, Montréal's other big fashion moment happens during the Montréal Fashion and Design Festival (p13), a free, outdoor fashion show held in mid-June (open to the public) where you can see Québécois, Canadian and international designers show off their collections outdoors, usually on stages set up on Ave McGill College.

It's been said that Montréal fashion boutiques have the right styles but the wrong country, ie the local market is limited. But in recent years that's changed. The ultra-classy men's boutique Kamkyl (p106) sells to an international clientele including boutiques in London, Belgium and Japan, while Montrealer Siphay Southidara, known as YSO (ee-sew), is one of Canada's most exciting designers and has an eponymous label (the moniker YSO is derived from the last letter of his first name and the first two of his last name – it's easier for Canadians to pronounce).

After immigrating to Canada from Laos in 1979, YSO attended fashion school in Montréal and later apprenticed with designer Marie Saint-Pierre. Heaps of awards followed, and by 1996 he was making samples for designer Tod Lynn and designing costumes for U2's Bono. Later he made the costumes for Cirque du Soleil's show *Alegria* and presented to catwalks in Montréal and Toronto. You can find his creations at the U&I boutique (p112).

Georges Lévesque is another designer making waves – he's designed stage costumes for Céline Dion and Québec singing superstar Diane Dufresne. You can check out his designs at Scandale (p111).

E-zines and blogs proliferate in this growing cyber-hub. For a survey of the country's news and media links, see www.canada.com. The *Web Citylog* (via www.montreal.com) routes to a discerning choice of stories from various electronic media. *Maisonneuve* (www.maisonneuve.org) is a sophisticated general-interest magazine with a good e-zine.

FASHION

One of the things visitors first notice here is how well dressed people are – and it's not just the women that stop traffic. The navy suit reigns supreme in the rest of Canada and only in Montréal do men sport business suits that merit a double-take – perhaps a chic, sober shade like olive-green with a lavender tie – that their counterparts in Vancouver, Toronto or even New York wouldn't dream of donning.

Whether artists, students or entrepreneurs, it seems like everybody knows the look they're going for and pulls it off well. Label watchers put it down to the perfect fusion of European and American fashion – the daringness and willingness to experiment from Paris coupled with a kind of American practicality that makes people choose what's right for them and not what's just of the moment. Probably most of all, Montrealers have a love of culture and an enjoyment of life that feeds right into their garments. In short, they just have fun with clothes and are happy to flaunt this.

Québec fashion magazines like *Clin d'Oeil, Lou Lou* and *Elle Québec* are excellent places to check out for exciting new boutiques and up-and-coming Québec designers.

After Los Angeles and New York, Montréal is the third-largest garment-making city in North America, and its fashion industry has annual sales of over $4 billion to the USA.

LANGUAGE

French is the official language of Québec and French Quebecers are passionate about it, seeing their language as the last line of defense against Anglo-Saxon culture. What makes Montréal unique in the province is the interface of English and French – a mix responsible for the city's dynamism as well as the root of many of its conflicts.

Until the 1970s it was the English minority (few of whom spoke French) who ran the businesses, held positions of power and accumulated wealth in Québec; more often than not a French Quebecer going into a downtown store couldn't get service in his or her own language.

But as Québec's separatist movement arose, the Canadian government passed laws in 1969 that required all federal services and public signs to appear in both languages. The separatists

SIGNS OF PRIDE

Québec's French Language Charter, the (in)famous Bill 101, asserts the primacy of French on public signs across the province. Stop signs in Québec read 'ARRÊT,' a word that actually means a stop for buses or trains (even in France, the red hexagonal signs read 'STOP'), apostrophes had to be removed from storefronts like Ogilvy's in the 1980s to comply with French usage, and English is allowed on signage provided it's no more than half the size of the French lettering. Perhaps most comical of all is the acronym PFK (Poulet Frit Kentucky) for a leading fast-food chain – even communist China still allows signs for KFC (Kentucky Fried Chicken).

The law is vigorously enforced by language police who roam the province with tape measures (yes – for real!) and hand out fines to shopkeepers if a door says 'Push' more prominently than 'Poussez.' These days, most Quebecers take it all in their stride, and the comical language tussles between businesses and the language police that were such regular features of evening newscasts and phone-in shows have all but disappeared in recent years.

took things further and demanded the primacy of French in Québec, which was affirmed by the Parti Québécois with the passage of Bill 101 in 1977 (see the boxed text, above). Though there was much hand-wringing, the fact is that Bill 101 probably saved the French language from dying out in North America. If you're at a party with five Anglophones and one Francophone these days, chances are everyone will be speaking French, something that would have been rare 10 years ago.

These days Montrealers with French as their mother tongue number 928,905, and native English speakers 300,580. Fifty-seven per cent of Montrealers from a variety of backgrounds speak both official languages.

Québec settlers were relatively cut off from France once they arrived in the New World, so the French you hear today in the province, known colloquially as Québécois, developed more or less independently from what was going on in France. The result is a rich local vocabulary, with its own idioms and sayings, and words used in everyday speech that haven't been spoken in France since the 1800s.

Accents vary widely across the province, but all are characterized by a delicious twang and rhythmic bounce unique to Québec French, and the addition of the word *lá* repeated from one to three times at the end of each spoken sentence.

The French spoken in Montréal most closely resembles that of France and will be easiest for French speakers from elsewhere to understand.

To francophone Quebecers, the French spoken in France sounds desperately posh. To people from France, the French spoken in Québec sounds terribly old-fashioned, quaint and at times unintelligible – an attitude that ruffles feathers here in an instant, as it's found to be condescending.

Quebecers learn standard French in school, hear standard French on newscasts and grow up on movies and music from France, so if you speak standard French, locals will have no difficulty understanding you – it's you understanding them that will be the problem. Remember, even when French-language Québécois movies are shown in France, they are shown with *French* subtitles.

Young Montrealers today are less concerned about language issues, so visitors shouldn't worry too much. Most residents grew up speaking both languages, and people you meet in daily life – store owners, waiters, bus drivers – switch effortlessly between French and English.

NEIGHBORHOODS

top picks

- Parc du Mont-Royal (p79)
- Basilique Notre-Dame (p47)
- Musée des Beaux-Arts (p60)
- Marché Jean-Talon (p82)
- Musée McCord (p60)
- Parc Jean-Drapeau (p57)
- Rue St-Denis (p75)
- Musée d'Art Contemporain (p60)

NEIGHBORHOODS

Montréal has a complicated soul. Elements of Europe and North America, along with an alluring spirit of bohemianism, all play a role in shaping the elusive identity of La Belle Ville.

This is a city of grand cathedrals, old-world markets and cobblestone streets still lined with 17th-century stone buildings. European virtues aside, Montréal retains her North American roots – from the love of a good sports bar to adulation of the latest trends emerging from Québec's southern neighbor. Add to this the fascinating blend of Anglophones and Francophones mixing on the streets, plus the surprising diversity of Montréal's newest arrivistes, and the city begins to reveal herself in all her dynamic beauty.

Each neighborhood of Montréal presents a distinct world of its own, complete with its own color, character and energy (not to mention language). For the flaneur, Montréal offers boundless intrigue, in the form of avant-garde art galleries, kitsch-loving boutiques, bohemian-style jazz bars and flower-filled parks for taking a respite from the streets.

On the edge of the St Lawrence River, Old Montréal is the city's birthplace with picturesque squares, grand old-world architecture and a dense concentration of camera-toting tourists. The narrow Rue St-Paul, the old main street, teems with art galleries, shops and eateries, while the broad concourse of the Old Port is lined with green parkland and cafés along Rue de la Commune. North of Old Montréal lies the pint-sized but colorful Chinatown, with a delightful selection of restaurants from all corners of Asia.

'Each neighborhood of Montréal presents a distinct world of its own, complete with its own color, character and energy'

The buzz of downtown lies just west. At the feet of its modern skyscrapers and condo developments lie heritage buildings and old-time mansions, top-notch museums and numerous green spaces. The two most common species here are businesspeople and students from McGill and Concordia Universities. The city's major shopping district is downtown, as is the performing-arts complex, Place des Arts.

East of downtown you'll find the Quartier Latin, gateway to lively cafés and low-key bars packed with students from the French-speaking Université du Québec à Montréal. Continue west to reach the Village, a major icon for gay travelers. Shops, restaurants and bars proudly fly the rainbow colors here, and the nightlife and café scene rarely slows down.

Further north is the Plateau Mont-Royal, a once-immigrant neighborhood that houses an unbelievable wealth of sidewalk cafés, restaurants, clubs and boutiques. For many Montrealers and visitors alike, exploring the Plateau is what Montréal is all about. The Plateau is handily located next to Montréal's beloved 'Mountain,' Mont-Royal, home to walking and biking trails, a pretty lake and great views over the city.

Just up from the Plateau are Mile End and Outremont, two leafy neighborhoods with upscale boutiques and restaurants; nearby, Little Italy is a slice out of the old world, with classic Italian trattorias and espresso bars, plus neighborhood churches and the sprawling Marché Jean-Talon, the city's best market.

Parc Jean-Drapeau stretches across two leafy islands in the midst of the mighty St Lawrence about 1km east of the Old Port. The prime draws are outdoor activities like cycling and jogging, though you'll also find some noteworthy museums plus lakeside swimming and weekly dance parties in the summer.

Other areas worth exploring include up-and-coming neighborhoods in the Southwest borough like Petite-Bourgogne and St-Henri. The eastern part of the city also has some popular attractions, including Olympic Park, which is home to botanical gardens, a kid-friendly ecosystems museum and the costly stadium that lends the area its name.

lonelyplanet.
Little Italy,
Mile End
& Outremont
(p82)
Plateau
Mont-Royal
(p75)
Quartier Latin
& The Village
(p71)
Downtown
(p60)
Old Montréal
& Chinatown
(p47)
Parc
Jean-Drapeau
(p57)
St Lawrence River
0
1 km
0
0.5 miles

ITINERARY BUILDER

Montréal is a great city in which to put away the map and do a bit of spontaneous exploring. Sometimes, however, you want to make sure you don't miss the iconic attractions, whether it's the city's best smoked-meat sandwich or that tucked-away bistro that everyone's talking about. This chart should help you make the most of your time.

AREA / ACTIVITIES	Sights	Shopping	Eating
Old Montréal & Chinatown	Basilique Notre-Dame (p47) Musée d'Archéologie Pointe-à-Callière (p50) Centre d'Histoire de Montréal (p50)	Yves Laroche Galerie d'Art (p105) Reborn (p105) Marché Bonsecours (p106)	Olive + Gourmando (p123) Garde-Manger (p120) L'Orignal (p120)
Parc Jean-Drapeau	Biosphère (p57) Musée Stewart (p58)		
Downtown	Musée d'Art Contemporain (p60) Musée des Beaux-Arts (p60) Musée McCord (p60)	Les Antiquités Grand Central (p114) Holt Renfrew (p107) Galeries d'Art Contemporain du Belgo (p106)	Toqué! (p120) Joe Beef (p124) Ferreira Café (p124)
Quartier Latin & the Village	Écomusée du Fier Monde (p73) Bibliothèque et Archives Nationale du Québec (p73) Chapelle Notre-Dame-de-Lourdes (p73)	Archambault (p110) Renaud Bray (p110) Priape (p111)	O'Thym (p128) Au Petit Extra (p129) Le Commensal (p129)
Plateau Mont-Royal	Carré St-Louis (p75) Parc du Mont-Royal (p79) Boulevard St-Laurent (p75)	Coffre aux Trésors du Chainon (p112) Preloved (p111) Revenge (p111)	Au Pied de Cochon (p130) L'Express (p132) Schwartz's (p134)
Little Italy, Mile End & Outremont	Marché Jean-Talon (p82) Église St Michel (p82) Église St-Viateur (p85)	Drawn & Quarterly (p113) General 54 (p113) Le Marché des Saveurs (p114)	Milos (p135) Pizzeria Napoletana (p137) Juliette et Chocolat (p137)
Southwest & Outer Montréal	Oratoire St-Joseph (p88) Jardin Botanique (p90) Biodôme (p90)	Les Antiquités Grand Central (p114) Parisian Laundry (p114) Lucie Favreau Antiques (p115)	La Louisiane (p128) Magnan (p128) Chez Nick (p128)

HOW TO USE THIS TABLE

The table below allows you to plan a day's worth of activities in any area of the city. Simply select which area you wish to explore, and then mix and match from the corresponding listings to build your day. The first item in each cell represents a well-known highlight of the area, while the other items are more off-the-beaten-track gems.

Drinking	Clubs & Live Music	Sports & Activities
Café des Éclusiers (p141) **Terrasse 701** (p141)	**Tribe Hyperclub** (p156) **Cherry** (p154)	**AML Cruises** (p172) **Calèche rides** (p168)
	Piknic Électronik (p57)	**Plage des Îles** (p174) **Casino de Montréal** (p158) **Circuit Gilles-Villeneuve** (p169)
Pub Ste-Élisabeth (p143) **Sir Winston Churchill Pub Complexe** (p143) **Brutopia** (p142)	**House of Jazz** (p153) **SAT** (p155) **Tokyo Bar** (p156)	**Atrium Le 1000** (p170) **Istori** (p158) **Montréal Canadiens** (p176)
Le St-Sulpice (p144) **Les Trois Brasseurs** (p144) **Club Date Piano-Bar** (p144)	**Parking Nightclub** (p155) **Mado Cabaret** (p155) **Stereo** (p157)	**Sunday tam-tam concerts** (p80) **Parc du Mont-Royal** (p79)
Reservoir (p147) **Bily Kun** (p145) **Blizzarts** (p145)	**Le Ballatou** (p153) **La Sala Rossa** (p154)	
Chez Serge (p148) **Le Cagibi Café** (p148) **Bu** (p149)	**Baldwin Barmacie** (p154) **Green Room** (p153) **Zoobizarre** (p156)	**Canal de Lachine** (p168) **L'École de Voile de Lachine** (p172) **Uniprix Stadium** (p173)
Burgundy Lion (p149)	**The Wheel** (p157)	

CITY OF MONTRÉAL

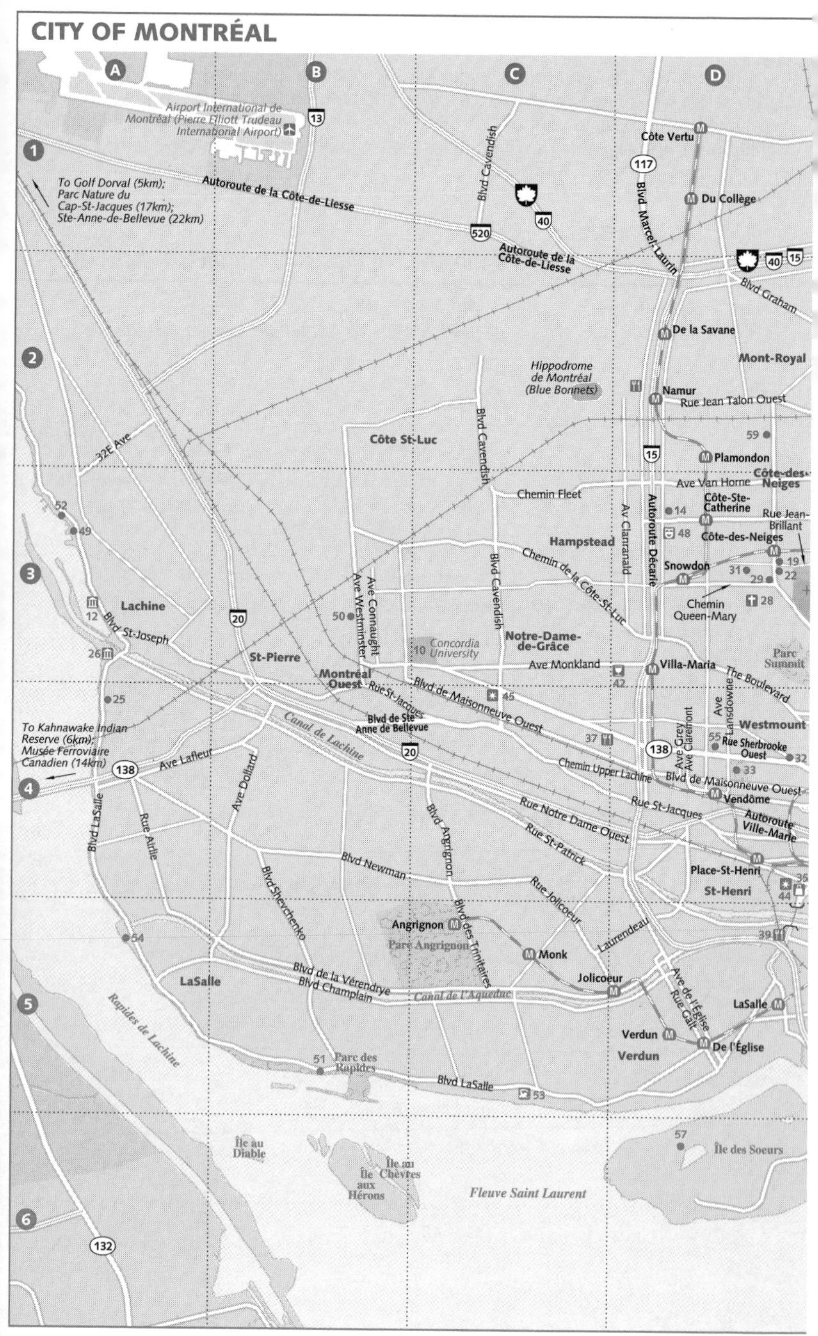

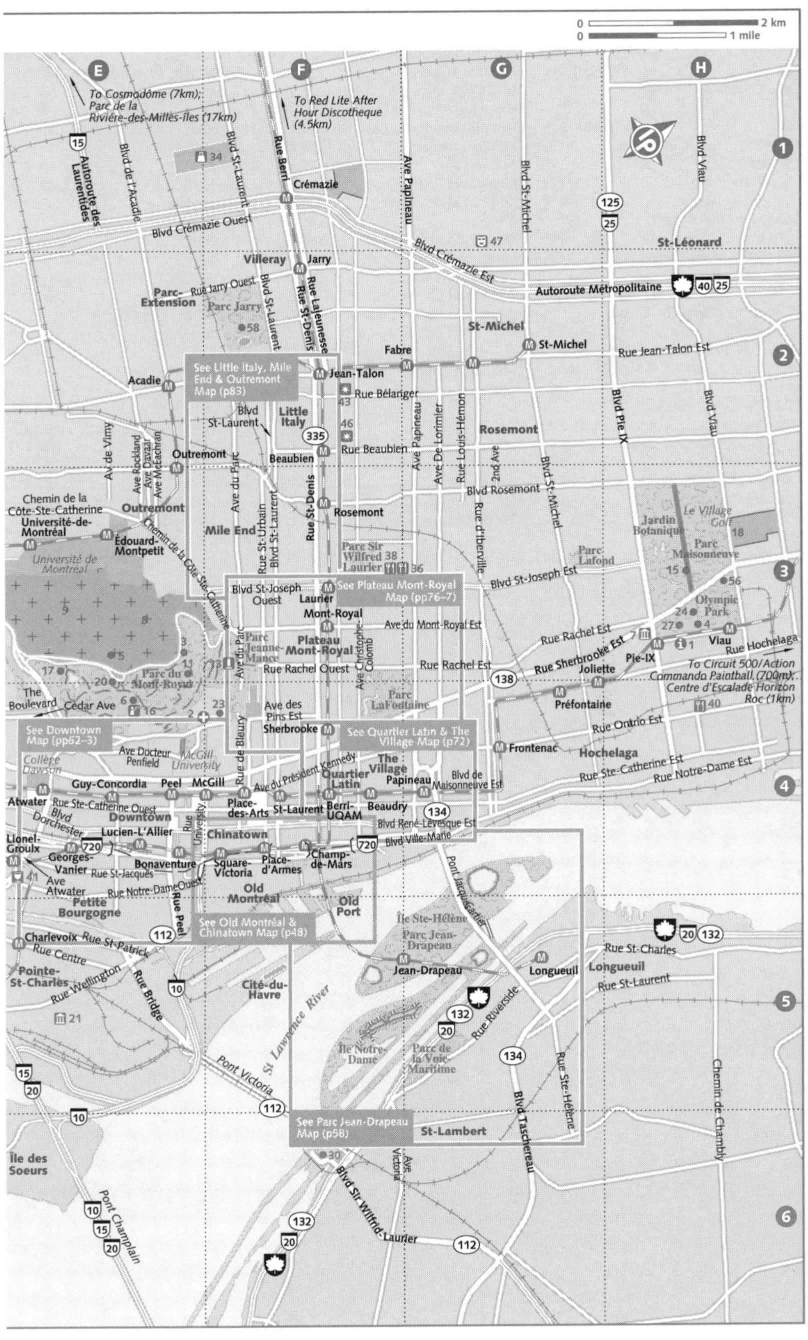

0 2 km
0 1 mile
To Cosmodôme (7km); Parc de la Rivière-des-Milles-Îles (17km)
To Red Lite After Hour Discotheque (4.5km)
Autoroute des Laurentides
Blvd de l'Acadie
Blvd St-Laurent
Rue Berri
Crémazie
Ave Papineau
Blvd St-Michel
Blvd Viau
Blvd Crémazie Ouest
Blvd Crémazie Est
St-Léonard
Villeray
Jarry
Parc-Extension
Rue Jarry Ouest
Parc Jarry
Rue Lajeunesse
Rue St-Denis
Autoroute Métropolitaine
St-Michel
Fabre
Rue Jean-Talon Est
Acadie
See Little Italy, Mile End & Outremont Map (p83)
Jean-Talon
Rue Bélanger
Little Italy
Rosemont
Beaubien
Rue Beaubien
Outremont
Ave De Lorimier
Rue Louis-Hémon
2nd Ave
Blvd Pie-IX
Blvd Rosemont
Chemin de la Côte-Ste-Catherine
Université-de-Montréal
Édouard-Montpetit
Mile End
Ave du Parc
Rue St-Urbain
Rue d'Iberville
Parc Sir Wilfred Laurier
Jardin Botanique
Le Village Golf
Parc Maisonneuve
Parc Lafond
Université de Montréal
Blvd St-Joseph Ouest
Laurier
See Plateau Mont-Royal Map (pp76–7)
Blvd St-Joseph Est
Mont-Royal
Ave du Mont-Royal Est
Olympic Park
Plateau Mont-Royal
Parc Jeanne-Mance
Rue Rachel Ouest
Ave Christophe-Colomb
Rue Rachel Est
Rue Sherbrooke Est
Viau
Rue Hochelaga
Joliette
Pie-IX
To Circuit 500/Action Commando Paintball (700m); Centre d'Escalade Horizon Roc (1km)
Parc du Mont-Royal
The Boulevard
Cedar Ave
Parc LaFontaine
Préfontaine
Ave des Pins Est
Sherbrooke
See Downtown Map (pp62–3)
See Quartier Latin & The Village Map (p72)
Rue Ontario Est
Ave Docteur Penfield
McGill University
Collège Dawson
Rue de Bleury
Ave du Président Kennedy
The Village
Quartier Latin
Frontenac
Hochelaga
Rue Ste-Catherine Est
Rue Notre-Dame Est
Guy-Concordia
Peel
McGill
Papineau
Blvd de Maisonneuve Est
Atwater
Rue Ste-Catherine Ouest
Place-des-Arts
St-Laurent
Berri-UQAM
Beaudry
Blvd Dorchester
Downtown
Rue University
Blvd René-Lévesque Est
Lionel-Groulx
Lucien-L'Allier
Chinatown
Blvd Ville-Marie
Georges-Vanier
Rue St-Jacques
Bonaventure
Square-Victoria
Place-d'Armes
Champ-de-Mars
Pont Jacques-Cartier
Ave Atwater
Rue Notre-Dame Ouest
Old Montréal
Old Port
Petite Bourgogne
Rue Peel
See Old Montréal & Chinatown Map (p48)
Île Ste-Hélène
Parc Jean-Drapeau
Charlevoix
Rue St-Patrick
Rue Centre
Jean-Drapeau
Longueuil
Rue St-Charles
Pointe-St-Charles
Rue Wellington
Rue Bridge
Cité-du-Havre
Rue St-Laurent
St Lawrence River
Rue Riverside
Île Notre-Dame
Parc de la Voie Maritime
Pont Victoria
Rue Ste-Hélène
Blvd Taschereau
Chemin de Chambly
See Parc Jean-Drapeau Map (p58)
St-Lambert
Île des Soeurs
Ave Victoria
Blvd Sir Wilfrid-Laurier
Pont Champlain

CITY OF MONTRÉAL

INFORMATION

Kéroul....1 H3
Royal Victoria Hospital....2 E4

SIGHTS (pp86–93)

Belvédère Camillien-Houde....3 E3
Biodôme....4 H3
Cemetery Office....5 E3
Centre Aquatique....(see 27)
Chalet du Mont-Royal....6 E4
Château Dufresne....7 H3
Cimetière Mont-Royal....8 E3
Cimetière Notre-Dame-des-Neiges....9 E3
Concordia University, Loyola Campus....10 C3
Croix du Mont-Royal....11 E3
Fur Trade in Lachine National Historic Site....12 A3
George Étienne Cartier Monument....13 F3
Holocaust Memorial Centre....14 D3
Insectarium....15 H3
Kondiaronk Lookout....16 E4
Lac des Castors Pavillion....17 E3
Le Village Golf....18 H3
Librairie Olivieri....19 D3
Maison Smith....20 E3
Maison St-Gabriel....21 E5
Marché Côtes-des-Neiges....22 D3
Molson Stadium....23 F4
Montréal Tower....24 H3
Moulin Fleming....25 A4
Musée de Lachine....26 A3
Olympic Stadium....27 H3
Oratoire St-Joseph....28 D3
Pharmaprix....29 D3
St Lawrence Seaway Observation Tower....30 F6
TOHU....(see 47)
Tourist Hall....(see 27)
Université de Montréal Adult Education Department....31 D3
Westmount City Hall....32 D4
Westmount Park & Library....33 D4

SHOPPING (pp114–15)

Chabanel Warehouses....34 E1
Surface Jalouse....35 D4

EATING (p128)

Byblos....36 G3
La Louisiane....37 C4
Le Fromentier....38 F3
Magnan....39 D5
Marché de Maisonneuve....40 H4

DRINKING (p149)

Burgundy Lion....41 E4
Typhoon Lounge....42 D3

NIGHTLIFE (pp151–8)

DoReMi....43 F2
La Va-Et-Vient....44 D4
The Wheel....45 C4
Zoobizarre....46 F2

THE ARTS (pp159–66)

Cirque du Soleil....47 G1
Olympic Stadium....(see 27)
Saidye Bronfman Centre....48 D3

SPORTS & ACTIVITIES (pp167–77)

Centre Aquatique....(see 27)
Club de Canoë de Course de Lachine....49 A3
Diz....50 B3
Kayak Sans Frontiéres....51 B5
L'École de Voile de Lachine....52 A3
Natatorium....53 C5
Olympic Stadium....(see 27)
Rafting Montréal....54 A5
Running Room....55 D4
Saputo Stadium....56 H3
Strøm Nordic Spa....57 D6
Uniprix Stadium....58 F2

TRANSPORT (pp251–5)

Rent-A-Wreck....59 D2

OLD MONTRÉAL & CHINATOWN

Drinking p141; Eating p120; Shopping p104; Sleeping p180

Most visitors to the city begin their trips in Vieux-Montréal (Old Montréal), drawn by its imposing churches, photogenic streets and fascinating museums relating the early days of French and British settlement in Canada. Ville-Marie, the settlement that was to become Montréal, has gone through numerous incarnations, from hub of the fur trade to financial giant of Canada to kitschy tourist trap. In more recent days, it's become a trendy destination in its own right, with a crop of boutique hotels, award-winning restaurants and converted lofts attracting a younger, savvier crowd than in decades past.

Grand architecture lurks around every corner in Old Montréal, including the city's iconic Basilique Notre-Dame, the photogenic Hôtel de Ville and the silver-domed Marché Bonsecours, among many other buildings. All played a role in the history of this grand neighborhood. There are several excellent museums tucked away in the backstreets, as well as plenty of lowbrow fare to be had, starting on Pl Jacques-Cartier, a magnet for spray-painted performance artists and Top 40–singing guitar players.

The main thoroughfare crossing the neighborhood is old, narrow Rue St-Paul, which is lined with art galleries, plush boutiques and eateries; bigger, busier Rue Notre-Dame runs parallel and to the north. The Old Port lies just downhill from the cobblestones. Here you'll find grassy open expanses, a grand science museum and a smattering of cafés (with many more along nearby Rue de la Commune). In summer numerous tourist cruises sail in and out all day, and the Promenade du Vieux-Port gathers strollers and waterfront lovers of all stripes. For boat rides and outdoor adventure (biking, running, in-line skating along the Canal de Lachine), this is a good place to start. There's also *calèche* (carriage) rides around Old Montréal, and ice-skating near the waterfront come wintertime. For loads of info on the area, stop in the ever-popular Old Montréal tourist office at the end of Pl Jacques-Cartier (on Rue Notre-Dame).

Despite its diminutive size, Montréal's Chinatown percolates with energy. Just a few blocks north of Old Montréal, you'll find bustling eateries attracting diners from all parts of the globe, incense-filled shops, curio stalls and Taiwanese bubble-tea parlors. Entry to the district is through one of two gold-leaf ceremonial gates – one on Blvd St-Laurent and the other at Rue Viger – both gifts from the city of Shanghai. The main attraction here is the plethora of atmospheric restaurants serving Cantonese, Szechuan and Vietnamese delicacies. Blvd St-Laurent and pedestrian-only Rue de la Gauchetiére are good starting points on the culinary journey.

Like most neighborhoods in Montréal, it's easy to get around on foot. To reach the area, take the metro to Square-Victoria, Place-d'Armes or Champ-de-Mars. Bus 14 runs along Rue Notre-Dame in Old Montréal between Rue Berri and Blvd St-Laurent; bus 55 stops on Blvd St-Laurent. Place-d'Armes is the most convenient station for going to Chinatown.

BASILIQUE NOTRE-DAME Map p48

☎ 514-842-2925; 110 Rue Notre-Dame Ouest; adult/child $5/4; 🕑 7am-4:30pm Mon-Sat, 8am-4pm Sun, extended hrs in summer; Ⓜ Place-d'Armes

The grand dame of Montréal's ecclesiastical treasures, this basilica is a must-see when exploring the city. The looming neo-Gothic church can hold up to 3000 worshippers and houses a collection of finely crafted artworks, including an elaborately carved altarpiece, vibrant stained-glass windows and an intricate pulpit.

The Sulpicians had an ever-growing congregation and no one in the soon-to-be Canadian colonies schooled in neo-Gothic architecture. So they commissioned James O'Donnell, a New York architect and Irish Protestant, to design what would be the largest church north of Mexico. Such was O'Donnell's dedication to the project that he converted to Catholicism so he could have his funeral in the basilica. Today, he's buried in the basement under the gift shop.

Opened in 1829, the basilica has a spectacular interior with a forest of ornate wood pillars and carvings made entirely by hand (and constructed without the aid of a single nail). Gilt stars shine from the ceiling vaults and the altar is backlit in evening-sky blues. The massive Casavant organ with 5772 pipes provides the powerful anthem at the famous Christmas concerts; the church bell, the Gros Bourdon, is the largest on the continent. The stained-glass windows, which depict scenes from Montréal's

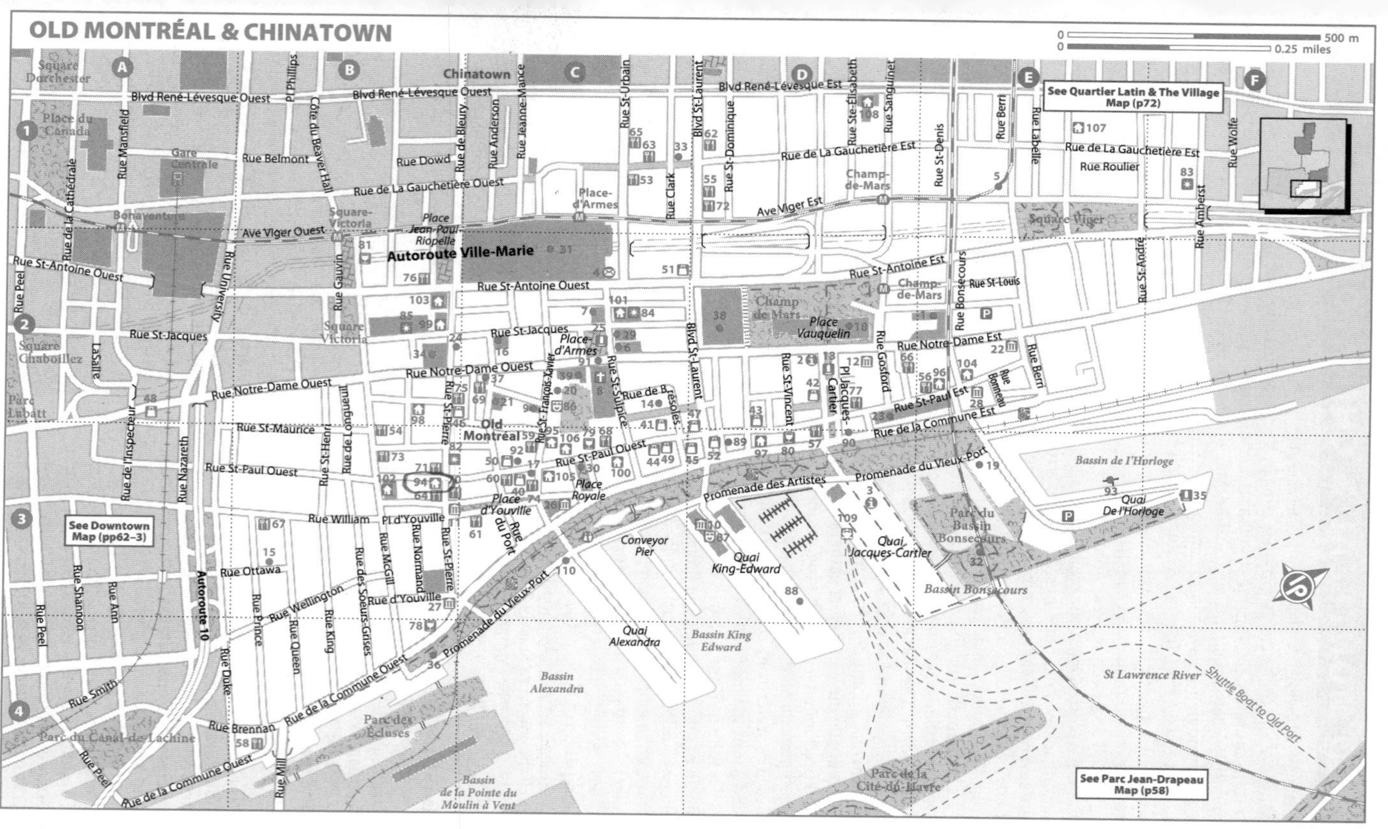
OLD MONTRÉAL & CHINATOWN
0 500 m
0 0.25 miles
See Quartier Latin & The Village Map (p72)
See Downtown Map (pp62–3)
See Parc Jean-Drapeau Map (p58)
Chinatown
Old Montréal
Autoroute Ville-Marie
Autoroute 10
Blvd René-Lévesque Ouest
Blvd René-Lévesque Est
Rue de La Gauchetière Ouest
Rue de La Gauchetière Est
Ave Viger Ouest
Ave Viger Est
Rue St-Antoine Ouest
Rue St-Antoine Est
Rue St-Jacques
Rue Notre-Dame Ouest
Rue Notre-Dame Est
Rue St-Paul Ouest
Rue St-Paul Est
Rue de la Commune Ouest
Rue de la Commune Est
Promenade du Vieux-Port
Promenade des Artistes
Rue St-Maurice
Rue William
Pl d'Youville
Rue d'Youville
Rue Wellington
Rue Ottawa
Rue Brennan
Rue Smith
Rue Peel
Rue de la Cathédrale
Rue Mansfield
Rue University
Rue Belmont
Côte du Beaver Hall
Pl Phillips
Rue Gauvin
Rue Dowd
Rue de Bleury
Rue Anderson
Rue Jeanne-Mance
Rue St-Urbain
Rue Clark
Blvd St-Laurent
Rue St-Dominique
Rue Ste-Élisabeth
Rue Sanguinet
Rue St-Denis
Rue Berri
Rue Labelle
Rue Roulier
Rue Wolfe
Rue Amherst
Rue St-André
Rue Bonsecours
Rue St-Louis
Rue Gosford
Rue Bonneau
Pl Jacques-Cartier
Rue St-Vincent
Rue de Brésoles
Rue St-Sulpice
Rue St-François-Xavier
Rue St-Pierre
Rue de Longueuil
Rue St-Henri
Rue de l'Inspecteur
Rue Nazareth
Rue Duke
Rue Prince
Rue Queen
Rue King
Rue des Soeurs-Grises
Rue McGill
Rue Normand
Rue du Port
Rue Mill
Rue Shannon
Rue Ann
LaSalle
Square Dorchester
Place du Canada
Gare Centrale
Bonaventure
Square-Victoria
Square Victoria
Place Jean-Paul-Riopelle
Place-d'Armes
Place d'Armes
Champ-de-Mars
Champ de Mars
Place Vauquelin
Place Royale
Place d'Youville
Square Viger
Square Chaboillez
Parc Labatt
Parc du Canal-de-Lachine
Parc des Écluses
Parc du Bassin Bonsecours
Parc de la Cité-du-Havre
Bassin de la Pointe du Moulin à Vent
Bassin Alexandra
Quai Alexandra
Bassin King Edward
Quai King-Edward
Conveyor Pier
Quai Jacques-Cartier
Bassin Bonsecours
Bassin de l'Horloge
Quai De l'Horloge
St Lawrence River
Shuttle Boat to Old Port

OLD MONTRÉAL & CHINATOWN

INFORMATION

Académie Culinaire du Québec ... 1 E2
Old Montréal Tourist Office ... 2 D2
Old Port Tourist Kiosk ... 3 D3
Station Placed'Armes Post Office ... 4 C2
Union Français ... 5 E1

SIGHTS (pp47–56)

Aldred Building ... 6 C2
Bank of Montréal ... 7 C2
Basilique Notre-Dame ... 8 C2
Canadian Pacific Telegraph Chambers ... 9 C2
Centre des Sciences de Montréal ... 10 D3
Centre d'Histoire de Montréal ... 11 B3
Chapelle du Sacré Coeur ... (see 8)
Chapelle Notre-Dame-de-Bonsecours ... (see 28)
Château Ramezay ... 12 D2
Colonne Nelson ... 13 D2
Cours le Royer ... 14 C2
Fonderie Darling ... 15 B3
Guardian Insurance Building ... 16 C2
Guidatour ... 17 C3
Hôtel de Ville ... 18 D2
Labyrinth ... 19 E3
Les Fantômes du Vieux-Montréal ... 20 C2
Lewis Building ... 21 C2
Lieu Historique de Sir George- Étienne-Cartier ... 22 E2
Marché Bonsecours ... 23 D2
Molson Bank Building ... 24 B2
Money Museum ... (see 7)
Montréal Stock Exchange Building ... (see 86)
Monument Maisonneuve ... 25 C2
Musée d'Archéologie Pointe-à-Callière ... 26 C3
Musée des Soeurs Grises ... 27 B3
Musée Marguerite-Bourgeoys ... 28 E2
New York Life Insurance Building ... 29 C2
Old Customs House ... 30 C3
Palais des Congrès ... 31 C2
Parc du Bassin Bonsecours ... (see 32)
Pavillon du Bassin Bonsecours ... 32 E3
Place Sun Yat Sen ... 33 C1
Royal Bank Building ... 34 B2
Sailors' Memorial Clock Tower ... 35 F3
Silo Phone ... 36 B4
Sun Life Annex & Old Sun Life Building ... 37 C2
Three Courthouses ... 38 D2
Vieux Séminaire de St-Sulpice ... 39 C2

SHOPPING (pp104–6)

Betty's Bazaar ... (see 50)
Diffusion Griff '3000 ... (see 23)
Fourrures Dubarry ... 40 C3
Galerie 2000 ... 41 C2
Galerie Le Chariot ... 42 D2
Galerie Orange ... 43 D2
Galerie Pangée ... 44 C3
Galerie St-Dizier ... 45 D3
Kamkyl ... 46 B2
La Guilde Graphique ... 47 D2
Le Baron ... 48 A2
Librissime ... 49 C3
Marché Bonsecours ... (see 23)
Reborn ... 50 C3
Simon's Camera ... 51 C2
Yves Laroche Galerie D'art ... 52 D3

EATING (pp120–4)

Beijing ... 53 C1
Boris Bistro ... 54 B3
Cali ... 55 D1
Chez L'Épicier ... 56 E2
Chez Queux ... 57 D3
Cluny Artbar ... (see 15)
Da Emma ... 58 B4
Garde-Manger ... 59 C3
Ghandi ... 60 C3
Gibby's ... 61 C3
Hoang Oanh ... 62 D1
Jardin de Jade ... 63 C1
La Gargote ... 64 B3
La Maison Kam Fung ... 65 C1
Le Club Chasse et Pêche ... 66 D2
Le Local ... 67 B3
Le Petit Moulinsart ... 68 C3
L'Orignal ... 69 C2
Marché de la Villette ... 70 B3
Olive + Gourmando ... 71 B3
Phô Bang New York ... 72 D1
Restaurant Holder ... 73 B3
Scola Pasta ... (see 37)
Stash Café ... 74 C3
Titanic ... 75 B2
Toqué! ... 76 B2
Usine de Spaghetti Parisienne ... 77 D2

DRINKING (p141)

Café les Éclusiers ... 78 B4
Cluny Artbar ... (see 15)
Garde-Manger ... (see 59)
Le Pharaon Lounge ... 79 C3
L'Orignal ... (see 69)
Pub St-Paul ... 80 D3
Terrasse 701 ... (see 101)
Vauvert ... (see 102)
Wunderbar ... 81 B2

NIGHTLIFE (pp151–8)

Cherry ... 82 B3
Club Bolo ... 83 F1
Suite 701 ... 84 C2
Tribe Hyperclub ... 85 B2

THE ARTS (pp159–66)

Centaur Theatre ... 86 C2
Cinéma IMAX du Centre des Sciences de Montréal ... 87 D3

SPORTS & ACTIVITIES (pp167–77)

AML Cruises ... 88 D3
Ça Roule Montréal ... 89 D3
Calèche Rides ... 90 D3
Calèche Rides ... 91 C2
Centre Luna Yoga ... 92 C3
Le Bateau Mouche ... (see 109)
Le Petit Navire ... (see 109)
Saute Moutons ... 93 E3

SLEEPING (pp180–3)

Auberge Alternative ... 94 B3
Auberge Bonaparte Inn & Restaurant ... 95 C3
Auberge Bonsecours ... 96 E2
Auberge du Vieux-Port ... 97 D3
Hôtel Gault ... 98 B2
Hôtel Le St-James ... 99 B2
Hôtel Nelligan ... 100 C3
Hôtel Place-d'Armes ... 101 C2
Hôtel St-Paul ... 102 B3
InterContinental Montréal ... 103 B2
La Maison Pierre du Calvet ... 104 E2
Le Petit Hôtel ... 105 C3
Les Passants du Sans Soucy B&B ... 106 C3
Maison Brunet ... 107 E1
UQAM Residences ... 108 D1

TRANSPORT (pp251–5)

Ça Roule Montréal ... (see 89)
Navettes Maritimes ... 109 D3
Zap World Scooters ... 110 C3

history rather than the usual biblical stories, were the brainchild of the Sulpicians who wanted to teach the mostly illiterate French Canadians about the founding of the colony.

The **Chapelle du Sacré Coeur** (Sacred Heart Chapel), located behind the main hall, is nicknamed the Wedding Chapel. It's so popular that couples might have to wait two years to tie the knot here. The curious mix of styles emerged after a 1978 fire, when the chapel was rebuilt with a brass altar with abstract-modern motifs.

An evening **sound and light display** (adult/child $10/5; 6:30pm Tue-Thu, 6:30pm & 8:30pm Fri, 7pm & 8:30pm Sat) uses cutting-edge technology to tell the story of the church and the city.

MUSÉE D'ARCHÉOLOGIE POINTE-À-CALLIÈRE Map p48

☎ 514-872-9150; www.pacmuseum.qc.ca; 350 Pl Royale; adult/child $14/6; 🕑 10am-6pm Mon-Fri, 11am-6pm Sat & Sun late Jun–early Sep, 10am-5pm Tue-Fri, 11am-5pm Sat & Sun rest of year; Ⓜ Place-d'Armes

Built on the spot where European settlers set up their first camp, the Pointe-à-Callière Museum of Archaeology and History provides a good overview of Montréal's beginnings. Visitors should start with *Montreal, Tales of a City,* a 20-minute multimedia show that takes visitors back through the centuries.

For the most part the museum is underground. Head to the archaeological crypt in the basement where you can explore the remains of the city's ancient sewage and river system and the foundations of its first buildings and first public square. Interactive exhibits allow visitors to hear what life was like in the 17th and 18th centuries from characters on video screens.

The lookout at the top of the tower provides an excellent view of the Old Port.

CENTRE D'HISTOIRE DE MONTRÉAL Map p48

☎ 514-872-3207; 335 Pl d'Youville; adult/child $6/4; 🕑 10am-5pm Tue-Sun; Ⓜ Square-Victoria

Housed in a handsome old fire hall on Pl d'Youville, the Montréal History Center has 300-plus artifacts that illustrate the city's eventful past with the aid of models and videos. You can listen to the tales of real people while sitting in a period kitchen, or travel back in time while watching archival footage from the '40s and '60s. For sweeping views, head to the rooftop.

CHÂTEAU RAMEZAY Map p48

☎ 514-861-3708; www.chateauramezay.qc.ca; 280 Rue Notre-Dame Est; adult/child $9/4.50; 🕑 10am-6pm Jun 1–Thanksgiving, 10am-4:30pm Tue-Sun rest of year; Ⓜ Champ-de-Mars

A home of French governors in the early 18th century, this mansion is one of the finest examples from the ancien régime. It was built for the 11th governor, Claude de Ramezay, and includes 15 interconnecting rooms with a ballroom of mirrors and mahogany galore. Ramezay went broke trying to maintain it. American generals used it as a headquarters during the revolution, and Benjamin Franklin stayed here attempting (and failing) to convince the Canadians to join the cause. In 1903 turrets were added to give the 'château' its fanciful French look.

The building is a repository of Québec history with a collection of 20,000 objects, including valuable Canadian art and furniture. The Governor's Garden in the rear recreates a horticultural garden from the 18th century, including many original varieties of fruit trees and vegetables.

top picks

OLD MONTRÉAL

- Basilique Notre-Dame (p47) Magnificent carvings, kooky lighting.
- Marché Bonsecours (p52) Wander the shops in this historic building.
- Château Ramezay (left) Opulent mansion that ruined a doting governor.
- Musée d'Archéologie Pointe-à-Callière (left) Plunge into the depths (literally) of Montréal's earliest days.
- Old Port (p55) Performers, picnics and paddleboats in summer; ice-skating in winter.

FONDERIE DARLING Map p48

☎ 514-392-1554; www.fonderiedarling.org; 745 Rue Ottawa; 🕑 noon-7pm Wed & Fri-Sun, until 10pm Thu; admission $3, free on Thu; Ⓜ Square-Victoria

Tucked away in a little-visited corner of Old Montréal, the Darling Foundry hosts avant-garde, often large-scale exhibitions in its two sizable showrooms. The brick industrial building, which dates back to the early 1900s, once housed a prosperous iron foundry and is today home to the gallery and live-work studios for artists. The space also houses the Cluny Artbar (p122; entrance around the corner on Rue Prince), a fine spot for coffee, desserts or light lunch fare. In the summertime, the foundry hosts occasional Thursday-night street parties (when admission is free). Check the website for upcoming exhibitions.

CHAPELLE NOTRE-DAME-DE-BONSECOURS Map p48

☎ 514-282-8670; www.marguerite-bourgeoys.com; 400 Rue St-Paul Est; chapel free, museum

THE NEW FACE OF OLD MONTRÉAL

An interview with Dimitri Antonopoulos, president of the Société de Développement Commercial for Old Montréal, and one of the leaders in the movement to revitalize Old Montréal.

Where do you live? In Old Montréal. I walk to work. That's one of the great things about Montréal, you don't need a car. You can walk everywhere.
What makes Montréal different from other cities? It's these dual cultures – French and English – but also the new immigrants, who have contributed so much culturally in the last 100 years.
How has Old Montréal changed since you were a kid? The streets used to be empty; no one lived down here. Slowly, it started becoming a destination – first for tourists in the summer, but now it's becoming a year-round destination. And some 5000 to 6000 people live in the neighborhood.
What are your hopes for the future of Old Montréal? I'd like to see more people moving here to live and work, and to see more neighborhood life. The Old Port will play a role: this is federally controlled land looking to modernize, and it will be an integral part of the city.
What are the things you most like about the city? Montréal has many charms. It has great restaurants – at all prices. There are lots of different types of cuisine, which has everything to do with its immigrant history. And the city is very creative. At Hôtel Nelligan (p182), we're working with a number of prominent artists who are painting interpretations of Nelligan's poems.
Where are you favorite places to go out in the city? In Old Montréal my favorite spots are Suite 701 (p156), L'Orignal (p120) and Garde-Manger (p120); I also like going out around Ave du Parc and Ave du Mont-Royal heading east – lots of cool bars and cafés, and some excellent brunch places.

adult/child $8/5; 10am-5:30pm Tue-Sun May-Oct, 11am-3:30pm Tue-Sun Nov–mid-Jan & Mar-Apr; M Champ-de-Mars
Known as the Sailors' Church, this enchanting chapel derives its name from the sailors who left behind votive lamps in the shapes of ships in thanksgiving for safe passage. The restored interior has stained-glass windows and paintings depicting key moments in the life of the Virgin Mary (for whom Montréal – aka Ville-Marie – was originally named).

The attached Musée Marguerite-Bourgeoys relates the story of Montréal's first teacher and the founder of the Congregation of Notre-Dame order of nuns. The crypt has artifacts dating back 2000 years and foundations of the original chapel from 1773. The observation tower offers grand views of the Old Port.

HÔTEL DE VILLE Map p48

☎ 514-872-3355; 275 Rue Notre-Dame Est; 8am-5pm Mon-Fri, free tours 10am-4pm late Jun–mid-Aug; M Champ-de-Mars
Montréal's handsome City Hall was built between 1872 and 1878. Far from being a humdrum administrative center, it's actually steeped in local lore. Most famously, it's where French leader Charles de Gaulle took to the balcony in 1967 and yelled to the crowds outside *'Vive le Québec libre!'* ('Long live a free Québec!') Those four words fueled the fires of Québécois separatism and strained relations with Ottawa for years.

Peer into the Great Hall of Honor for some scenes of rural Québec and busts of Jacques Viger, the first French-speaking mayor (1833–36), and Peter McGill, the first English-speaking mayor (1840–42).

LIEU HISTORIQUE DE SIR GEORGE-ÉTIENNE-CARTIER Map p48

☎ 514-283-2282; www.parkscanada.gc.ca/cartier; 458 Rue Notre-Dame Est; adult/child $4/2; 10am-5:30pm late Jun–Aug, 10am-noon & 1-5pm Sep-Dec & May–late Jun
The Sir George-Étienne Cartier National Historic Site consists of two historic houses owned by the Cartier family. Exhibitions in the first detail the life of Sir George-Étienne Cartier, one of the founders of the Canadian Confederation, and illustrate the changes that society saw in his lifetime. The other house is a faithful reconstruction of his home during the Victorian era. Staff in period costume run guided tours throughout the day and hold dramatic presentations on etiquette and a servant's life. In season the program includes a Victorian Christmas.

MARCHÉ BONSECOURS Map p48

☎ 514-872-7730; 350 Rue St-Paul Est; 10am-6pm Jan-Mar, 10am-6pm Sat-Wed & 10am-9pm Thu & Fri Apr-Jun & Labour Day–Dec, 10am-9pm Mon-Sat & 10am-6pm Sun Jul–Labour Day; Ⓜ Champ-de-Mars

Opened in 1847, this sprawling neoclassical building has been everything from a farmers' market to a concert theater, and even served briefly as Montréal's city hall (1852–78). It's also where the government of United Canada retreated, in order to continue the legislative session after the parliament buildings nearby were burned down by an angry anglo mob in 1849.

Today's *marché* plays a somewhat less heroic role. The restored building reopened in 1992 as a gallery for shops selling arts and crafts, leather goods and garments. Restaurants line the facade on Rue St-Paul.

COURS LE ROYER Map p48

Ⓜ Place-d'Armes

Montréal's first hospital was founded on this narrow lane by Jeanne Mance in 1644. Later on, a huge commercial complex was built here, leaving several beautiful 19th-century warehouses behind. The buildings caught the eyes of developers in the 1970s and were converted into apartments and offices. Today, the buildings line this quiet pedestrian mall pocked with lush greenery.

MUSÉE DES SOEURS GRISES Map p48

☎ 514-842-9411; 138 Rue St-Pierre; admission free; appointment only; Ⓜ Square-Victoria

Dedicated to Ste Marguerite d'Youville, founder of the community of the Sisters of Charity, better known as the Grey Nuns, this museum has a small but wonderfully presented set of exhibits. The sisters set out by canoe and founded a mission in what was to become Manitoba in western Canada in 1850. Folk legend has it that the nuns sold moonshine to the Aboriginals, getting them *gris* (grey) or tipsy. Tours of the museum in French and English are available by appointment only.

PLACE-D'ARMES Map p48

Ⓜ Place-d'Armes

This square is framed by some of the finest buildings in Old Montréal, including its oldest bank, first skyscraper and Basilique Notre-Dame (p47). The square's name references the bloody battles that took place here as religious settlers and First Nations tribes thrashed out control of what would become Montréal. At its center stands the Monument Maisonneuve (Map p48), dedicated to city founder Paul de Chomedey, *sieur* de Maisonneuve.

The red sandstone building on the east side of the square is the New York Life Insurance Building (Map p48), Montréal's first skyscraper (1888). It's said to be built with the blocks used for ballast on ships bringing goods to Montréal. Next door, the Aldred Building (Map p48) is made of limestone and was designed to emulate the Empire State Building. Completed in 1931, it has an opulent, L-shaped, art-deco lobby. On the north side of the square, the Bank of Montréal (p54) was Canada's first permanent bank.

top picks

FOR CHILDREN

- Biodôme (p90) A giant indoor zoo with forest, river and marine habitats.
- Biosphère (p57) Make a dam and walk on water at this hands-on multimedia museum in Parc Jean-Drapeau.
- Centre des Sciences de Montréal (p56) Technological wonders, unusual games and an IMAX cinema.
- Labyrinth (p56) Amazing maze with obstacles, traps and play zones.
- La Ronde Amusement Park (p57) Chills and thrills galore – plus fireworks some nights – at Québec's largest amusement park.
- Montréal Planetarium (p64) Quarks, black holes and celestial shows.
- Musée Ferroviaire Canadien (p92) Stationary, moving, new, old...trains of every type that thrill adults as much as children.
- Musée Stewart (p58) Oversized cannons, military parades and guides in period costumes inside an old British garrison.
- Old Port (p55) Hop into a paddleboat, go jet boating on the St Lawrence or tootle along in a minitrain for a grand tour.
- Parc Nature du Cap-St-Jacques (p93) Verdant park with trails, a beach, a sugar shack and a working farm.

PLACE JACQUES-CARTIER Map p48

Ⓜ Champ-de-Mars

The liveliest spot in Old Montréal, this gently inclined square hums with performance artists, street musicians and the animated chatter from terrace restaurants linings its borders. A public market was set up here after a château burned down in 1803. At its top end stands the Colonne Nelson, a monument erected to Admiral Nelson after his defeat of Napoleon's fleet at Trafalgar. The great likeness is now a fiberglass replica.

Nelson's presence is a thorn in the side of many French Quebecers, and there have been many attempts to have it removed (the last was by mayor Pierre Bourque in 1998). Francophones later installed a statue of an obscure French admiral, Jean Vauquelin, in the nearby Place Vauquelin, just west of Hôtel de Ville on Rue Notre-Dame.

PLACE ROYALE Map p48

M Place-d'Armes

This little square in the west of Old Montréal marks the spot where the first fort, Ville-Marie, was erected. Defense was a key consideration due to lengthy fighting with the native Iroquois. In the 17th and 18th centuries this was a marketplace; it's now the paved forecourt of the 1836 Old Customs House (Vieille Douane; Map p48) and linked to the Musée d'Archéologie Pointe-à-Callière (p50) via an underground passage. The neoclassical building looks much the same today as when it was built, but now serves as the museum's gift shop.

RUE DE L'HÔPITAL & AROUND Map p48

M Place-d'Armes

Named for a hospice set up by nuns in the 17th century, the Rue de l'Hôpital and adjoining streets are full of architectural quirks and highlights. On the corner of Rue St-François-Xavier, the Canadian Pacific Telegraph Chambers (Map p48) was the 19th-century equivalent of a national internet provider. It houses condominiums today but the wild-eyed keystone over the entrance remains. The Lewis Building (Map p48) was built as the head office of the Cunard Shipping Lines. One mischievous character on the facade is holding a bag full of loot; a more scholarly colleague is taking notes.

The Sun Life Annex & Old Sun Life Building (Map p48) is an ornate 1920s structure covered in beautiful granite with stately columns on the upper floors. In WWII the British crown jewels were moved here for safekeeping as well as the gold reserves of several European countries. The building is equipped with one of the Montréal's few carillons, which you can hear being played daily at noon.

The Centaur Theatre (p164) performs English-language plays in the old Montréal Stock Exchange Building (Map p48). Opened in 1903, the huge columns recall imperial Rome while the interior has sumptuous marble and wood paneling. The building backs onto the Secret Garden of the Sulpicians'

MONTRÉAL'S LITERARY STAR

Émile Nelligan (1879–1941) is one of Québec's literary icons, a star like Oscar Wilde or Lord Byron whose mix of talent and tragedy keeps them in the public consciousness long after their era is over. A poetic genius, Nelligan created most of his famous works by the age of 20 before being committed and spending the rest of his life in mental institutions.

Born in Montréal of an Irish father and a Québécois mother, his bohemian traits were in evidence from the time he was a teenager. He sailed in and out of school to the dismay of his parents and seemed interested in little other than romantic poetry. After submitting two samples of his work, he was accepted by the l'École Littéraire de Montréal (Literary School of Montréal); public readings followed and his poems exploring love and loneliness were regularly published in French-language magazines around Montréal. Nelligan had always marched to a different drum but by 1899 it was apparent his problems were more than just those of a temperamental artist and there was something seriously wrong.

His father had him committed to a mental institution that year. Though he tried briefly to rejoin society in 1925, he was back in care within days. What was wrong with him? Historians who've examined his hospital records believe he may have suffered from schizophrenia.

Though there has been both a movie and play about Nelligan's life, and he was immortalized in a painting by master Québec artist Jean-Paul Lemieux, there is no museum devoted to his work or life. Hunting his ghost around town is the best you'll be able to do. The Château Ramezay (p50) is where l'École Littéraire de Montréal used to meet and where Nelligan's poems were first read in public. Nelligan lived in a house on the west side of Carré St-Louis (p75). The square is also the setting for the famous Lemieux painting. Further along, St Patrick's Basilica (p67) is where Nelligan was baptized; there's a plaque at the back commemorating this event, along with a plaque devoted to Montréal's other famous Irishman, D'Arcy McGee.

seminary, but forget about visiting – the Sulpicians are a secretive bunch.

RUE ST-JACQUES Map p48

M Place-d'Armes

Known as the Wall Street of Canada into the 1930s, Rue St-Jacques was lined with the head offices of insurance companies and banks that proclaimed Montréal's prosperity for the best part of a century. In those days it was known as St James Street.

Some great edifices are veritable temples to capitalism. The 1902 Guardian Insurance Building (Map p48) has helmeted women guarding the entrance while lions and mermaids watch over on the 2nd floor. The beer-brewing dynasty had its own bank, but the Molson Bank Building (Map p48) looks more like a royal residence; heads of founder William and his two sons grace the doorway.

The most glamorous of the lot is the Royal Bank Building (Map p48), the city's tallest building (22 stories) when it was built in 1928. Pass under the royal coat of arms into a banking hall that resembles a Florentine palace; the coffered ceilings are of Wedgwood and the walls display insignias of eight provinces, Montréal (St George's Cross) and Halifax (a yellow bird).

RUE ST-PAUL Map p48

This narrow cobblestone street, the oldest in Montréal, was once a dirt road packed tight by horses laden with goods bound for the Old Port. Today it's a shopping street with galleries, boutiques and restaurants, touristy in spots but undeniably picturesque and enjoyable to wander.

BANK OF MONTRÉAL Map p48

☎ 514-877-7373; 119 Rue St-Jacques; 9am-5pm Mon-Fri; M Place-d'Armes

Modeled after the Pantheon in Rome, the grand colonnaded edifice of Canada's oldest chartered bank, built in 1847, dominates the north side of Place-d'Armes (p52) and is still a working bank. The imposing interior has 32 marble columns and a coffered 20m ceiling in Italian Renaissance style over a long row of tellers behind glass partitions. The helmeted marble lady is Patria, representing a minor Roman god of patriotism to honor the war dead. A snoozy money museum inside the bank has a replica of a cashier's window, old banknotes and an account of early banking in Canada.

THREE COURTHOUSES Map p48

M Place-d'Armes

Along the north side of Rue Notre-Dame Est near Pl Jacques-Cartier, three courthouses stand bunched together. The most fetching is the neoclassical Vieux Palais de Justice, Montréal's old justice palace and oldest courthouse (1856) that's now an annex of the Hôtel de Ville. It's a popular backdrop for wedding photos. The Édifice Ernest Cormier from the 1920s was used for criminal trials before being turned into a conservatory and later a court of appeal. The ugly stepsister is the oversized Palais de Justice, built in 1971 when concrete and smoked glass were all the rage.

VIEUX SÉMINAIRE DE ST-SULPICE Map p48

116 Rue Notre-Dame Ouest; M Place-d'Armes

The Catholic order of Sulpicians was given title to the entire Island of Montréal in 1663. The order built the seminary in 1684 and the 3rd-floor apartments of the old seminary have been occupied ever since. The clock on the facade was a gift from French king Louis XIV in 1701; it is believed to be the oldest working clock in North America. Ancient oaks shade the rear garden laid out in 1715. The seminary and grounds are closed to the public.

PLACE SUN-YAT-SEN Map p48

cnr Rue de la Gauchetière & Rue Clark; M Place-d'Armes

Dedicated to Sun Yat Sen, the ideological father of modern China, this small square was opened in 1988. The space was later refashioned by eight craftsmen from Shanghai who used traditional methods and materials. The mural on the north and east walls is made of grey slate. There's a small concrete stage for performances and a pavilion from which souvenirs or knick-knacks are sold.

On any given day here you will find old-timers sitting on stone stools laughing and gossiping in Cantonese while a handful of Falun Gong demonstrators hand out their literature nearby.

PLACE JEAN-PAUL-RIOPELLE Map p48

cnr Ave Viger Ouest & Rue de Bleury; ring of fire every hr 6:30-10:30pm mid-May–mid-Oct; M Place-d'Armes

The big draw of this square is the fountain that releases a ring of fire (and an ethereal mist) at certain times of year. The fountain and sculpture by Jean-Paul Riopelle (1923–2002), called *La Joute* (The Joust), was inaugurated here in 2003. During the day this area is filled with nearby office workers having lunch, but summer nights are a big draw as that's when the pyrotechnics take place.

SQUARE VICTORIA Map p48

Ⓜ Square-Victoria

In the 19th century this was a Victorian garden in a swanky district of Second Empire homes and offices. Today, Sq Victoria is a triangle of manicured greenery and water jets in the midst of modern skyscrapers. The only vestige of the period is a statue of Queen Victoria (1872). The art-nouveau entrance railing to the metro station was a gift from the city of Paris for Expo '67.

PALAIS DES CONGRÈS Map p48

☎ 514-871-8122; www.congresmtl.com; 201 Ave Viger Ouest; Ⓜ Place-d'Armes

Entering the hall of this convention center with its facade of popsicle-colored panes is akin to strolling through a kaleidoscope. Day brings out the colors, night the transparency. The cutting-edge Palais integrates several historic buildings: a 1908 fire station, the art-deco Tramways building from 1928 and a Victorian-era office complex. Immediately east of the Palais lies a landscape garden with stone pathways linking 31 heaps of earth, each topped off with Montréal's official tree, the crab apple.

OLD PORT

The Old Port is a requisite stop during a visit to Old Montréal. Its four piers have many worthwhile sites, with numerous river cruises departing from here. In warm weather the Promenade du Vieux-Port is a favorite recreation spot for joggers and in-line skaters, while cyclists can take in the view from the city bike path that runs parallel. There is plenty of green space for those seeking a little relaxation or for phenomenal views of the Loto Québec International Fireworks Competition (p14). In winter, skating at the outdoor rink, with the St Lawrence River shimmering nearby, may warm your soul – while leaving the rest of you quite cold.

There are a few cafés (with outdoor seating in the summer) sprinkled around the port area. The nearby Rue de la Commune, a street still lined with many 18th-century buildings, faces the Old Port and has snack stands, restaurants and gear rental.

QUAI ALEXANDRA & AROUND

Map p48

Ⓜ Place-d'Armes

This easternmost pier in the port is home to the Iberville Passenger Terminal, the dock for cruise ships that ply the St Lawrence River as far as the Magdalen Islands out in the Gulf of St Lawrence. Nearby the Parc des Écluses (Park of Locks; Map p48) holds exhibitions of landscape architecture, shows and concerts. A bicycle path starts here and runs southeast along the pretty Canal de Lachine (p86).

The abandoned 17-story-tall concrete silo on the south side of the locks is the last big relic of Montréal's heyday as a grain port. On the promenade just west of Café des Éclusiers (p141) is the Silo Phone (Map p48), a set of speakers and microphones hooked up to the grain silo across the locks. Say something and the sound will be transmitted into four of the huge grain chambers and bounced back at you.

QUAI JACQUES-CARTIER & AROUND

Map p48

Ⓜ Champ-de-Mars

This pier is the anchor of the Old Port area, home to restaurants, an open-air stage and a handicraft center. Every year the port stages a number of temporary exhibits, shows and events.

Montréal's Cirque du Soleil troupe of acrobats will perform here in early summer through 2011. Tours of the port area also depart from here, and a ferry goes to Parc Jean-Drapeau (p57). The ferry can also stop at Parc de la Cité-du-Havre (Map p48), where there's a restaurant and picnic tables.

Just east of Quai Jacques-Cartier is the Parc du Bassin Bonsecours, a grassy expanse enclosed by a waterway and crisscrossed with footbridges. In summer you can rent paddleboats ($6.50 per half-hour) or remote-control model sailboats; in winter the ice-skaters take over.

There's a café at the Pavilion du Bassin Bonsecours (Map p48) with outdoor seating in the summer.

A CAPITAL EXPERIMENT

Montréal would have a very different place in history but for a boozy rabble and a few newspaper articles. When the city became the capital of the United Provinces of Canada in 1844, the government moved into a two-story limestone building on the elongated Place d'Youville (Map p48), which at the time was a public market. It was here that Canada's first prime minister, John A Macdonald, made his inaugural speech to a joint French-English parliament.

Montréal's tenure as capital came to an abrupt end in 1849. Egged on by inflammatory editorials in the *Gazette*, an anglophone mob set fire to the assembly and the building burned to a crisp. The crowd was protesting a law that would require the Crown to compensate French Canadians for damages inflicted by the British army in the rebellion of 1837. As a consequence Montréal lost its status as capital, and the seat of government shifted back and forth between Québec City and Toronto until 1858, when Queen Victoria declared Ottawa the new capital.

Nothing was saved from the Montréal flames except a legislative mace and a portrait of Queen Victoria; the latter now hangs in the federal parliament building in Ottawa. The location of the first Canadian parliament (the east end of the square) is today a parking lot.

CENTRE DES SCIENCES DE MONTRÉAL Map p48

☎ 514-496-4724; www.centredessciencesdemontreal.com; Quai King-Edward; admission $12-23; 🕑 9am-4pm Mon-Thu, 10am-9pm Fri & Sat, 10am-5pm Sun; Ⓜ Place-d'Armes

This sleek, glass-covered science center houses virtual and interactive games, technology exhibits and an 'immersion theater' that puts a video game on giant screens. There's a huge range of different admission prices depending on which combinations of films and/or exhibits you want to take in. The center includes an IMAX cinema (p160) showing vivid nature and science films.

RUE DE LA COMMUNE Map p48

Ⓜ Champ-de-Mars

Set back from the waterfront, 'The Common' is a showcase of the rejuvenation that has swept Old Montréal. Compare it with old photos and you'll see the warehouses and factory buildings haven't changed much on the outside, but the tenants are upmarket hotels, restaurants and converted condos. Though the street has lost its raw, industrial feel, the original stone walls can still be viewed inside many buildings.

SAILORS' MEMORIAL CLOCK TOWER Map p48

Quai de l'Horloge; 🕑 10am-7pm; Ⓜ Champ-de-Mars

At the eastern edge of the historic port stands the striking white Tour de l'Horloge. This notable clock commemorates all of the sailors and shipmen who died in the world wars. Visitors can climb the 192 steps for a view over Old Montréal and the river.

LABYRINTH Map p48

☎ 514-499-0099; www.labyrintheduhangar16.com; Quai de l'Horloge; adult/child $14/11; 🕑 11am-9pm late Jun–late Aug, 11:30am-5:30pm Sat & Sun late Aug–Sep & mid-May–late Jun; Ⓜ Champ-de-Mars

Located in an old aircraft hangar, the winding corridors, obstacles and surprises of the Labyrinth are a kid's delight, whether English or French. Themes change regularly. It takes about one hour to get through the maze; small children may be frightened.

PARC JEAN-DRAPEAU

In the middle of the mighty St Lawrence, this alluring green space spreads across Île Ste-Hélène and Île Notre-Dame. Together, the two islands offer a fine choice of recreational activities, along with some worthwhile museums. The park is also home to a Vegas-sized casino, a Formula One racetrack, an old-fashioned amusement park and a popular electronic music fest in summer.

Despite its obvious appeal, the park remains little visited by locals. As fans of the park explain, something about it still feels very distant to the big city across the water – which, of course, is part of the charm. The best way to get around the park is by bicycle – access is via the busy Pont Jacques-Cartier bridge or the circuitous but far more peaceful route via Cité du Havre. There's also a metro stop on Île Ste-Hélène, while ferries depart from the Old Port in the summer. Boats operated by Navettes Maritimes (☎ 514-281-8000; www.navettesmaritimes.com; one way $6; 🕒 Sat & Sun mid-May–late Jun & Sep–early Oct, Fri-Sun late Jun–Aug) travel between Quai Jacques-Cartier and Île Ste-Hélène every hour from about 9:30am to 6:30pm. On the islands, information kiosks open during the summer and provide detailed info on events.

ÎLE STE-HÉLÈNE

Walkways meander around this island, past gardens and among the old pavilions from the World's Fair. The western part of the island was transformed into an open-air stage for shows, concerts and even after-hour parties. A large metal sculpture, L'Homme (Humankind; Map p58), was created by American artist Alexander Calder for Expo '67. It's also here, near the sculpture, that the fantastic Piknic Électronik (Map p58; www.piknicelectronik.com; Belvedere, Île Ste-Hélène; admission $10; 🕒 1-8pm Sun mid-May–Sep) takes place. DJs spin techno and electronic music while you can dance or lounge on the grass.

BIOSPHÈRE Map p58

☎ 514-283-5000; www.biosphere.ec.gc.ca; adult/child $10/free; 🕒 10am-6pm daily Jun-Oct, 10am-6pm Tue-Sun Nov-May; Ⓜ Jean-Drapeau

Located in the striking spherical dome of the former American pavilion in the '67 World's Fair, the center has the most spectacular collection of hands-on displays in the entire city. Exhibits focus on the world of water, the St Lawrence River ecosystem (which, together with the Great Lakes, makes up 25% of the planet's freshwater reserves) and emerging ecotechnologies. Hands-on exhibits all involve real water, and though primarily geared to kids, big people will also find it worthwhile. The upstairs Visions Hall offers a great view of the river.

LA RONDE AMUSEMENT PARK Map p58

☎ 514-397-2000; www.laronde.com; adult/child $39/26; 🕒 11am-8pm Jun-Aug; Ⓜ Jean-Drapeau, then bus 167; Ⓟ $13

Québec's largest amusement park, La Ronde has a battery of impressive rides, including

top picks

IT'S FREE

- Musée des Beaux-Arts (p60) There's never a charge to visit the permanent collection of Montréal's stellar art museum.
- Tam-tam jam (p80) Dance, pound your drums or simply gawk at this Sunday-afternoon bongo-banging bash held all summer long.
- Centre Canadien d'Architecture (p61) The fascinating exhibits of this beautifully designed museum are free on Thursday nights (from 6pm to 9pm).
- Musée d'Art Contemporain (p60) Wednesday nights (6pm to 9pm) are free at this showcase to modern art.
- Musée Redpath (p61) Check out a full-sized dinosaur skeleton, Egyptian mummies and tons of other curiosities at this free natural history museum.
- Oratoire St-Joseph (p88) The world's largest shrine to Jesus' dad offers captivating views over Mont-Royal.
- Canal de Lachine (p86) Enjoy a waterside stroll or bike ride along the peaceful canal – the Atwater market is a good destination.
- Musée de Lachine (p87) Follow the canal path far enough (14km) and you reach the oldest house in Montréal, now a cozy museum depicting early colonial days among settlers and fur traders.
- Sailors' Memorial Clock Tower (opposite) Climb to the top of the clock tower for fine views over the port and the churning St Lawrence.
- Fonderie Darling (p50) This avant-garde art gallery offers free admission on Thursdays – when it's open until 10pm. Keep an eye out for summertime parties on the street in front.

Le Monstre, the world's highest wooden roller coaster; and Le Vampire, a corkscrew roller coaster with gut-wrenching turns. For a more peaceful experience, there's a Ferris wheel and a gentle minirail that offers views of the river and city. Concerts and shows are held throughout the summer, and fireworks explode overhead on weekend evenings (when the park stays open later).

MUSÉE STEWART Map p58

☎ 514-861-6701; www.stewart-museum.org; adult/child under 7/student $10/free/7; 🕐 10am-5pm late May–early Oct, 10am-5pm Wed-Mon early Oct–late May; Ⓜ Jean-Drapeau

Inside a former British garrison (where troops were stationed in the 19th century), this museum displays relics from Canada's past as well as a multimedia model of Old Montréal. Demonstrations are given outside by actors in period costume, and there's a military parade every day in summer. It's a 15-minute walk from metro Jean-Drapeau station.

ÎLE NOTRE-DAME

This isle emerged in 10 months from the riverbed, atop millions of tons of earth and rock excavated from the new metro created in 1967. The planners were creative with the use of water, carving out canals and pretty garden walkways amid the parklands that stretch across the isle. The Formula One Grand Prix racetrack no longer hosts the high-octane event (see the boxed text, p177). Instead, bikers and in-line skaters take to the Circuit Gilles-Villeneuve (Map p58) in droves.

PLAGE DES ÎLES Map p58

☎ 514-872-2323; adult/child $8/4; ⌚ 10am-7pm mid Jun–late Aug; Ⓜ Jean-Drapeau, then bus 167

On warm summer days this artificial sandy beach can accommodate up to 5000 sunning and splashing souls. It's safe, clean and ideal for kids; picnic facilities and snack bars serving beer are also on-site. There are also several professional-standard volleyball courts for anyone to use.

CASINO DE MONTRÉAL Map p58

☎ 514-392-2746; 1 Ave du Casino; ⌚ 24hr; Ⓜ Jean-Drapeau, then bus 167

Based in the former French pavilion from the World's Fair, the Montréal Casino opened in 1993 and was so popular (and earned so much money) that expansion occurred almost instantly. It remains Québec's biggest casino. You can gather your winnings at 3000 slot machines and 120 gaming tables, but drinking isn't allowed on the floor. See also p158 for more information about the casino.

Arched footbridges link the casino to the Jardin des Floralies (Map p58), a rose garden that is wonderful for a stroll.

CENTRE OPTION PLEIN AIR Map p58

☎ 514-872-0199; informations@optionpleinair.com; 1 Circuit Gilles-Villeneuve; Ⓜ Jean-Drapeau, then bus 167

Competitive rowers and kayakers, among other amateur athletes, train at this former Olympic rowing basin. It's not open to the public except during special events like the famous dragon boat rowing races held here in late July.

HABITAT '67 Map p58

The artificial peninsula called Cité-du-Havre was created to protect the port from vicious currents and ice. Here, in 1967, architect Moshe Safdie designed a set of futuristic cubelike condominiums for the World's Fair when he was just 23 years old. If you're utterly taken with the site, units are available for rental or purchase (check out www.habitat67.com), but prices aren't cheap. A narrow spit of land connects Île Ste-Hélène with Old Montréal via the bridge Pont de la Concorde.

top picks

GREEN SPACES

- Jardin Botanique (p90) A bonsai forest, Ming dynasty garden and hundreds of orchids make for some memorable meandering.
- Parc LaFontaine (p75) The perfect year-round park with performances at the bandstand in summer and ice-skating on the pond in winter.
- Parc du Mont-Royal (p79) Climb up 'the Mountain' for sweeping views of the city below.
- Parc Jean-Drapeau (p57) Trails, paths, gorgeous views of Montréal and plenty of unique sights (like a giant Alexander Calder sculpture) along the way.
- Canal de Lachine (p86) Picnic, stroll or cycle alongside the picturesque canal, a stunning success in the realm of urban renewal.
- Carré St-Louis (p75) A tiny square surrounded by stately mansions with impromptu Django Reinhardt–playing guitarists, a summertime café and grassy areas on which to unwind.
- Parc Outremont (p82) Little known neighborhood park with a picturesque pond, yarmulke-wearing tots and a great little ice-cream shop (Le Bilboquet, p138) a few blocks away.
- Centre Canadien d'Architecture (p61) Peaceful grassy lawn located on the center's grounds, plus a curious sculpture garden with views across busy Blvd René-Lévesque.

DOWNTOWN

Drinking p141; Eating p124; Shopping p106; Sleeping p183

Downtown Montréal hums with energy. Its mix of wide boulevards, glass skyscrapers and shopping galleries give the area a decidedly North American flavor, while numerous green spaces, eye-catching heritage buildings and 19th-century churches add a more-European character to the bustling city streets. On weekdays, downtown draws an equally diverse crowd to the neighborhood, from businesspeople power-lunching at high-end restaurants to backpack-toting students who flood the district each day en route to McGill or Concordia Universities.

Downtown is also home to some of Montréal's best museums, and is a popular place with the after-work crowd for a wide variety of urban distractions. With numerous shopping galleries, multifloor department stores and underground malls, downtown is also a magnet for shoppers. A few key destinations include the long thoroughfare of Rue Ste-Catherine, which is packed with boutiques and shopping galleries (particularly between Rue Crescent and Rue University). Meanwhile, Rue Crescent and Rue Bishop are the traditional anglophone centers of nightlife with an array of bars and restaurants. Rue Sherbrooke Ouest features upscale shops and turn-of-the-century residences with a pronounced English flavor. At the east end of downtown is the Place des Arts, the performing-arts complex and hub of the jazz festival. To the west of downtown, you'll find the picturesque neighborhood of upscale Westmount (p69).

Downtown has an abundance of public transit options. By metro, the green and orange lines have over a dozen stops; Peel and McGill are both central and convenient. If you prefer to bus it, bus 15 runs on Rue Ste-Catherine and Blvd de Maisonneuve, bus 24 on Rue Sherbrooke and bus 150 on Blvd René-Lévesque. Bixi bike (p169) is also a great way to get around, with numerous bike stations in the area. If you're cycling, head to Blvd de Maisonneuve, which has a separate protected bike lane, running both directions.

MUSÉE DES BEAUX-ARTS Map pp62–3

☎ 514-285-2000; www.mbam.qc.ca; 1380 Rue Sherbrooke Ouest; permanent collection free, special exhibits adult/student $15/7.50; 🕒 11am-5pm Tue, 11am-9pm Wed-Fri, 10am-5pm Sat & Sun; Ⓜ Peel

Montréal's Museum of Fine Arts, the oldest in the country and the city's largest, is housed in two buildings: the classical, marble-covered Michal and Renata Hornstein Pavilion at 1379 Rue Sherbrooke Ouest, and the modern annex across the street at the Jean-Noël Desmarais Pavilion. The latter plays host to works by European and Canadian masters but also ancient artifacts from Egypt, Greece, Rome and the Far East, Islamic art and works from Africa and Oceania. The Old Masters collection has paintings from the Middle Ages stretching through the Renaissance and classical eras up to contemporary works.

The classical pavilion is accessible via an underground tunnel and houses the Musée des Arts Décoratifs, with works and handicrafts from some of the world's most influential designers. The eclectic collection includes glass vases, Victorian chests and an Inuit gallery as well as industrial and graphic design exhibits. After 5pm Wednesday entry for adults is half-price. Regular English tours are given on various subjects. Call ahead for the schedule.

MUSÉE D'ART CONTEMPORAIN Map pp62–3

☎ 514-847-6226; www.macm.org; 185 Rue Ste-Catherine Ouest, Place des Arts; adult/student $8/4, free 6-9pm Wed; 🕒 11am-6pm Tue & Thu-Sun, 11am-9pm Wed, English tours 6:30pm Wed, 1pm & 3pm Sat & Sun; Ⓜ Place-des-Arts

This showcase of modern Canadian and international art has eight galleries divided between past greats (since 1939) and exciting current developments. A weighty collection of 6000 permanent works includes Québec legends Jean-Paul Riopelle, Paul-Émile Borduas and Geneviève Cadieux, but also temporary exhibitions of the latest trends in current art from Canadian and international artists. Forms range from traditional to new media, from painting, sculpture and prints to installation art, photography and video. The sculpture garden is also worth a look.

The pleasant restaurant upstairs has a great dining terrace.

MUSÉE MCCORD Map pp62–3

☎ 514-398-7100; www.mccord-museum.qc.ca; 690 Rue Sherbrooke Ouest; adult/child/student

$13/5/7; ⌚ 10am-6pm Tue-Fri, 10am-5pm Sat & Sun; Ⓜ McGill

With hardly an inch to spare in its cramped but welcoming galleries, the McCord Museum of Canadian History houses nearly one million artifacts and documents illustrating Canada's social, cultural and archaeological history from the 18th century to present day. The eclectic collection has large sections on Canada's earliest European settlement and the history of Québec's indigenous people; other display highlights include embroidered gowns, toys, prints and First Nations' works. The 2nd-floor gallery neatly encapsulates French-Canadian history in Québec. There's also a gift shop and an inviting café. In summer it's also open Monday.

MARCHÉ ATWATER Map pp62–3

☎ 514-937-7754; 138 Ave Atwater; ⌚ 7am-6pm Mon-Wed, 7am-8pm Thu & Fri, 7am-5pm Sat & Sun; Ⓜ Lionel-Groulx

Just off the Canal de Lachine, this fantastic market has a mouthwatering assortment of fresh produce from local farms, excellent wines, crusty breads, fine cheeses and other delectable fare. The market's specialty shops operate year-round, while outdoor stalls open from March to October. The excellent Première Moisson (p131) is a popular café and bakery. It's all housed in a 1933 brick hall, topped with a clock tower. The grassy banks overlooking the nearby Canal de Lachine make a great spot for a picnic.

CENTRE CANADIEN D'ARCHITECTURE Map pp62–3

☎ 514-939-7026; www.cca.qc.ca; 1920 Rue Baile; adult/child $10/free, free after 5:30pm Thu; ⌚ 11am-6pm Wed & Fri-Sun, 11am-9pm Thu; Ⓜ Guy-Concordia

A must for architecture fans, this center is equal parts museum and research institute. The building incorporates the Shaughnessy House, a 19th-century grey limestone treasure. Highlights in this section include the conservatory and an ornate sitting room with intricate woodwork and a massive stone fireplace. There's also a busy, well-stocked bookstore. The exhibition galleries focus on remarkable architectural works of both local and international scope, with a particular focus on urban design. The CCA's sculpture garden is located on a grassy lot overlooking south Montréal, but separated from the main grounds by busy Blvd René-Lévesque.

top picks

DOWNTOWN

- Musée McCord (opposite) Learn about the rich cultural history of this fascinating city.
- Musée d'Art Contemporain (opposite) Eclectic showcase of modern Canadian art.
- Musée des Beaux-Arts (opposite) New- and old-world masterpieces, plus great temporary exhibitions.
- Centre Canadien d'Architecture (left) Excellent cutting-edge temporary exhibits delving into the world of urban architecture and green design, plus surveys of world-renowned architects.
- Rue Ste-Catherine (p67) The need-to-know/go street for unreformed shopping addicts.
- Marché Atwater (left) Heavenly scents and tempting fruits, crusty baguettes, artisanal cheeses and much more at this beautiful market.
- Cathédrale Marie-Reine-du-Monde (below) Scaled-down version of St Peter's in Rome.

MUSÉE REDPATH Map pp62–3

☎ 514-398-4086; 859 Rue Sherbrooke Ouest, McGill University; admission free; ⌚ 9am-5pm Mon-Thu, 1-5pm Sun; Ⓜ McGill

A Victorian spirit of discovery pervades this old natural history museum, though you won't find anything more gruesome than stuffed animals from the Laurentians hinterland. The Redpath Museum houses a large variety of specimens, including a dinosaur skeleton and seashells donated from around the world. A highlight is the 3rd-floor Ethnology Gallery, which traces the beginnings of human civilization. It includes Egyptian mummies, shrunken heads and artifacts from ancient Mediterranean, African and East Asian communities. In winter it's also open Friday.

CATHÉDRALE MARIE-REINE-DU-MONDE Map pp62–3

☎ 514-866-1661; 1045 Rue de la Cathédrale; ⌚ 7:30am-6pm; Ⓜ Bonaventure

The Cathedral of Mary Queen of the World is a smaller but still magnificent version of St Peter's Basilica in Rome. The architects

DOWNTOWN

Lac des Castors (Beaver Lake)
Parc du Mont-Royal
Chalet Lookout
Chemin Trafalgar
The Boulevard
Ave Cedar
Chemin de la Côte-des-Neiges
Chemin McDougall
Ave Montrose
Ave Mountain
Ave Clarke
Redpath Crescent
Chemin St-Sulpice
Chemin de la Vigne
Ave Holton
Chemin Barat
Parc Percy Walters
Ave Docteur-Penfield
Collège Dawson
Atwater
Place Alexis Nihon
Square Cabot
Rue Sherbrooke Ouest
Blvd de Maisonneuve Ouest
Rue Ste-Catherine Ouest
Downtown
Guy-Concordia
Ave Lincoln
Rue Tupper
Rue Baile
Blvd Dorchester
Rue Staynor
Rue Prospect
Rue Selby
Lionel-Groulx
Rue Souvenir
Ave Hawarden
Autoroute Ville-Marie
Rue St-Antoine Ouest
Georges-Vanier
Lucien-L'Allier
Rue Coursol
Rue Quesnel
Parc Campbell-Centre
Rue Torrance
Rue Delisle
Rue Workman
Ave Lionel Groulx
Rue St-Jacques
Parc Vinet
Antique Alley
Parc Herb-Trawick
Parc Labatt
Pl Victor Hugo
Rue Duvernay
Rue Notre-Dame Ouest
Rue Ste-Cunégonde
Rue Barré
Rue William
Canal de Lachine
Charlevoix

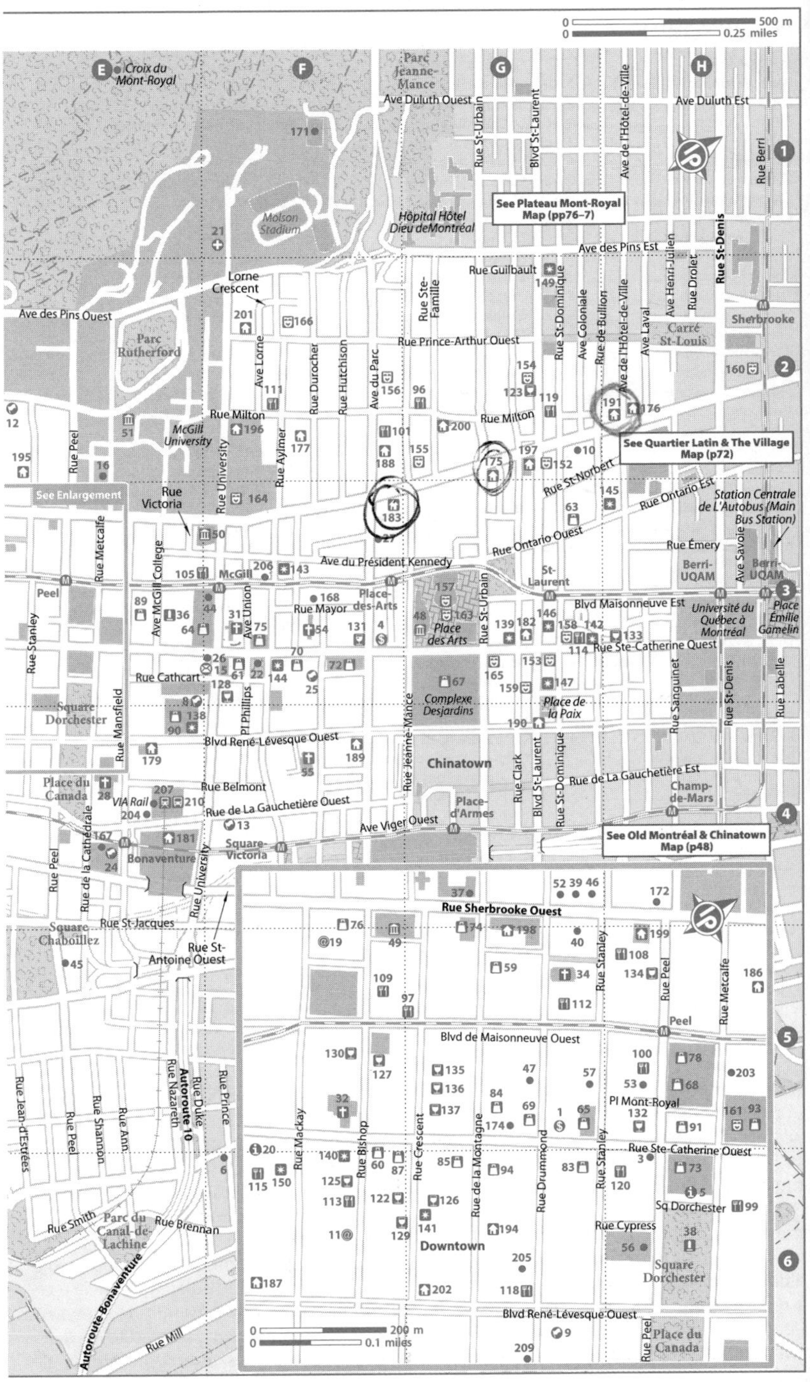

See Plateau Mont-Royal Map (pp76–7)
See Quartier Latin & The Village Map (p72)
See Old Montréal & Chinatown Map (p48)
See Enlargement
Croix du Mont-Royal
Parc Jeanne-Mance
Molson Stadium
Hôpital Hôtel Dieu deMontréal
Parc Rutherford
McGill University
Carré St-Louis
Station Centrale de L'Autobus (Main Bus Station)
Université du Québec à Montréal
Place Émilie Gamelin
Place des Arts
Complexe Desjardins
Place de la Paix
Chinatown
Place-d'Armes
Place du Canada
Square Dorchester
Square-Victoria
Bonaventure
Square Chaboillez
Parc du Canal-de-Lachine
Champ-de-Mars
Downtown
Ave Duluth Ouest
Ave Duluth Est
Ave des Pins Ouest
Ave des Pins Est
Rue Prince-Arthur Ouest
Rue Milton
Rue Sherbrooke Ouest
Ave du Président Kennedy
Blvd Maisonneuve Est
Blvd de Maisonneuve Ouest
Rue Ste-Catherine Ouest
Blvd René-Lévesque Ouest
Rue de La Gauchetière Ouest
Rue de La Gauchetière Est
Ave Viger Ouest
Rue Ontario Est
Rue Ontario Ouest
Rue St-Denis
Blvd St-Laurent
Rue St-Urbain
Rue Peel
Rue University
Rue Mill
Autoroute Bonaventure
Autoroute 10

DOWNTOWN

INFORMATION

Bank of Montreal ... 1 G5
Battlenet 24 ... 2 C3
British Council ... (see 24)
Calforex ... 3 H6
Canada Trust ... 4 F3
Centre Infotouriste ... 5 H6
Chapters Bookstore ... (see 65)
Cité Multimedia ... 6 F6
CLSC (Community Health Center) ... 7 C3
Danish Consulate ... (see 8)
French Consulate ... 8 E3
German Consulate ... 9 G6
Héritage Montréal ... 10 G2
Intertainment Café ... 11 F6
Italian Consulate ... 12 E2
Japanese Consulate ... 13 F4
Jean Coutu ... 14 C3
Main Post Office ... 15 F3
McGill Legal Information Clinic ... 16 E2
Montréal General Hospital ... 17 C2
Montréal International Language Centre ... 18 C3
Net.24 ... 19 F5
Pharmaprix ... 20 F5
Royal Victoria Hospital ... 21 F1
Square Phillips ... 22 F3
Swiss Consulate ... 23 C2
Thomas Cook ... (see 64)
UK Consulate ... 24 E4
US Consulate ... 25 F3

SIGHTS (pp60–70)

Alouettes Box Office ... 26 F3
Black Watch Highlanders Regimental Museum & Archives ... 27 F3
Cathédrale Marie-Reine-du-Monde ... 28 E4
Centre Canadien d'Architecture ... 29 C3
Chalet du Mont-Royal ... 30 D1
Christ Church Cathedral ... 31 F3
Church of St James the Apostle ... 32 F5
Concordia University, Sir George Williams Campus ... 33 C3
Emmanuel Congregation Church ... 34 G5
Gare Windsor ... (see 208)
Grand Séminaire de Montréal ... 35 C2
Illuminated Crowd ... 36 E3
Le Château ... 37 G4
Les Cours Mont-Royal ... (see 78)
Lord Strathcona Statue ... 38 H6
Louis-Joseph Forget House ... 39 G4
Maison Alcan ... 40 G5
Maison Smith ... 41 C1
Marché Atwater ... 42 A5
Masonic Memorial Temple ... 43 C3
McGill University Centre for Continuing Education ... 44 F3
Montréal Planetarium ... 45 E5
Mount Royal Club ... 46 G4
Mt Stephen Club ... 47 G5
Musée d'Art Contemporain ... 48 G3
Musée des Arts Décoratifs ... (see 49)
Musée des Beaux-Arts ... 49 F5
Musée McCord ... 50 F3
Musée Redpath ... 51 E2
Reid Wilson House ... 52 G4
Seagram House ... 53 H5
St James United Church ... 54 F3
St Patrick's Basilica ... 55 F4
Windsor Hotel ... 56 H6
YMCA ... 57 G5

SHOPPING (pp106–10)

Adrenaline ... 58 D3
Andy The-Anh ... 59 G5
Betsey Johnson ... 60 F6
Birks Jewellers ... 61 F3
Blue Marine Cie ... 62 A2
Boutique Eva B ... 63 G3
Centre Eaton ... 64 E3
Chapters Bookstore ... 65 G5
Chaussures Tony ... 66 A3
Complexe Desjardins ... 67 G3
Face London ... 68 H5
Felix Brown ... 69 G5
Future Shop ... 70 F3
Galerie de Bellefeuille ... 71 A2
Galeries d'Art Contemporain du Belgo ... 72 F3
HMV ... 73 H6
Holt Renfrew ... 74 G4
Hudson Bay Co ... 75 F3
Indigo ... (see 89)
La Casa del Habano ... 76 F4
Les Antiquités Grand Central ... 77 B5
Les Cours Mont-Royal ... 78 H5
Librairie Astro ... 79 C3
Lili-les-Bains ... 80 D5
Lucie Favreau Antiques ... 81 C5
Lululemon Atheletica ... 82 A2
Maison de la Press Internationale ... 83 G6
Nadya Toto ... 84 G5
Ogilvy ... 85 G6
Oink Oink ... 86 A3
Olam ... 87 F6
Parisian Laundry ... 88 A4
Place Montréal Trust ... 89 E3
Place Ville-Marie ... 90 E4
Roots ... 91 H5
Sexe Cité ... 92 C3
Simons ... 93 H5
Urban Outfitters ... 94 G6
Westmount Square ... 95 B3

EATING (pp124–8)

Amelio's ... 96 G2
Beaver Club ... (see 179)
Boustan ... 97 G5
Café Méliès ... (see 154)
Chez Nick ... 98 A2
Dunn's ... 99 H6
Ferreira Café ... 100 H5
Isakaya ... 101 F2
Joe Beef ... 102 B5
Kaizen ... 103 B3
La Gargote des Antiquaries ... 104 C5
Le Caveau ... 105 E3
Le Faubourg ... 106 C3
Le Paris ... 107 C3
Le Taj ... 108 H5
Les Chenêts ... 109 F5
Liverpool House ... 110 B5
Lola Rosa ... 111 F2
M:Brgr ... 112 G5
Mango Bay ... 113 F6
Marché Atwater ... (see 42)
Ong Ca Can ... 114 G3
Phayathai ... 115 F6
Pizzeria Gepetto ... 116 B5
Premiére Moisson ... (see 42)
Provigo ... 117 C3
Queue de Cheval ... 118 G6
Restaurant Globe ... 119 G2
Reuben's ... 120 H6
Three Amigos ... 121 C3

scaled it down to one-quarter size, mindful of the structural risks of Montréal's severe winters. This landmark was built from 1870 to 1894 as a symbol of Catholic power in the heart of Protestant Montréal.

The 13 statues of saints over the entrance are sculpted in wood and covered with copper; at nighttime they're brilliantly illuminated. The neobaroque altar canopy, a replica of Bernini's masterpiece in St Peter's, is fashioned of gold leaf and copper with swirled roof supports.

MONTRÉAL PLANETARIUM Map pp62–3

☎ 514-872-4530; www.planetarium.montreal.qc.ca; 1000 Rue St-Jacques; adult/child $8/4; 12:30-5pm Mon, 9:30am-5pm Tue-Thu, 9:30am-4:30pm & 7-9:30pm Fri, 12:30-4:30pm & 7-9:30pm Sat & Sun, closed Mon Sep-Jun; M Bonaventure

This 20m-high dome offers a window on the stars, space and solar system via a celestial projector. The 50-minute shows run in shifts: mornings are geared toward kids and school groups, afternoons are for all

DOWNTOWN

DRINKING (pp141–4)

- Brutopia 122 F6
- Buonanotte 123 G2
- Cock 'n Bull Pub 124 C3
- Grumpy's Bar 125 F6
- Hurley's Irish Pub 126 G6
- Le Social 127 F5
- Le Vieux Dublin Pub & Restaurant 128 F3
- Mad Hatter Saloon 129 F6
- McKibbin's 130 F5
- NYK'S 131 F3
- Peel Pub 132 H5
- Pub Ste-Élisabeth 133 H3
- Restaurant Globe (see 119)
- Ristorante Cavalli 134 H5
- Sir Winston Churchill Pub Complexe 135 G5
- Thursday's 136 G5
- Ziggy's 137 G5

NIGHTLIFE (pp151–8)

- Club 737 138 E4
- Club Opera 139 G3
- Comedyworks 140 F6
- Cubano's Club 141 G6
- Electric Avenue (see 135)
- Ernie Butler's Comedy Nest (see 162)
- Foufounes Electriques 142 G3
- House of Jazz 143 F3
- Istori 144 F3
- Jello Bar 145 H3
- Le Loft 146 G3
- Salsathèque (see 5)
- SAT 147 G3
- Sharx 148 C3
- Tokyo Bar 149 G2
- Upstairs 150 F6

THE ARTS (pp159–66)

- AMC Forum (see 162)
- Bell Centre 151 D4
- Cabaret Music-Hall 152 G2
- Club Soda 153 G3
- Ex-Centris Cinema 154 G2
- I Musici de Montréal 155 G2
- Le Nouveau Cinéma du Parc 156 F2
- L'Opera de Montréal 157 G3
- Metropolis 158 G3
- Monument-National 159 G3
- Orchestre Métropolitan du Grand Montréal 160 H2
- Orchestre Symphonique de Montréal (see 157)
- Paramount & IMAX Cinemas 161 H5
- Pepsi Forum 162 B3
- Place des Arts 163 G3
- Pollack Concert Hall 164 F3
- Théâtre du Nouveau Monde 165 G3
- Yellow Door 166 F2

SPORTS & ACTIVITIES (pp167–77)

- Ashtanga Yoga Studio (see 72)
- Atrium Le 1000 167 E4
- Bell Centre (see 151)
- Croisiére Patrimoniale du Canal (see 42)
- Gamma - Gelinas Academy of Mixed Martial Arts 168 F3
- H2O Adventures 169 A5
- Lac des Castors 170 C1
- McConnell Winter Stadium 171 F1
- Moretti Studio 172 H4
- My Bicyclette 173 A5
- Nautilus Plus 174 G5

SLEEPING (pp183–7)

- Alacoque B&B Revolution 175 G2
- Armor Manoir Sherbrooke 176 H2
- Castel Durocher 177 F2
- Château Versailles 178 C3
- Fairmont Le Reine Elizabeth 179 E4
- HI Auberge de Montréal 180 D4
- Hilton Montréal Bonaventure 181 E4
- Hôtel Abri du Voyageur 182 G3
- Hôtel Casa Bella 183 F3
- Hôtel du Fort 184 C3
- Hôtel du Nouveau Forum 185 D4
- Hôtel Le Germain 186 H5
- Hotel Maritime Plaza 187 F6
- Hotel Parc Suites 188 F2
- La Tour Centre Ville 189 F4
- Le 1 René Lévesque 190 G4
- Le Gîte du Plateau Mont-Royal 191 H2
- Le Petit Prince 192 D4
- Les Bons Matins 193 D4
- Loew's Hotel Vogue 194 G6
- Manoir Ambrose 195 E2
- McGill University Residence Halls 196 F2
- Opus Montréal 197 G2
- Ritz-Carlton 198 G5
- Sofitel 199 H5
- Trylon Apartments 200 G2
- University Bed & Breakfast Apartments 201 F2
- Y des Femmes 202 G6

TRANSPORT (pp251–5)

- AMT commuter rail station (see 207)
- Avis 203 H5
- Budget 204 E4
- CAA (Canadian Automobile Club) 205 G6
- Discount Car 206 F3
- Gare Centrale 207 E4
- Gare Windsor 208 D4
- Hertz 209 G6
- My Bicyclette (see 173)
- Station Aérobus 210 E4

ages, and evenings are reserved for adult programs. Seasonal presentations run at Christmas and other times of the year.

PLACE DES ARTS Map pp62–3

☎ box office 514-285-4200; 175 Rue Ste-Catherine Ouest; Ⓜ Place-des-Arts

Montréal's performing-arts center is the nexus for artistic and cultural events. Several renowned musical companies call the Place des Arts home, including the Montréal Symphony Orchestra and the McGill Chamber Orchestra; it's also center stage for the International Jazz Festival (p14) and Les Francofolies (p15). The complex embraces an outdoor plaza with fountains and an ornamental pool and is attached to the Complexe Desjardins shopping center via an underground tunnel. The five halls include the 3000-seat Salle Wilfrid-Pelletier and the 1500-seat Théâtre Maisonneuve, and there's a small experimental space called the Cinquième Salle. At research time, construction of a new concert hall for the Montréal Symphony Orchestra was under way, and is scheduled for completion by 2011.

MCGILL UNIVERSITY Map pp62–3

☎ 514-398-4455; www.mcgill.ca; 845 Rue Sherbrooke Ouest; Ⓜ McGill

Founded in 1828 by James McGill, a rich Scottish fur trader, McGill University is one of Canada's most prestigious learning institutions, with 15,000 students. The university's medical and engineering faculties have a fine reputation and many campus buildings are showcases of Victorian architecture. The campus, at the foot of Mont-Royal, is rather nice for a stroll around and also incorporates the Musée Redpath (p61).

CHRIST CHURCH CATHEDRAL

Map pp62–3

☎ 514-843-6577;1444 Ave Union; 🕑 7:30am-5:45pm; Ⓜ McGill

Montréal's first Anglican bishop had this cathedral built (modeled on a Salisbury, England, church) and it was completed in 1859. The church was the talk of the town in the late 1980s when it allowed a shopping center, the Promenades de la Cathédrale, to be built underneath it. Spectacular photos show the house of worship resting on concrete stilts while construction went on underneath.

The interior is sober apart from the pretty stained-glass windows made by William Morris' studios in London. In the rear cloister garden stands a memorial statue to Raoul Wallenberg, the Swedish diplomat who saved 100,000 Jews from the concentration camps in WWII.

SQUARE DORCHESTER Map pp62–3

Ⓜ Peel

This leafy expanse in the heart of downtown was known until 1988 as Dominion Square, a reminder of Canada's founding in 1867. A Catholic cemetery was here until 1870 and bodies still lie beneath the grass. Events of all kinds have taken place here over the years – fashion shows, political rallies and royal visits. The square still exudes the might of the British Empire, with statues of Boer-War booster Lord Strathcona, Queen Victoria and poet Robert Burns, plus Wilfrid Laurier, Canada's first francophone prime minister, who faces off a statue of John A Macdonald, the first anglophone prime minister, in Place du Canada (right) across Blvd René-Lévesque.

The city's main tourist office (p263) lies on the square's northwest side.

GARE WINDSOR Map pp62–3

☎ 514-287-8726; 1160 de la Gauchetière Ouest; Ⓜ Bonaventure

The massive Victorian building hugging the slope west of the Marriott Château Champlain is the old Windsor Station, opened in 1889 as the headquarters of the Canadian Pacific Railway. The Romanesque structure inspired a château style for train stations across the country; its architect, Bruce Price, would later build the remarkable Château Frontenac (p205) in Québec City. The station is no longer the terminus of the transcontinental railway but still serves commuter trains. Much of the building today houses offices and shops.

LES COURS MONT-ROYAL Map pp62–3

1455 Rue Peel; Ⓜ Peel

This elegant shopping mall is a reincarnation of the Mount Royal Hotel (1922), at the time the largest hotel in the British Empire. The 1000-room hotel was converted into a snazzy mix of condos and fashion boutiques (see p109) in 1988. Under the skylight you'll see six birdmen sculptures by Inuit artist David Pioukuni. These were shamans who transformed themselves into winged creatures and were powered by a wind god. The spectacular chandelier is from Monte Carlo's old casino.

MT STEPHEN CLUB Map pp62–3

☎ 514-849-7338; www.clubmountstephen.com; 1440 Rue Drummond; Ⓜ Peel

The Mt Stephen Club, dating from 1880, was an exclusive businessmen's club named for the first president of the Canadian Pacific Railway. The 15 rooms of this Renaissance-style mansion have been completely renovated by a private foundation and are rich with quality materials and skillful artistry, including a splendid mahogany staircase, marble mantelpieces and rather swanky furnishings. It's still one of the swishest private clubs in town. The public can take it all in on weekends, during a seven-course Saturday-evening feast ($70) or a Sunday-morning brunch ($45); both feature live music. Free guided tours are included with Sunday brunch. Reservations and proper attire essential.

PLACE DU CANADA Map pp62–3

Ⓜ Bonaventure

This park immediately southeast of Sq Dorchester is best known for its monument of John A Macdonald, Canada's first prime minister, who addressed the maiden session of parliament in Montréal. The two cannons around the base were captured in the Crimean War; if you look closely you'll see the dual-headed eagle of Czar Nicholas I. The statue was decapitated by vandals in 1992 and the head vanished for two years.

The overpass across Blvd René-Lévesque leads to the Marriott Château Champlain Hotel, known as the 'cheese grater' for its windows shaped like half-moons.

ST PATRICK'S BASILICA Map pp62–3

☎ 514-866-7379; 460 Blvd René-Lévesque Ouest; 🕑 9am-6pm; Ⓜ Square-Victoria

Built for Montréal's booming Irish population in 1847, the interior of St Patrick's Basilica contains huge columns from single pine trunks, an ornate baptismal font and nectar-colored stained-glass windows. The pope raised its status to basilica in 1989, in recognition of its importance to English-speaking Catholics in Montréal. It's a sterling example of French-Gothic style and, as you might expect, is classified a national monument. The Irish-Canadian patriot D'Arcy McGee was buried here after his assassination in 1868; his pew (number 240) is marked with a small Canadian flag.

WINDSOR HOTEL Map pp62–3

☎ 514-393-3588; 1170 Rue Peel; Ⓜ Peel

The palatial Windsor was Canada's first grand hotel (1878) and played host to all manner of international guests and celebrities, including Mark Twain, Winston Churchill, King George VI, Queen Elizabeth II and John F Kennedy. The original Windsor had six restaurants and 382 sumptuous guest rooms, but a fire that devastated the hotel in 1957 left only the annex – the portion still standing today. You can stroll down the magnificent main hall, Peacock Alley, and peek at the vast wooden dance floors, chandeliers and high windows that recall turn-of-the-century splendor.

RUE STE-CATHERINE Map pp62–3

Lively Rue Ste-Catherine is one endless orgy of shops, restaurants, bars and cafés on the hyperactive stretch between Rue Crescent and Rue St-Urbain. Shopping malls, department stores and multiplex cinemas are sprinkled along the way. Shoppers flood the streets on weekends, slowing pedestrian traffic to a mere shuffle.

CHURCH OF ST JAMES THE APOSTLE Map pp62–3

☎ 514-849-7577; 1439 Rue Ste-Catherine Ouest; Ⓜ Guy-Concordia

Built in 1864 on a sports field for the British military, this Anglican church used to be called St Crickets in the Fields for the matches that unfolded here. The stained glass in the east transept, the Regimental Window, was donated in memory of the WWI fallen.

ST JAMES UNITED CHURCH Map pp62–3

☎ 514-288-9245; 463 Rue Ste-Catherine Ouest; 🕑 11am Sun; Ⓜ McGill

The excellent acoustics at St James United are coveted for organ and choir concerts as well as performances of the International Jazz Festival (p14). The church was originally opened in 1889.

RUE SHERBROOKE OUEST Map pp62–3

Until the 1930s the downtown stretch of Rue Sherbrooke Ouest was home to the Golden Square Mile, then one of the richest residential neighborhoods in Canada. You'll see a few glorious old homes along this drag, though most of them have been torn down to make way for skyscrapers. Those still standing serve mostly as private clubs, but there are good interpretation panels outside them explaining their history. The route is also home to visit-worthy churches, some first-rate museums and strings of energetic students en route to McGill University.

GRAND SÉMINAIRE DE MONTRÉAL Map pp62–3

☎ 514-935-1169; 2065 Rue Sherbrooke Ouest; admission by donation; 🕑 tours 1pm & 3pm Tue-Sat Jun-Aug; Ⓜ Guy-Concordia

The immense complex was built in 1860 to train priests for the Roman Catholic diocese. Shortly after construction the main instruction building, the Collège de Montréal, was requisitioned by the British army to house soldiers (who departed in 1870 after petitioning by the archdiocese). The seminary has a pretty Romanesque chapel, with hand-carved oak pews and walls covered with imported stone from Caen, France. Several shaded canals on the property are lovely for a stroll. Tours last about 1½ hours and the guides are excellent.

ILLUMINATED CROWD Map pp62–3

1981 Ave McGill College; Ⓜ McGill

The Illuminated Crowd is one of Montréal's most talked-about sculptures and arguably its most photographed piece of public art. The inscription reads in part: 'A crowd has gathered…the strong light casts shadows, and as light moves toward the back and diminishes, the mood degenerates; hooliganism, disorder and violence occur.' The group placed on four giant steps ranges

THE UNDERGROUND CITY

Brilliant marketing that conjures up images of subterranean skyscrapers and roads has made the underground city one of the first things visitors seek out when they travel to Montréal.

The underground city doesn't actually have any of these things. What it does have is a network of 2600 shops, 200 restaurants and 40-odd cinemas, theaters and exhibition halls, all hidden neatly beneath the surface of the congested city upstairs. For most travelers, it's a major letdown, because no matter what tourism officials call it, it is basically just a kind of colossal network of interlocking shopping malls. Where it does get interesting, however, is for residents living in downtown Montréal, as it gives them a reprieve from winter.

The 60-odd distinct complexes that make up this network are linked by brightly lit, well-ventilated corridors; fountains play to maintain humidity and the temperature hovers around 20°C. Add the metro and you've got a self-contained world, shielded from the subarctic temperatures. If you move to Montréal and pick the right apartment building, it could literally be the middle of winter and you would be able to go to work, do your grocery shopping, go see a movie and take in a performance at Place des Arts and never need more than a T-shirt.

The underground city was started, albeit inadvertently, when the Canadian National Railway laid a track through Montréal in 1918, splitting downtown in two and creating an ugly divide. Forty years later architect IM Pei was commissioned to build a skyscraper, Place Ville-Marie, to bridge the gap and link the Queen Elizabeth Hotel with CNR headquarters. Part of the new complex was underground, and in 1962 workers tunneled from the building to the hotel. The underground city was born. The metro was finished just in time for the Expo '67 World's Fair, and as 1% of the construction costs went into art, the entire network was conceived as a huge art gallery (see the boxed text, p71).

The underground city continues to evolve but with no master blueprint, making it easy to get lost. Plans are emerging to provide more artificial light and post more signposts to guide the perplexed. The easiest thing, however, is to seek out the info points at main crossroads that will print you a plan of how to get to your destination.

from wide-eyed, upstanding citizens in the front to miscreants in the rear as the steps descend downwards. They're made of polyester resin with a vanilla-yellow coating.

LE CHÂTEAU Map pp62–3

1321 Rue Sherbrooke Ouest; Ⓜ Guy-Concordia

This fortresslike apartment complex was designed by the famed Montréal architects George Ross and Robert MacDonald. The style would do Errol Flynn proud: Scottish and French Renaissance with stone battlements, demons and pavilion roofs. In the early 20th century these were some of Montréal's most elegant apartments. You can walk into the romantic courtyard for a closer look at the walls; fossilized shells are visible in the granite blocks.

LOUIS-JOSEPH FORGET HOUSE

Map pp62–3

1195 Rue Sherbrooke Ouest; Ⓜ Peel

This Victorian mansion was built in the late 19th century for the first francophone chairman of the Montréal Stock Exchange. Forget was also a founding member of the Mont-Royal Club and ran the Canadian Pacific Railway – much like George Stephen, an earlier CPR president who founded the Mt Stephen Club (p66).

MAISON ALCAN Map pp62–3

1188 Rue Sherbrooke Ouest; Ⓜ Peel

This mélange of four carefully restored 19th- and 20th-century buildings is not only an architectural wonder, but also the symbolic headquarters of the Alcan aluminum concern. It integrates the old Berkeley Hotel and four houses, including the Atholstan House, a Québec historic monument. To the rear is an intriguing atrium with a pretty garden. Also on the property stands the Emmanuel Congregation Church (Map pp62–3), which belongs to the Salvation Army.

MASONIC MEMORIAL TEMPLE

Map pp62–3

☎ 514-933-6739; 2295 Rue St-Marc; Ⓜ Guy-Concordia

This Grand Lodge of Québec is one of the most imposing monuments on Rue Sherbrooke, built in 1929 to honor the fallen in WWI. Huge classical columns frame the facade while two mysterious obelisks with dragons and globes guard the entrance. Free guided tours are offered on an irregular basis; check ahead for a worthwhile glimpse into the secretive world of Freemasonry.

MOUNT ROYAL CLUB Map pp62–3

☎ 514-933-6739; 1193 Rue Sherbrooke Ouest; Ⓜ Peel

Founded as an exclusive men's society, the Mount Royal Club was formed in the 19th century as a one-up on the older Beaver Club (p124) across town. It's essentially a business-people's club today, and both men and women are welcome.

PLACE VILLE-MARIE Map pp62–3

1 Pl Ville-Marie; Ⓜ McGill

Known for its rotating rooftop beacon that illuminates downtown at night, the Pl Ville-Marie tower marked the beginning of Montréal's underground city (opposite) over four decades ago. Its cruciform shape was chosen to commemorate Maisonneuve's planting of a great cross on Mont-Royal in 1642. The 42-story skyscraper is home to high-powered offices as well as a chic rooftop bar, Club 737 (p155). The intriguing fountain in the fore-court is called *Feminine Landscape* (1972) by Toronto artist Gerald Gladstone.

REID WILSON HOUSE Map pp62–3

1187 Rue Sherbrooke Ouest; Ⓜ Peel

This is one of Montréal's finest old mansions, built in 1902 with an old coach

WANDERING IN WESTMOUNT

Though short on traditional sites, the leafy, upper-class neighborhood of Westmount makes a fascinating destination for a day's exploring. Here you'll find a mix of sleepy backstreets set with Victorian mansions and manicured parks, while the main boulevard, Rue Sherbrook Ouest, has high-end boutiques, cafés and bistros. The extents of Westmount are roughly Ave Atwater in the east, Autoroute Ville-Marie in the south, Ave Devon in the north and Ave Claremont in the west.

Westmount has a long and colorful history, starting in the 1670s as an outpost of the Catholic order of Sulpicians and growing into a village called Côte St-Antoine. After Canadian Confederation in 1867 the village grew rapidly and the influx of anglophone families led the name to be changed to Westmount in 1895. However, it was only after WWII that this anglo enclave assumed its poshness after some of the most moneyed families of the day decided to settle down in the neighborhood. Today the area is still largely a bastion of wealthy anglos.

Though there is little left of the time when it was just a village made up of farms and a sprinkling of stately homes, several of Westmount's green spaces are actually the grounds of former estates that have been turned into parks.

For the most impressive mansions, you can start at Westmount Park and walk north of Rue Sherbrooke Ouest. The closer you get to Parc du Mont-Royal, the bigger and more imposing the houses get, and this is where many of the city's, and indeed the country's, movers and shakers reside, including former prime ministers.

South of Rue Sherbrooke Ouest, between Ave Greene and Ave Lansdowne, there are some wonderful examples of houses from the late 1800s, though many of them have been converted or modified since then. You can often still pick out interesting carvings on the facades and elegant windows that were once such a fixture on residential homes in this area. Ave Elm has several two- and three-story residential houses dating from the late 1800s.

Some of the most impressive houses are along Boulevard Dorchester east of Ave Greene. There you'll find a clump of almost castlelike greystone residences dating from around 1890. Many of these homes still have original doors, stained-glass windows and facades decorated with elaborate carvings.

For a bite to eat, sidewalk cafés and window-shopping, take a stroll along pedestrian-friendly Ave Greene just south of Rue Sherbrooke. The western edge of Westmount, along Rue Sherbrooke Ouest, also has a growing number of trendy shops and restaurants.

A few key sights in the neighborhood:

- Westmount Square (Map pp62–3; cnr Ave Wood & Blvd de Maisonneuve Ouest; Ⓜ Atwater) Famed architect Ludwig Mies van der Rohe, a disciple of the Bauhaus movement, made a bold statement in 1966 with this black metal-and-glass office-apartment-shopping complex. It is linked to a section of the underground city (see the boxed text, opposite), and its exclusive stores are frequented by well-heeled Westmounters.
- Westmount City Hall (Map pp44–5; ☎ 514-989-5200; 4333 Côte St-Antoine; ⏲ 8:30am-4:30pm; Ⓜ Atwater) The faux medieval towers of Westmount City Hall come as a surprise after the skyscrapers of downtown. This Tudor gatehouse in rough-hewn stone looks like something from an English period drama. A lawn-bowling green lies in the rear.
- Westmount Park & Library (Map pp44–5; ☎ 514-989-5300; 4575 Rue Sherbrooke Ouest; ⏲ 10am-9pm Mon-Fri, to 5pm Sat & Sun; Ⓜ Atwater) The lovely Westmount Park encompasses pathways, streams and concealed nooks that recall the whimsical nature of English public gardens. At the western boundary the Westmount Public Library stands stolid, with its Romanesque brickwork, leaded glass and delightful bas-reliefs dedicated to wisdom. Two fine buildings are attached: the Westmount Conservatory (a Victorian greenhouse) and the Victoria Jubilee Hall, fronted by a beautiful floral clock. Both can be visited during business hours.

house out back and an attached conservatory – rare features among the remaining Golden Square Mile homes. Architecture buffs will have a good time here picking out the Gothic, Italian and Romanesque Revival elements.

BLACK WATCH HIGHLANDERS REGIMENTAL MUSEUM & ARCHIVES

Map pp62–3

☎ 514-496-1686; 2067 Rue de Bleury; 🕑 11am-3pm Tue Jun-Aug, 7-9pm Tue Sep-May or by appointment; Ⓜ Place-des-Arts

The presence of the legendary Highlanders is usually reserved for holidays and official ceremonies, but military buffs can delve deeper at this small museum of military memorabilia that includes medals, insignia, munitions and small arms from prior to 1969. The fanciful building – a faux Gothic castle, complete with turrets – also houses a national military archive and takes numerous requests for personnel documents. Few Montrealers know about this place because it never advertises and almost never opens.

SEAGRAM HOUSE Map pp62–3

1430 Rue Peel; Ⓜ Peel

For almost seven decades this faux château served as headquarters for the world's largest distilling company – a child of the Prohibition era. When Seagram was sold to France's Vivendi in 2000 the building was donated to McGill University; its new moniker is Martlet House (named after the mythical birds on the university coat of arms).

QUARTIER LATIN & THE VILLAGE

Drinking p144; Eating p128; Shopping p110; Sleeping p187

The young, boisterous neighborhood of the Quartier Latin is a lively if unpolished district packed with buzzing bars, bistros and record shops. Anchor of the neighborhood is the Université du Québec à Montréal, which brings thousands of students streaming in every day and gives the neighborhood its vibrancy.

In the 19th century, the neighborhood was an exclusive residential area for wealthy Francophones. Although many original buildings burned in the great fire of 1852, there are a number of Victorian and art-nouveau gems hidden on the tree-lined streets. Today, the quarter is a hotbed of activity, especially during summer festivals, when energy spills from the streets 24 hours a day.

Gay-friendly doesn't even begin to describe the Village, one of the world's most exuberant communities for people of all persuasions. Packed with eclectic eateries, shops and nightspots, Rue Ste-Catherine is the main thoroughfare, and it closes to traffic in the summer. August is the most frenetic time as hundreds of thousands of international visitors gather to celebrate Divers/Cité (p14), the massive annual Gay Pride parade.

But though Rue Ste-Catherine seethes with fun, and condo development is taking off on the side streets, this is not an area without social problems. Homelessness is prevalent, panhandlers are on most corners east of metro Berri-UQAM, and used syringes are commonly discarded in alleys and residential parking lots.

The handiest access to the area is the green metro line, with stops at Berri-UQAM (close to Rue St-Denis), Beaudry (near the heart of the Village) and Papineau. Bus 30 runs along Rue St-Denis.

THE METRO MUSEUM OF ART

Primarily a mover of the masses, the Montréal metro was also conceived as an enormous art gallery, although not all stations have been decorated. Here are a few highlights from the central zone; many more await your discovery.

Berri-UQAM

A set of murals by artist Robert La Palme representing science, culture and recreation hangs above the main staircase leading to the yellow line. These works were moved here from the 'Man and His World' pavilion of Expo '67 at the request of mayor Jean Drapeau, a buddy of La Palme.

Champ-de-Mars

The station kiosk boasts a set of antique stained-glass windows by Marcelle Ferron, an artist of the Refus Global movement. The abstract forms splash light down into the shallow platform, drenching passengers in color as their trains roll through.

Peel

Circles, circles everywhere: in bright single colors on advertising panels, in the marble of one entrance, above the main staircases, as tiles on the floor – even the bulkhead vents are circular. They're the work of Jean-Paul Mousseau of the Québécois art movement Les Automatistes.

Place-des-Arts

The station's east wall has a back-lit stained-glass mural entitled *Les Arts Lyriques*, by Québécois artist and Oscar-winning filmmaker Frédéric Back. It depicts the evolution of Montréal's music from the first trumpet fanfare played on the island in 1535 to modern composers and conductors.

Further afield, there are plenty of interesting artistic quirks if you decide to ride along the blue line; check out the geometric stained glass by Claude Bettinger at metro Côte-des-Neiges, the colored brick designs by Gilbert Poissant at metro Outremont, or the elaborate hanging grills by Jean-Louis Beaulieu at metro Snowdon.

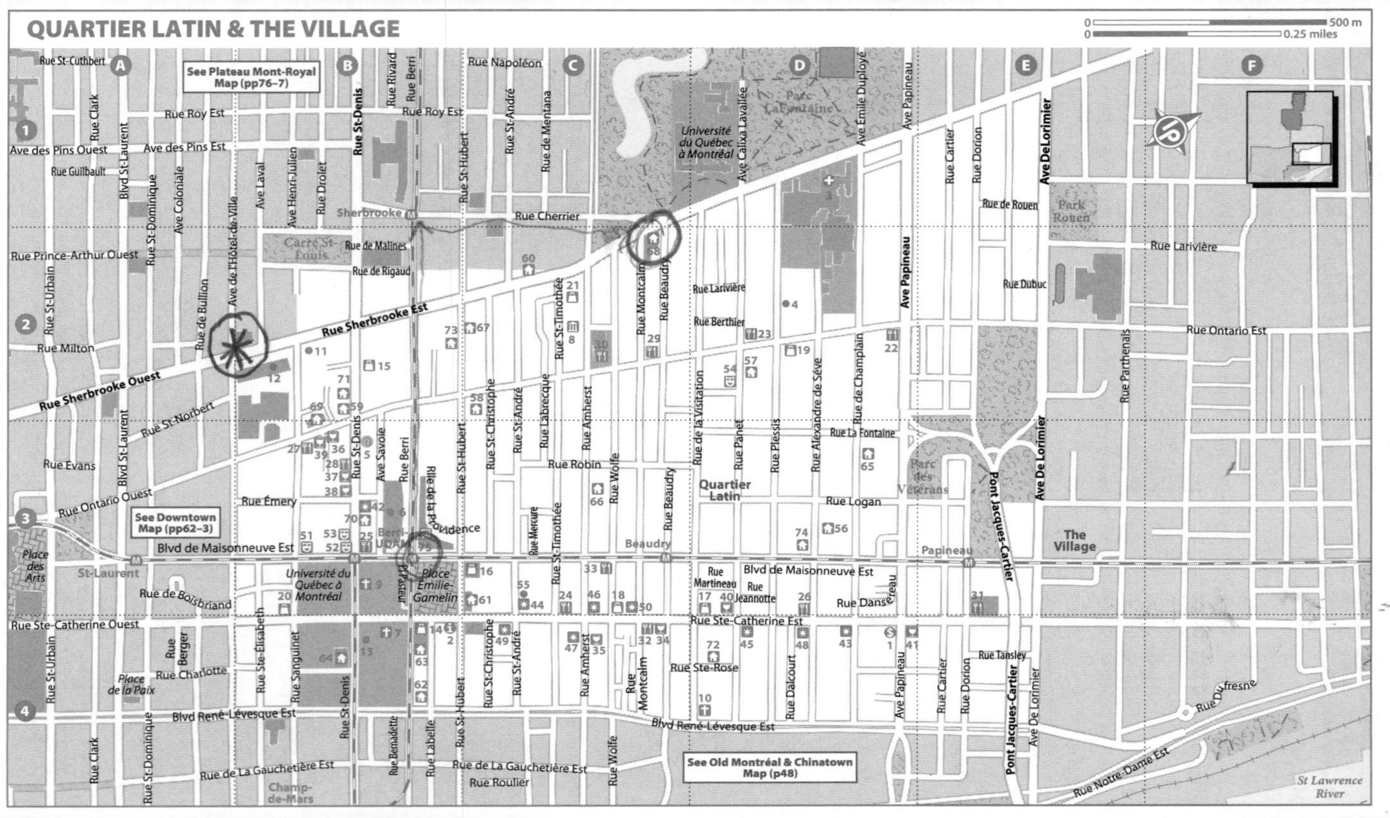

QUARTIER LATIN & THE VILLAGE
0 500 m
0 0.25 miles
See Plateau Mont-Royal Map (pp76–7)
See Downtown Map (pp62–3)
See Old Montréal & Chinatown Map (p48)
St Lawrence River
Rue Sherbrooke Ouest
Rue Sherbrooke Est
Rue Ontario Est
Rue Ontario Ouest
Blvd de Maisonneuve Est
Rue Ste-Catherine Ouest
Rue Ste-Catherine Est
Blvd René-Lévesque Est
Rue Notre-Dame Est
Rue de La Gauchetière Est
Rue St-Cuthbert
Rue St-Urbain
Rue Clark
Blvd St-Laurent
Rue St-Dominique
Ave Coloniale
Rue de Bullion
Ave de l'Hôtel-de-Ville
Ave Laval
Ave Henri-Julien
Rue Drolet
Rue St-Denis
Rue Rivard
Rue Berri
Rue St-Hubert
Rue St-Christophe
Rue St-André
Rue St-Timothée
Rue Labrecque
Rue Mercure
Rue Amherst
Rue Wolfe
Rue Montcalm
Rue Beaudry
Rue de la Visitation
Rue Panet
Rue Plessis
Rue Alexandre de Sève
Rue de Champlain
Ave Papineau
Rue Cartier
Rue Dorion
Ave DeLorimier
Ave De Lorimier
Rue Parthenais
Rue Larivière
Rue Cherrier
Rue Roy Est
Ave des Pins Ouest
Ave des Pins Est
Rue Guilbault
Rue Prince-Arthur Ouest
Rue Milton
Rue Evans
Rue Napoléon
Rue de Mentana
Ave Calixa Lavallée
Ave Émile Duployé
Rue de Rouen
Rue Dubuc
Rue Berthier
Rue La Fontaine
Rue Robin
Rue Logan
Rue Émery
Ave Savoie
Rue St-Norbert
Rue de Malines
Rue de Rigaud
Rlle de la Providence
Pl Pasteur
Rue Martineau
Rue Jeannotte
Rue Dansereau
Rue de Boisbriand
Rue Ste-Élisabeth
Rue Sanguinet
Rue Berger
Rue Charlotte
Rue Ste-Rose
Rue Dalcourt
Rue Tansley
Rue Dufresne
Rue Bernadette
Rue Labelle
Rue Roullier
Pont Jacques-Cartier
Université du Québec à Montréal
Parc Lafontaine
Park Rouen
Carré St-Louis
Parc des Vétérans
Quartier Latin
The Village
Place des Arts
Place Émilie-Gamelin
Place de la Paix
Champ-de-Mars
Sherbrooke
Berri-UQAM
Beaudry
Papineau
St-Laurent

QUARTIER LATIN & THE VILLAGE

INFORMATION		
Bank of Montreal	1	D4
Centre d'Information Gay Touristique du Village	2	B4
Hôpital Notre Dame	3	D1
Montreal Gay & Lesbian Community Centre & Library	4	D2
Netopia	5	B3
SIGHTS (pp71–4)		
Bibliothèque et Archives Nationale du Québec	6	B3
Chapelle Notre-Dame-de-Lourdes	7	B4
Ecomusée du Fier Monde	8	C2
Église St-Jacques	9	B3
Église St-Pierre Apôtre	10	D4
Maison Fréchette	11	B2
Mont St-Louis	12	B2
Université du Québec à Montréal	13	B4
SHOPPING (pp110–11)		
Archambault	14	B4
La Capoterie	15	B2
Le Château	16	C3
Priape	17	D3
Renaud Bray	18	C3
Tabagie Pat & Robert	19	D2
Underworld	20	B3
Zéphyr	21	C2
EATING (pp128–30)		
Au Petit Extra	22	D2
Bistro le Porto	23	D2
Chez Cora	24	C3
Juliette et Chocolat	25	B3
Kilo	26	D3
La Paryse	27	B3
Le Commensal	28	B3
Le Spirite Lounge	29	C2
Marché St Jacques	30	C2
Metro (Supermarket)	31	E3
Mozza	32	C4
O'Thym	33	C3
DRINKING (p144)		
Bistro Kilo	(see 26)	
Club Date Piano-Bar	34	C4
Donjon	35	C4
Le Magellan Bar	36	B3
Le St-Sulpice	37	B3
Les Trois Brasseurs	38	B3
Quartier Latin Pub	39	B3
Saloon	40	D3
Stud Bar	41	D4
NIGHTLIFE (pp151–8)		
Bistro à Jojo	42	B3
Bourbon Complex	43	D4
Circus After Hours	44	C3
La Track	(see 43)	
Le Drugstore	45	D4
Le National	(see 34)	
Mado Caberet	46	C3
Mississippi Club	(see 43)	
Parking Nightclub	47	C4
Sky Pub & Club	48	D4
Stereo	49	C4
Unity II	50	C3
THE ARTS (pp159–66)		
Cinémathèque Québécoise	51	B3
National Film Board	52	B3
Théâtre St-Denis	53	B3
Usine C	54	D2
SPORTS & ACTIVITIES (pp167–77)		
Nautilus Plus	55	C3
Underworld	(see 20)	
SLEEPING (pp187–90)		
Alexandre Logan	56	D3
Atmosphere	57	D2
Au Gît'Ann	58	C2
Auberge Le Jardin d'Antoine	59	B2
Hôtel de Paris	60	C2
Hôtel Gouverneur Place Dupuis	61	C3
Hôtel Le Roberval	62	B4
Hôtel Lord Berri	63	B4
Hôtel St-Denis	64	B4
La Claire Fontaine	65	D3
La Loggia	66	C3
La Maison St Hubert	67	C2
Le Gîte du Parc Lafontaine	68	C2
Le Jazz Hostel St-Denis	69	B2
Le Relais Lyonnais	70	B3
Montréal Espace Confort	71	B2
Ruta Bagage B&B	72	D4
Studios du Quartier Latin	73	B2
Turquoise B&B	74	D3
TRANSPORT (pp251–5)		
Station Centrale de l'Autobus (Main Bus Station)	75	B3

BIBLIOTHÈQUE ET ARCHIVES NATIONALE DU QUÉBEC Map p72

☎ 514-873-1100, 800-363-9028; 475 Blvd de Maisonneuve Est; ⏲ 10am-10pm Mon-Fri, to 5pm Sat & Sun; Ⓜ Berri-UQAM

Opened in 2005, this stunning building houses both the library and national archives of Québec. The library itself is 33,000 sq meters, connected to the metro and underground city. Since 1968, everything published in Québec (books, brochures, sound recordings, posters) has been deposited here. Bibliophiles can enjoy free guided tours.

ÉCOMUSÉE DU FIER MONDE Map p72

☎ 514-528-8444; 2050 Rue Amherst; admission $6; ⏲ 11am-8pm Wed, 9:30am-4pm Thu & Fri, 10:30am-5pm Sat & Sun; Ⓜ Berri-UQAM

This magnificent ex-bathhouse explores the history of Centre-Sud, an industrial district in Montréal until the 1950s and now part of the Village. The museum's permanent exhibition, 'Triumphs and Tragedies of a Working-Class Society,' puts faces on the industrial revolution through a series of excellent photos and multimedia displays. The 1927 building is the former Bain Généreux, an art-deco public bathhouse modeled on one in Paris. Frequent modern-art exhibitions are also held here.

CHAPELLE NOTRE-DAME-DE-LOURDES Map p72

☎ 514-842-4704; 430 Rue Ste-Catherine Est Ⓜ Berri-UQAM

Now hidden among the university buildings, this Romanesque gem was built by the Sulpicians in 1876 to cement their influence in Montréal. The chapel was designed by Rue St-Denis resident, artist Napoléon Bourassa, whose frescoes dotted about the interior are regarded as his crowning glory.

ÉGLISE ST-PIERRE-APÔTRE Map p72

☎ 514-524-3791; 1201 Rue de la Visitation; Ⓜ Beaudry

The Church of St Peter the Apostle belonged to the monastery of the Oblate fathers who settled in Montréal in the mid-19th century. The neoclassical church in the Village has a number of fine decorations – flying buttresses, stained glass, statues in Italian marble – but nowadays the house of worship is more renowned for its gay-friendly Sunday services. It also houses the Chapel of Hope, the first chapel in the world consecrated to the memory of victims of AIDS.

MAISON FRÉCHETTE Map p72

306 Rue Sherbrooke Est; Ⓜ Sherbrooke

Louis Fréchette, a 19th-century poet, journalist and member of parliament, lived in this striking Second Empire residence just off Rue St-Denis. The French actress (and one-time courtesan) Sarah Bernhardt stayed here during her North American tours in the 1890s.

MONT ST-LOUIS Map p72

244 Rue Sherbrooke Est; Ⓜ Sherbrooke

This charming greystone was converted into a Christian boys' school. The long, segmented facade is one of the best examples of French Second Empire style, with a mansard roof, arches and pavilions.

RUE STE-CATHERINE EST Map p72

Montréal's embrace of the gay community is tightest along the eastern end of Rue Ste-Catherine, a one-time bed of vice and shabby tenements. This strip of restaurants and clubs has been made so presentable that middle-class families mingle with drag queens on the pavements, all part of the neighborhood scenery. One of the anchors of the street is Mado Cabaret (p155), famed for its campy, tongue-in-cheek shows.

UNIVERSITÉ DU QUÉBEC À MONTRÉAL Map p72

☎ 514-596-3000; 405 Rue Ste-Catherine Est; Ⓜ Berri-UQAM

The modern, rather uninspiring buildings of Montréal's French-language university blend into the cityscape and are linked to the underground city and the Berri-UQAM metro station. The most striking aspect here is the old Gothic steeple of the Église St-Jacques (Map p72), which has been integrated into the university's facade.

PLATEAU MONT-ROYAL

Drinking p144; Eating p130; Shopping p111; Sleeping p190

East of the verdant Parc du Mont-Royal, the Plateau captures the city's imagination like no other neighborhood. Writers set their novels in it, filmmakers use the photogenic streets as a backdrop, and young Québécois from all over daydream about pulling up stakes and moving here – if only real-estate prices weren't so high.

Originally a working-class neighborhood, in the 1960s and '70s the Plateau became the place where writers, singers and all manner of artists lived. The district was made famous by playwright Michel Tremblay, who took an unvarnished look at some of its more colorful residents. Pockets of the district were famously poor. But over recent years, gentrification has arrived in full force, transforming the quarter into a highly coveted destination.

The main drags are Blvd St-Laurent ('the Main'), Rue St-Denis and Ave du Mont-Royal, with a wealth of sidewalk cafés, restaurants and shops. The streets of Rue Prince-Arthur and Ave Duluth are lined with eateries proudly posting placards announcing '*apportez votre vin*'(bring your own wine), which only adds to the congenial atmosphere.

The Plateau is also a good access point for entering the lush Parc du Mont-Royal (p79).

Transport to the Plateau is via the orange metro line, at the stations of Sherbrooke, Mont-Royal and Laurier. Bus 55 runs along Blvd St-Laurent; bus 30 coasts along Rue St-Denis.

BOULEVARD ST-LAURENT Map pp76–7

A dividing line between the city's east and west, Blvd St-Laurent – 'the Main' – has always been a focus of action, a gathering place for people of many languages and backgrounds. In 1996 it was declared a national historic site, for its role as ground zero for so many Canadian immigrants and future Montrealers. The label 'the Main' or 'Rue Principale' has stuck in the local lingo since the 19th century. Today it's a gateway into the Plateau and a fascinating street to explore.

CARRÉ ST-LOUIS Map pp76–7

cnr Rue St-Denis & Rue Prince-Arthur; Ⓜ Sherbrooke

This lovely green space with a three-tiered fountain is flanked by beautiful rows of Second Empire homes. In the 19th century a reservoir here was filled, and a neighborhood emerged for well-to-do French families. Artists and poets gathered in the area back then, and creative types like filmmakers and fashion designers now occupy houses in the streets nearby. The café, which opens in the summer, is a good spot for a pick-me-up, with occasional musicians creating the soundtrack for the square. Nearby students and local residents take in precious rays, while others linger puffing on strange smokes.

Carré St-Louis feeds west into Rue Prince-Arthur, a former slice of 1960s hippie culture that has refashioned itself as a popular restaurant-and-bar strip.

RUE ST-DENIS Map pp76–7

The backbone of Montréal's francophone shopping district, Rue St-Denis is lined with hat and garment shops, überhip record stores and terrace cafés designed to keep people from getting any work done. Summer crowds flock to the inviting bistros and bars on both sides of the street.

PARC LAFONTAINE Map pp76–7

cnr Rue Sherbrooke Est & Ave du Parc LaFontaine; Ⓜ Sherbrooke

This great verdant municipal park is the city's third-largest, after Parc du Mont-Royal and Parc Maisonneuve. In the warmer months weary urbanites flock to leafy LaFontaine to enjoy the walking and bicycle paths, the attractive ponds and the general air of relaxation that pervades the park. The view down the steep banks from Ave du Parc LaFontaine is impressive, especially if the fountains are in play. You can rent paddleboats in the summer and go ice-skating in winter. The open-air Théâtre de Verdure (p165) draws a laid-back crowd on summer evenings.

ÉGLISE ST-JEAN-BAPTISTE Map pp76–7

309 Rue Rachel Est; Ⓜ Mont-Royal

Dedicated to St John the Baptist, the patron saint of French Canadians, this church was the hub of working-class Catholic families in the late 19th and early 20th centuries. Plateau residents weren't rich but they channeled large sums of money into

PLATEAU MONT-ROYAL

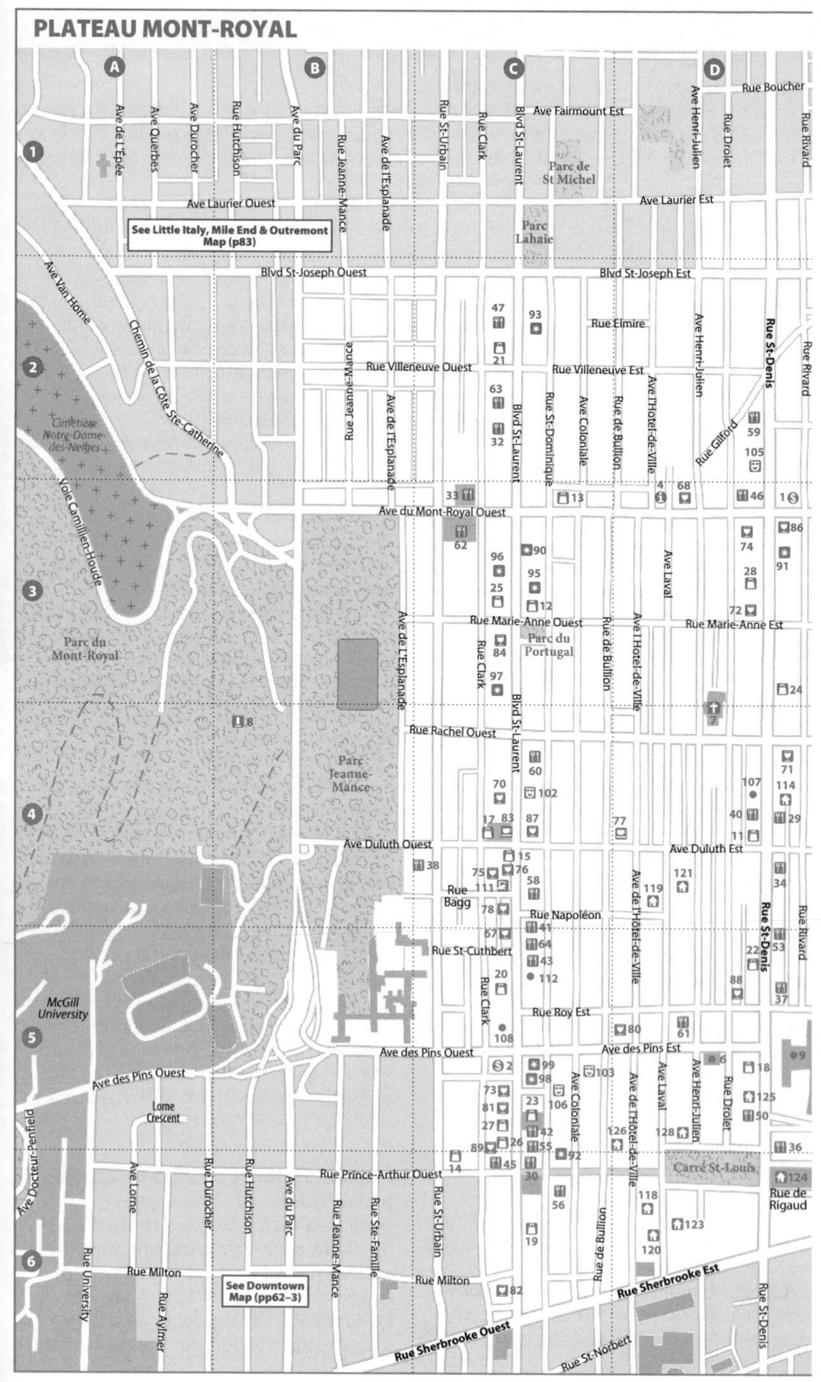

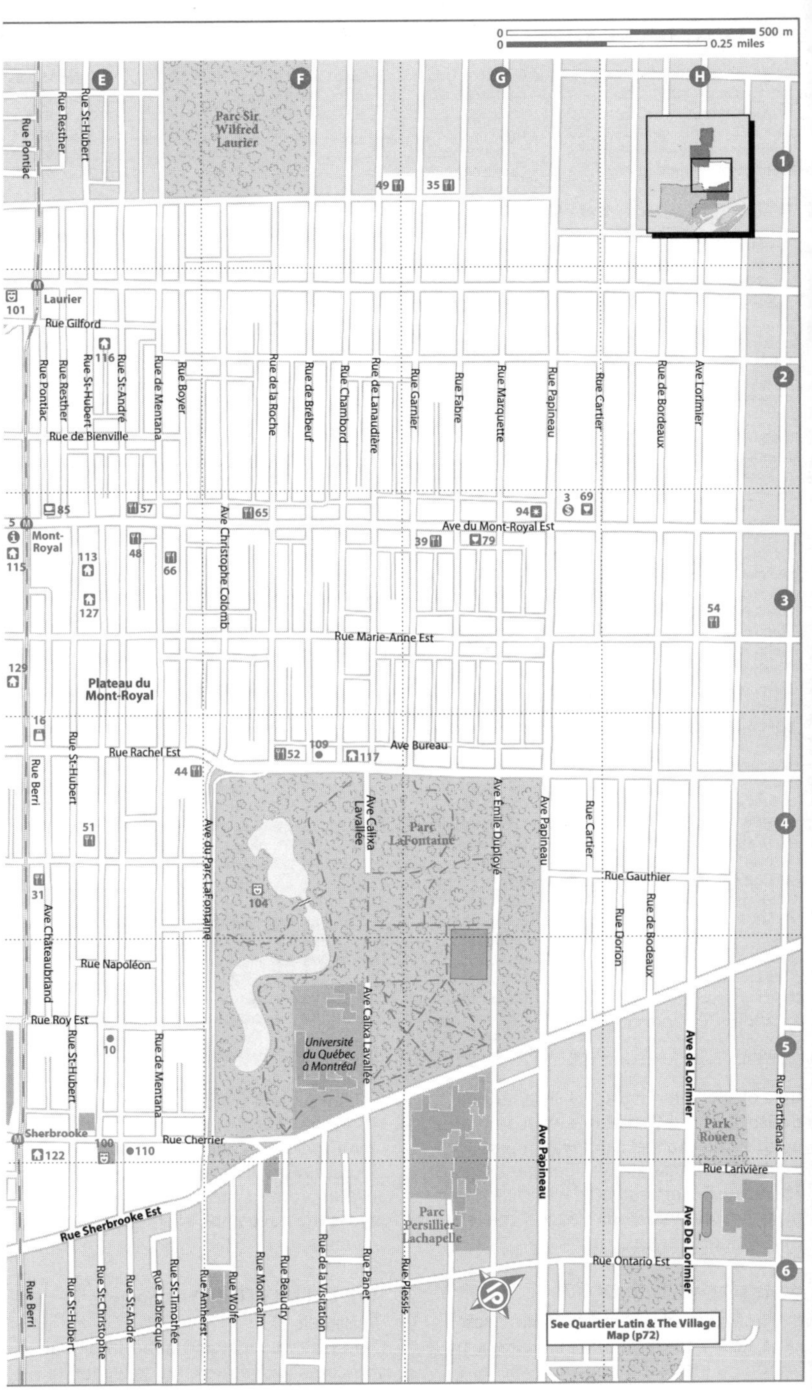

See Quartier Latin & The Village Map (p72)

PLATEAU MONT-ROYAL

INFORMATION

Banque Desjardins 1 D3
Banque Laurentienne 2 C5
Banque Laurentienne 3 G3
Boutique Tourisme Jeunesse 4 D3
Mont-Royal Information Booth 5 E3

SIGHTS (pp75–81)

Armoury of the Mount Royal Fusiliers 6 D5
Aveda Montréal Lifestyle Salon Spa & Academy (see 30)
Église St-Jean-Baptiste 7 D4
George Etienne Cartier Monument 8 B4
Institut des Sourdes-Muettes 9 D5
Palestre Nationale (see 100)
Place Roy 10 E5

SHOPPING (pp111–13)

Boutique Le Marcheur 11 D4
Coffre Aux Trésors du Chainon 12 C3
Cruella 13 C3
Duo 14 C6
Friperie St-Laurent 15 C4
Kanuk 16 E4
Le Point Vert 17 C4
Librairie Michel Fortin 18 D5
Lola & Emily 19 C6
Moog Audio 20 C5
Preloved 21 C2
Revenge 22 D5
Scandale 23 C5
Scarpa 24 D3
Schreter 25 C3
Space FB 26 C5
U&I 27 C5
Zone 28 D3

EATING (pp130–5)

Au Festin de Babette 29 D4
Au Pain Doré 30 C6
Au Pied de Cochon 31 E4
Aux Vivres 32 C2
Beauty's 33 C3
Brûlerie St Denis 34 D4
Byblos 35 G1
Café Cherrier 36 D5
Café Fruits Folie 37 D5
Café Santropol 38 C4
Chez Cora 39 G3
Chu Chai 40 D4
Coco Rico 41 C4
Euro Deli 42 C5
Jano 43 C5
La Banquise 44 E4
La Belle Province 45 C6
La Binerie Mont Royal 46 D3
La Sala Rosa 47 C2
L'Avenue 48 E3
Le Fromentier 49 F1
Le Nil Bleu 50 D5
Le Piton de la Fournaise 51 E4
Le Poisson Rouge 52 F4
L'Express 53 D5
Ma-am-m Bolduc 54 H3
Maestro SVP 55 C5
Mazurka 56 C6
Misto 57 E3
Moishe's 58 C4
Ouzeri 59 D2
Patati Patata 60 C4
Pintxo 61 D5
Provigo Supermarket 62 C3
Robin des Bois 63 C2
Schwartz's 64 C5
St-Viateur Bagel & Café 65 F3
Tampopo 66 E3

DRINKING (pp144–8)

Bar Korova 67 C5
Bar Plan B 68 D3
Bar Salon La Porte Rouge 69 G3
Barfly 70 C4
Barouf 71 D4
Bières & Compagnie 72 D3
Bifteck 73 C5
Bily Kun 74 D3
Blizzarts 75 C4
Bluedog Motel 76 C4
Chez José 77 D4
Copacabana 78 C4
Edgar Hypertaverne 79 G3
Else's 80 D5
Go Go Lounge 81 C5
Koko 82 C6
Laïka 83 C4
Les Bobards 84 C3
Les Folies 85 E3
L'Escogriffe (see 74)
Quai Des Brumes 86 D3
Reservoir 87 C4
Salon Officiel 88 D5
Ye Olde Orchard Pub & Grill 89 C5

NIGHTLIFE (pp151–8)

Belmont 90 C3
Cactus 91 D3
Café Campus 92 C6
Casa del Popolo 93 C2
La Tulipe 94 G3
L'Académie de Tango Argentin 95 C3
Le Ballatou 96 C3
Le Divan Orange 97 C3
Saphir 98 C5
Tokyo Bar 99 C5

THE ARTS (pp159–66)

Agora de la Danse 100 E5
Espace Tangente (see 100)
Grands Ballets Canadiens de Montréal 101 E2
Mainline Theatre 102 C4
Théâtre de Quat' Sous 103 C5
Théâtre de Verdure 104 F4
Théâtre du Rideau Vert 105 D2
Théatre La Chapelle 106 C5

SPORTS & ACTIVITIES (pp167–77)

Altitude Sports Plein Air 107 D4
Coupe Bizzarre 108 C5
La Maison des Cyclistes 109 F4
Le Grand Cycle 110 E5
Piscine Schubert 111 C4
Studio Bliss 112 C5

SLEEPING (pp190–2)

À la Bonne Heure B&B 113 E3
Anne ma Soeur Anne 114 D4
Au Piano Blanc 115 E3
Auberge de Jeunesse Maeva 116 E2
Auberge de la Fontaine 117 F4
Aux Portes de la Nuit 118 D6
Bienvenue B&B 119 D4
Bob & Mariko's Bed & Breakfast 120 D6
Chez Brasil 121 D4
Couette et Café Cherrier 122 E5
Gingerbread Manor B&B 123 D6
Hôtel de l'Institut 124 D6
Kutuma Hotel & Suites 125 D5
Le Gîte 126 D5
Le Grand Cycle (see 110)
Le Rayon Vert 127 E3
Pierre et Dominique B&B 128 D5
Shézelles 129 E3

the colorful interior, especially after two disastrous fires. The altar is white imported marble, the chancel canopy is in pink marble and there are two Casavant organs. The acoustics are splendid and the church plays host to numerous classical concerts throughout the year.

PLACE ROY Map pp76–7

cnr Rue Roy Est & Rue St-André; M Sherbrooke

On a sleepy corner of the Plateau sits an intriguing installation by artist Michel Goulet. A giant stone map of the world sits in the center of the small square, with water trickling alongside the continents. Goulet finished off the piece by scattering several bronze chairs of different types across the pavement, each facing a different direction.

AVE DU MONT-ROYAL Map pp76–7

M Mont-Royal

Old-fashioned five-and-dime stores rub shoulders with a growing collection of trendy restaurants and fashion boutiques on Ave du Mont-Royal. The nightlife here has surged to the point that it rivals Blvd St-Laurent, with bars and nightclubs ranging from the sedate to uproarious. Intimate shops, secondhand stores and ultramodern boutiques offer eye-catching apparel.

PALESTRE NATIONALE Map pp76–7

840 Rue Cherrier; Ⓜ Sherbrooke

The neobaroque National Palace (1918) was formerly a sports center for local youth, drawing crowds to amateur athletic events in the 1980s. Note the horn-of-plenty motif above the portico. It now houses the university dance troupe Agora de la Danse (p162).

PARC DU PORTUGAL Map pp76–7

cnr Blvd St-Laurent & Rue Marie-Anne

This quaint little park dedicated to Portuguese immigrants was spruced up in 2003, the 50th anniversary of the official founding of the Portuguese community in Montréal. At the rear of the park, next to the little summer pavilion, a plaque reads in translation: 'We arrived in this area seeking a new life and ample horizons.' The gates and fountain are covered with colorful glazed tiles.

INSTITUT DES SOURDES-MUETTES Map pp76–7

☎ 514-284-2581; 3600 Rue Berri; Ⓜ Sherbrooke

The little silver-plated cupola of the Deaf and Dumb Institute has reigned over the Plateau since 1900. An earlier building was built on clay, a problem typical to the area, and the soft ground gave way. The architects didn't take any chances the second time around and the newer version sits on 1700 stakes and a concrete slab 60cm deep. The building still houses a private communications institute for the deaf, along with other offices.

AVE CHÂTEAUBRIAND Map pp76–7

This shady little lane is a classic story of Plateau renovation. Until the early 1990s this was one of the Plateau's poorer streets where residents painted murals on the facades to disguise the deterioration. The murals have long since gone and in their place have emerged colorful homes with trim little gardens and potted plants hanging under the windows.

ARMOURY OF THE MOUNT ROYAL FUSILIERS Map pp76–7

☎ 514-283-7444; 3721 Ave Henri-Julien; Ⓜ Sherbrooke

The former munitions depot of this Canadian Black Watch regiment is a miniature château complete with steel turrets and battlements. Today it's an administrative center and a museum of old military gear, but you'll be hard-pressed to find it open.

PARC DU MONT-ROYAL AREA

Montrealers are proud of their 'mountain,' so don't call it a hill as Oscar Wilde did when he visited the city in the 1880s. The charming, leafy expanse of Mont-Royal Park is charged for a wide range of outdoor activities. The wooded slopes and grassy meadows have stunning views that make it all the more popular for jogging, picnicking, horseback riding, bicycling and throwing Frisbees. Winter brings skating, tobogganing and cross-country skiing. Binoculars are a good idea for the bird feeders that have been set up along some walking trails.

The park was laid out by Frederick Law Olmsted, the architect of New York's Central Park. The idea came from bourgeois residents in the adjacent Golden Square Mile who fretted about vanishing greenery. Note that walking in the park after sunset isn't such a safe idea.

Contrary to what people may try to tell you, this place is *not* an extinct volcano. Rather, Parc du Mont-Royal is a hangover from when magma penetrated the earth's crust millions of years ago. A kind of erosion-proof rock was formed, so while time and the elements were wearing down the ground around it, the 232m-high hunk of rock, which locals affectionately refer to as 'The Mountain,' stood firm.

On the north side of the park lie two enormous cemeteries, Cimetière Notre-Dame-des-Neiges (Catholic) and the Cimetière Mont-Royal (Protestant and nondenominational).

For more info on the park visit www.lemontroyal.qc.ca.

BELVÉDÈRE CAMILLIEN-HOUDE Map pp44–5

Voie Camillien-Houde; Ⓜ Mont-Royal, then bus 11

This is the most popular lookout on Mont-Royal thanks to its accessibility and large parking lot. Naturally enough, it's a

TAM-TAM JAM

Huge crowds of alternative-loving free spirits gather every Sunday afternoon in summer for the legendary 'tam-tam' concerts at the edge of Parc du Mont-Royal, when the pounding rhythms and whirling dancers seem to put everyone in a trance. The action takes place at the George-Étienne Cartier monument (Map pp76–7) opposite Parc Jeanne-Mance, at the corner of Ave du Parc and Ave Duluth. The percussionists are tireless in their dedication, with some riffs going on for an hour or more, and other instruments join in on the odd occasion. Vendors along the grass sell alternative handicrafts (eg Indian dream catchers, crystals and bead jewelry) and sarongs, plus percussion instruments if you left your tambourine and conga drum at home.

magnet for couples once night falls, making it nearly impossible on summer nights to find a parking space.

You can walk to Chalet du Mont-Royal about half an hour away. To get to this lookout, take the stairs that lead from the parking lot. There's also a quick alternative: after the first set of stairs turn left and walk a few meters to an unofficial lookout point. The protruding boulder gives a fantastic panorama free of guard rails.

CHALET DU MONT-ROYAL Map pp62–3

stairs up from Redpath Cres; seasonal

Constructed in 1932, this grand old white villa, complete with bay windows, contains canvases that depict scenes of Canadian history. Big bands strut their stuff on the huge balcony in summer, reminiscent of the 1930s. Most people, however, flock here for the spectacular views of downtown from the Kondiaronk lookout nearby. It's about a 20-minute walk from the park entrance on Ave de Pins.

LAC DES CASTORS Map pp62–3

Created in a former marsh as part of a work-creation project, Beaver Lake is a center of activity year-round. You can rent paddleboats on the lake or, in winter, ice skates and sleds from the pavilion, and refreshments are sold in summer. The slopes above are served by a ski lift when it snows.

MAISON SMITH Map pp62–3

Voie Camillien-Houde; 9am-5pm Mon-Fri, 10am-6pm Sat & Sun; 11

Constructed in 1858 by a merchant who wanted to get away from the pollution and overpopulation of the rest of Montréal, this house was one of 16 private properties on the mountain that were expropriated by the government in 1869 once the land was officially designated for a park. The building houses a small permanent exhibition on the history of the park, a visitors center and a café selling soups and sandwiches. There's also a gift shop selling bird-watching paraphernalia, maps of the park and souvenirs.

CROIX DU MONT-ROYAL Map pp44–5

About 1km northeast of Kondiaronk lookout stands the Mont-Royal Cross, one of Montréal's most familiar landmarks. Thirty-one meters tall and made of reinforced steel, the cross was erected in 1924 on the very spot where Maisonneuve placed a wooden cross.

According to legend, when floods threatened the fledgling colony in 1643, Maissonneuve prayed to the Virgin Mary to save the town. When the waters receded, out of gratitude, Maisonneuve carried a cross up the steep slopes and planted it there. The white illuminated cross is visible from anywhere downtown.

CIMETIÈRE NOTRE-DAME-DES-NEIGES Map pp44–5

514-735-1361; www.notredamedesneiges cemetery.ca; 4601 Chemin de la Côte-des-Neiges; 8am-7pm Apr-Oct, 8am-5pm Nov-Mar; M Côte-des-Neiges

More than one million people have found their final resting place here since this Catholic cemetery opened in 1854, making it the largest cemetery in Canada. It has a few intriguing mausoleums that emit solemn music, including that of Marguerite Bourgeoys, a nun and teacher who was beatified in 1982 (see Chapelle Notre-Dame-de-Bonsecours, p50).

The catalog of permanent guests includes 20 Montréal mayors, several ex-passengers of the *Titanic*, and Calixa Lavallée, the composer of 'O Canada.' The cemetery office (Map pp44–5; 8:30am-4:30pm Mon-Fri, 9am-4pm Sat) has brochures for self-guided tours around the tombs but there's also a map posted at the entrance.

CIMETIÈRE MONT-ROYAL Map pp44–5

☎ 514-279-7358; 1297 Chemin de la Forêt; ⌚ 10am-6pm; Ⓜ Édouard-Montpetit

Much smaller than Notre-Dame-des-Neiges, this cemetery was founded in 1852 for the last journey of non-Catholic Montrealers – Presbyterians, Anglicans, Unitarians, Baptists and nondenominationals. The most famous tomb is of Anna Leonowens, the inspiration for the heroine in the musical *The King and I*. The cemetery is laid out like a landscape garden and is perfect for the Goth-historically interested.

LITTLE ITALY, MILE END & OUTREMONT

Drinking p148; Eating p135; Shopping p113

The zest and flavor of the old country find their way into the lively Little Italy district, where the espresso seems stiffer, the pasta sauce thicker and the chefs plumper. Italian football games seem to be broadcast straight onto Blvd St-Laurent, where the green-white-red flag is proudly displayed. Drink in the atmosphere on a stroll and don't miss a visit to the magnificent market of Jean-Talon (below), always humming with activity.

Though Little Italy is a fairly compact area, Italians are the third-largest ethnic group in Montréal, after the French and British, and many of them have been here just as long. Many families settled in the late 19th century and after WWII. Stroll through this neighborhood and you'll encounter a riot of dialects spilling from apartment balconies and mom-and-pop cafés. The main arteries are Blvd St-Laurent, with its row of restaurants, shops and cafés, and Rue Dante. Tiny, manicured Parc Martel is the main square but it's dwarfed by Marché Jean-Talon, where almost everyone converges. The whole district is less than 1 sq km around and easily walkable.

Mile End has been dubbed 'the new Plateau' by the exodus of students and artists seeking a more affordable, less polished hangout, and has quickly become a trendsetter in its own right. Mile End has upscale dinging along Ave Laurier, the best bagels in town, and increasingly trendy hangouts at its epicenter: Rue St-Viateur and Blvd St-Laurent. Mile End is bordered roughly by Blvd St-Joseph to the south, Ave Henri-Julien to the east, Ave du Parc to the west and Rue Bernard to the north. The main strips for bars, cafés and restaurants are Ave Fairmount and Ave St-Viateur (both running east–west) as well as Ave du Parc (north–south).

Outremont is largely a residence for wealthy Francophones, with few attractions aside from pretty streets and some upscale dining and shopping. Fabulous old mansions and oversized family homes lie on leafy streets northwest of Rue Bernard. There is also a significant Hassidic community in Outremont, though most of the synagogues and community centers are in neighboring Mile End.

Outremont is bordered by Parc du Mont-Royal to the west, Ave du Parc to the east, Blvd St-Joseph to the south and Ave Van Horne to the north. The two most interesting streets for travelers for boutiques, browsing and eating are Ave Laurier Ouest and Rue Bernard Ouest.

Little Italy is about the only neighborhood where it's not a pleasant walk to reach the next neighborhood of interest, it being too far and the scenery unremarkable. Hop on the orange metro line at either de Castelnau or Jean-Talon stations to zip down to Rosemont or Laurier stations (for access to Mile End). Outremont has its own eponymous station lying on the blue line, meaning you'll have to transfer at Jean-Talon or Snowdon to get to points south.

Bus 55 runs along Blvd St-Laurent.

MARCHÉ JEAN-TALON Map p83

☎ 514-277-1588; 7075 Ave Casgrain; ⏰ 7am-8pm Mon-Fri, 7am-6pm Sat & Sun; Ⓜ Jean-Talon

The pride of Little Italy, this huge covered market is Montréal's most diverse. Many chefs buy ingredients for their menus here or in the specialty food shops nearby. Three long covered aisles are packed with merchants selling fruit, vegetables and flowers as well as baked goods. The market is flanked by delis and café-restaurants with tiny patios. Even in winter the market is open under big tents.

Be sure to stop by the Marché des Saveurs, one of the few large stores in town devoted entirely to Québec specialties like wine and cider, fresh cheeses, smoked meats, preserves and a huge number of tasteful gifts.

PARC OUTREMONT Map p83

cnr Ave Outremont & Ave St-Viateur; Ⓜ Rosemont

One of Montréal's best-kept secrets, this small leafy green space is a great place for a bit of quiet time after exploring the neighborhood. Lovely Victorian homes ring the park, and benches provide a nice vantage point of the small pond with fountain. Hassidic residents and their children play on the grass or make their way toward the playground. This is a good spot to go, ice cream in hand, after a visit to Le Bilboquet (p138) two blocks northwest.

ÉGLISE ST MICHEL Map p83

☎ 514-277-3300; 5580 Rue St-Urbain; Ⓜ Rosemont

This Byzantine-style church dominates the corner of Rue St-Urbain and Rue St-Viateur.

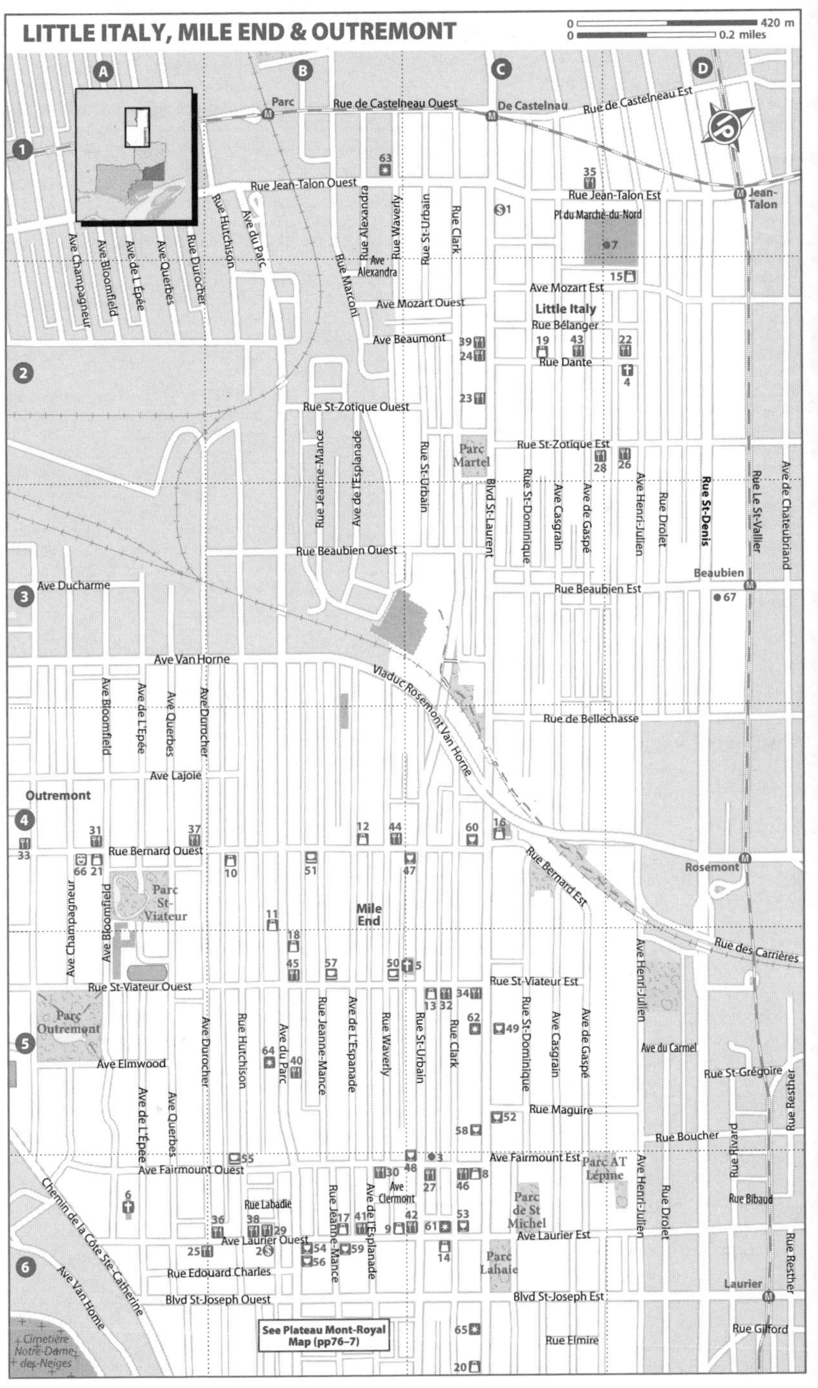
LITTLE ITALY, MILE END & OUTREMONT
0 420 m
0 0.2 miles
Rue de Castelneau Ouest
De Castelnau
Rue de Castelneau Est
Parc
Rue Jean-Talon Ouest
Rue Jean-Talon Est
Jean-Talon
Pl du Marché-du-Nord
Little Italy
Ave Mozart Est
Ave Mozart Ouest
Rue Bélanger
Ave Beaumont
Rue Dante
Rue St-Zotique Ouest
Rue St-Zotique Est
Parc Martel
Rue Beaubien Ouest
Rue Beaubien Est
Beaubien
Ave Ducharme
Ave Van Horne
Viaduc Rosemont Van Horne
Rue de Bellechasse
Ave Lajoie
Outremont
Rue Bernard Ouest
Rue Bernard Est
Rosemont
Rue des Carrières
Parc St-Viateur
Mile End
Rue St-Viateur Ouest
Rue St-Viateur Est
Parc Outremont
Ave Elmwood
Ave du Carmel
Rue St-Grégoire
Rue Maguire
Rue Boucher
Ave Fairmount Ouest
Ave Fairmount Est
Parc AT Lépine
Ave Clermont
Rue Labadie
Parc de St Michel
Ave Laurier Ouest
Ave Laurier Est
Rue Bibaud
Rue Edouard Charles
Parc Lahaie
Laurier
Blvd St-Joseph Ouest
Blvd St-Joseph Est
Chemin de la Côte Ste-Catherine
Ave Van Horne
Cimetière Notre-Dame-des-Neiges
See Plateau Mont-Royal Map (pp76–7)
Rue Elmire
Rue Gilford
Ave Champagneur
Ave Bloomfield
Ave de L'Épée
Ave Querbes
Rue Durocher
Rue Hutchison
Ave du Parc
Rue Marconi
Rue Alexandra
Ave Alexandra
Rue Waverly
Rue St-Urbain
Rue Clark
Rue Jeanne-Mance
Ave de l'Esplanade
Blvd St-Laurent
Rue St-Dominique
Ave Casgrain
Ave de Gaspé
Ave Henri-Julien
Rue Drolet
Rue St-Denis
Rue Le St-Vallier
Ave de Chateaubriand
Rue Rivard
Rue Resther

LITTLE ITALY, MILE END & OUTREMONT

INFORMATION

Banque Laurentienne	1	C1
Banque Nationale	2	B6
Laundry	3	C6

SIGHTS (pp82–5)

Église Madonna della Difesa	4	D2
Église St Michel	5	C5
Église St-Viateur	6	A6
Marché Jean-Talon	7	D1
Mezza Luna Cooking School	(see 19)	

SHOPPING (pp113–14)

Au Papier Japonais	8	C6
Billie	9	B6
Boutique Safran	10	B4
Chez Rose Marie Lingerie	11	B4
Drawn & Quarterly	12	B4
General 54	13	C5
Jet-Setter	14	C6
Le Marché des Saveurs	15	D2
Local 23	16	C4
Mimi & Coco	17	B6
Phonopolis	18	B5
Quincaillerie Dante	19	C2
Rachelle-Béry	20	C6
Un Amour des Thés	21	A4

EATING (pp135–8)

Alati-Caserta	22	D2
Café International	23	C2
Caffè Italia	24	C2
Chez Lévêque	25	A6
Da Enrico	26	D2
Fairmount Bagel	27	C6
Il Mulino	28	C2
Juliette et Chocolat	29	B6
La Khaïma	30	B6
La Moulerie	31	A4
La Panthère Verte	32	C5
Le Bilboquet	33	A4
Le Cagibi Café	34	C5
Le Petit Alep	35	C1
Lémeac	36	B6
Lester's	37	A4
Marché Jean-Talon	(see 7)	
Mikado	38	B6
Milano Supermarket	39	C2
Milos	40	B5
Pâtisserie de Gascogne	41	B6
Phayathai	42	C6
Pizzeria Napoletana	43	C2
Senzala	44	B4
St-Viateur Bagel	45	B5
Wilensky's Light Lunch	46	C6

DRINKING (pp148–9)

Assomoir	47	C4
Bond Lounge Grill	48	C6
Bu	49	C5
Café Olimpico	50	B5
Café Romolo	51	B4
Chez Serge	52	C5
Dieu du Ciel	53	C6
La Buvette Chez Simone	54	B6
La Croissanterie Figaro	55	B6
La Petite Idée Fixe	56	B6
Le Cagibi Café	(see 34)	
Le Club Social	57	B5
Snack'n Blues	58	C5
Toi Moi & Café	59	B6
Whiskey Café	60	C4

NIGHTLIFE (pp151–8)

Baldwin Barmacie	61	C6
Green Room	62	C5
Il Motore	63	B1
Kola Note	64	B5
La Sala Rossa	65	C6

THE ARTS (pp159–66)

Théâtre Outremont	66	A4

SPORTS & ACTIVITIES (pp167–77)

Ovarium	67	D3

Its dome and soaring turret make it one of the more unique examples of church architecture in Montréal.

Completed in 1915, St Michel served a mostly Irish community up through the 1960s (when it was known as 'St Mike's' and was the largest English-speaking parish in Montréal). Intriguing elements include the massive dome with a depiction of St Michael vanquishing the seven-headed serpent (representing the seven deadly sins), figures of downward-descending angels (representing the fallen angels cast into hell) painted on the pendentives, and the shamrocks hidden in the design elements. Today, the church serves a largely Polish community, the latest wave of immigrants to the area.

RETURN OF THE MONTRÉAL MELON

In its heyday it was truly the Queen of Melons. A single specimen might easily have reached 9kg and its spicy flavor earned it the nickname 'Nutmeg Melon.' The market gardeners of western Montréal did a booming business in the fruit.

After WWII small plots vanished as Montréal expanded, and industrial farms had little interest in growing a melon with ultrasensitive rind. By the 1950s the melon was gone – but not forever. In 1996 an enterprising Montréal journalist tracked down Montréal melon seeds held in a US Department of Agriculture collection in Iowa. The first new crop was harvested a year later in a new collective garden in Notre-Dame-de-Grâce, the heart of the old melon-growing district. To sample this blast from the past, visit local markets such as Marché Atwater (p61) or Marché Jean-Talon (p82) after the harvest every September.

ÉGLISE MADONNA DELLA DIFESA

Map p83

6800 Ave Henri-Julien; Ⓜ Jean-Talon

Our Lady of Protection Church was built in 1919 according to the drawings of Florence-born Guido Nincheri (1885–1973), who spent the next two decades working on the Roman-Byzantine structure. The artist painted the church's remarkable frescoes, including one of Mussolini on horseback with a bevy of generals in the background. The work honored the formal recognition by Rome of the pope's sovereignty over Vatican City in 1929 and was unveiled a few years later as Hitler came to power. During WWII, Nincheri and others who had worked on the building were interned by the Canadian authorities. The fresco, still controversial, can be viewed above the high marble altar.

ÉGLISE ST-VIATEUR Map p83

cnr Ave Laurier & Ave Bloomfield; Ⓜ Laurier, then bus 51

If you are already on Ave Laurier for the shopping and food, poke your head into this church, opened in 1910. The interior is pure Gothic Revival with ornate paintings, stained glass, hand-crafted cabinets and sculptures by renowned Montréal artists; the impressive ceiling vaults depict the life of St Viateur. Funeral services for former prime minister Pierre Trudeau were held here in 2000.

SOUTHWEST & OUTER MONTRÉAL

Drinking p149

Sud-Ouest Montréal encompasses many neighborhoods, including Petite-Bourgogne, St-Henri and Pointe-St-Charles. These mainly working-class districts have some worthwhile sights, even though the areas don't make it onto many visitors' itineraries. The Canal de Lachine, which weaves through many of the districts, is lined by a cycling path, making a bike tour (p98) a great way to experience this area's highlights. The rough borders are Old Montréal to the east, the St Lawrence River to the south and west, and the Canal de Lachine to the north.

In this section we've also included several outer neighborhoods, including Côtes-de-Neiges and nearby Notre-Dame-de-Grâce, as well as the Olympic Park and surrounding area.

Côte-des-Neiges, which lies off the western slope of Parc du Mont-Royal, has always been home to an eclectic mix of residents. Even in the 19th century you'd find both upper-crust bankers and low-wage tannery workers. The magnificent Oratoire St-Joseph and the buzzing campus of the prestigious Université de Montréal are the main draws here.

Southwest of Côte-des-Neiges, Notre-Dame-de-Grâce (or simply NDG) is a sleepy residential district, livened up by the cafés and restaurants along Ave Monkland. Few visitors make the trip here, though you will find plenty of students from Concordia University's Loyola campus. You'll hear more English spoken on these streets than in other Montréal neighborhoods. Notre-Dame-de-Grâce is marked by Ave Connaught in the west, Chemin de la Côte-St-Luc in the north, Rue St-Jacques in the south and the jagged line of Ave Grey to the east.

Metro access to the area is via Villa-Maria station for NDG and Côte-des-Neiges station for the neighborhood of the same name.

On the east side of town, the Olympic Park area lies nestled in the heart of the blue-collar Hochelaga-Maisonneuve district. The big draw here is the massive Olympic Stadium, the kid-friendly Biodôme and the verdant Botanical Gardens. To get here, take the green metro line to either Pie-IX or Viau.

SOUTHWEST MONTRÉAL

CANAL DE LACHINE Map pp44–5

The Lachine Canal was built in 1825 as a means of bypassing the treacherous Lachine Rapids on the St Lawrence River. It was closed to shipping in 1970, but the area has been transformed into a 14km-long cycling and pedestrian pathway, with picnic areas and green spaces. Since the canal was reopened for navigation in 2002, flotillas of pleasure and sightseeing boats glide along its calm waters (see p172). Old warehouses converted into luxury condos line the canal near Atwater market.

It's well worth hiring a bike or in-line skates and heading out along the canal path, but try to avoid summer weekends, when it's particularly crowded. For bike rental, see p168; for kayak rental, see p171; for other boating outings, see p172.

FUR TRADE IN LACHINE NATIONAL HISTORIC SITE Map pp44–5

☎ 514-637-7433; 1255 Blvd St-Joseph, borough Lachine; adult/child $4/2; 🕓 9:30am-12:30pm & 1-5pm daily May-Sep, 9:30am-12:30pm & 1-5pm Mon-Fri Apr & Oct-Nov; Ⓜ Jarry, then bus 193 est

This 1803 stone depot is now an engaging little museum telling the story of the fur trade in Canada. The Hudson Bay Company made Lachine the hub of its fur-trading operations because the rapids made further navigation impossible. Visitors can view the furs and old trappers' gear, and costumed interpreters show how the bales and canoes were schlepped by native trappers.

A little office display near the Fur Trade site relates the history of the Canal de Lachine, and guided tours are conducted along the canal on request.

This museum has a gorgeous little location, kissing Lac St-Louis, making it lovely to wander the side streets, particularly behind the Collège Ste-Anne nunnery and the Hôtel de Ville, both along Blvd St-Joseph.

MAISON ST-GABRIEL Map pp44–5

☎ 514-935-8136; www.maisonsaint-gabriel.qc.ca; 2146 Pl Dublin; adult/child/student $8/2/4; 🕓 1-5pm Tue-Sun early Jan–mid-Jun & early Sep–mid Dec; Ⓜ Charlevoix

This magnificent farmhouse in Pointe St-Charles is one of the finest examples of

MONTRÉAL'S FAVORITE GARBAGE-POWERED CIRCUS CITY

If you decide to take a jaunt to Montréal's circus mecca in its working-class St-Michel district, be prepared to be wowed. This innovative complex, named TOHU (which comes from the French expression *tohu-bohu*, for hustle and bustle), includes an arena designed only with the circus arts in mind, Cirque du Soleil's international headquarters and artists' residence and the National Circus School. Moreover, it was built on the sight of North America's second-largest waste dump and the whole complex is now powered completely by methane gas from the landfill garbage beneath it.

The 192 hectares started out as a limestone quarry before being turned into a landfill. By the end of the 1980s it was receiving about one million tons of waste a year. The whole project was taken over by the city in 1988 and one of Montréal's most exciting rehabilitation projects was in the works soon afterwards.

TOHU, rather than being imposed on the neighborhood, has made a real effort to be part of it. Priority is given to residents of St-Michel for jobs and TOHU has already won numerous environmental prizes.

You can visit the complex on your own (via guided audio tour), or on a guided 90-minute tour. TOHU also hosts special exhibitions and outdoor activities (like *petanque* tournaments and bike rallies), and you can catch live performances here throughout the year. Visit the website or contact TOHU (☎ 514-376-8648; www.tohu.ca; 2345 Rue Jarry Est & Rue d'Iberville; admission $6-7; 🕑 9am-5pm Mon-Fri). Get there by taking the blue metro line to d'Iberville station and then hopping onto bus 94 north (or walking 1km northwest up Rue d'Iberville).

traditional Québec architecture. The house was bought in 1668 by Marguerite Bourgeoys to house a religious order. Young women, called the Filles du Roy, who were sent from Paris to Montréal to find husbands also stayed here. The 17th-century roof of the two-story building is of particular interest for its intricate beam work, one of the few of its kind in North America. The museum has an excellent collection of artifacts going back to the 17th and 18th centuries, with unusual items including sinks made from black stone and a sophisticated water-disposal system. It all gives visitors a wonderful idea of how people *really* lived way back when. It also hosts fantastic temporary exhibits that are beautifully executed and can cover anything from the history of French schools in North America to the art of making candy in the 1700s.

MUSÉE DE LACHINE Map pp44–5

☎ 514-634-3471; http://lachine.ville.montreal.qc.ca; 110 Chemin LaSalle; admission free; 🕑 11:30am-4:30pm Wed-Sun Apr-Dec; Ⓜ Angrignon, then bus 110

Practically right on the Lachine Canal, it's a great bike ride to this museum, also one of the oldest houses (1669) in the Montréal region, with shooting holes inserted for defense. Back then Lachine was the last frontier for trappers heading west and the final stop for fur shipments. You can see and smell the old fur-storage building from the original trading days. Adjacent to the museum is a huge waterfront sculpture garden that you can visit anytime from dawn to dusk.

PARC DES RAPIDES Map pp44–5

☎ 514-367-6540; cnr Blvd LaSalle & 6e Ave; Ⓜ De l'Église, then bus 58

This space on the St Lawrence is the spot to view the Lachine Rapids (and the jet boats that ride them). The park attracts hikers, anglers and cyclists who pedal the riverside trail, and it's a renowned bird sanctuary – located on a small peninsula, with what's said to be Québec's largest heron colony. The 30-hectare sanctuary is an important site for migratory birds, with some 225 species passing through each year. Some information displays relate the history of the rapids and of the old hydroelectric plant on the grounds.

You can rent kayaks and sign up for classes where you'll learn to surf or kayak the Lachine Rapids – scaredy-cats need not apply. Kayak Sans Frontières (p172) can get you in the water. Another adrenaline-rushing experience can be had with Rafting Montréal (p171), a jet-boating and rafting outfit located 2km west of the Parc des Rapides.

MOULIN FLEMING Map pp44–5

☎ 514-367-6439; 9675 Blvd LaSalle, borough LaSalle; admission free; 🕑 1-5pm Sat & Sun May-Aug; Ⓜ Angrignon, then bus 110

This restored five-story windmill was built for a Scottish merchant in 1816, and a multimedia exhibit inside covers its two centuries of history. It's a nice diversion if

THE ELUSIVE AND EVER-CHANGING CITY

An interview with Daniel Weinstock, who holds the Canada Research Chair in Ethics and Political Philosophy in the Department of Philosophy at the Université de Montréal. He has written extensively on a wide range of issues, including democratic theory, multiculturalism and global justice.

Where do you live? I've always lived in NDG, which stands for Notre-Dame-de-Grâce, but NDG is sometimes affectionately – or unaffectionately – said to stand for 'No Damn Good.' Growing up there, I wouldn't describe it as much more than a family neighborhood. I later lived in the Plateau, but then drifted back to NDG over the years, and lo and behold, in my absence, the neighborhood has become a vastly more interesting part of the city, with cafés and galleries and cultural bohemia bubbling under Sherbrooke.

What is it about Montréal that makes it different from other cities? The governing tension in Montréal has always been linguistic in nature. Bilingualism is what gives the city its character and makes it so rich. You have this cultural life occurring in both languages, and people can benefit from both. A lot of cultural aspects of the city reflect this linguistic duality. In both literature and in everyday street life, the creative tension plays a role. How one experiences this creative tension certainly distinguishes Montréal from other cities in Canada and many other cities in the world.

How has the city changed in your lifetime? I grew up in a francophone household in an anglophone neighborhood. It used to be that immigrants would send their kids to anglophone schools. That was definitely the norm. Today, immigrants send kids to French schools – and even anglophones do. Had we retained that 1960s-era mentality, French would be much more fragile, have a much less secure place in North America. Montréal should never be exclusively francophone or anglophone.

Montréal has seen a decline in its role as an industrial powerhouse. When the Parti Québécois (a party that advocated secession) came to power in 1976, it sent Anglophones and a fair bit of industry over to Toronto. Montréal has had an interesting time over the last 10 years reinventing itself. *Wallpaper* magazine, among other publications, has rated Montréal as the future cutting-edge and trendy, hip place to be. This wasn't intentional. It just sort of happened. As industry left, there was a sort of vacuum, and other energy – cultural, creative, dance, design – filled it.

How do you rate the intellectual community? Incredible. We have four real world-class PhD-granting universities – two in English, two in French. Whatever your field, you'll be able to find it. My intellectual community is richer than any other city I've lived in – and I've lived in Oxford and Boston. I've even heard that Montréal has the highest number of university students per capita in North America. The big debate is on underfunding.

What role – if any – does religion play in the city these days? The Roman Catholic religion stamps the city. There's a church every three streets or so; the landscape is dominated by a cross – the cross on Mont-Royal – that can be seen from miles and miles away. There are two opposing groups. A French-Canadian majority who've felt like they've just spent the last 200 years getting rid of the priests and don't want to bring back the 'dark ages.' Then there's the dwindling minority of practicing Catholics who are saying that at some point we have to reassert ourselves as Catholics. Despite the trappings of religion, Montréal is a secular society. Quebecers are the least likely people in Canada to get married and today the level of knowledge about Catholicism is actually quite low.

My stock question: How do you survive the winter here? I find something invigorating about winter. There's something magical about a fresh snowfall – 20 to 30cm. Kids go out and play in this beautiful white snow. I wouldn't trade it for anything. I wouldn't mind one less month of it, however. I'd definitely give up March.

you're out here visiting the other Lachine sites, and a great photo op.

CÔTE-DES-NEIGES & NOTRE-DAME-DE-GRÂCE

ORATOIRE ST-JOSEPH Map pp44–5

☎ 514-733-8211; 3800 Chemin Queen-Mary; admission free; church & votive chapel 6:30am-9:30pm, museum 7am-5pm; Ⓜ Côte-des-Neiges; Ⓟ $5

The gigantic oratory honors St Joseph, Canada's patron saint. The largest shrine ever built in honor of Jesus' father, this Renaissance-style building was completed in 1960 and commands fine views of the northern slope of Mont-Royal. The oratory dome is visible from anywhere in this part of town.

The oratory is also a tribute to the work of Brother André, the determined monk who first built a little chapel here in 1904. André was said to have healing powers and as word spread, a larger shrine was needed so the church began gathering funds to build one. Rows of discarded crutches and walking sticks in a votive chapel testify to this belief and the shrine is warmed by hundreds of candles. Brother André's heart is on view too. It was stolen by a zealot some years ago but later returned intact. Film buffs will know that scenes of *Jésus of Montréal* were shot along the Way of the Cross outside the oratory.

Religious pilgrims might climb the 300 wooden steps to the oratory on their knees, praying at every step; other visitors take the stone stairs or one of the free shuttle buses from the base parking lot.

There's a small museum dedicated to Brother André, who was beatified in 1982.

HOLOCAUST MEMORIAL CENTRE

Map pp44–5

☎ 514-345-2605; www.mhmc.ca; 5151 Chemin de la Côte-Ste-Catherine; adult/child $8/5; 🕑 10am-5pm Mon, Tue & Thu, to 9pm Wed, to 4pm Fri & Sun; Ⓜ Côte-Ste-Catherine

The Montréal Holocaust Memorial Centre provides a record of Jewish history and culture from pre-WWII Europe and holds seminars, exhibitions and other events. The museum has many powerful exhibits, including testimonies by Holocaust survivors that mix video interviews with archival footage. There's also a Jewish library open to the public. The museum is closed on Jewish holidays; call to confirm Friday hours between November and March.

AVE MONKLAND Map pp44–5

Over the past decade or so Ave Monkland has been transformed, with coffee bars, restaurants and condominiums springing up like mushrooms after a warm rain. Called Monkland Village by anglo real-estate agents, it certainly has a village character as many people walk to the shops from their homes.

Among the nightspots here is Ye Olde Orchard Pub & Grill (p147), a Celtic pub known for its waiters in kilts.

CONCORDIA UNIVERSITY, LOYOLA CAMPUS Map pp44–5

☎ 514-848-2424; 7141 Rue Sherbrooke Ouest; Ⓜ Vendôme, then bus 105

Concordia's western campus started out as Loyola College, built by Jesuits on melon fields they had bought from the famous Décarie family. Its main building is an impressive Tudor-style structure built in 1913.

Loyola College fused with downtown's Sir George Williams University in 1974 to form Concordia University. Today, the Loyola campus is home to Concordia's journalism, communications and music departments.

SAIDYE BRONFMAN CENTRE

Map pp44–5

☎ 514-739-2301; www.segalcentre.org; 5170 Chemin de la Côte-Ste-Catherine; 🕑 gallery 9am-9pm Mon-Thu, 9am-2pm Fri, 10am-5pm Sun; Ⓜ Côte-Ste-Catherine

There's a tremendous gallery in this performing-arts center that focuses on art both by well-known and emerging talent in a variety of mediums and styles. Frequent talks and lectures are also given.

HARVARD DE MONTRÉAL

For all the Francophiles among you, the Université de Montréal is kind of like the French-speaking Harvard in Canada. In fact, this is the second-largest French-speaking university in the world (after the Sorbonne in Paris), with more than 55,000 students. Maybe because it's on the mountain far from downtown and feels removed from the rest of the city, but you'll find an array of cultural events and happenings that remain virtually unknown to those outside the area. DJs working the campus radio station at 89.3FM are among the best sources in the city – aside from *Voir* weekly mag – for getting the lowdown on up-and-coming francophone bands. Those who can speak French can join Québec's best and brightest in attending wonderful colloquiums and public talks by French academics and intellectuals.

Anglophones can also enjoy the area. Chemin de la Côte-des-Neiges is a lively street for strolling, with cafés, bookstores and a green market, the Marché Côtes-des-Neiges (cnr Chemin de la Côte-des-Neiges & Rue Jean-Brillant) open 24 hours a day in summer. A splendid place to while away a few hours is the indie bookstore Librairie Olivieri (☎ 514-739-3639; 5219 Chemin de la Côte-des-Neiges), which also has an excellent bistro serving poached salmon, *magret de canard* (duck breast) and changing daily specials.

From here you're also within walking distance of the Oratoire St-Joseph (opposite) – a great spot to visit at sunset. Two handy metro stations – Côte-des-Neiges and Université de Montréal – provide easy access to the area.

UNIVERSITÉ DE MONTRÉAL Map pp44–5

☎ 514-343-6111; 2900 Blvd Édouard-Montpetit; Ⓜ Université-de-Montréal

This is the second-largest French-language university in the world, after the Sorbonne in Paris. Located on the north side of Mont-Royal, its most recognizable building is an art-deco tower and pale-yellow brick structure. The university was founded in 1920.

OLYMPIC PARK & AROUND

JARDIN BOTANIQUE Map pp44–5

☎ 514-872-1400; www.ville.montreal.qc.ca/jardin; 4101 Rue Sherbrooke Est; adult/child $16/8; 9am-6pm mid-May–early Sep, to 9pm early Sep–Oct, to 5pm Tue-Sun rest of the year; Ⓜ Pie-IX

Montréal's Jardin Botanique is the third-largest in the world, after London's Kew Gardens and Berlin's Botanischer Garten. Since its 1931 opening, the 75-hectare garden has grown to include tens of thousands of species in 30 thematic gardens, and its wealth of flowering plants is carefully managed to bloom in stages. The rose beds in particular are a sight in summer. Climate-controlled greenhouses house cacti, banana trees and 700 species of orchid. Bird-watchers should bring their binoculars.

A popular draw is the landscaped Japanese Garden with traditional pavilions, tearoom and art gallery; the bonsai 'forest' is the largest outside Asia. The twinning of Montréal with Shanghai gave impetus to plant a Chinese Garden. The ornamental *penjing* trees from Hong Kong are up to 100 years old. A Ming-dynasty garden is the feature around Lac de Rêve (Dream Lake). In the northern part of the Jardin Botanique you'll find the Maison de l'Arbre (Tree House), a permanent exhibit on life in the 40-hectare arboretum. Displays include the yellow birch, part of Québec's official emblem. The First Nations Garden reveals the bonds between 11 Amerindian and Inuit nations and indigenous plants such as silver birches, maples, Labrador and even tea. The Orchidée Gift Shop in the main building has a wonderful selection, including handmade jewelry and crafts, stuffed animals and beautifully illustrated books.

In fall (mid-September to early November) the Chinese garden dons its most exquisite garb for the popular Magic of Lanterns, when hundreds of handmade silk lanterns sparkle at dusk. Montrealers are devoted to this event and it can feel like it's standing-room only even though it's held in a huge garden.

Creepy crawlies get top billing at the bug-shaped Insectarium. Most of the 250,000 specimens are mounted but live displays include bees and tarantulas.

The admission ticket includes the gardens, greenhouses and the Insectarium.

BIODÔME Map pp44–5

☎ 514-868-3000; www.biodome.qc.ca; 4777 Ave Pierre-de-Coubertin; adult/child $16/8; generally 9am-6pm mid-Jun–Aug, 9am-5pm Sep–mid-Jun; Ⓜ Viau

At this captivating, kid-friendly exhibit you can amble through a rainforest, the Arctic Circle, rolling woodlands or along the raw Atlantic oceanfront – all without ever leaving the building. Be sure to dress in layers for the temperature swings.

The four ecosystems house many thousands of animal and plant species; follow the self-guided circuit and you will see everything. Penguins frolic in the pools a few feet away from groups of goggle-eyed children; the tropical chamber is a cross-section of Amazonia with mischievous little monkeys teasing alligators in the murky waters below. The Gulf of St Lawrence has an underwater observatory where you can watch cod feeding alongside lobsters and sea urchins in the tidal pools. The appearance of the Laurentian Forest varies widely with the seasons, with special habitats for lynx, otters and around 350 bats.

The Biodôme is wildly popular so try to visit during the week, avoiding the middle of the day if possible. Plan two hours to do it justice. You can bring a packed lunch for the picnic tables or dine in the cafeteria. In summer there are educational day camps for kids.

OLYMPIC STADIUM Map pp44–5

☎ 514-252-8687; www.rio.gouv.qc.ca; 4141 Ave Pierre-de-Coubertin; tower adult/child $15/7.50; 9am-7pm mid-Jun–Aug, to 5pm rest of the year, closed for maintenance Jan–mid-Feb; Ⓜ Viau

The Stade Olympique seats 56,000 and remains an architectural marvel, though these days it hosts mostly concerts and trade shows and only rarely hosts sports events.

The best thing to do is take the bilevel cable car up the Montréal Tower (Tour de Montréal, also called the Olympic Tower) that lords over the stadium. It's the world's tallest inclined structure (190m at a 45-degree angle), making it a whisper taller than the Washington Monument. The glassed-in observation deck (with bar and rest area) isn't for the faint of heart but affords a bird's-eye view of the city. In the distance you'll see the pointy modern towers of the Olympic Village, where athletes stayed in 1976.

The Centre Aquatique (p174) is the Olympic swimming complex with six pools, diving towers and a 20m-deep scuba pool.

The Tourist Hall is a three-story information center with a ticket office, restaurant and souvenir shop, as well as the cable-car boarding station. There are regular English-language tours (adult/child $8/4) from 10am in spring and summer, and five tours a day starting at 11am in fall and winter.

CHÂTEAU DUFRESNE Map pp44–5

☎ 514-259-9201; www.chateaudufresne.qc.ca; 2929 Ave Jeanne-d'Arc; adult/child $7/3.50; 10am-5pm Wed-Sun; M Pie-IX

Brothers Oscar and Marius Dufresne commissioned this beautiful beaux-arts mansion, along the lines of the Versailles Palace in France, in 1916 and moved in with their families – Oscar on one side and Marius on the other. The interiors are stunning – tiled marble floors, coffered ceilings in Italian Renaissance style, stained-glass windows – and are open for the public to explore. Italian artist Guido Nincheri was in charge of interior decoration and painted many murals, including one of dainty nymphs in the Petit Salon. Marius' side of the building is furnished in a more masculine style, with a smoking room fitted to look like a Turkish lounge with hookah pipes. The furniture, art and other objects reflect the tastes of Montréal's bourgeoisie of the period, and the building has been declared a national monument.

The frequent temporary exhibits explore all aspects of early-20th-century culture, from art to lifestyle.

OUTER DISTRICTS

KAHNAWAKE INDIAN RESERVE

off Map pp44–5

The Kahnawake (gon-a-*wok*-ee) Indian Reserve is home to 6000 Mohawks. The best time to visit is the traditional powwow every year on the weekend closest to July 11, the anniversary of the Oka crisis. Over two days you can enjoy a variety of dances performed by indigenous people in traditional costume.

THE BIG OWE

Built for the 1976 Olympic Games, Montréal's Olympic Stadium was plagued with difficulties right from the start. A strike by construction workers meant the inclined tower wasn't finished on time – in fact it took another 11 years to complete. The stadium's affectionate nickname, the 'Big O' (in reference to the huge oval stadium), was redubbed the 'Big Owe' by irate Montrealers.

The 65-ton stadium roof took another two years to complete but never worked properly. Made of Kevlar, the material used in bulletproof vests, the striking orange dome worked like a huge retractable umbrella that opened and closed by the tower cables. It was a sight to behold (if you were so lucky), but winds ripped the 'bulletproof' Kevlar and mechanical glitches led to its permanent closure. Even when the roof was functioning, there were problems. For instance, the roof could not be retracted when winds gusted greater than 40km/h. This resulted in the occasional rain delay during baseball season – an irritating event for fans who were waiting for the roof to simply be closed.

In 1998 the umbrella was folded up for good and replaced with a set model (costing $37 million) that didn't open – though this roof too malfunctioned, collapsing one year later, dumping snow and ice on workers setting up for the Montréal Auto Show (the roof installers were later sued by the stadium). Another unfortunate event over the years was the collapse of a 55-ton support beam in 1991, though luckily no one was injured.

Provincial officials calculated that the total price tag of the stadium (including construction, repairs etc) when it was finally paid off in late 2006 amounted to $1.6 billion (or $1000 per person, if every man, woman and child in the city of Montréal had to pay up). The irony of the Big O is that now that it's paid off and the roof is no longer broken, no one is interested in using the stadium. The city's baseball team, the Montréal Expos, played its last game in the stadium in 2004 (when it was trounced 9-1 by the Florida Marlins in front of a crowd of some 31,000), before it was packed off to Washington DC and rechristened the Capitals. Today, the stadium remains empty save for the odd trade show, big-name concert and the occasional visitors (maybe you) who find themselves staring up at the empty seats, the unretractable roof and the absent baseball team wondering how such a place could ever be so cursed.

In the summer of 1990 the reserve was the site of a standoff between the Mohawks and the Québec and federal governments in a bitter territorial dispute. Local support of the Mohawks in Oka exploded into a symbolic stand against the mistreatment of First Nations people across the country, and the reverberations are still felt today.

The cultural center (☎ 450-638-0880; 8:30am-noon & 1-4pm Mon-Fri) contains an extensive research library relating to the nations of the Iroquois Confederacy. Temporary exhibitions show off work by local Mohawk artists. The permanent display on the reserve and its history was taken down at the time of research, however it will likely be set up again by the time you read this. The St Francis Xavier Church (☎ 450-632-6031; 9am-5pm daily Jun-Sep, 9am-5pm Mon-Fri rest of the year, Sunday Mass year-round) was established as a Catholic mission for the Aboriginal people and has a small museum with drawings and religious artifacts. Sunday Mass at 10:30am is in English but the choir sings in Mohawk.

The largest Iroquois art gallery in the country is in the Five Nations Village (☎ 450-632-1059; Rte 138 east; 9am-5pm) and you can also take an hour's guided tour (adult/child $10/5, English guides weekends only) of the reserve; kids in particular will enjoy seeing the deer and buffalo that wander the pastures. Traditional dance performances are staged for tour groups and independent travelers can call ahead for the schedule and are welcome to take part.

The reserve is located about 18km southwest of Montréal. By car take Route 138 west and cross the St Lawrence River over the Mercier bridge; the reserve is below and to the right, on the riverbank. Then take Hwy 132 and turn off at Old Malone, the main road. You can also take the metro to the Angrignon station and have a taxi pick you up (about $11 one way).

COSMODÔME off Map pp44–5

☎ 450-978-3600; www.cosmodome.org; 2150 Autoroute des Laurentides; adult/child under 6/student/family $11.50/free/7.50/29.50; 10am-5pm late Jun–early Sep, 10am-5pm Tue-Sun & holidays rest of year

You (or your kids) can experience the thrill of space flight in this interactive museum of space and new technologies. Exhibits focus on the solar system, satellite communications, teledetection and space travel, and there are mock-ups of rockets, the space shuttle *Endeavor* and planets. A multimedia show, *Reach for the Stars*, simulates space travel with special effects on a 360-degree screen. The center also runs space camps for one to five days for kids aged nine and up in a sort of mini-NASA training.

The center is a 25-minute drive north of downtown Montréal. It's a bit of a push by public transportation, but you can take the metro to Henri-Bourassa station and then bus 60 or 61 from Laval bus station outside (ask to be let out at the Cosmodôme).

MORGAN ARBORETUM off Map pp44–5

☎ 514-398-7811; Chemin des Pins, Ste-Anne-de-Bellevue; adult/child $5/2; 9am-4pm

This arboretum holds the country's largest grouping of native trees: fragrant junipers, cedars and yews but also exotic species like ginkgo, cork and yellowwood. There's a wonderful trail map and the area is perfect for a long hike in the woods, strolling through magnolia blossoms or having a family picnic. Spring and fall offer the best colors.

The grounds of the arboretum serve as an educational facility for McGill's MacDonald agricultural school. There are several species of wildlife and reptile, and it's also a stop for 170 species of wintering or migratory birds, making it a thrill for birdwatchers.

In winter, this is a beautiful location for cross-country skiing.

Located about 15km west of Montréal on the western tip of the island, the arboretum can be reached most easily from Autoroute 40. Take exit 41 and follow signs for Chemin Ste-Marie; at the stop sign at the top of the hill, turn left onto Chemin des Pins for the registration office.

MUSÉE FERROVIAIRE CANADIEN off Map pp44–5

☎ 450-632-2410; www.exporail.org; 110 Rue St-Pierre (rte 209), St-Constant; adult/child/student/senior $12/6/7/9.50; 10am-6pm daily mid-May–early Sep, 10am-5pm Wed-Sun early Sep–late Oct, 10am-5pm weekends & holidays Nov-Apr

The Canadian Railway Museum contains more than 150 historic vehicles, ranging from locomotives, steam engines, Old Montréal streetcars and passenger cars to snow plows. It's widely acknowledged as one of North America's most outstanding collections. Not particularly well known by Montrealers, this museum gets raves from those who make the trek, especially families, and many claim it's the best museum in the Montréal area.

The aerodynamic steam engine *Dominion of Canada* broke the world speed record in 1939 by clocking over 200km/h. A special sight is Montréal's famous *Golden Chariot,* an open-air streetcar with tiers of ornate seats and gilt ironwork. Another good exhibit is the school car, a Canadian invention that served the railway towns of northern Ontario: two cars of each teaching train had a kitchen, living area and classroom with 15 desks.

There always seems to be something special going on here, whether it's the miniature railway or streetcar rides, weather permitting.

By car, take the Pont Champlain from Montréal to Autoroute 15, then Hwy 132 at the Châteauguay cutoff to rte 209. It's a 20-minute drive.

PARC NATURE DU CAP-ST-JACQUES off Map pp44–5

☎ 514-280-6871; 20099 Blvd Gouin Ouest, borough Pierrefonds; admission free; 🕑 10am-7pm Jun-Aug, 10am-5pm May, Sep & Oct; Ⓜ Henri-Bourassa, then bus 69; Ⓟ $5

Arguably the most diverse of Montréal's nature parks, Cap-St-Jacques has a huge beach, 27km of trails for hiking and skiing, a farm and even a summer camp. The maple and mixed deciduous forest in the interior is a great patch for a ramble, and in spring a horse-drawn carriage brings visitors to a sugar shack to watch the maple sap boil. On the north shore there's the Eco-Farm, a working farm with two barns and horses, pigs and chickens, as well as a large greenhouse for viewing. Picnic tables abound and a restaurant serves the farm's produce. The beach (adult/child $4.50/3) is a comfortably wide stretch of fine white sand, and the shallow water is wonderful for splashing with kids, but bear in mind it gets as popular as Cape Cod on summer weekends. You can also rent canoes, kayaks and pedal boats.

By car, take Autoroute 40 west from Montréal to exit 49 (Rue Ste-Marie Ouest), turn north on Rue l'Anse-à-l'Orme and continue on to Blvd Gouin Ouest.

STE-ANNE-DE-BELLEVUE off Map pp44–5

Situated on the western tip of Montréal Island, this old-fashioned anglo town occupies a wonderful spot at the locks of the Ste-Anne-de-Bellevue Canal, also known as the Becker Dam (1877). The boardwalk is dotted with terrace restaurants and boutiques, and a green space along the canal is wonderful for a stroll.

For a meal with a view, try the Marco Restaurant (☎ 514-457-3850; 82 Rue Ste-Anne; 🕑 lunch & dinner), serving pasta, veal scallop-pini and steaks along with popular pizzas for $9 to $18.50. Grab a table overlooking the canal on the raised open-air terrace.

Drive the 20km from Montréal along Autoroute 20 west, getting off at exit 39 (Ste-Anne-de-Bellevue) and drive 200m into town, where you can park on the edge of the canal and boardwalk.

ST LAWRENCE SEAWAY Map pp44–5

admission free; 🕑 9am-9:30pm Apr-Dec

This system of locks, canals and dams that opened in 1959 along the St Lawrence River enables oceangoing vessels to sail 3200km inland via the Great Lakes. Across Pont Victoria from the city is an observation tower over the first locks of the system, the St Lambert Locks, where ships are raised/lowered 5m. From January to March, the locks are closed – they're frozen like the river itself until the spring thaw.

The site can be reached by the bike trail on the south shore of the St Lawrence, about 300m southwest of Pont Jacques-Cartier.

WALKING TOURS

RELIVING HISTORY IN OLD MONTRÉAL

Wigged colonists, top-hatted financiers and scheming spies are just some of the characters you'll run into in Old Montréal. It's a treasure trove of period sets for visiting film crews and there's an historic building at every turn. You can recall what you've seen in the atmospheric cafés and restaurants of this very walkable district.

1 Place-d'Armes One of the most captivating little squares in the city is the small, handsome Place-d'Armes (p52). According to legend, on this spot Paul de Chomedey, one of Montréal's early settlers, is believed to have met the Iroquois in battle. Today, iconic buildings surround the square.

2 Basilique Notre-Dame On the southeast side of the plaza, you'll see the city's most celebrated cathedral, the magnificent Basilique Notre-Dame (p47). Go inside for a look at the spectacularly carved pulpit and richly hued stained-glass windows relating key events from the city's founding.

3 Bank of Montréal Back out on the square, walk across to the Bank of Montréal (p54), the country's oldest bank, with a grand, colonnaded edifice modeled after the Pantheon in Rome. Peek inside at the glittering ornate interior with a ceiling in Italian Renaissance style.

4 Royal Bank Building Head southwest along Rue St-Jacques, which was known as the Wall Street of Canada until the 1930s. On your left, you'll soon see the great temple of mercantilism, the Royal Bank Building (p54). When completed in 1928, it was Montréal's

WALK FACTS

Start Place-d'Armes
End Place-d'Armes
Distance 2.5km
Time One to three hours
Fuel Stop Le Petit Moulinsart

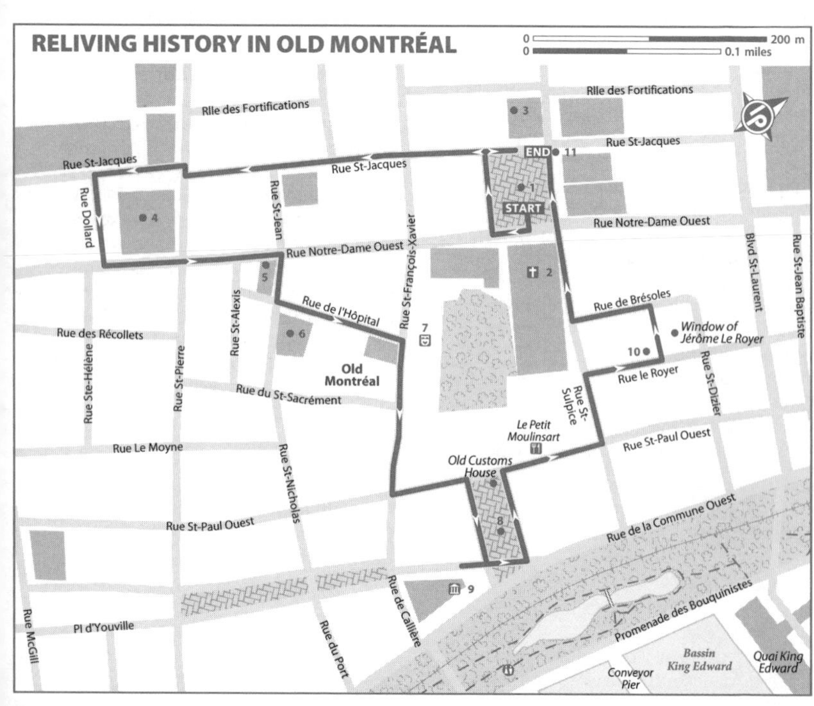

tallest building. Inside, the lobby resembles a Florentine palace.

5 Old Sun Life Building On Rue Dollard turn left, and left again on Rue Notre-Dame Ouest. Continue past the Old Sun Life Building (p53), which was once the storehouse for gold reserves of some European countries and the British crown jewels in WWII.

6 Lewis Building Cut down Rue St-Jean and turn left on Rue de l'Hôpital. On the corner stands the Lewis Building (p53), which was built as the head office of the Cunard Shipping Lines, a steamship company founded in 1840. Note the dragons and mischievous gargoyles adorning the facade.

7 Montréal Stock Exchange Building Continue one block down Rue de l'Hôpital until reaching the impressive Montréal Stock Exchange Building (p53), which opened in 1903. Now home to the Centaur Theatre (p164) its stately columns and sumptuous marble interior recall imperial Rome.

8 Place Royale Head southeast down Rue St-François-Xavier and turn left on Rue St-Paul Ouest, where you then cut past the Old Customs House to Place Royale (p53), the square believed to be where the first settlers landed. In the 17th and 18th centuries, this was the city's marketplace.

9 Musée d'Archéologie Pointe-à-Callière The Old Customs House is connected by underground tunnel to the Musée d'Archéologie Pointe-à-Callière (p50), a fascinating museum devoted to the city's history and archaeology. Head inside for a look at the city's ancient foundations. On the top floor is a fine vantage point over the Old Port.

10 Cours Le Royer Exiting the museum, walk north to Rue St-Sulpice. Turn right onto Rue le Royer and take the first left. This leads to the lovely Cours Le Royer (p52), a tranquil pedestrian mall with fountains and lush greenery. The passageway on the north side features a stained-glass window of Jérôme Le Royer, one of the founders of Montréal.

11 New York Life Insurance Building Continue through the passage to Rue de Brésoles and take a left back out onto Rue St-Sulpice, where you'll make a right to return to Place-d'Armes. Before leaving the area, note the New York Life Insurance Building (p52), Montréal's first skyscraper, built in 1888.

DELVING INTO DOWNTOWN

Skyscrapers give downtown Montréal a distinctly North American feel, but the area is also dotted with historic buildings with plenty of stories to tell. Rue Ste-Catherine and Rue Sherbrooke slice through the area in a blaze of trendy boutiques and department stores, and some are attractions in their own right.

1 Square Dorchester The official center of town is leafy Square Dorchester (p66). The statue on the northeast side represents Lord Strathcona, a philanthropist who helped to sponsor Canada's efforts in the South African Boer War. Wander south to see the neglected rendition of Sir Wilfrid Laurier (1841–1919), one of Canada's most respected prime ministers.

2 Les Cours Mont-Royal Take a peek at the Windsor Hotel (p67), opened in 1878, before cutting over to Rue Metcalfe and walking northwest to the upscale shopping complex Les Cours Mont-Royal (p109). The central atrium features bird sculptures with human heads and a chandelier from a Monte Carlo casino.

3 Emmanuel Congregation Church Head down to action-packed Rue Ste-Catherine Ouest, then turn onto Rue Drummond, where you'll soon come to the architecturally impressive Emmanuel Congregation Church (p68). The highlight here is the peaceful rear garden, reachable by turning into the little passageway leading to Rue Stanley.

4 Mount Royal Club In the garden, you can refuel at the pleasant Brûlerie St Denis with outdoor tables. Otherwise continue up to Rue Sherbrooke Ouest. This was Montréal's most prestigious residential street in the early 20th century. Turn left to reach the Mount Royal Club (p68), founded as an exclusive men's society.

WALK FACTS

Start Sq Dorchester
End Musée des Beaux-Arts
Distance 2.5km
Time Two to three hours
Fuel Stop M:Brgr, Brûlerie St Denis

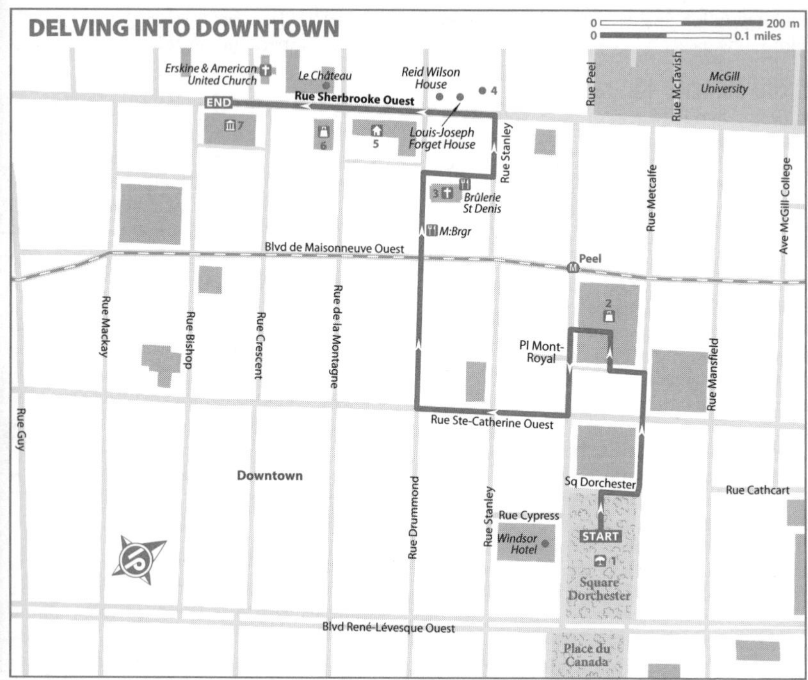

5 Ritz-Carlton Nearby are two other impressive mansions: the Louis-Joseph Forget House (p68) and the Reid Wilson House (p69). Continue along Sherbrooke and you'll soon reach the lavish Ritz-Carlton (p183). The afternoon tea here is legendary (reservations recommended).

6 Holt Renfrew Further along Sherbrooke, you'll pass Le Château (p68), a fortresslike apartment complex with vestiges of shell fossils in the brick. Directly opposite, the department store with art-deco motifs is Holt Renfrew (p107), official supplier of furs to Queen Elizabeth.

7 Musée des Beaux-Arts Take a peek inside one of the area's most imposing churches, the Erskine & American United Church. End your tour with a look at Québec's finest painters at the Musée des Beaux-Arts (p60).

BOHEMIAN LIFE IN THE QUARTIER LATIN

Much of the charm of the compact Latin Quarter lies not in official sights but in soaking up the laid-back atmosphere – allow yourself to linger, especially along the café-filled terraces of Rue St-Denis. Today a nexus of student and alternative life, the neighborhood has French and Roman Catholic roots dating back to the early 19th century.

1 Place Émilie-Gamelin Begin your walk in the somewhat unkempt Place Émilie-Gamelin, the site of spontaneous concerts, wacky metal sculptures, outdoor chess matches and dozens of punks with their beleaguered pets. The square is named for the Catholic nun Émilie Gamelin, founder of the Sisters of Providence.

2 Chapelle Notre-Dame-de-Lourdes Head southwest along Rue Ste-Catherine, and take a peek inside the Chapelle Notre-Dame-de-Lourdes (p73), commissioned in 1876. This Romanesque gem is filled with imaginative frescoes painted by Napoléon Bourassa and is regarded as his crowning glory.

3 Église St-Jacques Back on Rue Ste-Catherine, turn right up Rue St-Denis, where you'll be in the midst of the – sadly uninspiring – campus of the Université du Québec à Montréal (p74). The most striking building here is the old facade of the Église St-Jacques, with its magnificent Gothic steeple.

WALK FACTS

Start Pl Émelie-Gamelin
End Maison Fréchette
Distance 1.5km
Time One to two hours
Fuel Stop Juliette et Chocolat

4 Bibliothèque et Archives Nationale du Québec Turn right down Blvd de Maisonneuve and continue to the massive Bibliothèque et Archives Nationale du Québec (p73), home to an astounding collection of all things Québécois. Head into the main hall and downstairs to a sunken gallery, which often hosts fascinating (and free) exhibitions.

5 Théâtre St-Denis Return to Rue St-Denis and turn right. You'll soon pass two of the neighborhood's cultural mainstays. The Théâtre St-Denis (p164) is the city's second-largest theater. Next door you can watch independent cinema at the National Film Board (p161), occupying an ultramodern cinema and production complex.

6 Terrasse St-Denis Continue up the street, noting the terrace cafés, lively pubs and quirky shops for which the neighborhood is so well known. The little side street, Terrasse St-Denis, used to be a meeting place of Montréal's bohemian set at the turn of the 20th century.

7 Maison Fréchette On busy Rue Sherbrooke, turn left and have a look at the Maison Fréchette (p74), the former home of Louis Fréchette, a well-known Québec poet of the day. French actor (and courtesan) Sarah Bernhardt stayed in his home during her North American tours in the late 1800s.

STROLLING THE PLATEAU

The Plateau Mont-Royal area is best known for its eclectic restaurants, colorful bars and cafés and fashion-forward boutiques, but its leafy residential streets are a great place to stroll. This area epitomizes Montréal diversity, offering a wide mix of grunge and chic, and it's packed with places of historical interest.

1 Carré St-Louis Start at the Carré St-Louis (p75), a pleasant, green, shady oasis with a splashing

WALK FACTS

Start Carré St-Louis
End Palestre Nationale
Distance 3km
Time Two to three hours
Fuel Stop L'Express

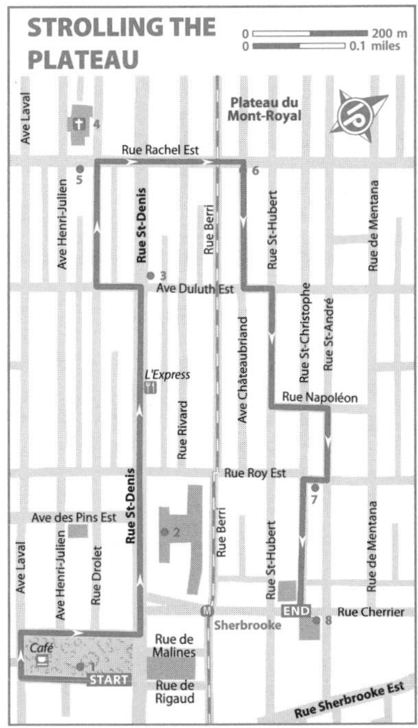

fountain that's a popular spot for lazing and people-watching. It's surrounded by beautiful old houses that were built for wealthy French residents in the 19th century.

2 Institut des Sourdes-Muettes Walk around the park (stopping perhaps for a coffee at the summertime café near Ave Laval), then walk up Rue St-Denis. On your right you'll pass the majestic buildings of the former Institut des Sourdes-Muettes (p79) – note the little silver cupola.

3 Terraced Houses Continuing up Rue St-Denis, stay on the left-hand side of the street to see the pretty facades of the bars and shops to the east. Note the row of terraced houses with slate mansards and lantern roofs above the entrances on the northeast corner of Ave Duluth Est.

4 Église St-Jean Baptiste Turn left onto Rue Duluth and right onto Rue Drolet. At the end of the street, you'll reach the baroque Église St-Jean Baptiste (p75), its enormous interior decorated with gilded wood and pink marble. The acoustics are excellent, making it a popular venue for concerts.

5 Les Cours Rachel Exiting the church, look right to see the winged angel on the imposing Sir George-Étienne Cartier monument (p51), way down at the end of the street at the leafy base of Mont-Royal. Directly opposite the church stands Les Cours Rachel, which was once a boarding school but has been converted into condos.

6 Ave Châteaubriand Walk northeast along Rue Rachel Est and turn right on Ave Châteaubriand. A rundown street through the 1970s, today this narrow lane has been spruced up with blue, green and turquoise paint and potted plants hanging outside the windows. Here too you'll spot another of this town's signature objects: the external staircase.

7 Place Roy Zigzag over to Rue St-Hubert, turn right on Rue Napoléon and right again on Rue St-André. One block down you'll reach Place Roy (p78), an intriguing art installation with a fountain in a quiet corner of the neighborhood.

8 Palestre Nationale Continue down Rue Roy and turn left on Rue St-Christophe. At St-Hubert, you'll see the Italian Renaissance Palestre Nationale (p79), built in 1918. Today it's home to one of Montréal's leading dance theaters, Agora de la Danse (p162).

CYCLING THE CANAL DE LACHINE

The prettiest cycle path in Montréal stretches along the Canal de Lachine and has easy access from downtown and the Old Port. Warm days draw everyone outdoors: sunbathers flop on the grass to read and take in the view, families lunch at picnic tables, while cyclists and in-line skaters glide along the path. For info on bicycle hire and Bixi bikes, see p168 and p169.

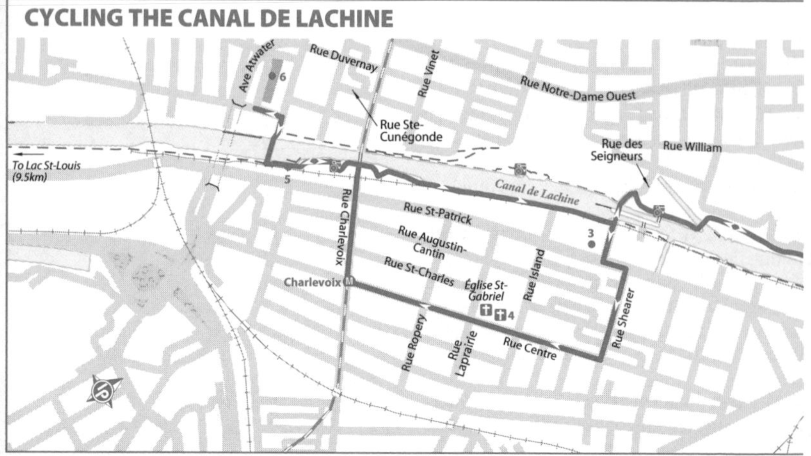

1 Canal Locks Start at the Canal Locks at the southwestern end of the Old Port. This part of town has an industrial feel thanks to the abandoned grain silo just southeast of the locks.

2 Farine Five Roses Pedaling southwest along Rue de la Commune Ouest, you'll pass under Autoroute 10 and continue along the downtown side of the canal where strips of greenery line both sides. Keep an eye out for the enormous neon sign Farine Five Roses, which crowns a former flour mill.

3 Former silk mill The path switches sides at the bridge at Rue des Seigneurs, where you come to a former silk mill that ran its operations on hydraulic power from the canal. The red-brick factory has been reborn as lofts – one of many such conversions alongthe canal.

4 Église St-Charles Continue south on Rue Shearer and turn right on Rue Centre where soon you'll come to the massive, Romanesque Église St-Charles on your right. Next push your bike over to the French-style Église St-Gabriel, taking in the charm of this little-visited neighborhood.

CYCLE FACTS

Start Canal Locks
End Canal Locks
Distance 7km (27km including Lac St-Louis)
Time Two to four hours
Fuel Stop Marché Atwater

5 H2O Adventures Cycle to Rue Charlevoix and turn right and you'll soon meet up with the bike path again. Turn left, and you'll come to H2O Adventures (p171), a kayak-rental outfit. If you're interested in getting out on the water, this is the place to do it.

6 Marché Atwater Continue on the bike path and turn right at the pedestrian bridge to head to the Marché Atwater (p61), one of the city's best markets. This is a great spot to assemble a picnic, which you can then enjoy by the water, followed by an easy pedal back to the port. If you're keen for more exploring, head west of the market. Another 10km along the path will take you to a sculpture garden at the edge of scenic Lac St-Louis – a favorite spot at sunset. To head back, simply follow the canal path back to the Canal Locks.

MONTRÉAL'S FAVORITE MOUNTAIN

Many of Montréal's neighborhoods hug the foot of the Parc du Mont-Royal, making everyone feel like they've got a bit of green space in their backyard. 'The Mountain,' as Mont-Royal is affectionately known by locals, is cherished for its winding trails, fresh air and terrific views.

1 Ave de Pins Ouest The starting point for this walk is on Ave des Pins Ouest at the staircase into the park. It's a fairly brisk 10- to 15-minute climb that alternates between steps and inclined trail.

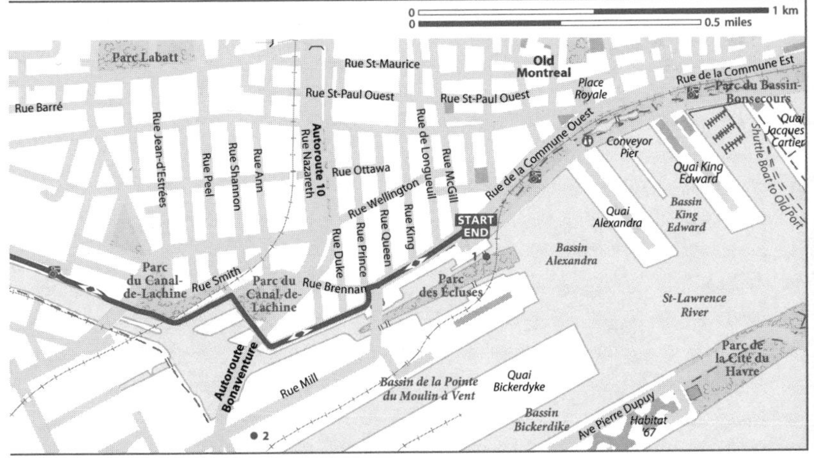

2 Kondiaronk Lookout You cross a large path and continue climbing to the signposted Kondiaronk lookout (p80). The lookout offers stunning views of the downtown area, best seen in the early evening when the skyscrapers begin to light up.

3 Chalet du Mont-Royal Just up the steps from the lookout is the Chalet du Mont-Royal (p80), which contains paintings of some key scenes from Canadian history. It's decorated like a ski lodge and has a few vending machines for grabbing a quick drink.

4 Croix du Mont-Royal From the chalet, walk north along the trail named Chemin Olmsted about 600m to the Cross of Mont-Royal (p80), the Montréal landmark that's illuminated at night. This is where city founder Maisonneuve allegedly planted a cross in thanksgiving for saving the city from flood.

WALK FACTS

Start Ave des Pins Ouest
End Ave des Pins Ouest
Distance 6km
Time Two to three hours
Fuel Stop Maison Smith

5 Belvédère Camillien-Houde Further along you can descend a set of stairs to reach the scenic lookout of Belvédère Camillien-Houde (p79), one of the most romantic views in the city. If you're traveling with someone you feel like kissing, here's the place to do it.

6 Maison Smith Returning to the path, head south toward Maison Smith (p80), an 1858 heritage building that houses a permanent exhibition on the history and ongoing conservation of Mont-Royal. A visitors center doles out information on the park; the on-site café is a good spot to grab a bite or a cold drink.

7 Lac des Castors Another 500m further south, the artificial pond Lac des Castors (p80) is a haven of toy-boat captains in summer and ice-skaters in winter. Refreshments are available at the pavilion, and in warm weather the meadows around the pond is full of sunbathers.

8 Cimetière Notre-Dame-des-Neiges To the north you can venture across the wide road called Chemin Remembrance into

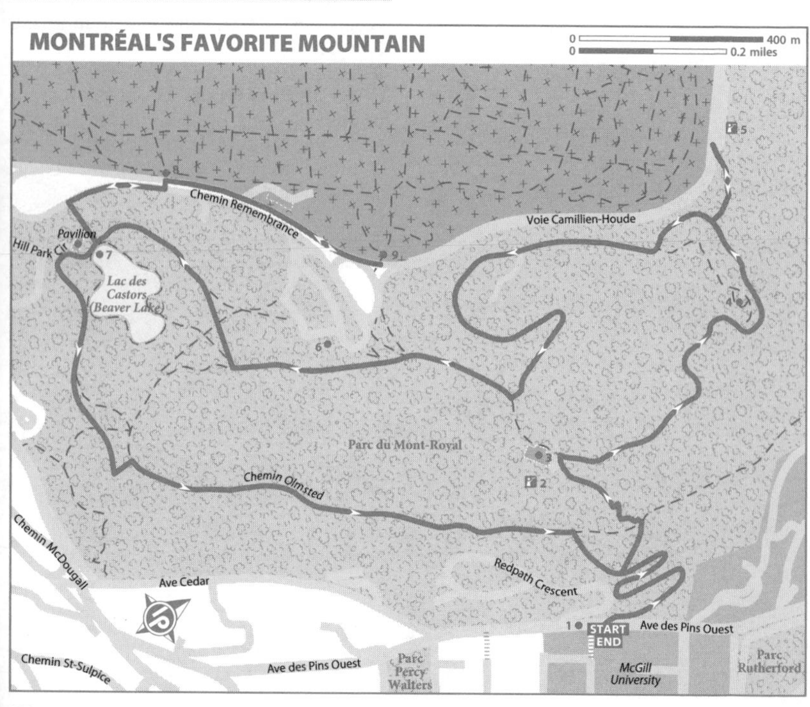

Montréal's largest cemetery, the very Catholic Cimetière Notre-Dame-des-Neiges (p80), which has some intriguing mausoleums (some filled with music). The entrance map reveals the plots of the famous departed.

9 Cimetière Mont-Royal The smaller, mainly Protestant Cimetière Mont-Royal (p81) lies just to the north. Both cemeteries are on rolling, leafy terrain and ooze Montréal history. Afterwards, retrace your steps to Lac des Castors and follow the lake around to the east, until meeting up with the main path (Chemin Olmsted) that leads back to your starting point on Ave des Pins Ouest.

EXPLORING MILE END & OUTREMONT

Still off the radar for many visitors, Mile End and Outremont are creatively charged neighborhoods with multicultural pasts. A large Hassidic community rubs shoulders with Francophones, Anglophones, Portuguese, Greeks and Italians. The community atmosphere is just one part of the equation when visiting the neighborhood. You'll also find eclectic cafés, eye-catching boutiques, vegetarian restaurants, lively bars, leafy parks and great bagels.

1 St-Viateur Bagel Start the walk off with a bit of energy food: fresh-from-the-oven bagels at one of Montréal's most famous bagel shops, St-Viateur Bagel (p138), which first opened its doors in 1957. After sampling the much-touted poppy- and/or sesame-seed bagel, head northeast along Rue St-Viateur.

2 Église St Michel You'll soon reach the massive Byzantine-style Église St Michel (p82). A neighborhood icon, this Roman Catholic church (with an unusual minaret-like tower) was built for Irish parishioners (evidenced by the shamrocks in the stained-glass windows). Today, it serves a mostly Polish community.

WALK FACTS

Start St-Viateur Bagel, Rue St-Viateur
End Drawn & Quarterly, Rue Bernard
Distance 4km
Time Two to three hours
Fuel Stop Le Cagibi Café

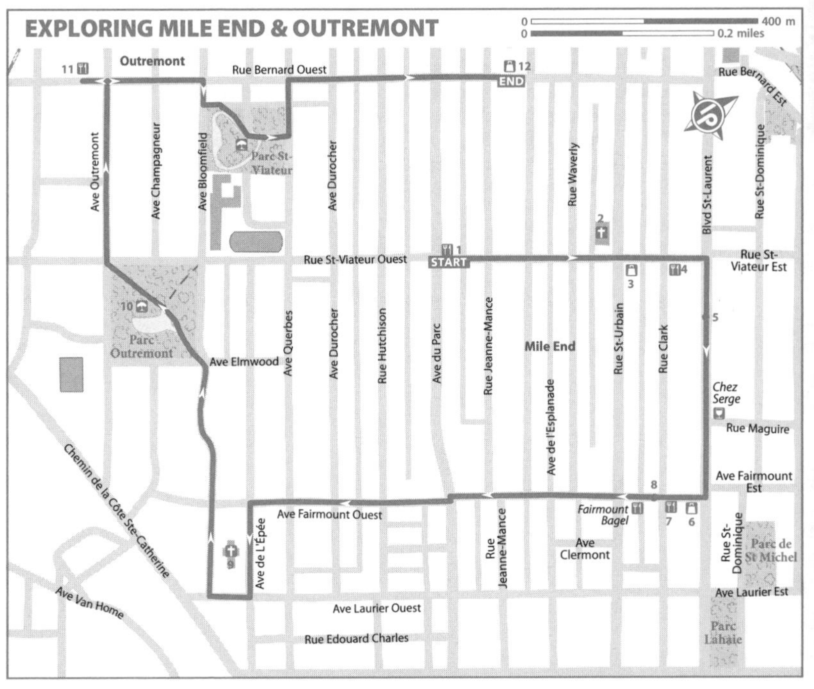

3 General 54, Across the street lies one of Mile End's excellent clothing shops, General 54 (p113). Nearly everything here was created by local designers. You'll see plenty of eye-catching, one-of-a-kind items – T-shirts, handbags, accessories – you won't find elsewhere.

4 Le Cagibi Café Continuing along Rue St-Viateur you'll pass one of Mile End's great little bohemian spots, Le Cagibi Café (p137). Stop in for satisfying plates of veggie Tex-Mex, or return at night for film screenings, live bands, book launches and other eclectic fare.

5 Blvd St-Laurent Turn right along Blvd St-Laurent and take in some of the galleries and curio shops that have recently opened their doors. You'll also pass Chez Serge (p148), a whimsical sports bar with a bra-covered moose head and a mechanical bull. If hockey is on, go here.

6 Au Papier Japonais Continue along Blvd St-Laurent and turn right onto Ave Fairmount. Near the corner is Au Papier Japonais (p114), a sweet little store specializing in gorgeous handmade paper (over 500 kinds), plus paper lanterns, Japanese-style blinds and more. It also offers short workshops for budding artisans.

7 Wilensky's Light Lunch Next door is the traditional Mile End deli Wilensky's Light Lunch (p138). Made famous in a Mordecai Richler novel, the place hasn't changed much since opening in 1937. For grilled salami and bologna sandwiches, Wilensky's is your place. Otherwise, continue on!

8 Ave Fairmount Ouest Continue the walk along Ave Fairmount, stopping for a bagel taste-test at the famous Fairmount Bagel (p138), archrival of St-Viateur Bagel.

9 Église St-Viateur Continuing on Fairmount, turn left on Ave de l'Épee and right on Ave Laurier. The magnificent church on the corner is Église St-Viateur (p85), an icon of the neighborhood. Funeral services for prime minister Pierre Trudeau were held here in 2000.

10 Parc Outremont Exiting the church, turn right up Ave Bloomfield and in two blocks you'll reach Parc Outremont (p82), a beautiful park with a tiny lake and a playground that's used mostly by Hassidic children from the neighborhood. Lovely Victorian homes surround the park.

11 Le Bilboquet Exit the park onto Ave Outremont and continue up this street until reaching Rue Bernard. Go left to reach Le Bilboquet (p138), one of the best ice-cream shops in Montréal. Grab a sidewalk table or zigzag over to Parc St-Viateur, another peaceful green space in the neighborhood.

12 Drawn & Quarterly Go back onto Rue Bernard and make your way toward Blvd St-Laurent. Rue Bernard is yet another great street for exploring, with enticing cafés and shops, including the bookstore and indie publisher Drawn & Quarterly (p113), with a well-curated selection of graphic novels and literary fare.

SHOPPING

top picks

What's your recommendation? www.lonelyplanet.com/canada/montreal

SHOPPING

Style is synonymous with Montréal living. The city itself is beautiful and locals live up to the standard it sets. Maybe it's that much-touted European influence, but most Montrealers seem to instinctively lead stylish lives regardless of income level, enjoying aesthetic pleasures like food, art and, of course, fashion.

Montréal is Canada's unofficial fashion capital and many of the country's most talented and internationally successful designers have roots here. Gorgeous locally based lines to look for include Denis Gagnon, Nadya Toto, Marie Saint-Pierre, YSO and up-and-comer Travis Taddeo. For more information, check out Québec fashion magazines like *Clin d'Oeil, Lou Lou* and *Elle Québec*. Or visit during **Montreal Fashion Week** (www.montrealfashionweek.ca), which takes place every March and October to showcase new collections. With hot local artisans dressing locals, it's no wonder Montréal is known for its beautiful citizens. Of course, hunting in vintage bins can produce looks just as cool, and locals are adept at putting together killer ensembles that combine the best of both worlds.

Even beyond fashion, Montréal is an ideal shopping city, full of goods you'll want to take home. You'll find the cream of the crop in this shopping paradise – from big international department stores to high fashion designers, vintage clothing boutiques to weird one-of-a-kind antique shops, used music- and booksellers, chic home decor and more. American visitors in particular tend to appreciate the reasonable prices, made even more affordable by the US–Canada money exchange rate. As well, many international megastore chains (including Urban Outfitters, H&M, Zara and American Apparel – which, incidentally, was started by a Montrealer) have set up shop here, but with a local or European flair.

Since Montréal is also a walking city, strolling down any of its prime outdoor shopping strips is a perfect way to spend a sunny afternoon. Upscale Rue St-Paul in Old Montréal (below) is full of art galleries, designer furnishings and clothing shops. The district's touristy streets also house souvenir shops that sell maple syrup T-shirts and random Canadiana. Busy Rue Ste-Catherine in the heart of Downtown (p106) has all the big names, department stores, and some specialty shops and local fashion boutiques. For antiques, head southwest to Rue Notre-Dame Ouest. The trendy Plateau (p111) and artsy Mile End (p113) are full of hip clothing and home-decor boutiques, many located on Blvd St-Laurent and Rue St-Denis. Rue Mont-Royal has lots of vintage shops. Little Italy (p113) is terrific for grocery shopping and cooking items. Prices and style quotient soar on Rue Laurier and Ave Bernard in Outremont (p113), as well as on elegant Ave Greene in the wealthy Westmount neighborhood (see the boxed text, p110).

Most stores open 9:30am or 10am to 6pm Monday to Wednesday; clothing boutiques usually open their doors at 11am. Thursday and Friday are late opening days, usually until 9pm; Saturday hours are 10am to 5pm. Opening hours on Sunday afternoon (noon to 5pm) are standard along Rue Ste-Catherine and Blvd St-Laurent as well as in the large malls. Some convenience stores such as the chain Couche Tard stay open 24 hours. In summer you may find extended weekday hours at many stores.

OLD MONTRÉAL & CHINATOWN

GALERIE 2000 Map p48 — Art Gallery

☎ 514-844-1812; 45 Rue St-Paul Ouest; 🕑 10am-9pm; Ⓜ Champ-de-Mars

Always fresh and entertaining, this eclectic gallery has large, flashy, tasteful displays from classic landscapes to neocubist portraits, with the occasional well-charted flight into the alternative.

GALERIE LE CHARIOT Map p48 — Art Gallery

☎ 514-875-4994; 446 Pl Jacques-Cartier; Ⓜ Champ-de-Mars

This arts emporium claims to have the largest Inuit collection in Canada. Choose from First Nations art carved mainly from soapstone, as well as walrus tusks, fur hats, mountain-goat rugs and fleecy moccasins.

GALERIE ORANGE Map p48 — Art Gallery

☎ 514-396-6670; 81 Rue St-Paul Est; Ⓜ Champ-de-Mars

top picks

SHOPPING STRIPS

- Ave du Mont-Royal (p78) For gritty, off-the-rack style, and surprising specialty stores.
- Blvd St-Laurent (p75) Funky new designer boutiques mixed in with secondhand fashion.
- Rue Sherbrooke Ouest (p67) For furs, stogies and expense accounts.
- Rue St-Denis (p75) Classy European-style boutiques galore.
- Rue Ste-Catherine (p67) Upscale clothing boutiques and popular chain stores.

Bright gallery representing established and up-and-coming contemporary artists like Francine Simonin and Elmyna Bouchard and a terrific collection of works on paper.

GALERIE PANGÉE Map p48 — Art Gallery

☎ 514-845-3368; 40 Rue St-Paul Ouest; ⏲ 10am-7pm; Ⓜ Place d'Armes

This wonderful, bright space is devoted to showing off contemporary art, as well as literature and art consulting. Relationships with European galleries allow Québécois artists to enjoy international exposure, while local collectors can purchase works from abroad.

GALERIE ST-DIZIER Map p48 — Art Gallery

☎ 514-845-8411; 24 Rue St-Paul Ouest; Ⓜ Champ-de-Mars

This spacious Old Town gallery has always been at the forefront of the avant-garde scene in Montréal. Works are split between local and heavyweight artists known abroad, including Besner, Missakian and Tetro. Its forte is naïve and modernist art and sculpture.

LA GUILDE GRAPHIQUE

Map p48 — Art Gallery

☎ 514-844-3438; 9 Rue St-Paul Ouest; Ⓜ Champ-de-Mars

This place exhibits works of more than 200 contemporary artists in a variety of media and techniques. Most works are sketches, woodcuts, etchings and lithographs on paper, and you can visit the artists working in the upstairs studio.

YVES LAROCHE GALERIE D'ART

Map p48 — Art Gallery

☎ 514-393-1999; 4 Rue St-Paul Est; Ⓜ Champ-de-Mars

High and low culture collide at this fantastic gallery that showcases the best in upscale contemporary and urban art. From surrealist to pop, tattoo to illustration, this local institution twice a year presents massive collective shows of local and international artists.

SURFACE JALOUSE

Map pp44–5 — Art & Furniture

☎ 514-303-6220; 2672 Rue Notre-Dame Ouest; Ⓜ Lionel-Groulx

Graphic art and home decor meet at this slick and innovative boutique that sells murals, vinyl decals and custom designs to emboss on walls, furnishings, mirrors and any other surface that takes your fancy (instead of wallpaper!). Unique furniture is also for sale, and many decals are removable.

LIBRISSIME Map p48 — Books

☎ 514-841-0123; 62 Rue St-Paul Ouest; Ⓜ Place-d'Armes

It bills itself as more than just a bookstore, and it's right, there really is no other place like this in the city. Gorgeous books here are imported from all over the world including Italy and India and white gloves are laid on the displays for you to don before touching the tomes, including giant-sized books that cost upwards of $1000.

BETTY'S BAZAAR

Map p48 — Fashion

☎ 514-285-2212; 218 Rue St-Paul Ouest; Ⓜ Square-Victoria

This innovative boutique is an ideal hunting ground to find fashions by rising Montréal design stars, whose unique and stylish gear isn't yet available on department store racks. Girly and feminine, the space also stocks nonlocal brands. A true shopping treat!

REBORN Map p48 — Fashion

☎ 514-499-8549; 231 Rue St-Paul Ouest; Ⓜ Place-d'Armes

Upscale lines like Harakiri, Complexgeometries, Filippa K, Opening Ceremony and Nom de Guerre meet accessories and a slick, old-meets-new feel at this must-see fashion laboratory.

ROONEY Map p48 Fashion

☎ 514-543-6234; 395 Rue Notre-Dame Ouest; Ⓜ Square-Victoria

Jeans, jeans and more jeans are the highlight of this high-end streetwear headquarters. Coveted international brands in stock include True Religion, Rock & Republic and Seven. Rooney also sells other fashion items.

KAMKYL

Map p48 Fashion, Men's

☎ 514-281-8221; 439 Rue St-Pierre; Ⓜ Place -d'Armes

Kamkyl has a fine Italian-made collection of men's suits with understated lines that beam self-confidence. Son of a German master tailor, designer Douglas Mandel (formerly of Hugo Boss and DKNY) also snagged a design award for this stylish post-industrial atelier of parquet, light and space.

DIFFUSION GRIFF '3000

Map p48 Fashion & Fur

☎ 514-398-0761; Marché Bonsecours, 350 Rue St-Paul Est; Ⓜ Champ-de-Mars

French fashion diva Anne de Shalla studied fashion in Paris and came to Montréal in the 1970s. She now selects from up to 30 Québec designers every year for her exclusive shop collection – stretchy leathers, semi-sheer dresses, blouses and wraparound casuals.

FOURRURES DUBARRY

Map p48 Fashion & Fur

☎ 514-844-7483; 206 Rue St-Paul Ouest; Ⓜ Place-d'Armes

This place carries off-the-rack fur jackets, hats, fur-trim capes and coats, plus a selection of sheepskin coats and leather jackets. There are no middlemen, which keeps prices low, and you can trade in your old garment toward your purchase.

LE BARON Map p48 Outdoors

☎ 514-381-4231; 932 Rue Notre-Dame Ouest; Ⓜ Square-Victoria

For survival, sporting and leisure gear this is the top address in town in a spanking-new warehouse location. Backpack buyers should set aside a few hours just to look.

SIMON'S CAMERA Map p48 Photography

☎ 514-861-5401; 11 Rue St-Antoine Ouest; Ⓜ Place-d'Armes

> **TAXES & REFUNDS**
>
> Federal goods and services tax (called TPS in Québec, or GST in the rest of Canada) applies on just about every transaction except groceries. Québec also charges sales tax (TVQ) of 6% to 12% on top of that. Keep your receipts because foreign visitors can apply for a partial refund – see p109 for details of where to apply.

A real shopping icon in the Old Town, Simon's has one of the city's best selections of photography equipment. New and used digital cameras, darkroom gear, video and sound equipment go at competitive prices, with trade-ins possible. It also rents equipment.

MARCHÉ BONSECOURS

Map p48 Shopping Mall

☎ 514-872-7730; 350 Rue St-Paul Est; Ⓜ Champ-de-Mars

This majestic old building has housed the Canadian parliament, city hall and, now, a collection of cute boutiques selling Québec-made wares, goodies like fashion, accessories, jewelry and crafts. Restaurants and terraces are also on-site, and the *marché* is often used for trade shows and art events.

DOWNTOWN

GALERIES D'ART CONTEMPORAIN DU BELGO Map pp62–3 Art Gallery

372 Rue Ste-Catherine Ouest; Ⓜ Place-des-Arts

Over a decade ago the Belgo building was a run-down haven for struggling artists. It quickly earned a reputation as one of Montréal's most important exhibition spaces with galleries, dance, yoga and photography studios. Designers, art dealers and architects now make up three-quarters of the tenancy.

LIBRAIRIE ASTRO

Map pp62–3 Books & Comics

☎ 514-932-1139; www.astrolib.com; 1844 Rue Ste-Catherine Ouest; ⏲ noon-7pm Mon-Wed, noon-8pm Thu & Fri, noon-6pm Sat, noon-5pm Sun; Ⓜ Guy-Concordia

Rollicking wit and helpful service are as ubiquitous as the collectible comics, books, cards and CDs stocked at this little family-run shop. They know their customers by name and will email you if they come across something you might like.

CHAPTERS BOOKSTORE

Map pp62–3 Books & Music

☎ 514-849-8825; 1171 Rue Ste-Catherine Ouest; 9am-10pm; M Peel

Peruse three huge floors of English- and French-language books and a fantastic choice of travel-related items in the sunken floor at the back. There's a coffee bar and internet café on the 2nd floor.

INDIGO Map pp62–3 Books & Music

☎ 514-281-5549; 1500 Ave McGill College, Place Montréal Trust; M Peel

This sister store of Chapters is a three-floor emporium with comfy reading chairs that keep you browsing for hours. It has a great selection of Canadian and Montréal literature, a good CD section and Starbucks coffee bar. A wonderful travel and map section is on the 2nd floor at the back.

LA CASA DEL HABANO Map pp62–3 Cigars

☎ 514-849-0037; 1434 Rue Sherbrooke Ouest; M Guy-Concordia

This well-stocked stogie temple has 50 brands of Cuban cigar. Be aware that taking these across the border into the USA is illegal although some travelers separate the bands when packing. Cigaraphernalia sold here includes cutters, humidors, lighters and books. The lounge and espresso bar attracts young important puffers.

HOLT RENFREW

Map pp62–3 Department Store

☎ 514-842-5111; 1300 Rue Sherbrooke Ouest; M Peel

This Montréal institution is a godsend for label-conscious, cashed-up professionals and upscale shoppers. From fragrance to cosmetics, jewelry and men's and women's fashion, 'Holt's' is the go-to spot for prestigious brands like Gucci and Prada. Services include personal shoppers and concierges, and an on-site café.

HUDSON BAY CO

Map pp62–3 Department Store

☎ 514-281-4422; 585 Rue Ste-Catherine Ouest; M McGill

La Baie, as it's called in French, found fame three centuries ago for its striped wool blankets used to measure fur skins. Pass the legions of perfumery stands on the ground floor and take the escalators to the clothing boutiques on the 2nd floor, or make a strategic move for the cut-price garments on the 8th floor.

CLOTHING SIZES

Women's clothing

Aus/UK	8	10	12	14	16	18
Europe	36	38	40	42	44	46
Japan	5	7	9	11	13	15
USA	6	8	10	12	14	16

Women's shoes

Aus/USA	5	6	7	8	9	10
Europe	35	36	37	38	39	40
France only	35	36	38	39	40	42
Japan	22	23	24	25	26	27
UK	3½	4½	5½	6½	7½	8½

Men's clothing

Aus	92	96	100	104	108	112
Europe	46	48	50	52	54	56
Japan	S		M	M		L
UK/USA	35	36	37	38	39	40

Men's shirts (collar sizes)

Aus/Japan	38	39	40	41	42	43
Europe	38	39	40	41	42	43
UK/USA	15	15½	16	16½	17	17½

Men's shoes

Aus/UK	7	8	9	10	11	12
Europe	41	42	43	44½	46	47
Japan	26	27	27½	28	29	30
USA	7½	8½	9½	10½	11½	12½

Measurements approximate only; try before you buy

OGILVY Map pp62–3 Department Store

☎ 514-842-7711; 1307 Rue Ste-Catherine Ouest; M Peel

Once a Victorian-era department store, Ogilvy has transformed itself into a collection of high-profile boutiques. When it was remodeled in the late 1920s the owner had a concert hall built on the 5th floor called 'The Tudor' that's still open for viewing. Ogilvy's front window displays mechanical toys that are a Montréal fixture at Christmas.

SIMONS Map pp62–3 Department Store

☎ 514-282-1840; 977 Rue Ste-Catherine Ouest; M Peel

This Québec City chain is a phenomenon of which everyone, no matter their age or style, seems a fan. The selection runs from $15 T-shirts to $5000 designer coats, with the former (cheap, fashionable creations and basics with which you can't go wrong) a hit with basically everyone.

FUTURE SHOP Map pp62–3 Electronics

☎ 514-393-2600; 470 Rue Ste-Catherine Ouest; 9am-9pm Mon-Fri, 10am-9pm Sat, noon-9pm Sun; Ⓜ Place-des-Arts

Canada's one-stop shop for music systems, computers and software, printers, cell phones, video cameras and entertainment gadgets. Watch out for the weekly flyers with awesome sales.

ANDY THE-ANH Map pp62–3 Fashion

☎ 514-842-4208; 2120 Rue de la Montagne; Ⓜ Peel

The flagship boutique of this Montréal design star is bursting at the seams with the daring geometrical silhouettes that have made him a hit in Kuwait, Greece and Asia. Stylish professionals and glamorous girls with money to spend, this is the shop for you.

BETSEY JOHNSON Map pp62–3 Fashon

☎ 514-392-9786; 1382 Rue Ste-Catherine Ouest; Ⓜ Peel

Yes, the iconic New York designer has oodles of fans across the border, and her dresses are a smashing hit with the Montréal set. Browse through layers of feminine bliss, ruffles and perfectly fitted silhouettes in satin and lace. While frocks can run upwards of $3000, they'll last a lifetime and the half-old sale rack is always crammed with pretty bargains.

FACE LONDON Map pp62–3 Fashion

☎ 514-282-4527; Les Cours Mont-Royal, 1455 Rue Peel; Ⓜ Peel

This lovely little dress shop specializes in carefully selected dresses, blouses and jewelry, much of the stock imported from England. Prices are reasonable and you're sure to find a dress that fits just right.

NADYA TOTO Map pp62–3 Fashion

☎ 514-350-9090; 2057 Rue de la Montagne; Ⓜ Peel

Defined by a unique recipe of spandex and wool in asymmetric cuts, Nadya's garments offer a wonderful mixture of flexibility, comfort and warmth. Not to mention that just about every woman looks great in these gems that cost only about $150 each.

OLAM Map pp62–3 Fashion

☎ 514-875-9696; 1374 Rue Ste-Catherine Ouest; Ⓜ Peel

This classy little boutique carries gorgeous threads by French and European brands like Miss Sixty as well as local designers including Mackage outerwear.

FELIX BROWN

Map pp62–3 Fashion & Footwear

☎ 514-287-5523; 1233 Rue Ste-Catherine Ouest; Ⓜ Peel

Black pumps with 10cm heels, ego-stroking staff and suits that mean business are the hallmarks of a shopping trip to this place. All items are imported from Italy and styles are sharp as a tack.

URBAN OUTFITTERS

Map pp62–3 Fashion & Housewares

☎ 514-874-0063; 1246 Rue Ste-Catherine Ouest; Ⓜ Peel

An impossibly trendy garment store for the teens and 20-somethings. Music thumps from morning to night throughout the warehouse-style building and the front mini-boutique is full of amusements and apartment furnishings and decor pieces.

LILI-LES-BAINS

Map pp62–3 Fashion & Swimwear

☎ 514-937-9197; 1336 Rue Notre-Dame Ouest; 150

Montréal's larger-than-life swimsuit maker started out making cruise-ship gear. Her philosophy is: every woman should have the dress of her dreams – size makes no difference. Cuts can reveal or conceal. Lili uses gorgeous fabrics flown in from Europe and has clients from all over the world.

ROOTS Map pp62–3 Fashion & Streetwear

☎ 514-845-7995; 1035 Rue Ste-Catherine Ouest; Ⓜ Peel

Its reputation is now soooo big worldwide that customers may forget Canada's own Roots started off as a humble shoemaker in the '70s. Now its range includes Roots for kids, Roots athletics, leather and home accessories. Tastes are easily accessible and geared to teens and 20-somethings, fashionable and at times even innovative.

BIRKS JEWELLERS Map pp62–3 Jewelry

☎ 514-397-2511; 1240 Square Phillips; Ⓜ McGill

For more than a century this upscale vendor of baubles and bangles has been Montréal's answer to Tiffany's of New York. Henry Birks opened his first store in 1879 and expanded throughout Canada. By 1936 the store won the right to supply the British royal family. Just the coffered ceiling in Wedgwood blue warrants a visit to the sales floor.

HMV Map pp62–3 Music & DVDs

☎ 514-875-0765; 1020 Rue Ste-Catherine Ouest; Ⓜ Peel

Entertainment headquarters. This cavernous, multilevel store is like a department store for music with fantastic sections of everything you could ever want, from classical, world music, techno and francophone to pop and jazz, as well as DVDs and video games.

MAISON DE LA PRESSE INTERNATIONALE Map pp62–3 Newsagent

☎ 514-861-6767; 1166 Rue Ste-Catherine Ouest; 🕓 7:30am-11pm Mon-Wed, 7:30am-midnight Thu-Fri, 8am-midnight Sat, 8am-11pm Sun; Ⓜ Peel

This is a slick international newspaper chain with papers from a couple of dozen countries, row upon row of magazines on every imaginable subject, and best-selling novels.

SEXE CITÉ Map pp62–3 Sex & Fetish

☎ 514-937-3678; 1821 Rue Ste-Catherine Ouest; 🕓 10am-midnight daily; Ⓜ Guy-Concordia

Spicy, sexy gear is all over this place, one of the most popular sex boutiques in town. It also stocks the gamut of sex toys, games and joke items. It's all so upfront that any inhibitions are checked at the door.

CENTRE EATON Map pp62–3 Shopping Mall

☎ 514-288-3708; 705 Rue Ste-Catherine Ouest; Ⓜ McGill

This five-story retailing palace on the main shopping drag is home to 175-plus stores and restaurants, and six movie screens. The tax-refund service Global Refund Canada is on the 4th floor. The Promenade de la Cathédrale is an underground passage of the complex that runs beneath the Cathédrale Christ Church.

COMPLEXE DESJARDINS

Map pp62–3 Shopping Mall

150 Rue Ste-Catherine Ouest; Ⓜ Place-des-Arts

This 1970s multifunctional complex links three office towers, a shopping mall and a big public plaza with atrium, trees and tinkling waterfalls in what's still Montréal's largest commercial building. The food court in the basement is usually buzzing with shoppers exhausted by the selection from 110 stores.

LES COURS MONT-ROYAL

Map pp62–3 Shopping Mall

cnr Rue Peel & Blvd de Maisonneuve Ouest; Ⓜ Peel

This capitalist emporium was once the jewel in the crown of the Mount Royal Hotel, and is now the city's most posh and airy shopping mall, with a bright atrium and winding staircase. With midrange and high-end shops like Club Monaco, DKNY and Armani, as well as spas and restaurants, there's something for everyone.

PLACE MONTRÉAL TRUST

Map pp62–3 Shopping Mall

1500 Ave McGill College; Ⓜ Peel

One of downtown's most successful malls, with enough rays from the skylights to keep shoppers on their day clock. Major retailers here include Athletes World Superstore, Indigo books, Mexx, Winners and Zara. It has a tremendous water fountain with a spout 30m high, and during the holidays a Christmas tree illuminates the five-story space.

TATTOOS & PIERCING

Many of the city's tattoo and piercing places are in the 'seedier' or more alternative parts of town like Blvd St-Laurent or Rue Ste-Catherine Est. But oddly enough Adrenaline (Map pp62–3; ☎ 514-938-8884; www.adrenalinetattoos.com; 1541 Rue Sherbrooke Ouest; 🕓 11am-8pm Mon-Wed, 11am-9pm Thu-Sat, 11am-7pm Sun; Ⓜ Guy-Concordia) chose to set up right next to upper-crust Westmount in the shadow of a university and a hospital. It's considered one of the best tattoo and piercing places in town. For those who aren't ready to make a lifetime commitment to body art, Adrenaline offers red henna 'tattoos,' lasting anywhere from two to eight weeks. Other options include temporary 'airbrushed' tattoos, lasting three to five days, and body glitter designs that can last up to two weeks.

WESTMOUNT

Just west of downtown is the aptly named Westmount, a wealthy residential part of Montreal where the hills are lined with ornate mansions. Beneath these regal homes is a fancy little shopping district where residents walk their pooches and peruse specialty wares. While many Westmount shops appeal exclusively to those with money to burn, they often carry cool items you can't find elsewhere, and quality is always top-notch. Plus, where else can you ogle at Montreal's rich and famous?

Even Montrealers may not know that Galerie de Bellefeuille (Map pp62–3; ☎ 514-933-4406; 1367 Ave Greene; Ⓜ Atwater) is one of the top private agents of Canadian art abroad, representing the likes of Nicola Hicks, Stephen Conroy and Jim Dine. Sculpture, paintings and limited-edition prints are given excellent space in this grand ex-bank with its winding staircase. The manager, Anthony Collins, is a gold mine of knowledge on the local arts scene.

Blue Marine Cie (Map pp62–3; ☎ 514-488-6366; 1383 Ave Greene; Ⓜ Atwater) sports designer jeans and stylish imported sportswear and jewelry. It's lovely, expensive, and very Greene Avenue!

At Chaussures Tony (Map pp62–3; ☎ 514-935-2993; 1346 Ave Greene; Ⓜ Atwater) the gracious, professional staff aren't afraid to measure your feet and have made this elegant, old-fashioned shoe store popular among Westmount locals of all ages since 1937. The family-owned business stocks mostly high-end and comfortable footwear with a few trendy pairs for the fashionistas.

Westmount Square (Map pp62–3; cnr Rue Ste-Catherine Ouest & Ave Wood; Ⓜ Atwater), designed by Bauhaus architect Ludwig Mies Van der Rohe, is a modern complex with office towers, terrace and shopping concourse that opened in 1967. It has a variety of boutiques, gift shops and art galleries, plus a food court.

The prime Westmount location of Lululemon Athletica (Map pp62–3; ☎ 514-937-5151; 1394 Ave Greene; Ⓜ Atwater), the big, bright branch of the massive yoga brand, makes it the community hangout of choice for stay-at-home moms, university students, and ladies who lunch. It sells a great selection of yoga attire, sportswear, mats and accessories, and offers a diverse schedule of classes that includes Indian dancing.

Westmount parents rush to Oink Oink (Map pp62–3; ☎ 514-939-2634; 1343 Ave Greene; Ⓜ Atwater) for the latest and greatest in toy gadgets and fashionable clothing for children. You'll find that pink mini-ghetto blaster, Barbie wig set or Sunday picnic garb in this adorable little shop.

PLACE VILLE-MARIE
Map pp62–3 Shopping Mall

☎ 514-861-9393; cnr Ave McGill College & Rue Cathcart; Ⓜ Bonaventure

Begun in the late 1950s, Montréal's first shopping complex marked the start of the underground city, was Montréal's most important skyscraper for years and set the standards for similar complexes around the city. It now hosts around 80 boutiques, restaurants and service stores.

QUARTIER LATIN & THE VILLAGE

ARCHAMBAULT Map p72 Books & Music

☎ 514-849-6202; 500 Rue Ste-Catherine Est; Ⓜ Berri-UQAM

Behind the art-deco portals you'll find Montréal's oldest and largest book and record shop, an emporium that boasts CDs, books, plus assorted musical supplies such as pianos and sheet music. Some recordings sold here are hard to find outside Québec.

RENAUD BRAY Map p72 Books & Music

☎ 514-876-9119; 1376 Rue Ste-Catherine Est; 🕐 9am-midnight; Ⓜ Beaudry

One of 14 branches in greater Montréal, this bright 'n' cheery bookstore specializes in French titles but has a decent choice of English best-sellers, travel and literature titles. A good portion of the store is dedicated to CDs in both languages, with a choice of local rock and pop.

TABAGIE PAT & ROBERT Map p72 Cigars

☎ 514-522-8534; 1474 Rue Ontario Est; Ⓜ Beaudry

Pat & Robert has a marvelous selection of the aromatic leaf – canned, rolled, displayed in plastic dispenser bins, with whatever accessory to make those rising coils a heavenly trip.

ZÉPHYR Map p72 Retro Art & Furniture

☎ 514-529-9199; 2112 Rue Amherst; 🕐 noon-6pm Mon-Fri, noon-5pm Sat & Sun; Ⓜ Berri-UQAM, then bus 61

Breathtakingly cramped, this bright emporium on the fringe of the Village is dedicated to showing art from Montréal artists. The proprietor, Daniel Roberge, will also rent his stock of prized faux Victorian mirrors, beanbags and cube chairs for movie shoots.

LA CAPOTERIE Map p72 Sex & Fetish
☎ **514-845-0027; 2061 Rue St-Denis;** Ⓜ **Berri-UQAM**
If you're wondering what to wear for that special occasion, then trot on down to the Capoterie for late-night fashion advice. Its exhaustive array of condoms comes in all giggly shapes, colors and sizes.

PRIAPE Map p72 Sex & Fetish
☎ **514-521-8451; 1311 Rue Ste-Catherine Est;** Ⓜ **Beaudry**
Montréal's biggest gay sex store has made a career out of parodying itself in great style. It's been on the scene for a quarter of a century so it's plugged into the mainstream erotic wares (videos and DVDs, mags and books) but has branched into high-quality clothing with a titillating edge – shrink-wrapped jeans, but also a vast choice of black leather gear in the basement studio.

LE CHÂTEAU Map p72 Streetwear
☎ **514-279-6391; 6729 Rue St-Hubert;** Ⓜ **Berri-UQAM**
This trendy concept store is where to go for one-season fashion and cheaper versions of designer trends. Very popular for buying cheap, trendy club wear. There's also a shop in the Centre Eaton (☎ 514-288-3708; 705 Rue Ste-Catherine Ouest), as well as others around town.

UNDERWORLD Map p72 Streetwear
☎ **514-284-6473; 251 Rue Ste-Catherine Est;** 🕙 **10am-6pm Mon-Wed, 10am-10pm Thu & Fri, 11am-5pm Sun;** Ⓜ **Berri-UQAM**
Underworld is a first-class punk refuge and supply house on an appropriately grungy stretch of Rue Ste-Catherine. It's got jeans, a big CD and record store in the basement and a killer selection of skates and snowboards.

PLATEAU MONT-ROYAL

LIBRAIRIE MICHEL FORTIN
Map pp76–7 Books
☎ **514-849-5719; 3714 Rue St-Denis;** Ⓜ **Sherbrooke**
A mecca for every foreign-language student and linguist freak in town. You can find books, cassettes or novels on just about every language in the world from Thai to Basque to Georgian.

MOOG AUDIO
Map pp76–7 Electronics & Computers
☎ **514-527-4494; 3823 Blvd St-Laurent;** Ⓜ **Mont-Royal**
This electronic and audio-equipment boutique used to house the legendary techno DNA record shop. These days, it sells synthesizers, amps, speakers, mics and sampler-type gear to rock stars, DJs and producers, both aspiring and established. Moog also rents audio equipment (for concerts and events) and is an authorized Mac dealer.

LOLA & EMILY Map pp76–7 Fashion
☎ **514-288-7598; 3475 Blvd St-Laurent;** Ⓜ **Sherbrooke**
Less is more at this whimsically girly shop designed like your dream vintage apartment. Carefully selected clothes by brands like Swedish designer Filippa K, Denmark's Designers Remix, Belgium's Essential and Canada's Ca Va de Soi are displayed in antique Indian furniture, which is also for sale.

PRELOVED Map pp76–7 Fashion
☎ **514-499-9898; 4832 Blvd St-Laurent;** Ⓜ **Mont-Royal**
Recycling takes on a whole new meaning at this adorable old-made-new boutique, which deconstructs used clothing, then transforms the old fabrics into brand-new cuts and designs. Bedsheets become sundresses, jeans are transformed into purses, and skirts into T-shirts.

REVENGE Map pp76–7 Fashion
☎ **514-843-4379; 3852 Rue St-Denis;** Ⓜ **Sherbrooke**
This renowned showcase store for Québécois designers displays subtle designs for professional women who want to balance chic with audacious. The men's ready-to-wear garments have a less challenging task, stressing confidence and masculinity in direct, commanding lines.

SCANDALE Map pp76–7 Fashion
☎ **514-842-4707; 3639 Blvd St-Laurent;** Ⓜ **St-Laurent, then bus 55**
The magnificent Marie-Josée Gagnon has been running this boutique since 1977,

bringing in exotic Parisian imports and more recently showing off the creations of Georges Lévesque, one of Québec's most exciting designers known for cutting-and-pasting shapes and fabrics.

SCHRETER

Map pp76–7 Fashion

☎ 514-845-4231; 4358 Blvd St-Laurent; M Mont-Royal

This Jewish-run store has been going strong since 1928 thanks to its inexpensive brand-name clothing in all sizes: winter coats and boots, socks, underwear, jeans, sportswear. Parents remember how *their* parents brought them here to stock up on the equivalent of Nike, Reebok and Adidas at great savings. It's still the place to get your basics.

SPACE FB

Map pp76–7 Fashion

☎ 514-282-1991; 3632 Blvd St-Laurent; M Sherbrooke

Local sportswear designer Francois Beauregard's eponymous line of casual mix-and-match separates is a stylish and authentic alternative to American Apparel, and Montréal scenesters wear the stuff in spades. With sexy-sporty T-shirts and hoodies sharing racks with tailored jackets and slacks, the shop's clean design suits the simple silhouettes of its wares.

U&I

Map pp76–7 Fashion

☎ 514-844-8788; 3650 Blvd St-Laurent; M Sherbrooke

Local designers like YSO, Morales and Denis Gagnon are in the spotlight at this award-winning boutique, peppered with offerings from Paris and other fashion meccas. Brands include Vivienne Westwood, Fred Perry, Marlboro Classics and Comme des Garcons accessories.

DUO

Map pp76–7 Fashion, Men's

☎ 514-845-0882; 30 Rue Prince-Arthur Ouest; M Sherbrooke

If you're a suave fellow looking to dress sharp, head directly to this well-stocked little shop, staffed (it would appear) by models with a penchant for men's fashion. Duo carries hot brands like Swedish suitmaker J.Lindeberg, and Canada's own DSquared, as well as designer sneakers and accessories. Fedora, anyone?

KANUK

Map pp76–7 Fashion, Outerwear

☎ 514-527-4494; 485 Rue Rachel Est; M Mont-Royal

When people in Québec say 'Kanuk' they mean the winter coats that last a lifetime, and although they're available throughout the province, this flagship store has the best selection, and seasonal sales. Most jackets stay toasty in temperatures dipping to -30°C. Kanuk also carries raincoats, swimsuits, backpacks and hiking gear.

BOUTIQUE EVA B

Map pp62–3 Fashion, Vintage

☎ 514-849-8246; 2013 Blvd St-Laurent; 10am-7pm or later Mon-Sat, noon-5pm Sun; M St-Laurent

In a space reminiscent of a theater's backstage, this boutique is a riot of recycled women's clothing, retro gear and new streetwear. It's the kind of place where 1950s bowling shoes are proudly arranged beneath a flock of floaty feather boas and yet it all seems very normal.

COFFRE AUX TRÉSORS DU CHAINON

Map pp76–7 Fashion, Vintage

☎ 514-843-4354; 4375 Blvd St-Laurent; M St-Laurent, then bus 55

There are several *friperies* (used clothing stores) in this area, where Chainon takes the cake for its vintage hipster accoutrements. Browse through endless racks for five-dollar gold pumps and monogrammed bowling shirts, tea sets, horn-rimmed glasses, houndstooth ties and other treasures.

FRIPERIE ST-LAURENT

Map pp76–7 Fashion, Vintage

☎ 514-842-1308; 3972 Blvd St-Laurent; M Sherbrooke

This is another favorite *friperie* because of its small but extremely well-chosen selection. Famous 1940s ties, cowboy and motorcycle boots and Gothic-flavored blouses adorn fresh and colorful window displays.

BOUTIQUE LE MARCHEUR

Map pp76–7 Footwear

☎ 514-842-3007; 4062 Rue St-Denis; M Sherbrooke

A stomping ground of quality walking shoes for urban treks around town. Montréal is a walking city, and this aptly named boutique keeps local feet happy year-round. Admittedly, it can be tough to find footwear both stylish and comfortable but you've got a decent shot here.

SCARPA Map pp76–7 Footwear

☎ 514-282-6363; 4257 Rue St-Denis; Ⓜ Mont-Royal

A bounty of gorgeous, runway-worthy shoes for men and women, from sexy pumps to smart boots, strappy sandals to sneakers and leather handbags imported from Brazil, Italy and Scandinavia. Shoe-shopping heaven.

CRUELLA Map pp76–7 Gothic & Fetish

☎ 514-844-0167; 257 Ave du Mont-Royal Est; Ⓜ Mont-Royal

With a coffin centerpiece and one of the biggest arrays of Gothic and fetish clothing in Montréal, Cruella is the biggest apparition in the Plateau grave-digger's scene. Slip into a chain-link miniskirt, dominatrix leggings or a Victorian shroud to give your party that something extra, or pick up vampire fangs and bondage icons.

ZONE Map pp76–7 Housewares

☎ 514-845-3530; 4246 Rue St-Denis; Ⓜ Sherbrooke

Affordably chic housewares and home accents is the name of the game at this chain of shops. The simple and pretty kitchen accessories, picture frames, linens, lamps, lighting and bathroom stuff make terrific gifts for yourself or someone else.

LE POINT VERT Map pp76–7 Newsagent

☎ 514-982-9195; 4040 Blvd St-Laurent; Ⓜ Sherbrooke

Part magazine shop, part hangout, this family-run establishment in the Portuguese are of the Plateau carries hard-to-find literature as well as the essentials. You're apt to spot bespectacled hipsters perusing the latest issue of *Adbusters* alongside vintage fashionistas leafing through French *Vogue*.

LITTLE ITALY, MILE END & OUTREMONT

DRAWN & QUARTERLY

Map p83 Books & Comics

☎ 514-279-2224; 211 Rue Bernard Ouest; Ⓜ Rosemont

The flagship store of this cult independent comic-book and graphic-novel publisher has become somewhat of a local literary haven. Cool book launches take place here, and the quaint little shop sells all sorts of reading matter.

QUINCAILLERIE DANTE

Map p83 Cooking & Hardware

☎ 514-271-2057; 6851 Rue St-Dominique; Ⓜ De Castelnau

This quirky little Italian-owned hardware and cooking supply store is a household name, selling everything from first-class pots and pans to espresso makers, fishing rods and hunting gear.

BILLIE Map p83 Fashion

☎ 514-270-5415; 141 Ave Laurier Ouest; Ⓜ Laurier

Carefully selected Brazilian shoes, imported dresses, designer jeans, jewelry and luxurious cashmere sweaters make this treasure-filled boutique a must-see on the fashion circuit. Prices aren't cheap but the fits and high fashion are worth the cost.

GENERAL 54 Map p83 Fashion

☎ 514-270-9333; 54 Ave St-Viateur Ouest; Ⓜ Laurier

The hats! The bags! The community consciousness! Mile End artists have created almost everything stocked at this great little boutique. Goods are sold on consignment with creators getting proceeds from the store. You'll find stuff you won't find anywhere else, including funky T-shirts and leather handbags.

MIMI & COCO Map p83 Fashion

☎ 514-906-0349; 201 Ave Laurier Ouest; Ⓜ Laurier

The third boutique of this elegant T-shirt brand sells the Mimi & Coco line, plus dresses and knits, and chic sportswear for men, women and children. m0851 leather goods can also be found here, and Mandy's on-site salad bar serves yummy snacks and lunchtime treats.

LOCAL 23 Map p83 Fashion, Vintage

☎ 514-270-9333; 23 Rue Bernard Ouest; Ⓜ Laurier

This tart little *friperie* stocks recycled clothing and heaps of interesting vintage finds.

Even if you are not a secondhand clothing freak, this is an interesting place to stop by. There's nothing junky about it and pieces have been carefully chosen and arranged.

BOUTIQUE SAFRAN Map p83 Home Decor

☎ 514-271-0042; 1116 Ave Bernard Ouest; Ⓜ Rosemont

Of the fancy little home-decor shops lining Ave Bernard, Safran is one of the cutest and most affordable. With a clientele of interior designers and civilians alike, you can find one-of-a-kind fabrics, pillows, lamps, chandeliers and furnishings.

CHEZ ROSE MARIE LINGERIE

Map p83 Lingerie

☎ 514-272-0347; 5614 Ave du Parc; Ⓜ Rosemont

Run by a no-nonsense mother-daughter duo, this old-school lingerie boutique is serious about its underwear. It may not be as slick as the downtown lingerie boutiques, but this fantastic little shop has a great selection of support bras as well as sexy, frilly unmentionables, all at unbeatable prices.

PHONOPOLIS Map p83 Music

☎ 514-270-4442; 5403A Ave du Parc; Ⓜ Laurier

Indie rock, jazz, blues and classical sounds – and hybrids thereof – are the manifesto of this little record shop, which buys and sells CDs and LPs.

AU PAPIER JAPONAIS Map p83 Origami

☎ 514-276-6863; 24 Ave Fairmount Ouest; Ⓜ Laurier

You'd never have guessed how many guises Japanese paper can come in until you visit this gorgeous little shop. The lamps and kites make great gifts and you can fold them for easy transport. This store has also become an arts and crafts hub and offers workshops and seminars.

LE MARCHÉ DES SAVEURS

Map p83 Québécois Products

☎ 514-271-3811; 280 Pl du Marché du Nord; ⌚ 9am-6pm; Ⓜ Jean-Talon

Everything here is Québécois, from the food to the handmade soaps to one of the best collections of artisanal local beer in the city. The store was established so local producers could gain wider exposure for their regional products, and it's a joy to browse.

UN AMOUR DES THÉS Map p83 Tea

☎ 514-279-2999; 1224 Rue Bernard Ouest; Ⓜ Rosemont

Over 160 types of loose tea sit in canisters behind the counter of this charming shop. It stocks leaf varieties and flavors you've likely not only never heard of, but never imagined (red-berries and maple syrup, tea with chocolate oils, cream of Earl Grey). Regular tea tastings and ceremonies are also held.

JET-SETTER Map p83 Travel Goods

☎ 514-271-5058, 800-271-5058; http://jet-setter.ca; 66 Ave Laurier Ouest; Ⓜ Laurier

An orgy of state-of-the-art luggage and every travel gadget known to man, it's got luggage alarms, pocket-sized T-shirts, 'dry-in-an-instant' underwear and towels, mini-irons and hairdryers. You can also shop online.

RACHELLE-BÉRY

Map p83 Vitamins & Health Food

☎ 514-849-4118; 4810 Blvd St-Laurent; Ⓜ Laurier

An incredible selection of vitamins, teas, supplements, aromatherapy and homeopathic products to nourish and beautify your body inside and out make this well-stocked organic grocery shop stand out from the herd.

SOUTHWEST & OUTER MONTRÉAL

LES ANTIQUITÉS GRAND CENTRAL

Map pp62–3 Antiques

☎ 514-935-1467; 2448 Rue Notre-Dame Ouest; ⌚ 9am-6pm Mon-Sat; Ⓜ Lionel-Groulx

The most elegant store on Antique Row is a pleasure to visit for its English and continental furniture, lighting and decorative objects from the 18th and 19th centuries. Get buzzed in to see the Louis XIV chairs, full dining-room suites and chandeliers in Dutch cathedral or French Empire style, with price tags in the thousands.

PARISIAN LAUNDRY

Map pp62–3 Art Gallery

☎ 514-989-1056; www.parisianlaundry.com; 3550 Rue St-Antoine Ouest; ⌚ noon-5pm Tue-Sat; Ⓜ Lionel-Groulx

A former industrial laundry turned monster gallery, this 15,000-sq-ft space is worth a trip for the building itself even if you're not a fan of large-format contemporary art. Natural light floods through enormous 19th-century-era windows into two floors of exhibition rooms. Exhibitions have included print artist Francine Simonin and international star Jean-Paul Riopelle. It also holds occasional artists' talks and lectures.

LUCIE FAVREAU ANTIQUES

Map pp62–3 Collectibles

☎ 514-989-5117; 1904 Rue Notre-Dame Ouest; closed Sun; M Georges-Vanier

This colorful, museumlike store is brimming with giggle-inducing housewares, advertising plaques, toys and sports memorabilia like signed baseballs, among other collectibles.

OUTER DISTRICTS

CHABANEL WAREHOUSES

Map pp44–5 Garments & Textiles

900 Blvd St-Laurent; 9am-1pm Sat; M Crémazie

Bargain-sniffers from far and wide flock to the Chabanel, an eight-block expanse of old factory buildings in northern Montréal west of Blvd St-Laurent. Inside are hundreds of 'suites' or warehouse storage rooms stuffed with locally made and imported items. From Buffalo jeans to Monte Calvo coats to Indian skirts, the choice is so huge it's almost paralyzing. Just start on a top floor (the buildings have up to nine floors) and work your way down. Bring cash and be prepared to bargain. The shops open their doors on Saturday morning only, when something of a funfair atmosphere prevails. A few buildings are open normal hours during the week.

EATING

top picks

What's your recommendation? www.lonelyplanet.com/canada/montreal

EATING

Montréal is one of the great foodie destinations of the north. Here you'll find an outstanding assortment of classic French cuisine, hearty Québécois fare and countless ethnic restaurants from 80-odd nationalities. Today's haute cuisine is as likely to be conjured by talented young Italian, Japanese or British chefs as graduates from the Académie Culinaire du Québec.

Montréal has more eating choices per capita than anywhere in North America except for New York City, and boasts more than 5000 restaurants. The dining scene is marked by dazzling variety and quality, and brash chefs who attack their creations with innovative gusto. Life in Montréal revolves around food, and it's as much about satisfying your sensual fantasies as it is about nourishment.

Nearly every neighborhood has its culinary stars, which makes for rewarding dining no matter where you wander. The challenge, however, is knowing where to begin. A few good entry points into Montréal's dining scene follow.

Downtown and Plateau Mont-Royal are a diner's nirvana, linked by arteries Blvd St-Laurent and Rue St-Denis. 'The Main,' as locals call Blvd St-Laurent, teems with trendy establishments but shades into the alternative as you move north. Still in the Plateau, Rue Prince-Arthur Est and Ave Duluth Est are popular for their good-time BYOB (bring your own bottle) places. Mile End and Outremont also have a great selection of bistros and ethnic fare, with new places popping up all the time. The key streets here are Ave Laurier, Ave St-Viateur and Rue Bernard. Little Italy has great Italian trattorias along Blvd St-Laurent and Rue Dante. Old Montréal, meanwhile, is the latest setting for the city's culinary showdown, with a number of award-winning restaurants hidden in the old streets, particularly west of Blvd St-Laurent.

SPECIALTIES

Montrealers enjoy an enormous variety of locally produced ingredients and delicacies: raw cheeses, foie gras, game and maple syrup, to name a few. The outdoor markets carry exotic foodstuffs that weren't available even a decade ago alongside the tasty produce from local farms. Marché Atwater and Marché Jean-Talon (see the boxed text, opposite) are the city's two biggest markets, and are great places to assemble a picnic.

Residents argue heatedly over which places serve the best of anything – chewy bagels, espresso, comfort soup, fluffy omelet or creamy cakes. Montréal smoked meat and bagels, of course, have a formidable reputation that stretches across the country and is a constant source of friendly rivalry with New Yorkers. Montréal loyalists insist the secret to the hometown bagel's success is all in the time-tested preparation (see the boxed text, p138, for more).

Traditional Québécois cuisine is classic comfort food, heavy and centered on meat dishes. The fact that the ingredients are basic is said to be a historical legacy, as French settlers only had access to limited produce. A classic Québécois meal might center on game meat (caribou, duck, wild boar) or the *tourtière,* a meat pie usually made with pork and another meat like beef or veal along with celery and onions. Another favorite lowbrow staple is *poutine* (fries smothered in cheese curds and gravy), with many inventive versions served across the city (see the boxed text, p135).

There's also a fine choice of French food in the city, with bistros and brasseries of all types and price ranges. Many of them incorporate the best of Québec's produce and market ingredients, and you'll find everything from no-nonsense French food to experimental takes on the classics.

PARDON?

Menus in Montréal are often – but not always – bilingual; regardless, if you need help with *le français,* don't be shy to ask (the waiters are used to it). Important note: in French, an *entrée* is an appetizer, not a main course – that's *le plat principal.* Another thing to watch out for is recognizing the difference between *pâte,* which means pasta, and pâté, which means that spreadable stuff often made of goose liver (though there's also vegetarian pâtés, such as *pâté aux champignons et tofu,* which is made of mushrooms and tofu).

PRICE GUIDE

Prices in this chapter are based on a two-course meal (appetizer and main), excluding drinks.

$$$	over $30
$$	$16-$30
$	under $16

For local recipes and tips on mastering the great dishes of the province, pick up the cookbook *A Taste of Québec* by Julian Armstrong.

PRACTICALITIES

Opening Hours & Meal Times

Standard opening hours for restaurants are 11am to 2:30pm and 5:30pm to 11pm. Some places close on Monday. Breakfast cafés open around 8am (9am on Sundays) and close by late afternoon. On weekends two dinner sittings are common at 5:30pm to 6pm and 8pm to 8:30pm. Places tend to fill up from 8pm onwards.

How Much?

Depending on where you go (and sometimes what time you go), dining out in Montréal doesn't have to be a costly venture. On average, a multicourse dinner for two (including a glass of wine and taxes and tip) at a midrange place will set you back about $80 to $120. At the city's more famous establishments, expect to pay about twice that for a multicourse meal. At the other end of the scale, it's possible to eat some delicious fare at casual spots – vegetarian cafés, Jewish delis and down-market ethnic eateries (like a number of places in Chinatown) – for under $40 for two.

Keep an eye out for the table d'hôte, a fixed-price meal – usually three or four courses – that can be a good way to sample the chef's top dishes of the day. Prices start at around $20. Some restaurants offer a discount menu for late dining (usually starting at 10pm), while others have a policy of *apportez votre vin*, or bring your own wine. There's rarely a corkage fee, so take advantage of this. Pick up your tipple from an

GREAT MARKETS OF MONTRÉAL

Montréal is famed for its impressive year-round food markets, where you can sample the great bounty of the north. The biggest and best are Marché Jean-Talon in Little Italy and Marché Atwater just west of downtown near the Canal de Lachine. These are excellent places to wander, with a tempting array of fruit and veggies, artisanal cheeses, fresh baked baguettes, pure maple syrup, fragrant herbs, colorful flowers, glistening fish and meat counters and much more. There's no better place to assemble a picnic, and for those who'd rather eat and go, there are food stands, cafés and bakeries on-site.

For more on the market phenomenon visit Marchés Publics de Montréal (www.marchespublics-mtl.com).

- **Marché Jean-Talon** (Map p83; ☎ 514-277-1588; 7075 Ave Casgrain; 7am-6pm Mon-Wed & Sat, 7am-8pm Thu-Fri, 7am-5pm Sun; M Jean-Talon) The city's largest market, right in the heart of Little Italy. There are several hundred market stalls on a huge square ringed by shops that stock all manner of produce year-round including fruits, vegetables, potted plants, herbs and (of course) maple syrup. Food stalls whip up fresh juices, tender crepes, baguette sandwiches and more. Don't miss the Québécois specialty store Le Marché des Saveurs (p114).
- **Marché Atwater** (Map pp62–3; 138 Ave Atwater; 7am-6pm Mon-Wed, 7am-8pm Thu-Fri, 7am-5pm Sat & Sun; M Lionel-Groulx) Located right on the banks of the Canal de Lachine, with scores of vendors outside and high-class delicatessens and specialty food shops inside, in the tiled, vaulted hall under the art-deco clock tower. Try the Boucherie Claude & Henri for beautiful racks of lamb, the bakery Première Moisson (see the boxed text, p131) for baguettes or the astounding Fromagerie du Marché Atwater, whose hundreds of cheeses reach from runny triple crèmes to hard goudas.
- **Marché de Maisonneuve** (Map pp44–5; ☎ 514-937-7754; 4445 Rue Ontario Est; 7am-6pm Mon-Wed & Sat, 7am-8pm Thu-Fri, 7am-5pm Sun; M Pie-IX, then bus 139) About 20 farm stalls, and inside, a dozen vendors of meat, cheese, fresh vegetables, tasty pastries and pastas in a beautiful beaux-arts building (1912–14) in Maisonneuve, girded by pretty gardens.
- **Marché St-Jacques** (Map p72; 2035 Rue Amherst; 6am-9pm Mon-Fri, 6am-6pm Sat & Sun; M Beaudry) Traditional food and vegetable stalls and shops still occupy their 1931 art-deco home, in the northern reach of the Village. In the spring and summer, the market keeps longer hours (6am to midnight daily).

outlet of the government's alcohol retailer, SAQ (Société des Alcools du Québec).

Taxes amounting to 15% apply at all restaurants. Most don't include the taxes in their menu prices, but check the fine print.

Booking Tables

Reserve on weekends to avoid disappointment. During the week you needn't book a table unless the place is quite popular (or formal). Note that most budget eateries don't take reservations.

Tipping

A tip of 15% of the pretax bill is customary in restaurants. Some waiters may add a service charge for large parties; in these cases, no tip should be added unless the service was extraordinary. Leave the tip on the table or hand it directly to staff.

Groceries

The largest supermarket chains in Montréal are Provigo (p128) and Metro (p130), always well stocked and open long hours. In Mont-Royal, the section of Blvd St-Laurent between Ave des Pins and Ave Mont-Royal is renowned for its ethnic food shops. Little Italy has a multitude of small groceries and deli shops on Blvd St-Laurent, a few blocks south of Rue Jean-Talon.

There are four open-air food markets (see the boxed text, p119) where farmers, butchers and cheese makers sell their produce directly. Most sites also have indoor sections that stay open all winter. You'll find other good food shopping at the shopping centers of Le Fauborg (p127) and Westmount Square (see the boxed text, p110).

OLD MONTRÉAL & CHINATOWN

Vieux-Montréal has experienced a culinary renaissance in recent years, with a number of acclaimed restaurants winning over discerning diners and food critics alike. Here you'll find top-notch Québécois and fusion fare, among some of the city's most atmospheric dining rooms (hard to beat the 18th-century backdrop). That said, Old Montréal still has plenty of touristy restaurants (ie all the restaurants along Pl Jacques-Cartier) where quantity not quality is the name of the game. The touristy–local divide is roughly Blvd St-Laurent, with the better restaurants lying to the west of this iconic street.

Billowy steam and scrumptious odors waft out of kitchens and into the streets of Montréal's tiny but lively Chinatown. Cantonese, Szechuan and Vietnamese restaurants dominate Blvd St-Laurent and the pedestrian Rue de la Gauchetière.

GIBBY'S Map p48 — Steak House $$$

☎ 514-282-1837; Pl d'Youville 298, Old Montréal; mains $30-45; M Square-Victoria

A purveyor of the good old-fashioned steak, Gibby's serves excellent grilled meats and seafood, including a respected rack of lamb. A mix of corporate types clink glasses inside the elegant stone building (former stables, actually) dating back to the 1700s. There's an open courtyard in the back.

GARDE-MANGER Map p48 — International $$$

☎ 514-678-5044; 409 Rue St-François-Xavier, Old Montréal; mains $25-35; 🕑 6pm-3am Tue-Sun; M Place-d'Armes

The buzz surrounding Garde-Manger hasn't let up since its opening in 2006. This tiny upscale restaurant attracts a mix of local scenesters and haute-cuisine-loving out-of-towners who come for the lobster risotto, short ribs, succulent snow crab and other changing specials. After midnight, the soundtrack gets cranked up a notch and the candlelit dining room becomes a party place for the A-list. Reservations essential.

L'ORIGNAL Map p48 — Québécois $$$

☎ 514-303-0479; 479 Rue St-Alexis, Old Montréal; mains $28-36; 🕑 6-11pm Mon-Sat; M Place-d'Armes

This cozy chalet-style restaurant specializes in exquisitely prepared game meat and fresh seafood. Start off with oysters before moving on to braised wild boar or poached turbot in a lobster bisque. The service is excellent here. On weekend nights, L'Orignal gets packed and attracts a festive crowd when the kitchen closes.

TOQUÉ! Map p48 — French $$$

☎ 514-499-2084; 900 Pl Jean-Paul-Riopelle, Old Montréal; mains $38-42; 🕑 5:30-10:30pm Tue-Sat; M Place-d'Armes

Chef Normand Laprise has earned rave reviews for his innovative recipes based on products sourced from local farms. Even his desserts excite, created around fresh fruit with surprises like basil highlights. The bright, wide-open dining room has high ceilings accented by playful splashes of color, with a glass-enclosed wine cave with suspended bottles looming front and center. The seven-course menu dégustation ($92) is the pinnacle of dining in Montréal – allow three hours for the feast.

LE CLUB CHASSE ET PÊCHE Map p48 French $$$

☎ 514-861-1112; 423 Rue St-Claude, Old Montréal; mains $29-31; Ⓜ Champ-de-Mars
One of the pillars of Old Montréal's grand dining scene, this elegant restaurant serves fantastic new-wave French fare, including grilled Wagyu beef, sautéed scallops with fennel and a succulent lamb. Given the prices, it's a favorite among lunching execs, and Montrealers celebrating a special occasion. In the summer at lunchtime, dine alfresco in the historical Château Ramezay garden across the street.

LE LOCAL Map p48 French $$$

☎ 514-397-7737; 740 Rue William, Old Montréal; mains $20-30; Ⓜ Square-Victoria
On the western edge of Old Montréal, this captivating newcomer (opened in 2008) serves delectable fare in an architecturally stunning dining room. Well-moneyed 20- and 30-somethings feast on inventive (critics say overly complicated) dishes with rich, market-fresh ingredients to the backdrop of unobtrusive electronica. There's an outdoor terrace and an extensive wine list (and an award-winning sommelier). Reservations recommended.

CHEZ L'ÉPICIER Map p48 French $$$

☎ 514-878-2232; 311 Rue St-Paul Est, Old Montréal; mains $16-36; ⏲ restaurant 11:30am-10pm; Ⓜ Champ-de-Mars
Helmed by chef Laurent Godbout, Chez L'Épicier remains a solid choice when eating in Old Montréal. Inside the bright and cozy dining room with big windows overlooking the street, you'll find a menu that changes regularly, but features handsomely presented dishes like maple-syrup glazed pork, duo of lobster and scallops with sweet potato risotto, or seared filet mignon with smoked red wine sauce. For dessert, try the famous chocolate club sandwich with pineapple fries. The gourmet delicatessen attached is a fine spot for assembling a picnic.

CHEZ QUEUX Map p48 French $$

☎ 514-866-5194; 158 Rue St-Paul Est, Old Montréal; mains $30-42; ⏲ 11:30am-3pm & 5-11pm; Ⓜ Champ-de-Mars
Housed in an historic warehouse from 1862, with stone walls, polished paneling and Third Empire furnishings, this gem offers the epitome of old-fashioned French cuisine. Settle into a thronelike chair, order the delicious chateaubriand and prepare for a pampering. The little-known rear terrace overlooking the Old Port is a lovely dining spot in summer. The wine list features 300-plus varieties.

BORIS BISTRO Map p48 Bistro $$

☎ 514-848-9575; 465 Rue McGill, Old Montréal; mains $16-32; ⏲ 11:30am-midnight Mon-Fri, noon-midnight Sat & Sun; Ⓜ Square-Victoria
You'll be elbowing your way through everyone from Armani-clad executives and disheveled artists to maple-syrup-toting tourists in order to get a table at this popular bistro. Once settled, however, you can feast on a mouthwatering assortment of dishes, including artfully presented salads, a much-touted duck risotto with mushrooms or uncomplicated bistro favorites like pasta with spicy chorizo. Whether you want to eat inside or underneath the high ceilings and exposed heat conductors or in the outdoor courtyard, it's a good idea to reserve ahead during the lunch rush.

RESTAURANT HOLDER Map p48 Bistro $$

☎ 514-849-0333; 407 Rue McGill, Old Montréal; mains $18-28; ⏲ 11:30am-11pm Mon-Fri, 10am-3pm & 5:30-11pm Sat & Sun; Ⓜ Square-Victoria
High ceilings, a warm color scheme and beautifully turned-out dishes are just part of the appeal of this classic bistro on busy Rue McGill. It's a buzzing place (sometimes quite noisy), where the crowd – good-looking media and corporate types – dines on tuna niçoise, grilled hangar steak, pan-seared tilapia and other bistro classics.

DA EMMA Map p48 Italian $$

☎ 514-392-1568; 777 Rue de la Commune Ouest, Old Montréal; mains $15-28; Ⓜ Square-Victoria
The old stone walls and beamed ceiling of this atmospheric place – a former women's

prison – today provide the backdrop to delicious Italian cooking. Osso buco, fresh grilled fish, *agnolotti* with stuffed veal and satisfying homemade pastas are top picks from the changing menu. Reservations recommended.

LE PETIT MOULINSART
Map p48 Belgian $$

☎ 514-843-7432; 139 Rue St-Paul Ouest, Old Montréal; mains $16-29; ⏰ 11:30am-3pm & 5-11pm summer, Mon-Sat winter; Ⓜ Place-d'Armes
Fans of Tintin comic books will feel right at home here in a restaurant inspired by the Belgian hero and his sidekick Capt Haddock. There's a range of good dishes but it's the mussels (served 18 different ways) that play a starring role. It also has an extensive beer list and an inviting back terrace open in summer.

LA GARGOTE Map p48 French $$

☎ 514-844-1428; 351 Pl d'Youville, Old Montréal; mains $17-25; ⏰ noon-2:30pm & 5:30-10pm, closed Sun off-season; Ⓜ Square-Victoria
An Old Montréal standard, this bistro pumps along with quality bistro fare served in a cozy dining room with stone walls and beamed ceilings. There's nothing particularly inventive about the menu, but the fresh salads, grilled meats and crème brûlée are hard to fault. Good people-watching from the outdoor tables in summer.

GANDHI Map p48 Indian $$

☎ 514-845-5866; 230 Rue St-Paul Ouest, Old Montréal; mains $14-26; ⏰ noon-2pm Mon-Fri, 5:30-10:30pm daily; Ⓜ Square-Victoria
Gandhi has a core of loyal fans who come here for classics like tandoori chicken as well as the extensive curry menu with adventurous fare like *malaya,* a curry of pineapple, lychees and cream. Appetizers like pakoras or vegetable samosas are finely spiced, and faves such as tandoori duck, butter chicken and lamb korahi also go down nicely. Reservations are recommended.

USINE DE SPAGHETTI PARISIENNE
Map p48 Italian $$

☎ 514-866-0963; 273 Rue St-Paul Est, Old Montréal; mains $10-20; ⏰ 11am-11pm; Ⓜ Champ-de-Mars
Near the circuslike Pl Jacques-Cartier, this restaurant attracts loads of tourists who come for satisfying standard dishes like fettuccini with baby clams and grilled filet mignon. Although the crowds can be a bit much, the setting is congenial (stone walls and wood details, with an open hearth) and the price-to-quality ratio is decent. Mains include all the bread and salad you can eat.

STASH CAFÉ Map p48 Polish $$

☎ 514-845-6611; 200 Rue St-Paul Ouest; mains $12-19; ⏰ 11:30am-11pm; Ⓜ Place-d'Armes
Hearty Polish cuisine is served up with good humor in a dining room with seats made of church pews and daringly low red lights illuminating the tables. Staff range from warm and gregarious to completely stand-offish, but the food is consistent, with quality fare like pierogy (dumplings stuffed with meat or cheese, with sour cream) and potato pancakes with apple sauce. An enthusiastic pianist hammers away from time to time.

LA MAISON KAM FUNG
Map p48 Chinese $$

☎ 514-878-2888; 1111 Rue St-Urbain, Chinatown; mains $8-14; ⏰ 7am-3pm & 4:30-10pm; Ⓜ Place-d'Armes
This is generally considered the best place in town for dim sum, and is especially popular for Saturday and Sunday brunch. Waiters circle the tables with carts of dim sum ($4 to $6 each) – you pick and choose from tender dumplings, spare ribs, mushrooms, spicy shrimp and much more. The entrance is hidden in the rear of a shopping passage up an escalator.

TITANIC Map p48 Café $

☎ 514-849-0894; 445 Rue St-Pierre, Old Montréal; mains $5-10; ⏰ 8am-4:30pm Mon-Fri; Ⓜ Square-Victoria
The sandwiches here have office workers scurrying to these cramped basement quarters from all over Old Montréal on their lunch breaks. The varieties are endless and can include pepper pâté, smoked mackerel or spicy Calabrese sausage. Excellent salads, pastas, quiche and antipasto misto are popular takeouts that round out the mix.

CLUNY ARTBAR Map p48 Café $

☎ 514-866-1213; 257 Rue Prince, Old Montréal; mains $6-13; ⏰ 8am-5pm Mon-Fri, until 10pm Thu; Ⓜ Square-Victoria
Industrial style dominates at this renovated factory shared with the Fonderie Darling art space. Tables are made of recycled bowling

lanes, while exposed beams and pipes snake overhead. The menu features a daily special, along with reliably good deli sandwiches, soups, salads and antipasti. The breakfast menu includes flaky croissants and heartier *huevos rancheros* (fried eggs, tortillas and salsa).

OLIVE + GOURMANDO

Map p48 Deli-Bakery $

☎ 514-285-2493; 351 Rue St-Paul Ouest, Old Montréal; mains $9-12; 🕑 8am-6pm Tue-Sat, until 8pm summer; Ⓜ Square-Victoria

Named after the owners' two cats, this bakery/café is legendary in town for its sandwiches and baked goods. Excellent choices include the smoked trout with herbed cream cheese and the Cuban (ham, roast pork, Swiss cheese and house-made chipotle mayo). You'll also find good coffee, tempting desserts and fresh loaves for takeout (including olive and rosemary bread). Try to avoid the busy weekday lunch rush (11:30am to 1:30pm).

MARCHÉ DE LA VILLETTE

Map p48 Deli $

☎ 514-807-8084; 324 Rue St-Paul Ouest, Old Montréal; mains $8-20; 🕑 9am-6pm Mon-Fri, 9am-5pm Sat & Sun; Ⓜ Square-Victoria

Here you'll find a convivial traditional deli serving made-to-order sandwiches with homemade pâté, cured ham, sausages, foie gras and an array of pungent cheeses. Also does meat and seafood mains to go, best followed by its flavorful ice cream or sherbet.

PHÓ BANG NEW YORK

Map p48 Vietnamese $

☎ 514-954-2032; 970 Blvd St-Laurent, Chinatown; mains $10-15; 🕑 10am-10pm; Ⓜ Place-d'Armes

Near the gateway to Chinatown, Phó Bang New York has decor and service geared more toward Westerners who want to have their pho (noodle soups) in swisher digs. The food here is still good and regularly makes people's 'top' lists, but it lacks the kind of manic energy that makes the other Vietnamese places on this drag so atmospheric. The pho here tends to be leaner than at other Chinatown spots.

BEIJING Map p48 Chinese $

☎ 514-861-2003; 92 Rue de la Gauchetière Ouest, Chinatown; mains $8-15; 🕑 11am-3am; Ⓜ Place-d'Armes

Every Montrealer has a favorite Chinatown restaurant, a familiar place where a warm welcome awaits when turning up in the neighborhood. The unassuming and always-buzzing Beijing tops many lists, with a reputation built on tasty, fresh Cantonese and Szechuan dishes, friendly service and its late-night hours.

JARDIN DE JADE Map p48 Chinese $

☎ 514-866-3127; 67 Rue de la Gauchetière Ouest, Chinatown; buffet $9-14; 🕑 11am-10:30pm daily; Ⓜ Place-d'Armes

The chaotic, free-for-all Jardin de Jade buffet should be a must on your list if only to see it in action. Vegetarian, sushi, dumplings, fish, ribs, desserts and even pizza. To see it in its full elbow-bumping glory, try weekdays when locals, business people and students battle it out over the stir-fry. One of the town's best deals. Prices vary depending on day and time.

CALI Map p48 Vietnamese $

☎ 514-876-1064; 1011 Blvd St-Laurent, Chinatown; mains $6-12; 🕑 10am-10pm; Ⓜ Place-d'Armes

Cali is a decent hole-in-the-wall place, with friendly, good-humored waitstaff no matter how busy things get. The deal with this place is to get you in and out as quickly as possible, so don't be surprised if your order lands in front of you, piping hot, literally moments after you order it.

NECTAR OF THE GODS

Québec produces about three-quarters of the world's maple syrup, which is perhaps why it enjoys such pride of place, appearing on everything from meat and desserts to foie gras, blended with smoothies and of course in maple beer. French settlers began producing it regularly in the 1800s after learning how to make it from maple tree sap by Canadian Aboriginals. Sap is usually extracted in spring after enzymes convert starch into sugars over the winter. Once the weather warms and the sap starts flowing, Quebecers head to *cabanes à sucre* (sugar shacks) out in the countryside. There they sample the first amber riches of the season and do the taffy pull, where steaming maple syrup is poured into the snow and then scooped up on a popsicle stick once it's cooled.

HOANG OANH Map p48 Vietnamese $

☎ 514-954-0053; 1071 Blvd St-Laurent, Chinatown; sandwiches $3-4; 🕑 11am-3am; Ⓜ Place-d'Armes

The Vietnamese baguette sandwiches here are the very best in Chinatown. There's an endless choice of fillings but the grilled chicken or tofu varieties topped with mayonnaise, veggies and coriander are pretty unbeatable.

DOWNTOWN

Downtown Montréal has some of the most diverse dining options in the city. You can find frozen-in-time 1950s diners, classic Parisian brasseries, award-winning five-star dining rooms serving haute cuisine and scores of ethnic eateries for both budget-minded students and well-moneyed executives.

A few key dining areas to keep in mind when you're out exploring: Rue Ste-Catherine is a major shopping and dining strip, with the densest concentrations of decent restaurants (some of which lie off the main boulevard) between about Rue Guy and Rue University. In this area, you'll find Rues Crescent and Bishop, which are packed with pubs, bistros and cafés. These two parallel streets attract a mix of students, office workers and out-of-towners who pack the sidewalk-fronting terraces for dining and cocktails in the summertime.

Another area worth exploring is Petit Bourgogne (Little Burgundy), which is leading the way in a culinary renaissance, with stylish but delightfully unpretentious restaurants along Rue Notre-Dame (a street also known for its antique shops) just west of Rue Vinet.

West of Downtown lies lovely Westmount, which also has some impressive dining options (see the boxed text, p128).

BEAVER CLUB Map pp62–3 Canadian $$$

☎ 514-861-3511; Fairmont Reine Elizabeth, 900 Blvd René-Lévesque Ouest; table d'hôte $58-78; 🕑 6-10:30pm Thu-Sat; Ⓜ Bonaventure

The original Beaver Club was formed in 1785 by a group of Montréal fur barons, and to join you had to have wintered in the Northwest Territories. Membership is still elite – ask to see the pic of Bill Gates in trapper's furs – but anyone with the right currency can reserve in the impeccably serviced, old-fashioned dining room to enjoy a cross-section of Canadian luxury edibles. The *menu découverte* is a multi-course meal highlighting Québec produce like Îles de la Madeleine scallops, Marieville foie gras and Île d'Orléans raspberries. Reservations and proper attire are essential (no jeans; a jacket for men).

FERREIRA CAFÉ Map pp62–3 Portuguese $$$

☎ 514-848-0988; 1446 Rue Peel; mains $26-40; Ⓜ Peel

This warm and inviting restaurant serves some of Montréal's best Portuguese fare. The *cataplana* (bouillabaisse-style seafood stew) is magnificent, tender morsels of grilled fish comes to the table cooked to perfection, while meat lovers can feast on rack of lamb or spice-rubbed Angus rib-eye steak. There's an extensive wine list and a lively atmosphere.

QUEUE DE CHEVAL

Map pp62–3 Steak House $$$

☎ 514-390-0090; 1221 Blvd René-Lévesque Ouest; mains $28-46; 🕑 11:30am-2:30pm Mon-Fri, 5:30-10:30pm Sun-Wed, 5:30-11:30pm Thu-Sat; Ⓜ Lucien-L'Allier

This mecca of expense-account carnivores serves up delectable prime beef that's dry-aged on the premises. Order from a dozen varieties of mammoth-sized steaks that span filet mignon, T-bone and thick slabs of marbled tenderloin, and then watch as it's char-broiled in the pyrotechnics of the open kitchen. Service is impeccable, with attention paid to little details – chunky-handled steak knives for male clientele, thin and sleek models for women. Reservations are a must.

JOE BEEF Map pp62–3 Québécois $$$

☎ 514-935-6504; 2491 Rue Notre-Dame Ouest; mains $22-35; Ⓜ Lionel-Groulx

In the heart of the Little Burgundy neighborhood, Joe Beef is the current darling of food critics for its unfussy, market-fresh fare. The rustic, country-kitsch setting is a great spot to linger over fresh oysters, tender Wagyu beef, fresh fish and a changing selection of hearty Québécois dishes – all served with a dollop of good humor and a welcome lack of pretension.

LE CAVEAU Map pp62–3 French $$$

☎ 514-844-1624; 2063 Rue Victoria; mains $24-36; 🕑 11:30am-11pm Mon-Fri, 5-11pm Sun; Ⓜ McGill

Nestled amid a forest of skyscrapers, this Victorian villa has been a Montréal institution since 1949. A few popular dishes

LOCAL VOICES: DINING À LA QUÉBÉCOIS

Frédéric Morin, one of the chef-owners of Joe Beef (opposite), has garnered much attention for his innovative Québécois fare. He's at the forefront of a movement to bring attention to the great *produits du terroir* (foods sources from local markets and farms).

What keeps you in Montréal? It's cool to be in such a culturally rich place – growing up, your best friends are Italian and Lebanese, there's a Jewish neighborhood up the street, and you're the only Québécois kid on your block. You move between French and English – not just linguistically, but culturally. I like that quote by the PM during the independence drive: 'We're all ethnics here; it just depends on your date of arrival.'

What are your favorite dishes? I really love beef – a braised meat in winter, a thick steak in the summer. Sometimes I crave oysters and get the urge for greens. And I love Dover sole.

So what's the story behind the new garden you've created behind your restaurant? I get some things for the restaurant in there, but most of my greens come from the Atwater market (see the boxed text, p119). I do the garden for me. I love working in there. It's my happy place.

What's your take on the restaurant scene here? I love Paris and New York, but it's competitive. Cooks in restaurants here are friends. People rarely come to work pissed off. Maybe it's this laid-back city – the Canal de Lachine, the parks…

include bison with wild berries, duck confit, grilled marinated salmon and rack of lamb, plus escargot to start things off. The upper dining floors are most atmospheric, stuffed as they are with paintings and antiques, though in the summer you can also dine alfresco on the front terrace. Reservations recommended.

RESTAURANT GLOBE

Map pp62–3 French-International $$$

☎ 514-284-3823; 3455 Blvd St-Laurent; mains $24-38; 🕑 6-11pm Sun-Wed, 6pm-midnight Thu-Sat; Ⓜ St-Laurent, then bus 55

This stylish see-and-be-seen place features an imaginative menu combining high- and low-brow ingredients to create a decadent kind of comfort food. Recent standouts include lobster mac'n'cheese, calamari stuffed with goat cheese and chorizo, and mashed potatoes alongside slow-cooked rabbit with crispy fried pancetta. Reservations are essential.

CAFÉ MÉLIÈS

Map pp62–3 Media Café $$

☎ 514-847-9218; 3536 Blvd St-Laurent; mains $18-32; 🕑 11am-1am Mon-Wed, 11am-3am Thu & Fri, 8:30am-3am Sat & Sun; Ⓜ St-Laurent, then bus 55

This chic, modern restaurant and wine bar located in the Ex-Centris cinema and multimedia complex is tailor-made for Montréal's flashy showbiz types. It's an excellent place to be seen over lunch, dinner or afternoon coffee in front of the windows on the Main. The brunch is particularly upscale and popular. At night, movie-goers and politicians rub shoulders over plates of marinated salmon or roasted scallops.

LIVERPOOL HOUSE

Map pp62–3 Québécois $$

☎ 514-313-6049; 2501 Rue Notre-Dame Ouest; mains $18-26; Ⓜ Lionel-Groulx

From the same anti-establishment chefs that launched Joe Beef next door, this charming little eatery with touches of farmhouse decor serves an ever-changing menu of fresh-from-the-market fare. If you can't score a table, try next door at McKiernan's, also part of the Joe Beef group.

KAIZEN

Map pp62–3 Japanese $$

☎ 514-932-5654; 4075 Rue Ste-Catherine Ouest; mains $18-25; 🕑 noon-3pm & 5:30-10:30pm Mon-Sat, 5:30-10:30pm Sun; Ⓜ Atwater

The price is high but so is the quality at this fine-dining Japanese restaurant near Westmount. Here you'll find artfully presented sushi and sashimi platters along with much-touted tempura dishes served amid stylish ambience. For extra smoothness, there's also live jazz on Monday and Tuesday evenings (from 7pm). Reservations recommended.

LES CHENÊTS

Map pp62–3 French $$

☎ 514-844-1842; 2075 Rue Bishop; mains $16-32; 🕑 11:30am-2pm Mon-Fri, dinner 5:30pm-late daily; Ⓜ Guy-Concordia

Magnificent French food is served here by chef and owner Michel Gillet in an intimate, ornate dining room. Gillet is also owner of the world's largest cognac collection (830 different labels). The menu is written out on the chalkboard with classics like herring appetizers and mains like *steak frites* (steak and French fries). For dessert try the highly addictive chocolate profiteroles.

LE PARIS Map pp62–3 French $$

☎ 514-937-4898; 1812 Rue Ste-Catherine Ouest; mains $15-29; 11:30am-2:30pm & 5:30-10:30pm Mon-Sat, 5:30-10:30pm Sun; M Guy-Concordia

It's the quintessential neighborhood bistro and, refreshingly, there's nothing particularly trendy about this place. The old-fashioned decor and core of loyal customers give it a casual, family, community feel. The menu showcases no-frills French food, with classics like duck confit and *flétan menieur* (halibut dusted in flour and cooked in butter).

LE TAJ Map pp62–3 Indian $$

☎ 514-845-9015; 2077 Rue Stanley; mains $15-22; M Peel

Proving that Montréal is more than just a bistro and brasserie kind of town, Le Taj throws down the gauntlet for some excellent Indian dishes. The time to go is at lunch, when downtowners line up for a succulent buffet featuring a bounty of rich flavors from the East – tandoori chicken, vegetable korma, palaak paneer and tender lamb, along with steaming piles of naan bread, custardlike desserts and many other temptations.

ISAKAYA Map pp62–3 Japanese $$

☎ 514-845-8226; 3469 Ave du Parc; mains $14-23; 11:30am-2pm & 6-9:30pm Wed-Fri, 5:30-10pm Sat, 5:30-9pm Sun; M Place-des-Arts, then bus 80 or 129

This authentic, unpretentious Japanese restaurant has fairly simple decor but the fish is incredibly fresh. The owner, Shige Minagawa, is known for handpicking his seafood and preparing it in classic Japanese fashion. Daily specials such as lobster sashimi, tuna belly or yellowtail are listed on the chalkboard by the kitchen. Reservations are essential.

LA GARGOTE DES ANTIQUAIRES Map pp62–3 French $$

☎ 514-678-6429; 1708 Rue Notre-Dame Ouest; mains $14-22; noon-9pm Mon-Sat; M Lucien-L'Allier

In the heart of Montréal's antique district, this warm and inviting bistro prepares tasty galettes, chalkboard specials and flavorful desserts (sweet crepes). In addition to the antique-filled dining room, there's a plant-filled outdoor terrace for soaking up this peaceful little stretch of Rue Notre-Dame.

PHAYATHAI Map pp62–3 Thai $$

☎ 514-933-9949; 1235 Rue Guy; mains $12-18; M Guy-Concordia

Just off the beaten path, this casual little Thai restaurant serves good, fresh-tasting curries, satisfying duck and seafood plates and plenty of other delicacies from the East. The lunchtime and after-work crowds can be thick, so try to avoid arriving at prime time.

PIZZERIA GEPETTO Map pp62–3 Pizza $$

☎ 514-903-3737; 2504 Rue Notre-Dame Ouest; mains $12-16; 11:30am-midnight Mon-Fri, 5:30pm-midnight Sat & Sun; M Lionel-Groulx

New in 2009, Pizzeria Gepetto brings yet another star to the burgeoning restaurant scene in Petite Bourgogne, in the form of delicious thin-crust pizzas, fresh-from-the-market salads and a small but well-curated beer and wine selection. The interior is classically set with gilt-edged mirrors on one wall, low-lit art-deco-style lamps, dark wood details and a chalkboard listing daily specials. Red chairs add a touch of whimsy and match Gepetto's real star – the brick oven behind the bar. On warm summer nights, join the laid-back neighborhood crowd for alfresco dining at sidewalk tables in front.

MANGO BAY Map pp62–3 Caribbean $$

☎ 514-875-7082; 1202 Rue Bishop; mains $13-18; 11:30am-10pm Sun-Thu, to midnight Fri & Sat; M Guy-Concordia

Situated in a converted Victorian house with pretty stained-glass windows, Mango Bay serves up authentic chicken jerky or stew, curried goat or island chicken fajitas with a terrific side order of plantain. Watch out for the incendiary hot sauces, and be sure to save room for a slice of the signature mango cheesecake or rum cake. There's live Jamaican music from time to time.

LOLA ROSA Map pp62–3 Vegetarian $$

☎ 514-287-9337; 545 Rue Milton; mains $12-24; 11:30am-9:30pm; M McGill

On a leafy street near McGill, students, profs and the odd neighborhood regular not associated with the university flock to this charming and low-key vegetarian café.

A chalkboard menu lists the day's offerings: couscous with fresh vegetables, walnuts and goat cheese, rich tempeh-based stews and bountiful salads with juicy tomatoes and crisp rocket. Fresh juices, desserts and decent coffee complete the picture. Lola Rosa also hosts a popular weekend brunch.

M:BRGR Map pp62–3 Hamburgers $$

☎ 514-906-2747; 2025 Rue Drummond; mains $10-20; ⌚ 11:30am-11pm Mon-Sat, noon-9pm Sun; Ⓜ Peel

Bringing a gourmet touch to the humble hamburger, this stylish place serves juicy patties that can be dressed with smoked gouda, apple-smoked bacon and other high-end toppings. You can opt for organic, grass-fed beef or even Kobe beef. To complete, add in sweet potato fries and a thick milkshake – or better yet, a cocktail.

THREE AMIGOS Map pp62–3 Tex-Mex $$

☎ 514-939-3329; 1657 Rue Ste-Catherine Ouest; mains $10-16; ⌚ noon-11:30pm Sun-Thu, 11:30am-1:30am Fri & Sat; Ⓜ Guy-Concordia

This festive, Tex-Mex place is all trumpets and sombreros, but can be good fun if you know what you're in for. Burritos, chimichangas and enchiladas are all decent, and the margaritas flow fast and freely beneath the piñatas. Three Amigos becomes particularly festive on weekends when students from nearby universities pack the place.

ONG CA CAN Map pp62–3 Vietnamese $$

☎ 514-844-7817; 79 Rue Ste-Catherine Est; mains $10-16; ⌚ 11:30am-2pm & 6-10:30pm Tue-Sun; Ⓜ St-Laurent

Despite its crisp white linens and intricate artwork, this bustling Vietnamese restaurant only looks pricey. The kitchen staff gets most things right, although the lemongrass rolls and anything involving beef get especially high marks from loyal patrons.

AMELIO'S Map pp62–3 Italian $-$$

☎ 514-845-8396; 201 Rue Milton; pizzas $10-23; ⌚ 11:30am-9pm Tue-Fri, 4-9pm Sat; Ⓜ Place-des-Arts

Smack in the middle of the McGill student ghetto, this well-known joint has fed generations of students with generous portions of pizza and pasta. A medium pizza (always crisp and heaped with toppings) is enough to stuff two people. And the pasta dishes come with sumptuous bread and crisp salads. Lineups outside the plain flat-top structure are common around 6pm.

REUBEN'S Map pp62–3 Smoked Meat $

☎ 514-861-1255; 888 Rue Ste-Catherine Ouest; mains $9-18; ⌚ 6:30am-midnight Mon-Wed, 6:30am-1:30am Thu & Fri, 8am-1:30am Sat, 8am-midnight Sun; Ⓜ Peel

Another favorite deli in downtown, Reuben's has squishy booths and a long counter, where patrons line up for towering smoked-meat sandwiches served with big-cut fries. Burgers, smoked pork chops and other old-school favorites round out the menu. Try to avoid the busy lunch rush. Service is so-so.

DUNN'S Map pp62–3 Smoked Meat & Deli $

☎ 514-395-1927; 1249 Rue Metcalfe; mains $6-16; ⌚ 24hr; Ⓜ McGill

One of Montréal's oldest smoked meat institutions with satisfying sandwiches slapped down on wax paper and served in baskets piled with fries. In addition to classics (like the smoked-meat club sandwich with Swiss cheese and bacon), you'll find burgers, char-grilled steaks and bagels with lox and cream cheese.

BOUSTAN Map pp62–3 Lebanese $

☎ 514-843-3576; 2020 Rue Crescent; mains $5-10; ⌚ 11am-4am; Ⓜ Guy-Concordia

This friendly little Lebanese joint scores high in popularity on the city's *shwarma* circuit. Its late hours make it a favorite with pub crawlers in need of sustenance between bars. Can't-go-wrong picks include baba ghanoush, hummus, falafel, stuffed grape leaves with yogurt and tabbouleh salad with warm pita.

LE FAUBOURG Map pp62–3 Food Court

☎ 514-939-3663; 1606 Rue Ste-Catherine Ouest; ⌚ 7:30am-9pm daily; Ⓜ Guy-Concordia

The best food court in the city is here on the 3rd floor. Among the smorgasbord of international cuisines are German, Japanese and crepe stands. Keep your eye out for Cuisine Bangkok on the 3rd floor for quality Thai food better than in many restaurants. Also on the 3rd floor try the fabulous Taiwanese stall Bao Dao Taiwan as well as La Maison du Bédouin for refreshing Moroccan mint tea served in silver pots. The Parisian-style multilevel mall-cum-market also includes fruit vendors, a bakery, a bagel shop and a liquor store and is perfect for a meal or picnic goodies.

OUTER NEIGHBORHOODS

For a purely local experience, head to some of Montréal's outer neighborhoods. The stately neighborhood of Westmount has beautifully set bistros, inviting patisseries and stylish international restaurants along Rue Sherbrooke Ouest and Ave Greene.

Nôtre-Dame-de-Grâce, another historically Anglo area, houses an array of good restaurants west of the Blvd Décarie expressway, along the main strips of Rue Sherbrooke Ouest and Ave Monkland.

Just west of downtown along the Canal de Lachine, lofts and condos have transformed the old brick warehouses into Montréal's next up-and-coming district. Keep an eye out for new restaurants, which are sure to make a splash in coming years.

- La Louisiane (Map pp44–5; ☎ 514-369-3073; 5850 Rue Sherbrooke Ouest; mains $14-28; 5:30-9:30pm Sat, Sun, Tue & Wed, 5:30-10:30pm Thu & Fri; M Vendôme, then bus 105) Montréal meets the Deep South in this casual Cajun eatery, with amazing results. The menu bears the hearty, delicious flavors of jambalaya, shrimp Creole or chicken étoufée, all armed with mysterious peppers and spices. The rich 'voodoo pasta' has spicy Cajun sausage and tomatoes in white wine and cream. While you're here, be sure to check out paintings of street scenes by New Orleans native James Michelopoulos.
- Magnan (Map pp44–5; ☎ 514-935-9647; 2602 Rue St-Patrick; mains $12-20; 11am-11pm; M Charlevoix) Founded in the 1930s as a blue-collar diner, Taverne Magnan has long since raised meat and potatoes to an art form. Its reputation is fantastic roast beef – long-marinating, speckled with peppercorns and served in its own juice. This is the place to refuel after a day's cycling along the Canal de Lachine (just around the corner). There's open-air seating (next to a parking lot) in back.
- Chez Nick (Map pp62–3; ☎ 514-935-0946; 1377 Ave Greene; mains $10-16; 7am-8pm Mon-Sat, 8am-6pm Sun; M Atwater) This perfect little diner has been smack in the middle of swish Westmount since 1920. Despite the trendy stores and galleries that have mushroomed around it, it has stayed unabashedly dated and square. The Montréal diner staples are all here from burgers and fries, smoked meat and desserts so high and rich they threaten to topple over. But it's got something for everyone, including the foodies and fusion fanatics, and you'll find health fare like brie and Granny Smith apple sandwiches with balsamic vinaigrette on black Russian bread. Lunchtime is rush time and lineups stretch out the door.

PROVIGO
Map pp62–3 Supermarket

☎ 514-932-3756; 1953 Rue Ste-Catherine Ouest; 8am-2am; M Guy-Concordia

Montréal's well-known supermarket chain has huge, well-stocked stores with plentiful deli counters serving fried chicken and smoked-meat sandwiches. In addition to this large Rue Ste-Catherine branch, there's another outlet in the Plateau (Map pp76–7; ☎ 514-849-8028; 50 Ave du Mont-Royal Ouest).

QUARTIER LATIN & THE VILLAGE

The terraced cafés and restaurants of the Quartier Latin are great spots to watch the world go by, over coffee, croissants or even a bowl of borscht. Popular with students, the Quartier Latin is unrivaled when it comes to budget dining, inexpensive bistro fare and meals in a hurry. There are also abundant bars nearby, making for an easy transition from dinner to nighttime amusement.

Great new eateries open (and close) frequently in the Village. But you'll always find an exciting mix of eating options, from Italian trattorias to cozy cafés to Asian-fusion bistros. Most diners in this neighborhood concentrate on the kitchens around metro Beaudry, but consider getting off at Papineau instead (one stop east of Beaudry). It was formerly a bit of a run-down area, but stylish and flashy little restaurants are slowly popping up on this stretch of Rue Ste-Catherine Est.

O'THYM Map p72
French $$

☎ 514-525-3443; 1112 Blvd de Maisonneuve Est; mains $24-31; noon-2:30pm Tue-Fri, 6-10pm daily; M Beaudry

O'Thym is a delightful new addition to the neighborhood, with an elegant but understated dining room (exposed brick walls, floodlit windows, oversized mirrors), and beautifully presented plates of fresh seafood and grilled game. A well-heeled neighborhood crowd frequents the spot. Bring your own wine.

BISTRO LE PORTO Map p72 Portuguese $$

☎ 514-527-7067; 1365 Rue Ontario Est; mains $17-26; ⌚ 11am-10:30pm Mon-Fri, 5-10pm Sat & Sun; Ⓜ Beaudry

This is a charming and cozy bistro with rich, flavorful Portuguese cuisine and a fantastic selection of ports. The menu features changing daily specials as well as reliable favorites like *cataplana,* as well as a baked cod dish, grilled sardines and squid. The waitstaff are friendly and knowledgeable and give great advice about pairing wine with food.

AU PETIT EXTRA Map p72 French $$

☎ 514-527-5552; 1690 Rue Ontario Est; mains $16-28; ⌚ 11:30am-2:30pm & 6-10pm Mon-Wed, 6-10:30pm Thu-Sat, 5:30-9:30pm Sun; Ⓜ Papineau

This sweet little place serves traditional bistro fare to a garrulous local crowd. The blackboard menu changes frequently but features simple, flavorful dishes (*steak frites,* foie gras, duck confit, mahimahi), and staff can expertly pair wines with food. Reservations are advised, but you can linger over a glass of wine at the handsome wooden bar if you have to wait.

LE GRAIN DE SEL

Map pp44–5 Bistro $$

☎ 514-522-5105; 2375 Rue Ste-Catherine Est; mains $18-25; ⌚ 11:30am-2pm Mon-Fri, 6-10pm Tue-Sat; Ⓜ Papineau, then bus 34

This tiny, friendly bistro just beyond the eastern edge of the Village exudes old-world ambience with a small bar and open kitchen. The menu has bistro favorites such as pheasant terrine, *bavette* (undercut steak), mussels cooked in beer and goat cheese salad, but with Asian accents. The waiters will marry the right wines with your meal.

MOZZA Map p72 Italian $$

☎ 514-524-0295; 1208 Rue Ste-Catherine Est; mains $16-22; ⌚ 5-10pm Tue-Sun; Ⓜ Beaudry

One of the Village's best kept secrets, Mozza is a breadbox-sized restaurant serving delicious Caesar salads, thin-crust pizzas and pastas (try the penne a la vodka). Reservations are recommended at this bring-your-own-wine spot.

LE SPIRITE LOUNGE Map p72 Vegan $$

☎ 514-522-5353; 1205 Rue Ontario Est; mains $16; ⌚ 6pm-midnight Tue-Sun; Ⓜ Beaudry

This eccentric restaurant with over-the-top decor (Christmas lights and tinfoil) is good fun, but requires a bit of preparation. There's no menu, but the meal consists of soup, a hot crepe and cake. Eat every bite; if you don't, the chef will angrily tell you 'no cake for you!', then deliver the bill and ask you to leave (no kidding!).

LE COMMENSAL Map p72 Vegetarian $-$$

☎ 514-845-2627; 1720 Rue St-Denis; buffet per kg $20; ⌚ 11am-10:30pm Sun-Thu, 11am-11pm Fri & Sat; Ⓜ Berri-UQAM

A requisite stop for vegetarian diners in Montréal, this handsomely rustic dining room stocks an impressive variety of high-quality vegetarian cuisine, including baked dishes (lasagna, casseroles, quesadillas), salads, fresh fruits and desserts, sold by weight.

LA PARYSE Map p72 Diner $

☎ 514-842-2040; 302 Rue Ontario Est; mains $8-12; ⌚ 11am-11pm Mon-Fri, 2-10:30pm Sat & Sun; Ⓜ Berri-UQAM

Often credited with the thickest, juiciest burgers and best fries in town, this smart little retro diner offers an excellent variety of toppings and thick, rich milkshakes. This place is an integral part of the neighborhood and when owner Madame Paryse recently celebrated 25 years in business, employees and customers alike sent her a flood of congratulatory emails.

JULIETTE ET CHOCOLAT Map p72 Café $

☎ 514-287-3555; 1615 Rue St-Denis; mains $8-12; ⌚ 11am-11pm; Ⓜ Berri-UQAM

When the urge to devour something chocolaty arrives, make straight for Juliette et Chocolat, a bustling little café where chocolate is served in every shape and form – drizzled over crepes, blended into creamy milkshakes and coffees, or straight up in a blood-sugar-boosting chocolate 'shot.' The setting is charming but small and busy. For less hustle and bustle, visit the Laurier location (p137).

KILO Map p72 Café $

☎ 514-596-3933; 1495 Rue Ste-Catherine Est; mains $5-11; ⌚ 5-11pm Mon, 10:30am-11pm Tue-Thu, 10:30am-2am Fri, 1pm-2am Sat, 1-11pm Sun; Ⓜ Papineau

The house specialties are creamy cakes and tarts with a shot of Grand Marnier or some other liquid decadence, as well as hot

PRODUITS DU TERROIR

If you hang around the Montréal food scene for any length of time, it won't be long before you start hearing about *produits du terroir* ('produce from the earth,' loosely translated). While Québécois cuisine has typically been heavy, using only a small number of ingredients, these days more and more young chefs and cooks are heading to the markets and the farms, and constructing menus around what they find. In foodie circles, it's also influencing menus and making minor celebrities out of small producers and farmers who weren't on anyone's radar even a few years ago. The mania for these types of local ingredients aren't just for star chefs however. More and more Montrealers are heading outside of town, to hit the farms to tote back jams, spreads, cheese and red pepper jellies from local producers – more than are raiding the shelves at their local Provigo.

sandwiches, snacks and salads. This favored Village meeting point is great for recharging before the evening gets going.

METRO Map p72 Supermarket

☎ 514-525-5090; 1955 Rue Ste-Catherine Est; 7:30am-2am; M Papineau

This cavernous supermarket in the Village is perfectly situated for picking up late-night snacks and party goods.

PLATEAU MONT-ROYAL

Plateau Mont-Royal has a fantastic variety of bistros, upscale restaurants and bohemian-style cafés. Rue Prince-Arthur Est is a narrow residential street that has been converted into a dining and entertainment enclave. The restaurant segment runs west from leafy Carré St-Louis (just north of Rue Sherbrooke) to a block west of Blvd St-Laurent. Many of the small, inexpensive and mostly ethnic restaurants here aren't licensed to serve alcohol, so bring your own wine.

Further north on Blvd St-Laurent, Ave Duluth is a former red-light district that has been transformed into a restaurant center. And if you like Portuguese food, veer east when you reach Rue Marie-Anne. This area is packed with tiny family-run Portuguese eateries, the scent of charcoal-grilled fish and meat lingering in the air.

AU PIED DE COCHON Map pp76–7 French $$$

☎ 514-281-1114; 536 Ave Duluth Est; mains $20-45; 5pm-midnight Tue-Sun; M Sherbrooke

One of Montréal's most respected restaurants (it's so well known that there's no sign) features extravagant pork, duck and steak dishes, along with its signature foie gras plates. Award-winning chef Martin Picard takes simple ingredients and transforms them into works of art. The famous and surprisingly magnificent *canard en conserve* ('duck in a can'), for instance, is half a roasted duck magret served with foie gras, cabbage, bacon, venison and spices, sealed and cooked in a can – then opened tableside and dumped over celery root puree on toast. Dishes are rich and portions are large, so bring an appetite. Reservations essential.

MOISHE'S Map pp76–7 Steak House $$$

☎ 514-845-1696; 3961 Blvd St-Laurent; mains $24-38; 11:30am-2:30pm & 5:30-11pm Mon-Fri, 5-11pm Sat & Sun; M St-Laurent, then bus 55

Moishe's feels a bit like a social club, although guests from all backgrounds come to consume its legendary grilled meats and seafood. Closely set tables and old-fashioned hardwood paneling set the backdrop to the feasting. Skip the appetizers and launch straight into a gargantuan rib steak served with tasty fries or a Monte Carlo potato. Reservations are essential.

LE POISSON ROUGE Map pp76–7 Seafood $$$

☎ 514-522-4876; 1201 Rue Rachel Est; mains $24-28; 5:30-11pm Tue-Sat; M Mont-Royal

This seafood specialist with the cozy front terrace is renowned among market vendors for picking the best, freshest cuts. The pan-seared red tuna is juicy as can be with Cajun spices, but the ray braised in butter will also take your fancy. The five-course table d'hôte ($37) is a good value. There are two sittings on Friday and Saturday, at 6pm and 9pm. Bring your own wine.

MAESTRO SVP Map pp76–7 Seafood $$

☎ 514-842-6447; 3615 Blvd St-Laurent; mains $20-30; 11am-11pm Mon-Fri, 5-11pm Sat & Sun; M St-Laurent, then bus 55

Hundreds of oyster shells are nailed to the wall in this seafood bistro with high-backed chairs and halogen spots. The calamari is a great appetizer and the oysters – a palette

TOP BAKERIES IN MONTRÉAL

The bakeries in Montréal are bearers of light, crispy French-tradition goodies and, as in France, you'll see residents walking home with a baguette tucked under one arm. There are so many great bakeries scattered around town it's a wonder the supermarkets can still sell the mass-produced stuff.

- Au Pain Doré (Map pp76–7; ☎ 514-982-9520; 3611 Blvd St-Laurent; 8am-7pm Mon-Wed, 8am-9:30pm Thu & Fri, 8am-6pm Sat & Sun; M St-Laurent, then bus 55) Homemade and organic bread, Viennese pastries and sandwiches. There are 13 outlets around Montréal.
- Le Fromentier (Map pp44–5; ☎ 514-527-3327; 1375 Ave Laurier Est; 7am-7pm Mon-Fri, 7am-5pm Sat & Sun; M Laurier) High-quality artisanal bakery where you can pick up some of Montréal's best baked goods.
- Pâtisserie de Gascogne (Map p83; ☎ 514-490-0235; 237 Ave Laurier; 8am-7pm Mon-Fri, 8am-5:30pm Sat & Sun; M Laurier) Elegant bakery and café with heavenly pastries, baguettes and other baked temptations. There's another branch in Westmount (Map pp44–5; ☎ 514-932-3511; 4825 Rue Sherbrooke; M Vendôme).
- Olive + Gourmando (p123) The best baked items in the Old Town; it's particularly famous for fig loaves and olive and rosemary bread.
- Première Moisson (Map pp62–3; ☎ 514-931-6540; Marché Atwater, 137 Ave Atwater; M Lionel-Groulx) This legendary bakery (also with 13 branches) displays its 30-odd marvelous breads in wicker baskets, Parisian-style. Its cheery café inside the Atwater market is a great spot for a flaky croissant and a cup of dark-roast coffee.

of 15 varieties – are served in a bewildering number of ways. Try the oyster shooter – a raw specimen in jalapeño vodka, cocktail sauce and horseradish – and you'll never have to prove your courage again.

PINTXO Map pp76–7 Spanish $$

☎ 514-844-0222; 256 Rue Roy Est; mains $20-22; noon-2pm Wed-Fri, 6-10pm daily; M Sherbrooke

Tiny plates of tapas rule the day at this petite, artfully decorated Basque restaurant. Start off with poached octopus carpaccio or scallops with olive tapenade before moving onto heartier plates of duck breast risotto and lamb shank with couscous. It's on a peaceful street in the Plateau and gets packed on weekend nights.

OUZERI Map pp76–7 Greek $$

☎ 514-845-1336; 4690 Rue St-Denis; mains $18-30; 11:30am-11:30pm; M Mont-Royal

Recommended for its contemporary twist on traditional Greek food, Ouzeri is a sleek and stylish restaurant that attracts a garrulous, festive crowd. Favorites include moussaka (baked dish of minced meat, eggplant and tomato), charcoal-grilled mint-flavored meat patties, or calamari or veal cutlets. There's an extensive wine list and Greek dancing on Friday nights.

LE NIL BLEU Map pp76–7 Ethiopian $$

☎ 514-285-4628; 3706 Rue St-Denis; mains $18-28; 6pm-late; M Sherbrooke

Set with an interior fountain and a relaxing ambience, Le Nil Bleu is a fine place to go for a long, lingering meal. The dishes are traditional Ethiopian fare and include a range of stews all served with *injera* (a giant flatbread-like crepe), which you tear into small pieces to pick up the food. Service can be painfully inadequate at times.

ROBIN DES BOIS Map pp76–7 French $$

☎ 514-288-1010; 4653 Blvd St-Laurent; mains $16-26; 11:30am-11pm Mon-Fri, 5-11pm Sat; M Mont-Royal

Montréal's own Robin Hood, restaurateur Judy Servay donates all profits and tips from this St-Laurent hotspot to local charities. Ever-changing dishes scribbled on the chalkboard could include a succulent venison steak or a creamy wild mushroom risotto.

LE PITON DE LA FOURNAISE Map pp76–7 African $$

☎ 514-526-3936; 835 Ave Duluth Est; 3-course prix-fixe $25-30; 5:30-10pm Tue-Sun; M St-Laurent

Le Piton de La Fournaise introduces Montréal to the cuisine of Île de la Réunion (which lies off the east coast of Madagascar). For a taste of the exotic, this bamboo- and flower-filled restaurant is it. The fragrant cuisine (spiced with turmeric, ginger, garlic and red pepper) shows influences of African, French and Indian dishes, though goes easy on the heat. The menu features only seven dishes, all expertly prepared, though shark curry and octopus stew are perennial favorites. BYOB. Reservations recommended.

L'EXPRESS Map pp76–7 French Bistro $$

☎ 514-845-5333; 3927 Rue St-Denis; mains $14-28; 8am-3am; M Sherbrooke

L'Express has all the hallmarks of Parisian bistro – black-and-white checkered floor, art-deco globe lights, papered tables and mirrored walls. High-end bistro fare completes the picture with excellent seafood dishes (like grilled salmon dressed with sea salt or almond-crusted sole), and even standards such as *confit de canard* (roast duck) are consistently delicious. The waiters can advise on the extensive wine list. Reservations are essential.

JANO Map pp76–7 Portuguese $$

☎ 514-849-0646; 3883 Blvd St-Laurent; mains $14-16; 5-11pm Mon-Wed, 11am-11pm Thu-Sun; M St-Laurent, then bus 55

The scent of charcoal-grilled meats and seafood lingers in the air at this welcoming, family-friendly Portuguese restaurant. The menu features straightforward selections of fresh fish, pork and steak, all grilled to choice tenderness. Warm colors, small tables and a buzzing atmosphere draw in the crowds, particularly on weekends, when waits can be long.

MISTO Map pp76–7 Italian $$

☎ 514-526-5043; 929 Ave du Mont-Royal Est; mains $13-24; 11:30am-midnight; M Mont-Royal

Misto was one of the first 'see-and-be-seen' restaurants to open on Ave du Mont-Royal. It's set with exposed brick walls and polished wood details, with a sleek curved bar, while electronic music plays overhead. Like moths to the flame, a fashion-conscious crowd dines here, eyeing one another over organic pastas, thin-crust pizzas, grilled salmon and other tasty but unsurprising fare. Sidewalk dining in the summer.

LA SALA ROSA Map pp76–7 Spanish $$

☎ 514-844-4227; 4848 Blvd St-Laurent; mains $12-18, tapas $5-10; 5-11pm Tue-Sun; M St-Laurent, then bus 55

A festive, local and often Spanish-speaking crowd comes to this little Iberian gem. Sala Rosa is best know for its five tasty varieties of paella (including vegetarian) as well as numerous tapas dishes and a changing lineup of Spanish specials. On Thursday nights there's a live flamenco show, and the place gets packed.

CHU CHAI Map pp76–7 Vegetarian Thai $$

☎ 514-843-4194; 4094 Rue St-Denis; mains $12-22; M Mont-Royal

A stylish but unpretentious restaurant of the mock-meat variety, Chu Chai cooks up an impressive variety of Thai dishes. In summer, grab a table on the terrace and choose from plump vegetable-and-mushroom dumplings, crispy seaweed and spiced red curries with vegetarian 'duck,' 'chicken' or 'beef.'

L'AVENUE Map pp76–7 Bistro $-$$

☎ 514-523-8780; 922 Ave du Mont-Royal Est; mains $8-26; 7am-11pm Mon-Fri, 8am-11pm Sat, 8am-10pm Sun; M Mont-Royal

This self-consciously hip restaurant is a magnet for the young, post-party brunch crowd. Over a dozen different types of omelets, plus all the classics – French toast, waffles, eggs Benedict – all arrive nicely prepared. Lunch and dinner, with middling veggie burgers and salads, are less of a draw. Electronic music plays overhead at all hours, and artwork and urban murals adorn the walls. The surreal multimedia-infused washroom is an experience in itself.

CAFÉ CHERRIER Map pp76–7 Café $-$$

☎ 514-843-4308; 3635 Rue St-Denis; mains $7-18; 7:30am-10pm; M Sherbrooke

Locals flock to the shady, wraparound terrace of this comfy café with the long marble serving counter that wouldn't be out of place in Paris. This is an especially lively place after a performance at the nearby L'Agora de la Danse. A huge percentage of the audience usually swings by here for dinner or a drink, setting the whole place abuzz. Breakfast is popular as is classic French bistro fare like *steak frites*.

BYBLOS Map pp44–5 Iranian

☎ 514-523-9396; 1499 Rue Laurier Est; meals $14-18, tapas $4.20-7.50; 9am-11pm; M Laurier

This Iranian café does such good food and is so charming, people who come here tend to make a day of it. The big windows and tables invite lingering and though there are wonderful main courses, most people end up grazing on the Iranian tapaslike dishes all day and into the evening. The feta omelet is by far the most popular followed by the eggplant or chickpea purees. It's all served with pita bread perfect for dipping. The mint tea is the perfect way to finish it all off.

MAZURKA Map pp76–7 Polish $

☎ 514-844-3539; 64 Rue Prince-Arthur Est; mains $9-16; 11:30am-11pm; M Sherbrooke

This Polish place has kept generations of students filled with cheap and hearty fare. The menu features pierogy and meat or cheese blintzes (filled pancake rolls), Polish sausage, potato latkes, or the restaurant's namesake, *mazurkas* (potato latkes filled with beef goulash). Make sure to wash it all down with one of Poland's most famous exports, Zubrowka, a vodka flavored with bison grass. The restaurant is a sprawling place, with nearly 200 seats over four levels and paintings from the Old Country on the walls.

BEAUTY'S Map pp76–7 Diner $

☎ 514-849-8883; 93 Ave Mont-Royal Ouest; breakfast $10-16; 7am-4pm; M Mont-Royal

This sleek, retro '50s diner serves what many consider Montréal's best breakfast – all day long. Owner Hymie Sckolnick greets everyone with 'How are you, dahling.' Ask for 'The Special' – a toasted bagel with lox, cream cheese, tomato and onion. From the freshly squeezed juice to the piping-hot eggs, sausages and pancakes, it'll be hard to go anyplace else once you've tried it. Lineups on Saturday and Sunday mornings can run up to 40 minutes long, even in winter (go early).

TAMPOPO Map pp76–7 Asian $

☎ 514-526-0001; 4449 Rue de Mentana; mains $8-14; 11am-11pm; M Mont-Royal

Plateau residents love this cozy place for its aromatic Vietnamese soups and filling noodle dishes with flank steak, grilled pork and rice vermicelli. Take a seat at one of three low tables with bamboo matting, or at the long wavy counter with a view of the open kitchen.

CAFÉ SANTROPOL Map pp76–7 Café $

☎ 514-842-3110; 3990 Rue St-Urbain; mains $7-12; 11:30am-midnight; M St-Laurent, then bus 55

This is an iconic Montréal eatery known for its towering and creative sandwiches, its colorful digs, and lush outdoor garden patio. Its creations range from the sweet root (carrots, raisins, coriander, nuts, mayo and fresh apple) to pepper island with ham (which comes with jalapeño pepper jelly, pesto and cream cheese spread).

EURO DELI Map pp76–7 Italian $

☎ 514-843-7853; 3619 Blvd St-Laurent; mains $7-10; 8:30am-midnight; M St-Laurent, then bus 55

One of the lower Main's gems, for people-watching and its fresh pastas. Students and punks flop on the outside steps with pizza slices, inside regulars shoo away newcomers from 'their' tables. This bustling eatery is cafeteria-style and food changes daily – just go up and choose your pasta from the counter. If chocolate cake is on offer when you visit, pounce! It's pure decadence.

AUX VIVRES Map pp76–7 Vegetarian $

☎ 514-842-3479; 4631 Blvd St-Laurent; mains $7-10; 11am-11pm Tue-Sun; M Mont-Royal

Serving some of Montréal's best vegan fare, Aux Vivres whips up tasty fresh salads, soups and sandwiches, a hearty daily special and homemade desserts. You can also stop in for fresh juices and teas, and dine alfresco in the back garden.

BRÛLERIE ST-DENIS Map pp76–7 Café $

☎ 514-286-9158; 3967 Rue St-Denis; coffees $2-5, sandwiches $7-9; 8am-11pm Mon-Fri, 9am-midnight Sat & Sun; M Sherbrooke

This is coffee heaven: iced coffees, frappés, special blends like Café Dante (mocca espresso with whipped cream, cinnamon, chocolate and grated orange peel), made from beans fresh out of the big roaster. The front terrace is a great place to nurse a cup with a hot veggie sandwich or slice of cake.

CHEZ CORA Map pp76–7 Café $

☎ 514-525-9495; 1396 Ave du Mont-Royal Est; mains $6-14; 6am-3pm Mon-Fri, 7am-4pm Sat & Sun; M Mont-Royal

With locations across Canada, Chez Cora is the trusted breakfast standard. Like all others, the Mont-Royal outpost has cheerful decor and generous portions. To start the day with a bang, try 'Récolte 90,' featuring French toast with raisins served with bacon, an egg and an avalanche of fruit. There are several other branches around town including one in The Village (Map p72; ☎ 514-285-2672; 1017 Rue Ste-Catherine Est).

LA BANQUISE Map pp76–7 Québécois $

☎ 514-525-2415; 994 Rue Rachel Est; mains $6-12; 24hr; M Mont-Royal

A Montréal legend since 1968, La Banquise is probably the best place in town to sample *poutine* (if you've never heard of this dish, see the boxed text, opposite). More than two dozen varieties are available, including a veggie *poutine* (peppers, mushrooms, sautéed onions) and straight-up classic *poutine*. There's an outdoor terrace, a full breakfast menu and a selection of microbrews, plus the kitchen never closes.

LA BINERIE MONT ROYAL
Map pp76–7 Fast Québécois $

☎ 514-285-9078; 367 Ave du Mont-Royal Est; mains $6-10; 🕒 6am-8pm Mon-Fri, 7:30am-3pm Sat & Sun; Ⓜ Mont-Royal

Authentic Québécois cuisine is served from this dinerlike counter. The menu is full of typical traditional comfort fare including *tourtière* (meat pie) and *pudding chômeur* (a bread pudding with brown sugar syrup), plus hearty egg-and-sausage breakfasts.

SCHWARTZ'S Map pp76–7 Smoked Meat $

☎ 514-842-4813; 3895 Blvd St-Laurent; mains $5-16; 🕒 8am-12:30am Sun-Thu, 8am-1:30am Fri, 8am-2:30am Sat; Ⓜ St-Laurent, then bus 55

Known far and wide, this old-time Hebrew deli is widely considered to serve the best smoked meat in Montréal whether it's brisket, duck, chicken or turkey, all piled high on sourdough rye bread. The Romanian-style meat is cured on the premises and aged without chemicals. You can order it fat, medium (recommended) or lean. Expect long lines.

CAFÉ FRUITS FOLIE Map pp76–7 Café $

☎ 514-840-9011; 3817 Rue St-Denis; mains $5-14; 🕒 7am-11pm; Ⓜ St-Laurent, then bus 55

This agreeable café has a long list of crepes, bagels, burgers and sandwiches, plus good vegetarian choices. The front terrace (one of many in this neighborhood) has a great view of the happenings on Rue St-Denis, and people love to linger here over breakfast while watching the world go by.

SMOKED PERFECTION

Called pastrami elsewhere in the world, smoked meat is made by smoking beef brisket with garlic, herbs and spices and then steaming it. The iconic recipe was first introduced to Montréal in the 1900s by Ben Kravitz, a Jewish immigrant from Lithuania, who found success by following the recipe his grandparents used to make beef last longer without refrigeration. There's terrific smoked meat all over the city but Schwartz's (above) is the undisputed king. Reuben Schwartz, a Romanian Jew, opened the soon-to-be Montréal icon in 1928, and it's been going strong ever since. Schwartz's meat goes through a 14-day regime of curing and smoking before landing on your plate after a final three-hour steam.

MA-AM-M BOLDUC Map pp76–7 Québécois $

☎ 514-527-3884; 4351 Ave de Lorimier; mains $5-12; 🕒 7am-9pm Mon-Fri, 8am-10pm Sat, 9am-10pm Sun; Ⓜ Papineau, then bus 10

This neighborhood eatery with piped-in punk and New Age music still serves mainstays of Québécois cuisine: meatball stew, *tourtière,* and more *poutine* than you can shake a trotter at. Long departed, Mme Bolduc's friendly round face still graces the marquee above the terrace tables.

PATATI PATATA Map pp76–7 Québécois $

☎ 514-844-0216; 4177 Blvd St-Laurent; mains $5-8; 🕒 8am-11pm Mon-Fri, 11am-11pm Sat & Sun; Ⓜ St-Laurent, then bus 55

This matchbox-sized, bohemian-style eatery is known for its *poutine,* borscht and mini burgers. It's a Montréal classic with rocking music and young efficient staff, and there's almost always a line snaking out front. Grab a seat at the window and watch the city stroll past.

ST-VIATEUR BAGEL & CAFÉ
Map pp76–7 Bagels $

☎ 514-528-6361; 1127 Ave du Mont-Royal Est; sandwiches $4-8; 🕒 6am-midnight; Ⓜ Mont-Royal

A splendid café that serves its signature bagels, grilled or *nature,* with soup or salad. There are about a dozen sandwiches but most popular are the traditional smoked lox with cream cheese, and roast beef with Swiss cheese and tomato. You can also find breakfast bagels with eggs and ham.

COCO RICO Map pp76–7 Fast Chicken $

☎ 514-849-5554; 3907 Blvd St-Laurent; mains $4-8; 🕒 10am-11pm Mon-Fri, 9am-11pm Sat & Sun; Ⓜ St-Laurent, then bus 55

People strolling the Main pop into this no-frills Portuguese place all day for piping-hot plates of juicy rotisserie chicken, roasted potatoes and custard tarts. With only one long counter and flimsy bar stools inside, this place always looks empty; most people order their birds to go.

POUTINE!

Broach the topic of *poutine* with a native Montrealer, and either a look of utter rapture or vomitous disgust will likely cross the face of your interlocutor. One of the world's most humble dishes, *poutine* was invented in rural Québec sometime in the 1950s. According to legend, a restaurateur experienced an epiphany while waiting on a customer who ordered fries while waiting for his cheese curds. The word *'poutine'* itself derives from an Acadian slang term for 'mushy mess' or 'pudding.'

For the uninitiated, *poutine* at first glance looks like the leftovers from a large dinner party all slopped into one giant pile, scraped onto a plate and plunked down on the table. While recipes and imaginations run wild when it comes to *poutine*, the basic building block of the Québécois dish is fries smothered in cheese curds and gravy. Varieties include 'all dress' (sautéed mushrooms and bell peppers), 'richie boy' (ground beef), Italian (beef and spaghetti sauce), barbecue or even smoked meat. In the past, going out for *poutine* had about as much sex appeal as chowing down on boiled hotdogs and tap water; these days, however, even exalted restaurants like Au Pied de Cochon serve the well-known dish.

- **La Banquise** (p133) Serving 25 different type of *poutine* round the clock, this is the gold standard for classic *poutine*.
- **Au Pied de Cochon** (p130) Elevates the simple dish to respectability with its famous *poutine* foie gras.
- **Ma-am-m Bolduc** (opposite) Try *poutine* Italian style, with spaghetti sauce or red wine and garlic.
- **Patati Patata** (opposite) The house special is Patat-ine, with cheese curds served in an edible crispy potato basket.
- **La Belle Province** (Map pp76–7; ☎ 514-845-0700; 1018 Rue Ste-Catherine Est; 24hr; M Beaudry) For *poutine* in a hurry, stop by Québec's most famous greasy spoon. While not winning any culinary awards, Belle Province's Italian variety is particularly satisfying. Dozens of locations.

AU FESTIN DE BABETTE

Map pp76–7 — Ice Cream $

☎ 514-849-0214; 4085 Rue St-Denis; ice cream $3-5; 10am-6pm Sun-Wed, to 10pm Thu-Sat; M Mont-Royal

This charming café with sidewalk terrace is famed for its homemade ice cream. The supremely satisfying *crème glacée molle à l'ancienne* is chocolate or vanilla ice cream blended on the spot with fresh mango, blueberries, raspberries, lychee, kiwi and other fruits.

LITTLE ITALY, MILE END & OUTREMONT

Little Italy is the neighborhood of old-fashioned trattorias and lively little cafés, where the heavenly aroma of freshly brewed espresso hangs in the air. Beloved bakeries, family-style restaurants and outdoor tables packing the sidewalk in summer are all part of the charm of this food-loving neighborhood. Stylish new eateries are slowly edging their way into the neighborhood, but there are plenty of classic favorites that have withstood the test of time, including Italian grocery stores, well-worn diners and an authentic bakery that attracts cannoli lovers from miles around. The prime streets here are Blvd St-Laurent (between Parc Martel and Rue Jean-Talon) and the side streets of Rue Dante and Rue St-Zotique Est.

Mile End and Outremont are duly blessed in the dining department. Strewn with an impressive variety of Parisian-style bistros, high-end ethnic eateries and low-key cafés, these neighborhoods also boast two oven-baked stars of the city's culinary history: the famous Montréal bagel shops. The best exploring is along Ave Fairmount and Ave St-Viateur, which are packed with restaurants. Ave Laurier is another excellent dining strip, with slightly higher-end options to match the swish boutiques lining the street.

MILOS Map p83

Greek $$$

☎ 514-272-3522; 5357 Ave du Parc; mains $28-42; noon-3pm Mon-Fri, 5:30-11pm daily; M Place-des-Arts, then bus 80

Rock stars, socialites and business leaders flock to this fashionable restaurant with Mediterranean stucco, big urns filled with dried flowers and refrigerated counters of mouthwatering fish and fruits. Dinner for two (eg range of Greek appetizers, grilled *loup de mer* (seabass), fried veggies with tzatziki and honey-laced milk yogurt) could set you back $150 with wine. Reservations are essential.

LÉMEAC Map p83

French $$$

☎ 514-270-0999; 1045 Ave Laurier Ouest; mains $20-36; noon-midnight Mon-Fri, 10am-midnight Sat & Sun; M Laurier

A well-respected name among the well-heeled Laurier crowd, Lémeac has a light and airy setting with huge windows overlooking the street, a lively ambience and beautifully turned-out plates. Culinary standouts include salad of smoked salmon (made on-site), lobster ravioli, Angus beef filet mignon, duck leg confit and the veal liver with caramelized onions. It's a popular brunch spot on weekends, and at night – the after-10pm three-course prix-fixe menu is an excellent value at $22.

IL MULINO Map p83 — Italian $$

☎ 514-273-5776; 236 Rue St-Zotique Est; mains $18-28; 6-10pm Tue-Sat; M Jean-Talon

Arguably the best Italian restaurant in town. This family-style restaurant is low-key and homey with old black-and-white photos on the walls. Lamb chops are the house specialty and the vegetarian starter plate with sautéed peppers and olives, stuffed eggplant and grilled mushrooms is still considered a classic.

CHEZ LÉVÊQUE Map p83 — French $$

☎ 514-279-7355; 1030 Ave Laurier Ouest; mains $19-26; 10:30am-midnight; M Place-des-Arts, then bus 80

This classic bistro attracts the beautiful people of Mile End and Outremont to chat about fashion, movies and business under irreverent religious art. Paris-born owner Pierre Lévêque presents a superb choice of traditional French cuisine with grilled meats (rack of lamb or caribou) and fresh seafood (red snapper, Atlantic salmon or bouillabaisse). Many of the fine wines are sold by the glass.

LA MOULERIE Map p83 — Mussels $$

☎ 514-273-8132; 1249 Rue Bernard Ouest; mains $16-24; 11:30am-11pm Mon-Fri, 10am-11pm Sat & Sun; M Outremont

The mussels here seem bigger than elsewhere and the restaurant is renowned for its almost two-dozen varieties. Try the Greek mussels done up with umpteen ingredients including feta and ouzo or the Indian version with coriander and ginger. Outremont locals usually crowd the simple dining room and the patio outside.

MIKADO Map p83 — Japanese $$

☎ 514-279-4809; 399 Ave Laurier Ouest; mains $16-25; 11:30am-2:30pm Mon-Fri, 5:30-10pm daily; M Laurier

Sadly, good Japanese fare is a rarity in Montréal, which makes respectable Mikado all the more of a standout in this sushi-challenged city. Step inside and you'll find an elegant, Zenlike dining room with a lively wraparound sushi counter. Sashimi is mouthwateringly fresh, while the tuna tempura and grilled organic salmon teriyaki are other highlights. For dessert, try the refreshing green-tea nougat glacé.

LA KHAÏMA Map p83 — Mauritanian $$

☎ 514-948-9993; 142 Fairmount Ouest; mains $14-18; 6pm-midnight; M Laurier

For a taste of West Africa, head to this warm and welcoming Mauritanian spot. The friendly owner, in traditional dress, cooks up tasty slow-cooked recipes like spiced lentil soup and lamb or vegetables in peanut sauce over couscous. The menu changes regularly and features only a few dishes per day.

LE PETIT ALEP Map p83 — Middle Eastern $$

☎ 514-270-9361; 191 Rue Jean-Talon Est; mains $12-28; bistro 11am-11pm Tue-Sat, restaurant 5-10pm Tue & Wed, 5-11pm Thu-Sat; M De Castelnau

The complex flavors of Syrian-Armenian cuisine draw diners from all over Montréal. A big menu includes hummus, salads and *muhammara* (spread made of walnuts, garlic, breadcrumbs, pomegranate syrup and cumin), plus beef kabobs smothered in tahini, spices and nuts. Dine in the bright bistro (the front wall opens up onto the street during nice weather) or, in the evening, the slightly swish dining room next door.

CAFÉ INTERNATIONAL Map p83 — Italian $$

☎ 514-495-0067; 6714 Blvd St-Laurent; mains $12-22; 9am-1am; M Jean-Talon

The name may be generic, but the food is far from canned at this lively eatery on Little Italy's main drag. Carefully prepared but unfussy dishes draw in the crowds to feast on homemade pastas, thin-crust pizzas, satisfying sandwiches, calamari salad and superb cappuccinos. In the summer, try to snag a sidewalk table for prime people-watching.

SENZALA Map p83 — Brazilian $$

☎ 514-274-1464; 177 Rue Bernard Ouest; mains $12-18; 6-10pm Mon-Wed, 9am-late Thu-Sun; M Place-des-Arts, then bus 80

This colorful restaurant with a leafy terrace cooks up tasty Brazilian dishes, including hearty plates of *moqueca* (seafood stew with coconut milk), and *churrasquinho mixto* (sizzling platters of grilled beef, chicken and shrimp). Weekend brunches are also good.

DA ENRICO Map p83 Italian $$

☎ 514-388-0719; 264 Rue St-Zotique Est; mains $12-14; ⏲ 5-10pm Tue-Sat; Ⓜ Jean-Talon

A well-loved local trattoria, Da Enrico has a loyal following who come for freshly made pizzas and pastas, followed by tiramisu and good cappuccino. It's a small, unpretentious BYOB place, set with red-and-white checked tablecloths and old photos, where families, old-timers and the odd Plateau couple fill the air with chatter. While the menu offers no surprises, it's decent quality for the price.

PHAYATHAI Map p83 Thai $$

☎ 514-272-3456; 107 Ave Laurier Ouest; mains $10-18; ⏲ noon-2:30pm & 5:30-10:30pm; Ⓜ Laurier

Although the jury is out on who serves the city's best Thai food, this elegant little restaurant on Laurier is a strong contender. It's hard to go wrong with anything on the menu, with delicious and flavorful seafood soup, tender roasted duck and whole red snapper basted in red chili.

PIZZERIA NAPOLETANA Map p83 Italian $

☎ 514-276-8226; 189 Rue Dante; mains $10-18; ⏲ 11am-midnight Mon-Sat, noon-midnight Sun; Ⓜ De Castelnau

Homemade pasta sauces and thick-sauced pizzas (over 30 different types of each) draw Italian-loving crowds here all year long. The pizza crust – nice and crunchy – is the secret to Napoletana's success. The dining room is simple with neat wood tables and chairs. Lines can be long, particularly in summer, so avoid peak hours. Bring your own wine.

JULIETTE ET CHOCOLAT

Map p83 Café $

☎ 514-510-5651; 377 Ave Laurier Ouest; mains $8-12; ⏲ 11am-11pm; Ⓜ Laurier

Montréal's chocolate lovers unite at this sweet two-level café on Laurier. The menu is built around chocolate, from decadent piping-hot crepes to milkshakes, smoothies and chocolate 'shots,' not to mention cups of creamy hot chocolate. The varieties (rated by bitterness, country of origin, percentage of cocoa levels etc) are endless. Black-and-white tile floors and an inviting ambience seduce lingerers. There's another location in the Quartier Latin (p129).

LA PANTHÈRE VERTE

Map p83 Vegetarian $

☎ 514-903-7770; 66 Rue St-Viateur Ouest; mains $7-11; ⏲ 11am-3pm & 5-9pm Mon-Sat; Ⓜ Rosemont

Green in every sense of the word, La Panthère Verte is a small casual vegetarian spot, where you can stop in for delicious falafel sandwiches, energy-charging juices and fresh salads that change daily (salad of quinoa, rocket and sweet potato was one recent option). Hanging plants, a zippy green paint job and curious colander lamps set the scene.

CAFFÈ ITALIA Map p83 Café $

☎ 514-495-0059; 6840 Blvd St-Laurent; sandwiches $8, coffees $2-3; ⏲ 6am-11pm; Ⓜ Jean-Talon

This old-time Italian café has a loyal neighborhood following for its unpretentious charm. Plain Formica counters and faded Italian soccer posters set the stage for lingering over excellent espresso and unfussy sandwiches. Depending on how things are going (with AC Milan football club), staff can be grumpy and terse or enthusiastically welcoming.

LE CAGIBI CAFÉ Map p83 Vegetarian $

☎ 514-509-1199; 5490 Blvd St-Laurent; mains $7-10; ⏲ 10:30am-2:30am; Ⓜ Rosemont

Music-loving bohemians and Plateau eccentrics hold court at this plant- and antique-filled vegetarian restaurant by day, bar by night. The menu features tasty soups, salads, baked goods and Tex-Mex (burritos, chili, empanadas), all served on kitsch, lovingly mismatched crockery. There's a good entertainment lineup by night: DJs, live bands, film screenings, book readings, slide shows and other eclectic fare.

LESTER'S Map p83 Smoked Meat $

☎ 514-213-1313; www.lestersdeli.com; 1057 Rue Bernard Ouest; mains $6-14; ⏲ 9am-9pm Mon-Fri, 9am-8pm Sat; Ⓜ Outremont

Serving some of the city's best smoked meat for nearly 60 years, this deli is as much a part of Montréal lore as the three-hour lunch. With its art-deco yet 1950s diner-style decor, the restaurant attracts a loyal following of locals looking for the perfect smoked-meat sandwich (the dry-aged is formidable), but also smoked salmon or salads and awesome *karnatzel* (type of dried sausage) in fresh, medium or dry.

THE GREAT BAGEL DEBATE

The Montréal bagel has a long and venerable history. It all started in 1915 when Isadore and Fanny Shlafman, Jews from Ukraine, opened a tiny bakery on Rue Roy in the Plateau. They made the yeast bread rings according to a recipe they'd brought from the bakery where Shlafman's father worked. By 1919 they started the Montréal Bagel Bakery in a wooden shack just off Blvd St-Laurent, a few doors down from Schwartz's deli.

After WWII many Holocaust survivors emigrated to Montréal and the bagel market boomed. Isadore Schlafman decided to build a bakery in the living room of his house at 74 Ave Fairmount, where he opened Fairmount Bagel (below) in 1950. Meanwhile Myer Lemkowicz, a Polish Jew who had survived Auschwitz, went on to establish St-Viateur Bakery (below) in 1957. A legendary rivalry was born and scores of other bagel bakeries sprang up in their wake.

Ask any Montrealer whose bagel is best and passions will flare. Year-in and year-out tireless critics tour the main bagel bakeries to chat, chew and cogitate. In recent years St-Viateur has edged out Fairmount for the number-one slot. Lesser entries are dismissed with scorn – 'hockey puck' is a common assessment. But locals do agree that Montréal's bagels are superior to their New York cousins. The Montréal bagel is lighter, sweeter and crustier, and chewy but not dense thanks to an enriched eggy dough that looks almost like batter. The dough hardly rises and the tender rings are formed by hand and boiled in a honey-and-water solution before baking in a wood-burning oven.

LE BILBOQUET Map p83 Ice Cream $

☎ 514-276-0414; 1311 Rue Bernard Ouest; cones $3-6; ⌚ noon-midnight; Ⓜ Laurier

A legendary institution in Montréal, Le Bilboquet whips up highly addictive homemade ice cream and refreshing sorbets. On warm summer nights (and even on chilly evenings), long lines snake out the door. Although there's no seating inside, there are a couple of sidewalk tables, and some lovely little parks nearby.

WILENSKY'S LIGHT LUNCH

Map p83 Diner $

☎ 514-271-0247; 34 Ave Fairmount Ouest; sandwiches $3-5; ⌚ 9am-4pm Mon-Fri; Ⓜ Laurier

It's like walking onto a 1950s movie set the moment you step in the door here. Terminally grumpy staff make no effort to hide the fact that cranking out your hand-pumped soda and Wilensky's special is likely the most disagreeable task they've ever experienced. Rickety wooden stools line the counter and photographs from the 1930s adorn the walls. This place was immortalized in Mordecai Richler's novel *The Apprenticeship of Duddy Kravitz* and the subsequent film, but it's equally famous for grilled meat sandwiches and its chopped egg sandwich.

ALATI-CASERTA Map p83 Bakery $

☎ 514-271-3013; 277 Rue Dante; dessert $3-5; ⌚ 8am-7pm Tue-Fri, 8am-5pm Sat & Sun; Ⓜ Jean-Talon

For over four decades, this marvelous family-owned pastry shop in Little Italy has wowed Montrealers with its deliciously decadent cannoli, almond cake, tiramisu and *sfogliatelle* (pastries stuffed with orange and ricotta cheese). Master baker Ernesto Bellinfante prepares many types of pastries and cakes each day, though arrive early for the best selection.

ST-VIATEUR BAGEL Map p83 Bagels $

☎ 514-276-8044; 263 Ave St-Viateur Ouest; bagels $0.75; ⌚ 24hr; Ⓜ Place-des-Arts, then bus 80

Currently the bagel favorite of Montréal, St-Viateur Bagel has a reputation stretching across Canada and beyond for its perfectly crusty, chewy and slightly sweet creations – check out the newspaper articles from around the world.

FAIRMOUNT BAGEL Map p83 Bagels $

☎ 514-272-0667; 74 Ave Fairmount Ouest; bagels $0.75; ⌚ 24hr; Ⓜ Laurier

One of Montréal's famed bagel places – people flood in here around the clock to scoop them up the minute they come out of the oven. Bagels are one thing Montrealers don't get creative with. They stick to classic sesame or poppy seed varieties, though you can pick up anything from chocolate-chip to sundried tomato bagels here too.

MILANO SUPERMARKET

Map p72 Supermarket

☎ 514-273-8558; 6862 Blvd St-Laurent; ⌚ 8am-6pm Mon-Fri, 8am-5pm Sat & Sun; Ⓜ De Castelnau

This local food store has a mouthwatering selection of fresh pasta, antipasto and olive oil. The fun here is seeing the old-timers do the rounds. Stop, watch, listen, stalk (but do so politely) and buy what they buy. You'll be on your way to an authentic Italian meal.

DRINKING

top picks

What's your recommendation? www.lonelyplanet.com/canada/montreal

DRINKING

Montrealers love to drink. Maybe it's the European influence or that classic French joie de vivre but this is a town where it's perfectly acceptable, even expected, to begin cocktail hour after work and continue well into the night.

On a sunny Friday afternoon, the *5-à-7* festive tradition often becomes 5-*à*-last-call. (Legal closing time is 3am and most establishments stay open until then.) In warm weather, the bars, cafés, pubs and terraces that line Blvd St-Laurent and Rue St-Denis, for example, are all packed with friends enjoying each other's company and the city's charm over a glass of wine, beer or other festive libation. Come wintertime, Montrealers are undaunted by snowstorms and long, frigid nights. In fact, that's when there's not much else to do but find yourself a warm, cozy bar and drink and laugh the night away.

As for places to sip, the city is brimming with options, from grungy holes-in-the-wall to glamorous lounges. You'll find Irish pubs, artsy French watering holes, elegant wine bars, microbreweries, pool halls, student taverns, dancey bars, bohemian teahouses, European cafés and everything in between. Many hip restaurants unofficially become bars after about midnight, some even pushing aside tables to make room for the influx of revelers.

As in Europe, espresso coffee is big here, and most locals start the day with strong, espresso-based drinks at their neighborhood cafés. It's not uncommon for artists, students and self-employed types to spend days hanging out at their favorite cafés, laptops in tow. Many cafés roast their own beans, and fair trade and specialty blends to brew at home are sold in shops around town.

Ultimately, Montréal is a city of characters and personalities who interact over drinks day and night. French, English or other, there are as many choices of where to drink as there are drinkers. What better way to get to know them than by sharing some friendly libations?

WHERE TO DRINK

Just like its people, every Montréal neighborhood has its own unique personality and style. So, where you go usually depends on the vibe you're looking for on any given night (or day). Old Montréal, for example, has become quite a happening area. Its chichi boutique hotels and the new media industry boom centered around the Old Port have resulted in posh new lounges, wine bars and upscale restos where international celebrities canoodle with local scenesters and the fashion crowd.

Downtown's many bars, clubs and cafés tend to cater to tourists and students (Dawson College and McGill and Concordia Universities are all located downtown). In particular, the busy strip of Rue Crescent between Rue Ste-Catherine and Blvd de Maisonneuve is très touristy, especially weekend nights. However, hidden among these more mainstream establishments are some vibrant taverns and quirky little pubs that are part of the city's cultural energy.

Finally, the Plateau Mont-Royal and Mile End 'hoods house quite a variety of drinking spots, from snazzy to dive, though most do appeal to an arty, hip crowd of English and French speakers. Both districts are loaded with pubs, bars and cafés within walking (or stumbling) distance, so are ideal for bar-hopping. The long strip of Blvd St-Laurent, known as 'the Main,' is lined with bars, pubs and restaurants (in the Plateau, the part of 'the Main' south of Ave des Pins tends to be fancier and pricier, with things mellowing out as you head north).

PRACTICALITIES

The legal drinking age in the province of Québec is 18. Bars must close at 3am, so last call is usually about 15 minutes prior. Generally, you're expected to tip your server or bartender the greater of 15% of your bill, or between \$1 and \$2 for each drink you order.

To buy alcohol to drink at home, Société des Alcools du Québec (SAQ) are government-run liquor stores all over town, selling wines from around the world and most brands of liquor and beer. Their opening hours vary, but *dépanneurs* (corner stores) sell a selection of wine and beer until 11pm, including popular locally produced microbrews like Boréale, St-Ambroise, Cheval Blanc and Belle Gueule. Cheers!

OLD MONTRÉAL & CHINATOWN

CLUNY ARTBAR Map p48 Café

☎ 514-866-1213; 257 Rue Prince; 🕑 8am-5pm Mon-Wed & Fri, 8am-10pm Thu; Ⓜ Square-Victoria

Tucked into the loft-like Fonderie Darling gallery is this charmingly hip café that serves breakfast, lunch and coffee to an artsy-chic, bilingual, Old Montréal clientele. It's open later Thursdays for dinner and drinks, and can be rented for private parties, but Cluny's is really a daytime scene. It doesn't get more Montréal than this.

CAFÉ DES ÉCLUSIERS Map p48 Lounge

☎ 514-496-0109; 400 Rue de la Commune Ouest; 🕑 11:30am-11pm Mon-Wed, Fri & Sat, 11:30am-1am Thu May-Sep; Ⓜ Place-d'Armes

This Old Port summertime staple is open from May to September only. Always crowded, it has a restaurant, bar, lounge, sprawling outdoor terrace and beach club of sorts. Although the scene can be a bit much, the after-work crowd adores the lounge, house music DJs and elaborate cocktails.

LE PHARAON LOUNGE Map p48 Lounge

☎ 514-843-4779; 139 Rue St-Paul Ouest; 🕑 4-10pm; Ⓜ Place-d'Armes

The Tintin theme of its neighboring restaurant spills over into this small, laid-back, casual lounge. Like the nearby office workers who frequent it, you won't come here for gimmicks, pickups or trendiness, but rather for a place to hang out with friends when all you really want is a drink while you chat or unwind at the end of the day. It often hosts jazz acts.

WUNDERBAR Map p48 Lounge

☎ 514-395-3195; 901 Square-Victoria; 🕑 10pm-3am Wed-Sat; Ⓜ Square-Victoria

While hotel bars can be iffy, this modern room is among the city's safest bets for a soiree on the town. Wunderbar was developed by New York–based nightlife impresarios, who blended local and international culture with the ease of a dry martini. Weekly DJ nights attract a dancey, trendy crowd.

PUB ST-PAUL Map p48 Pub

☎ 514-874-0485; 124 Rue St-Paul Est; 🕑 11am-3am; Ⓜ Champs-de-Mars

In the heart of Old Montréal's most touristy drag is this rock pub, a hit among students, jocks and passersby. A lunch and dinner menu of upscale pub fare (think yummy chicken wings) is served, live bands rock out weekend nights, and drink specials complete the Top 40 formula.

GARDE-MANGER Map p48 Restaurant-Bar

☎ 514-678-5044; 409 Rue St-Francois-Xavier; 🕑 6pm-3am Tue-Sun; Ⓜ Place-d'Armes

After midnight this tiny, upscale restaurant becomes party central as scenesters, actors and gourmands-turned-merrymakers gyrate around. You'll probably find yourself dancing on the bar, or in the kitchen making out with some hottie. Be warned: the music is loud and getting in on weekends is tough – unless you're a close pal with the cool, beautiful staff.

L'ORIGNAL Map p48 Restaurant-Bar

☎ 514-303-0479; 479 Rue St-Alexis; 🕑 6pm-3am Mon-Sat; Ⓜ Place-d'Armes

Just a parking-lot's stumble away from Garde-Manger (above) is L'Orignal, a slightly larger restaurant that's perhaps a tad less debaucherous but just as much fun – in fact, its owners are Garde expats and the spots share virtually the same clientele, music and vibe. Nearing midnight, things get crazy as pretty people dance and flirt the night away.

TERRASSE 701 Map p48 Terrace

🕑 514-842-1887; 55 Rue St-Jacques Ouest; 🕑 noon-midnight Sun-Thu, until 2am Fri & Sat mid-Jun–mid-Sep)

The rooftop terrace above the boutique Hôtel Place-d'Armes is a requisite stop on the nightlife circuit if you're around during the summer. Nicely mixed cocktails, eclectic cuisine and a fantastic view over Old Montréal never fail to bring in the beauty crowd.

DOWNTOWN

MAD HATTER SALOON Map pp62–3 Bar

☎ 514-987-9988; 1220 Rue Crescent; 🕑 11am-3am; Ⓜ Guy-Concordia

With happy-hour specials and a kooky, anything-goes feel, this longtime Rue Crescent tavern is so uncool it's cool. Concordia and McGill University students have been flocking here for years, and during

RESTO DISCO?

When is a restaurant more than a restaurant? When it's also a bar, or a lounge, or a club, or whatever other festive euphemism may tickle your fancy. As in many cosmopolitan cities, Montréal's hippest restos stay hot long after their kitchens close. The popular spots are loud, sexy and rambunctious, so get a table and order bottle service, or be prepared to be pushed into sweaty bodies and picked up by hot-to-trot locals.

On the lower Main, if you're up for flirting, celeb-spotting and a scene that's about being seen, strut into **Restaurant Globe** (Map pp62–3; ☎ 514-284-3823; 3455 Blvd St-Laurent; Ⓜ St-Laurent) After-midnight highlights of this upscale local institution include gorgeous staff, DJ music and Euro-flavored clientele. Across the street is **Buonanotte** (Map pp62–3; ☎ 514-848-0644; 3518 Blvd St-Laurent; Ⓜ St-Laurent), an Italian resto staffed by scantily clad models that becomes a loud, pulsing nightclub, complete with flashing lights and a dance floor. A handsome doorman handpicks clients from the mad throng of young hopefuls gathered at the entrance.

Downtown, **Ristorante Cavalli** (Map pp62–3; ☎ 514-843-5100; 2040 Rue Peel Parc; Ⓜ Peel) is the spot. This fine Italian restaurant gets its DJ party on with upscale tourists and a good-looking crowd in their 20s and 30s.

In Old Montréal, head to the Hotel St-Paul to hang at **Vauvert** (Map pp62–3; ☎ 514-876-2823; 355 Rue McGill; Ⓜ McGill) The vibe is sophisticated and French, full of Old Montréal residents and hotel guests. For a more intimate but exciting scene full of interesting characters and lo-pro celebs, try **Garde-Manger** (p141) or **L'Orignal** (p141), though both are hard to get into unless you're a regular.

summertime its 2nd-floor terrace is a lo-pro, affordable spot to unwind.

THURSDAY'S Map pp62–3 Bar

☎ 514-288-5656; 1449 Rue Crescent; 🕑 11:30am-3am Mon-Sat; Ⓜ Guy-Concordia

This lively singles bar attracts hordes of fun-loving tourists and Montrealers looking for an easy place to paint the town red. Smoked bagels with cream cheese are the specialty on a menu that spans gourmet bites. The mammoth bars and two-level dance floor appeal to the after-work crowd. Not the coolest but does the job.

TYPHOON LOUNGE Map pp44–5 Lounge

☎ 514-482-4448; 5752 Ave Monkland; 🕑 4pm-3am; Ⓜ Vendôme, then 🚌 105

Young yuppies, anglo- and francophone, slip in to this Côte-des-Neiges watering hole for a beer and chicken legs on the way home, or camp out for jazz, blues and world beats. It's hard to shake the office-worker ambience but on summer nights it's a good pit stop while cruising Ave Monkland.

BRUTOPIA Map pp62–3 Pub

☎ 514-393-9277; 1219 Rue Crescent; 🕑 3:30pm-3am Sun-Fri, noon-3am Sat; Ⓜ Guy-Concordia

This fantastic brewpub has eight varieties of suds on tap, including honey beer, nut brown and the more challenging raspberry blonde. The brick walls and wood paneling are conducive to chats among the relaxed student crowd. Live blues bands play some evenings. It really picks up after the night classes from nearby Concordia get out.

COCK 'N BULL PUB Map pp62–3 Pub

☎ 514-933-4556; 1944 Rue Ste-Catherine Ouest; 🕑 11am-3am; Ⓜ Guy-Concordia

This weird joint is part dive bar, part Irish pub and all good times for students and low-rent party seekers. Located on a semi-seedy strip of Rue Ste-Catherine, its not-so-Irish food menu is – wait for it – Chinese. But cheap beers and theme nights like karaoke and bingo attract a fun, smart crowd.

GRUMPY'S BAR Map pp62–3 Pub

☎ 514-866-9010; 1242 Rue Bishop; 🕑 noon-3am; Ⓜ Guy-Concordia

This unassuming basement bar is a former stomping ground of Anglo intellectuals of an era gone by. Open-mic night presents stand-up comedy and spoken word on Wednesday, and most nights feature live blues, jazz, rock, country or folk. Grumpy's Moonshine on Thursday nights is legendary, with acoustic bluegrass jam sessions reeling in famous local musicians.

HURLEY'S IRISH PUB Map pp62–3 Pub

☎ 514-861-4111; 1125 Rue Crescent; 🕑 11am-3am; Ⓜ Guy-Concordia

This cozy place features live rock and fiddling Celtic folk on the rear stage and beer-soaked football and soccer matches on big-screen TVs. Standard pub grub – fish 'n' chips, meat pies and burgers – is also served.

LE VIEUX DUBLIN PUB & RESTAURANT Map pp62–3 Pub

☎ 514-861-4448; 1219a Rue University; ⏰ noon-3am Mon-Sat, 5pm-3am Sun; Ⓜ McGill

The city's oldest Irish pub has the expected great selection of brews (about $6 per pint) and live Celtic or pop music nightly. Curries rub shoulders with burgers on the menu. Fifty single malts.

MCKIBBIN'S Map pp62–3 Pub

☎ 514-288-1580; 1426 Rue Bishop; ⏰ 11:30am-3am; Ⓜ Guy-Concordia

With its garage-sale furniture, McKibbin's cultivates a familiar, down-at-heel pub atmosphere. Its live entertainment varies from Celtic, pop and punk music to drinking contests. The office crowd pops in at lunch for burgers, chicken wings and salads.

NYK'S Map pp62–3 Pub

☎ 514-866-1787; 1250 Rue de Bleury; ⏰ 11am-3am Mon-Fri, 4pm-3am Sat; Ⓜ Place-des-Arts

Its artsy-chic vibe makes this warm bistro pub the preferred lunch and after-work spot of Plateau cool kids who happen to work in downtown offices. Daily happy hours and pub finger-foods are a joy to downtowners seeking an authentic experience. Sometimes it even has live jazz.

PEEL PUB Map pp62–3 Pub

☎ 514-844-7296; 1107 Rue Ste-Catherine Ouest; ⏰ 7am-3am; Ⓜ Peel

This barn of a pub is a student institution for its cheap pitchers of beer and greasy-spoon menu. Happy hour is lengthy, from 3pm to 7pm. During televised sporting events fans hurl vocal abuse at the 30 big-screen TVs and it gets so crowded it's hard to move.

PUB STE-ÉLISABETH Map pp62–3 Pub

☎ 514-286-4302; 1412 Rue Ste-Élisabeth; ⏰ 3pm-3am; Ⓜ Berri-UQAM

Tucked off a side street, this awesome little pub is positively revered by Montrealers for its heavenly vine-covered courtyard and drink menu that includes beers galore, whiskies and ports. It's got a mind-whirring repertoire of beers on tap, including imports and rare-to-find microbrewery fare like Boréale Noire and Cidre Mystique.

SIR WINSTON CHURCHILL PUB COMPLEXE Map pp62–3 Pub

☎ 514-288-3814; 1459 Rue Crescent; ⏰ 11:30am-3am; Ⓜ Guy-Concordia

This Rue Crescent staple is the go-to spot of the block. Winnie's cavernous, split-level pub draws a steady crowd of tourists and students and an older Anglo crowd. In fact, the late, great author Mordecai Richler used to knock back cold ones in the bar upstairs. With multiple bars, pool tables and pulsating music, meals are served all day and happy-hour drink specials abound.

ZIGGY'S Map pp62–3 Pub

☎ 514-285-8855; 1470 Rue Crescent; ⏰ 1pm-3am; Ⓜ Guy-Concordia

Walking into this European-style pub and sports bar, you'd never guess it was once the watering hole of some of Montréal's most infamous writers and journalists (boisterous late newspaper columnist Nick Auf der Maur practically lived here). These days, Ziggy's features imported draft beer, nine televisions and celebrity memorabilia, included a hockey jersey autographed by Habs hero Maurice 'The Rocket' Richard.

QUÉBEC'S TOP ARTISANAL BEERS

McAuslan Brewing – keep an eye out for its apricot wheat ale and especially its St-Ambroise oatmeal stout.

Boréale – everything from black beer to blond, but the red variety is by far the preferred.

Unibroue – Fin du Monde (The End of the World) is a triple-fermented monster with 9% alcohol that more than lives up to its name; La Maudite (The Damned) is a rich, spicy beer that clocks in a close second at 8%.

L'Alchimiste – this Joliette-based brewer (about 60km northeast of Montréal) turns out a stable of different brews but its Bock de Joliette, an amber beer, is the star of the bunch.

Lion d'Or – this Lennoxville brewer (p249) is one of the best in the province and does an outstanding, *very* bitter, bitter beer. For some reason, finding the label in Montréal these days is a bit like searching for a needle in a haystack (you know it's there somewhere but…) so if you come across this mark, scoop it up fast.

PULLMAN Map pp76–7 Restaurant-Bar
☎ 514-288-7779; 3424 Ave du Parc; 4:30pm-1am Tue-Sat; M Place-des-Arts
This beautifully designed wine bar is a favorite haunt of the 30-something set. It's primarily a restaurant, but the downstairs bar of this two-level space gets jammed (or *jammé*, as they say in Franglais) after work and becomes quite a pickup spot, so be prepared to engage in some flirting. Sommeliers can help you choose from the sprawling wine list.

QUARTIER LATIN & THE VILLAGE

LE MAGELLAN BAR
Map p72 Bar
☎ 514-845-0909; 330 Rue Ontario Est; 11am-midnight; M Berri-UQAM
Once past the mock lighthouse out front you can enjoy a pleasant evening of eclectic offerings, from jazz to chansons. The interior is sprinkled with maritime doodads and the front terrace is great for people-watching. Good food, too.

LE ST-SULPICE Map p72 Bar
☎ 514-844-9458; 1680 Rue St-Denis; 11am-3am; M Berri-UQAM
This student evergreen is spread over four levels in an old Victorian stone house – a café, several terraces, disco and a sprawling back garden for drinks 'n' chats. The music changes with the DJ's mood, from hip-hop and ambient to mainstream rock and jazz. It use recyclable glasses and also sells alcohol-free beer.

SALOON Map p72 Bar
☎ 514-522-1333; 1333 Rue Ste-Catherine Est; 11:30am-11pm Mon-Fri, 10am-3am Sat & Sun; M Beaudry
This recently revamped gay bar-bistro earned a spot in Village hearts for its chilled atmosphere, cocktails and 'five-continents' menu, including some good vegetarian options. A stylish pre-club pit stop.

STUD BAR Map p72 Bar
☎ 514-598-8243; Rue Ste-Catherine Est; 10am-3am; M Papineau
This Village meat market has poor visibility and lots of guys with no hair and persistent hopes for the night ahead.

BISTRO KILO Map p72 Café
☎ 514-596-3933; 1495 Rue Ste-Catherine Est; 12:30-11:30pm; M Papineau
Known for its decadent desserts and ginormous salads and sandwiches, this gay café is also a convenient daytime hangout. Grab a table beside the huge windows, sip your coffee and watch life go by. Kilo also has tons of flyers for events nearby. Staff are friendly.

CLUB DATE PIANO-BAR
Map p72 Pub
☎ 514-521-1242; 1218 Rue Ste-Catherine Est; 8am-3am; M Beaudry
This gay tavern knew what it was doing when it karaoke-fied the spot. A mixed crowd cheers on aspiring vocalists from all walks of life, from hilariously awful to downright star-worthy. Cheap drinks and a weird saloon vibe guarantee you a night to remember – or forget.

LES TROIS BRASSEURS
Map p72 Pub
☎ 514-845-1660; 1660 Rue St-Denis; 11am-1am; M Berri-UQAM
This chain of European brewers has set up a great locale in the Quartier Latin. Four homegrown beers are always on tap and the menu has a number of great bistro-style bites. During summertime, sliding garage doors let in the cool night air.

QUARTIER LATIN PUB Map p72 Pub
☎ 514-845-3301; 318 Rue Ontario Est; 3pm-3am; M Berri-UQAM
This cool bar with 1950s lounge-style decor has a small dance floor and a DJ playing new wave on weekends. A great, reliable hangout any night of the week.

PLATEAU MONT-ROYAL

BAR KOROVA Map pp76–7 Bar
☎ 514-904-6444; 3908 Blvd St-Laurent; 10pm-3am; M St-Laurent, then 55
Boozy, smiley fun with the city's arty Anglo musicians and the girls (and boys) who love them. With DJ nights spanning soul, funk and rock, impromptu hipster dance parties go down at this no-frills watering hole almost every night. What else do you expect from a bar whose clientele refers to itself as Korova Kids, though most are on the upside of 30?

BAR PLAN B Map pp76–7 Bar

☎ 514-845-6060; 327 Ave du Mont-Royal Est; 🕑 3pm-3am; Ⓜ Mont-Royal

Warm decor, elegant snacks and a liquor menu showcasing absinthe make this high-end bar a perfect date and pickup spot. It's also perfect for drinking with friends, and usually not too loud to talk. A sophisticated French-speaking crowd flocks here after work and on weekends. As its name decrees, when there's nowhere else to go, try Plan B.

BAR SALON LA PORTE ROUGE Map pp76–7 Bar

☎ 514-522-8244; 1834 Ave du Mont-Royal Est; 🕑 5pm-3am Mon-Fri, 9pm-3am Sat & Sun; Ⓜ Mont-Royal

This historical old saloon has been fancied up into a trendy hangout. Old-fashioned decor pays tribute to the space's illustrious past, as do drink names like Scarlett O'Hara and Pink Lady. Sunday nights, electro DJs draw a trashy-glam fashion crowd, both gay and straight.

BARFLY Map pp76–7 Bar

☎ 514-284-6665; 4062 Blvd St-Laurent; 🕑 4pm-3am; Ⓜ St-Laurent, then bus 55

Cheap, gritty, loud, fun and a little bit out of control – just the way we like our dive bars. Live punk bands and bedraggled hipsters hold court alongside aging rockers at this St-Laurent hole-in-the-wall. A Montréal must.

BAROUF Map pp76–7 Bar

☎ 514-844-0119; 4171 Rue St-Denis; 🕑 1pm-3am; Ⓜ Mont-Royal

This French watering hole is the perfect spot to stop for a drink or three while cruising the Plateau. Brews can be ordered in giant plastic towers with a tap at the bottom. More conventional vessels are available for the 25 draft beers, including extra-potent brands from Belgium.

BIFTECK Map pp76–7 Bar

☎ 514-844-6211; 3702 Blvd St-Laurent; 🕑 2pm-3am; Ⓜ St-Laurent, then bus 55

Pool, popcorn and indie rockers hold court alongside students and random weirdos at this legendary dive bar that's as much part of the Main's culture as smoked meat and bagels. Drinks are cheap, the faux country-and-western decor hasn't budged for decades and the rough-around-the-edges staff keep it real. A great place to kick off a night out.

BILY KUN Map pp76–7 Bar

☎ 514-845-5392; 354 Ave du Mont-Royal Est; 🕑 3pm-3am; Ⓜ Mont-Royal

One of the pioneers of 'tavern chic,' Bily Kun is a favorite local hangout for a chilled DJ-spun evening. First-time visitors usually gawk at the ostrich heads that overlook the bar but soon settle into the music groove of DJs and sometimes bands. Upstairs, O Patro Vys (☎ 514-845-3855) is a performing-arts hall that features anything from electronic installations to Patagonian song and Haïku art.

BLIZZARTS Map pp76–7 Bar

☎ 514-843-4860; 3956a Blvd St-Laurent; 🕑 8pm-3am; Ⓜ St-Laurent, then bus 55

Blizz is one of the Plateau's coolest little spots. Part bar, part pub and part club (at least, when the small dance floor fills up – which is fairly often), local DJs spin house, techno, electro, breaks, jazz, funk, hip-hop, roots and dub to a small crowd both trendy and friendly. The artwork on the walls, exhibited by local artists, changes every month or so.

BLUEDOG MOTEL Map pp76–7 Bar

☎ 514-845-4258; 3958 Blvd St-Laurent; 🕑 4pm-2am; Ⓜ St-Laurent, then bus 55

Next door to Blizzarts is Bluedog, painted – you guessed it – blue. With a younger but equally inebriated crowd of arty urban revelers, music varies from hip-hop to trendy post-electro and dancey beats. Sunday nights, there's a free keg on the dance floor!

EDGAR HYPERTAVERNE Map pp76–7 Bar

☎ 514-521-4661; 1562 Ave du Mont-Royal Est; 🕑 3pm-3am Tue-Sat, 4pm-3am Sun & Mon; Ⓜ Mont-Royal

Once a trashy dive, Edgar's appeals to the well-educated, cognac-sipping crowd of the Plateau. When they're not air-kissing groupies, the DJs serve up a discriminating mix of acid jazz and New Age music. The wine list is copious.

ELSE'S Map pp76–7 Bar

☎ 514-286-6689; 156 Rue Roy Est; 🕑 10am-3am; Ⓜ Sherbrooke

A warm and welcoming neighborhood bar where, as the saying goes, everyone knows your name. Settle into one of the worn chairs for an order of nachos, a tasty microbrew and a big portion of chat in front of the ceiling-high windows. Late-night jazz is a joy on weekends.

GOGO LOUNGE Map pp76–7 Bar

☎ 514-286-0882; 3682 Blvd St-Laurent; 5pm-3am; M St-Laurent, then bus 55

The retro-kitsch decor here looks like it was copied from an Austin Powers movie: '60s psychedelics, flower-power motifs, glistening vinyl and teardrop chairs. Friendly, flirty staff shake martinis and dance on the bar, while regulars jump the long lineups for a guaranteed party any night of the week. Though the loud music tends to get a bit Top 40, the festive formula works.

LES BOBARDS Map pp76–7 Bar

☎ 514-987-1174; 4328 Blvd St-Laurent; 3pm-3am; M St-Laurent, then bus 55

This good-natured bar in the Portuguese area of the Plateau draws a hyper-fun 20s crowd for its sizzling Latin American beats with French lyrics. It's pretty dead until around 10pm when it becomes standing-room only. There are free peanuts and modern-art exhibits. Expect a cover charge when bands are brought in.

L'ESCOGRIFFE Map pp76–7 Bar

☎ 514-842-7244; 4467 Rue St-Denis; 1pm-3am; M Mont-Royal

Though you're apt to see some dubious characters staggering into this small, dungeon-like bar, the 'um, what?' factor is part of L'Esco's punk-rock charm. Over the years many amazing bands have graced its tiny stage, and the bar continues to book bands some nights. Sundays, resident DJs spin laid-back new wave, indie rock and rockabilly, making this deliciously dark hole-in-the-wall ideal for knocking a few back with friends.

QUAI DES BRUMES Map pp76–7 Bar

☎ 514-499-0467; 4481 Rue St-Denis; 3pm-3am; M Mont-Royal

BEHIND THE BAR: FACES OF MONTRÉAL

Always sporting his trademark glasses, Paulo Branco's grin is a familiar sight to any Montréal barfly. He knows the city's bar scene inside out, having cheerfully been in the business since the early 1990s. He shook things up as a bartender before he co-opened Gogo Lounge (above) in 1999, and is also one of the forces behind Chez Serge (p148) and Candy. When he's not manning the post at his own places, he can be spotted gallivanting around town spreading 'good vibes.'

What do you love about the bar business? The pleasure my bars bring to people. I love to see people letting loose, singing at the top of their lungs, dancing like no one is watching. Life is unfortunately sometimes stressful and complicated, so I love making people forget about their routines.

What makes a good bartender? A good bartender is someone who always acknowledges customers at the bar, who is always good vibes, someone who can handle working more than one day at a time, who knows all the products he or she sells, and never raises their eyes when someone orders what could be a 'weird' drink. Someone who stays discreet, we see a lot of things like husbands with women other than their wives, girlfriends who have many boyfriends, and it's not for us to judge.

How about getting personally entangled with customers? As tempting as it can be, a good bartender generally doesn't sleep with patrons or colleagues. Very, very bad for business. Seducing and flirting is essential but more than that is a very big faux pas.

What makes Montréal's bar culture unique? We live in a city that is very open to all cultures, therefore I feel like our scene is a product of this great mix. Montrealers are very, very open-minded people.

How can visitors to the city best experience that special part of it? Walk around more in different neighborhoods, ask people of their age groups where they should go out, what is cool, what to avoid. Not always stick to the regular tourist circuits.

Any downside to this city? Montréal has only one flaw: cold weather in the winter. That's it.

What's the highlight of your career so far? I love what I do, I haven't worked a day in 15 years. I still can't believe I make a good living having fun. I've taken care of a lot of celebrities in my life but the most rewarding thing is finding out that couples who met in one of my bars are now married and have children. I've helped many people get laid throughout the years but I have also helped many people find true love. And that's hot!

A Parisian-style café with ornate framed mirrors, curlicue moldings and paneling that's been toasted brown by a million cigarettes. This fine venue for live jazz, rock and blues also has DJ-spun techno in the upstairs disco.

SALON OFFICIEL Map pp76–7 Bar
☎ 514-510-1733; 351 Rue Roy Est; 8pm-3am Tue-Sat; M Sherbrooke
This small neighborhood bar-meets-club hosts DJ nights with the city's best up-and-comers. Depending on the night, you can get rock, electro, punk or dancey stuff. Local club kids are well acquainted with this location in its former incarnation as Roy Bar, a skateboarder scene until 2007. Drinks are still cheap.

CHEZ JOSÉ Map pp76–7 Café
☎ 514-845-0693; 173 Ave Duluth Est; 7am-7pm Mon-Fri, 9am-7pm Sat, 10am-7pm Sun; M Sherbrooke
Jolly owner José often mans the small kitchen of this tiny, colorful café. Besides serving some of the 'hood's best and strongest espresso, it's lauded for its breakfasts, seafood soup and Portuguese sausage. A young, bohemian clientele tends to spill onto the sidewalk to chat while eyeing the cast of characters that meanders by.

LAÏKA Map pp76–7 Café
☎ 514-842-8088; 4040 Blvd St-Laurent; 9am-3am; M St-Laurent, then bus 55
This local hot spot is a favorite haunt of the electronic-music and new-media crowds. Peering in from the huge street-level windows, you can glimpse patrons tapping away on laptops over morning espresso, lunchtime tapas or evening libations. At night, DJs play electronica.

LES FOLIES Map pp76–7 Café
☎ 514-528-4343; 70 Ave du Mont-Royal Est; 9am-10:30pm Sun-Thu, 9am-12:30am Fri & Sat; M Mont-Royal
A cross between a bar, café and club, the oh-so-chic Folies has a DJ every night spinning trendy music and, much more importantly, the only sidewalk terrace on Ave du Mont-Royal. Too-thin models and creative types breeze in for a quick Zen sandwich or a Buddha salad with mineral water before evaporating into the night.

BIÈRES & COMPAGNIE
Map pp76–7 Pub
☎ 514-844-4394; 4350 Rue St-Denis; 3pm-1am; M Mont-Royal
This relaxed pub has a great choice of European and local microbrews alongside excellent pub grub and mussels.

RESERVOIR Map pp76–7 Pub
☎ 514-849-7779; 9 Ave Duluth Est; 3pm-3am Mon, noon-3am Tue-Fri, 10:30am-3am Sat & Sun; M St-Laurent, then bus 55
We adore this low-key, friendly brasserie. It's nice but not too pricey and the mixed crowd is artsy but unpretentious. If you appreciate good beer, the owners brew their own on the premises. A small kitchen prepares gourmet lunch, after-work snacks and weekend brunch. Come summertime, the 2nd-floor terrace overlooks the bustle of this busy corner.

YE OLDE ORCHARD PUB & GRILL
Map pp76–7 Pub
☎ 514-845-7772; 20 Rue Prince-Arthur Ouest; 11:30am-1am Mon, 11:30am-2am Tue & Wed, 11:30am-3am Thu & Fri, 8:30pm-3am Sat, 8:30pm-1am Sun; M Sherbrooke
A Celtic pub in the middle of the Plateau, who knew? Yes, the third Montréal location of this popular chain is a lucky charm for its diverse clientele. Beers on tap, good food, waiters in kilts, live music, sports broadcast on TV, poker tournaments and other fun events keep this place rollicking from afternoon to night.

COPACABANA Map pp76–7 Restaurant-Bar
☎ 514-982-0880; 3910 Blvd St-Laurent; noon-3am; M St-Laurent, then bus 55
Referred to simply as 'Copa' by the scruffy writers, actors, directors, artists and wannabes who frequent the place, this Blvd St-Laurent fixture is, in actuality, a restaurant. Plastic palm trees notwithstanding, it's more of a drinking hole for the broke and interesting. You're apt to eavesdrop on some fascinating conversationalists, most of whom aren't too bad to look at, either.

KOKO Map pp76–7 Restaurant-Bar
☎ 514-657-5656; 8 Rue Sherbrooke Ouest; 11am-3pm Mon-Fri, 6-10pm Sun-Thu, 6-11pm Fri & Sat, bar stays open later on weekends; M St-Laurent
The specialty cocktails and luxe surroundings of this loungey restaurant inside the

Opus Hotel attract jet-setters and the city's fashion crowd. DJs mix house music on weekends and there's a massive outdoor terrace for a swanky soiree with hip downtown flair.

LITTLE ITALY, MILE END & OUTREMONT

CHEZ SERGE Map p83 Bar

☎ 514-270-3262; 5301 Blvd St-Laurent; 5pm-3am Mon-Sat; M St-Laurent, then bus 55

Hockey games, unbridled kitsch and a mechanical bull reel in neighborhood kids, jocks and sports fans hankering for the bells and whistles of the sports arena – without actually being there. With cold beer, flashing lights and dancing staff, this homey bar gets out of control during hockey and soccer seasons.

LA PETITE IDÉE FIXE Map p83 Bar

☎ 514-272-1734; 4857 Ave du Parc; 11am-3am; M Laurier

Tucked inconspicuously among cheap apartments, swanky cafés and discount stores is your new favorite dive bar. It's got no frills but all the essentials: affordable drinks, genial staff, dim lights, barstools, a pool table and, best of all, a jukebox (a rarity in Montréal).

SNACK'N BLUES Map p83 Bar

☎ 514-278-8844; 5260 Blvd St-Laurent; 9pm-3am Mon-Sat; M St-Laurent, then bus 55

Does the name of this dive bar indicate a combination ridiculous or genius? Probably both. The 'snack' consists of an assortment of salty treats poured from a bag – pretzels, beer nuts, cheese crackers – all conspiring to satisfy your sodium-laced fantasies. The 'blues' is pretty good too, though played on a CD – and loudly.

CAFÉ OLIMPICO Map p83 Café

☎ 514-495-0746; 124 Rue St-Viateur Ouest; 7am-11:30pm; M Laurier

Its espresso is among the city's best, yet this no-frills Italian café is all about atmosphere, as hipsters and unassuming local rock stars rub elbows with elderly gentlemen and quirky regulars. Spring and summer, the benches of the sunny outdoor terrace, a people-watching paradise, are jammed.

CAFÉ ROMOLO Map p83 Café

☎ 514-272-5035; 272 Rue Bernard Ouest; 8am-3am; M Rosemont

This affordable Italian café is a beacon to the city's coolest artists, musicians and those in search of a welcoming place to sip a beer or coffee. Romolo's big-screen TV broadcasts international sports events such as soccer and hockey. Don't be intimidated by the shouting fans; if you can't beat 'em, join 'em.

LA CROISSANTERIE FIGARO Map p83 Café

☎ 514-278-6567; 5300 Rue Hutchison; 7am-1am; M Laurier

A charming Parisian bistro popular with well-heeled locals. Located in a converted old house in a beautiful residential neighborhood, its terrace is among the city's prettiest. Although it can be a bit of a scene, La Croissanterie is a lovely spot to nurse a coffee or cocktail all afternoon or evening. It also serves homemade croissants, salads and other goodies.

LE CAGIBI CAFÉ Map p83 Café

☎ 514-509-1199; 5490 Blvd St-Laurent; 10:30am-2:30am; M Laurier

Music-loving bohemians and Plateau eccentrics hold court at this vegetarian restaurant by day (see p137), bar by night. The large space is filled with a hodgepodge of plants and antique furnishings reminiscent of your great-grandmother's living room gone wild. Some nights, live bands play in the back room, while thrift-store-clad DJs spin on others.

LE CLUB SOCIAL Map p83 Café

☎ 514-495-0114; 180 Rue St-Viateur Ouest; 8am-2am; M Laurier

Another character-filled mecca literally a block away from Olimpico (left). Its terrace is equally sun-kissed, its coffee as flavorful, its ambience as lively. (Most patrons split their time between these two legendary establishments.) You're apt to spot a rock star or two bicycling down Rue St-Viateur or ordering a cappuccino after rolling out of bed at noon.

TOI MOI & CAFÉ Map p83 Café

☎ 514-279-9599; 144 Ave Laurier Ouest; 7am-11:30pm Mon-Fri, 8am-11:30am Sat & Sun; M Laurier

It's best known for breakfasts, but this chic Laurier café embodies Montréal's European flair from morning to night. As you sip your café au lait on the outdoor terrace (alongside sophisticates of all ages) you'll feel as if you've crossed the pond yourself. It also serves tasty lunch and dinner, and its specialty coffee, roasted on-site, is sold around town.

WHISKEY CAFÉ Map p83 — Lounge

☎ 514-278-2646; 5800 Blvd St-Laurent; 🕑 5pm-3am Mon-Fri, 6pm-3am Sat, 7pm-3am Sun; Ⓜ St-Laurent, then bus 55

Cuban cigars and fine whiskies are partners in crime at this classy joint, hidden near the industrial sector of the Mile End. The well-ventilated cigar lounge is separated from the main bar, which stocks 150 Scotch whiskies, plus wines, ports and tasting trios. Snacks range from foie gras to Belgian chocolates. Music is as sexy-smooth as the leather chairs.

DIEU DU CIEL Map p83 — Pub

☎ 514-490-9555; 29 Ave Laurier Ouest; 🕑 3pm-3am; Ⓜ Laurier

Packed every night with a young, francophone crowd of students, this unpretentious bar serves a phenomenal rotating menu of microbrew beers, running from classic ales to stouts that taste like chocolate or espresso, to a beer so smoky it's like sucking ash.

ASSOMOIR Map p83 — Restaurant-Bar

☎ 514-272-0777; 112 Rue Bernard Ouest; 🕑 11am-11pm (or later) Sun-Thu, 11am-2am Fri & Sat; Ⓜ Laurier

The science and art of bartending is the inspiration behind this bustling neighborhood resto. Professional staff know their drinks, mixing more than 250 cocktail choices, plus an extensive wine and beer selection. It even offers bartending classes. World cuisine features seviches and tartares. DJs complete the recipe.

BOND LOUNGE GRILL

Map p83 — Restaurant-Bar

☎ 514-759-6607; 101 Ave Fairmount Ouest; 🕑 11am-1am Mon-Wed, 11am-3am Thu & Fri, 10am-3am Sat, 10am-1am Sun; Ⓜ Laurier

Plush couches, comfy booths and a long bar make this tapas restaurant a chic-yet-affordable lounge where everyone feels welcome. It's ideal for large groups, the kitchen is open late and an outdoor smoking balcony lets you puff away in all weather, year-round.

BU Map p83 — Restaurant-Bar

☎ 514-276-0249; 5245 Blvd St-Laurent; 🕑 5pm-1am; Ⓜ Laurier

This elegant, Italy-inspired wine bar is where Montréal's real wine aficionados go to drink. The 500-strong list features approximately 25 wines by the glass, and the excellent service is worth the steep price. The kitchen whips up fine Italian antipasto dishes.

LA BUVETTE CHEZ SIMONE

Map p83 — Restaurant-Bar

☎ 514-750-6577; 4869 Ave du Parc; 🕑 4pm-3am; Ⓜ Laurier

An artsy-chic crowd of (mostly) francophone bon vivants and professionals loves this cozy wine bar. The staff know their vino, and the extensive list is complemented by a gourmet tapas menu. Weekends, the place is jammed from *5-à-7* into the wee hours. Alone, you can comfortably park it on a barstool, though you probably won't be solo for long.

SOUTHWEST & OUTER MONTRÉAL

BURGUNDY LION

Map pp44–5 — Bar-Pub-Restaurant

☎ 514-934-0888; 2496 Rue de Notre-Dame Ouest; 🕑 11:30am-3am Mon-Sat, 10am-3am Sun; Ⓜ Lionel-Groulx

This trendy take on the English pub features British pub fare, beers and whiskies galore and an attitude-free vibe where everyone (and their parents) feels welcome to drink, eat and be merry. Things get the good kind of crazy late-night weekends. Tip your cap to Queen Elizabeth, whose portrait adorns the bathroom door.

NIGHTLIFE

top picks

What's your recommendation? www.lonelyplanet.com/canada/montreal

NIGHTLIFE

Montréal nightlife is the stuff of legends; it's a vibrant, exciting and ever-evolving scene on the cutting edge of international trends. That's why touring bands and DJs rave about Montréal audiences: crowds here aren't afraid to let loose and really get into the musical experience. At live shows, they hoot, holler and sing along, and even in cooler-than-thou clubs people get down and dirty on the dance floor.

Its worldwide party-town reputation may make Montréal a bachelor-party and frat-weekend destination, but beyond such mainstream titillation is the real deal. From underground dance clubs to French hip-hop, dub reggae to breakbeat; comedy shows to supper clubs and the still-exciting Anglo indie rock so hyped in the recent past, Montréal after dark holds something for everyone. You just have to know where to look.

To plan your soirée, Montréal's weekly newspapers (*Hour, Mirror* and the French-language *Voir*) are good places to start. All three report on nightlife happenings including club events, live music, film, theater, comedy, spoken word, installation art and hybrids of the above.

Pick up event flyers stacked in cafés, clothing and record shops throughout the Plateau, Mile End and the Village. Check out websites and blogs like www.midnightpoutine.com, www.montrealstateofmind.com, www.33mag.com and www.nightlifemagazine.ca. But the best way to get the goods is simply to ask around.

While established events and club nights have their followings, when it comes to one-off concerts and parties (including raves), an event's appeal has little to do with where it's happening and everything to do with who is putting it on. (And, of course, the talent on the bill!) Beloved party brands throw events regularly, while indie concert promoters book shows of all musical genres virtually every night. You can catch big names and local up-and-comers before they top the charts.

Social dancing, especially tango, has also found a home in Montréal, and burlesque is big as well, with cabaret shows and dance classes. And then there are the music festivals – not just the big kahunas like the International Jazz Festival (www.montrealjazzfest.com), but also the little guys: Pop Montreal (www.popmontreal.com), Osheaga (www.osheaga.com) and Suoni del Popolo (www.casadelpopolo.com), as well as major gay and lesbian festivals like Divers/Cité (www.diverscite.org) and Black & Blue (www. bbcm.org).

Whatever your pleasure, grab a disco nap and be prepared to go all night. Although clubs close at 3am, there's always an after-party – just ask around.

PRACTICALITIES

Tickets & Reservations

Many pop and rock concerts take place in additional venues and clubs around town, so check local listings for shows you're interested in.

To purchase tickets for concerts, shows and festivals, go to the venue box office or call Admission (☎ 514-790-1245; www.admission.com) or Ticketmaster (☎ 514-790-1111; www.ticketmaster.ca). Admission has a dozen sales points around town including the Centre Infotouriste (Map pp62–3; ☎ 514-873-2015, 877-266-5687; 1255 Rue Peel).

Tickets for smaller shows and parties are sold in various shops around town, and details can be found on event flyers.

LIVE MUSIC

JAZZ, BLUES & LATIN

BISTRO À JOJO Map p72

☎ 514-843-5015; 1627 Rue St-Denis; 🕓 11am-3pm; Ⓜ Berri-UQAM

This smoky venue in the Quartier Latin is the nightly place for down 'n' dirty French and English blues and rock groups. Sit close enough to see the band members' sweat.

CUBANO'S CLUB Map pp62–3

☎ 514-878-9009; 1186 Rue Crescent; 🕓 10pm-3am; Ⓜ Place-des-Arts

This undisputed hub of salsa, Afro-Cuban and Latin jazz gives dance classes during the day and sets standards of dexterity at night. Highlights here are the big Cuban orchestras and mambo competitions during the International Jazz Festival.

HOUSE OF JAZZ Map pp62–3

☎ 514-842-8656; 2060 Rue Aylmer; 11:30am-12:30am Mon-Wed, 11:30am-1:30am Thu, 11:30am-2:30am Fri, 6pm-2:30am Sat, 6pm-12:30am Sun; M McGill

Formerly known as Biddle's, this mainstream-but-excellent jazz club and restaurant changed names when owner-bassist Charlie Biddle passed away in 2003. Today, Southern-style cuisine and live jazz are on the menu daily. Prepare to wait if you haven't reserved. Cover is usually only $5.

JELLO BAR Map pp62–3

☎ 514-285-2621; 151 Rue Ontario Est; 9pm-3am; M St-Laurent

Though it's not as trendy as it once was, this retro martini lounge has evolved into a lovely intimate jazz venue. Its glitzy decor of love seats and lava lamps feels like moseying backwards in time. Order one of 50-plus martinis.

LE VA-ET-VIENT Map pp44–5

☎ 514-940-2330; 3706 Rue Notre-Dame Ouest; 11am-11pm; M Lionel-Groulx

This popular 'cultural bistro' straddles the boundaries between restaurant, music venue and exhibition space. Order a tasty microbrew and special bistro burger and settle down to an evening of jazz, Irish folk or roadhouse funk.

UPSTAIRS Map pp62–3

☎ 514-931-6808; 1254 Rue Mackay; 5:30pm-2am, music from 8:30pm; M Guy-Concordia

This slick downtown bar hosts quality jazz and blues acts nightly, featuring both local and touring talent. The walled terrace behind the bar is enchanting at sunset, and the dinner menu features inventive salads and grilled meats and seafood.

SOUL & WORLD MUSIC

LE BALLATOU Map pp76–7

☎ 514-845-5447; 4372 Blvd St-Laurent; 9pm-2am Tue-Sun; M Mont-Royal

This dark, smoky Afro-Caribbean nightclub draws a multi-ethnic crowd and dancers of awesome sophistication. Shows are presented on weeknights for a varied cover; on weekends the cover (around $7) includes one drink. Check out the happy dancers in the photo gallery out front.

POP, ROCK & HIP-HOP

CAFÉ CAMPUS Map pp76–7

☎ 514-844-1010; 57 Rue Prince-Arthur Ouest; 3pm-3am; M Sherbrooke

This eternally popular student club has great live acts, mostly French rock and live Québécois bands. In summer people wander in from the cafés and restaurants along Rue Prince-Arthur for music and extra-cheap beer.

CASA DEL POPOLO Map pp76–7

☎ 514-284-3804; 4873 Blvd St-Laurent; noon-3am; M St-Laurent, then bus 55

One of Montréal's cutest live venues, this place is also known for its vegetarian platters, its talented DJs, and as an exhibition space for showing art-house films and spoken-word performances. It's associated with the tapas bar La Sala Rosa (p132) and concert venue La Sala Rossa (p154).

FOUFOUNES ÉLECTRIQUES Map pp62–3

☎ 514-844-5539; 87 Rue Ste-Catherine Est; 3pm-3am; M St-Laurent

A one-time bastion of the alternafreak, this cavernous quintessential punk venue still stages some neat events (eg a DJ 'star-maker' night or indoor skateboard contest). On weekends the student-grunge crowd plays pool and quaffs brews with electro kids and punk stragglers.

GREEN ROOM Map p83

☎ 514-284-6665; 5386 Blvd St-Laurent; 9pm-3am; M St-Laurent, then bus 55

Attitude-free DJs get this small bar hopping on weekends, and a loyal crowd of music-scene partiers, pub crawlers and Anglo hipsters packs the tiny dance floor and throws their hands in the air. Green Room also hosts rock and pop shows by local and out-of-town bands.

IL MOTORE Map p83

☎ 514-284-0122; 179 Rue Jean-Talon Ouest; M De Castelnau

The baby of the Casa del Popolo family and indie concert promoters Blue Skies Turn Black is a show venue hidden in an unsuspecting warehouse building. The well-planned space is perfect for catching the latest indie rock, alternative and pop acts.

KOLA NOTE Map p83

☎ 514-274-9339; 5240 Ave du Parc; box office noon-5pm Tue-Sat; M Laurier

This cozy Mile End hall fits 450 people and hosts world music, rock, jazz and comedy acts.

LA SALA ROSSA Map p83

☎ 514-284-0122; 4848 Blvd St-Laurent; M Mont-Royal, then bus 55

This lovely old performance hall is known for the touring bands that regularly take the stage. Housed in a former community center, the venue is affiliated with the Spanish bar and tapas restaurant downstairs (p132). A popular neighborhood hangout.

LA TULIPE Map pp76–7

☎ 514-526-4000; 4530 Ave Papineau; M Mont-Royal

Many of the city's coolest concerts take place in this beautifully restored and intimate theater. Located in the French-speaking east area of the Plateau.

LE DIVAN ORANGE Map pp76–7

☎ 514-840-9090; 4234 Blvd St-Laurent; 4pm-3am Tue-Sat; M St-Laurent, then bus 55

This fantastic space was launched as a kind of restaurant–entertainment venue co-op. There's a terrific artistic vibe here. On any given night there may be a DJ, world music performer or record launch.

LE NATIONAL Map p72

☎ 514-845-2014; 1220 Rue Ste-Catherine Est; M Beaudry

A 750-capacity concert venue situated in the Village. Since the cavernous old theater is only open when events are booked, it's best to check local listings.

CLUBBING

Blvd St-Laurent and Rue St-Denis are the two main club strips, with Rue Ste-Catherine in the Village housing a strip of gay clubs. Blvd St-Laurent, known as the Main, is traditionally more English-speaking and St-Denis more French, though the lines have blurred. It's best to dress snappy at nicer clubs, which have selective door policies and cover charges, but anything goes at most underground spots. Things tend to start late (after midnight) and close at 3am, but Montréal's after-hours scene is very happening, with clubs and private warehouse and loft parties. The scene on the sidewalk of Blvd St-Laurent at 3am is pretty interesting, as revelers pour onto the street, in search of 99-cent pizza (the late-night snack of choice) and after-parties.

> **GAY & LESBIAN SPOTS**
>
> The majority of gay and lesbian entertainment is in the Village along Rue Ste-Catherine Est, with a smattering of venues elsewhere in the city. For event listings, *Fugues* is a free monthly booklet for the gay and lesbian scene. Posters and flyers are also posted everywhere, announcing new clubs, raves, and gay-friendly events.

BALDWIN BARMACIE Map p83

☎ 514-276-4282; 115 Ave Laurier Ouest; 5pm-3am Mon-Sat, 7pm-3am Sun; M Laurier

Loud music, live DJs and beautiful 20- and 30-somethings rule this small, apothecary-themed lounge and club. Showy staff mix specialty cocktails while poppy 1960s-inspired design fills your party prescription for flirting. Don't let its location in a quiet, residential neighborhood fool you; this joint goes off.

BELMONT Map pp76–7

☎ 514-845-8443; 4483 Blvd St-Laurent; 9pm-3am; M Mont-Royal

This pub-meets-club is packed on weekends with yuppie Francophones in jeans and leather jackets who dig the laser light shows and hit-spinning DJs. Some don't get past the pool table, cheap beer and big-screen sports in the front bar.

BOURBON COMPLEX Map p72

☎ 514-268-4679; 1574 Rue Ste-Catherine Est; 3pm-3am; M Beaudry

This gay entertainment complex looks big enough to get lost in. There's La Track, a popular disco-bar with a leather boutique, and the Mississippi Club for dancing, live cabaret and drag shows.

CHERRY Map p48

☎ 514-841-9669; 417 Rue St-Pierre; 10pm-3am Thu-Sat; M Square-Victoria

Danceable old-school house music and decadent antics are *de rigueur* at this upscale party spot known for its red leather booths and on-fire dance floor. Things tend to get going late at night, thanks to DJs who keep the energy grooving.

CLUB 737 Map pp62–3

☎ 514-397-0737; 1 Pl Ville-Marie; 🕑 5pm-3am; Ⓜ McGill

Try pre-dinner drinks with the glam set on the 43rd floor – the romantic skyline never disappoints. Serious cruising goes on among the office crowd of 30-somethings.

CLUB OPERA Map pp62–3

☎ 514-842-2836; 32 Rue Ste-Catherine Ouest; 🕑 10pm-3am Sat & Sun; Ⓜ St-Laurent

This massive dance club is adored for its bells, whistles and glitz. The spiffed-up clientele tends to be mostly young suburbanites and sexy students, but the promise of world-class DJs and VIP guests fill this hot spot week after week.

ELECTRIC AVENUE Map pp62–3

☎ 514-285-8885; 1469 Rue Crescent; 🕑 10pm-3am Thu-Sat; Ⓜ Guy-Concordia

Duran Duran, INXS, Depeche Mode…the spirit of '80s video pop lives on in this basement club in party-down Rue Crescent. A few mirrors and lamps on satin-covered walls make up the decor, but no matter; from around 11pm on weekends you'll find the dance floor is packed with nostalgic 30-somethings.

LE DRUGSTORE Map p72

☎ 514-524-1960; 1366 Rue Ste-Catherine Est; 🕑 8am-3am; Ⓜ Beaudry

This cavernous eight-story complex has nine theme bars, boutiques, a large delicatessen and a dance club in the basement. For bad hair days there's even a hairdresser. Lesbians and gays have staked out their terrain on different floors.

LE LOFT Map pp62–3

☎ 514-281-8058; 1405 Blvd St-Laurent; 🕑 9pm-3am Tue-Sat; Ⓜ St-Laurent

A spiffed-up crowd of 18-to-25s turns up for mainstream rock and alternative on two dance floors, rough-edged murals and a great rooftop terrace. The wide metal staircase and ventilation ducts give the place a warehouse feel; the usual gear is jeans and T-shirts.

LE SOCIAL Map pp62–3

☎ 514-849-8585; 1445 Rue Bishop; 🕑 10pm-3am Tue-Sat; Ⓜ Guy-Concordia

Inside a converted 19th-century mansion, Le Social is fun spot to while away the night among its three floors. Chandeliers, stained-glass windows and wild locally crafted artwork all add to the eclectic ambience. The crowd is hit-or-miss, depending on the night, with DJs spinning old-school funk, house, electropunk or straight-up rock.

MADO CABARET Map p72

☎ 514-525-7566; 1115 Rue Ste-Catherine Est; 🕑 2pm-3am; Ⓜ Beaudry

Mado is a flamboyant celebrity who writes a column in *Fugues*, the gay entertainment mag. Her cabaret is a local institution, with drag shows featuring an assortment of hilariously sarcastic performers in eye-popping costumes. Shows take place weekend and Tuesday nights.

PARKING NIGHTCLUB Map p72

☎ 514-282-1199; 1296 Rue Amherst; 🕑 3pm-3am; Ⓜ Berri-UQAM

Located in an old garage repair shop, this multilevel New York–ish club is one of the city's best underground dance spots. Though it's definitely a gay cruising joint, Parking Nightclub attracts a mixed, eclectic crowd of dance-ready partiers. The long-standing Thursday 'Overdose' nights are especially fun.

SAPHIR Map pp76–7

☎ 514-284-5093; 3699 Blvd St-Laurent; 🕑 10pm-3am Tue, Thu, Fri & Sat; Ⓜ St-Laurent, then bus 55

Underground punk, Goth, glam and industrial are in full effect at this cavernous two-story club. Cheap drinks, unbridled dance floors and no attitude make this club experience a dark and dirty free-for-all.

SAT Map pp62–3

☎ 514-844-2033; 1195 Blvd St-Laurent; Ⓜ St-Laurent

Officially called La Société des Arts Technologiques, this slick warehouse and new media space promotes partying as much as digital art. DJs and performance artists push the envelope with banks of multimedia installations, while cult party brands like NEON throw parties here. Dancing and carousing with the arty, electro-loving glam set.

top picks

CLUBS

- La Sala Rossa (p154) Anything from punk to world music.
- Parking Nightclub (p155) Gay meat market with Halloween flair.
- Tokyo Bar (below) Trendy cool club with a great terrace.
- Baldwin Barmacie (p154) Chic flirting and excellent service.
- SAT (p155) Avant-garde dance parties and slick multimedia.

SKY PUB & CLUB Map p72

☎ 514-529-6969; 1474 Rue Ste-Catherine Est; 2pm-3am Mon-Fri, noon-3am Sat & Sun; M Beaudry

This is one of those popular Village complexes designed to suck you in for an entire Saturday night of partying. If you're a gorgeous guy or looking for one, start the evening in the 1st-floor pickup pub before heading up to the dance floors (disco and energized house/hip-hop). The roof terrace is a perfect place to catch the Loto-Québec International Fireworks Competition (p14) in summer.

SUITE 701 Map p48

☎ 514-904-1201; 701 Côte de la Place-d'Armes; 5pm-3am; M Place-d'Armes

Housed in the former lobby of posh Hôtel Place-d'Armes, which in turn is located in a former bank, this elegant marble-filled space attracts a corporate crowd ready to get their party on.

TIME SUPPERCLUB Map p48

☎ 514-392-9292; 997 Rue St-Jacques Ouest; 7:30pm-3am Thu-Sat; M Square-Victoria

Dress for success at this Miami-inspired supper club, where models and wannabes shake their booties upon a lit-up catwalk. Special events featuring international DJs and celebrities attract paparazzi-seekers who dig high-energy house music and overall gorgeousness.

TOKYO BAR Map pp76–7

☎ 514-842-6838; 3709 Blvd St-Laurent; 10pm-3am; M Sherbrooke

This successful little club reels in scenesters and suburbanites in their 20s and early 30s, who dance up a storm on two dance floors. Weekends are more mainstream, while a cool crowd hangs out Wednesdays for 'rock night.' The huge rooftop bar and patio rules on summer nights! Great staff, too.

TRIBE HYPERCLUB Map p48

☎ 514-845-3066; 390 Rue St-Jacques Ouest; 10pm-3am Thu-Sun; M Square-Victoria

Celebrity guests like P-Diddy and Paris Hilton, house, trance and techno DJs, and sexy patrons make this very hyper nightclub the go-to spot of thousands. Don't forget the monstrous 100,000-watt sound system. If you're ready for bottle service, book a table in advance.

UNITY II Map p72

☎ 514-523-2777; 1171 Rue Ste-Catherine Est; 10pm-3am Thu-Sun; M Beaudry

This old Village favorite tragically burned down just before the 2006 World Outgames, but has come back with a bang. The rebuilt version features not only a club and pub but kitsch Bamboo bar, pool tables and rooftop terrace.

ZOOBIZARRE Map p83

☎ 514-270-9331; 6388 Rue St-Hubert; M Rosemont

One of Montréal's coolest party rooms, this intimate venue hosts special DJ nights and concerts featuring amazing local and international talents. You have to be 'in the know' to know about it, so consider yourself informed.

AFTER-HOURS CLUBS

After-hours clubs pick up the slack once the bars close at 3am. They don't serve alcohol but are made for dancing and all-night club experiences.

CIRCUS AFTER HOURS Map p72

☎ 514-844-3626; 1439 Rue St-André; 1:30am-10am Thu-Sat; M Berri-UQAM

Sometimes featuring circus performers and dancers, this hot spot is more glamorous than you might expect from an after-hours joint. Big-name DJs join local residents behind the decks, to the dancing thrills of glo-stick-brandishing ravers, and city clubbers not yet ready to call it a night. Get there early to avoid the long line; alcohol served before 3am.

RED LITE AFTER HOUR DISCOTHEQUE Map p72

☎ 450-967-3057; 1755 Rue de Lierre, Laval; hours vary, generally 2am-11am Fri & Sat

This 1850-sq-meter club has been around for decades, and the sketch factor – dark, pulsing, trippy – is through the roof. Its remote location in the French suburbs of Laval adds to the other-world feeling, and also explains its clientele, mostly people who live or work nights in Laval. With house and hip-hop rooms, it gets great DJs from around the world. A cab from the city should take about 20 minutes.

STEREO Map p72

☎ 514-286-0325; 858 Rue Ste-Catherine Est; 2am-11am Fri & Sat; M Berri-UQAM

Montréal's underground house-music giant has opened and closed for various reasons throughout the years. Still featuring a sound system so amazing regulars gush about out-of-body-experience, Stereo is open for business once again, attracting anyone – gay, straight, students, drag queens – looking to lose sleep in style.

BALLROOM & WESTERN DANCE CLUBS

CLUB BOLO Map p48

☎ 849-4777; 960 Rue Amherst; 7pm-midnight Fri only; M Beaudry

This is a one-of-a-kind, gay country-and-western line-dancing bar in the Village.

DOREMI Map pp44–5

☎ 514-274-5456; 505 Rue Bélanger Est; 6pm-midnight Thu-Sun; M Beaubien

If you want to keep your fox-trot fresh and your polkas perky, this all-round dance club in north Montréal has excellent music for ballroom dancing. The crowd is 30s and 40s, dedicated amateurs.

THE WHEEL Map pp44–5

☎ 514-489-3322; 3373 Blvd Cavendish; 8pm-1am Mon; M Vendome, then bus 105

Hosted by bluegrass star Bob Fuller, Hillbilly Night has been going strong for more than 40 years. Monday nights, this members-only NDG dart club is open to anyone

BEHIND THE DECKS: FACES OF MONTRÉAL

Hardworking Evelyne Drouin, also known as DJ Mini, plays around the city and has been the resident DJ and artistic director of Overdose Thursdays at Parking Nightclub (p155) for six years. She's earned her cred in the city's scene and knows it like the back of her hand.

What do you love about DJing? Expressing myself through music, the energy I get from it and give with it, sharing the music I enjoy. There's a really powerful thrill when you have a big crowd in front of you, screaming, bouncing and dancing like crazy, nothing beats it. It's kinda like an amusement ride that can last hours, same kind of rush. It can really make a crowd feel magical and really gives me the chills…

When and how did you get started? I started DJing at Blue Dog about nine years ago. The owner thought I had the ear, I always paid so much attention to music. She gave me my first record bag and the bar keys, and said, 'When you're feeling ready, you can have you own night. For now, practice when we're closed, or before the DJs show up.' I did, and started inviting people to see me play. Eventually, I got better, saved up money to buy equipment, and more promoters asked me to work with them.

What's the best part of Montréal nightlife? There's a bit of everything, we're pretty spoiled, which means we really get the cream of the crop. The DJs we hear here will remind you more of Europe than North America, at least, in the underground scene… There are so many local DJs, which creates a positive competition, and you've got to get very good until you can consider making a living out of it.

How can visitors to the city best experience that special part of it? Go underground! Come to the Plateau, the Village, the Mile End. That's where you'll find the fun parties and the friendly crowds. Go see some shows, ask around. and enjoy tech-house, techno and electro at will! There's also a very cool breakbeat scene, and drum 'n' bass, but you've got to dig harder to find those events…

Is there a challenge to being a DJ in Montréal? For a DJ, it's not easy, it may be discouraging at times. And for the party-goers, there's so much choice, sometimes you just wish you could clone yourself!

What's the highlight of your career so far? Putting out my first original album, *Audio Hygiene* (2006). It made people understand I was not only a DJ, but also an artist on the production level. We're now putting out remixes of it in Europe, and have a lot more coming.

hankering for some old-time bluegrass, cowboy and fiddle music. Montréal isn't exactly a cowboy capital, but local heroes are full of smiles and authenticity. Yeehaw!

LATIN DANCE CLUBS

CACTUS Map pp76–7

☎ 514-849-0349; 4461 Rue St-Denis; 🕑 10pm-3am Thu-Sat; Ⓜ Mont-Royal

Two floors of infatuation with things Latin, the Cactus is always packed with dancers ready to strut their stuff. Salsas and merengues are performed with astonishing ease by patrons poured into sexy outfits. Regulars are more than happy to show you the moves if your timing is off after a few *cervezas* (beers).

L'ACADÉMIE DE TANGO ARGENTIN Map pp76–7

☎ 514-840-9246; www.academietangoargentin.com; 4445 Blvd St-Laurent; 🕑 hours vary; Ⓜ Mont-Royal

Tango dancing has enjoyed a surge of popularity in Montréal and the Academy is an excellent place to learn all the moves. Ascend through the beat-up door to the 325-sq-meter studio and learn this sensual dance in private and intensive workshops as well as private parties. Prices and schedules vary.

SALSATHÈQUE Map pp62–3

☎ 514-875-0016; 1220 Rue Peel; 🕑 9pm-3am Wed-Sun; Ⓜ Peel

This bright, busy, dressy place presents large live Latin bands pumping out tropical rhythms. During the breaks slurp a margarita in one of the movie-theater seats and watch the 25-to-50s crowd gyrate into exhaustion.

BILLIARDS

ISTORI Map pp62–3

☎ 514-396-2299; 486 Rue Ste-Catherine; 🕑 11am-midnight Mon-Wed, 11am-3am Thu-Sat; Ⓜ McGill

Unwind at two bars or 20 pool tables in this loft-style pool hall on the 2nd floor, a world away from Rue Ste-Catherine below. Beers are tasty (Hoegaarden, Leffe, Stella Artois) and you can obliterate an order of nachos or tacos before your next full clearance.

SHARX Map pp62–3

☎ 514-934-3105; 1606 Rue Ste-Catherine Ouest; 🕑 11am-3am; Ⓜ Guy-Concordia

This underground cavern has no less than 36 pool and billiard tables, rows of TV screens beaming sports and a post-apocalyptic feel. The cool bowling alley is bathed in fluorescent light with glowing balls and pins.

COMEDY

COMEDYWORKS Map pp62–3

☎ 514-398-9661; 1238 Rue Bishop; 🕑 8pm-3am Mon-Sat; Ⓜ Guy-Concordia

This intimate comedy club has been around forever and is a fun place to catch emerging and established comedy talent. Mondays are open mic, while on Tuesdays and Wednesdays noted improv troupe On the Spot Players takes the stage. Reservations required.

ERNIE BUTLER'S COMEDY NEST Map pp62–3

☎ 932-36378; 2313 Rue Ste-Catherine Ouest; 🕑 8pm-3am Wed-Sat; Ⓜ Guy-Concordia

Named after its late founder, who passed away in 2007, this Montréal comedy club, based in the Pepsi Forum, remains the place to catch the hottest touring and local comedy talent, from improv to stand-up. Wednesdays are open-mic night, and the club serves dinner and a full bar.

CASINOS

CASINO DE MONTRÉAL Map p58

☎ 514-392-2746; Île Notre-Dame; 🕑 24hr; Ⓜ Jean-Drapeau, then bus 167

One of the 10 largest casinos in the world, occupying the former French pavilion from the Expo '67. The dress code is not very strict but turning up in shorts and beachwear is a definite no-no in this government-run good-time establishment, operated by provincial agency Loto-Québec. Glitzy Las Vegas–style shows are staged here too.

CASINO DE MONT-TREMBLANT

☎ 514-392-2746; 300 Chemin des Pléiades, Mont-Tremblant; 🕑 11am-1am Sun-Wed, 11am-3am Thu-Sat

Another government-run luxury casino is just a dice-roll away from the city in the posh Laurentian resort town of Mont-Tremblant (p245). With 400 slot machines, baccarat, poker, roulette, blackjack and craps, the new casino (opened in 2009) provides glitz and glamour in a stunning country setting. It's located on the mountain.

THE ARTS

top picks

What's your recommendation? www.lonelyplanet.com/canada/montreal

THE ARTS

Montréal is definitely Canada's unofficial arts capital, with both French- and English-language theater, dance, classical and jazz music and all sorts of interesting blends of the above on stage virtually every night of the week. The city's bilingualism makes it creatively unique and encourages opportunity for creative collaborations and cross-pollinations that light up the performing arts scene.

While the city may be small compared to other artistic capitals (like New York and London), Montréal boasts some world-class companies that are renowned on the international circuit: a symphony orchestra, the Orchestre Symphonique de Montréal (p166); an opera, L'Opera de Montréal (p165); and a ballet company, Les Grands Ballets Canadiens (p162). And don't forget Cirque du Soleil (see the boxed text, p162), the magical, Québec-born circus of dance, music and acrobatics that forever changed the art form. The presence of Québec's massive French-language film and TV industry, and US productions that shoot here, have made the picturesque city a hotbed of film and TV production. Especially during spring and summer, you're likely to see movie shoots taking place on downtown streets and Hollywood stars nonchalantly roaming around.

Montréal is referred to as 'festival city' come summertime, since literally dozens (if not hundreds) of culture and arts festivals take over city life. The festivals are special because they tend to showcase international stars alongside local up-and-comers. As well, most of these festivals offer free public events in addition to privately ticketed shows, so the arts are truly accessible to everyone, regardless of social class or income. Some festival highlights include literary festival **Blue Metropolis** (www.bluemetropolis.org); French-language song-and-dance festival **Les Francofolies** (www.francofolies.com); the artistic and gastronomic **Montréal High Lights Festival** (www.montrealenlumiere.com); the **Montréal Chamber Music Festival** (www.festivalmontreal.org); Montréal Fringe Festival (p165); Just for Laughs (p165) comedy festival; and, of course, the Montréal International Jazz Festival (p14). This huge unconventional jazz festival brings jazz, blues and pop legends like Stevie Wonder and Aretha Franklin to stages throughout the city, shared with cool, cutting-edge younger artists from Montréal and the world, many of whom don't fall into conventional musical categories. Thousands of tourists come to town for this event, considered one of the world's top music festivals. Every year, a massive free outdoor gala show turns the city into one big concert.

The *Montreal Gazette* and French-language *La Presse* daily newspapers are great resources for arts and culture listings, as are the city's three free weeklies: *Mirror, Hour* (in English) and *Voir* (in French). Or call **Info-Arts Bell** (☎ 514-790-2787) for information about plays, concerts and various cultural events.

CINEMAS

Montréal has its share of multiplex cinemas, but many also include foreign or independent films in their repertoire. More interesting are the several independent movie houses and repertory theaters. The website www.cinema-montreal.com is excellent, with reviews and details of discount admissions. The repertory houses offer double bills and midnight movies on weekends. These cinemas are sometimes cheaper than the chains showing first-run films.

AMC FORUM Map pp62–3

☎ 514-904-1250; cnr Rue Ste-Catherine Ouest & Ave Atwater; Ⓜ Atwater

This may seem like just another multi-theater monster cinema, but it's worth keeping an eye on these 22 screens. They are likely to have the most recent locally produced indie smash, foreign hit or subtitled Québécois film hit, as well as Hollywood blockbusters.

CINÉMA IMAX DU CENTRE DES SCIENCES DE MONTRÉAL

Map p48

☎ 514-496-4629; Quai King-Edward; Ⓜ Place-d'Armes

Located in the Centre des Sciences de Montréal (p56), this theater brings specially produced adventure, nature and historical films to oversized screens. Watch Cirque du Soleil, dinosaurs or marine life come tumbling into your lap with the aid of 3-D glasses and translation headsets. Great for kids.

FILM CITY MONTRÉAL

With its European ambience and big-city energy, Montréal is a movie-maker's dream. Since the 1970s the city has hosted hundreds of productions, helped by the favorable exchange rate and government tax credits, all of which make shooting here a bargain for US filmmakers. Hollywood celebrities like Robert de Niro, Cate Blanchett and Halle Berry can often be spotted dining in the sleek restaurants along Blvd St-Laurent, or sipping a cognac at the scenic Old Port. The stars feel comfortable mixing in public because Montrealers don't make a fuss about them. They're used to it!

The diversity of the urban landscape hands the producers a great variety of scenery choices. Especially popular are Old Montréal, the Plateau and the McGill University campus where you'll run across 'film-in-progress' signs throughout the year. In George Clooney's *Confessions of a Dangerous Mind* (2002) the cobblestone streets of Old Montréal stood in for East Berlin and Helsinki.

Of course, locally produced film and TV productions in French and English comprise an important part of the city's cinema industry. The French-language sphere, in particular, is a mini-Hollywood in and of itself. But everyone loves it when big US productions come shoot in 'Hollywood North' because it creates extra work for everyone: local film crews, hotels, bars, restaurants and the city's pool of actors.

While gala awards events like the annual Prix Gémeaux celebrate the best of French-language TV production in Canada, Montréal's largest and most glamorous film event is the Montréal World Film Festival (p15), attracting fans from around the globe to view 400-plus films from six continents.

CINÉMATHÈQUE QUÉBÉCOISE

Map p72

☎ 514-842-9763; 335 Blvd de Maisonneuve Est; admission $4; 🕑 1-9pm Tue-Sun; Ⓜ Berri-UQAM

A university-flavored venue noted for its French and Québécois avant-garde films. In the lobby there's a permanent exhibition on the history of filmmaking as well as a TV and new-media section.

EX-CENTRIS CINEMA Map pp62–3

☎ 514-847-2206; 3536 Blvd St-Laurent; Ⓜ St-Laurent

A showcase for independent films from around the world. It's sleek and geared to provide pure movie enjoyment (popcorn and soft drinks are banned, for example, because they distract from the movie-watching experience). Besides several cinemas, this place is full of high-tech film gadgetry you have to see to believe, starting with the box-office cashier whose disembodied head speaks to you through electronic portholes when you buy your tickets.

LE NOUVEAU CINÉMA DU PARC

Map pp62–3

☎ 514-281-1900; 3575 Ave du Parc; tickets $10; Ⓜ Place-des-Arts, then bus 80

Located in the lower level of La Cité mall complex, Montréal's English-language repertory cinema is a tried-and-true favorite of Plateau cinephiles. It shows cult classics as well as cool new releases and lots of foreign films. Despite the shabby decor, its charm and authenticity add to the cinematic experience.

NATIONAL FILM BOARD

Map p72

☎ 514-283-9000; www.nfb.ca; 1564 Rue St-Denis; 🕑 noon-9pm Tue-Sun; Ⓜ Berri-UQAM

This cutting-edge cinema in the Quartier Latin offers regular screenings from an archive of 6000 films, documentaries and animated shorts, but the real attraction is its Cinérobothèque – make your choice and a robot housed in a huge, glass-roofed archive plucks your selection from the stacks. Then relax and settle back into individual, stereo-equipped chair units to watch your personal monitor. There is also a huge Canadian video and DVD collection available.

PARAMOUNT & IMAX CINEMAS

Map pp62–3

☎ 514-842-5828; 977 Rue Ste-Catherine Ouest; Ⓜ Peel

An entertainment monstrosity with crowds darting through junk-food kiosks amid a riot of flashing lights and booming sounds to get to the IMAX theater and screens showing Hollywood blockbusters in this multilevel cinema.

FILM FESTIVALS

Montréal has so many film festivals that it's hard to keep track. In addition to Fantasia (p14), the Montréal World Film Festival (p15) and Festival du Nouveau Cinéma de Montréal (p15), check out the following festivals.

FESTIVAL INTERNATIONAL DU FILM SUR L'ART

www.artfifa.com

A March festival devoted to films and documentaries about art from all over the world.

CINEMANIA

www.cinemaniafilmfestival.com

This November festival features films from French-speaking countries, all subtitled in English for non-native speakers.

DANCE & PERFORMING ARTS

Considered Canada's dance capital, Montréal has always boasted an avant-garde and extremely vibrant dance scene. These days, styles like ballet, modern, jazz, hip-hop, Latin social dancing and tango exist side by side with cutting-edge contemporary dance that fuses various styles and incorporates theater, music and digital art. As such, Montréal is home to many internationally renowned companies, such as La La La Human Steps (☎ 514-277-9090), O Vertigo Danse (☎ 514-251-9177), Tangente (☎ 514-525-5584) and the popular theatrical touring dance company Cirque Eloize (☎ 514-596-3838). The fact that Canada's National Circus School (☎ 514-982-0859) is based here certainly helps feed fresh, unconventional talent into the dance and performing-arts scene.

CIRQUE DU SOLEIL

Over the past two decades Cirque du Soleil (literally 'Circus of the Sun') has pushed the boundaries of traditional circus arts with its astounding acts of dexterity, emotional story arcs, ethereal costume and Vegas-worthy spectacles. While Cirque's touring shows remain the company's bread and butter, Montrealers often enjoy first look at new shows in the Old Port. If you need further proof of the company's visionary approach to arts and life, consider that founder Guy Laliberté was the first private Canadian space explorer thanks to Space Adventures, blasting off alongside Russian and American astronauts. For more information on current shows, call ☎ 514-722-2234 or visit www.cirquedusoleil.com.

For more about Cirque du Soleil, see the boxed text, p29.

AGORA DE LA DANSE Map pp76–7

☎ 514-525-1500; www.agoradanse.com; 840 Rue Cherrier; Ⓜ Sherbrooke

Based in the striking old Palestre National building in the Plateau, this contemporary dance center explores and promotes modern and experimental forms. Two studios are open for instruction to the public, and its student and independent dance companies stage regular performances.

ESPACE TANGENTE Map pp76–7

☎ 514-525-5584; 840 Rue Cherrier; Ⓜ Sherbrooke

For more than 25 years, this cutting-edge contemporary-dance company (now with a 91-seat theater within the Agora de la Danse, above) presents regular and touring shows, classes and weekly artist talks. One of the city's best.

LES BALLETS JAZZ DE MONTRÉAL

☎ 514-982-6771

This Montréal modern-dance troupe has achieved international acclaim since its birth in the 1970s. Performances are full of sensual grace and physical fireworks. When it's not out on an international tour it plays at it home stage in Place des Arts (p164) and venues like the Théâtre de Verdure (p165) in Parc LaFontaine, where it often kicks off the fall arts season.

LES GRANDS BALLETS CANADIENS

Map pp76–7

☎ 514-849-8681; www.grandsballets.qc.ca; 4816 Rue Rivard; Ⓜ Mont-Royal

You can be assured of a treat with tickets to Québec's leading ballet troupe. Aside from playing four shows annually in Montréal, the 34 dancers play a major role on the world stage, with two tours every year. Its classical and modern programs are both innovative and accessible to general audiences. Dance classes for children are also available.

USINE C Map p72

☎ 514-521-4493; 1345 Ave Lalonde, off Rue Panet; Ⓜ Beaudry

This former jam factory in the Village is home to the award-winning Carbone 14 theatrical dance troupe that performs here regularly. Its two flexible halls (450 and 150 seats) can be rejigged to accommodate circuses or raves. To bump into its talented performers, head for the cozy basement café next to the changing rooms.

CONCERT HALLS & ARENAS

BELL CENTRE

Map pp62–3

☎ 514-790-2525, 877-668-8269; www.centrebell.ca; 1260 Rue de la Gauchetière; ⏲ noon-6pm Mon-Fri, box office to 9pm on event days; Ⓜ Lucien-L'Allier or Bonaventure

When it's not hosting matches of the city's beloved Montréal Canadiens hockey team, this 21,000-seat arena in downtown hosts all the big concerts. The likes of U2 and Céline Dion usually end up here when they're in town.

CLUB SODA Map pp62–3

☎ 514-286-1010; 1225 Blvd St-Laurent; adult/student $5/3; ⏲ 9pm-3am; Ⓜ St-Laurent

This venerable club hosts some of the city's coolest concerts as well as offbeat performances of all musical genres. Call for concert schedule.

METROPOLIS

Map pp62–3

☎ 514-844-3500; 59 Rue Ste-Catherine Est; Ⓜ St-Laurent

Housed in a former art-deco cinema, this beautiful old space (capacity 2300) features live bands and hip touring concerts, and is one of our favorite venues to see a rock show. It's sometimes used as a party or rave venue with DJs and dancing. Buy tickets at the box office (1413 Rue St-Dominique) around the corner.

OLYMPIC STADIUM

Map pp44–5

☎ 514-252-8687; 4141 Ave Pierre-de-Coubertin; Ⓜ Viau

Since the Montréal Expos baseball team moved to Washington DC this stadium isn't getting the same workout it used to, but it still occasionally hosts a variety of other events such as rock concerts, stunt-car shows, trade fairs and the occasional Canadian Football League game.

MUSIC MAN: FACES OF MONTRÉAL

Jordan Officer plays guitar and mandolin as a solo artist and with jazz musician Susie Arioli, and produces, arranges and writes jazz, blues and country music. Born in 1976, this warmhearted redhead honed his musical skills in the city's blues bars before gaining international acclaim alongside Arioli as a jazz musician to be reckoned with. Together, they've released six albums, and Jordan also has his own band.

How did you get started as a musician? As a kid I played violin and other instruments; guitar in bands in high school. My actual career started when I was 18, playing in blues, jazz, country, rock and folk bands. My first albums were with singer Susie Arioli, and our big break was a show at the Montréal Jazz Festival in 1998. Two days later, we opened for Ray Charles! That brought lots of attention to the band, we released our first album and toured Canada, the US, Europe and Japan.

Do you remember your first time on stage? Playing violin recitals at the age of three – I started very young. My first time with my band was at a place called L'Extérieur, previously the G-Sharp bar, a tiny but legendary blues venue (it has reopened as the Barfly; see p145). We played there once a week for about a year. It was also a place where, back in high school, I would go often to see my favorite local blues bands, in particular the Stephen Barry Band as well as blues legends like Hubert Sumlin, Jimmie Rogers, Pinetop Perkins, Gatemouth Brown…

How has being from Montréal influenced you? As a place to learn, exposure to tons of great musicians and artists! There has always been a strong music scene in Montréal, full of people to be inspired by. Also, there are a lot of music programs at universities here, which bring in young players from throughout the country. However, there are no real paying gigs in Montréal for local bands. So, rather than settle into a career of playing bars one is obliged to put out albums, tour and build a career internationally, which ends up being a blessing. In the meantime, the local gigs are fun and a great laboratory where you feel free to try stuff out and develop, take risks.

How can visitors best experience Montréal's unique music scene, both French and English? Local bars where people try stuff out, where musicians go to see what other musicians are up to. Barfly, L'Escogriffe, Quai Des Brumes, Le Divan Orange (I notice that place in particular has lots of both English and French bands), Verre Bouteille, Casa del Popolo. And slightly bigger venues like Le Lion D'Or, La Sala Rossa and others. Also, Montréal's festival culture features both big names and local acts.

What are your favorite Montréal music/arts events? The Montréal Jazz Festival, Monday nights at the Wheel Club, George Jones playing live in Montréal…if ever that happens.

PEPSI FORUM Map pp62–3

☎ 514-933-6786; 2313 Rue Ste-Catherine Ouest; M Atwater

This flashy entertainment arena is built on the site of the old Canadiens hockey rink. Cinemas with 22 screens, restaurants, a Jillian's pool and game emporium as well as Ernie Butler's Comedy Nest (p158) rank among the biggest tenants.

PLACE DES ARTS Map pp62–3

☎ 514-842-2112; Rue Ste-Catherine Ouest; M Place-des-Arts

Montréal's spacious municipal center for the performing arts has excellent acoustics. There are five theaters: the biggest, the 3000-seat Salle Wilfrid-Pelletier, hosts the city's symphony as well as ballet, opera and dance troupes. The eponymous square is the focal point of Montréal's International Jazz Festival (p14).

POLLACK CONCERT HALL
Map pp62–3

☎ 514-398-4547; 555 Rue Sherbrooke Ouest; M McGill

McGill University's main music hall features concerts and recitals from its students and faculty, notably the McGill Chamber Orchestra. It's in the stately 19th-century building behind the statue of Queen Victoria.

THÉÂTRE OUTREMONT Map p83

☎ 514-495-9944; 1248 Rue Bernard Ouest; box office noon-6pm Tue-Fri, to 5pm Sat; M Outremont

Built in 1929, this theater was both a repertory cinema and a major concert hall until it was shuttered in the late 1980s. The municipality of Outremont later brought it back to life and the theater was reopened in 2001. Now, everything from pop concerts and dance performances to Monday-evening film screenings take place here.

THÉÂTRE ST-DENIS Map p72

☎ 514-849-4211; 1594 Rue St-Denis; box office noon-9pm; M Berri-UQAM

This Montréal landmark and historic movie house hosts touring Broadway productions, rock concerts and various theatrical and musical performances. Its two halls (930 and 2200 seats) are equipped with the latest sound and lighting gizmos and figure prominently in the Just for Laughs festival (opposite).

THEATER

CENTAUR THEATRE
Map p48

☎ 514-288-3161; 453 Rue St-François-Xavier; M Place-d'Armes

Montréal's chief English-language theater presents everything from Shakespearean classics to works by experimental Canadian playwrights. It occupies Montréal's former stock exchange (1903), a striking building with classical columns.

MAINLINE THEATRE
Map pp76–7

☎ 514-849-3378; 3997 Blvd St-Laurent; M Mont-Royal

Located on the Main (hence the name) this intimate indie theater presents mostly new plays. It also serves as headquarters for the annual Montréal Fringe theater festival.

MONUMENT-NATIONAL
Map pp62–3

☎ 514-871-2224; 1182 Blvd St-Laurent; M St-Laurent

Shows here run the gamut from Oscar Wilde to Sam Shepard with everything from acting, directing and technical production performed by graduating students of the National Theatre School. There are two halls, one with 800 seats, the other with 150. The smaller theater stages about three original works a year by student playwrights.

SAIDYE BRONFMAN CENTRE
Map pp44–5

☎ 514-739-2301; 5170 Chemin de la Côte-Ste-Catherine; M Côte-Ste-Catherine

Montréal's Jewish theater stages dramatic performances in English, Yiddish and Hebrew – although as one of the city's most prominent professional theater venues, plays presented are by no means exclusively Jewish. The center also hosts a variety of other arts events throughout the year, including dance and musical recitals, puppet shows and readings.

THÉÂTRE DE QUAT' SOUS Map pp76–7

☎ 514-845-7277; 100 Ave des Pins Est; M Sherbrooke

Housed in a former synagogue, this cozy theater is a launchpad for the careers of young singers, directors and playwrights. Its forte is intellectual and experimental drama.

THÉÂTRE DE VERDURE Map pp76–7

☎ 514-872-2644; Parc LaFontaine; ⏲ Jun-Aug; Ⓜ Sherbrooke

This open-air theater hosts musical, dance and drama events in the summer months, and something of a folk-festival atmosphere prevails. Movies are also shown on a big pondside screen, and everyone shows up with blankets and ice chests.

THÉÂTRE DU NOUVEAU MONDE

Map pp62–3

☎ 514-866-8668; 84 Rue Ste-Catherine Ouest; Ⓜ St-Laurent

The New World Theater specializes in classic dramas like Shakespeare's *Hamlet* or Molière's *Les Précieuses Ridicules*. The French-language venue is a 1912 movie house and theater renovated in 1996, now with snappy technical gear. There are matinee and evening performances.

THÉÂTRE DU RIDEAU VERT

Map pp76–7

☎ 514-845-0267; 4664 Rue St-Denis; Ⓜ Mont-Royal

This quality French-language venue has an elegant stage that's well suited to classic plays. Its lineup includes both repertory and contemporary works with a preference for timeless works, like a French-language performance of the Jewish classic *Fiddler on the Roof*! The theater's stage designs, costumes and lighting have earned accolades.

THÉÂTRE LA CHAPELLE Map pp76–7

☎ 514-843-7738; 3700 Rue St-Dominique; Ⓜ Sherbrooke

This little mecca of contemporary works presents cutting-edge theater and dance. It's also a studio space for artistic creation, aiming to mentor and encourage young, cutting-edge artists while contributing new energy to the city's cultural life.

THÉÂTRE STE-CATHERINE Map p72

☎ 514-284-3939; 264 Rue Ste-Catherine Est; Ⓜ Berri-UQAM

From improv to theater, stand-up comedy to music concerts, this relatively new venue presents a variety of shows: Oscar Wilde one night, burlesque dance the next. Its Sunday Night Improv (sketch and comedy) performances are quite popular with the city's theatrical community. Admission for the improv is $7, $5 for students.

THEATER FESTIVALS

FESTIVAL DE THÉÂTRE DES AMÉRIQUES

⏲ 514-842-0704; www.ftq.qc.ca, in French

Around 160 shows from countries throughout the western hemisphere are featured at this festival from late May to early June.

FESTIVAL JUSTE POUR RIRE (JUST FOR LAUGHS)

☎ 514-845-2322; www.hahaha.com

This festival draws big names like Jerry Seinfeld or Drew Carey, plus Canadian comics (in both French and English) in late July.

MONTRÉAL FRINGE FESTIVAL

☎ 514-849-3378; www.montrealfringe.ca

This famous festival features avant-garde dancing, music and plays in intimate venues around town during the second half of June.

CLASSICAL MUSIC

I MUSICI DE MONTRÉAL Map pp62–3

☎ 514-982-6038; 279 Rue Sherbrooke Ouest; Ⓜ Place-des-Arts

Under the leadership of Moscow-born violinist-cellist Yuri Turovsky, this 15-member chamber ensemble has won many awards for its baroque and contemporary performances. Over the past 20 years I Musici, which has its home stage at the Place des Arts (opposite), has recorded almost 50 CDs and toured the world.

L'OPERA DE MONTRÉAL Map pp62–3

☎ 514-985-2258; Place des Arts; ⏲ box office 9am-5pm Mon-Fri; Ⓜ Place-des-Arts

Holds lavish stage productions that feature big names from Québec and around the world. The specialty is classics such as *Mefistofele, Aïda* and *Carmen;* translations (French or English) are run on a video screen above the stage. Tickets cost around $50 to $125 during the week and slightly more on Saturday.

MCGILL CHAMBER ORCHESTRA

☎ 514-487-5190

Founded in 1939, this fine chamber ensemble is one of Canada's oldest. Concerts series are held at McGill University's Pollack Concert Hall (opposite) and other venues around the city. Its annual performance of the *Messiah* is extremely popular.

ORCHESTRE MÉTROPOLITAIN DU GRAND MONTRÉAL Map pp62–3

☎ 514-598-0870; 505 Rue Sherbrooke Est; Ⓜ Sherbrooke

This hip 58-member orchestra is made up of young professional musicians from all over Québec led by conductor Yannick Nézet-Séguin. The orchestra's mission is to democratize classical music, so besides the swish Place des Arts, you may see it playing Mahler or Hayden in churches or colleges in even the city's poorest neighborhoods for reduced admission.

ORCHESTRE SYMPHONIQUE DE MONTRÉAL Map pp62–3

☎ 514-842-9951; Place des Arts, 260 Blvd de Maisonneuve Ouest; Ⓜ Place-des-Arts

This internationally renowned orchestra plays to packed audiences in its Place des Arts home. Its Christmas performance of *The Nutcracker* is legendary. Rock-star conductor Kent Nagano, a Californian with a leonine mane and stellar credentials, took over as music director in 2006. Until then the Orchestre Symphonique de Montréal (OSM) was performing under the baton of guest conductors. Check for free concerts at the Basilique Notre-Dame (p47), the Olympic Stadium (p90) and in municipal parks in the Montréal area.

COFFEEHOUSES & SPOKEN WORD

The spoken-word scene is quite popular in Montréal, often linked to the hip-hop community. Some of the most exciting and interesting stuff is being done on university campuses. Since these events tend to move around from bar to bar, it's best to check out the bulletin boards or flyers at McGill or Concordia Universities where new and underground performances are regularly announced. Bars such as Barfly (p145) also hold spoken-word events, and hip-hop crews and improvisational music collectives like Kalmunity (www.kalmunity.com) organize special spoken-word and improv events.

YELLOW DOOR Map pp62–3

☎ 514-398-6243; 3625 Rue Aylmer; 🕑 Sep-Jun; Ⓜ McGill

This earthy university-hangout coffeehouse claims to be Canada's oldest, having given refuge to US draft dodgers in the '60s. The program is English-language folk and blues acts, poetry and literature readings, but the schedule is erratic; call for upcoming events. There's no alcohol license and smoking is taboo.

SPORTS & ACTIVITIES

top picks

- **Jogging** (p170), **bird-watching** (p171), **ice-skating** (p170) or **cross-country skiing** (p171) in **Parc du Mont-Royal**
- **Rafting the Lachine Rapids** (p171)
- **Kayaking the Canal de Lachine** (p171)
- **Watching a Montréal Canadiens hockey game at the Bell Centre** (p176)
- **Strøm Nordic Spa** (p176)

What's your recommendation? www.lonelyplanet.com/canada/montreal

SPORTS & ACTIVITIES

No matter the season, Québecers are an active bunch, out jogging, cycling and kayaking on warm summer days, with cold wintry days bringing ice-skating, cross-country skiing and pickup hockey games on frozen lakes.

Sporting events – which can essentially be subcategorized as glorious hockey followed by those *other* activities – draw huge numbers of Montrealers. The essential experience – whether you're a fan or not – is to journey into the great hockey hall of the Bell Centre to catch the Canadiens glide to victory (or perhaps shuffle soberly away in defeat – as has more often been the case in recent years).

Other key spectator moments include joining the roaring crowds at Molson Stadium, home to the mighty Alouettes (a Canadian football team with plenty of muscle despite being named after a songbird). You can also root for the Montréal Impact as it reaches for soccer stardom at its new home stadium, built in 2008. Last of all is the famed Grand Prix du Canada Formula One race, which may or may not be on the calendar when you read this (see p177).

For those who'd rather join the fray than sit and watch, there are plenty of big events where you can channel your inner Armstrong. The Tour de l'Île (p13), for instance, is one of Montréal's best-loved participatory bike rides, when tens of thousands fill the streets for a fun cycle (but 50km, mind you) around Montréal. There's a palpable energy in the city that even nonpedalers enjoy.

In winter, green spaces become cross-country ski trails, and ponds and lakes transform into outdoor skating rinks at places like the Old Port and Parc LaFontaine.

Other great ways to enjoy the scenery include white-water rafting down the Lachine Rapids (or surfing them if your life insurance policy is in order), kayaking idly down the Canal de Lachine, or simply heading to 'the Mountain' (Parc du Mont-Royal) for a bit of unplanned activity (running, pedal-boating, ice-skating, snowshoeing, bird-watching or – if it's Sunday – gyrating and/or pounding your drums with hippie folk at the free-spirited tam-tam jam, p80). There's much to do in this grand little city.

After all the physical activity, it's good to know Montréal won't leave you hanging when your gams are aching. There are plenty of places around town where you can drop in for a yoga class or book in for a massage at a beautifully set spa on the edge of a lake.

ACTIVITIES

Like elsewhere in Canada, the choice of outdoor activities in Montréal is impressive, no matter when you're visiting. Lovely waterfront strolls and jogs through tree-lined neighborhoods are part of the fun. You can also find aquatic adventures – rafting, kayaking, sailing and canoeing, as well as walking on water (winter only).

CALÈCHE

Horse-drawn carriages are one of the most popular (and romantic – assuming Silver didn't go overboard on the morning oats) ways to see downtown. Calèche drivers pony up in front of Place-d'Armes and next to Pl Jacques-Cartier by the Old Port. You can even sometimes score sleigh rides through Parc du Mont-Royal once the winter weather arrives. Drivers have a fair bit of knowledge about the old quarters, and will happily rattle off some history along the way. A half-hour ride is $45, one hour is $75.

CYCLING & IN-LINE SKATING

Montréal teems with cycling and skating paths; more than 600km of paths in total. One very fine route leads 14km southwest from the edge of Old Montréal along the Canal de Lachine (p86) with a lot of history en route. Tables are scattered along the canalside park, which makes a fine place to relax with a picnic. The path continues all the way out to Lac St-Louis and beyond for those who want a serious workout. You can also head to the Atwater market (p61), just a few steps from the canal, where you can assemble a delicious meal of fresh goodies.

There are also cycling paths along the Canal de l'Aquedoc (south of the Canal de Lachine), and a route that follows the St Lawrence River, passing by the Lachine Rapids.

If you're biking across town, there's a good bike path (physically separated from traffic) along Blvd de Maisonneuve. Other bike lanes lie along Rue Berri (between the port and Sherbrooke), Rue McGill and Rue St-Urbain, among other places.

Île Notre-Dame (p58) offers lovely views of Old Montréal, plus the chance to speed around a Formula One track – the smooth Circuit Gilles-Villeneuve (Map p58) is the speediest track in town for in-line skating and cycling. It's open and free to all except when Nascar races come to town (and during the Grand Prix du Canada).

In the river northeast of downtown at Parc des Îles de Boucherville, there are 22km of trails around a string of island parks connected by bridges. A ferry departs from Quai Jacques-Cartier in the Old Port hourly in the summer.

For an overview of all the routes in Greater Montréal, pick up a cycling map at the tourist office or at any bicycling shop. Québec's bicycling portal (www.velo.qc.ca) has loads of information – bicycling events, bike-friendly accommodations, local cycling clubs and other *velo* (bicycle) news.

Gear Rental

ÇA ROULE MONTRÉAL Map p48

☎ 514-866-0633, 877-866-0633; www.caroulemontreal.com; 27 Rue de la Commune Est; bicycle per hr/day from $8/25, in-line skates from $9/20; 🕑 9am-8pm Apr-Oct; Ⓜ Place-d'Armes

Nicely located near the Old Port, Ça Roule Montréal has a wide selection of bicycles, in-line skates, spare parts and a good repair shop. Each rental includes a lock, helmet, patch kit, cycling map and (in the case of in-line skates) full protective gear. Prices listed are for weekday rentals; weekends cost more. You can also rent a fat-tired cruiser for tootling around the Port for $5 per hour. You can also hire children's bikes, tandems and bike trailers for pulling the little ones along while you pedal.

LE GRAND CYCLE Map pp76–7

☎ 514-525-1414; www.legrandcycle.com; 901 Rue Cherrier Est; bicycle per hr/day $10/30; 🕑 9am-7pm Mon-Fri, 9am-5pm Sat, noon-5pm Sun; Ⓜ Sherbrooke

Le Grand Cycle is another fine place to get you rolling, with good eight-speed hybrids for rent plus all the extras. The diner-like counter is a nice touch: you can grab a sandwich, cold drink or espresso and get the latest on Montréal's rapidly changing bike scene.

LA MAISON DES CYCLISTES Map pp76–7

☎ 514-521-8356; www.velo.qc.ca; 1251 Rue Rachel Est; bicycle per day $30; 🕑 9am-6pm Mon-Fri, 10am-5pm Sat & Sun; Ⓜ Mont-Royal

Described as the nerve center of Québec's biking culture, this three-story house in the Plateau is an essential stop for avid cyclists in the city. Here you'll find a shop with

MONTRÉAL BY BIXI

Montréal is one of the most bike-friendly cities in North America, with hundreds of kilometers of bicycle paths across the city. In 2009 the city unveiled Bixi (www.bixi.com), an extensive network of bike-renting stations around town, with bikes available from May to November. For short jaunts, it's great value (one-day/one-month subscription fee is $5/28; bikes are free the first half-hour and $1.50 for the next half-hour). The network includes more than 5000 bikes scattered around 400 stations. Although some citizens were skeptical when Bixi first appeared, the project was quickly hailed as a success as Montrealers took to the bikes in droves. Other cities also took notice. In late 2009 Bixi was contracted by officials from other cities to set up networks in both Boston and London.

If you plan to use a Bixi bike, you probably won't have to walk far to find a station. Once there, it's fairly simple to obtain a bike – a solid (heavy) three-speeder with puncture-resistant tires that make for a surprisingly smooth ride. You insert your credit card (unless you have a monthly or annual membership) and are then granted a code to unlock any of the bikes. You then have 30 minutes free to get to your destination (after that, you'll start to receive incremental charges). The majority of Bixi stands display a network map showing other docking stations across the city. Once you dock the bike, you must wait five minutes before checking out another one. Just reinsert your credit card and you'll be ready to go. (Bixi tallies up the charges at the end of a 24-hour period. As long as you always return a bike within 30 minutes, you'll only be charged the one-time fare.) Although the bikes are fine for short hops, the pricing structure discourages longer trips (it costs $1.50 for the second 30 minutes, $3 for the next 30 minutes and $6 for every 30 minutes thereafter). If you're planning a long day's outing along the Canal de Lachine or a trip of any distance, it's better to rent from a more conventional outfit.

cycling books, maps and guides; the Velo Québec association (involved in developing one of the largest bicycling networks in North America); a travel agency for planning biking trips; and loads of info on upcoming events. There's also a cozy café here. It's right along the bike path that runs above Parc LaFontaine.

MY BICYCLETTE Map pp62–3

☎ 514-998-6252; www.mybicyclette.com; 2985 Rue St-Patrick; bicycle per hr/day $10/30; 10am-7pm mid-May–mid-Oct; M Charlevoix

Located along the Canal de Lachine (just across the bridge from the Atwater market), this place rents bikes and other gear during the warmer months. It also sponsors city bike tours, and the repair shop next door is a good place to go if your bike conks out on the Lachine Canal path.

WALKING & JOGGING

Montréal has terrific places for jogging. Dedicated runners favor Parc du Mont-Royal (p79), which is laced with walking and jogging trails. Parc LaFontaine (p75) and Île Ste-Hélène (p57) offer less challenging terrain. You can also jog the pathways lining the Canal de Lachine (p86).

RUNNING ROOM Map pp44–5

☎ 514-483-4495; www.runningroom.com; 4873 Rue Sherbrooke Ouest; 9:30am-9pm Mon-Fri, 9:30am-6pm Sat, 8:30am-5pm Sun; M Vendôme

This terrific Canadian chain store is devoted completely to running: clothing, gadgets, everything. It holds all kinds of clinics, touching on everything from walking to marathon training. If you are just looking for some company, it has free group runs Wednesday at 6pm and Sunday at 8:30am (just show up at the store). Its website has handy downloadable running-route maps (including the best route to get to its store!), plus routes for all the cities in which it has stores.

ICE-SKATING

ATRIUM LE 1000 Map pp62–3

☎ 514-395-0555; www.le1000.com; 1000 Rue de la Gauchetière Ouest; adult/child $6/4, skate rental $5.50; M Bonaventure; P

Enjoy year-round indoor ice-skating at this excellent glass-domed rink near Gare Centrale. On weekends, kids and their families have a special session from 10:30am to 11:30am. Special events change regularly – like the summertime 'Bermudas Madness,' a cheesy good time of skating in shorts and T-shirts while DJs spin Hawaiian and summer-inflected beats. Call for operating hours as the schedule changes frequently.

LAC DES CASTORS Map pp62–3

☎ 514-843-8240; Parc du Mont-Royal; admission free, skate rental $7; 10am-9pm weather permitting; 11; P

Nestled in the woods near the large parking lot and pavilion, the 'Beaver Lake' makes for wonderful ice-skating in the bucolic surrounds of Mont-Royal. The season usually runs from late December to mid-March.

PARC DU BASSIN BONSECOURS Map p48

☎ 514-496-7678; Old Port; adult/child $5/4, skate rental $7; 10am-9pm Mon-Wed, until 10pm Thu-Sun weather permitting; M Champ-de-Mars, 14; P

This is one of Montréal's most popular outdoor skating rinks, located on the shore of the St Lawrence River next to the Pavilion du Bassin Bonsecours. DJs add to the festivities. At Christmas time there's a big nativity scene.

SKIING & SNOWBOARDING

Though Montrealers often flock to the nearby mountains to ski and snowboard, several areas within the city limits have cross-country trails. Parc du Mont-Royal (p79) has 20km of marked, groomed ski trails and a couple of slopes; it's best to go during the week as the crowds wear the snow thin on weekends. Parc LaFontaine (p75), Île Ste-Hélène (p57) and the trails along the Canal de Lachine (p86) are easy for beginners. The Parc Nature du Cap-St-Jacques (p93) to the west of Montréal is one of the prettiest options, with 46km of trails about a half-hour's drive northwest of downtown.

Gear Rental/Purchase

ALTITUDE SPORTS PLEIN AIR Map pp76–7

☎ 514-847-1515; www.altitude-sports.com; 4140 Rue St-Denis; 10am-6pm Mon-Wed, 10am-9pm Thu & Fri, 10am-5pm Sat, noon-5pm Sun; M Mont-Royal

This well-stocked Montréal sports boutique has various outdoor and ski gear available for hire.

BIRD-WATCHING ON 'THE MOUNTAIN'

Parc du Mont-Royal has some fantastic bird-watching opportunities, particularly in the spring. A great number of migrators use the area as a passage on their way to breeding grounds. In both the park and in nearby Cimetière Mont-Royal keep a lookout for screech owls, red-shouldered hawks, northern orioles, rose-breasted grosbeaks, bluebirds, olive-sided flycatchers, indigo buntings and many more species. In the winter hardy bird lovers come out for walks along the bird-feeder circuit that goes around the Summit Loop (the park places feeders out from November to April). Guided walks with a member of the park's conservation staff are held on Saturdays from January to mid-March. Contact Les Amis de la Montagne (☎ 514-843-8240; www.lemontroyal.qc.ca; 1260 Chemin Remembrance), located at Maison Smith (p80), for more information.

DIZ Map pp44–5

☎ 514-486-9123; 48 Ave Westminster, Montréal West; noon-6pm Mon-Wed, noon-9pm Thu & Fri, noon-5pm Sat & Sun

If you're not a snowboarder it's kind of hard to figure out what the fuss is about just by looking around, but fans of the sport say if you're in Montréal and need a board or any kind of accessory under the sun, then this place is it. A good smattering of skateboards rounds out the offerings but they're clearly a sideline. By car, take the Décarie Expressway to the Westminster exit.

LAC DES CASTORS PAVILION Map pp44–5

☎ 514-843-8240; Parc du Mont-Royal; 10am-6pm Wed-Sun in winter; 11; P

This place rents out ski equipment, snowshoes and toboggans right on the slopes of 'the Mountain.'

RAFTING & JET BOATING

RAFTING MONTRÉAL Map pp44–5

☎ 514-767-2230; www.raftingmontreal.com; 8912 Blvd LaSalle; jet boat adult/teen/child $49/39/29, rafting adult/teen/child $40/34/23; 9am-6pm May-Sep; M Angrignon, then bus 110; P

Located near the Lachine Rapids in LaSalle, this outfit offers the same brand of adrenaline-charged white water as Saute Moutons (below). In addition to 75-minute jet-boat trips, you can sign up for 12-person rafting adventures (which last 2¼ hours). A new service is the 8km self-guided descent down the St Lawrence in either a kayak ($34) or a five-person mini-raft ($125). The trip includes transport to the headwaters, equipment and instruction. Reserve ahead.

SAUTE MOUTONS Map p48

☎ 514-284-9607; www.jetboatingmontreal.com; 47 Rue de la Commune Ouest, Old Port; jet boat adult/teen/child $65/55/45, speedboat adult/teen/child $25/20/18; 10am-6pm May-Oct; M Champs-de-Mars; P

Thrill seekers will get their money's worth on these fast, wet and bouncy boat tours to the Lachine Rapids. The aluminum jet boats take you through foaming white water, from Quai de l'Horloge, on hour-long tours. There are also speedboats that take half-hour jaunts around the Parc des Îles from the Jacques Cartier pier. Reservations are a must.

KAYAKING & CANOEING

CLUB DE CANOË DE COURSE DE LACHINE Map pp44–5

☎ 514-634-4402; www.canoelachine.com; 2105 Blvd St-Joseph; kayak/canoe per hr $10/15; 4-8pm Mon-Fri & 10am-8pm Sat & Sun mid-May–mid-Jun, 10am-8pm daily mid-Jun–mid-Aug, 4-7pm Mon-Fri & 1-7pm Sat & Sun mid-Aug–early Sep

Out near the edge of Lac St-Louis, this canoeing club rents out canoes as well as single and double kayaks. Visitors are welcome, though it's more geared to folks in the club who come to train or participate in dragon boat races (canoe instruction is also available). If you really want a workout, it's a lovely bike ride to the club, following along the canal.

H2O ADVENTURES Map pp62–3

☎ 514-842-1306; www.aventuresh2o.com; 2985B Rue St-Patrick; kayak/pedal boat per hr $15/10; 9am-9pm Jun-Aug; M Charlevoix

Located across from the Atwater market on the banks of the Canal de Lachine, H2O rents out kayaks and pedal boats for a gentle glide along the water. There is a variety of courses on offer – white-water, rolling clinic, introductory two-hour classes ($39 to $45). H2O has multi-day trips throughout the summer to an island in the Rouge River.

KAYAK SANS FRONTIÈRES

Map pp44–5

☎ 514-595-7873; www.ksf.ca; 7770 Blvd LaSalle; 9am-9pm Jun-Aug; M De l'Église, then bus 58

Adrenaline junkies should head straight for this 'school of river surfing and kayaking.' Utilizing the rushing white water of the Lachine Rapids, KSF will get you out on the river and taking on the beast, in the safety of a tiny snub-nosed kayak or atop a surfboard. You can take instruction in beginner, intermediate or advanced surfing or kayaking. Day-long surf courses cost $100, and a three-hour kayak class costs $50. Wet suits are available for hire. Those with skills can rent kayaks for $15 to $20 for four hours.

PARC DE LA RIVIÈRE-DES-MILLE-ÎLES

Map pp44–5

☎ 450-622-1020; www.parc-mille-iles.qc.ca; 345 Blvd Ste-Rose; kayak/canoe per hr $11/12, per day $37/40; 1-7pm Mon-Fri, 9am-7pm Sat & Sun May, Jun & Sep, 9am-8pm daily Jul & Aug; M Cartier, 73; P

This is one of the most beautiful spots for canoeing and kayaking. This park on the Rivière des Mille-Îles near Laval has 10 islands where you can disembark on self-guided water tours, and about 10km of the river (including calm inner channels) are open for paddling. You can rent a wide range of watercraft, including 20-seat *rabaskaw* – canoes like those used by fur trappers.

CRUISES

AML CRUISES Map p48

☎ 514-842-3871, 866-856-6668; www.croisieresaml.com; Quai King-Edward; 1½hr tour adult/child $27/14; 11:30am, 2pm & 4pm; M Champ-de-Mars

These 1½-hour river tours in a glassed-in sightseeing boat take in the Old Port, Île Ste-Hélène (p57) and Îles de Boucherville. Other options include night cruises with a band, dancing and a gourmet dinner. Early and late cruises are in high season only.

CROISIÉRE PATRIMONIALE DU CANAL Map pp62–3

☎ 514-283-6054; www.pc.gc.ca/lachinecanal; Marché Atwater; 2hr tour adult/child $18/11; 1pm & 3:30pm Sat & Sun mid-May–late Jun & Sep, 1pm & 3:30pm daily late Jun–Aug; M Lionel-Groulx

Operated by the Parks Canada service, this sightseeing cruise offers a good overview of one of North America's most dramatic urban renewal projects. A Parks Canada interpreter brings to life the canal's industrial and commercial history and you visit an archaeological site. The two-hour round trip begins at the canal dock near the pedestrian footbridge just south of Atwater market and goes all the way to the Old Port locks.

LE BATEAU MOUCHE Map p48

☎ 514-849-9952, 800-361-9952; www.bateaumouche.ca; Quai Jacques-Cartier; 1hr tour adult/child $23/11, 1½hr tour adult/child $27/11; 1hr tour 1:30pm, 3pm & 4:30pm, 1½hr tour 11:30am mid-May–mid-Oct; M Champ-de-Mars

This comfortable, climate-controlled sightseeing boat with a glass roof offers narrated cruises of the Old Port and Parc Jean-Drapeau. Dinner cruises of 3½ hours are also available. Phone ahead for reservations and make sure you board the vessel 15 minutes before departure.

LE PETIT NAVIRE Map p48

☎ 514-602-1000; www.lepetitnavire.ca; Quai Jacques-Cartier; 45min tour adult/child $16/8, 2hr tour adult/child $25/15; mid-May–Aug; M Champ-de-Mars

Aside from rowing a boat yourself, this outfit offers the most ecologically friendly boat tours in Montréal. The silent, electric-powered Le Petit Navire takes passengers on 45-minute tours departing hourly around the Old Port area. Equally intriguing are the 1½-hour cruises up the Canal de Lachine (departing weekends at 2pm).

SAILING & WINDSURFING

L'ÉCOLE DE VOILE DE LACHINE

Map pp44–5

☎ 514-634-4326; www.voilelachine.com, in French; 3045 Blvd St-Joseph, Lachine; boat rental per hr $20-35, per 3hrs $35-80; 10am-6pm Mon-Thu, 9am-8pm Sat & Sun May-Sep; M Lionel-Groulx, then 173; P

Located on the edge of Lac St-Louis, the Lachine Sailing School organizes regattas on the St Lawrence River, gives free boat tours in late June and early July and rents light craft (windsurf boards, small sailboats and catamarans). Qualified instructors give windsurfing and sailing courses in summer. One-week sailing courses cost $160.

ROCK CLIMBING

CENTRE D'ESCALADE HORIZON ROC

Map pp44–5

☎ 514-899-5000; www.horizonroc.com; 2350 Rue Dickson; admission from $15; 5-11pm Mon-Fri, 9am-6pm Sat, 9am-5pm Sun; M L'Assomption, 85; P

This enormous 2600-sq-meter climbing gym features 12m walls and hundreds of lead and top-rope routes. Indeed, it's one of the world's largest indoor climbing facilities and even hosted the 2008 North American Continental Climbing Championship. Whether or not you have experience, you'll have to take an accreditation test in order to receive ongoing access to the center. You can also sign up for lessons. All the gear (rope, harness, climbing shoes, etc) is on hand for hire. There's also a café on-site.

TENNIS

Scattered across the Island of Montréal are hundreds of outdoor tennis courts open to the public during warmer months (typically from late April until mid-October). Some are free, others require fees to use them. Handy courts for visitors include Parc LaFontaine (Map pp76–7; ☎ 514-872-3626; 9am-11pm Mon-Fri, 9am-9pm Sat & Sun), with 14 courts, and Parc Jeanne-Mance (Map pp76–7; ☎ 514-872-5520; 4422 Ave de l'Esplanade; 9am-11pm Mon-Fri, 9am-9pm Sat & Sun), with 12 courts. Fees at these courts are $9 per hour; call ahead to reserve a space.

For the location of other courts, visit Montréal's official city portal at www.ville.montreal.qc.ca.

UNIPRIX STADIUM Map pp44–5

☎ 514-273-1234; www.stadeuniprix.com; 285 Rue Faillon Ouest; court per hr outside/inside from $10/25; 7am-11pm; M de Castelnau, 55; P

This modern complex inside Jarry Park near Little Italy is home to 12 indoor and 10 outdoor courts, plus an 11,000-seat center court that hosts the Rogers Cup. Rates vary depending what time of year – and more importantly what time of day – you want to reserve a court (peak times are weekends and after 5pm on weekdays). There's an early-riser special ($10 per hour inside or outside) from 7am to 8am. Racket rental is available.

GOLF

The Montréal region has some fine courses but most are outside the city proper, such as in the resort areas of the Laurentians. Tourisme Québec (☎ 514-873-2015; www.bonjourquebec.com) has a complete listing.

GOLF DORVAL Map pp44–5

☎ 514-631-6624; www.golfdorval.com; 2000 Rue Reverchen; Mon-Fri $24-39, Sat & Sun $27-43; dawn-dusk May-Oct; P

This semiprivate club near Pierre Trudeau Airport has a fairly challenging 18-hole course, a lighted driving range and two putting greens. It's a 20-minute drive northwest of downtown; take Autoroute 20 Ouest to exit 53, Blvd des Sources Nord.

LE VILLAGE GOLF Map pp44–5

☎ 514-872-4653; 4235 Rue Viau; 9 holes $22; 6:30am-7pm; M Viau, 132; P

Hone your drives and putts at this straightforward municipal course just east of Olympic Stadium.

SKATEBOARDING

UNDERWORLD Map p72

☎ 514-284-6473; www.underworld-shop.com; 251 Rue Ste-Catherine Est; 11am-6pm Sat-Wed, 11am-9pm Thu & Fri; M Berri-UQAM

Skateboarding is popular in Montréal and devotees come out with a vengeance after winter. Pl Émile-Gamelin is nearby and is the first place kids head after swinging by here.

SPEED KARTING & PAINTBALL

CIRCUIT 500/ACTION COMMANDO PAINTBALL Map pp44–5

☎ 514-254-4244; www.action500.com; 5592 Rue Hochelaga; karting 24hr, paintball noon-midnight Mon-Sat, noon-10pm Sun; M L'Assomption, 85; P

Canada's largest indoor go-kart center provides plenty of amusement for gearheads. Sharpen your skills in 10-minute races on a large indoor karting track. The racers blaze around the circuit at speeds of up to 75km/h. Uniforms and safety helmets are provided. True addicts sign up for all-you-can-drive specials ($75 for 24 hours); otherwise, it's $23 to $26 per race.

You can also let off steam in a round of paintball on four terrains strewn with obstacles, bunkers, pyramids and catacombs. The games pit security agents against thieves in a dozen splattering scenarios. A one-hour package ($38) includes mask, paint gun and 100 paintballs.

HEALTH, FITNESS & BEAUTY

Fitness fanatics won't have to give up their routine when they come to Montréal. You'll find the same quality of elliptical trainers, wood-floored yoga studios and spinning classes as you have back home – though instructors may be barking at you in French rather than English. Swimmers can get their laps in at neighborhood pools or world-class facilities like Parc Jean-Drapeau's aquatic complex (there's also an artificial beach nearby if you'd rather just sit and soak).

Part of your cooldown might consist of hitting the beauty salon, booking a day at the spa or hitting a meditation class. Those who want to change things up a bit can score a tattoo (maybe a temporary one to start) from one of Montréal's many great ink artists.

SWIMMING

CENTRE AQUATIQUE Map pp44–5

☎ 514-252-4622; www.rio-gouv.qc.ca; 4141 Ave Pierre-de-Courbertin; adult/child $5/4; 6:30am-9pm Mon-Fri, 9am-4pm Sat & Sun; M Viau; P

The competition pools at the Olympic Stadium are great for laps – they're among the fastest in the world thanks to a system that reduces water movement. The six indoor pools include a wading pool for tots, a water slide and a diving basin. Call or check online for the current schedule, which can change owing to events and competitions.

COMPLEXE AQUATIQUE DE L'ÎLE STE-HÉLÈNE Map p58

☎ 514-872-2323; www.parcjeandrapeau.com; Île Ste-Hélène, Parc Jean-Drapeau; adult/child $5/3; 10am-8pm daily mid-Jun–late Aug, 11am-4pm Sat, Sun & holidays mid-May–mid-Jun & Sep; M Jean-Drapeau

Originally constructed in 1953, this outdoor pool complex was completely demolished and rebuilt when Montréal scored the 2005 World Aquatic Championships. The state-of-the-art facilities are now open to the public. The diving pool (complete with underwater viewing windows) and competition pool are mainly reserved for hosting competitions or for training competitive swimmers and athletic teams. But the championships' magnificent 55m-by-44m warm-up pool is open for recreational swimming. There's also a bay-like portion of the pool with a shallow, gently sloping bottom that's great for kids and families.

NATATORIUM Map pp44–5

☎ 514-765-7230; 6500 Blvd LaSalle, Verdun; adult/child $2/1; 11am-8pm mid Jun–late Aug; M de l'Église, then bus 58; P

Québec's first outdoor pool (1930) harks back to the era when bathing wasn't just about recreation. It occupies a beautiful spot on the banks of the St Lawrence River, reachable via a pretty bicycle trail through greenery.

PISCINE SCHUBERT Map pp76–7

☎ 514-872-2587; 3950 Blvd St-Laurent; admission free; 2-9:30pm Mon-Wed, noon-7:30pm Thu & Fri; M St-Laurent, then bus 55

This former bathhouse in the Plateau is chockablock with pretty art-deco details. There are special sessions throughout the day so call ahead to check the schedule.

PLAGE DES ÎLES Map p58

☎ 514-872-2323; Île Notre-Dame; adult/child $8/4; 10am-7pm mid-Jun–late Aug; M Jean-Drapeau, then bus 167

On warm summer days this artificial sandy beach can accommodate up to 5000 sunning and splashing souls. It's safe, clean and ideal for kids, and picnic facilities and snack bars serving beer are also on-site. Volleyball at the 2006 World Outgames was held here and there are still several professional-standard volleyball courts left over for anyone to use. The beach is closed on 'bad days,' but call to check if it's open – their idea of a bad day may not be the same as yours.

GYMS & HEALTH CLUBS

NAUTILUS PLUS Map pp62–3

☎ 514-843-5993; www.nautilusplus.com; 1231 Rue Ste-Catherine Ouest; nonmembers per session $15; 6am-10pm Mon-Fri, 9am-8pm Sat & Sun; M Peel

This high-tech fitness center offers a barrage of weight-lifting, cycling and climbing machines. Various courses like aerobics, spinning and targeted muscle training are available. There are a number of other branches around town including one in the **Village** (Map p72; ☎ 514-905-9999; 1231 Rue St-André; 6am-11pm Mon-Fri, 9am-8pm Sat & Sun; M Beaudry).

YOGA & PILATES

ASHTANGA YOGA STUDIO

Map pp62–3

☎ 514-875-9642; www.ashtangamontreal.com; 372 Rue Ste-Catherine Ouest, ste 118; 1½hr class $15; M Place-des-Arts

Ashtanga, also known as'power' yoga, is an intense, aerobic form of the exercise. This professional center has big, bright studios, very friendly staff and offers 30-plus classes for all age groups and skill levels. Multiclass discount cards available (five classes $70).

CENTRE LUNA YOGA Map p48

☎ 514-845-1881; www.centrelunayoga.com; 231 Rue St-Paul Ouest, ste 200; 1½hr class $16; M Square-Victoria

Conveniently located in Old Montréal, this yoga center offers a small selection of daily Vinyasa classes. Go online or stop in to find out its latest schedule. Five-class cards cost $70.

MORETTI STUDIO Map pp62–3

☎ 514-285-4884; www.pilates-montreal.com; 1115 Rue Sherbrooke Ouest; private session $65; M Peel

This is a relaxed pilates studio providing a practical, down-to-earth approach to getting and staying in shape. Private one-hour instruction is tailored to suit personal needs, with an emphasis on abdominal work, joints and spinal articulation. If you're in town a while, you can also sign up for an eight-week group class.

STUDIO BLISS Map pp76–7

☎ 514-286-0007; www.studiobliss.ca; 3841 Blvd St-Laurent; 1hr class $10; M Sherbrooke

Equal parts spa and yoga studio, Studio Bliss aims to rejuvenate the body by a variety of passive and kinetic means. A full lineup of yoga classes runs throughout the week, along with prenatal yoga and meditation workshops. You can also opt for vitality wraps, therapeutic baths and various massages.

MARTIAL ARTS

GAMMA – GELINAS ACADEMY OF MIXED MARTIAL ARTS

Map pp62–3

☎ 514-281-9928; www.montrealmartialarts.com; 1121 Rue Ste-Catherine Ouest; 10am-9pm Mon-Fri, 10am-4pm Sat & Sun; M Peel

This large, well-equipped center offers an awesome choice of on-demand courses in martial arts like jujitsu, Muay Thai, Kuntao Silat and Jeet Kune Do (Bruce Lee's art) by fully qualified instructors. There's Western-style boxing, too.

SPAS & BEAUTY SALONS

AVEDA MONTRÉAL LIFESTYLE SALON SPA & ACADEMY Map pp76–7

☎ 514-499-9494; www.avedamontreal-lifestyle.com; 3613 Blvd St-Laurent; 9am-5pm Mon, 9am-8pm Tue & Wed, 10am-9pm Thu & Fri; M St-Laurent, then bus 55

This newly renovated 930-sq-meter spa and salon offers a wide range of treatments and pampering packages. A favorite is the Rejuvenating Experience ($170), featuring a rosemary-mint body wrap, a 30-minute massage and a manicure and pedicure. You can also opt for facials, various massages (Chakra balancing massage, stone massage), waxing, peels and hair cuts.

COUPE BIZZARRE Map pp76–7

☎ 514-843-3433; 3770 Blvd St-Laurent; 10am-8pm Mon-Fri, noon-8pm Sat, noon-7pm Sun; M St-Laurent, then bus 55

One of Montréal's funkiest hairdressers. Apart from wash-cut-blown, you can order sculpted, vicious, voluptuous or whatever suits your mood.

OVARIUM Map p83

☎ 514-271-7515; 877-356-8837; www.ovarium.com; 400 Rue Beaubien Est; 9am-9pm; M Beaubien

The excellent staff and the Ovarium weightlessness experience have garnered a loyal following at this day spa. Packages are available, such as the half-day 'Essential', a flotation bath followed by a massage ($115). Ovarium's flotation tanks are egg-shaped tubs filled with water and 2000 cups of Epsom salts, making you gravity-free.

STRØM NORDIC SPA Map pp44–5

☎ 514-761-2772, 877-761-2772; www.stromspa.com; 1001 Blvd de la Forêt; ⏰ 10am-10pm; Ⓜ Square-Victoria, then bus 168

For a get-away-from-it-all experience, it's hard to top this beautifully set spa located on the Île des Soeurs, a few kilometers south of downtown. The trim Nordic-style buildings overlook a watery and tree-lined expanse, with grassy lawns and outdoor pools and tiny waterfalls from which to enjoy the pretty scenery. A good range of treatments and packages is available, and there's also a good bistro on hand. Hour-long Swedish massages are $80, and you can add in the 'thermal experience' for $34 – featuring use of outdoor Jacuzzis, thermal and Nordic baths, Finnish sauna and eucalyptus steam bath.

SPECTATOR SPORTS

Montréal lost its professional baseball team, the Montréal Expos, in 2005 but to be honest, no one really cared for the sport. I mean, where' s the ice, the body checking, the gloves-off-I'm-going-to-punch-you-in-the-face-now aesthetic? If you haven't noticed, Canada is hockey country, and while there are other cities in Canada that play hockey (and there are other sports, it's true), Montréal is home to the greatest legends of the sport – and for this town, no other event really comes close. Don't pass up an opportunity to join the roaring crowds (as colorful as the game itself) as the famous Canadiens take to the ice. If you can't make it to the stadium, you can always stop in a sports bar, where the excitement can be just as palpable.

Tickets for many sporting events can be purchased from Admission (☎ 514-790-1245, 800-361-4595; www.admission.com). It has dozens of sale outlets in Montréal, including Centre Infotouriste (Map pp62–3; ☎ 514-873-2015, 877-266-5687; www.tourisme-montreal.org; Sq Dorchester; Ⓜ Peel) and Place des Arts (Map pp62–3; ☎ 514-285-4200; 175 Rue Ste-Catherine Ouest; Ⓜ Place-des-Arts) concert halls.

While hockey is king in this town, there is a growing love for other sports like Canadian Football and even soccer – with pro teams of each packing stadiums on opposite sides of town. Catch a hockey, football, soccer or volleball match of the McGill Redmen. Another hometown team to root for is the basketball team Concordia Stingers (☎ 514-848-2424; www.stingers.ca). It'll probably lose, but it's great fun watching it do so among the cheering university-student fans.

HOCKEY

MONTRÉAL CANADIENS Map pp62–3

☎ 514-790-2525, 877-668-8269; http://canadiens.nhl.com; tickets $30-180; ⏰ season Oct-Apr, playoffs until Jun; Ⓜ Lucien-L'Allier or Bonaventure

The Canadiens of the National Hockey League have won the Stanley Cup 24 times. Although the team has struggled in recent years, Montrealers have a soft spot for the 'Habs' and matches at the Bell Centre (☎ 514-790-2525, 877-668-8269; www.centrebell.ca; 1250 Rue de la Gauchetière Ouest) sell out routinely. Scalpers hang around the entrance on game days, and you might snag a half-price ticket after the puck drops. Bring your binoculars for the rafter seats. The center also hosts big-name concerts, boxing matches, Disney on Ice and visits by the Dalai Lama.

MCGILL REDMEN Map pp62–3

☎ ticket office 514-398-1539; www.mcgill.ca/athletics/varsitysports; Redbird Sports Shop, McGill Sports Centre, 475 Pine Ave; adult/student/child $7/4/free; ⏰ Oct-Mar; Ⓜ McGill

The indoor McConnell Winter Stadium (☎ 514-398-1539; 3883 Rue University) is the perfect place to experience a classic rivalry when the McGill Redmen face off against the Toronto Varsity Blues. It's a pleasure to warm the comfy seats.

AUTO RACING

NASCAR: BUSCH SERIES EVENT Map p58

www.nascar.com; Île Notre-Dame; ⏰ Aug; Ⓜ Jean-Drapeau

In 2009 Nascar signed another three-year agreement with the city of Montréal to stage the race at the legendary Circuit Gilles-Villeneuve. Since first appearing in 2007, the event has become a major draw for Nascar lovers from all corners of North America and beyond. If all goes well, it may become a permanent fixture on Montréal's event calendar. The race is typically held toward the end of August.

FOOTBALL & SOCCER

MONTRÉAL ALOUETTES Map pp62–3

☎ 514-871-2255; www.montrealalouettes.com; Molson Stadium, 475 Ave des Pins Ouest; tickets $37-140; ⏰ Jun-Nov; Ⓜ McGill; Ⓟ

THE GRAND RACE

In 2009, for the first time in 22 years, Montréal lost the right to host the famous Grand Prix – North America's biggest Formula One event. The loss happened in late 2008 when the city and race organizers couldn't agree on financial details. As this book went to press Montréal's mayor Gérald Tremblay was in heated negotiations with Formula One boss Bernie Ecclestone to try to bring the race (and its accompanying prestige) back to Montréal. If plans work out, count on the world's flashiest drivers, crews and entourages to hit the city sometime in June for the three-day event. The race would be held on Parc Jean-Drapeau's Circuit Gilles-Villeneuve, but the festivities spill over into the city core until late.

The Montréal Alouettes, a once-defunct football team of the Canadian Football League, is the unlikely star of the city's sports scene. The Alouettes (French for 'larks') folded several times before going on to win the league's Grey Cup trophy in 2002. Rules are a bit different from American football: the field is bigger and there are only three downs. Games are held at Molson Stadium. The **Alouettes box office** (Map pp62–3; ☎ 514-790-1245, 800-361-4595; 1260 Rue University, 2nd fl; 9am-5pm Mon-Fri) sells advance tickets. Look for the big red sign.

MONTRÉAL IMPACT Map pp44–5

☎ 514-328-3668; www.montrealimpact.com; Saputo Stadium, 4750 Rue Sherbrooke Est; tickets $10-40; Apr-Sep; M Viau; P

Although Canadians aren't known for doling out the soccer love, the Montréal Impact has played its heart out to earn a local following. In 2008, its labors bore fruit in the form of Stade Saputo, a brand-new 14,000-seat stadium, located east of Olympic Stadium, that was built in its honor. The Impact's big rivals are Toronto FC and, more surprisingly, the US team the Rochester Rhinos.

SLEEPING

top picks

- **Hôtel Le St-James** (p181)
- **La Maison Pierre du Calvet** (p180)
- **Auberge du Vieux-Port** (p182)
- **University Bed & Breakfast Apartments** (p186)
- **La Loggia** (p188)
- **Hôtel Gault** (p181)
- **Hôtel Nelligan** (p182)
- **Gingerbread Manor B&B** (p192)
- **Atmosphere** (p188)
- **Auberge Alternative** (p183)

Montréal's accommodation scene is blessed with a tremendous variety of rooms and styles. Though rates aren't particularly cheap, they are reasonable by international standards – or even compared with Canadian cities like Toronto or Vancouver. French- and Victorian-style inns and independent hotels cater to a variety of budgets. The many B&Bs, in particular, offer heaps of character – the precious commodity that can make all the difference – and their owners are often invaluable sources of travel advice. There are many comfortable but bland chain hotels in town, which may be useful in peak season, when the B&Bs and guesthouses are booked solid.

Planning in advance is key to finding accommodation during big events. The summertime festival season, beginning with the Montréal International Jazz Festival (late June to mid-July) and ending with Les Francofolies (August) is the peak period, and conventions can crimp availability in late summer.

ACCOMMODATION STYLES

Small, European-style hotels are a Montréal specialty. Located downtown and in the Quartier Latin, they occupy Victorian-era homes that are plain and functional or comfy and charming. Prices are graded by facilities (eg with sink, toilet and/or full bathroom), but note that not all places have air-conditioning.

B&Bs are a wonderful alternative. Many of them are set in attractive, 19th-century stone houses close to the Plateau's bar-and-restaurant strips of Blvd St-Laurent and Rue St-Denis, or near Rue Ste-Catherine Est in the Village.

Almost every establishment serves some kind of continental breakfast, and quantities can be lavish – croissants or rolls, jam, cheese, several cereals and a selection of coffee. More upscale hotels also offer hot English breakfasts with eggs, bacon and sausage.

The luxury hotels have a surprising number of rooms that fall into the midrange category, even if you book at the last minute and especially in low season. Keep an eye out for cut-rate weekend and internet specials.

Montréal has an abundance of good budget accommodation. Apart from the usual dorm beds, hostels may offer basic single and double rooms – though these are often booked out months in advance. In addition, the universities throw open their residence halls to nonstudents in summer and prices are competitive.

ROOM RATES

In Montréal, the average room rate is around $140, with some seasonal fluctuations (lowest in January through March, when rates fall by about 30%). Prices listed in this book are for peak-season travel (June to September) and do not include taxes, which add another 16% or so (6% GST, 7.5% provincial sales tax plus a 'hospitality tax' of anywhere from 2% to 4%) to the bill.

OLD MONTRÉAL & CHINATOWN

Old Montréal has the most atmospheric – and highest priced – rooms in town. Over the last decade or so, many of the area's old buildings have been converted into impeccable boutique hotels with unique ambience and careful, confident service. The proliferation of such distinctive hotels has also inflated the area's B&B and inn rates.

Tiny Chinatown has no hotels to speak of, though there are plenty of places nearby.

LA MAISON PIERRE DU CALVET

Map p48 Historic Inn $$$

☎ 514-282-1725, 866-544-1725; www.pierreducalvet.ca; 405 Rue Bonsecours; d $265-295; Ⓜ Champ-de-Mars; Ⓟ

THE B&B CONNECTION

For an overview of the many charming B&Bs across Montréal, visit B&B Canada (www.bbcanada.com). It currently has over 110 Montréal B&Bs listed on its network, with photos, room descriptions and reviews.

If you show up in Montréal without a reservation and don't feel like making the rounds, you can always book a place through the city's main tourist office, Centre Infotouriste (Map pp62–3; ☎ 514-873-2015, 877-266-5687; www.tourisme-montreal.org; Sq Dorchester). Keep in mind that it can book you a room only with guesthouses with which it has an affiliation.

The heritage hotel experience par excellence! This historic landmark in Old Montréal was built right into the city defense walls in 1725, and staying here is like stepping back in time: massive stone fireplaces with original carvings, gilded picture frames, four-post beds surrounded by carefully preserved antiques. Benjamin Franklin stayed here in 1775 while trying to garner support for the American Revolution. The salon, library, wine cellar and dining rooms all drip the moneyed elegance of the period. There's also a Victorian greenhouse and pretty vine-covered terrace.

HÔTEL LE ST-JAMES

Map p48 Boutique Hotel $$$

☎ 514-841-3111; www.hotellestjames.com; 355 Rue St-Jacques; d from $249; Ⓜ Square-Victoria; Ⓟ

Housed in the former Merchants Bank, the Hôtel Le St-James is world-class. Lavish guest rooms are decorated in a heritage style complete with antique furnishings and oil paintings adorning the walls – covering five continents throughout the hotel. There's a candlelit spa, a library and high-tea service. The concierge and staff are particularly kind and helpful. The ornately decorated restaurant has lovely ambience but surprisingly unimpressive dishes – chefs tend to go a bit heavy on the complexity.

PRICE GUIDE

$$$	over $180 a night
$$	$80-180 a night
$	under $80 a night

HÔTEL GAULT Map p48 Boutique Hotel $$$

☎ 514-904-1616, 866-904-1616; www.hotelgault.com; 449 Rue Ste-Hélène; d from $239; Ⓜ Square-Victoria; Ⓟ

The Gault delivers both beauty and comfort in its 30 spacious rooms. The lovely heritage building figures in some rooms, with exposed stone walls, though for the most part the Gault boasts a fashion-forward, contemporary design. Rooms have extremely comfortable beds, ergonomic chairs, high ceilings, huge windows and spotless bathrooms (though most lack bathtubs) with heated tile floors.

HÔTEL ST-PAUL Map p48 Boutique Hotel $$$

☎ 514-380-2222, 866-380-2202; www.hotelstpaul.com; 355 Rue McGill; d from $209; Ⓜ Square-Victoria; Ⓟ

The lobby greets you with a fireplace flickering inside a wall of glowing alabaster – a fine introduction to this swanky beaux-arts hotel. The 120 rooms and 24 suites feature dark-wood furnishings, nice lighting, hardwood floors and large windows (in most

LONGER-TERM RENTALS

The universities offer good deals from May to August, though you should not expect much more than dormitory amenities.

For a taste of life in the 'real' Montréal, away from the hotel circuit, seek out these clean, trim Studios du Quartier Latin (Map p72; ☎ 514-845-0916; www.studiosquartierlatin.com; 2022 Rue St-Hubert; apt per day/week/month from $60/350/980; Ⓜ Berri-UQAM;) in the Quartier Latin, the Plateau and Little Italy. All studios generally have fully equipped kitchenette, TV, private telephone and bed linen, plus wireless access.

Although the brochures oversell things a bit ('a vast and comfortable room'), the studios and one-bedroom suites at La Tour Centre Ville (Map pp62–3; ☎ 514-866-8861, 800-361-2790; www.hotelcentreville.com; 400 Blvd René-Lévesque Ouest; studio/ste from $102/135; Ⓜ Square-Victoria) are roomy, each with a separate kitchen and your very own window. Unless you're a fan of beige carpeting and shiny floral fabrics, however, these clean, cookie-cutter quarters probably won't impress. The amenities are quite all right – indoor swimming pool, sauna and a gym with a city panorama. They're normally rented by the week, and prices are usually lower on weekdays.

The modern high-rise Trylon Apartments (Map pp62–3; ☎ 514-843-3971, 877-843-3971; www.trylon.qc.ca; 3463 Rue Ste-Famille; apt per day/week/month from $90/500/1410; Ⓜ Place-des-Arts) are a plush alternative to top-end hotels at a fraction of the price. The small studios (36 sq meter) and one-bedroom apartments (51 sq meter) all have contemporary furnishings with kitchenettes, and guests can enjoy the indoor swimming pool, sauna, exercise room and rooftop terrace. Some rooms have balconies.

but not all rooms). Excellent amenities available – from free high-speed internet, CD players, a fitness center and a high-end restaurant that becomes a popular nightspot on weekends (take note light sleepers near the bar). Staff receive mixed reviews.

INTERCONTINENTAL MONTRÉAL

Map p48 Luxury Hotel $$$

☎ 514-987-9900, 877-424-2449; www.montreal.intercontinental.com; 360 Rue St-Antoine Ouest; d from $200; M Square-Victoria; P

This enormous InterContinental has a unique location between a new high-rise and a restored annex of the 19th-century Nordheimer building. Photography and paintings by local artists adorn all 357 rooms; the turret suites are particularly attractive, with superb views to Mont-Royal. There are extensive facilities, including a piano bar and restaurant.

LE PETIT HÔTEL

Map p48 Boutique Hotel $$$

☎ 514-940-0360, 877-530-0360; www.petithotelmontreal.com; 168 Rue St-Paul Ouest; d from $200; M Place-d'Armes; P

This small, 24-room boutique hotel, which opened in 2009, dispenses with the inflated talk of 'superiors' and 'deluxes'. Instead, Le Petit Hôtel uses small, medium, large and extra-large to describe its four room classes – which are indeed identical save for the size. Like the Hôtel Place-d'Armes (which is owned by the same group), rooms here boast a sleek, contemporary design (polished wood floors, atmospheric lighting, dark woods and fluffy white duvets), while showcasing the old stone walls in some rooms. You'll also find iPod docking stations, wi-fi access and dashes of color – orange! – that give a creative tint to the overall look. There's a small spa here and an enticing little café, with down-tempo beats, on the ground floor.

AUBERGE BONSECOURS

Map p48 Inn $$$

☎ 514-396-2662; www.aubergebonsecours.com; 353 Rue St-Paul Est; s/d from $125/195; M Champ-de-Mars; P

The unusual ambience of the renovated stables lends this secluded hotel particular appeal. All seven rooms have bare brick walls, designer lighting and floral linen piled high, but each room is cut differently. The front-facing room with the pine floors and sloping ceiling is especially popular, and all quarters are set around an inner courtyard, remaining blissfully quiet at night.

HÔTEL PLACE-D'ARMES

Map p48 Boutique Hotel $$$

☎ 514-842-1887, 888-450-1887; www.hotelplacedarmes.com; 55 Rue St-Jacques Ouest; r/ste from $195/225; M Place-d'Armes; P

Spread among three regal buildings on the edge of Pl-d'Armes, this luxury hotel has earned many admirers for its stylish rooms, excellent service and historic location in Old Montréal. Rooms are set with first-class fittings – antique moldings, brick or stone walls, black granite and white marble in the bathrooms, and a CD player/entertainment system in every room. Even small quarters feel spacious thanks to the views of Mont-Royal or the Basilique Notre-Dame. There's a full-service spa, fitness center, restaurant and bar, but the crowning touch is the splendid rooftop terrace – Terrasse 701 (p141), which on a summertime night is a magnet for the beauty crowd.

AUBERGE DU VIEUX-PORT

Map p48 Boutique Hotel $$$

☎ 514-876-0081, 888-660-7678; www.aubergeduvieuxport.com; 97 Rue de la Commune Est; d/loft from $195/215; M Champ-de-Mars; P

Set in a stolid 1882 warehouse, the Auberge du Vieux-Port is a stylish boutique hotel with exposed brick or stone walls, wood beams, wrought-iron beds, high-quality furnishings (antiques here and there) and big windows overlooking the waterfront. For more space and seclusion (a kitchen, multiple rooms), you can book one of its minimalist lofts (www.loftsduvieuxport.com) in a separate building around the corner.

HÔTEL NELLIGAN

Map p48 Boutique Hotel $$$

☎ 514-788-2040, 877-788-2040; www.hotelnelligan.com; 106 Rue St-Paul Ouest; d/ste from $179/235; M Place-d'Armes; P

Housed in two restored buildings and named in honor of Québec's most famous and tragic poet Émile Nelligan (see the boxed text, p53), this is one of the Old Town's most enchanting boutique hotels. Rooms are decorated with warm woods, original details (like exposed brick or stone in some rooms) and luxurious fittings (down comforters, wi-fi, high-quality bath products, Jacuzzis in some rooms). Verses, a plush bar and restaurant, is next door, with a magnificent roof terrace.

AUBERGE BONAPARTE INN & RESTAURANT Map p48 Boutique Hotel $$

☎ 514-844-1448; www.bonaparte.com; 447 Rue St-François-Xavier; d from $170, ste $355; M Place-d'Armes; P

Wrought-iron beds and Louis Philippe furnishings lend a suitably Napoleonic touch to this historic 30-room inn, a former judge's residence built in 1886. The best rooms are warmly decorated and boast high ceilings, dormer windows and bronze lamps. Low-end rooms can seem a little dark and dowdy. Those at the rear overlook a pretty garden with views of the Basilique Notre-Dame. Breakfast (included) is served in the fine Bonaparte Restaurant, which has been done up in Napoleonic Imperial style. There's also a pleasant rooftop terrace.

LES PASSANTS DU SANS SOUCY B&B Map p48 B&B $$

☎ 514-842-2634; www.lesanssoucy.com; 171 Rue St-Paul Ouest; d/ste from $160/225; M Place-d'Armes

Built in 1723, this B&B feels more like a classic country inn straight out of the old country. It's set back from the road at the rear of a quiet courtyard in the heart of Old Montréal. Its comfy rooms are furnished with tasteful antiques and some have wood-beam ceilings, stone walls and other original details. The breakfast room has a stained-glass skylight above the dining table and the foyer doubles as an art gallery.

UQAM RESIDENCES Map p48 University Apartments $$

☎ 514-987-6669; www.residences-uqam.qc.ca; 303 Blvd René-Lévesque; studios $80-114; M Berri-UQAM; P

This UQAM residence hall offers tidy modern studio apartments with small, fully equipped kitchens in a convenient location not far from the club district along Blvd St-Laurent. Rooms are available only during the summer. There's laundry and a café on-site.

MAISON BRUNET Map p48 B&B $$

☎ 514-845-6351; www.maisonbrunet.ca; 1035 Rue St-Hubert; d with/without bathroom $85/80; M Berri-UQAM;

Not far from the Quartier Latin and the Village, this charming little guesthouse has a splash of old-fashioned decor with touches of sugary rococo. Rooms are spacious with polished-wood floors and colorful linens, and the congenial owner is full of local tips.

AUBERGE ALTERNATIVE Map p48 Hostel $

☎ 514-282-8069; www.auberge-alternative.qc.ca; 358 Rue St-Pierre; dm/d $23/60; M Square-Victoria;

This laid-back hostel near the Old Port has a bohemian vibe with an inviting café/restaurant where you can mingle with other travelers or enjoy an organic breakfast ($5 extra). Guests bunk in trim, colorfully painted dorms that accommodate anywhere from four to 20 people. There's also one simple but highly coveted private room. There's laundry and no curfew.

DOWNTOWN

The city center is the bastion of the business hotel and the large upper-end chain. There are some interesting independent hotels, B&Bs as well as budget establishments scattered throughout the area.

FAIRMONT LE REINE ELIZABETH Map pp62–3 Luxury Hotel $$$

☎ 514-861-3511; www.fairmont.com; 900 Blvd René-Lévesque Ouest; d from $240; M Bonaventure; P

This is the crème de la crème of Montréal business hotels with over 1000 tastefully renovated rooms and suites. Its celebrity guest list is longer than a stretch limousine, including Queen Elizabeth, the Dalai Lama and several presidents and prime ministers. The most famous was arguably John Lennon, who wrote the song *Give Peace a Chance* here during his 1969 bed-in – you can stay in the same suite, which contains memorabilia such as the framed seven-inch single.

RITZ-CARLTON Map pp62–3 Luxury Hotel $$$

☎ 514-842-4212; www.ritzmontreal.com; 1228 Rue Sherbrooke Ouest; M Peel

This classic grande dame of Montréal has been impressing guests ever since Liz Taylor and Richard Burton got married here. Its impeccable high-tea service – served by white-uniformed waiters – is famous. At research time, the Ritz was undergoing a long-overdue renovation. It is scheduled to reopen in 2010.

HILTON MONTRÉAL BONAVENTURE

Map pp62–3 Luxury Hotel $$$

☎ 514-878-2332, 800-445-8667; www.hiltonmontreal.com; 900 Rue de La Gauchetière Ouest; d from $240; Ⓜ Bonaventure; Ⓟ

Your standard business Hilton with deluxe amenities, but the best part is arguably the panoramic view of downtown. All rooms have on-command movies, mahogany furniture, marbled bathrooms and large working areas. The winning highlight is the one-hectare rooftop garden with a duck pond and heated pool. Ask about the famous UFO sighting here a few years back.

LOEW'S HOTEL VOGUE

Map pp62–3 Luxury Hotel $$$

☎ 514-285-5555, 888-465-6654; www.loewshotels.com; 1425 Rue de la Montagne; d from $219; Ⓜ Peel; Ⓟ

This upmarket hotel has managed to blend French-empire style with modern luxury. You'll find flat-screen TVs attached to the oversized marble Jacuzzi bathtubs, an iPod docking station and nicely furnished rooms (though somewhat lacking in individuality). Staff are friendly and efficient, and there's a stylish candlelit Italian restaurant and bar on-site.

HÔTEL LE GERMAIN

Map pp62–3 Boutique Hotel $$$

☎ 514-849-2050, 877-333-2050; www.hotelgermain.com; 2050 Rue Mansfield; d from $200; Ⓜ Peel; Ⓟ

This stylish hotel boasts luxurious rooms with dark wood details (headboard, wood blinds), cream-colored walls, sheer curtains and artful lighting. You'll find all the creature comforts, such as iPod docks and oversized showerheads; the bathrooms have a touch of the eccentric with one big window into the room. (Superior rooms have only a shower.) Service is friendly and professional with the occasional hiccup from time to time. The restaurant receives mixed reviews. The continental breakfast is generally substandard.

OPUS MONTRÉAL

Map pp62–3 Boutique Hotel $$$

☎ 514-380-3899, 866-744-6346; www.opushotel.com; 10 Rue Sherbrooke Ouest; d/ste from $200/330; Ⓜ St-Laurent

Set in a minimalist art-nouveau building, this new designer hotel features sleek, ultramodern rooms with all the trappings of luxury. You'll plenty of space (30 to 50 sq meters), daring color schemes, Zenlike bathrooms with rain showers, and atmospheric lighting (which can be a little inadequate at night). The Opus attracts a young, good-looking crowd and its stylish restaurant, Koko (better for drinks than food), becomes a party place on weekend nights. Unless you're a 24-hour party person, be sure to book a room well away from this action. Staff dole out earplugs – a kind but ultimately fruitless gesture.

LE PETIT PRINCE

Map pp62–3 Boutique Hotel $$$

☎ 514-938-2277; www.montrealbandb.com; 1384 Ave Overdale; d $200-225; Ⓜ Lucien-L'Allier;

Blessed with four picture-perfect guest rooms, this B&B features handpicked furniture (four-post beds, sleigh beds, handcrafted bedside tables), wood floors, paintings by local artists and creative but subdued use of color. Two rooms have private balconies. The open-style layout is intriguing, and several rooms have big bathtubs right in the rooms. Breakfast is a full gourmet affair, whipped up in a cool kitchen with fire-engine-red appliances.

SOFITEL Map pp62–3 Luxury Hotel $$$

☎ 514-285-9000; www.sofitel.com; 1155 Rue Sherbrooke Ouest; r from $200; Ⓜ Peel; Ⓟ

Yet another solid chink in the French luxury chain (and the only Sofitel in Canada), this hotel has stylish, modern rooms and European feel. Staff hit the right note of sophistication without too much snobbery and the rooms are modern and attractive – featuring either a cool black-and-white color scheme or all-white with blond-wood details. The best rooms are spacious and have separate tub and shower, while the least expensive rooms (the 'superiors') are too small to recommend and have showers only. The usual trappings of luxury are here – the fine lobby, excellent French restaurant, fitness center and sauna, and the stylish but curiously named Le Bar. You can bring your pet.

CHÂTEAU VERSAILLES

Map pp62–3 Hotel $$$

☎ 514-933-3611, 888-933-8111; www.chateauversaillesmontreal.com; 1659 Rue Sherbrooke Ouest; d from $180; Ⓜ Guy-Concordia

$75 2 Double

$75 2 Queen
Private Washroom
Croissant Coffee Tea, Muffin

Eva

Hôtel Casa Bella
Guest House

Maison Brunet
st. Zotique

The stately Château Versailles exudes class. Spread among three interconnected townhouses, the best rooms here are elegantly furnished with high-quality fabrics, a light and airy color scheme and handsome decorative details (framed art prints, crown moldings). Less-expensive rooms can be darker and less charmingly furnished. The street in front is a busy one, but traffic noise drops off at night.

CASTEL DUROCHER

Map pp62–3 Apart-Hotel $$$

☎ 514-282-1697; www.casteldurocher.com; 3488 Rue Durocher; 1-/2-bedroom apt from $180/250; M McGill; P

This family-run establishment occupies a tall, turreted stone house on a peaceful, tree-lined street near McGill University. Lodging is for those seeking self-sufficiency in one- or two-bedroom apartments with kitchen units, homey furnishings and artwork covering the walls (the multitalented Belgian owner is an artist, novelist and chocolate-maker extraordinaire). Discounts for long-term stays.

HÔTEL DU FORT Map pp62–3 Hotel $$

☎ 514-938-8333, 800-565-6333; www.hoteldufort.com; 1390 Rue du Fort; r/ste from $150/210; M Guy-Concordia; P

This fairly cookie-cutter business hotel has clean, modest rooms done in beige and creams, with carpeting, shiny fabric wallpaper and a few spruce touches like framed botanical prints on the walls. Some rooms also have kitchenettes. Staff can be quite friendly or sleepily apathetic, depending on the day.

HOTEL PARC SUITES

Map pp62–3 YWCA Hotel $$

☎ 514-985-5656, 800-949-8630; www.parcsuites.com; 3463 Ave du Parc; ste from $145; M Place-des-Arts; P

This eight-room all-suites guesthouse is a great place to decamp while exploring Montréal. The accommodations range from small studios to only marginally more expensive one-bedroom suites, with a furnished living/dining area and adjoining kitchenette, and a separate bedroom – all tastefully furnished in a trim, contemporary style. Staff and owner are friendly and helpful and deserve kudos for all the freebies thrown in – wi-fi, parking and long-distance calls to the US and Canada. Mind the steep stairway up to the lobby.

LES BONS MATINS

Map pp62–3 Boutique Hotel $$

☎ 514-931-9167,800-588-5280; www.bonsmatins.com; 1401 Ave Argyle; d/ste from $130/210; M Lucien L'Allier; P

Charming and seductive with exposed brick walls and vibrant colors (bed sheets, wall hangings), this classy establishment fills a series of adjoining turn-of-the-century walk-ups. Breakfasts are excellent, with gourmet quiche, homemade waffles and Italian-style espresso.

HOTEL MARITIME PLAZA

Map pp62–3 Hotel $$

☎ 514-932-1411, 800-363-6255; www.hotelmaritime.com, 1155 Rue Guy; r from $125; M Guy-Concordia; P

Inside a magnificently ugly concrete facade, you'll find neat rooms with blue-toned carpeting, striped wallpaper, thick white comforters and trim furnishings (brassy lamps, comfy armchairs). Minuses: overly noisy heating and air-conditioning units, showers that sometimes flood and slow elevators. There is also a bar with pool table.

MANOIR AMBROSE Map pp62–3 Hotel $$

☎ 514-288-6922, 888-688-6922; www.manoirambrose.com; 3422 Rue Stanley; s/d without bathroom from $95/110, s/d with private bathroom from $105/120; M Peel;

This hotel consists of two merged Victorian homes in a quiet residential area. Its 22 rooms are comfortably furnished, with a somewhat dated floral look. The economy and standard rooms are cramped, with equally small bathrooms. Upstairs rooms are best (avoid the dank basement quarters). Staff are friendly and the location is decent.

ARMOR MANOIR SHERBROOKE

Map pp62–3 Hotel $$

☎ 514-845-0915, 800-203-5485; www.armormanoir.com; 157 Rue Sherbrooke Est; d $99-149; M Sherbrooke

This conversion of two fine Victorian houses is replete with atmosphere. Its 30 rooms range from small standards to spacious deluxe rooms. The cheapest rooms have thick carpeting, floral details and ensuite showers – but toilets outside the room. The best rooms have oversized gilded mirrors, decorative fireplaces and Jacuzzi bathtubs.

HÔTEL DU NOUVEAU FORUM

Map pp62–3 Independent Hotel $$

☎ 514-989-0300, 888-989-0300; www.nouveau-forum.com; 1320 Rue St-Antoine Ouest; r from $90; M Lucien-L'Allier; P

The Hôtel du Nouveau Forum is ideally placed for visiting hockey fans, as it's right next to the Bell Centre where the Habs play (see p176). The hotel has an old stone facade and small but quaint rooms. The neighborhood can be a bit sketchy (car break-ins aren't uncommon).

UNIVERSITY BED & BREAKFAST APARTMENTS

Map pp62–3 B&B $$

☎ 514-842-6396; www.universitybedandbreakfast.ca; 623 Rue Prince Arthur Ouest; d with shared bathroom from $85, ste from $125; M McGill;

Tucked away on a leafy street near McGill University, this handsome three-story townhouse has abundant charm. Accommodations all vary in size and style, although you'll find wood floors, wrought-iron beds, classy furnishings and exposed brick, while the suites are roomier with modern touches like flat-screen TVs, kitchenettes and iPod docking stations to listen to your music. There's wireless access. Excellent location.

HÔTEL CASA BELLA

Map pp62–3 Guesthouse $$

☎ 849-2777, 888-453-2777; www.hotelcasabella.com; 264 Rue Sherbrooke Ouest; s/d without bathroom from $80/95, with bathroom from $100/110; M Place-des-Arts; P

This intimate greystone along busy Rue Sherbrooke offers humble, simply furnished rooms with frilly touches. Rooms in front are bright but open onto a noisy street. Cleanliness is an issue in some rooms, so have a look before committing. The free continental breakfast is served in the room. There's also free wi-fi.

HÔTEL ABRI DU VOYAGEUR

Map pp62–3 Hotel $$

☎ 514-849-2922; www.abri-voyageur.ca; 9 Rue Ste-Catherine Ouest; r with shared/private bathroom $61/98; M St-Laurent;

It's on a seedy stretch of Rue Ste-Catherine but if you're not turned off by the nearby sex clubs (no pun intended), you can enjoy clean, cozy rooms with exposed brick walls, wood floors and comfortable furnishings. Some rooms are spacious with tiny kitchenettes, while others could use more natural light. Befitting the neighborhood, there's a funky smell in the stairwell. Free wi-fi.

LE 1 RENÉ LÉVESQUE

Map pp62–3 Hotel $$

☎ 514-871-9696, ext 5500; www.le1renelevesque.com; 1 Blvd René Lévesque Est; s/d from $65/90; M St-Laurent;

Relive your college days at this modern 12-story high-rise near the gates to Chinatown. In a former student dormitory, Le 1 offers clean minimalist rooms that come in small, medium and large. Aside from size considerations, all offer the same style and equipment, namely tile floors, kitchen units, new mattresses, tubs in the bathrooms, sizable windows (with nice views from upper floors) and cable-modem internet access. Brightly painted corridors attempt to break up the otherwise institutional feel.

ALACOQUE B&B REVOLUTION

Map pp62–3 B&B $$

☎ 514-842-0938; www.bbrevolution.com; 2091 Rue St-Urbain; s/d without bathroom $75/85; M Place-des-Arts; P

This little place offers good rates for its simply furnished rooms. Exposed brick walls and homey touches create a warm ambience, but some beds and furnishings need a refresh. Guests have access to the whole house (kitchen, terrace, garden, dining room, laundry). There's free parking and free wi-fi.

Y DES FEMMES

Map pp62–3 YWCA Hotel $$

☎ 514-866-9942; www.ydesfemmesmtl.org; 1355 Blvd René-Lévesque Ouest; s/d without bathroom $60/70, with bathroom $75/85; M Lucien-L'Allier

The YWCA's hotel welcomes both sexes to rooms that are basic but clean – and decent value for the neighborhood. Each floor has a kitchen with refrigerator and microwave; shared bathrooms are decent for women but not in great shape for men. Unfortunately, the Y no longer lives up to its name – there's no fitness center or pool. The money goes to Y programs.

MCGILL UNIVERSITY RESIDENCE HALLS
Map pp62–3 University Dorms $

514-398-5200; www.mcgill.ca/residences; 3473 Rue University; s student/nonstudent $40/45, per month $700/800, Solin Hall per week from $180; mid-May–mid-Aug; M McGill; P

Over summer, McGill opens its student residence halls to travelers seeking budget accommodation. Lodging is in one of four different buildings, including the uninspiring 1960s New Residence Hall, the greystone Bishop Mountain Hall and the more inviting Solin Hall, near the Atwater market and the Lachine Canal. The latter offers studios and two-, three- and four-bedroom apartments (with no air-conditioning), rented either per room with shared facilities, or for the entire apartment. The other halls are basic student dorms, with a single bed and shared everything else (bathroom, kitchenettes). Bedding is usually not provided. Guests can use the university cafeteria, pool, gym and tennis courts.

HI AUBERGE DE MONTRÉAL
Map pp62–3 Hostel $

514-843-3317, 866-843-3317; www.hostellingmontreal.com; 1030 Rue Mackay; dm/r from $32/98; M Lucien-L'Allier;

This large, well-equipped HI hostel has bright, maintained dorm rooms (all with air-con) with four to 10 beds, and a handful of private ensuite rooms. Rooms are small and, depending on your bunkmates, can feel cramped. Energetic staff organize daily activities and outings (pub crawls, bike tours, day trips), plus there's a lively café on the ground floor. There's free wi-fi and no curfew. Reservations are strongly recommended in summer.

LE GÎTE DU PLATEAU MONT-ROYAL
Map pp62–3 Hostel $

514-284-1276, 877-350-4483; www.hostelmontreal.com; 185 Rue Sherbrooke Est; dm/d with shared bathroom from $27/60; M Sherbrooke

This popular youth hostel lies at the southern end of the Plateau (and the western edge of downtown). All the expected hostel features are here (kitchen access, laundry room, lounge), though rooms and facilities are basic. The staff are friendly. There's also bike rental.

QUARTIER LATIN & THE VILLAGE

You'll find a good mix of options in the nightlife-charged areas of the Quartier Latin and the Village. Delightful, superb-quality B&Bs dominate the choices in this part of town. This is also a good place to base yourself, with excellent metro connections and walking access to both downtown and Old Montréal – plus the Plateau is just up the hill.

HÔTEL GOUVERNEUR PLACE DUPUIS
Map p72 Hotel $$

514-842-4881, 888-910-1111; www.gouverneur.com; 1415 Rue St-Hubert; d from $150; M Berri-UQAM;

Set in a modern high-rise in the Village, this clean, well-maintained business hotel offers comfortable, fairly spacious rooms (though bathrooms tend to be small), some with fine views. Friendly staff make up for the somewhat generic feel overall. It's attached to the metro and the Village's Pl Dupuis.

LE RELAIS LYONNAIS
Map p72 Guesthouse $$

514-448-2999; www.lerelaislyonnais.com; 1595 Rue St-Denis; r/ste from $145/225; M Berri-UQAM

The small, seven-room Le Relais Lyonnais provides excellent value for money. Exposed brick and dark woods give the rooms an elegant but masculine look, while white goose-down duvets provide a soft complement. High ceilings, oversized windows, rain showers and DVD players add to the allure. Light sleepers beware: front-facing rooms get lots of street noise

GAY STAYS

Any guesthouse located in the Village will be gay-friendly – welcoming gay as well as straight travelers. A few perennial favorites include the following:

- **Alexandre Logan** (p188) Splendid 19th-century ambience.
- **Atmosphere** (p188) Receives rave reviews from readers.
- **Turquoise B&B** (p189) Like stepping into a glossy magazine.
- **Alacoque B&B Revolution** (opposite) Gorgeous antiques in an 1830s setting.
- **Ruta Bagage B&B** (p189) Exquisitely decorated rooms and an inviting terrace for sunbathing.

from lively Rue St-Denis. Suites face the rear and are quieter.

HÔTEL LE ROBERVAL

Map p72 Independent Hotel $$

☎ 514-286-5215, 877-552-2992; www.leroberval.com; 505 Blvd René-Lévesque Est; d/ste from $140/160; Ⓜ Berri-UQAM; Ⓟ

On the southern edge of the Quartier Latin, perky Roberval has nicely appointed doubles with either carpeting or tile floors and the usual features (coffeemaker, satellite TV, mini-refrigerator). There's also a work desk and free internet access. The suites add a bit more space and also come with kitchenettes.

ATMOSPHERE Map p72 B&B $$

☎ 514-510-7976; www.atmospherebb.com; 1933 Rue Panet; d with shared/private bathroom from $129/179; Ⓜ Beaudry

Set in a beautifully restored 1875 home, Atmosphere lives up to its name. Rooms here feature exposed brick, polished wood floors, artful lighting and handsome design flourishes. Rooms and common areas are kept meticulously clean, and the friendly host receives rave reviews for the three-course breakfasts (dessert included) he prepares. Only gripe is that the ensuite room (the Sensation) has no door to the bathroom.

MONTRÉAL ESPACE CONFORT

Map p72 Hotel $$

☎ 514-849-0505; www.montrealespaceconfort.com; 2050 Rue St-Denis; s/d from $90/120; Ⓜ Berri-UQAM;

Back in the 1990s this stretch used to be the stomping ground for the transient and the confused, and this address was a notorious flophouse. Things have changed dramatically since then, with this new hotel being a shiny example of urban renewal in action. Rooms boast trim Ikea-style furnishings, with desk and a kitchenette, but are quite small. Street-facing rooms can be noisy (especially on weekends). Gay-friendly.

HÔTEL LORD BERRI Map p72 Hotel $$

☎ 514-845-9236, 888-363-0363; www.lordberri.com; 1199 Rue Berri; d from $114; Ⓜ Berri-UQAM; Ⓟ

This modern high-rise is a heartbeat away from the nightlife of Rue St-Denis. Furnishings are tasteful and contemporary in its 154 rooms, with big comfy beds and in-room movies. It lies along busy Rue Berri. Wi-fi costs extra.

AU GÎT'ANN Map p72 B&B $$

☎ 514-523-4494; www.augitann.com; 1806 Rue St-Christophe; d with shared/private bathroom from $100/180; Ⓜ Beaudry

This small B&B has just three rooms, all painted in deep dreamlike hues (lavender, canary yellow), with abstract artwork on the walls and comfortable furnishings. The best room has a private bathroom and a balcony. While the host is very friendly, some guests complain that the doting attention can be a bit stifling at times.

ALEXANDRE LOGAN Map p72 B&B $$

☎ 514-598-0555, 866-895-0555; www.alexandrelogan.com; 1631 Rue Alexandre-de-Sève; s/d from $100/110; Ⓜ Beaudry;

The friendly host Alain has an eye for details like original plaster moldings, ornate woodwork and art-deco glass patterns at this award-winning B&B. This splendidly renovated home dates from 1870 and has hardwood floors, high-quality mattresses (some rooms have king-size beds) and big windows, making the rooms bright and cheerful. Common spaces are also beautifully designed, from the breakfast room to the outdoor terrace complete with tiki torches.

LA LOGGIA Map p72 B&B $$

☎ 514-524-2493; www.laloggia.ca; 1637 Rue Amherst; s/d with shared bathroom from $90/110, s/d with private bathroom from $125/145; Ⓜ Beaudry

This beautifully maintained B&B has a handful of charming rooms, each with artwork on the walls and attractive furnishings. The best rooms are light and airy with Persian carpets, antique armoires and private bathrooms. Lower-level rooms are a little dark, but still clean. Good firm mattresses and soundproof windows ensure a decent night's rest. The hosts offer a warm and friendly welcome. Buffet-style breakfasts are simple but adequate.

HÔTEL ST-DENIS Map p72 Hotel $$

☎ 514-249-4526, 800-291-5927; www.hotel-st-denis.com; 1254 Rue St-Denis; d from $100; Ⓜ Berri-UQAM; Ⓟ

In a good location in the Village, this hotel receives positive reviews for its clean, well-maintained rooms with wood floors, trim modern furnishings and comfortable beds.

Sizes vary from cramped to rather spacious – avoid the budget rooms if you need space. The King Suite has a Jacuzzi tub tiled right into the living area. Free wi-fi.

AUBERGE LE JARDIN D'ANTOINE

Map p72 B&B $$

☎ 514-843-4506, 800-361-4506; www.hotel-jardin-antoine.qc.ca; 2024 Rue St-Denis; d/ste from $95/137; Ⓜ Berri-UQAM;

Romantic Victorian decor is the chief selling point at this welcoming four-story hotel, handily located in the thick of the Quartier Latin action. Rooms sport a classic old-world look with wrought-iron bedsteads and antique wallpaper (exposed brick in some rooms), with the florals a bit heavy-handed at times. Budget rooms have showers only (toilets outside the room). There's free wi-fi.

HÔTEL DE PARIS

Map p72 Independent Hotel $$

☎ 514-522-6861, 800-567-7217; www.hotel-montreal.com; 901 Rue Sherbrooke Est; d $90-170; Ⓜ Sherbrooke;

Inside a turreted Victorian mansion, you'll find a range of rooms and suites. The most picturesque have balconies overlooking Rue Sherbrooke (though noise can be a factor). Budget rooms are small and rather worn, though some travelers find them fair for the price. In the annex across the street are a mix of 'premium rooms,' including several with wood floors, tall ceilings and wood details.

LA MAISON ST HUBERT Map p72 B&B $$

☎ 514-529-5541; www.bbhubert.com; 2017 Rue St-Hubert; d with shared bathroom $80-105; Ⓜ Berri-UQAM

Set in a gingerbread turn-of-the-century Victorian, La Maison St Hubert (formerly known as Hébergement Temara) provides a friendly welcome to the neighborhood. Its five rooms have hardwood floors and high ceilings and each is painted in warm tones. Street noise can be an issue for light sleepers. Ask for the quietest room with a balcony overlooking the garden. There are no private bathrooms, and the queue can be long at times.

TURQUOISE B&B Map p72 B&B $$

☎ 514-523-9943, 877-707-1576; www.turquoisebb.com; 1576 Rue Alexandre-de-Sève; s/d with shared bathroom from $80/90; Ⓜ Beaudry

The decor in this plush two-story greystone looks like something out of *Better Homes & Gardens*. Each of the five bedrooms has a queen-size bed, original moldings, shiny wood floors and carved faux gables (yes, indoors). Breakfast is served in the large backyard. Bathrooms are shared.

RUTA BAGAGE B&B Map p72 B&B $$

☎ 514-598-1586; www.rutabagage.qc.ca; 1345 Rue Ste-Rose; s/d with shared bathroom from $70/85; Ⓜ Beaudry

Tucked away in a quiet side street near bustling Rue Ste-Catherine Est, this old Victorian house is a true Village charmer. There are only four rooms, impeccably decorated – including the 'Russian room' with dark-wood furnishings and swirling carved bedstead. There are two outdoor terraces, one designated for breakfast and the other for sunbathing.

LA CLAIRE FONTAINE Map p72 B&B $$

☎ 514-528-9862; www.laclairefontaine.com; 1652 Rue La Fontaine; s/d from $70/85; Ⓜ Papineau

This place is minutes away from the Village nightlife, but tucked away in a quiet corner with its own lush, spacious patio garden so you get the best of both worlds. Rooms are on the old-fashioned side but still cheery and bright.

LE JAZZ HOSTEL ST-DENIS

Map p72 Hostel $

☎ 514-448-4848; www.jazzhostels.com/jazzstdenis; 329 Rue Ontario Est; dm $30; Ⓜ Berri-UQAM;

This small hostel, which opened in 2008, enjoys a good location near the nightlife action along Rue St-Denis. The amenities are decent (backyard with BBQ, in-room wi-fi, guest kitchen), though sometimes the place could use a firmer hand in the cleaning department.

LE GÎTE DU PARC LAFONTAINE

Map p72 Hostel $

☎ 514-522-3910, 877-350-4483; www.hostelmontreal.com; 1250 Rue Sherbrooke Est; dm/d with shared bathroom from $27/60; Ⓜ Sherbrooke

This converted Victorian house has an atmosphere more like that of a guesthouse or inn than a hostel. It's located just a 10-minute walk from the main bus station and close to bar-filled Rue St-Denis. Continental breakfast (included in the price) is served on the terrace and guests can use the kitchen, TV room and laundry. There's also bike rental for exploring the city.

PLATEAU MONT-ROYAL

Staying in the most fashionable district of Montréal means being close to some of the best eateries and nightlife in town. Like the Village, the Plateau is packed with B&Bs; hotels are few and far between.

AUBERGE DE LA FONTAINE

Map pp76–7 Inn $$

☎ 514-597-0166, 800-597-0597; www.aubergedelafontaine.com; 1301 Rue Rachel Est; d from $166; Ⓜ Mont-Royal

A gem of an inn on the edge of Parc LaFontaine, this guesthouse has rooms painted in Provençal hues, with exposed brick walls (in some rooms) and cheerful art and furnishings. Staff are friendly and knowledgeable. The snack refrigerator with goodies free for the taking is a nice touch.

HÔTEL DE L'INSTITUT Map pp76–7 Hotel $$

☎ 514-282-5120; www.ithq.qc.ca; 3535 Rue St-Denis; s/d $129/144; Ⓜ Sherbrooke

Set in a sleek modern glass cube, this hotel is run as a training center for the Québec tourism and hotel board. The 42 rooms are spacious and comfortable, and all have tiny balconies – some offering decent views. Bathrooms are cramped, but otherwise clean and functional. The trim restaurant on-site is a well-kept secret, with excellent multicourse meals. Young attentive staff provide noteworthy service.

KUTUMA HOTEL & SUITES

Map pp76–7 B&B $$

☎ 514-844-0111; www.kutuma.com; 3708 Rue St-Denis; d/ste from $140/170; Ⓜ Sherbrooke

In an excellent location on lively Rue St-Denis, the Kutuma has the feel of a boutique hotel. Cozy, well-maintained rooms feature safari-theme decor, including animal-print fabrics, potted palms and colorful artwork on the walls. Bathrooms are modern and perhaps overly sleek, but the two-person tub in some bathrooms is a nice feature. Negatives: some rooms have tiny windows, and there's no elevator – though staff can help you lug your stuff up the stairs. The on-site Ethiopian restaurant, Le Nil Bleu (p131) is excellent.

À LA BONNE HEURE B&B

Map pp76–7 B&B $$

☎ 514-529-0179; www.alabonneheure.ca; 4425 Rue St-Hubert; s/d with shared bathroom $85/100, s/d with bathroom $115/135; Ⓜ Mont-Royal

This is a typical turn-of-the-century Montréal terrace home with five bright, spacious rooms that exude an old-fashioned charm. Breakfast is served in the elegant dining room with high ceiling, French doors and cornice molding. It's well located, just one block from the Mont-Royal metro station.

AUX PORTES DE LA NUIT

Map pp76–7 B&B $$

☎ 514-848-0833; www.auxportesdelanuit.com; 3496 Ave Laval; d $115-135; Ⓜ Sherbrooke;

In a lovely location near the lush Carré St-Louis, this five-room B&B offers abundant charm. Inside the beautifully maintained 1894 Victorian, you'll find a mix of elegantly decorated rooms, each done in a different color scheme, but featuring wood floors, a few antique furnishings and original artwork (painted by the owner's daughter). The Balcony Room has lovely views of the park; the Terrace Room has its own secluded terrace.

ANNE MA SOEUR ANNE

Map pp76–7 Studio Apartments $$

☎ 514-281-3187; www.annemasoeuranne.com; 4119 Rue St-Denis; s/d from $110/130; Ⓜ Mont-Royal;

These smart, fully equipped studios fill a valuable niche in the Plateau. They're suitable for short- or long-term stays, each unit having a 'microkitchen' with a microwave and stove, work space and Ikea-style furnishings built into the walls. The cheapest rooms are a little cramped, while others have private terraces, some overlooking the shady backyard. Croissants are delivered to your door as breakfast.

PIERRE ET DOMINIQUE B&B

Map pp76–7 B&B $$

☎ 514-286-0307; www.bbcanada.com/928.html; 271 Carré St-Louis; s without bathroom $75, s/d with bathroom from $95/110; Ⓜ Sherbrooke

This is one of several inviting B&Bs snuggled in the rows of stone Victorian houses overlooking Carré St-Louis. You'll find just three small, cozy bedrooms, all neatly set with

Swedish-style furniture and painted in cheery tones. The best room has a view of the park.

SHÉZELLES Map pp76–7 B&B $$

☎ 514-849-8694; www.shezelles.com; 4272 Rue Berri; s/d with shared bathroom $90/105, r with private bathroom $150; M Mont-Royal

Shézelles is a bastion of warmth with its paneled walls, wood floors and attractively furnished rooms. The en suite room has a king-size bed and a spacious bathroom with a Jacuzzi. There are smaller but welcoming doubles, as well as a 'love nest' behind a Japanese sliding door (the bed is directly under a skylight).

COUETTE ET CAFÉ CHERRIER
Map pp76–7 B&B $$

☎ 514-982-6848, 888-440-6848; www3.sympatico.ca/couette; 522 Rue Cherrier; s/d with shared bathroom from $80/95; M Sherbrooke

This pretty greystone with lantern gables is stacked with perks: a living room with a fireplace, a separate guest floor with private access, and English-language newspapers in the morning. The four rooms are immaculate and come with a variety of beds (double, queen, king) and personal touches, like dressing gowns. An open staircase leads to the 3rd floor, where breakfast is served.

LE RAYON VERT Map pp76–7 B&B $$

☎ 514-524-6774; www.lerayonvert.ca; 4373 Rue St-Hubert; s/d with shared bathroom $78/90; M Mont-Royal

This centennial greystone has three comfortable, individual rooms not far from the alternative bustle of Ave du Mont-Royal. Rooms have wood floors and classic wood furnishings (there's even a chandelier and cornice molding in the Victorian room). The breakfast room recalls a French country inn, but the clincher is the idyllic rear terrace – in summer it's as green as the tropics.

AU PIANO BLANC Map pp76–7 B&B $$

☎ 514-845-0315; www.aupianoblanc.com; 4440 Rue Berri; s/d with shared bathroom $80/95, s/d with private bathroom $115/130; M Mont-Royal; P 💻

The 'colors of the sun,' as owner Céline, a former singer, puts it, radiate from this delightful B&B a stone's throw from Mont-Royal metro station. Brightly painted rooms, colorful artwork and whimsical bedside lamps add to the good cheer. Some rooms are tiny while others have views of the back terrace.

BIENVENUE B&B Map pp76–7 B&B $$

☎ 514-844-5897, 800-227-5897; www.bienvenuebb.com; 3950 Ave Laval; s/d with shared bathroom from $77/87; M Sherbrooke

On a peaceful backstreet in the Plateau, Bienvenue is a 12-room Victorian B&B set with a range of small, clean rooms with homey furnishings. Decorative touches (artwork here and there and quilted bedspreads in some rooms) add to the appeal, though the carpeting is a little worn. All rooms get decent light and some have high ceilings.

LE GÎTE Map pp76–7 B&B $$

☎ 514-849-4567; www.legite.ca; 3619 Rue de Bullion; s/d from $75/85; M Sherbrooke;

In a row house just off restaurant-lined Rue Prince Arthur, Le Gîte is yet another charming Plateau B&B. The four rooms here have polished wood floors, an attractive Zenlike design and striking works of art covering the walls (created by the owner's son). Other nice touches are the small shaded terrace, wi-fi access, kitchen use and free laundry.

BOB & MARIKO'S BED & BREAKFAST
Map pp76–7 B&B $$

☎ 514-289-9749, 800-267-5180; www.bbmontreal.qc.ca; 3458 Ave Laval; s/d with shared bath from $75/85

Owners Bob and Mariko Finkelstein receive high marks for their warm hospitality. Set in a 100-year-old house, this small, cozy B&B has just four rooms, all with original maple floors and trim furnishings – some of which could use an update. Good location.

CHEZ BRASIL Map pp76–7 Hotel $$

☎ 514-581-8363; www.bbcanada.com/chezbrasil; 3945 Ave Laval; s/d with shared bathroom $60/85, apt $125-135; M Sherbrooke

Run by two welcoming expats from Brazil, this cozy B&B lies on a quiet street in the Plateau and offers comfortable rooms with splashes of color and homey furnishings. There are also two apartments, each with two bedrooms and kitchens – good value for families or those looking for a bit more space.

GINGERBREAD MANOR B&B

Map pp76–7 B&B $$

☎ 514-597-2804; www.gingerbreadmanor.com; 3445 Ave Laval; s/d with shared bathroom $74/84, d with private bathroom $109; Ⓜ Sherbrooke

A warm welcome to visitors is given by the hosts at this charming B&B near the leafy Carré St-Louis. The house itself is a stately three-story townhouse built in 1885 with bay windows, ornamental details and an attached carriage house. The elegant rooms – five in all – are uniquely furnished (only one has a private bathroom, the others share), and the best have king-size beds and a bay window. All have decent light. Hot cooked breakfasts (which may include banana walnut pancakes, French toast and fruit salad, croissants, etc) are a bonus.

AUBERGE DE JEUNESSE MAEVA

Map pp76–7 Hostel $

☎ 514-523-0840; www.aubergemaeva.com; 4755 Rue St-Hubert; dm $24, d without bathroom $65; Ⓜ Laurier;

This small, quaint, family-run hostel sits in a peaceful residential neighborhood not far from the action on Ave du Mont-Royal. Guests bunk in four- or six-bed dorms, with a bathroom in each. Guests enjoy free wi-fi access and free use of bikes, plus kitchen access and table soccer.

QUÉBEC CITY

top picks

- **Musée de la Civilisation** (p208)
- **La Citadelle** (p202)
- **Musée National des Beaux-Arts du Québec** (p211)
- **Parc des Champs de Bataille** (p209)
- **St-Jean-Baptiste** (p212)
- **Panache** (p221)

What's your recommendation? www.lonelyplanet.com/canada/quebec-city

QUÉBEC CITY

The crown jewel of French Canada, Québec City is one of the oldest European settlements in North America. Its picturesque Old Town is a Unesco world heritage site, a living museum of narrow cobblestone streets lined with 17th- and 18th-century houses, with narrow church spires soaring overhead. There's more than a glimmer of Old Europe in its classic bistros and brasseries, sidewalk cafés and manicured parks and plazas.

Located on a strategic cliff above the St Lawrence River, its massive citadel bears testament to the crucial role this settlement played in the history of the New World. Indeed, history lurks around every corner of this atmospheric city, and its historical superlatives are many. This is, after all, home to the continent's first parish church, its first museum, first Anglican cathedral and first French-speaking university, among many other firsts. When you flip through the *Quebec Chronicle-Telegraph*, you're reading North America's oldest newspaper, and if you have to pay a visit to L'Hôtel Dieu de Québec, console yourself with the thought that it's the continent's oldest hospital.

What this historical onslaught adds up to is an aged capital that still carries the spirit of its days past, with twinges of romance, melancholy, eccentricity and intrigue lurking in its windswept lanes. This is also a city that goes to great lengths to attract (and amuse) visitors. Although busloads of tourists arrive during the summer, the buzz in the air and lively street life somehow counterbalance the mayhem of the masses. Musicians, acrobats and actors in period costume take to the streets and squares, while fantastic festivals fill the city with song.

Fall and spring bring beautiful colors, dramatically reduced prices and thinner crowds. And in the winter, Caribou, an alcoholic drink enjoyed by the early settlers, is sold everywhere to keep people warm and toasty. Even in the darkest and coldest months of January and February, Quebecers have found a way to have fun: throwing the annual Winter Carnival, arguably the biggest, most colorful and most successful winter festival around.

Once past Le Château Frontenac, the most photographed hotel in the world, visitors find themselves torn between the various neighborhoods' diverse charms. In the Old Upper Town, the historical hub, there are some fine museums and restaurants among the T-shirt stores. The Old Lower Town, at the base of the steep cliffs, is a labyrinth, where it's a pleasure to get lost among street performers and cozy inns before emerging on the north shore of the St Lawrence.

One of the best ways to see these areas and to savor Québec's unique atmosphere is to grab a table at a sidewalk café and watch the lively street scene unfold.

Most visitors never venture outside the Old Town, but there is plenty to explore beyond the walls as well. The St-Jean-Baptiste neighborhood has wonderful shopping, cafés and bars as does *'le nouveau'* St-Roch, another downtown neighborhood that's become one of the most striking and exciting examples of urban renewal in the province's recent history.

About 622,000 people live in the Québec City municipality and the vast majority of them have French ancestry. The English minority is miniscule here, but everyone associated with the tourism industry, including staff at hotels, restaurants, shops and tourist sites, speaks English. Québec City is the capital of the province of Québec, which means once you leave those Old Town walls and head for the compact downtown you'll be rubbing shoulders with the province's elite: the rich, the powerful, the lobbyists, the wheelers, dealers and decision makers.

GETTING STARTED

Québec (as locals refer to the city) makes a great addition to a Montréal trip, though it has enough magnetism to justify the journey whether or not you visit that *other* town further downriver. Traveling here has ample rewards, not least of which is that uncertain feeling that you've surely left the continent – over 95% of the city is francophone. Big colorful festivals, rambling cobblestone streets full of history and that magnificent cliff-top setting overlooking the mouth of the mighty St Lawrence River – just a few reasons why a one- or two-day excursion here simply isn't enough.

WHEN TO GO

Winters here are a little colder and last just a bit longer than in Montréal. Even in May and early June, the weather can be a little unpredictable, with chilly bouts of rain and fog followed by days of clear blue skies. When summer arrives in full, so do the big crowds, which can overflow the narrow lanes of the Old Town. Still, this is one of the most festive and liveliest times to visit, with a packed events calendar from June to August. Even during the height of summer it's possible to avoid the crowds (by simply stepping outside of the Old Town, or rising early for a photographic journey around town).

Summer isn't the only time to visit. Québec's Winter Carnival is famous, and for those looking for a unique experience – sleeping in an ice hotel (p238), cross-country skiing through the parks, or visiting a *cabane à sucre* (sugar shack; p123) – off-season is the time to come.

Festivals & Events

JANUARY–FEBRUARY

WINTER CARNIVAL

www.carnaval.qc.ca

This famous annual event, unique to Québec City, bills itself as the biggest winter carnival in the world. Held sometime between late January and mid-February, there are parades, ice sculptures, a snow slide, boat races, dances, music and lots of drinking. Activities take place all over the Old Town (many at the Parc de l'Esplanade) and include a giant slide on the Terrasse Dufferin behind the Château. If you want to go, bring lots of warm clothes and organize the trip early, as accommodations fill up fast.

JUNE

FÊTE NATIONALE DU QUÉBEC

www.fetenationale.qc.ca

Québec City parties hard on June 24, honoring John the Baptist, the patron saint of French Canadians. The day has evolved into a quasi-political event celebrating Québec culture and nationalistic leanings. Major festivities on the Plains of Abraham start around 8pm, ending with a massive fireworks display.

LE GRAND RIRE

Comedy Festival; www.grandrire.com

Every year this big comedy fest gets bigger. In 2009, Le Grand Rire celebrated its 10th anniversary, with over 500,000 visitors streaming into town. The three-week fest features days of comedy, from stand-up shows to street performances. It usually kicks off in mid-June and continues into early July.

JULY–AUGUST

CANADA DAY

Yes, it's celebrated even here, smack on July 1. The event sometimes coincides with the big comedy fest Le Grand Rire (above). You can also expect at least one big outdoor concert, and a big fireworks show over the waterfront.

FESTIVAL D'ÉTÉ

Summer Festival; www.infofestival.com

Early July attracts musicians from all over Québec, Canada and even the world. The eclectic mix features everyone from Québec

BONHOMME CARNAVAL

You don't even need to be around for the winter festivities to know about Bonhomme. He's now as much a symbol of Québec as the Château Frontenac.

The official mascot of the Winter Carnival and the unofficial mascot of the provincial capital, Bonhomme was created with the founding of the carnival in 1954, along with a fantastical backstory. He lives in a land of ice and snow called Knulandis, whose residents are called Knuks; Grrrounches form a minority in the population. In the Knulandis tales, there is a town chief, ritualistic dances and natural elements like the wind, moon and sun that all play a formative role in the destiny of the land. The clear references to First Nations' beliefs and customs cleverly link Québec's past and present.

This friendly snowman dresses in a red Québécois *tuque* (winter hat) and an arrowed, colorful belt like those his *coureurs des bois* (fur-trader) ancestors wore, purportedly to 'support the kidneys' and prevent the cold from seeping into the cracks between the *coureurs'* pants and jackets.

He makes appearances at many of the festival's activities. A month before festivities begin, he unofficially sneaks into town, throws a big party, then reappears only at the solemn, official opening of the carnival, in which Québec City's mayor hands him the keys to the city.

According to his official description, Bonhomme loves to dance and be merry, expresses his feelings through gestures, loves everyone equally and without prejudice and represents the joy and the hardy spirit with which the Québécois handle their winters.

vedettes (stars) Garou and Éric Lapointe to German heavy-metal band the Scorpions. The 11-day festival is a fabulous place to see plenty of concerts by the province's stars.

LES GRANDS FEUX LOTO-QUÉBEC

www.lesgrandsfeux.com

A spectacular fireworks and music show at La Chute Montmorency, held between late July and mid-August.

FÊTES DE LA NOUVELLE-FRANCE

Festival of New France; ☎ 418-694-5560; www.nouvellefrance.qc.ca

A fab little festival in early August that commemorates Québec's colonial period. There are historical reenactments and people running around in period costumes along with a slew of performances and other events.

SEPTEMBER

FÊTE ARC-EN-CIEL

Gay Pride Festival; ☎ 418-809-3383; www.glbtquebec.org

The celebrations early in September end in an enthusiastic rally through downtown Québec City.

OCTOBER–NOVEMBER

FESTIVAL DES MUSIQUES SACRÉES DE QUÉBEC

Québec City Festival of Sacred Music; www.festivalmusiquesacree.ca

This terrific festival showcases everything from gospel and Celtic music to Gregorian chants and Inuit throat singing. Look for it in late October or early November.

COSTS & MONEY

For the most part, prices in Québec City are about the same as they are for Montréal. Lodging can run a bit higher here, if you want to stay in the old part of town. Most B&Bs and inns charge upwards of $150 per night for a room, and in high season, average rates top $200. Parking can also cost a little more – though you can save if you don't mind parking far out and taking a bus in (see p233). Some guesthouses also provide parking – usually for a fee.

INTERNET RESOURCES

Quebéc Region (www.quebecregion.com) The city's official tourism portal with events calendars, cycling maps and attractions in and around Québec City.

BACKGROUND

HISTORY

The first significant settlement that we have knowledge of, on the site of today's Québec City, was an Iroquois village of 500 called Stadacona. The Iroquois were seminomadic, building longhouses, hunting, fishing and cultivating crops until the land got tired, when they moved on.

French explorer Jacques Cartier traveled to the New World in 1534, but barely lasted the winter. He returned in 1535; by the time May 1536 rolled around Cartier and his remaining crew beat a retreat back to France, kidnapping some of the Iroquois, along with the chief of Stadacona, to take with them. The Iroquois all died in France but Cartier returned in 1541 to start a post upstream in the New World. Again, he faced a winter of scurvy and disastrous relations with the indigenous population so the plan failed, setting back France's colonial ambitions for 50 years.

Explorer Samuel de Champlain gets the credit for founding the city for the French in 1608, calling it Kebec, from the Algonquian word meaning 'the river narrows here.'

The English successfully attacked in 1629, but Québec was returned to the French under a treaty three years later and it became the center of Nouvelle-France (New France). Repeated English attacks followed. In 1759 General Wolfe led the British to victory over Montcalm on the Plains of Abraham. One of North America's most famous battles, it virtually ended the long-running conflict between Britain and France. In 1763 the Treaty of Paris gave Canada to Britain. In 1775 the American revolutionaries tried to capture Québec but were promptly pushed back. In 1864 meetings were held in the city that led to the formation of Canada in 1867. Québec City became the provincial capital.

In the 19th century the city lost its status and importance to Montréal. When the Great Depression burst Montréal's bubble in 1929, Québec City regained some stature as a government center. Some business-savvy locals launched the now-famous Winter Carnival in the 1950s to incite a tourism boom.

While the suburbs and outskirts of Québec City kept developing, they sucked the life out of much of the city center. Poor urban planning through to the 1980s led to an exodus to the suburbs, leaving the downtown core depopulated and prone to crime in some areas.

The megamalls being built in the suburbs were also a capital drain on the downtown businesses. The area started to turn around in the 1990s, with the rejuvenation of St-Roch and diversification of the economy. Laval University moved some of its apartments downtown as well, bringing an influx of young students into the neighborhood.

The improvements in urban renewal went hand in hand with growth and diversification of Québec's economy. The explosion of the high-tech sector brought new jobs, spurred the creation of start-ups and infused cash into growing research facilities. Québec City reached out to the high-tech industries and now there are research centers in everything from lasers and optics to health and biotechnology. The government established the National Center of New Technology (CNNTQ) in St-Roch and now there are over 20 IT firms that bring more than 800 workers into the neighborhood each day.

The 'rebranding' of Québec seems to be working. In a recent poll of North American and European cities, Québec City ranked number two for its software, plastics and metal manufacturing.

So like modern Montréal, Québec City has a new sheen, with both the pluses and minuses that brings: locals are struggling with their property taxes which are skyrocketing, just as they have in Montréal.

The other downside is what some consider the transformation of the Old Town. As recently as the early '90s, even students were able to afford to live there, and the place still had something of a community feel. However, rental increases have pushed out almost all but the very moneyed and fewer and fewer locals can actually afford to live in the area. It's also pushed out the day-to-day businesses like grocery stores that gave the neighborhood a sense of community. While the Old Town is still breathtaking it's hard not to be a little wistful about the change.

Speaking of the Old Town, in 2006 archaeologists made a startling discovery when they uncovered the failed site of Cartier-Roberval (1541–43), one of two forts that were built. Though historic records have long spoken of the site, no one had ever been able to find it. The team that uncovered it did so quite by accident when it was doing perfunctory exploratory work on a site that was slated to be turned into a parkway. Among the items unearthed were porcelain from Italy and Iroquois pottery, both dating from the 1550s. The historians and archaeologists involved believe they may also uncover the bodies of the first settlers who were wiped out by disease. If so, studying the remains will blow the lid off the mystery of early settlement of the colony. Researchers estimate there may be another 15 years of work before that happens, however. In the meantime, the site has opened to the public, which you can have a look at next to the Terrasse Dufferin (p203).

In 2008 Québec City threw its biggest bash in honor of the 400th anniversary of its founding. Meanwhile, the global economic downturn that began that same year has also affected Québec. It remains to be seen whether the optimism of recent years can counteract the rising unemployment and inflationary worries that continue to lurk on the horizon.

ARTS

Visual Arts

Many of Canada's top artists have been inspired by the beauty of Québec City and its surrounding scenery.

Jean-Paul Lemieux (1904–90) is one of Canada's most accomplished painters. Born in Québec City, he studied at L'École des Beaux-Arts de Montréal and later in Paris. He is famous for his iconic paintings of Québec's vacant and endless landscapes and Quebecers' relation to it. Many of his paintings are influenced by the simple lines of folk art. There's a whole hall devoted to his art at the Musée National des Beaux-Arts du Québec (p211) and it is definitely worth a visit.

Alfred Pellan (1906–88) was another renowned artist who studied at the local École des Beaux-Arts before moving to Paris. He later became famous for his portraits, still life, figures and landscapes, before turning to surrealism in the 1940s.

Other artists born elsewhere have moved to Québec City after being bewitched by its countryside.

Cornelius Krieghoff (1815–72) was born in Amsterdam but was acclaimed for chronicling the customs and clothes of Quebecers in his paintings. He is known especially for the portraits he did of the Wendats (p234) who lived around Québec City.

Francesco Iacurto was born in Montréal but moved to Québec City in 1938 and his acclaimed works are dominated by the town's streetscapes, landscapes and portrayals of Île d'Orléans (p234).

Music

Québec City has plenty to offer music lovers. For classical music fans there's the L'Orchestre Symphonique de Québec (p228), a respected 100-year-old symphony orchestra. Its season runs from September to May and it performs at Le Grand Théâtre de Québec (p229). There's also the terrific Opéra de Québec (p228), which performs at the same venue. Its season runs from October to May.

Some of the province's biggest rock stars started out here. Jean Leloup of rock and pop fame (see p25) was born here, and Loco Locass is a hip-hop group that formed in the city. But the scene here is so small, bands and singers end up relocating to Montréal at some point in their careers to be where the music industry is concentrated and to be closer to the thriving club scene.

If you're interested in original music, there's still enough here to keep you busy. Heavy metal and Goth are extremely popular (for advice on that area just ask the kids who hang out in the graveyard at Église St-Matthew off Rue St-Jean). For more off-the-wall stuff check out the electronic music of Millimetrik (www.millimetrik.com) and for New York Dolls/Hanoi Rocks–like dance music keep an eye out for Uberko.

There's a brash and independent spirit among the eclectic mix of active bands here so ask around at record stores about what's new and check out the weekly listings in *Voir Québec* every Thursday.

Cinema

The Québec film industry is firmly based in Montréal both from the production and creative angles.

The well-preserved state of the Old Town makes it extremely popular with foreign productions as it can easily stand in for medieval Europe. However, there is no production studio in Québec nor are there many Québec City–set stories being made today, strange for a capital and the second-biggest city in the province.

Robert Lepage's Ex Machina, a multidisciplinary performing-arts company, is still based here. Though Lepage had hoped to turn a giant tunnel under the city into a movie production studio, negotiations are stalled for the moment. Lepage is one of the only contemporary filmmakers who regularly sets his films in the city. See the boxed text, p229, for more on Lepage.

FILMS

All names listed here refer to the director of the film. Below are some films in which Québec City gets center stage.

Les Plouffe by Gilles Carle (1981) – based on a novel by Roger Lemelin, this film depicts a family's struggles in Depression-era Québec City. If you want to understand the turbulent changes going on in the province at that time, it's hard to find a better film.

Les Yeux Rouges (The Red Eyes, or Accidental Truths) by Yves Simoneau (1982) – a Québec City–set thriller with two cops on the trail of a deranged strangler.

Ma Vie en Cinémascope (My Life in Cinemascope) by Denise Filiatrault (2004) – singer Alys Robi was Québec's first international superstar (Never heard of her? Robi's 'Tico-Tico' was as well known in the 1940s as Céline's 'My Heart Will Go On' is 50 years later). Robi reached a level of fame that most Canadians could never dream of, let alone a French-speaking girl from conservative, isolated Québec City. The brilliant (as always) Pascale Bussières plays the adult Alys as she realizes her wildest dreams before mental illness sees her shut up for years in a mental institution where she receives electroshock treatments and a lobotomy.

I Confess by Alfred Hitchcock (1953) – a film-noirish suspense thriller, and Québec City has never looked better than when Hitchcock is caressing its atmospheric Old World edges with his lens. It's based on a French play about a priest who hears a murderer's confession that his covenant with God won't let him break, even when he finds himself accused of the murder instead. Hitchcock was so taken with Québec City he based the entire story here and made the characters Canadian (see the boxed text, p205).

Le Confessionnal (The Confessional) by Robert Lepage (1995) – an homage to the above Hitchcock film. Lepage's character starts off the film saying the days that had the most impact on his life were the re-election of Maurice Duplessis as premier of Québec, the arrival of TV, and Hitchcock arriving in Québec City. Sometimes retracing Hitchcock's steps, Lepage builds a beautiful portrait of Québec City through a man's quest to uncover a family secret that coincided with Hitchcock's arrival in town.

La Neuvaine (The Novena) by Bernard Émond (2005) – OK, so it's not *exactly* in Québec City, but if you're in this section, you may very well be nipping off to Ste-Anne-de-

Beaupré (p234), whose shrine has a starring role in this film. It brings together a young man who comes to the cathedral to pray for his grandmother's life and a guilt-ridden Montréal doctor who arrives to put an end to her own. It's all too easy to ridicule Ste-Anne-de-Beaupré's religious rock-concert vibe, but as the director Bernard Émond said so well of this film, 'I don't want to mock the crutches and ex-votos…you don't mock hope.'

Theater

Canada's French-language TV and film industries are firmly based in Montréal, but when it comes to theater, Québec City is still holding its own. Pretty much every actor who graduates from the local drama conservatory here asks themselves whether it's the big city and bright lights of Montréal they seek, or if they'll stick around in the capital's tight-knit theater community.

Actors in Québec City can't always completely support themselves just through performing so usually combine it with a related job like teaching or drama coaching. There's a lot that's attractive about staying. An actor here with a creative or original idea can write a script and have it produced – something that would take years, if it happened at all, in Montréal. One of the most infamous examples was the brilliant one-woman show *Gros et Détail* by Québec City actor Anne-Marie Olivier, about the different people who live in the St-Roch neighborhood. The show was a full-on hit in Québec City, France and several countries in francophone Africa, but when Olivier tried to get it produced in Montréal she was told 'no' because it focused too much on Québec City.

One of Québec City's most famous native sons is Robert Lepage, an award-winning playwright and director still quite active in the performing-arts scene today. While his best-known works feature Québec City, he has also collaborated on productions abroad, working on Cirque du Soleil's 2010 touring show and the Ring Cycle for New York's Metropolitan Opera. See p229 for more details on his artistic successes.

Literature

There are many wonderful Québec City writers but few are translated. For a great sense of the city that still applies today, read one of the horror/fantasy stories by American writer HP Lovecraft. Lovecraft was obsessed with cities in which the past and present exist on top of each other, and Québec City was one of his favorite locations.

ARCHITECTURE

You'll find a fascinating architectural mix here, ranging from 18th-century buildings to newer and more daring buildings springing up in the outer districts. The soaring cathedrals and basilicas encompassing everything from Gothic to neoclassical elements will likely be the highlights for many architecture buffs. These awesome religious structures are generally of such colossal size, they positively dwarf everything around them, whether it's the Église St-Jean-Baptiste (p212) casting shadows over the residential St-Jean-Baptiste neighborhood or the Église St-Roch (p213) that completely overpowers even the flashiest and ritziest boutiques of the St-Roch district.

Québec's Old Town is the place to head for a taste of what residential dwellings were like in New France. One feature you'll notice is the tiny doors on many of the buildings. While some people say their small size is because people were shorter in the 17th and 18th centuries, another explanation is that these doors were actually delivery ports, small only because they were meant for cargo deliveries and not for humans at all.

For some of the city's most interesting modern buildings, the up-and-coming St-Roch neighborhood is likely the most interesting. Even run-of-the mill buildings like parking garages have been given a makeover and are worth a look. Check out the Stationnement Odéon (Rue de la Chapelle) that got an overhaul in 2002.

ENVIRONMENT

There are wonderful parks and green spaces here, including Parc du Bois-de-Coulonge (p213), Jardin Jeanne-d'Arc and, of course, Battlefields Park (p209). The city says about 45% of greater Québec City is wooded territory. Recycling programs are high on the city's environmental to-do list. Presently, only 30% of household waste is recycled. Québec City recently spent $7 million on 110,700 recycling carts.

GOVERNMENT & POLITICS

Québec City has a great tradition of colorful, rabble-rousing mayors. Jean-Paul L'Allier,

THE QUÉBÉCOIS ETHOS

Québec City has a reputation for being square and conservative (that is, at least from the Montréal perspective) and locals often refer to Québec City as a 'village' with equal parts affection and derision. Though it has all the big-city trappings, the core downtown population numbers just 180,000.

Québec City locals are very proud but there's a time in pretty much all of their lives, usually after high school or university, when they decide whether they are going to 'try' Montréal or stay put. As the 'everything' capital of French Canada, from arts to business, science, technology and media, Montréal's pull is hard to resist. However, that means that those creative, dynamic people who chose to stay in Québec City are there because they really love the city and want to be there. So you'll find the way they identify with the city is very strong.

Québec City is also known in Montréal and the rest of Canada as being a notoriously challenging place for people born outside of the city to establish themselves in the long term.

With a near-homogenous French-Catholic background, community ties go way, way back. In fact, professional and future business networks are often established by the time the city's future citizens leave high school, if not primary school. Even French-speaking Quebecers from elsewhere in the province who come to Québec City to work or do business say these networks are extremely difficult to penetrate both professionally and socially.

mayor from 1989 to 2005, had a reputation as a bit of an egoist but he did wonders for the city by taking the initiative to diversify the economy and clean up the St-Roch neighborhood. Present mayor Andrée Boucher is arguably the most colorful in Canada. She was the mayor of Ste-Foy before it became part of Québec City during the province-wide mergers, then was elected mayor of Québec City in the best punk-rock tradition – Boucher pummeled her competition, which included a slick campaign by former provincial justice minister Marc Bellemare, with a grassroots campaign. She participated in public debates but did not do any advertising and limited her campaign spending to just $5000.

MEDIA

Weekly newspaper the *Quebec Telegraph-Chronicle* (www.qctonline.com) is Québec City's only English-language publication. It claims to be the oldest newspaper in North America, having published continuously since 1764. Though it does have some interesting editorials and columns, it is actually more of a community newspaper and has only limited distribution. The city's two daily newspapers are the French-language *Le Soleil* (www.cyberpresse.ca/le-soleil), which has the best coverage of the city, and the tabloid *Le Journal de Québec* (www.lejournaldequebec.com).

Voir Québec (www.voir.ca) is the city's free entertainment weekly with pages of listings each Thursday for what's going on around town. Though it shares some of the editorial content with its Montréal incarnation, the listings are all focused on the Québec City scene.

FASHION

Some of Canada's most famous and iconic clothing stores were founded in Québec City. Simons is a province-wide department-store chain, known for stocking fashions by its own designers that aren't available in the other major stores. It's particularly known for its Twik clothing line for women.

On the high-fashion front, Holt Renfrew, now the flagship of high fashion all across Canada, got its start in Québec City as a modest hat shop, established by an Irishman named William Samuel Henderson. However, it was only when the store started stocking furs that it drew national and then international attention. The store still proudly boasts that it received 'the prestigious honor of five generations of royal warrants under Queen Victoria's reign and was appointed Furrier-in-Ordinary to Her Majesty.'

Unlike Montréal, Québec City isn't known as a hotbed of fashion. With so many locals being government workers, the dark navy or grey suit reigns supreme among both men and women, leaving little room for spicy fashion or experimentation.

When the most recent fashion scandal did hit, it was iconoclastic Québec City mayor Andrée Boucher (see p199) of all people who set it off. Mayor Boucher was on a business trip to Paris when she was snapped wearing a bright lime-green sundress with red lace-up ballet flats. Quebecers were scandalized and the picture made its way across English Canada where she was pilloried as well.

In fine form as always, Mayor Boucher said it was a $3000 Yves St-Laurent dress and that the picture just didn't do it justice. Still, the story had legs for weeks and we'll go out on a limb here to give Mayor Boucher a standing ovation for taking a risk and for being the only person to get 'Québec City' and 'fashion' together in every single major national newspaper in recent memory.

LANGUAGE

Though many young people will be comfortable chatting to you in English, it is far less commonly spoken here than in Montréal. English is learned from primary school and locals grow up listening to anglophone music, but given the tiny English community in Québec City, if you venture outside the walls you may find many locals who are not used to speaking or listening to the language.

Within the walls, where almost all locals are somehow engaged with the tourist industry, you will have no problem finding English speakers.

If you speak some French and are coming from Montréal, you may find the accent here thicker and more challenging to understand. Montrealers and Québec City locals can easily recognize each other at parties just by their accents.

NEIGHBORHOODS

Québec City is a gorgeous old place whose compact size makes it ideal for walking and exploring. The Old Town is packed with museums, old architecture and fantastic scenery. It's hard to walk more than a few steps without coming across an interesting sight or cobblestone street just begging to be explored.

The city itself covers 93 sq km. Part sits atop the cliffs of Cap Diamant (Cape Diamond), and part lies below. Quebecers call the upper part the Haute Ville (Upper Town) and the lower part Basse Ville (Lower Town). Together, the 10 sq km of these historic upper and lower areas, within the stone walls, form the appealing Vieux-Québec (Old Town).

The Citadelle (p202), a fort and landmark, stands on the highest point of Cap Diamant. The other major landmark is the splendid, dominating, copper-topped, castle-style Fairmont Le Château Frontenac hotel (p233) dating from 1892. Behind the Château, a large boardwalk called the Terrasse Dufferin edges along

PARLEZ-VOUS FRANÇAIS?

Great as Montréal is, if you are serious about picking up French or improving the French you already have, there is no better place than Québec City. As more than one frustrated French-language student has remarked, once Montrealers realize you're from somewhere else they will do *le switch* into English and you've said goodbye to another chance to road test your verb conjugations. It's different in Québec City. Though Quebecers grow up learning English like they do in Montréal, because the anglophone minority in Québec is so tiny, they don't hear much of it or get the chance to practice. So, as long as you stay away from the tourist-centered businesses, you'll be able to practice away and get plenty of encouragement while you're at it.

If you do decide to come for a language trip, you will be one of hundreds of students who do so regularly. Don't be put off by the Québécois accent; the instructors both teach and speak standard international French.

École de langues de l'Université Laval (Map p204; ☎ 418-656-2321; www.elul.ulaval.ca; bureau 2301 2nd fl, Pavillon Charles-De Koninck, Laval University) is your best bet. It offers 15-week fall and winter courses or five-week spring and summer courses. You can be hooked up for accommodations with a Québécois family (from $88 per week with kitchen access to $180 a week with breakfast and dinner) or, in the spring and summer sessions, you can stay in residence (per week $88).

Another good place to study in Québec City is at Bouchereau Lingua International (☎ 418-692-1370; www.bli.ca; 43 Rue de Buade). In business for over 25 years, BLI offers small-group (four to nine students) immersion courses – generally 20 hours per week. BLI can also set you up with a host family or an apartment. Courses run year-round and you can often join an ongoing class at your level without having to wait for another to begin.

If you are set on Montréal, your best chance at full French immersion is on 'the Mountain' at Université de Montréal. Université de Montréal Adult Education Department (☎ 514-343-6090, 800-363-8876; www.fep.umontreal.ca/langues; Pavilion 3744, Rue Jean-Brillant, room 320; Ⓜ Côte-des-Neiges) has terrific programs that include night or weekend courses, courses in everything from beginners' French to Québec culture to advanced courses in written French. This is a very proud French-language campus so people are not prone to making *le switch* so feared by French-language students. Many Americans and South Americans attend this program in summer as a kind of study vacation as it's cheaper than flying to Europe.

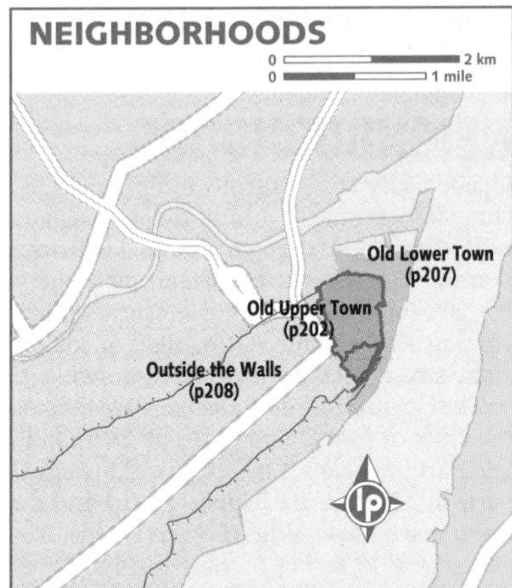

the cliff, providing fabulous views across the river. Below the Château Frontenac is the Old Lower Town, the oldest section of the city.

The two main streets heading southwest from the Old Upper Town are Blvd René-Lévesque and, to the south, Grande Allée, which eventually becomes Blvd Wilfrid-Laurier.

The wider area of Lower Town has the highways leading north, east and west. If you're driving, your plan should be to get to Vieux-Québec, then park the car for the duration of your stay. To the extreme southwest of the city are Pont de Québec and Pont Pierre-Laporte, both bridges leading to the south shore.

To get oriented, Observatoire de la Capitale (p213) gives views from 31 floors up.

Lévis, a suburb and a town, is seen directly across the river from the Old Town.

The borough of Ste-Foy-Sillery is the location of Université Laval. The area has a large student population and all the great bars and cheap eats that come with it. But there won't be much here of interest to the average traveler that you wouldn't be able to easily find in and around the Old City, other than enormous box malls.

OLD UPPER TOWN

The heart of Québec City, the Old Town is where you will be spending most of your time because it's packed with the city's blockbuster sites and numerous museums on everything from history and the military to religious life in New France. The narrow, winding roads are lined with extraordinary old architecture, with some buildings dating from the 1600s. The grandest military structures, churches and buildings are concentrated in the Old Upper Town.

LA CITADELLE Map p206

☎ 418-694-2815; www.lacitadelle.qc.ca; 201 Côte de la Citadelle; adult/child/student $10/5.50/9;

QUÉBEC CITY FOR CHILDREN

With the entire place heaving with history, there is plenty to hold kids' attention in Québec City. While some of the weightier religious museums and sights won't be of much appeal, kids go giddy over the guides in period costume and are mesmerized by the antique cannons sprinkled everywhere from the Old Town to Battlefields Park (p209).

Much of the accommodations and restaurants are geared to adults, but several of even the poshest French bistros we've listed in our Eating section have children's menus. There are good things to do with younger ones in the central core, while around the edges are other sites fully designed for kids' enjoyment.

In the historic area, walking the Fortifications (opposite) suits all ages. The Citadelle (above) ceremonies, with uniformed soldiers beating the retreat for example, are winners too. Martello Tower 1 (p209) in Battlefields Park has terrific interactive exhibits and parents swear the small size is perfect for children's attention spans. Terrasse Dufferin (opposite), with its view and abundance of buskers, always delights children. Place d'Armes and Place-Royale are also good for street performers. The cheap ferry to Lévis (p230) and any boat cruise always appeals to the whole family, as would a slow tour of the Old Town in a horse-drawn calèche (p230).

For a break from all the history, try the newly overhauled Aquarium du Québec (p213). It focuses on the water life of the St Lawrence River as well as the waterways and coasts of the rest of Canada. Different family rates are offered depending on the children's ages.

A little further afield, northeast of Québec City on Hwy 138 is honey store and bee museum Musée de l'Abeille (off Map p204; ☎ 418-824-4411; www.musee-abeille.com; 8862 Blvd Ste-Anne, Château Richer; admission museum free, bee safari adult/child $5/3; 🕒 9am-6pm Jun 24–early Sep, to 5pm other times except 11am-5pm Mon-Fri & 9am-5pm Sat & Sun Jan & Feb). It gets good reviews from families (kids for the 'safari,' parents for the honey wine!).

10am-4pm Apr & Sep, 9am-5pm May & Jun, 9am-6pm Jul & Aug, 10am-3pm Oct; 3, 11
This massive, star-shaped fort towers above the St Lawrence River on Cap Diamant. French forces started construction here in the late 1750s leaving a gunpowder building and a redoubt, the beginnings of a defensive structure. But the Citadelle we know today was actually built by the British, who feared two things: an American invasion of the colony and a possible revolt by the local French-speaking population (that's why the cannons point not only at the river, but at Québec City itself). However, by the time the Citadelle was completed (construction began in 1820 and was finished about 30 years later) things were calming down. Twenty years later, in 1871, the Treaty of Washington was signed between the United States and the newly minted Dominion of Canada (on behalf of Her Majesty the Queen of England, of course), ending the threat of American invasion.

The Citadelle now houses about 200 members of the Royal 22e Régiment (the rest live with their families at the nearby Valcartier base). The Vandoos, a nickname taken from the French for 22 (*vingt-deux*), is the only entirely French-speaking battalion in the Canadian Forces. It has a reputation among the Forces as the toughest (ie badass) regiment in the army.

The hour-long guided tours are excellent and will give you the lowdown on the spectacular architecture and get you into exhibits on military life from colonial times to today.

The changing of the guard ceremony takes place at 10am each day in the summer months. The beating of the retreat, which features soldiers banging on their drums at shift's end, happens every Friday at 7pm from July 6 until early September.

The second official residence of the governor general (the Queen of England's representative in Canada) has been located here since 1872 (the other residence is in Ottawa and called Rideau Hall). There are free one-hour tours of the Citadelle residence.

ARTILLERY PARK Map p206

418-648-4205, 800-463-6769; 2 Rue d'Auteuil; adult/child $4/2; 10am-6pm Mon-Sat Apr-Oct; 3, 7, 11, 28

The French chose this location for their army barracks because of its strategic view of the plateau west of the city and the St Charles River, both of which could feed enemy soldiers into Québec City. English soldiers moved in after the British conquest of New France. The English soldiers left in 1871 and it was changed into an ammunition factory for the Canadian army. The factory operated until 1964 and thousands of Canadians worked there during the World Wars. Now you can visit the Officers' Quarters and the Dauphine Redoubt where guides greet you in character (ie the garrison's cook) and give you the scoop on life in the barracks. There's also a huge model of Québec City in the old Arsenal Foundry.

FORTIFICATIONS OF QUÉBEC

Map p206

418-648-7016; Rue d'Auteuil, near Rue St-Louis; admission to interpretive center adult/child $4/2; 10am-6pm May-Oct; 3, 11
These largely restored old walls are a national historic site. You can walk the complete 4.6km circuit on top of it all around the Old Town for free. From this vantage point, much of the city's history is within easy view. The fortifications' interpretive center is by the Porte St-Louis where you can visit a small but interesting exhibit on the history of the walls as well as an old gunpowder building from 1815. It also offers 90-minute guided walks (adult/child/student $10/5/7.50; 2pm Jun-Sep & 10am & 2pm late Jun–Aug) that include the Old Town.

TERRASSE DUFFERIN Map p206

Outside the Château Frontenac, along the riverfront, this 425m-long promenade is a marvelous setting for a stroll, with dramatic views over the river from its cliff-top perch, 60m above the water. In the summer it's peppered with street performers, and you can stop at a well-placed snack stand for ice cream or a cold drink. Just past the statue of Samuel de Champlain, you can see recent excavations of Champlain's second fort that stood here from 1620 to 1635. Nearby, you can take the funicular (Map p206, $2 one way; 7:30am-11pm Sep–mid-Jun, until midnight mid-Jun–Aug) to the Old Lower Town. Just above the Terrasse Dufferin is the leafy Jardin des Gouverneurs, a peaceful refuge from the holidaying masses.

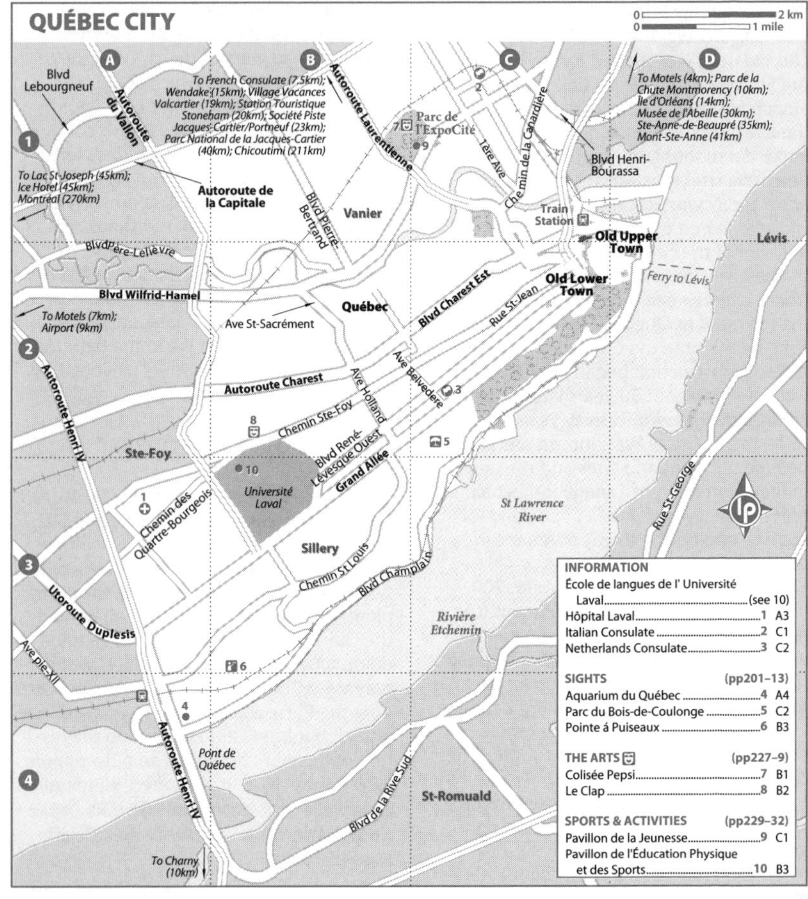

Latin Quarter

The Latin Quarter refers to a section of the Old Upper Town wedged into the northeast corner. The site of both the Québec Seminary and Laval University, the neighborhood got its name because the religious communities and those at the university all conversed in Latin.

BASILIQUE-CATHÉDRALE NOTRE-DAME-DE-QUÉBEC Map p206

☎ 418-694-0665; 20 Rue de Buade; admission free, guided tours $4; 8am-4pm Mon-Fri, 8am-6pm Sat & Sun; 3, 7, 11

This basilica got its start as a small church in 1647. In the ensuing years, the churches built here suffered everything from frequent fires to battle damage, especially during fighting between British and French armies in 1759. But no matter what, the church was rebuilt and repaired. Each replacement was bigger than the last until it reached the size you see today – a structure completed in 1925. The interior is appropriately grandiose, though most of the basilica's treasures didn't survive the 1922 fire that left behind only the walls and foundations. To have a look at the crypt, you'll have to sign on to a guided tour. Everyone from governors of New France to archbishops and cardinals has been laid to rest there.

CATHEDRAL OF THE HOLY TRINITY Map p206

☎ 418-692-2193; 31 Rue des Jardins; admission free; 10am-5pm late May–mid-Oct; 3, 7, 11

Built from 1800 to 1804, this cathedral was designed by two officers from the British army's military engineering corps and modeled on St Martin-in-the-Fields Church in London, England. This elegantly handsome Anglican cathedral was the first ever built outside the British Isles, with oak imported from Windsor Castle's Royal Forest just to make the pews. Upon its completion, King George III sent the cathedral a treasure trove of objects, including candlesticks, chalices and silver trays. The elaborateness of the gifts heading toward the New World sent London's chattering classes atwitter. The royal box for the reigning monarch or her representative is located in the upper left balcony if you are facing the altar. (Look for the royal coat of arms.) The cathedral's bell tower, an impressive 47m high, competes for attention with the Basilique Notre-Dame located nearby. You will find that a guide is usually around in the summer months and conducts free 10-minute tours of the cathedral.

MUSÉE DE L'AMÉRIQUE FRANÇAISE

Map p206

☎ 418-692-2843; 2 Côte de la Fabrique; adult/child/student $7/2/5, free Tue Nov 1–May 31; 🕑 9:30am-5pm daily Jun 24–early Sep, 10am-5pm Tue-Sun Sep-Jun; 🚌 3, 7, 11

On the grounds of the Séminaire de Québec (the Québec Seminary), this excellent museum is purported to be Canada's oldest. (The Musée Scientifique du Séminaire de Québec opened here in 1806.) The museum that stands here today has brilliantly atmospheric exhibits on life in the seminary during the colonial era as well as religious artifacts and temporary exhibitions on subjects like endangered species. The priests from the Québec Seminary were avid travelers and collectors and there are some magnificent displays of the scientific objects they brought back with them from Europe, such as old Italian astronomical equipment. The exhibits are capped off by a wonderful short film on New World history from a Quebecer's perspective.

MUSÉE DES URSULINES Map p206

☎ 418-694-0694; 12 Rue Donnacona; adult/student $8/5; 🕑 10am-noon & 1-5pm Tue-Sat & 1-5pm Sun Jun-Sep, 1-5pm Tue-Sun Oct; 🚌 3, 7, 11

The fascinating story of the Ursuline nuns' lives and their influence in the 17th and 18th centuries is told in this thoughtful, well-set-out museum. The sisters established the first girls' school on the continent in 1641, educating both aboriginal and French girls. Marie de l'Incarnation, the founder, was one of the most intriguing figures from the order. Leaving a young son in France after she was widowed, she joined the Ursulines and moved to New France and lived well into old age. She taught herself aboriginal languages and her frequent and eloquent letters to her son back in France are held by historians to be some of the richest and most valuable

CHÂTEAU FRONTENAC

The Château Frontenac (Map p206) is not only the city's most luxurious hotel, but is so iconic it has become a tourist site in and of itself. Its winding halls and dramatic location have lured everyone from politicians and movie stars to movies and TV shows.

It's probably one of the rare hotels where you can be walking through the lobby and discover the majority of people there aren't even guests but tourists visiting to get close to the history and architecture and see what all the commotion is about (this is the world's most photographed hotel, after all).

Designed by New Yorker Bruce Price (father of manners maven Emily Post), the Château was named after the mercurial Count of Frontenac, Louis de Buade, who governed New France in the late 1600s. Completed in 1893, the Château Frontenac was one of the Canadian Pacific Railway's series of luxury hotels built across Canada. One-part medieval and one-part Renaissance, the hotel has had regular extensions over the years, the most recent one in 1993.

Its turrets and multiple imposing wings top off its dramatic location on Cap Diamant, atop a cliff that swoops down into the St Lawrence River. The setting alone is so powerful that Alfred Hitchcock opened his 1953 Québec City–set mystery *I Confess* with that very shot.

During WWII, the Québec Conferences involving British prime minister Winston Churchill, US president Franklin Roosevelt and Canadian prime minister William Lyon Mackenzie King were all held here. Other illustrious guests have included King George VI, Chiang Kaishek and Princess Grace of Monaco. For details on lodging, see p233.

Guides in period costume give 50-minute tours (☎ 418-691-2166; www.tourschateau.ca; adult/child $9/6; 🕑 10am-6pm May–mid-Oct, noon-5pm Sat & Sun mid-Oct–Apr) on the hotel's history. Call for reservations.

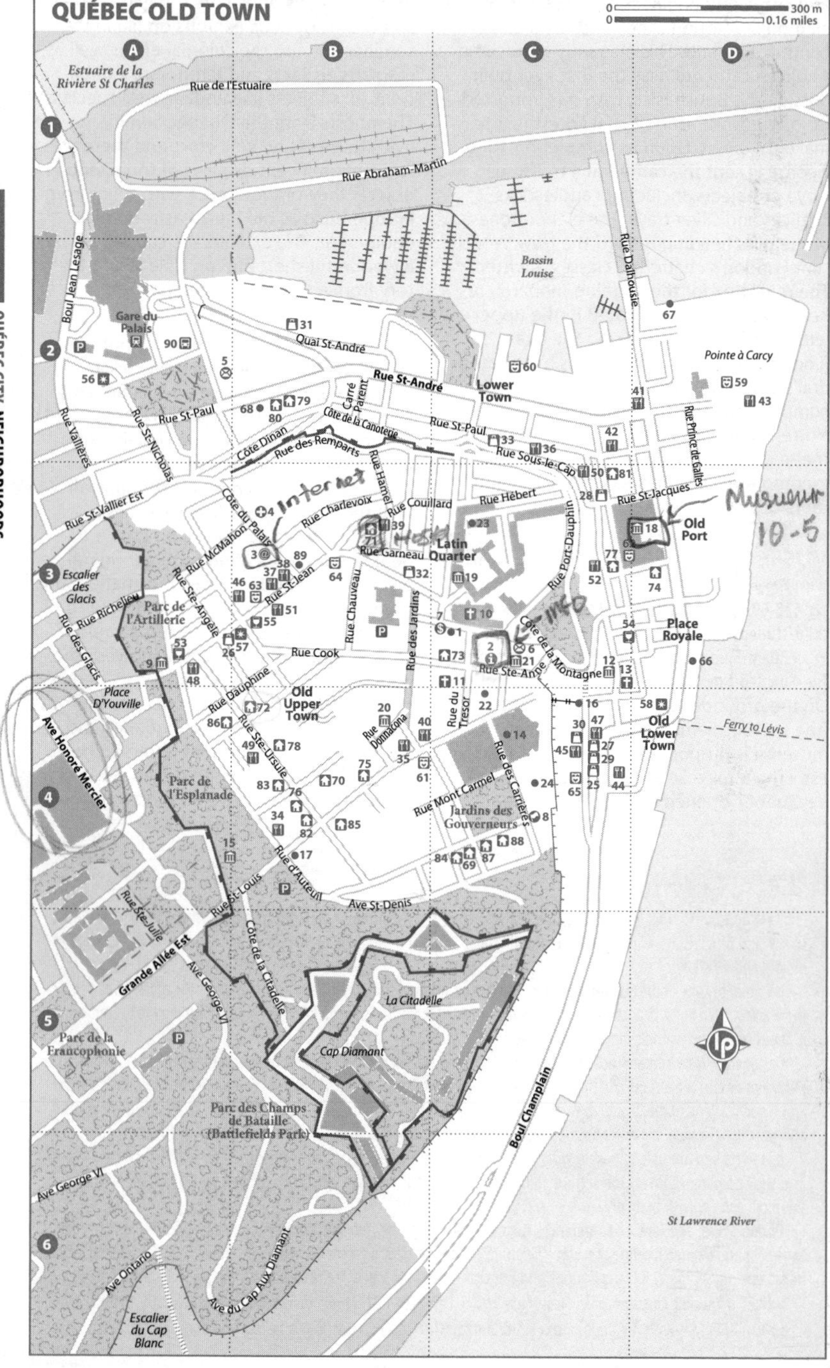
QUÉBEC OLD TOWN
300 m
0.16 miles
Estuaire de la Rivière St Charles
Rue de l'Estuaire
Rue Abraham-Martin
Bassin Louise
Rue Dalhousie
Boul Jean Lesage
Gare du Palais
Quai St-André
Rue St-André
Lower Town
Pointe à Carcy
Carré Parent
Rue St-Paul
Côte de la Canoterie
Rue des Remparts
Côte Dinan
Rue Vallières
Rue St-Nicholas
Rue Sous-le-Cap
Rue Prince de Galles
Rue St-Vallier Est
Côte du Palais
Rue Charlevoix
Rue Hamel
Rue Couillard
Rue Hébert
Rue St-Jacques
Old Port
Rue McMahon
Rue Garneau
Latin Quarter
Rue Port-Dauphin
Escalier des Glacis
Rue St-Jean
Rue Richelieu
Parc de l'Artillerie
Rue Ste-Angèle
Rue Chauveau
Rue des Jardins
Côte de la Montagne
Place Royale
Rue des Glacis
Rue Cook
Rue Ste-Anne
Place D'Youville
Rue Dauphine
Old Upper Town
Rue du Tresor
Ferry to Lévis
Old Lower Town
Ave Honoré Mercier
Rue Donnacona
Rue Ste-Ursule
Rue Mont Carmel
Rue des Carrières
Parc de l'Esplanade
Jardins des Gouverneurs
Rue d'Auteuil
Rue St-Louis
Ave St-Denis
Rue Ste-Julie
Grande Allée Est
Ave George VI
Côte de la Citadelle
La Citadelle
Cap Diamant
Parc de la Francophonie
Parc des Champs de Bataille (Battlefields Park)
Boul Champlain
St Lawrence River
Ave Ontario
Ave du Cap Aux Diamant
Escalier du Cap Blanc
Internet
Museum 10-5
Info

QUÉBEC OLD TOWN

INFORMATION
Bouchereau Lingua International....1 C3
Centre Infotouriste....2 C3
Centre Internet....3 B3
L'Hôtel Dieu de Québec....4 B3
Main Post Office....5 A2
Post Office....6 C3
Transchange International....7 C3
US Consulate....8 C4

SIGHTS (pp201–8)
Artillery Park....9 A3
Basilique-Cathédrale Notre-Dame-de-Québec....10 C3
Cathedral of the Holy Trinity....11 C3
Centre d'Interpretation de Place-Royale....12 C3
Discovery Centre du Vieux-Port de Québec....(see 60)
Église Notre-Dame-des-Victoires....13 C3
Fairmont Le Château Frontenac....14 C4
Fortifications of Québec....15 A4
Funicular....16 C4
Ghost Tours of Québec....17 B4
Gunpowder Building....(see 15)
Les Tours Voir Québec....(see 2)
Musée de la Civilisation....18 D3
Musée de l'Amérique Française....19 C3
Musée des Ursulines....20 B4
Musée du Fort....21 C3
Place d'Armes (Calèches)....22 C4
Seminaire de Québec....23 C3
Terrasse Dufferin....24 C4

SHOPPING (pp215–16)
Boutique Oclan....25 C4
Excalibur Québec....26 A3
Fruits & Passion....27 C4
Galerie d'Estampe Plus....28 C3
Joaillerie Jules Perrier....29 C4
La Petite Cabane A Sucre Du Québec....30 C4
Marché du Vieux-Port....31 B2
Simons....32 B3
Vêtements 90 Degrés....33 C2

EATING (pp218–22)
Apsara....34 B4
Aux Anciens Canadiens....35 B4
Buffet de l'Antiquaire....36 C2
Casse-Crêpe Breton....37 B3
Chez Ashton....38 B3
Chez Temporel....39 B3
Conti Caffe....40 B4
Epicerie de la Rue Couillard....(see 39)
Laurie Raphaël....41 D2
Le 48 International....42 C2
Le Café du Monde....43 D2
Le Cochon Dingue....44 C4
Le Lapin Sauté....45 C4
Le Pain Béni....(see 73)
Le Patriarche....46 B3
Le Petit Cochon....47 C4
Le Petit Coin Latin....48 A3
Le Saint-Amour....49 B4
L'Échaudé....50 C3
Paillard Café-Boulangerie....51 B3
Panache....(see 74)
Toast!....52 C3

DRINKING (pp224–7)
L'Alterno....53 A3
L'Oncle Antoine....54 C3
Pub St-Alexandre....55 B3

NIGHTLIFE (pp224–7)
Aviatic Club....56 A2
Chez son Père....57 B3
Le Pape-Georges....58 D4

THE ARTS (pp227–9)
Agora....59 D2
Espace 400....60 C2
Galerie Art Inuit....61 B4
Galerie d'Art Beauchamp....62 C3
Le Théâtre Capitole....63 B3
Les Gros Becs....64 B3
Théâtre Petit-Champlain....65 C4

SPORTS & ACTIVITIES (pp229–32)
AML Cruises....66 D3
Croisiéres le Coudrier....67 D2
Cyclo Services....68 B2
Patinoire de la Terrasse....(see 24)

SLEEPING (pp233–6)
Au Château Fleur-de-Lys....69 C4
Au Petit Hôtel....70 B4
Auberge de la Paix....71 B3
Auberge Internationale de Québec....72 B4
Auberge Place D'Armes....73 C3
Auberge St-Antoine....74 D3
Auberge St-Louis....75 B4
Chez Hubert....76 B4
Fairmont Le Château Frontenac....(see 14)
Hôtel 71....77 C3
Hôtel Acadia....78 B4
Hôtel Belley....79 B2
Hôtel des Coutellier....80 B2
Hôtel Dominion 1912....81 C3
La Maison Demers....82 B4
La Maison Sainte Ursule....83 B4
La Marquise Bassano....84 C4
Le Clos Saint Louis....85 B4
L'Hôtel du Capitole....(see 63)
Manoir La Salle....86 A4
Manoir Sainte-Geneviéve....87 C4
Manoir Sur le Cap....88 C4

TRANSPORT (pp251–5)
AML Cruises....(see 66)
Budget....89 B3
Bus Station....90 A2

material available to scholars studying life in the French colony. The Ursulines were also expert embroiderers and many examples of their work are on display. There's a lovely chapel (admission free; 10am-noon & 1-5pm Tue-Sat, 1-5pm Sun May-Oct) at the same address. It dates from 1902 but retains some interiors from 1723.

MUSÉE DU FORT Map p206

418-692-1759; www.museedufort.com; 10 Rue Ste-Anne; adult/student $8/5; 10am-5pm Apr-Oct, 11am-4pm Jan-Mar; 3, 7, 11

Not really a museum at all, the Musée du Fort houses a 30-minute multimedia show on the many attempts over the centuries to take Québec City. It's all played out on a model/diorama that lights up in the middle of a minitheater. The breathless narration and anemic smoke-puffs that pass for special effects are a bit hokey but it does give a quick, enjoyable, easy-to-grasp audiovisual survey of the city's battles and history, making a good introduction to it. English-language shows are held on the hour (French-language versions on the half-hour).

OLD LOWER TOWN

Sandwiched between the Upper Town and the waterfront, this area has yet more intriguing museums and sites of historical interest, plus plenty of outdoor cafés and restaurants along its pedestrian-friendly streets, as well as numerous plaques and statues. Street performers in period costume help recapture life in distant centuries.

Teeming Rue du Petit-Champlain is said to be, along with Rue Sous-le-Cap, the narrowest street in North America, and is also one of the oldest. Look for the incredible wall paintings that feature on the 17th- and 18th-century buildings.

Place-Royale, the principal square of Québec City's Lower Town, has 400 years of history behind it. When Samuel de Champlain founded Québec, it was this bit of shoreline that was first settled. In 1690 cannons placed here held off the attacks of the English naval commander Phipps and his men. Today the name 'Place-Royale' often generally refers to the district.

Built around the old harbor in the Old Lower Town northeast of Place-Royale, the Vieux-Port (Old Port) is being redeveloped as a multipurpose waterfront area.

From the Upper Town, you can reach the Lower Town in several ways. Walk down Côte de la Canoterie from Rue des Remparts to the Old Port or edge down the charming and steep Rue Côte de la Montagne. About halfway down on the right there is a shortcut, the Break-Neck Stairs (Escalier Casse-Cou), which leads down to Rue du Petit-Champlain. You can also take the funicular (p203).

CENTRE D'INTERPRETATION DE PLACE-ROYALE Map p206

☎ 418-646-3167; 27 Rue Notre-Dame; adult/child/student $6/2/4; 9:30am-5pm late Jun–early Sep, 10am-5pm Tue-Sun early Sep–late Jun; 1

This interpretive center touts the area as the cradle of French history. The exhibits focus on the individual people, houses and challenges of setting up on the shores of the St Lawrence River. It goes a bit heavy on the random artifact displays (though pottery shards do have their charm), but also has some worthwhile displays that help illuminate what life was like from the 1600s to the 20th century. Children can dress up in costumes on the bottom floor and tours of the Lower Town are offered by guides in period dress during summer.

ÉGLISE NOTRE-DAME-DES-VICTOIRES Map p206

☎ 418-692-1650; 32 Rue Sous-le-Fort; admission free; 9:30am-4:30pm; 1

Dating from 1688, Our Lady of Victories Church, a modest house of worship on the square, is the oldest stone church in the USA and Canada. It stands on the spot where Champlain set up his 'Habitation,' a small stockade, 80 years prior to the church's arrival. Inside are copies of works by Rubens and Van Dyck. Hanging from the ceiling is a replica of a wooden ship, the *Brézé,* thought to be a good-luck charm for ocean crossings and battles with the Iroquois. The church earned its name after British ships were unable to take Québec City in 1690 and again in 1711.

DISCOVERY CENTRE DU VIEUX-PORT DE QUÉBEC Map p206

☎ 418-648-3300; 100 Quai St-André; 1

This sparkling new exhibition hall was unveiled in 2008 for use during the city's 400th birthday celebrations. In 2010, the center, now under the auspice of Parks Canada, will open a permanent exhibit on immigration along the St Lawrence River. Displays will touch on Champlain's early explorations as well as the First Nations people who preceded him.

MUSÉE DE LA CIVILISATION Map p206

☎ 418-643-2158; www.mcq.org; 85 Rue Dalhousie; adult/child/student $11/4/8, free Tue Nov-May; 9:30am-6:30pm late Jun–early Sep, 10am-5pm Tue-Sun early Sep–late Jun

The Museum of Civilization wows you even before you've visited the exhibitions. It is a fascinating mix of modern design that incorporates pre-existing buildings with contemporary architecture. The permanent exhibits, like the one on the cultures of Québec's Aboriginals and the one titled 'People of Québec: Then and Now,' are unique and well worth seeing. Many of the exhibits include clever interactive elements. The changing shows are also outstanding and this is really the only museum in town that regularly focuses on contemporary issues and culture. This is a big place with lots to see, so you should concentrate on only one or two exhibitions if you're not planning to make a full day of it.

OUTSIDE THE WALLS

A stroll west of the Old Town leads to several impressive sites, including the historic Battlefields Park and one of the province's best fine-arts museums. The other big draw is the bohemian neighborhood of St-Jean-Baptiste. Here, you'll find lively cafés, record shops, gourmet grocers and bistros, with a welcome lack of elbow-jousting tourists. St-Roch, to the northwest of the Old Town, is an up-and-coming neighborhood sprinkled with bars, eclectic eateries and secondhand shops.

PARC DES CHAMPS DE BATAILLE (BATTLEFIELDS PARK) Map p210

One of Québec City's must-sees, this verdant, cliff-top park contains the Plains of Abraham (www.ccbn-nbc.gc.ca). This was the stage for the infamous 1759 battle between British General James Wolfe and French General Montcalm that determined the fate of the North American continent. The park, named for Abraham Martin, a Frenchman who was one of the first farmers to settle in the area, is packed with sites, old cannons, monuments and commemorative plaques. It also has a fine multimedia history museum and several impressive fortification towers (one with a small military museum inside). The park is also a draw for locals, who come for outdoor activities such as running, in-line skating and, in winter, cross-country skiing. There's also a stage that sees a good bit of action at open-air concerts at the Kiosque Edwin-Bélanger (p228) in the summer. On warm days, the tree-lined 'plains' make a good spot for picnics.

The area became an official park in 1908 and has been the site of many modern historical events as well: 'O Canada,' the Canadian national anthem, written by Sir Aldophe Routhier with music by Calixa Lavallée, was sung here for the first time on June 24, 1880.

There's no charge to wander through the park, but if you want to get the whole experience – and you have about four hours to spare – consider purchasing a day pass (adult/child/student $10/3/8). This is available in the high-season summer months and includes Abraham's Bus Tour, plus free admission to the Odyssey and the Martello Tower 1 (all described following). You can purchase day passes at the information desk on the lower level of the Discovery Pavilion. You can also buy tickets to individual sites if you don't have time to see it all. If you want to explore the grounds on your own, pick up a bilingual tourist map of the park ($3) from the Discovery Pavilion.

To get your bearings consider the 40-minute Abraham's Bus Tour (adult/child $4/free; 🕑 10:30am, noon, 12:45pm, 2pm & 3:30pm early May–early Sep) around the park. An actor in period costume points out historical sites of interest and throws in some colorful asides. It departs from the Discovery Pavilion (Map p210; ☎ 418-648-4071; 835 Ave Wilfrid-Laurier; 🚌 11), the main gateway to Battlefields Park, which houses a museum as well as the excellent Québec City tourist office, Centre Infotouriste (p263). The main draw here is the permanent exhibition entitled Odyssey (adult/child $8/7; 🕑 10am-5:30pm Jun 24–Sep 4, to 5pm Sep 5–Jun 23). In it, you move from theater to theater where the history of the Plains of Abraham are depicted through clever multimedia presentations and generous doses of good humor. There's a fine exhibit at the end devoted to French and British colonial military with displays depicting the lives of soldiers in the New World. The exhibit on their uniforms, which describes the significance of the designs and colors, is nicely done.

The British, however, never got to try the towers out, as the American army was defeated in 1812. Martello Tower 1 (Map p210; Battlefields Park; adult/child $4/3; 🕑 10am-5pm Jun 24–early Sep) is the only one of the original towers regularly open to the public. Because of its small size, many visitors balk at having to pay admission here. Those who do go in are often pleasantly surprised – packed into the compact tower are a number of fascinating exhibits, which delve into the engineering history of the structures and describe living conditions for the soldiers based here.

Martello Tower 2 (Map p210; cnr Ave Taché & Ave Wilfrid-Laurier, Battlefields Park) is nearby but opens to the public only during staged events, like the Convict's Last Drink (☎ 418-649-6157; admission

REBIRTH OF ST-ROCH

Once a gritty area better left unexplored, the neighborhood of St-Roch has gone through a remarkable rebirth in the last decade. Under an ambitious revitalization plan, the city created a public garden, restored a shuttered theater and hired artists to paint frescoes in the neighborhood. Artists and entrepreneurs began moving back into the area, bringing cafés and shops on their heels. Today, *'le nouveau'* St-Roch has become one of Québec City's trendiest neighborhoods. Rue St-Joseph has everything from art galleries and glitzy boutiques to junk shops and fine dining – all drawing a similarly eclectic mix of locals – while there's some excellent nightlife options on nearby Rue de l'Église. For a dynamic slice of contemporary Québec City, take a stroll, heading 1km west, outside the old quarters.

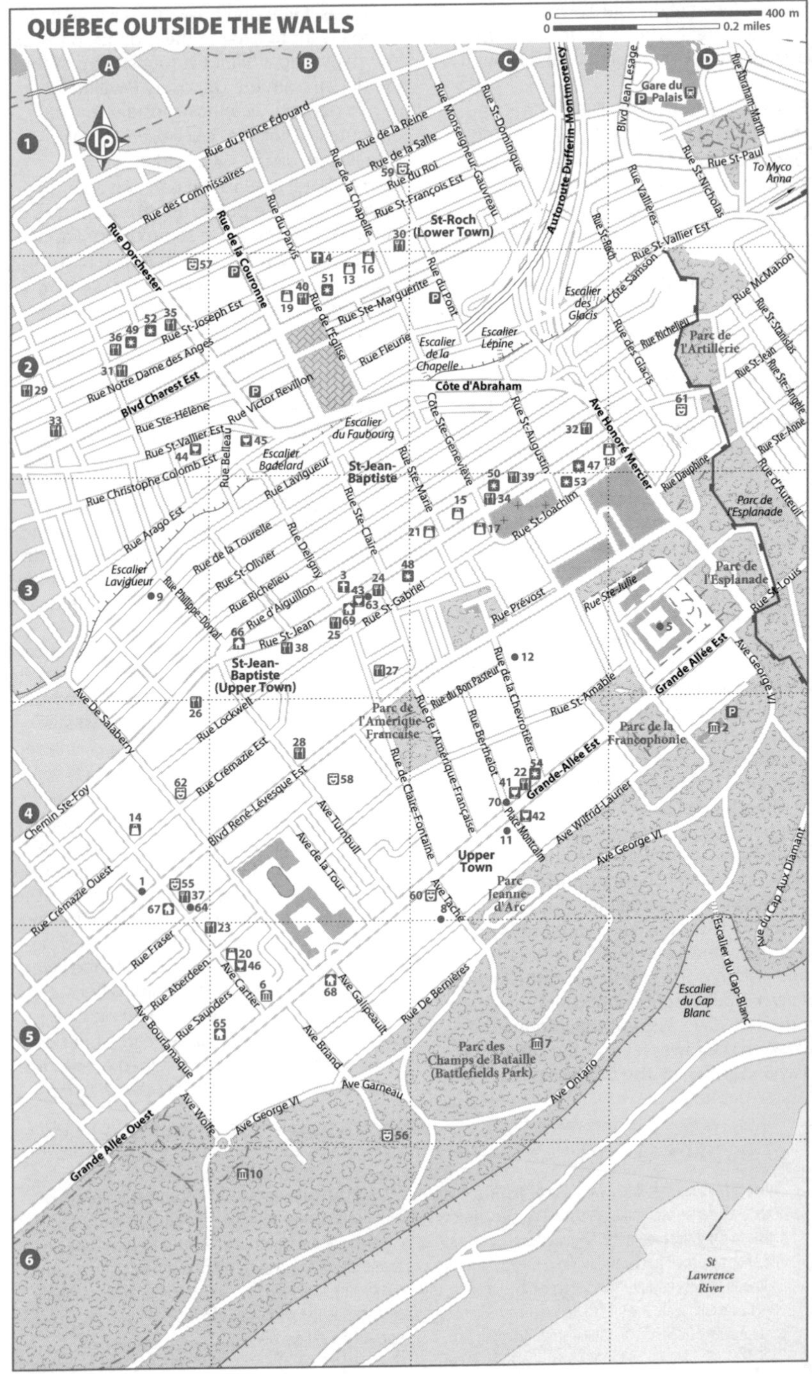
QUÉBEC OUTSIDE THE WALLS
0
400 m
0
0.2 miles
Rue du Prince Édouard
Rue de la Reine
Rue de la Salle
Rue du Roi
Rue des Commissaires
Rue St-François Est
Rue Dorchester
Rue de la Couronne
Rue du Parvis
Rue de la Chapelle
Rue Monseigneur-Gauvreau
Rue St-Dominique
Autoroute Dufferin-Montmorency
Blvd Jean Lesage
Gare du Palais
Rue Abraham-Martin
Rue St-Paul
To Myco Anna
Rue Vallières
Rue St-Nicholas
Rue St-Roch
St-Roch (Lower Town)
Rue St-Vallier Est
Côte Samson
Rue McMahon
Rue St-Joseph Est
Rue Ste-Marguerite
Rue du Pont
Rue de l'Église
Rue Fleurie
Escalier des Glacis
Escalier Lépine
Escalier de la Chapelle
Rue Richelieu
Parc de l'Artillerie
Rue des Glacis
Rue St-Stanislas
Rue St-Jean
Rue Ste-Angèle
Rue Notre Dame des Anges
Blvd Charest Est
Rue Victor Revillon
Côte d'Abraham
Rue Ste-Hélène
Escalier du Faubourg
Côte Ste-Geneviève
Rue St-Augustin
Ave Honoré Mercier
Rue Ste-Anne
Rue St-Vallier Est
Rue Christophe Colomb Est
Rue Belleau
Escalier Badelard
Rue Lavigueur
St-Jean-Baptiste
Rue Ste-Marie
Rue Dauphine
Rue d'Auteuil
Parc de l'Esplanade
Rue St-Joachim
Rue Arago Est
Rue de la Tourelle
Rue Deligny
Rue Ste-Claire
Escalier Lavigueur
Rue Philippe-Dorval
Rue St-Olivier
Rue Richelieu
Rue d'Aiguillon
Rue St-Gabriel
Rue Prévost
Rue Ste-Julie
Rue St-Louis
Rue St-Jean
St-Jean-Baptiste (Upper Town)
Ave De Salaberry
Rue Lockwell
Rue du Bon Pasteur
Rue de la Chevrotière
Grande Allée Est
Ave George VI
Parc de l'Amérique Française
Rue de l'Amérique-Française
Rue Berthelot
Rue St-Amable
Parc de la Francophonie
Rue Crémazie Est
Blvd René-Lévesque Est
Rue de Claire-Fontaine
Grande-Allée Est
Chemin Ste-Foy
Ave Turnbull
Ave de la Tour
Place Montcalm
Ave Wilfrid-Laurier
Ave George VI
Ave du Cap Aux Diamant
Upper Town
Parc Jeanne-d'Arc
Rue Crémazie Ouest
Ave Taché
Rue Fraser
Rue Aberdeen
Ave Cartier
Rue Saunders
Ave Galipeault
Rue De Bernières
Escalier du Cap-Blanc
Escalier du Cap Blanc
Ave Bourlamaque
Ave Briand
Parc des Champs de Bataille (Battlefields Park)
Ave Ontario
Ave Garneau
Ave Wolfe
Ave George VI
Grande Allée Ouest
St Lawrence River
A
B
C
D
1
2
3
4
5
6

QUÉBEC OUTSIDE THE WALLS

$12; 4:30pm daily mid-Jul–early Sep). This lively interactive theater (in English) gives a taste of 19th-century justice. It features a mock trial of a soldier accused of a crime, and the audience will decide his fate while – and this is the important part – sampling homemade beers. Because alcohol is served, those under 18 must be accompanied by an adult; reserve through the Discovery Pavilion or by phone. A French-language version (La Dernier Verre) takes place at 6:30pm daily (mid-July to early September). Other shows include an '1814, council-of-war-style' feast (adult/child $35/32), during which diners must discover who among them is the 'traitor.' It's in French only, but there are translated scripts so English speakers can follow along. Call for a schedule. Reserve ahead.

Martello Tower 3 was torn down in 1905 to make way for construction and Martello Tower 4 (Rue Lavigueur) is in the St-Jean-Baptiste neighborhood between Rue Félix-Gabriel-Marchand and Rue Philippe-Dorion.

MUSÉE NATIONAL DES BEAUX-ARTS DU QUÉBEC Map p210

418-643-2150, 866-220-2150; www.mnba.qc.ca; Battlefields Park; adult/child/student $15/4/7; 10am-6pm Thu-Tue & 10am-9pm Wed Jun-Aug, 10am-5pm Tue & Thu-Sun, 10am-9pm Wed Sep-May; 11; P

Anyone curious about Québec art needs to carve out at least half a day for a visit to this museum, one of the best in the province. There are expert permanent exhibitions that range from art and artists in the early French colonies to Québec's abstract artists. There are also individual halls devoted entirely to the province's artistic giants of the last century.

The do-not-miss permanent exhibitions include one devoted to Jean-Paul Lemieux (1904–90) and another to Jean-Paul Riopelle (1923–2002), which includes *L'hommage à Rosa Luxemburg* (Tribute to Rosa Luxemburg; 1986), his largest work.

The Brousseau Inuit Art Collection of 2639 pieces spanning 50 years was a personal collection of Inuit art acquired by the museum in 2005.

There are also frequent exhibitions from abroad and elsewhere in Canada. The museum is spread out through three halls including the Pavilion Charles-Baillairgé, Québec City's former prison. Audioguides are available for the permanent collections and often for temporary exhibitions as well.

Guides in period getup lead prison tours (☎ 418-643-2150; adult/youth under 17 $10/5) during the summer, though usually these are in French only. Call ahead for info and reservations.

Other ongoing events include film screenings (often documentaries on prominent international artists), drawing and painting classes open to the public, and a concert series.

LA MAISON HENRY-STUART Map p210

☎ 418-647-4347; www.cmsq.qc.ca; 82 Grande Allée Ouest; adult/child $7/3; daily Jun 25–early Sep, Sun only May–Jun 24 & Sep-Oct

This handsomely preserved cottage, built in 1849, once belonged to an upper-middle-class anglophone family, and contains period furnishings from the early 1900s. Guided tours help elucidate what life was like in those days, and tea and lemon cake makes it seem all the sweeter. A small but verdant garden surrounds the cottage. Visits are by guided tour, which take place every hour on the hour between 11am and 4pm. Call for the latest schedule.

St-Jean-Baptiste

The heart of this area is Rue St-Jean, which extends from the Old Town. It's one of Québec's best streets for strolling, with an excellent assortment of colorful shops and restaurants, hip little cafés and bars. Near the corner of Rue St-Augustin is also where you'll find the epicenter of the city's tiny, unofficial gay 'village.' From Rue St-Jean, take any side street and walk downhill (northwest) to the narrow residential streets like Rue d'Aiguillon, Rue Richelieu or Rue St-Olivier. Note the smattering of outside staircases and row-style houses, some with very nice entrances, typical of Québec City's residential landscape.

ÉGLISE ST-JEAN-BAPTISTE Map p210

☎ 418-688-0350; 400 Rue St-Jean; admission free; noon-5pm Mon-Sat, 11am-4pm Sun late Jun–early Sep, noon-4pm Mon-Sat, 11am-4pm Sun rest of the year

This colossus completely dominates its area on the southwest end of Rue St-Jean. The first church was built in 1842 but was destroyed by fire in 1881. It was completely rebuilt by architect Joseph-Ferdinand Peachy and open again for business by 1884. Peachy drew on well-known French churches for inspiration: Notre-Dame-de-Paris for the pillars, Église St-Sulpice for the vaults and Église de la Trinité for the facade. In summer, the church presents modest but well-researched exhibitions on church or neighborhood history.

HÔTEL DU PARLEMENT Map p210

☎ 418-643-7239; cnr Ave Honoré-Mercier & Grande Allée Est; admission free; 9am-4:30pm Mon-Fri year-round, 10am-4:30pm Sat & Sun Jun 24–early Sep; 11, 25, 28

The National Assembly building is a Second Empire structure completed in 1886. It's home to the Provincial Legislature. Free tours are given in English and French year-round. The 30-minute visits get you into the National Assembly Chamber, the Legislative Council Chamber and the Speakers' Gallery. The facade of the building is decorated with 23 bronze statues of significant provincial historical figures, including explorer Samuel de Champlain (1570–1635), early New France governor Louis de Buade Frontenac (1622–98) and battle heroes like James Wolfe (1727–59) and Louis-Joseph Montcalm (1712–59), the English and French generals who met, fought and received mortal wounds on the nearby Plains of Abraham (p209). On the grounds are more recent figures in Québec's tumultuous history, including Maurice Duplessis (1890–1959) who kept a stranglehold on the province during his 20-year-long premiership. The grounds here are also used for staging events during Winter Carnival. Note the fairly new flower-trimmed fountain facing the grounds, installed in celebration of the city's 400th anniversary. It's a fine vantage point for photographing the building.

NUNAVIK INFORMATION CENTRE Map p210

☎ 418-522-2224; www.nunavik.ca; 1204 Cours du Général-de-Montcalm; admission free; 11am-1pm & 2-7pm Jul-Sep, 9am-noon & 1-5pm Mon-Fri Oct-Jun; 11, 25, 28

Far in Québec's north, Nunavik (not to be confused with Canada's third territory, Nunavut) is almost completely inhabited by Inuit. With no trains or roads into Nunavik, even most Quebecers know little about the Inuit culture or this fascinating region. This modest center was opened mainly to promote tourism to the area's 14 villages, but it's an interesting place for a short stop just to look at the wall pictures or the small craft displays. It's an incredibly friendly place and the employees are more than willing to shoot the breeze for the genuinely curious, answering questions on anything from the Inuit language to Inuit culture.

OBSERVATOIRE DE LA CAPITALE

Map p210

☎ 418-644-9841, 888-497-4322; 1037 Rue de la Chevrotière, Édifice Marie-Guyart; adult/student $5/4; 🕑 10am-5pm daily Jun 24–mid-Oct, 10am-5pm Tue-Sun rest of year; 🚌 11, 25, 28

Head 221m up to the 31st floor for great views of the Old Town, the St Lawrence River and (if it's clear enough) even the Laurentian Mountains. It all helps to get your bearings, while the information panels along the way will get you up to speed on some of the local history.

St-Roch

This neighborhood went from a working-class district for factory and naval workers to an abandoned urban wasteland to an up-and-coming nightlife district. Urban renewal and ongoing gentrification has transformed a fairly derelict area, bringing a mix of stylish nightspots, eclectic restaurants and hidden boutiques and vintage shops. It's a great area for a bit of urban exploring, though not as established as the neighborhood of St-Jean-Baptiste to the south – some would say that's exactly the charm of St-Roch.

ÉGLISE ST-ROCH Map p210

☎ 418-524-3577; 590 Rue St-Joseph; admission free; 🕑 9am-5pm

There are giants and then there is this, the biggest church in Québec City. Measuring over 80m long, 34m wide and 46m high including the steeples, it was built between 1914 and 1923. When the original architects died, the neo-Gothic, neo-Roman structure was finished off by Louis-Napoléon Audet, the same man who worked on the Ste-Anne-de-Beaupré Basilica. The marble inside the church is from Saskatchewan. See if you can find faint fossil imprints in it. Around late October the St-Roch Church hosts the Festival des Musiques Sacrées de Québec (the Québec City Festival of Sacred Music; p196), a wonderful time to see it at its best.

Ste-Foy-Sillery

Ste-Foy and Sillery, separate before the municipal mergers, have two distinct characters. Ste-Foy, roughly north of Blvd Laurier, has a stranglehold on the city's malls but is enlivened by the student population at Laval University. Sillery, roughly south of Blvd Laurier, has leafy streets lined with affluent homes; places like Ave Maguire are lined with charming cafés. Aside from the aquarium, there isn't much here in the way of sights, but if you're in the neighborhood you should make sure to drop by the Pointe à Puiseaux down at the foot of Rue d'Église. Here you can take in a gorgeous view of the St Lawrence River.

AQUARIUM DU QUÉBEC Map p204

☎ 418-659-5264, 866-659-5264; 1615 Ave des Hôtels; adult/child $17/9; 🕑 10am-5pm Jun-Aug, 10am-4pm Sep-May; 🚌 13, 25, Ⓟ

Spread across 40 hectares, Québec's aquarium contains some 10,000 aquatic creatures, in the form of freshwater and saltwater fish, amphibians, reptiles, invertebrates and marine mammals. The park is divided into several habitats, including a wetlands region and an arctic sector (with an underwater observation window of the polar bears). There's also a food court with a terrace overlooking the river. You can catch daily events like walrus feeding (10:30am) and polar bear feeding (11am) or live shows with either a walrus (3:30pm) or a trained harbor seal (1:15pm and 4:15pm).

PARC DU BOIS-DE-COULONGE Map p204

☎ 418-528-0773, 800-442-0773; 1215 Chemin St-Louis; admission free; 🕑 dawn-dusk; 🚌 11, 25; Ⓟ

Not far west of the Plains of Abraham (p209) lie the colorful gardens of this park, a paean to the plant world and a welcome respite from downtown. Now open to the public, this wonderful woodland with extensive horticultural displays used to be the private property of a succession of Québec's and Canada's religious and political elite.

HISTORIC STROLL THROUGH THE OLD TOWN

Walking Tour

This tour will walk you through some of the best-known – as well as lesser-known – parts

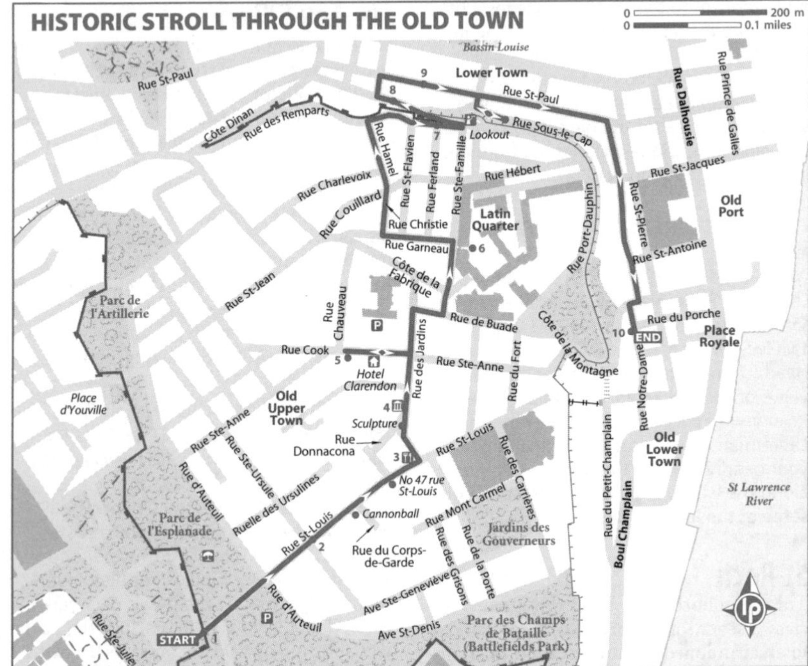

WALK FACTS

Start Porte St-Louis
End Fresque des Québécois
Distance 3km
Time Two to three hours
Fuel Stop Chez Temporel, Epicerie de la Rue Couillard

of Vieux-Québec and give you an introduction to the rich history that lurks in these cobblestone streets. Try to go early in the morning (you'll pass a marvelous bakery en route), before the tour buses fill the streets, when it's easy to lose yourself in an earlier epoch.

1 Porte St-Louis Begin at the Porte St-Louis, an impressive entrance gate first erected in 1693 (though this incarnation dates from 1878). As you walk up Rue St-Louis, you'll pass the Parc de l'Esplanade, which was a cow pasture before becoming the site of 18th- and 19th-century military exercises, concerts and parades.

2 Rue St-Louis On the corner of Rue du Corps-de-Garde, you'll see a cannonball embedded in a tree, supposedly lodged there since 1759. Number 47 Rue St-Louis is where General Montcalm was taken after being shot by the British during the destiny-changing Plains of Abraham Battle on September 13, 1759. He died here the next day.

3 Aux Anciens Canadiens Slightly further, at 34 Rue St-Louis, you'll see a 1676 home, which today houses the Québécois restaurant Aux Anciens Canadiens (p219). The name comes from the title of a novel by Philippe-Aubert de Gaspé, who lived here from 1815 to 1824. Its steeply slanted roof was typical of 17th-century French architecture.

4 Ursuline Convent Turn down Rue des Jardins. You'll soon reach a sculpture by Jules Lasalle honoring the nuns who came to Québec and educated both French and First Nations girls. The work was created to mark the 325th anniversary of the death of Marie de l'Incarnation, the Founder of the Ursuline convent in front of you.

5 Edifice Price Turn left on Rue Cook and have a look at Edifice Price, built in 1929 (at a then-stratospheric sum of $1 million), becoming one of Canada's first skyscrapers. Next to it is the elegant Hotel Clarendon, built in 1870, and Québec City's oldest hotel. The art-deco lobby is well worth a peek.

6 Québec Seminary Continue down Rue des Jardins and enter the grounds of the Québec Seminary. Founded in 1663, the seminary was a place of religious study and education; it's also where American officers were locked up after their unsuccessful siege of Québec in 1775–76. On the grounds there's interpretation trail, revealing the history of this place.

7 Rue des Remparts Head down Rue Ste-Famille and make a left onto the narrow, pretty Rue Garneau. Make your way down to Rue des Remparts and follow the wall to the fine overlook, complete with model cannons. Before you is the business end of QC, with factories along the waterfront.

8 Côte de la Canoterie Next head down along Côte de la Canoterie, which for centuries was the main link between the Lower and Upper Towns (and classes). Hope Gate stood at the top of the *côte* until 1873 to keep the riffraff from entering the Upper Town uninvited – or from hoping too much.

9 Rue St-Paul Turn right onto Rue St-Thomas and right on Rue St-Paul, the heart of Québec's antique district. Peek in atmospheric stores like Maison Dambourgès, where you can hold a bit of history in your hands. Also, take a peek at the tiny lane behind Rue St-Paul, Rue Sous-le-Cap, the narrowest street in the city and a former red-light district.

10 Fresque des Québécois Turn right onto Rue Sault-au-Matelot and jog over to Rue Notre-Dame. Here you'll see a marvelous 420-sq-meter trompe-l'oeil Fresque des Québécois, painted by 12 artists in 1999. Look for historical figures like Jacques Cartier, Samuel de Champlain and others before snapping the requisite tourist pic, planting yourself in the image.

SHOPPING

While it may not have as many big international stores and high-end designer fashion boutiques as larger cosmopolitan cities, Québec is a shopper's paradise in its own special way. Small, unique and authentic little boutiques are this touristy town's claim to retail fame. Think crafts and souvenirs, specialty foods, one-of-a-kind antiques, custom jewelry, furs and fantastic works of art – the city is full of world-class galleries. Of course, Québec does have its share of department stores, fashion boutiques and the usual retail suspects, but its small size makes it ideal for strolling around and shopping the day away hunting for surprises.

The Old Upper Town is full of quaint little shops perfect for browsing. Rue du Trésor by the Château Frontenac is crowded with tourists but worth a browse for meeting the (mostly) talented artists and perusing their works, which are surprisingly affordable. The Old Lower Town combines upscale fashion with old-fashioned architecture. Lower Town also has quite a few artisanal jewelers, regional crafts shops and gourmet food shops specializing in maple-syrup delights! Rue St-Paul is primed for gallery and antique lovers, while Le Quartier Le Petit-Champlain has charming shops as well, from specialty foods to high-end clothing and jewelry.

Most stores open Monday to Wednesday 9:30am or 10am to 6pm; clothing boutiques usually open their doors at 11am. Thursday and Friday, retailers have later opening hours, usually until 9pm. Saturday hours are 10am to 5pm and Sunday is afternoon only (noon to 4pm or 5pm). During high season, between May 1 and Labour Day, many stores in Québec City extend their hours well into the night whatever the day, often until 9pm or 10pm. Many stores will stay open as long as people are coming in. Conversely, you'll find several of the smaller, privately owned stores keep more European hours (11am to 4pm Tuesday to Saturday, closed Sunday and Monday) no matter the season.

OLD UPPER TOWN

EXCALIBUR QUÉBEC Map p206 Clothing

☎ 418-692-5959; 1055 Rue St-Jean; ⌚ 10am-9pm
Devoted to all things medieval, this Québec company sells clothes, jewelry and accessories. It also manufactures about 80% of its merchandise. Some of the outfits are pretty spectacular – and pricey. But plenty of items have been dialed down a notch and are actually wearable in public. This is one of many such stores around the province.

SIMONS Map p206 Department Store

☎ 418-692-3630; 20 Côte de la Fabrique
One of the city's business success stories, Simons was started by the son of a Scottish

immigrant who set up a dry-goods store in Québec City. By 1952 his descendants had turned the business into a successful clothing store. It's popular all over Québec for its trendy Twik label and for stocking items more cutting-edge than those at competing department stores. There's been a Simons at this location since 1870.

OLD LOWER TOWN

GALERIE D'ESTAMPE PLUS
Map p206 Art Gallery

☎ 418-694-1303; 49 Rue St-Pierre; ⏲ 11am-5:30pm Mon-Sat, noon-5pm Sun

A terrific gallery specializing in prints by Quebecers. The artists' biographies are pasted on the walls and there are plenty of postcards and greeting cards if you can't afford the real thing.

BOUTIQUE OCLAN Map p206 Clothing

☎ 418-692-1214; 67 et demi, Rue de Petit-Champlain; ⏲ 10am-6pm Sat-Wed, 10am-9pm Thu & Fri

International brands like Miss Sixty, Michael Kors, Buckler, JP Gaultier and more meet high-end Québec designers like Philippe Dubuc and Mackage at this little basement fashion cave. Charismatic owner Jean-Francois Renaud is quite a personality.

FRUITS & PASSION Map p206 Clothing

☎ 418-692-2859; 75 Rue de Petit-Champlain; ⏲ 10am-5:30pm Mon-Wed, 10am-9pm Thu & Fri, 10am-5:30pm Sat, 11am-5:30pm Sun

This well-known international chain of natural aromatherapy bath and beauty products sells lovely, familiar products whose scents and sense of pampering are a welcome relief to road warriors.

VÊTEMENTS 90 DEGRÉS Map p206 Clothing

☎ 418-694-9914; 141 Rue St-Paul; ⏲ usually 11am-6pm

Set up by a Québec City artist who decided to slap simple, strong images and cheeky French text onto T-shirts and tank tops, this store is now going gangbusters. Even non-French speakers are taken with the shirts.

LA PETITE CABANE À SUCRE DU QUÉBEC Map p206 Food

☎ 418-692-5875; 94 Rue de Petit-Champlain; ⏲ 10am-5:30pm Mon-Wed, 10am-9pm Thu & Fri, 10am-5:30pm Sat, 11am-5:30pm Sun

Maple syrup is a massive industry in Québec, and this adorable little shop sells it in every shape and form: candies, delicacies, ice cream, snacks, syrup-related accessories and, of course, the sweet stuff itself.

MARCHÉ DU VIEUX-PORT Map p206 Food

☎ 418-692-2517; 160 Quai St-André; ⏲ 8am-8pm

This is a local market where you can buy fresh fruits and vegetables as well as dozens of local specialties, from Île d'Orléans blackcurrant wine to ciders, honeys, chocolates, herbal hand creams and, of course, maple-syrup products. Weekends see huge crowds and more wine tastings than can be considered sensible.

JOAILLERIE JULES PERRIER
Map p206 Jewelry

☎ 418-692-0880; 39 Rue de Petit-Champlain; ⏲ 10am-5:30pm Mon-Wed, 10am-9pm Thu & Fri, 10am-5:30pm Sat, 11am-5:30pm Sun

Passion is the inspiration behind this well-known jeweler's stunning designs, unique earrings, brooches, pendants and more. It's full of precious stones, making browsing in this elegant locale – still a family business – feel like perusing art. The shop also carries brands like Movado.

OUTSIDE THE WALLS

St-Jean-Baptiste

SILLONS Map p210 Music

☎ 418-524-8352; 1149 Ave Cartier; ⏲ 10am-9pm Mon-Fri, 10am-5pm Sat, 11am-5pm Sun

This independent record store has been around for almost 20 years and specializes in jazz, world music and music from Québec and France. It's not the best place for metal or hip-hop but other than that this is a great place to come if you want advice on which Jean Leloup or Les Colocs CD you should be adding to your collection.

BOUTIQUE KETTÖ
Map p210 Ceramics/Jewelry

☎ 418-522-3337; 951 Ave Cartier; ⏲ 10am-10pm

Illustrator Julie St-Onge-Drouin started up Kettö after her illustrative designs kept finding their way onto ceramic surfaces. Now at this big, bright and beautifully set-up boutique, they're on everything from plates and mugs to ceramic jewelry and necklaces. Great gifts, her designs are sold in small boutiques throughout Québec, but here you'll find the best selection.

CHOCO-MUSÉE ÉRICO

Map p210 Chocolate

☎ 418-524-2122; www.chocomusee.com; 634 Rue St-Jean; ⌚ 10am-5:30pm Mon-Wed, 10am-9pm Thu & Fri, 10am-5:30pm Sat, 11am-5:30pm Sun, open longer in fine weather May–late Sep

The exotic smells and flavors here will send a chocolate lover into conniptions of joy. Try strawberry-and-basil truffles or the ice cream that comes in orange pekoe tea and beet-and-raspberry flavors. Or go for the chocolate-chip cookie packed with semi-sweet chocolate chunks, dates and black tea. There's a little museum in the back and a window where you can watch the chocolatiers work.

JA MOISAN ÉPICIER Map p210 Food

☎ 418-522-0685; 699 Rue St-Jean; ⌚ 9am-10pm

Established in 1871, this is considered the oldest grocery store in North America. The store is beautifully set up and fun just to browse – ever seen black-and-white, zebra-striped bow pasta? The products do generally fall on the 'You've got to be kidding!' side of expensive but there will be products here you've never seen before along with heaps of local goods.

TAXI Map p210 Men's Underwear

☎ 418-694-1828; 586 Rue St-Jean; ⌚ 9:30am-5:30pm

This is a funky little store devoted to men's underwear and lots of it. The T-shirts and briefs are colorful and cutting-edge. Well, as cutting- edge as men's cotton underwear can be without raising eyebrows. The company is based in the village of Ste-Anne-de-la-Pérade, about 1½ hours southwest of Québec City. Taxi underwear is 100% Canadian made.

KAMA SUTRA Map p210 Sex Toys

☎ 418-648-6286; 879 Rue St-Jean; ⌚ 10am-10pm

This low-key store was started up by a sexologist. Despite being surrounded by all manner of dildos and naughty bits done up in milk chocolate, the fresh-scrubbed, friendly staff mingle easily with everyone from students to middle-aged married couples from Toronto in this no-embarrassment environment.

St-Roch

MOUNTAIN EQUIPMENT CO-OP

Map p210 Clothing

☎ 418-522-8884; 405 Rue St-Joseph Est; ⌚ 10am-5:30pm Mon-Wed, 10am-9pm Thu & Fri, 9:30am-5pm Sat, 11am-5pm Sun

The mountain man (or woman) in all of us needs his fix, especially if you're planning to conquer the great Québec wilderness. Enter this sprawling shop, the largest from the renowned Canadian brand. It even has an outdoor resource center to help you plan your adventure.

MYCO ANNA Map p210 Clothing

☎ 418-522-2270; 615 Rue St-Vallier Ouest; ⌚ 10am-5:30pm Mon-Wed, 10am-9pm Thu & Fri, 9:30am-5pm Sat, 11am-5pm Sun

Old meets new at this bright and daring women's fashion line's signature shop. Launched in 1996, Myco Anna is known for bright, patchworky, flirty and sexy dresses – all made from at least some recycled material.

J.B. LALIBERTÉ Map p210 Furrier

☎ 418-525-4841; 595 Rue St-Joseph Est; ⌚ 10am-5:30pm Mon-Wed, 10am-9pm Thu & Fri, 9:30am-5pm Sat, 11am-5pm Sun

Founded in 1867, this furrier has grown into one of Canada's major players. You'll find fancy collections of furs, coats, accessories and more, quite reasonably priced.

BENJO Map p210 Toys

☎ 418-640-0001; www.benjo.ca, in French; 543 Rue St-Joseph Est; ⌚ 10am-5:30pm Mon-Wed, 10am-9pm Thu & Fri, 9:30am-5pm Sat, 11am-5pm Sun

This toy shop gives a glimpse into what the world would be like if kids ran the show. Even the front door is pint-sized (the adult-sized door for grown-ups is off to the side). There's a train that goes around the store on weekends, and arts and crafts for little ones during the week (usually around $10 to $15).

EATING

The restaurant scene in Québec City has never been better. The city has become a tiny eating mecca all its own. These days, interesting budget eateries share the foodie landscape with some of the most acclaimed restaurants in Canada. It's flipped the city's culinary reputation from overpriced and unvaried to exciting and inviting. Québec City has always excelled at classic French food but, excitingly, in the past couple of years, new places are diverging from the regular cozy bistro fare (as great as it is). These new additions to the food scene are sleek and hip and aren't afraid to take risks. They may not always be completely successful, but it's exciting to see the experimentation nonetheless.

The buzz it's created has also caused a reverse foodie migration. While before it was always Quebecers heading down to Montréal to eat, these days it's not unusual to see Montréal couples in the Québec City tourist office waving a national magazine or newspaper review in their hand and asking how to get to the latest, greatest resto.

Most of these new additions seem to land in the high range of people's budgets, but often you can get the same food for a much lower price just by going for the table d'hôte (set-course meal) at lunchtime when meals are cheaper.

The low immigrant population in Québec City means you won't see the range of ethnic restaurants that you do in a place like Montréal, but if you are a lover of French food, Québec City has a wonderful choice of bistros for you to work through.

PRACTICALITIES

Opening Hours & Meal Times

Most restaurants in Québec City are open for lunch and dinner in the off-season and from about 11am to late in high-season summer. During peak time, many restaurants close when the last customer leaves. Standard lunch hours are 11am to 2:30pm, with dinner 5:30pm to 10pm. Note that outside of Winter Carnival, many restaurants in winter may be closed Sunday and Monday or both. Breakfast cafés open around 7am (9am on Sunday) and close by 3pm. Places really tend to fill up from 8pm onwards in the francophone tradition.

PRICE GUIDE

Our restaurants are listed in order of price, from costliest to least expensive. The price icon represents the average cost of a main course without drinks.

$$$	over $30 a meal
$$	$16-30 a meal
$	under $16 a meal

THE QUÉBÉCOIS TABLE

French food is king in Québec City. The lack of a significant immigrant population means that there is not the kind of massive ethnic smorgasbord that you'll find in Montréal, though the quality of restaurants here is outstanding. While for years Québec City locals were known to drive to Montréal for fine dining, these days Montrealers are making their way to Québec City to dine in the more-than-half-dozen fine restaurants like L'Utopie (p224) or Panache (p221).

Then there's Caribou, something you won't find in Montréal. It's an alcoholic beverage that resembles a very powerful and sweet red wine, almost like a marriage of port and sherry, and warms the body – if not the soul. It's available for purchase on streets around Québec City during Winter Carnival.

How Much?

Midrange places in Québec City will, on average, charge $20 to $30 for a multicourse meal, including a glass of wine. Top-end restaurants run upwards of $25 for a main; a culinary temple of some renown might charge $60 to $100 or more for a four-course gourmet dinner, including wine. Count on $6 to $10 for a glass of drinkable red and $25 to $35 (and up) for a bottle from the house cellar. Taxes amounting to nearly 15% apply at all restaurants. Most do not include the taxes in their menu prices, but check the fine print.

Booking Tables

If you're in Québec City between May and October, or during Winter Carnival, definitely book ahead to dine in one of the finer restaurants. During this peak season, popular places can fill up quickly, even at odd times like Monday nights.

Tipping

A tip of 15% of the pretax bill is customary in restaurants. Some waiters may add a service charge for large parties; in these cases, no tip should be added unless the service was extraordinary. Leave the tip on the table or hand it directly to staff.

OLD UPPER TOWN

If you are not eating at the places we've listed below, be choosy about where you spend your money in the Old Town. Though many have gorgeous settings, and may be great places for coffee, tea or a beer, food at many of them can be disappointing (ie a chicken Caesar salad may turn out to be wilted lettuce with a slice of Spamlike processed chicken slapped on top of it). Your accommodations or the delightfully non-BS tourist office on Rue St-Anne in the Upper Town would be great places to ask for recommendations.

LE SAINT-AMOUR

Map p206 French/Québécois $$$

☎ 418-694-0667; 48 Rue Ste-Ursule; mains $38-52; 🕙 11:30am-2pm Mon-Fri, 6-10:30pm daily

One of the top-end darlings of the capital, Le Saint-Amour has earned a loyal following over the years for its beautifully prepared grills and seafood. Perhaps more impressive than the food is the excellent wine selection, with over 10,000 bottles in the cellar. The setting is warm and inviting beneath the glass-domed ceiling trimmed with hanging plants. The service, however, doesn't always come through.

AUX ANCIENS CANADIENS

Map p206 Québécois $$$

☎ 418-692-1627; www.auxancienscanadiens.qc.ca; 34 Rue St-Louis; mains $28-52; 🕙 noon-10pm

Housed in the historic Jacquet House, which dates from 1676, this place is all about robust country cooking and typical Québécois specialties. Here, waitstaff in historic garb serve dishes like caribou in blueberry wine sauce, duckling in maple-syrup sauce or Lac St-Jean meat pie served with pheasant and buffalo casserole. Lunch is served noon to 5:45pm and is by far the best deal (around $20 for three courses). The restaurant gets its name from the novel *Les Anciens Canadiens* by Philippe-Aubert de Gaspé, who lived in the house from 1815 to 1824. The original rooms have been left intact, resulting in several small, intimate dining areas.

LE PATRIARCHE Map p206 Québécois $$$

☎ 418-692-5488; 17 Rue St-Stanislas; mains $28-50; 🕙 11:30am-2pm Wed-Fri & 5:30-10pm daily, closed Mon & Tue Sep-Jun

The nouvelle cuisine echoes the contemporary art hanging on the 180-year-old stone walls in this top-class restaurant. Imaginative culinary creations seem almost too lovely to eat, but the feeling soon passes when you read the restaurants' roll call of local suppliers. Start off with coconut and lemongrass poached scallops before moving on to roasted rack of lamb, caribou steak or a garden-vegetable mushroom risotto.

LE PAIN BÉNI Map p206 Québécois $$$

☎ 418-694-9485; 24 Rue Ste-Anne; mains $20-32; 🕙 noon-10pm daily May-Oct, noon-2pm Mon-Fri & 6-10pm Tue-Sat Nov-Apr

Another great gourmet outing can be head at this small, unpretentious dining room inside the Auberge Place d'Armes. Le Pain Béni serves an excellent assortment of dishes with Québec highlights. Recent favorites include lamb-shank confit, lobster lasagna with sweetbread and morels, and beer-braised wild boar over parmesan risotto. Prices are reasonable compared with similar options. Delectable desserts are the coup de grâce.

APSARA Map p206 Asian $$

☎ 418-694-0232; 71 Rue d'Auteuil; mains $15-25; 🕙 11am-2pm & 5:30-10pm

This pan-Asian restaurant serves tasty, consistently good dishes and has been around since 1982. You'll find an enticing mix of Cambodian, Thai and Vietnamese plates utilizing lemongrass, spicy peanut sauces, rice and delicate noodles. The restaurant has the feel of a drawing room in an upmarket townhouse.

CONTI CAFFE Map p206 Italian $$

☎ 418-692-4191; Rue St-Louis; mains $14-25; 🕙 11am-11pm

Set on busy Rue St-Louis, the handsome Conti Caffe features an impressive selection of flavorful Italian classics. Start off with prosciutto and melon or the house antipasto, before moving on to penne with gorgonzola, apples and walnuts or the grilled halibut with mango salsa. The dining room is a warmly lit retreat, with exposed brick walls trimmed with art and big windows overlooking the street.

LE PETIT COIN LATIN Map p206 Bistro $

☎ 418-692-2033; 8½ Rue Ste-Ursule; mains $7-12; 🕙 7:30am-10:30pm

For a French-style breakfast, try this excellent, European spot near Rue St-Jean for croissants, muffins or eggs. In summer you can eat the low-priced lunch specials out on the patio. A wide variety of fresh salads and soups rounds out the menu.

PAILLARD CAFÉ-BOULANGERIE

Map p206 Bakery/Sandwiches $

☎ 418-692-1221; 1097 Rue St-Jean; mains $7-9; 7:30am-7pm

This bright and buzzy space has high ceilings, huge windows looking onto the street and a long wooden table down the middle where diners tuck into tasty gourmet sandwiches (ham with green apples and brie; hot roast beef sandwiches with blue cheese, caramelized onions and horseradish), satisfying soups and fresh salads. The attached bakery with its displays of sweet temptation is too hard to resist. It's a bit of a madhouse at lunchtime.

CHEZ TEMPOREL Map p206 Café $

☎ 418-694-1813; 25 Rue Couillard; mains $6-10; 7am-midnight

Hidden away on a side street just off the beaten path, this charming little café serves tasty sandwiches, homemade soups and quiches, plus prodigious salads, fresh-baked goods and excellent coffees. It attracts a curious mix of locals and travelers.

CASSE-CRÊPE BRETON Map p206 Creperie $

☎ 418-692-0438; 1136 Rue St-Jean; mains $6-8; 8am-6pm

Tiny and unassuming, this perennial favorite specializes in hot, fresh crepes of every kind starting as low as $4. Some diners like to sit at the counter and watch the chef at work.

CHEZ ASHTON Map p206 Fast Food $

☎ 418-692-3055; 54 Côte du Palais; mains $3-6; 11am-2am Sun-Wed, until 4am Thu-Sat

For a break from fine dining, head to Chez Ashton, a Québec City fast-food institution with dozens of restaurants across town. Some Québec City boosters swear it's *the* best *poutine* in the province (Montrealers, of course, would quickly dismiss such an idea). Though *poutine* is the draw, Ashton also whips up burgers and roast beef sandwiches.

EPICERIE DE LA RUE COUILLARD

Map p206 Bakery $

☎ 418-692-3748; 27 rue Couillard; pastries $2-3; 8am-10pm Mon-Fri, 9am-10pm Sat & Sun

Hidden on one of Upper Town's pretty backstreets, this pleasant little bakery and gourmet grocery whips up delicious fresh-baked goodies and tasty sandwiches, and is something of a local secret. Stop in early for the best selection.

OLD LOWER TOWN

Rue St-Paul is lined with restaurants. In warm weather, they fling their windows (and walls) wide open and set up outdoor seating on the streets. With the revelry overflowing outdoors there's terrific atmosphere – there's not one terrace that doesn't seem warm and inviting. In winter the streets outside may be deserted, but the revelry packs indoors, and windows positively glow with the warmth and good cheer inside. Many of the best bistros in town are located on this strip. Many can get a little pricey, but do not write them off. Do what the locals do; a carefully chosen table d'hôte at lunchtime will give you exactly the same food for a more manageable price.

TOAST! Map p206 Québécois $$$

☎ 418-692-1334; 17 Rue Sault-au-Matelot; 3-/4-course meal $65/75; 6-10:30pm

Inside Le Priori Hotel, Toast! is another contender for best restaurant in the city. The trim, attractive dining room with fireplace is the setting for an eclectic array of dishes, including poached lobster risotto, foie gras appetizers (one of the house specialties), seared black cod in an almond crust, and scallops with crispy pork belly. You'll find excellent wine selections, and generally good service. In the summer, you can dine alfresco in the vine-covered courtyard out back.

LAURIE RAPHAËL

Map p206 French/Québécois $$$

☎ 418-692-4555; 17 Rue Dalhousie; lunch table d'hôte $25, dinner mains $38-45; 11:30am-2pm Tue-Fri, 6-10pm Tue-Sat

This highly respected restaurant features a blend of *produits du terroir* (local Québec produce), along with international accents. Delectable favorites include giant scallops with coconut milk and exotic fruits, and lamb with mint and anise. Chef Daniel Vézina keeps menu descriptions to the minimum, saying he wants to 'leave room for imagination and discovery.' There's also a spontaneous chef's menu ($60) 'for those that like to be surprised.'

PANACHE Map p206 French/Québécois $$$

☎ 418-692-1022; 10 Rue St-Antoine; lunch mains $14-24, dinner mains $34-50; 7-10:30am & 6-10pm daily, noon-2pm Wed-Fri

One of Québec's most celebrated restaurants, Panache generally receives high marks for its delectable, imaginatively prepared Québécois cuisine and top-notch service. The feast, which can easily last three or four hours, might feature the likes of maple-glazed halibut, Appalachian red deer with wild berry sauce, spit-roasted duck or caramelized giant scallops. It's set in a 19th-century maritime warehouse, with rustic wood beams nicely complementing the elegant place settings. The price tag for all this, not surprisingly, is high. Some foodies say it's a memorable, worthwhile experience; others say Panache is overhyped.

L'ÉCHAUDÉ Map p206 Bistro $$

☎ 418-692-1299; 73 Rue Sault-au-Matelot; mains $18-38; 11:30am-2:30pm & 6-10pm

This classic little bistro has a refreshingly relaxed and nonstuffy waitstaff. All the classics are on offer – including duck confit, *steak frites* (steak with French fries), fresh fish of the day and braised lamb shank – along with more daring options like Cornish hen with braised shrimp, and pan-fried foie gras with grilled mushrooms. All come beautifully plated to the table and bursting with flavor, which is why L'Échaudé is one of the rare places in the Old Town where locals regularly outnumber tourists. The terrific wine list favors bottles from France.

LE LAPIN SAUTÉ

Map p206 French $$

☎ 418-692-5325; 52 Rue du Petit-Champlain; mains $15-24; 11am-10pm Mon-Fri, 9am-10pm Sat & Sun

This cozy, rustically set restaurant brings a breath of the French countryside into the Old Town. Naturally *lapin* (rabbit) plays a starring role on the menu, in dishes like rabbit cassoulet and rabbit pie, though you can also opt for bouillabaisse, marinated salmon cooked on cedar, filet mignon, smoked pork chops, or lighter fare like the *croque monsieur*, French onion soup and grilled vegetables with a goat cheese salad. In good weather, you can sit on the flowery patio overlooking tiny Félix Leclerc park.

LE CAFÉ DU MONDE Map p206 Bistro $$

☎ 418-692-4455; 84 Rue Dalhousie; mains $15-24; 11:30am-11pm Mon-Fri, 9:30am-11pm Sat & Sun

This Paris-style bistro is the only restaurant in town directly on the St Lawrence River. Bright, airy and casually elegant, it has been a local favorite for years, swearing by bistro classics like *steak frites* and *saucisse de Toulouse*. The menu is authentic and there's a great choice of other dishes like roasted pork rack with honey and lobster ravioli. The accent is on local Québec products.

LE 48 INTERNATIONAL Map p206 Bistro $$

☎ 418-694-4448; 48 Rue St-Paul; mains $14-20; noon-midnight

This stylish spot leans toward theatricality with its sleek black tables and chairs and Cirque du Soleil footage playing in the background. The menu features tasty global bistro fare (Asian noodle soups, gourmet burgers, salads, pizzas) and there's an outdoor patio. Service is hit-or-miss.

LE COCHON DINGUE Map p206 Café $$

☎ 418-692-2013; 46 Blvd Champlain; mains $11-17; 8am-1am

Since 1979 this ever-popular choice has been serving visitors and locals straight-ahead French standbys, from *café au lait en bôl* to *croque monsieur*, sandwiches, *steak frites*, salads, mussels or quiche. It's all good day-to-day food and a kid-friendly place to boot. There's outside seating in warm weather for crowd-watching.

BUFFET DE L'ANTIQUAIRE

Map p206 Diner $

☎ 418-692-2661; 95 Rue St-Paul; mains $10-15; 6am-10pm

Tucked in among the bistros and the galleries is this convivial little diner with an old-school vibe. Locals and tourists alike crowd in for hearty breakfasts, steaming plates of *poutine*, savory meat pies and other tasty comfort fare. Grab a seat at the narrow counter or, if the weather is warm, slip into one of the sidewalk tables out front.

LE PETIT COCHON DINGUE

Map p206 Café/Bakery $

☎ 418-694-0303; 24 Blvd Champlain; mains $7-12; 7:30am-10pm

Just down the street from Le Cochon Dingue, this dapper little café and patisserie is a fine destination for coffee, desserts, salads, baguette sandwiches or grilled panini. The helpful staff keep the crowds moving.

OUTSIDE THE WALLS

Beyond the walls, there are heaps of terrific eateries of all types and for all budgets.

St-Jean-Baptiste

Here, there are three small but terrific main eating districts: Rue St-Jean; Ave Cartier between Grande Allée Ouest and Blvd René-Lévesque Ouest; and west along Grande Allée from the Old Town where you'll find a popular and lively strip of more than a dozen alfresco, economic, visitor-oriented restaurants complete with touts.

VOODOO GRILL Map p210 Fusion $$

☎ 418-647-2000; 575 Grande Allée Est; mains $19-27; 11:30am-11pm Mon-Fri, 5:30-11pm Sat & Sun

Attractive young servers, thumping electronica and wildly elcectic decor set the stage for this buzzing fusion restaurant. African and Asian statues peer down at the tables and the dining room is done up in dark, rich tones. Specialties here include filet mignon from the Charlevoix region, mixed seafood platters and huge savory Asian soups. After a big meal, diners can burn off the calories at the Chez Maurice (p226) nightclub upstairs.

AUX VIEUX CANONS Map p210 International $$

☎ 418-529-9461; 650 Grande Allée Est; mains $15-25; noon-10pm

Set with a spacious front terrace on restaurant-lined Grande Allée, this place serves fairly mainstream bistro fare – roast chicken, spaghetti bolognaise, *steak au poivre* (pepper steak), grilled meats, French onion soup. The draw, however, is the beer; it's poured in yard-long glasses and served with a wooden brace. A fine place to refresh after a day exploring the city.

OH! PINO Map p210 Bistro $$

☎ 418-525-3535; 1019 Ave Cartier; mains $14-25; noon-10pm

One of the most authentic French bistros in town, the elegantly set Oh! Pino attracts a well-heeled, slightly older crowd that comes for tasty bouillabaisse, grilled filet mignon or roasted scallops in pear sauce with leek fondue; Oh! Pino also offers more than 20 different mussel dishes. The roomy terrace in front is a fine spot for people-watching. Thursday nights feature a live accordionist, to help give the place that Rive Gauche (Left Bank) feel.

ENZO SUSHI Map p210 Japanese $$

☎ 418-649-1688; 150 Blvd René-Lévesque; mains $14-24; 11:30am-2:30pm Mon-Sat, 5-10pm daily

One of Québec City's best (and priciest) sushi restaurants, Enzo receives rave reviews for its mouthwateringly fresh sushi and sashimi. In addition to the classics, house specialties feature inventive sushi combinations like *homard grillé* (grilled lobster with fish roe, cucumber, lettuce and spicy mayonnaise). There are a few tempura and teriyaki dishes for nonsushi lovers. Start the meal off with a sake martini or a soho martini (vodka and lychee juice) or head straight for the wine list.

LE HOBBIT Map p210 Bistro $$

☎ 418-647-2677; 700 Rue St-Jean; mains $14-20; 10am-10pm

This popular and inviting bistro on Rue St-Jean has outdoor seating, a casual atmosphere and good-value lunch and dinner specials (check out the chalkboard). The classics are all nicely done, including French onion soup, juicy duck confit and *steak frites* – plus Québécois specialties like elk with sautéed apples and leeks. There's a small but fairly priced wine list. Various fresh pasta dishes and salads round out the menu.

CARTHAGE Map p210 Tunisian $$

☎ 418-529-0576; 399 Rue St-Jean; mains $14-20; noon-3pm & 6-11pm

This BYOB (bring your own bottle) Tunisian restaurant offers couscous, meat and vegetarian specials, all lightly spiced. Tables and chairs fill the colorful room while at the tables by the windows patrons kneel on cushions in traditional Middle Eastern style.

CICCIO CAFÉ Map p210 Italian $$

☎ 418-525-6161; 875 Rue de Claire-Fontaine; mains $13-22; 11:30am-2pm Mon-Fri, 5-10pm Sun-Thu, until 11pm Fri & Sat

Tucked just off Rue St-Jean (up a steep hill), this hidden gem serves excellent Italian fare in a charming but low-key setting. Reliable old-world favorites include linguini with clams, as well as slightly creative touches like rib steak with Roquefort and a rich scallop and shrimp risotto.

LE COMMENSAL Map p210 Vegetarian $$

☎ 418-647-3733; 860 Rue St-Jean; per kg $21; 11am-9:30pm

An endless choice of strictly vegetarian food dishes, including vegan and organic options, lines the buffet counters in this huge and bright self-serve restaurant. The menu changes daily, but typically features lasagna, savory veggie pies, stews, curries, wraps, ratatouille, veggie pâté, soups, salads, fresh fruits and berries, plus a large dessert counter (the maple sugar pie is tops, as is the raspberry cheesecake). You can bring your own wine.

CAFÉ KRIEGHOFF Map p210 Café $

☎ 418-522-3711; 1091 Ave Cartier; mains $10-17; 7am-11pm

This brilliant little resto is a city classic, with a varied bistro menu, extensive breakfast choices and some of the best coffee in town. If it's warm, you can watch the comings and goings on Ave Cartier from a table on the massive front porch, or head to the laid-back terrace out back. Inside, the dining room is decorated with reproductions from the café's namesake artist, Cornelius Krieghoff (1815–72), one of Québec's master painters of the 20th century, who lived just down the street from here on Grande Allée.

RESTAURANT DANA Map p210 Asian $

☎ 418-523-0260; 269 Rue St-Jean; mains $10-15; noon-3pm & 6-11pm

This casual little pan-Asian restaurant serves a good selection of dishes from the East, including flavorful noodle soups, curries, pad Thai and, for dessert, pineapple beignet tapioca. It has a relaxed, family-friendly ambience, making it a destination to hit when the craving for spring rolls strikes and you happen to be in the neighborhood.

CHEZ VICTOR Map p210 Hamburgers $

☎ 418-529-7702; 145 Rue St-Jean; mains $8-14; noon-10pm

One of the best-loved little neighborhood eateries in the city, Chez Victor specializes in juicy burgers, served with more than a dash of creativity. Choose from ostrich, deer, elk, wild boar, straight-up beef or vegetarian, which you can then dress a number of ways (brie, smoked bacon, cream cheese etc). The sides are also nice, including fresh coleslaw and fries, which you can get with a variety of sauces (including the recommended curry sauce). There's a tiny outdoor patio or dine in the cozy, exposed-brick dining room. Service is sometimes frustratingly slow.

CAFÉ LE SULTAN Map p210 Lebanese $

☎ 418-525-9449; 467 Rue St-Jean; mains $6-12; noon-11pm Mon-Fri, 5pm-midnight Sat

This warm, cozy café is head and shoulders above the normal, soulless Lebanese fast-food restaurant. There are hookah pipes in the windows, music playing in the background, oriental tapestries and tiny tables. The service isn't particularly friendly but the atmosphere is terrific. Try the *merguez* (spicy lamb sausage), falafel or the leg of lamb.

TUTTO GELATO Map p210 Ice Cream $

☎ 418-522-0896; 716 Rue St-Jean; 1/2 scoops $2/3.25; 9:30am-10pm Sun-Thu, until 11pm Fri & Sat

There's a reason people line up halfway out the door at all hours for Tutto Gelato. The creamy, rich, homemade ice cream here is simply too good to pass up. Over two dozen varieties of the Italian-style gelato and nine different sorbets (plus four soy-based varieties for the vegan crowd) vie for attention behind the glass counters. Top picks include *fraise des champs* (wild strawberries), passion fruit, pistachio, Bacio (milk chocolate and hazelnut) and green tea. Young, efficient staff move things along quickly.

St-Roch

The rejuvenation of St-Roch means everything from shopping to entertainment has become more exciting – and the eating scene is no exception. What's refreshing here is that, despite the number of stylish and trendy eateries, not a trace of snobbery has entered into the mix (so far). There are some terrific eating experiences to be had and new places are opening all the time.

L'UTOPIE Map p210 French $$$

☎ 418-523-7878; www.restaurant-utopie.com; 226½ Rue St-Joseph Est; lunch $15-21, dinner mains $26-33; 11:30am-10pm Thu & Fri, 6-10pm Tue, Wed, Sat & Sun

L'Utopie is one of several critically acclaimed restaurants to open its doors in the last few years. Stylish yet refined, L'Utopie serves imaginative, artfully presented dishes by chef-owner Stéphane Modat. The menu changes regularly and features dishes like truffle risotto, scallops with warm foie gras, and grilled almond-crusted veal. The food-and-wine pairings are simply phenomenal. Everything is served in a bright, open dining room with an exposed wine cellar. Bunches of slender birch trees separate the tables and reach toward the ceiling.

LE GRAIN DE RIZ Map p210 Asian Fusion $$$

☎ 418-525-2227; 410 Rue St-Anselme; mains $26-32; lunch & dinner

A foodie favorite, this Western-Asian fusion restaurant lies just off Rue St-Joseph. Creative twists on Vietnamese and Chinese dishes appear in menu items like chicken with Earl Grey cream sauce served on couscous, or coconut shrimp with mango salsa. Helpful staff give tips on navigating the complex menu flavors. The attached store sells imported rice and tea.

LE CAFÉ DU CLOCHER PENCHÉ Map p210 Bistro $$

☎ 418-640-0597; 203 Rue St-Joseph Est; brunch around $16, mains $23-30; 8am-11pm Mon-Fri, 11am-11pm Sat & Sun

This café serves classy, classic bistro fare and proudly shows off local products like Québécois *fromages* (cheeses). What sets it apart are the one-of-a-kind weekend brunches. Brioche comes with caramelized pears, homemade *crème fraîche*, caramel sauce and almonds. An English muffin is served with veggie pâté, poached eggs, cheddar cheese, pesto vinaigrette, roasted potatoes and vegetarian chili. Reservations recommended.

LARGO RESTO-CLUB Map p210 International $$

☎ 418-529-3111; 643 Rue St-Joseph Est; mains $17-24; 11:30am-3pm & 6-11pm

Rich wood tones and exposed brick create a warm ambience at this welcoming restaurant in the heart of St-Roch. The menu is small, featuring simple ingredients, but the preparation is excellent, making for a rewarding dining experience. *Tartelette de canard* (savory duck pie), seafood linguini and grilled squid with vegetables and polenta are popular selections. Catch live music here Thursday through Saturday nights (opposite). The Largo Resto-Club also does gallery duty, showing off the work of local painters and sculptors.

YUZU Map p210 Japanese $$

☎ 418-521-7253; 438 Rue du Parvis; mains $14-25; 11:30am-2:30pm Mon-Fri & 5:30-10pm Sun-Wed, until 11pm Thu-Sat

This stylish but warmly lit restaurant (lightboxes, bonsai trees) spreads a tempting array of sushi and creative dishes (tempura soft-shell crab), plus a multicourse tasting menu with foie gras thrown in for good measure. A young, somewhat hip crowd stops in before hitting the nearby bars.

LE POSTINO Map p210 Italian $$

☎ 418-647-0000; 296 Rue St-Joseph Est; mains $12-18; 11:30am-10pm Mon-Fri, 8am-10pm Sat & Sun

Prime people-watching coupled with friendly, unpretentious waitstaff make this place a popular low-key option in St-Roch. There are plenty of classic pasta dishes on the menu for around $10 to $12 as well as a fantastic choice of risottos with genius combinations such as rabbit, roasted parsnips, caramelized shallots and wild mushrooms.

JAMAIS VU Map p210 Creperie $

☎ 418-529-0944; 46 Rue St-Joseph Est; mains $10; 11am-2pm & 5:30-9pm Tue-Fri, 10am-3pm & 6-10pm Sat, 10am-3pm Sun

On a quiet stretch of Rue St-Joseph, Jamais Vu is a cozy little restaurant that whips up tasty crepes, fresh salads and smoothies. Favorites include the ham with béchamel and asparagus, the Greek salad and a satisfying *croque monsieur*. Dessert crepes are a nice cap to the meal.

DRINKING & NIGHTLIFE

Let's be honest. Québec City isn't exactly considered a party town. Bars and clubs tend to close early, and although winter après-ski festivities can be just as debaucherous as the nightlife of any bigger city (especially when sexy snowboard and ski pros come out to play) you simply don't have as many options and variety. That said, what Québec City does offer after dark is quite special, fun and refreshingly attitude-free. You get the feeling that everyone is welcome, and although the swankier supper clubs and restaurants may lack a snooty urban edge, people are friendly and service and ambience are always top-notch. Perhaps Québec's true bon-vivant flair is best experienced in its older pubs, watering holes, and *boîtes à chanson* (Québec folk-music clubs), where generations of locals dance and sing with uncensored glee. Of course, the city's more contemporary music scene is equally cool. Daring French-language rock, metal, punk, hip-hop and electronica scenes rival those of any bigger North American metropolis, but the communities are perhaps tougher for outsiders to infiltrate because of the language barrier (rock star Jean Leloup got his start here!). Still, many touring bands from across Canada, the US and Europe do perform here, and it's not that hard to pick up the weekly *Voir Québec* newspaper (published every Thursday) to check out club and bar listings. *Scope* is a glossy monthly that focuses on movies and cinema, and *Fugues* is a free gay and lesbian entertainment guide. Have fun!

LIVE MUSIC

CHEZ SON PÈRE Map p206

☎ 418-692-5308; 24 Rue St-Stanislas; 🕒 8pm for show at 10pm (9pm Fri & Sat)

One of the city's best-loved *boîtes à chanson*, this spot boasts a great atmosphere and is probably the first place locals will send you if you're interested in seeing this rollicking kind of French folk music. Cover charge varies; sometimes it's free.

FOU-BAR Map p210

☎ 418-522-1987; 525 Rue St-Jean 🕒 3pm-3am

Laid-back and with an eclectic mix of bands, this is one of the town's classics for good live music.

GALERIE ROUJE Map p210

☎ 418-688-4777; 228 Rue St-Joseph Est

This place is a mini cultural heaven. Downstairs is gallery space while upstairs you'll find fantastic gigs ranging from electronic music to DJs.

LARGO RESTO-CLUB Map p210

☎ 418-529-3111; 643 Rue St-Joseph Est; 🕒 jazz shows 8pm

Thursday, Friday and Saturday, the music-mad Largo owner lets the jazz-club side of this resto shine, bringing in local bands, singers and musicians from as far away as Los Angeles. Upscale, ultrarelaxed, slightly swish vibe.

LE PAPE GEORGES Map p206

☎ 418-692-1320; 8 Rue de Cul-de-Sac; 🕒 3pm-3am

With live music at least three nights a week (more in the summer) from 10pm, this charming wine bistro located in a 300-year-old house also serves cheeses, meats and baguettes with a healthy dollop of Québécois culture.

LES VOÛTES DE NAPOLÉON Map p210

☎ 418-640-9388; 680A Grande Allée; 🕒 approx 8:30pm-late

Another jubilant *boîte à chanson*. Its impossible-to-find-on-your-own entrance means it will likely be just you and the locals – it's underneath the Restaurant Bonaparte. If you can't find the entrance, just ask a local to point you in the right direction.

BARS & CLUBS

LE SACRILÈGE Map p210 Bar

☎ 418-649-1985; 447 Rue St-Jean; 🕒 noon-3am

It's been around for over 10 years, but most night owls still start or end their weekend revelry at this watering hole. Even on Monday night, it's standing-room only. There's a popular terrace out back – get to it through the bar or the tiny brick alley next door. To find Le Sacrilège keep an eye out for the sign with a laughing, dancing monk saucily showing off his knickers.

LES SALONS D'EDGAR Map p210 Bar

☎ 418-522-1987; 263 Rue St-Vallier Est; 🕒 4:30pm-late Wed-Sun

The unofficial 'official' hangout for the city's theater community. The eavesdropping here is as much fun as the drinking – you'll be privy to conversations on roles lost and roles gained.

L'ONCLE ANTOINE Map p206 Bar

☎ 418-694-9176; 29 Rue St-Pierre; 🕒 11am-1am Sun-Thu, until 3am Fri & Sat

Set clandestinely in the stone cave-cellar of one of the city's oldest surviving houses (dating from 1754), this great tavern pours out excellent Québec microbrews (try the Barberie Noir stout or the strong Belgian-style Fin du Monde), several drafts *(en fût)* and various European beers.

PUB ST-ALEXANDRE Map p206 Bar

☎ 418-694-0015; 1087 Rue St-Jean; 11:30am–around 1am

High ceilings and dark wood house a regular mix of tourists and loyal locals. The pub grub is fine, though generally unremarkable. It's the atmosphere and the near encyclopedic range of suds (250 sorts!) and over three dozen types of single malt that will keep you coming back. Occasional live music (Celtic to jazz) on Friday and Saturday.

SCANNER Map p210 Bar

☎ 418-523-1916; 291 Rue St-Vallier Est; 11am-late Mon-Fri, 3pm-late Sat & Sun

Ask any local between the ages of 18 and 35 to suggest a cool place for a drink and this is where they might send you. Come see if you can figure it out. Live rock bands play every Saturday from September to May. There's a terrace outside in summer, Foosball and pool inside year-round.

TURF Map p210 Bar

☎ 418-522-9955; 1179 Ave Cartier; 11am-around 3am Mon-Fri, 9am-3am Sat & Sun

Come in, grab a bowl and walk to the enormous peanut-filled barrel in the middle of the room. Swipe your fill from the barrel and settle in at one of the most popular pubs in the St-Jean-Baptiste neighborhood. It's hugely popular with everyone in the 18-to-25-year-old range, from students to suits.

CHEZ DAGOBERT Map p210 Club

☎ 418-522-2645; 600 Grande Allée Est; 11am-late Mon-Fri, 3pm-late Sat & Sun

Multifloors, multibars, multiscreens – the capital's classic disco behemoth has everything from live rock to naughty DJs. The music may change; the young, randy crowd stays the same.

CHEZ MAURICE Map p210 Club

☎ 418-647-2000; 575 Grande Allée Est; 8pm-3am Wed, 10pm-3am Thu-Sat

Set up in a gutted, châteaulike mansion and cheekily named after hard-ass former Québec premier Maurice Duplessis, this entertainment complex has three separate partying spaces. There's a nightclub, and a cigar lounge with 200 sorts to choose from.

FIXION Map p206 Club

☎ 418-694-9669; 811 Rue St-Jean 3pm-3am

Québec's love affair with all things Latino is bizarre but heartfelt. This Latin nightclub features live bands, DJs and dancing to reggae, salsa, *bachata* and merengue. *Olé*.

L'ALTERNO Map p206 Club

☎ 418-692-2674; 1018 Rue St-Jean; 4pm-late

Regulars kept telling former Le Drague employee Benoît they wished there was another gay club in town to shake up the scene a little, so finally he opened one, tucked away just inside the Porte St-Jean. It's low-key during the day with people playing billiards, but wilder at night once the DJs come out. It's easy to miss this place – look for the pride flag and go up the stairs.

L'AMOUR SORCIER Map p210 Club

☎ 418-523-3395; 789 Côte Ste-Geneviève; 2pm-3am Thu-Sun

The tamer atmosphere at this café-bar is mainly enjoyed by lesbians, but gay men are welcome too. The gay community may be small but the lesbian one is even smaller and this is the only horse in town.

LE DRAGUE Map p210 Club

☎ 418-649-7212; 815 Rue Ste-Augustine; 10am-late

The star player on the city's tiny gay scene, Le Drague comprises a front outdoor terrace, a two-level disco where drag shows are held, a slightly more laid-back tavern – and then there's Base 3. The men-only Base 3 is…well…let's just say it turns the capital's conservative reputation on its head and has even seen-it-all Montrealers saying 'I didn't know they had that in Québec City.'

LE BOUDOIR Map p210 Lounge

☎ 418-524-2777; 441 Rue du Parvis; noon-3am Mon-Fri, 4pm-3am Sat & Sun

Part restaurant, part nightclub, all scene, this posh but low-key lounge in the hip St-Roch district is pretty much the place for well-heeled locals to party. On weekends, two DJs let you choose between downtempo and dancing, while games include billiards, Wii and Pac-Man!

GAY & LESBIAN VENUES

The city's gay and lesbian scene is tiny, with pretty much everything centered around Le Drague (opposite). A few additional clubs such as L'Alterno (opposite) and L'Amour Sorcier (opposite) complete the picture. For info on parties and other gay events, *Fugues* is the free gay and lesbian entertainment guide with listings for the entire province of Québec.

AVIATIC CLUB Map p206 Restaurant-Bar

☎ 418-522-3555; 104-450 Ave de la Gare-du-Palais; ⌚ noon-3am

This elegant wine bar and restaurant is nestled in the historic Gare du Palais train station and attracts a professional crowd. A rotating list of 50 wines is served by the glass, and a vibrant terrace, featuring live DJs, is open during summer.

LE CERCLE Map p210 Restaurant-Bar

☎ 418-948-8648; 228 Rue St-Joseph Est; ⌚ 11:30am-3am Mon-Fri, 2pm-3am Sat & Sun

Restaurant, art gallery and show venue, this very cool joint draws a hip crowd for its underground DJs and bands, ranging from indie rock to electronica. Affordable tapas sweeten the deal.

THE ARTS

Visual arts is in fine form in Québec City. Perhaps the region's scenic beauty inspires its painters and sculptors, whose contemporary works can be seen (and purchased) in the city's plethora of small, treasure-filled art galleries. Québec is also home to many museums. While some focus on culture, science, history and technology as opposed to art, it's worth buying a Québec City Museum Card ($50) to visit them all. The card can be purchased at all participating museums and at Québec City tourist information bureaus. Over a period of three consecutive days, you have access to 18 museums and two one-day bus passes. For additional seasonal locations and information, please call ☎ 1-877-783-1608.

The city also boasts a symphony orchestra, L'Orchestre Symphonique de Québec (p228), and an opera company, Opéra de Québec (p228). French-language theater is an interesting scene here, with tons of small companies producing a variety of shows for families and children, and lots of experimental multidisciplinary works. While Canada's French-language TV and film industries are mostly based in Montréal, you can see the latest Hollywood and French-language foreign films at the multiplex cinema or repertory theater. Note that French-language films are not subtitled in English.

ART GALLERIES

GALERIE ART INUIT Map p206

☎ 418-694-1828; 35 Rue St-Louis

Devoted to Inuit carvings from artists all over arctic Canada, this place is gorgeously set up and elaborately lit with well-trained staff who knowledgeably answer questions. Carvings range from the small to the large and intricate. Be prepared for both steep prices and fantastic quality. It ships internationally.

L'ESPACE CONTEMPORAIN Map p204

☎ 418-648-2002; 313 Rue St-Jean

This dynamic little art gallery has an ever-rotating showcase of beautiful contemporary works, and hosts many vernissages for solo and thematic group shows.

LE LIEU Map p210

☎ 418-648-2002; 345 Rue du Pont

With art installations, sound art, video art and other multidiscliplinary exhibitions, this St-Roch artist center is more than a gallery. Visitors are welcome to browse and experience this local art community hub, which also aims to share Québec art with the world.

LES GALERIES D'ART BEAUCHAMP Map p206

☎ 418-694-2244; www.galeriebeauchamp.com; 69 Rue St-Pierre

With seven galleries and counting, this important contemporary-art company features the work of Québécois, Canadian and international artists. While the works themselves never disappoint, the gallery also hosts special events like virtual exhibitions and a nonprofit organization to bring art to underprivileged children in Québec City. Artists also come to paint on-site in the Artist in Gallery program. Visit the website for other gallery locations.

CINEMA

CINÉMA CARTIER Map p210

☎ 418-522-1011; 1019 Ave Cartier; ⌚ 4pm-late

This huge building really was a former movie theater until it was sliced up with a store on the bottom and retail space up top. The 2nd floor houses an independent video shop with a little movie theater in the back showing independent films. It's deliciously old-world, completely pitch-black except for the screen, and set up with big comfy chairs. Subtitles in French only.

IMAX LES GALERIES DE LA CAPITALE Map p204

☎ **418-624-4629; 5401 Blvd des Galeries;** ⏲ **9am-11pm**

Like all IMAX theaters, this shopping-mall wonder screens specially produced adventure, nature and historical films on oversized screens. Most films are in French, and families love it.

LE CLAP Map p204

☎ **box office 418-653-2470 ext 229; 2360 Chemin Ste-Foy;** ⏲ **screenings from noon;** 🚌 **7, 79, 87, 93;** Ⓟ

Located in the Ste-Foy-Sillery borough, Le Clap's mandate is to show off the best of what's going on in the film world. On any given afternoon, you'll find an eclectic mix of films that could include the latest British hit, an old indie French film and probably one American blockbuster. Non-French-language films are almost always dubbed in French instead of subtitled but call ahead to double-check.

CLASSICAL MUSIC

L'ORCHESTRE SYMPHONIQUE DE QUÉBEC Map p206

☎ **418-643-8486; www.osq.org; 401 Grande Allée Est**

For more than a century, this internationally recognized symphony orchestra has performed for more than 100,000 people a year! Concerts are usually broadcast on the radio by public broadcaster Radio-Canada. Led by prolific Israeli maestro Yoav Talmi, the orchestra is also active in the community.

OPÉRA DE QUÉBEC Map p206

☎ **418-529-0688; www.operadequebec.qc.ca; 1220 Ave Taché**

Under the artistic direction of Grégoire Legendre, this world-class company presents classics like *Aida, Pagliacci, Madame Butterfly, La Traviata, Carmen* and more. Shows take place in the majestic Le Grand Théâtre de Québec (opposite)

CONCERT HALLS & ARENAS

AGORA Map p206

☎ **418-692-4672; 120 Rue Dalhousie, Vieux-Port**

Fantastic open-air rock shows are held here all summer.

COLISÉE PEPSI Map p204

☎ **418-691-7211, 418-525-1212; Parc de l'ExpoCité, 250 Blvd Wilfrid Hamel**

You are now on hallowed ground…home to the late, great Québec Nordiques (p232). May they RIP. The Nordiques started playing here in 1972 when the venue was known as the Québec Colisée. They played their last game here in 1995, after which the team was moved to Denver, Colorado. Today this 15,000-person arena gets the likes of Iron Maiden and Metallica, and hosts games of the Remparts, from the Québec Major Junior Hockey League.

ESPACE 400 Map p206

100 quai St-André, Vieux-Port

Revamped in 2008 to the tune of $24 million to create a fresh public venue for the city's 400th-birthday festivities, this Old Port waterfront pavilion is an official Parks Canada discovery center. Concerts, shows and performances of all sorts are held here.

KIOSQUE EDWIN-BÉLANGER Map p210

☎ **418-523-1916; Battlefields Park 418**

Each summer 35 free concerts are staged in the middle of Battlefields Park. Music covers everything from pop, jazz and world music to blues.

PALAIS MONTCALM Map p210

☎ **418-641-6411 ext 2606; 995 Pl d'Youville**

This place has slowly been falling off the radar since the Grand Théâtre was built in the 1970s. It was undergoing heavy renovations at the time of research and there's talk the new, improved model is gearing up to carve out its place on the entertainment scene. Keep your eye out, it should be open again by the time you read this.

DANCE

LA ROTONDE Map p210

☎ **418-649-5013; www.larotonde.qc.ca; 336 Rue du Roi**

This contemporary dance center presents shows from touring companies from around

ROBERT LEPAGE

Robert Lepage is not only Québec City's most famous playwright and director, but is also one of the world's most renowned contemporary directors and writers, having received a Governor General's Performing Arts Award in 2009 and many other international prizes. He's especially known for incorporating technology in creative new ways.

Born in Québec City in 1957, Lepage trained at the city's Conservatoire d'Art Dramatique. He joined the local Théâtre Repère and went on to create one award-winning play after another. He has gone on to stage or direct everything from opera to two of Peter Gabriel's world tours, and was the first North American director ever to do a Shakespeare play at London's Royal National Theatre (1992's *A Midsummer Night's Dream*). He founded his multidisciplinary performing-arts Ex Machina company in Québec City in 1993 – among his plays, he produced the award-winning *La Face Cachée de la Lune* that was later made into a film. He helped create Cirque du Soleil's *KA*, and his most recent project as a theater director, the nine-hour (no joke) play *Lipsynch*, an Ex Machina production, debuted in 2009 at Toronto's Luminato festival. *Lipsynch* explores the relationship between the individual and the collective set against the backdrop of the human voice. He is also creating an architectural projection against oversized grain silos in the Québec City harbor, called *The Image Mill*, which explores his hometown's history.

the world as well as local dancers, including experimental and cutting-edge works. It also offers workshops and classes, and is pivotal in keeping dance alive in Québec.

THEATER

LE GRAND THÉÂTRE DE QUÉBEC Map p210

☎ 418-643-8131, 877-643-8131 (toll-free in Québec only); www.grandtheatre.qc.ca; 269 Blvd René-Lévesque Est

Le Grand Théâtre is the city's main performing-arts center with a steady diet of top-quality classical concerts, dance and theater. The Opéra de Québec (opposite) also performs here.

LE THÉÂTRE CAPITOLE Map p206

☎ 418-694-4444; www.lecapitole.com; 972 Rue St-Jean

A terrific, historic old theater that now stages everything from musicals to concerts. Check out the sumptuous attached hotel (p233). This is where Hitchcock held his *I Confess* premiere.

LE THÉÂTRE DU TRIDENT Map p206

☎ 418-643-5873; www.letrident.com; 269 Blvd René-Lévesque Est

Another terrific company that regularly stages exciting modern works, including plays by the likes of Wajdi Mouawad.

THÉÂTRE PÉRISCOPE Map p210

☎ 418-529-2183, 418-648-9989; www.theatreperiscope.qc.ca; 2 Rue Crémazie Est

A terrific place to see creative and cutting-edge contemporary productions.

LES GROS BECS Map p206

☎ 418-522-7880; www.lesgrosbecs.qc.ca, in French; 1143 Rue St-Jean; shows Sep-Apr

Devoted to shows for children and young people, this is a brilliantly creative company. Even its website is stunning, full of animation and cartoons on how to get young people interested in live theater (unfortunately, it's in French only). All shows listed in its schedules have labels with suggested age limits.

THÉÂTRE PETIT-CHAMPLAIN Map p206

☎ 418-692-4744; 68 Rue du Petit-Champlain

Theater productions take place here in the summer. The rest of the year this is a great place to see Québec's most popular singing stars like Lynda Lemay.

SPORTS & ACTIVITIES

Aside from strolling the cobblestone streets of the Old Town, there's a whole range of activities on offer in Québec City.

There are great places to go bicycling, picturesque parks ideal for an early-morning jog, rafting along the Jacques Cartier River and a host of winter sports when the weather turns cold.

OUTDOOR ACTIVITIES

Whether summer or deepest, darkest winter, Québec City locals take to the outdoors. Outside the Château Frontenac, the scenic Terrasse Dufferin (p203) along the riverfront stages the giant toboggan slide (11am-11pm) during the winter.

CALÈCHE

For a scenic, old-fashioned journey about town, climb aboard a *calèche* (horse-drawn carriage). While rides are not cheap – about $80 for 45 minutes – drivers can give you an earful of history as they take you to historic points around the city. Find them by the entrance to the Port St-Louis.

Battlefields Park (p209) is a great spot for outdoor activity. There's a nature trail, footpaths, and the park is great for in-line skating. In winter, people come here for Québec's well-known winter activities like snowshoeing, cross-country skiing or a romantic moonlight sleigh ride.

Cycling & In-Line Skating

There's a large network of bike paths both by the Vieux-Port inside the city and out in the surrounding countryside. There's a free bike-route map available at the tourism offices.

For in-line skating in the city, there's a route in Battlefields Park (p209). Île d'Orléans can also be a fantastic setting for a bike outing, but because there are no bike paths and heaps of traffic in summer, this is not a recommended bike trip to do with children.

CYCLO SERVICES Map p206

☎ 418-692-4052; www.cycloservices.net; 298 Rue St-Paul; hybrid bike per hr/day $14/35; 🚌 1

This outfit rents bikes and organizes excellent bike tours of the city and outskirts to places like Wendake (p234) or La Chute Montmorency (p234). The knowledgeable and fun guides frequently give tours in English. There are good cycling maps covering the vicinity.

MUSÉOVELO Map p210

☎ 418-523-9194; 463 Rue St-Jean; bike rental per day $35

Located in the St-Jean-Baptiste neighborhood, this place rents, makes and repairs all sorts of bikes. It also has lots of high-quality Canadian-made bike accessories for sale.

SOCIÉTÉ PISTE JACQUES-CARTIER/PORTNEUF off Map p204

☎ 418-337-2900, 800-321-4992; admission day/season $6/12

Formerly a railway linking St-Gabriel-de-Valcartier and Rivière-à-Pierre, this 68km trail winds its way through country scenery. In winter it turns into a snowmobile track.

Cruises

You'll find boat-tour operators moored near Place-Royale, going downriver to Montmorency Falls and on to Île d'Orléans. For city views, you can't beat the cheap ferry to Lévis (adult/child $3/2); boats leave daily, every 20 minutes to an hour, from 6am to at least midnight.

CROISIÉRES AML Map p206

☎ 866-856-6668; www.croisieresaml.com; Quai Chouinard, Vieux-Port

You can get a new perspective of the city aboard these small vessels. AML offers a range of dining and sightseeing cruises, including a popular 1½-hour trip along the St Lawrence (adult/child $32/17) and a two-hour brunch cruise (adult/child $45/24).

CROISIÉRES LE COUDRIER Map p206

☎ 418-692-0107, 888-600-5554; www.croisierescoudrier.qc.ca; 180 Rue Dalhousie, Bassin Louise, Quai 19, Vieux-Port

Its sightseeing cruises (1½ hours) run all the way to Île d'Orléans (adult/child $32/15). Other offerings include dinner cruises (adult $75) and special three-hour cruises during Les Grands Feux Loto-Québec (p196).

Walking & Jogging

At Battlefields Park (p209) you can run along trails or pound the pavement of a terrific jogging track based on a former horse-racing course. Die-hard runners training for marathons like to take to the slopes of the Old Town for drills and hill training.

RUNNING ROOM Map p210

☎ 418-522-2345; www.runningroom.com; 1049 Ave Cartier; 🕒 free group runs 6pm Wed, 8:30am Sun

This Alberta-based chain sells running shoes and accessories but also has free group runs led by an employee. Just meet at the store. It also has fantastic route maps that you can download from its website.

Rafting

VILLAGE VACANCES VALCARTIER off Map p204

☎ 418-844-2200, 800-321-4992; www.raftingvalcartier.com; 1860 Blvd Valcartier; 3hr trip $50; 🕒 8am & 1pm May 6–Aug 1

For an adrenaline rush, head off on a white-water rafting trip down the Jacques Cartier River. This outfit also has guided trips for families, suitable for both beginners and experienced rafters. For the biggest thrills, come from May to June when the water is at its highest. You must reserve at least three days in advance. Canoe rental is also available (per three hours $25). It's a 20-minute drive from Québec City along Hwy 73 north (exit St-Émile/La Faune).

Ice-Skating

The following rinks appear in winter only, in the Old Upper Town.

PATINOIRE DE LA TERRASSE Map p206

☎ 418-829-9898; Terrasse Dufferin; end Oct–mid-Mar; 3, 11

A kind of ice rink gets set up here every winter and is ideal for families and children to putter around on. Skate rentals on-site.

PLACE D'YOUVILLE Map p206

☎ 418-641-6256; Porte St-Jean; end Oct–mid-Mar; 3, 7, 11, 28

One of the most popular places for ice-skating once winter rolls around. You can also rent skates here.

Skiing & Snowboarding

MONT-STE-ANNE off Map p204

☎ 418-827-4561, 888-827-4579; www.mont-sainte-anne.com; 2000 Blvd du Beau-Pré; mid-Nov–Apr

A hugely popular ski resort with 66 ski trails, 17 of which are set aside for night skiing (from 4pm to 9pm). You'll find all sorts of other winter activities here, including snowshoeing, skating and even dogsledding. You can rent skis and snowboards too.

PARC NATIONAL DE LA JACQUES-CARTIER off Map p204

☎ 418-528-8787, 800-665-6527; roughly Dec–late March

There's a range of snowshoeing and cross-country skiing trails and circuits here, from easy to difficult. Those who've done the trails say the winter scenery is picture-perfect. The park is about 40km from Québec City along Rte 175.

STATION TOURISTIQUE STONEHAM Map p204

☎ 418-848-2411, 800-463-6888; www.ski-stoneham.com; 1420 Chemin du Hibou, Stoneham-et-Tewkesbury

Smaller than Mont-Ste-Anne and only about 20 minutes from Québec City, there are 32 slopes here for downhill skiing and snowboarding. Night skiing runs are usually open from late November until around mid-March. Take Hwy 73 north until the Stoneham exit.

Swimming

PAVILLON DE L'ÉDUCATION PHYSIQUE ET DES SPORTS Map p204

☎ 418-656-7377; www.peps.ulaval.ca, in French; Pavillon de l'Éducation Physique et des Sports, Laval University; admission $5-10; 7, 11, 13, 18, 87

There's a huge Olympic-sized pool here – probably the best in town – that's also open to the public at certain times. Call for the latest times.

SPECTATOR SPORTS

The end of the Nordiques meant the end of beloved professional hockey in the city, though the Québec Remparts of the Québec Major Junior Hockey League are quite popular. You can see them at the Colisée Pepsi (p228). The latest news in sport is the arrival of the Kebs, a professional basketball team in the Premier Basketball League.

QUÉBEC KEBS

☎ 418-780-4850; www.kebsdequebec.com; admission $15-35

The city's brand-new basketball team, the Québec Kebs play at the 5000-seat stadium of Pavillon de la Jeunesse (Map p204; ☎ 418-643-8131; 250 Blvd Wilfrid-Hamel). In the Atlantic division of the Premier Basketball League, the Kebs play from December through March. Incidentally, the logo of the Kebs (a jumping frog that goes by the name 'Dunky') is a still a sore spot for some locals. 'Frog' has long been a derogatory name the English have used for French-speaking people and some consider it racist. When the man behind bringing the franchise to Québec City, businessman Réal Bourassa, said the new team name would be either the Québec Jumping Frogs or Kebekwa (how Québécois is pronounced in English), the uproar

THE LOSS OF (HOCKEY) IDENTITY

Until 1995 the Québec Nordiques hockey team was the sports sensation in town and the city alternately laughed with the team's every success and cried at its every defeat. When rumors began to seriously circulate that the team would be moved, protests were launched and gallons of ink spilled but it left town anyway. Pretty much any Quebecer you talk to will admit the loss of the city's National Hockey League team was the saddest day in sport. But there was also province-wide outrage, as the move put an end to one of the most infamous sports rivalries – between the Nordiques and the Montréal Canadiens. It was especially wrenching as pretty much every hockey fan felt the Nordiques' time had come and that they were on their way to Stanley Cup glory. And win they did. Exactly a year after they moved, the ex-Nordiques, now Colorado Avalanche, took home the 1996 trophy.

These days fans content themselves with supporting the Québec Remparts (www.remparts.qc.ca/eng), who play in the Québec Major Junior Hockey League. They play regularly at the Colisée Pepsi (p228). You can keep track of the team on its website.

There are ongoing rumblings that Québec City could get a Canadian Football Team (CFL) franchise, but so far there doesn't seem to be much interest in spending the kind of money needed to build a stadium for it (and CFL rules stipulate that only a 25,000-seat stadium would be sufficient).

was heard across the country and all the way to France. Bourassa told people they should just relax. 'We are in 2006 and we have to be able to laugh at ourselves,' he told the Canadian Press newswire service. Locals, however, didn't find it so funny and the Jumping Frogs was jettisoned in favor of the Kebs, although the frog was kept as the team's mascot.

SLEEPING

From old-fashioned B&Bs to stylish boutique hotels, Québec City has some fantastic overnight options. The best choices are the numerous small European-style hotels and Victorian B&Bs scattered around the Old Town. They offer character-filled rooms and common areas and a great location in the center of the historic district.

As you'd expect in such a popular city, the top choices are often full, so make reservations well in advance, especially for weekends. It's unwise to show up in the city on a Saturday morning in summer or during holidays and expect to find a room for the same night.

Prices rise in the high-season summer months and during Winter Carnival. At other times of year, you can usually save 30% or so off the high-season prices.

Budget accommodation also fills up quickly during high season – with student groups block-booking entire hostels. If you're in a bind, student dorms are available to travelers during the summer at **Université Laval** (Map p204; ☎ 418-656-5632; www.sres.ulaval.ca; Local 1618, Pavillon Alphonse-Marie Parent). Located in the borough of Ste-Foy-Sillery, about a 15- to 20-minute bus ride away from the Old Town, rooms are clean but very plain and have shared bathrooms.

Outlying motels are concentrated primarily in three areas. Beauport is just a 12-minute drive northeast of the city. To get there, go north along Ave Dufferin, then take Hwy 440 until the exit for Blvd Ste-Anne/Rte 138. The motels are located on a stretch between the 500 to 1200 blocks. A bike trail from the city passes nearby.

A second area is located west of the center on Blvd Wilfrid-Hamel (Rte 138) – head west on Hwy 440 to the Henri IV exit. The third area is Blvd Laurier in the borough of Ste-Foy-Sillery. To get there, follow Grande Allée west until it turns into Blvd Laurier.

City buses run to these areas, so whether you have a car or not, they may be the answer if you find everything booked up downtown. The further out you go, the more the prices drop. Prices are generally higher than usual for motels, averaging about $90 to $130 in high season.

A few other caveats: many guesthouses in the Old Town simply do not have elevators; be sure to inquire on the room location if you're packing a lot of luggage and not keen on walking up a few flights of stairs.

PRICE GUIDE

Accommodations in this section are listed from costliest to least expensive. The price icon represents the cost of a double room with private bathroom.

$$$	over $180 a night
$$	$80-180 a night
$	under $80 a night

Lastly, a minimum stay (usually of two nights) may be required at some places in the height of summer. This is particularly true if arriving on the weekend.

OLD UPPER TOWN

This area has the widest choice of accommodation in town, from hostels and familial B&Bs to cheap little hotels and intimate, luxurious inns.

FAIRMONT LE CHÂTEAU FRONTENAC

Map p206 Hotel $$$

☎ 418-692-3861, 866-540-4460; www.fairmont.com/frontenac; 1 Rue des Carrières; r from $329; Ⓟ

More than just a hotel, the iconic Château Frontenac is one of the enduring symbols of Québec City. It's also one of the busiest places in town, with over 600 rooms and busloads of guests and nonguests alike filling its halls. Rooms are elegantly decorated and come in all shapes and sizes with a number of views to choose from. Service is professional and generally staff are adept at handling the big crowds. Even if you aren't staying, the bar is a fine place for a drink while taking in the spectacular view of the St Lawrence River. While some guests enjoy connecting with a little slice of Québec City history, others say the grand dame doesn't quite live up to its storied reputation.

LE CLOS SAINT LOUIS

Map p206 Hotel $$$

☎ 418-694-1311, 800-461-1311; www.clossaintlouis.com; 69 Rue St-Louis; r from $210; Ⓟ

It's hard to tell which trait is more evident here: the obvious care that the owners devote or simply the natural 1844 Victorian charm. The 18 spacious, lavishly decorated rooms each have a Jacuzzi tub in a beautifully tiled bathroom. The suites are like Victorian apartments, apart from the TV in the mini drawing room.

L'HÔTEL DU CAPITOLE Map p206 Hotel $$$

☎ 418-694-4040, 800-363-4040; www.lecapitole.com; 972 Rue St-Jean; r from $209

Right on top of the stately Théâtre Capitole (p229), this hotel is one of the city's gems. Rooms vary, but may feature floor-to-ceiling windows, exposed brick walls and velvety red furniture with just a touch of old-fashioned theatricality. Some rooms are quite small, while others have in-room bathtubs and balconies overlooking the old city walls. Staff generally earn high marks for service. There's also a good Italian restaurant with terrace seating that's a major draw in the summer.

> **PARKING**
>
> If you have a car, some guesthouses provide discount vouchers for nearby parking garages. Another option is to park the car at one of the free lots outside the city center and take the bus in. One of the closest free lots is located at the Aquarium du Québec (p213), reachable by bus 400 (*navette du litoral*, $3) which travels along the riverfront road down Blvd Champlain. You can catch it along Rue Dalhousie by the Old Port.

AUBERGE PLACE D'ARMES

Map p206 Inn $$

☎ 418-694-9485, 866-333-9485; www.aubergeplacedarmes.com; 24 Rue Ste-Anne; r from $160

Overhauled from top to bottom after a change in ownership, this place now has some of the most dapper-looking rooms in town. Everything from the halls to the guest rooms is done up in rich crimsons, navy blues and golds and many of the rooms have exposed red-brick walls. The inn is located across from the Church of the Holy Trinity and is only a short stroll from the funicular to Lower Town.

LA MARQUISE BASSANO

Map p206 B&B $$

☎ 418-692-0316, 877-692-0316; www.marquisedebassano.com; 15 Rue des Grisons; r with shared/private bathroom $145/175; Ⓟ

The young, gregarious owners have set up a beautifully furnished home, outfitting its five rooms with thoughtful touches, whether it's a canopy bed or a claw-foot bathtub – the library room has wood floors, a writing desk and a wall of books. Despite being just minutes from the important sites, this house is located on a low-traffic street surrounded by period homes. Only two rooms have private bathrooms; the other three share a bath. The breakfasts are cold but worth getting out of bed for, with fresh croissants and pastries, meats, hard-boiled eggs, cheese and fruit.

THE WONDROUS BACKYARD OF QUÉBEC CITY

Québec City is surrounded by stunning countryside and there are fantastic attractions for every interest. If you're traveling by car, all the sights below, except for Wendake, can be reached by taking Rte 138 northwest of Québec City.

Île d'Orléans

This place is the stunner of the region. It can be visited on a day trip but is easily worth two days or more if you have the time. Cut off from the rest of Québec for centuries (the Taschereau Bridge was only built in 1935), the pastoral lifestyle of the islanders remains very much preserved. One of the first colonies of New France was established here, and thousands of North Americans can trace their roots back to one of the 300 original families that settled here. The island is divided into six parishes; there is plenty to see, from gorgeous scenery to old churches to 300-year-old stone homes. Local ciders and *produits du terroir* (Québec produce) also abound.

Don't miss Maison Drouin (☎ 418-829-0330; www.fondationfrancoislamy.org; 4700 Chemin Royal; admission $4; 10am-6pm daily mid-Jun–mid-Aug, 1-5pm Sat & Sun mid-Aug–late Sep). This old house was built in 1730 and is one of the most fascinating stops on the island as it was never modernized (ie no electricity or running water) even though it was inhabited until 1984. Guides in period dress give tours of the house in summer. Éspace Félix-Leclerc (☎ 418-828-1682; www.felixleclerc.com; 682 Chemin Royal, St-Pierre; adult/child $7/4; 9am-6pm spring & summer, 9am-5pm fall & winter) highlights the works of one of Québec's most popular singers, whose ancestors were among the original island settlers. At Parc Maritime de St-Laurent (☎ 418-828-9672; www.parcmaritime.ca; 120 Chemin de la Chalouperie, St-Laurent; adult/child $3/free; 10am-5pm late Jun–early Sep) you can learn about the parish's ship-building history.

There's a tourist office (☎ 418-828-9411, 866-941-9411; www.iledorleans.com; 490 Côte du Pont, St-Pierre; 8:30am-7:30pm late Jun–early Sep, 10am-5pm early Sep–late Jun) on the island just after you cross the bridge. It's a great place for info and finding accommodations. You can also buy a CD for $22 (or rent it for $17 plus a $5 deposit) that guides you on a two-hour tour of the island. Île d'Orléans is about a 15-minute drive from Québec City.

Parc de la Chute Montmorency

This waterfall is right by the Taschereau Bridge on the way to Île d'Orléans and is worth a stop if you're in the area. It's 83m high, topping Niagara Falls by about 30m, though it's not nearly as wide. What's cool is walking over the falls on the suspension bridge to see (and hear) them thunder down below. The park (☎ 418-663-3330; www.sepaq.com/chutemontmorency; 2490 Ave Royale, Beauport; year-round) is free but parking ($10 per car) and the cable car (adult/child $11/6) can add up over the average one-hour visit. You can opt to walk the circuit instead of taking the cable car up. This is an interesting stop even in winter. When the spray from the falls freezes, it creates a 30m-high toboggan hill. The falls are about 12km from Québec City.

MANOIR SAINTE-GENEVIÈVE

Map p206 Hotel $$

☎ 418-694-1666, 877-694-1666; www.quebecweb.com/msg; 13 Ave Ste-Geneviève; r $115-130; P

Gracious staff welcome guests to this Victorian manor dating from 1800. Rooms vary in size and style from bright and rather classically furnished to modern and small with rather unsightly color schemes. Most of the nine rooms are carpeted. This is ideal for those looking for slow-paced, old-fashioned accommodations.

MANOIR SUR LE CAP Map p206 Hotel $$

☎ 418-694-1987, 866-694-1987; www.manoir-sur-le-cap.com; 9 Ave Ste-Geneviève; r $105-175; P

Manoir sur le Cap is a lovely guesthouse with 14 rooms, some overlooking the Jardin des Gouverneurs, the Château or the river. It's in a wonderful, quiet location, well away from the tourist throngs on Rue St-Louis. Some rooms are on the small side with slightly dated furnishings. The best have tiny balconies and attractive stone or brick walls.

HÔTEL ACADIA Map p206 Hotel $$

☎ 418-694-0280, 800-463-0280; www.hotelsnouvellefrance.com; 43 Rue Ste-Ursule; r $90-200; P

This hotel is spread over three adjacent historic houses along a quiet, convenient side street. Rooms run the gambit from small with shared bathrooms to quite luxurious

Wendake

This Huron aboriginal reserve is only about 20 minutes west of Québec City (you'll know you're there when you start seeing the bilingual Huron/French traffic signs). The major attraction here is the Onhoúa Chetek8e (☎ 418-842-4308; www.huron-wendat.qc.ca; 575 Rue Stanislas-Kosca; adult/child $10/6; 9am-5pm, last tour 4pm; 72), a reconstructed Huron village (the 'letter' 8 in Huron is pronounced 'oua' like the 'wh' in 'what'). The guides are excellent (one is even a former land-claims negotiator) and take you round the village explaining Huron history, culture and daily life. It may be artificial, but visitors love this place and children go wild for the tipi, canoes and bow-and-arrow range. Several guides speak English but call ahead to make sure they aren't already assigned to a tour group or on their day off when you arrive. The onsite restaurant (noon-3pm) serves excellent aboriginal food and there's an enormous boutique selling mostly Wendake-made crafts. With activities and shows (at additional costs), you can easily end up spending the whole day here.

If you're coming by car, take Hwy 73 (exit 154). It's very well signed after that.

Ste-Anne-de-Beaupré

This village is known for the Goliath-sized Basilique Ste-Anne-de-Beaupré (☎ 418-827-3781; 10018 Ave Royale; admission free; church early–late, information center (southwest side of basilica) 8:30am-4:30pm) and its role as a shrine. Churches were built at this location since the mid-1600s but were frequently destroyed by fire. The awe-inspiring basilica of today was constructed after a devastating blaze in 1922 and has been open since 1934.

Ste-Anne's reputation as a shrine started to grow even before the first church had been completed. A crippled Louis Guimont had just started laying stones when he was suddenly cured by 'Good Ste-Anne,' Mary's mother and the patron saint of Québec. Legions of believers swear they have been cured after their pilgrimages here and over 1.5 million people do the trip each year.

On July 26, Ste-Anne's feast day, the place goes berserk. The church fills to capacity, the nearby camping grounds are swamped with pilgrims, hotels are booked full and the whole village starts feeling like a kind of religious Woodstock. You just have to catch a glimpse of the enormous Blessings Office, the first-aid station and what looks like 50-toilet bathrooms to understand the scale that things here can reach.

There's also a museum (☎ 418-827-3781 ext 754; adult/youth $4/2; early Jun–early Sep), Magasin Ste-Anne (a store) with shelves of Ste-Anne paraphernalia, religious medals and other souvenirs, and the Cyclorama of Jerusalem (☎ 418-827-3101), a coliseum-sized, 360-degree 'panoramic display' produced in Germany in 1882 of Jesus' Crucifixion. It's 14m high and 110m in circumference.

Saturday-night masses are a good time to visit. In the middle of the mass, the entire congregation lights lamps and is led out of the church carrying the flames along with their church banners, identifying the congregations they are representing on their pilgrimage. In particular, you'll see many are from New York, Boston and Ontario.

It's about 50km from Québec City.

with fireplaces or Jacuzzis, which means there's a refreshing cross-section of travelers crowding the lobby clamoring for the free newspapers each morning. Breakfast is served in a quaint little alcove and there's a peaceful garden overlooking the Ursuline convent.

AU CHÂTEAU FLEUR-DE-LYS

Map p206 Hotel $$

☎ 418-694-1884, 877-691-1884; www.quebecweb.com/cfl; 15 Ave Ste-Geneviève; r $90-150; P

Set on a quiet street, this towering Victorian home is just seconds from the Citadelle and the Terrasse Dufferin, yet it feels like it's far off the beaten track. Old-world details spruce up the rooms without going overboard. With laid-back, personable staff, this is an ideal place if you're looking for relaxed and uncomplicated accommodations. Just be warned, you may have to access your private bathroom through a door out in the hall, rather than from inside your room. There are 18 rooms but only 12 parking spaces so, if arriving by car, double-check availability when reserving.

CHEZ HUBERT Map p206 Hotel $$

☎ 418-692-0958; www.chezhubert.com; 66 Rue Ste-Ursule; s/d with shared bathroom from $85/100; P

This dependable choice is in a Victorian townhouse with chandeliers, fireplace mantels, stained-glass windows, a lovely rcase and oriental rugs. The ul rooms, one with a view of the me with a large buffet breakfast rking. Each are painted in warm le Hubert's English has a few rough edges, but he hasn't any.

AUBERGE ST-LOUIS Map p206 Hotel $$

☎ 418-692-2424, 888-692-4105; www.auberge stlouis.ca; 48 Rue St-Louis; r with shared/private bathroom from $80/140

Only a minute or so from the Citadelle and the Old Town's main sites, rooms in this little hotel are clean, wonderfully kept, and decorated in shades of light grey. This wouldn't necessarily be your first choice (some of the rooms are tiny or don't get much natural light) but it's a great place to keep in mind if the nearby B&Bs are full but you still want to stay in the Upper Town.

AU PETIT HÔTEL Map p206 Hotel $$

☎ 418-694-0965; aupetithotel@sympatico.ca; 3 Ruelle des Ursulines; r $75-125;

Sitting on a tranquil lane and decorated with flowers, this former rooming house has a range of clean, simply furnished rooms, each with a private bathroom. Some of the options are small and rather drab, while others are airy and borderline charming. Only a few rooms have air conditioning. Overall, it's good value for the Old Town.

LA MAISON SAINTE URSULE Map p206 Guesthouse $$

☎ 418-694-9794; 40 Rue Ste-Ursule; r with shared/private bathroom from $65/120

Nestled among other midrange options on central, tranquil Rue Ste-Ursule, this petite hotel has eight rooms in an 18th-century townhouse and seven in a modern extension opening onto a garden. Rooms are carpeted and fairly well maintained, though some are on the small side. The cheapest rooms share a bathroom, but have in-room sinks.

LA MAISON DEMERS Map p206 Guesthouse $$

☎ 418-692-2487, 800-692-2487; 68 Rue Ste-Ursule; r with shared/private bathroom from $75/100; P

Run by a friendly elderly couple, La Maison Demers has a handful of old-fashioned rooms that are great value for the area. Most are carpeted with homey touches – as if little junior has just gone away to college and you're letting his room. Several rooms have tiny balconies, just large enough to step out and watch the sunset. Room 1, on the ground floor, can be noisy; the other rooms (on the 2nd and 3rd floors) are quieter. Free parking included.

MANOIR LA SALLE Map p206 Guesthouse $

☎ 418-692-9953; 18 Rue Ste-Ursule; r with shared bathroom from $65

Four fat, fluffy cats patrol the halls of this simple, familial accommodation that's clean but unabashedly worn. You may prefer the upstairs rooms to avoid having to go through the lobby to the bathroom, as guests on the ground floor do. Some kitchenettes are available.

AUBERGE INTERNATIONALE DE QUÉBEC Map p206 Hostel $

☎ 418-694-0775, 866-694-0950; www.auberge internationaledequebec.com; 19 Rue Ste-Ursule; dm $28-34, r with/without bathroom $87/74;

Floors are creaky and the frustrating labyrinth of corridors goes on forever, but this lively place heaves with energy and bustle year-round. It attracts a wide mix of independent travelers, big families with small children and groups. Staff are friendly but usually harried just trying to keep up with all the comings and goings. It's usually full in summer, despite having almost 300 beds, so reserve ahead if you can.

AUBERGE DE LA PAIX Map p206 Hostel $

☎ 418-694-0735; www.aubergedelapaix.com; 31 Rue Couillard; dm incl breakfast $25;

On a quiet street, this funky hostel has relaxed, welcoming staff and 60 brightly colored rooms with comfortable wooden furniture. With the cheerfully painted halls and guests lounging in the garden, it feels less institutional than the official HI hostel nearby. There are also two highly coveted private rooms ($25 per person) that must be booked well in advance. A continental breakfast is served each morning and bedding is provided for $4 per stay.

OLD LOWER TOWN

A cluster of the most tantalizing boutique hotels in the city is found in this area, along with a handful of hip, small inns.

AUBERGE ST-ANTOINE Map p206 Hotel $$$

☎ 418-692-2211, 888-692-2211; www.saint-ant oine.com; 6 Rue St-Antoine; r from $300; P

The Auberge St-Antoine is simply one of the finest hotels in Canada. With phenomenal service, plush rooms and endless amenities, this hotel delivers near-perfect execution. The spacious rooms are elegantly set with high-end mattresses, goose-down duvets, luxury linens, atmospheric lighting, Bose sound systems and large windows (that you can actually open). Walking through the halls is like strolling through a gallery – when the neighboring parking lot was dug up to expand the hotel, thousands of historical relics from the French colony were discovered and put on display. Panache (p221) restaurant, the darling *du jour* of Canada's fine-dining scene, is located just off the hotel's lobby.

HÔTEL 71 Map p206 Hotel $$$

☎ 418-692-1171, 888-692-1171; www.hotel71.ca; 71 Rue St-Pierre; r from $270

Set in an imposing greystone building that dates to the 1800s, Hôtel 71 provides the boutique experience par excellence. Like a page torn from a design magazine, the lobby, with its flickering candles, black-clad young staff and artful details provides a suitable entry to the hotel. Rooms are sleek, with a Zenlike design, while not stinting on comfort (fantastic mattresses, plush down comforters, oversized TVs, dramatically lit bathrooms). The lobby café serves excellent (and beautifully presented) coffee along with a continental breakfast.

HÔTEL DOMINION 1912

Map p206 Boutique Hotel $$$

☎ 418-692-2224, 888-833-5253; www.hoteldominion.com; 126 Rue St-Pierre; r from $215;

The Dominion is yet another outstanding luxury option with great service in the Lower Town. Rooms are tastefully designed with high-end fittings (sumptuous mattresses, Egyptian cotton bedding, good lighting, big windows) and a few quirks – bathroom sinks that glow in the dark, eclectic continental breakfasts – complement the otherwise understated feel to the place. Located near the Old Port area, rooms here are quiet and cozy, and guests (understandably) are quite loyal.

HÔTEL DES COUTELLIER

Map p206 Hotel $$$

☎ 418-692-9696, 888-523-9696; www.hoteldescoutellier.com; 253 Rue St-Paul; r from $185

This handsomely set hotel offers style and comfort, and surprisingly friendly service as well. Refreshingly unpretentious rooms are bright and spacious with modern furnishings (flat-screen TVs, iPod docks and high-end coffeemaker). A tasty continental breakfast is packed up in a wicker basket for you every morning and hung outside your door. Reasonably priced minibar items are a rather nice – admittedly small – feature.

HÔTEL BELLEY Map p206 Hotel $$

☎ 418-692-1694; www.oricom.ca/belley; 249 Rue St-Paul; r $100-160

A great place for the young and hip who still like their creature comforts, this personable eight-room hotel offers spacious, uniquely designed rooms with features including brick walls or wood paneling; some have original details like beamed ceilings. You might also find French doors to the bathroom, a claw-foot tub – or, on the downside, a very tiny bathroom. Many rooms include microwave ovens or small refrigerators. The wonderful Belley Tavern is attached to the hotel.

OUTSIDE THE WALLS

St-Jean-Baptiste

Accommodation here means you'll be rubbing elbows with locals more than you would in the Old Town. Delightful B&Bs are scattered throughout the neighborhood. The B&B ban on Rue St-Jean has been lifted by the city, so it may be worth a stroll when you arrive to see if anything new and interesting has opened.

HOTEL RELAIS CHARLES-ALEXANDRE

Map p210 Hotel $$

☎ 418-523-1220; 91 Grande Allée Est; r from $130; P

This is a small, cozy hotel with a great location near both the Musée National des Beaux-Arts du Québec and Battlefields Park. Rooms here are all different and are best described as low-key and comfortable with modern furnishings. Standard rooms are bright and comfortably set, but with a view onto the parking lot. Some of the superior rooms have big bay windows and fireplaces (plus plasma-screen TVs). Staff are friendly and do a fine job keeping the place in tip-top shape.

QUÉBEC'S COOLEST HOTEL

Visiting North America's first ice hotel, which opened in 2001, is like stepping into a wintry fairy tale. Nearly everything here is made of ice: the reception desk, the pen with which you sign in, the sink in your room, your bed, even the cocktail glasses – all ice.

Some 500 tons of ice and 15,000 tons of snow go into the five-week construction of this perishable hotel. One of the most striking aspects is its size – over 3000 sq meters of frosty splendor. First impressions in the entrance hall are strangely overwhelming – tall, sculpted columns of ice support a ceiling where a crystal chandelier hangs, and carved sculptures, tables and chairs line the endless corridors.

Though the structure of the ice hotel remains the same from year to year, everything else changes, from the location of the chapel (at your disposal for cool winter weddings!) to the placement of the lounge.

The hotel is about a half-hour drive from central Québec City at Lac St-Joseph's Station Écotouristique Duchesnay, giving you easy access to icy activities like skiing, snowshoeing, dogsledding and ice fishing.

The ice hotel usually opens from January to April and offers packages starting at $320 per double, including a welcome cocktail and breakfast buffet. Overnight guests say the beds are not as frigid as they sounds, courtesy of thick sleeping bags laid on lush deer pelts.

If you're not staying, simply take the tour ($16). It lasts about 30 minutes. For information, contact the Ice Hotel (off Map p204; ☎ 418-875-4522, 877-505-0423; www.icehotel-canada.com; 143 Rte Duchesnay, Ste-Catherine-de-la-Jacques-Cartier). It's off exit 295 of Hwy 40, west of Québec City via Rte 367.

AUBERGE DU QUARTIER

Map p210 Hotel $$

☎ 418-525-9726, 800-782-9441; www.aubergeduquartier.com; 170 Grande Allée Est; r from $120; P ⊠ ☐

Around the corner from restaurant-lined Ave Cartier, this friendly hotel offers sleek modern rooms and professional service. Rooms range in size from small and modestly furnished to spacious numbers with nice extras – a fireplace! They're done up in masculine tones with rich burgundies, exposed steel beams or original brickwork adding to the atmosphere. There's an outdoor terrace (but no view). The Auberge is a gay-friendly guesthouse.

CHÂTEAU DES TOURELLES

Map p210 B&B $$

☎ 418-647-9136, 866-346-9136; www.chateaudestourelles.qc.ca; 212 Rue St-Jean; r from $120

On a great little strip of Rue St-Jean, lined with interesting stores and eateries, you'll notice this B&B's soaring turret long before you get to the door. The lovely owners have done a stunning job with this old house; it's cozy and rustic without straying into kitsch. Named after members of the owners' families, rooms are beautifully decorated and may have exposed red-brick walls or antique sinks. Delightfully lopsided stairs lead up onto a rooftop terrace with a smashing 360-degree view of, well, just about everything of note in town. Hot breakfast is included in the room rate.

LE CHÂTEAU DU FAUBOURG

Map p210 B&B $$

☎ 418-524-2902; www.lechateaudufaubourg.com; 429 Rue St-Jean; r from $120

Built by the massively rich Imperial Tobacco family in the 1800s, this is one of the city's most atmospheric B&Bs. The interior is pure British-Lord-of-the-Manor meets French-Marquis style, replete with old oil paintings, antique furnishings and shimmering chandeliers. While some rooms are packed with old-world details, others seem a little cramped (notably the Boudoir du Josephine in the attic). The hosts are kind and good-humored, and their dozen-or-so pet birds keep the halls filled with happy tweets (an annoyance for some guests).

AUBERGE CAFÉ KRIEGHOFF

Map p210 Guesthouse $$

☎ 418-522-3711; www.cafekrieghoff.qc.ca; 1091 Ave Cartier; s/d from $110/130; ☐

A gem hidden away in the old house above the Café Krieghoff (p223). Spacious rooms are simply decorated but blessed with offbeat flourishes like antique hat boxes or oversized wooden side tables. All rooms have private, modern bathrooms and flat-screen TVs but no phones. A common area on the main floor has a phone, umbrellas to borrow and a computer with internet, all free for guests. Another bonus is the breakfast voucher for Café Krieghoff each morning. Check-in is at the bar, open 7am to 11pm.

COUETTE & CAFÉ TOAST & FRENCH

Map p210 B&B $$

☎ 418-523-9365, 877-523-9365; 1020 Ave Cartier; s/d with shared bathroom $94/104, s/d with private bathroom $100/115

Located a few blocks from Grande Allée Ouest on a lively street of bars and bistros, this B&B turns Anglophones into crack French speakers. Residential courses are available, while short-term guests will also find a sympathetic environment in which to practice their lingo over morning toast and coffee. Five smart rooms with private and shared bathrooms are available, but test the beds because they have received complaints.

DAY TRIPS & EXCURSIONS

DAY TRIPS & EXCURSIONS

Packed with history and culture, both high and low, Montréal and Québec City can be difficult places to leave. But to really get a taste of this wondrous province, sometimes you need to hit the road. Just outside these two cities, you'll find some captivating getaways – from sweeping mountain panoramas to historic little villages and tiny lakeside settlements surrounded by forest. This is the great Canadian outdoors, and it lies right outside your doorstep.

Many of these destinations can be visited as pleasant one-day jaunts, though cozy B&Bs and charming country-style restaurants may entice you to linger overnight.

Leaving Montréal behind, traveling northeast toward Québec City, small-town life in Québec seems to unfold before you: stone houses with light-blue trim and tin roofs, the silver spires of churches lit by sunlight, old-fashioned main streets with big picture windows full of antiques. The most picturesque town here is Trois-Rivières (below) with a lovely riverside setting, charming dining and lodging options and an impressive prison (the country's oldest), where you can take a fascinating guided tour.

A short drive northwest of Montréal leads to the Laurentians (p244), a favorite weekend getaway for city folk yearning for a bit of fresh air. Sprinkled with small towns and resorts, this alpine area is a year-round destination offering hiking, cycling, golf and tennis in the summer, plus downhill and cross-country skiing in the winter. While some areas are quite commercialized (you've heard of Disneyland, no?), there are places to go where you can beat the crowds, and take in the splendid mountain scenery for which the Laurentians are famed. For camping, hiking, canoeing and other outdoor activities, head straight for the verdant Parc National du Mont-Tremblant (p245).

To the east of Montréal lie the rolling hills and pristine lakes of the Eastern Townships (p247). Sprinkled with villages and idyllic scenery, this region makes a refreshing getaway. A few highlights here are the pretty lake Memphrémagog (p248), the New England–style town of North Hatley (p248) and the sweet little town of Knowlton (p248). You can easily while away a few days exploring the countryside – and there are some great little inns in which to base yourself.

TROIS-RIVIÈRES

The pleasant town of Trois-Rivières boasts a history dating back to 1634, making it North America's second-oldest city north of Mexico. Unfortunately, little of its 350-year-old past remains: the historic center burned down in 1908. Still, its scenic location along the north shore of the St Lawrence River and its picturesque tree-lined streets have obvious appeal. There are also some worthwhile sites, including an intriguing museum and the old stone prison attached; are both essential stops if passing through the area.

Though the city's glory days as a major industrial player are past, it is still a pulp and paper center and the largest town between Québec's two main cities. The name Trois-Rivières is a bit of a misnomer. Don't bother looking – there aren't three rivers. The name refers to the way the St Maurice River divides as it approaches the St Lawrence.

After taking in a bit of the main street, stop in the sophisticated tourist office and pick up a map with a walking tour of key downtown sites; you can also join one of the office's many tours.

Events like the Festival International de la Poésie (☎ 819-379-9813; ww.fiptr.com), held over two weeks in October, or even one-day events like 'Italian Day' are great times to visit the town. There is a wonderful community atmosphere here and the locals turn out in droves to drink it all up.

Musée Québécois de Culture Populaire (☎ 819-372-0406; 200 Rue Laviolette; adult/child/student $9/5/7; 🕑 10am-5pm Tue-Sun, to 6pm Jun-Aug) is one of the most interesting stops in the area. Its changing exhibits cover the gamut from folk art to pop culture, delving into the social and cultural life of the Québécois. Recent exhibits include a quirky show on the social significance of garage sales and woodcarvings of birds commonly sighted in the area.

Also leaving from here are highly recommended 90-minute tours of the former Trois-Rivières prison, En Prison (☎ 819-372-0406; www.enprison.com; 200 Rue Laviolette; adult/child/student $9/5/7; 🕑 first tour 10am, last tour 4:45pm Jun-Aug). When it

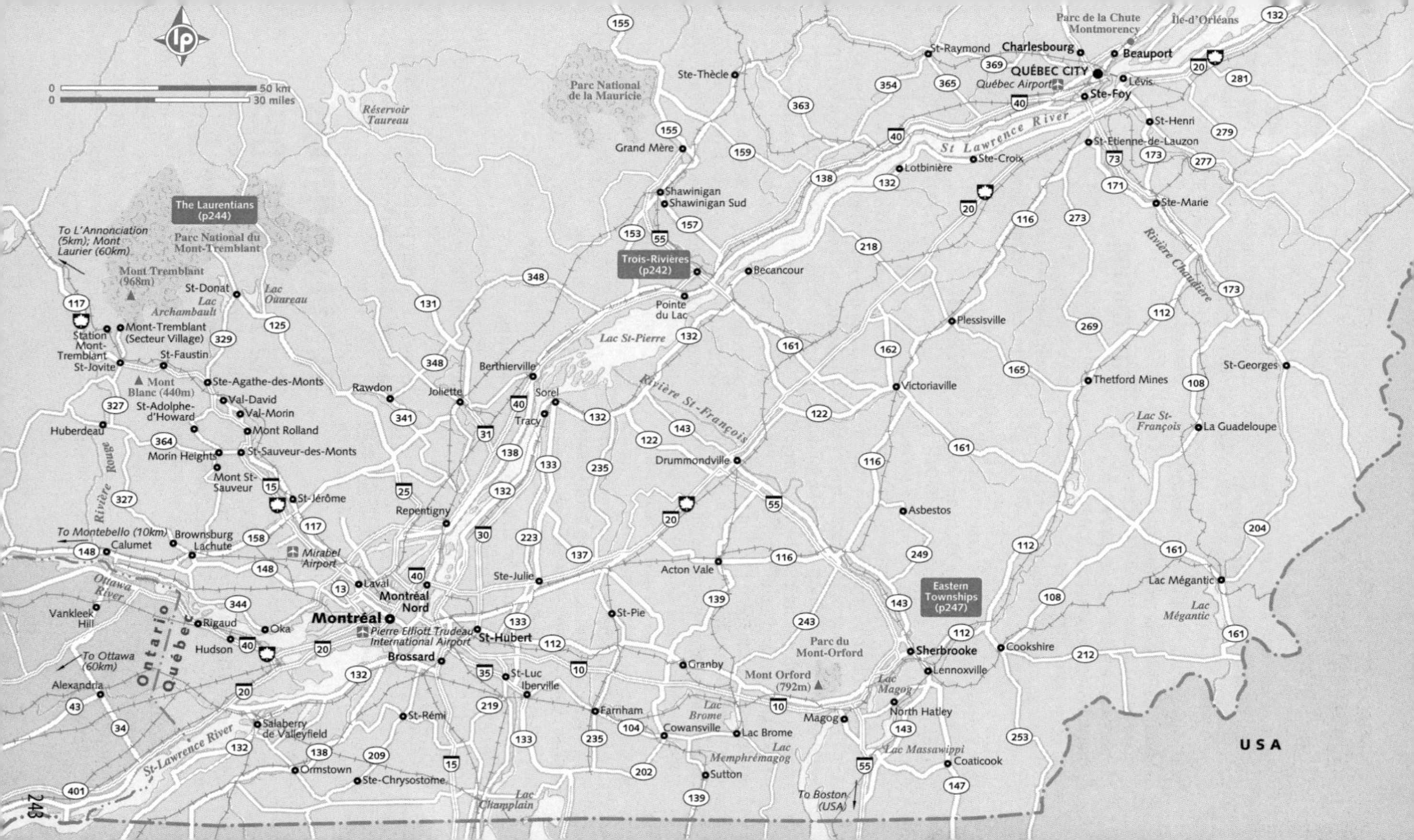

0 50 km
0 30 miles
The Laurentians (p244)
Parc National du Mont-Tremblant
Mont Tremblant (968m)
To L'Annonciation (5km); Mont Laurier (60km)
Réservoir Taureau
Parc National de la Mauricie
Trois-Rivières (p242)
Eastern Townships (p247)
Québec City
Charlesbourg
Beauport
Parc de la Chute Montmorency
Île-d'Orléans
Lévis
Ste-Foy
Québec Airport
St-Raymond
Ste-Thècle
Grand Mère
Shawinigan
Shawinigan Sud
St-Henri
St-Étienne-de-Lauzon
Ste-Croix
Lotbinière
Ste-Marie
St Lawrence River
Rivière Chaudière
Becancour
Pointe du Lac
Lac St-Pierre
Plessisville
Victoriaville
Thetford Mines
St-Georges
La Guadeloupe
Lac St-François
Rivière St-François
Drummondville
Asbestos
Acton Vale
Lac Mégantic
Lac Mégantic
Sherbrooke
Cookshire
Lennoxville
North Hatley
Lac Magog
Lac Massawippi
Coaticook
Magog
Mont Orford (792m)
Parc du Mont-Orford
Granby
Lac Brome
Lac Brome
Cowansville
Farnham
Lac Memphrémagog
Sutton
To Boston (USA)
USA
St-Donat
Lac Archambault
Lac Ouareau
Mont-Tremblant (Secteur Village)
Station Mont-Tremblant
St-Jovite
St-Faustin
Mont Blanc (440m)
Ste-Agathe-des-Monts
Val-David
Val-Morin
St-Adolphe-d'Howard
Mont Rolland
Huberdeau
Morin Heights
St-Sauveur-des-Monts
Mont St-Sauveur
Rivière Rouge
St-Jérôme
Rawdon
Joliette
Berthierville
Sorel
Tracy
Repentigny
To Montebello (10km)
Calumet
Brownsburg
Lachute
Mirabel Airport
Laval
Montréal Nord
Montréal
Pierre Elliott Trudeau International Airport
St-Hubert
Ste-Julie
St-Pie
Ottawa River
Vankleek Hill
Rigaud
Oka
Hudson
Ontario
Québec
To Ottawa (60km)
Alexandria
Brossard
St-Luc
Iberville
St-Rémi
Salaberry de Valleyfield
St-Lawrence River
Ormstown
Ste-Chrysostome
Lac Champlain

TRANSPORTATION: TROIS-RIVIÈRES

Distance from Montréal 134km northeast

Distance from Québec City 121km southwest

Car Autoroute 40

Bus From Montréal or Québec City, Orléans Express buses (☎ 514-842-2281; one way/return $33/52) leave from the main bus terminal in each respective city and go to Trois-Rivières; prices are the same from either city. Buses arrive at the main bus station, Gare d'Autobus (☎ 819-374-2944; 1075 Rue Champflour), in the old train station.

closed in 1986 it was the oldest continually in-use jail in Canada. The tours are led by former convicts – perhaps the only job in Canada where a criminal record is a prerequisite. The tours cover not only the history of this particular prison but life in Canada's prisons in general. It's fascinating but at times rather disturbing stuff, and guides try to lighten things up a bit by throwing in a few jokes now and again. Only a few of the guides speak English, so call ahead to make sure they'll be available when you drop by. Combined tickets (museum & prison adult/child/student $14/8/10) are also available.

Nearby, Rue des Ursulines is worth exploring, with its picturesque homes (some of which are now B&Bs) and its unseen history, which you can learn about in the Ursuline Museum (☎ 819-375-7922; 734 Rue des Ursulines; adult/student $3.50/2.50; 🕑 10am-5pm Tue-Sun May-Nov, 1-5pm Wed-Sun Mar & Apr). Founded by Ursuline nuns in 1639, the museum has a fine collection of textiles, ceramics, books and prints related to Catholicism. Frescoes adorn the chapel.

Church admirers should also pay a visit to the colossal Cathédrale de l'Assumption (☎ 819-374-2409; 362 Rue Bonaventure; admission free; 🕑 7am-noon & 2-5pm), a soaring neo-Gothic confection with exquisite sculpture and intricate Florentine stained-glass windows.

Two-hour cruises along the river aboard the MV Le Draveur (☎ 819-375-3000, 800-567-3737; www.croisieres.qc.ca; 1515 Rue du Fleuve; adult/child from $25/13) are available from the dock in Parc Portuaire, at the foot of Blvd des Forges in the center of the Old Town.

La Domaine Joly de Lotbinière (☎ 418-926-2462; Rte de Pointe-Platon, Hwy 132, Ste-Croix; adult/child/student $14/6/8; 🕑 10am-5pm mid-May–mid-Oct), a stately museum between Trois-Rivières and Québec City, was built for Henri-Gustave Joly de Lotbinière (1849–1908), a premier of Québec. This is one of the most impressive manors built during the seignorial period of Québec and has been preserved in its late-19th-century state. The outbuildings and huge cultivated garden are a treat, and the café serves lunch and afternoon teas.

Information

Trois-Rivières tourist office (☎ 819-375-1122; 1457 Rue Notre-Dame; 🕑 9am-8pm Jun–early Sep, 9am-5pm Mon-Fri, 10am-4pm Sat & Sun early Sep–Oct, 9am-5pm Mon-Fri Nov-May) Extremely helpful tourist office.

Sleeping

L'Emerillon B&B (☎ 819-375-1010; www.bbcanada.com/1949.html; 890 Terrasse Turcotte, Trois-Rivières; r $115) One of the classiest B&Bs in town, L'Emerillon has a grand wooden staircase leading up to the four rooms, the best of which has a four-post bed and balcony with river views.

Manoir De Blois (☎ 819-373-1090; www.manoirdeblois.com; 197 Rue Bonaventure, Trois-Rivières; r $140) This gorgeous family-run inn has beautifully furnished rooms. Breakfast is served in a spacious, antique-filled room, reminiscent of a Victorian drawing room.

Le Fleurvil (☎ 819-372-5195, 877-375-5190; www.lefleurvil.qc.ca; 635 Rue des Ursulines, Trois-Rivières; s/d $90/125; 💻 🏊) Operated by a gregarious Harley aficionado with a knack for decorating, this enchanting inn fronts a lush garden with pool. Most of the nine rooms have private facilities.

Auberge Internationale de Trois-Rivières (☎ 819-378-8010, 877-378-8010; www.hihostels.ca; 497 Rue Radisson, Trois-Rivières; dm/d $26/55; 💻) This wonderfully clean and friendly youth hostel is set in a two-story brick Georgian home.

THE LAURENTIANS (LES LAURENTIDES)

Named for their location along the northern side of the St Lawrence River, the Laurentians are one of the great outdoor playgrounds for Quebecers. In winter, outdoor enthusiasts and nature-lovers take to the clear lakes and forest-covered peaks for downhill and cross-country skiing, snowshoeing and snowmobiling. When the weather warms, hikers, cyclists, kayakers and campers come to soak up the natural beauty. People also come in fall to take in the changing leaves, with hues of ocher, gold and vermilion dramatically coloring the landscape. While it's possible to come up on a long day trip, some prefer to linger in the region's alpine-style villages, overnighting in cozy chalets, spa retreats and atmospheric B&Bs. There's also an excellent assortment of restaurants.

The rolling peaks of the Laurentian mountain range were once as high as the Rockies, but eroded over centuries to the more modest heights that you see today. In spite of their size, the skiing is truly outstanding – rivaled only by Whistler in the whole of Canada. Not surprisingly, the place is popular – expect higher prices and heavy crowds during the high season, which includes the summer months and Christmas holidays.

A good first stop in the region is the Laurentians Tourist Association (Association Touristique des Laurentides) at the Porte du Nord, off the highway north of Montréal. One of many such tourist information centers in the area, it has free maps, a reservation service and brochures galore to help you get started.

The region's blockbuster attraction is Parc National du Mont-Tremblant. Skiing and its rugged wilderness attracts everyone from families on vacation to Hollywood *vedettes* (stars) like Catherine Zeta-Jones and Michael Douglas, who own a pied-à-terre at Lac Desmarais.

The name Mont-Tremblant comes from the Algonquins, who felt the mountain 'trembled' to punish them. These days the name Tremblant conjures up a different kind of punishment, since several villages in the region were amalgamated into the City of Mont-Tremblant and given almost indecipherable variations of the same moniker. With every highway exit now labeled 'Tremblant,' tourists and locals alike play the game of trying to figure out if it's the actual Tremblant where they have their hotel reservations – the best solution is to get detailed directions from your accommodations before heading up.

In any case, these are the areas of interest to visitors: the ski resort known as Station Mont-Tremblant; the village of Mont-Tremblant now referred to as Secteur Village, a low-key area that has a main street lined with good eateries; and Secteur St-Jovite, an area worth noting only because you can often find a hotel room here even when accommodations in other regions of the city are full.

Station Mont-Tremblant has a chairlift at its base for winter skiing or summer transport up the mountain. There are also walking paths alongside pretty Lac Tremblant and a tourist cruise around the lake. The pedestrianized resort feels a bit like a miniaturized Disneyland, with shopping, cafés and restaurants plus towering hotel units next to the chairlift at the base of the mountain.

The village of Mont-Tremblant (Secteur Village), some 4km southwest of there, is spread along the shores of pretty Lac Mercier. You'll find shops, B&Bs, restaurants and a walking path around the lake. You can also take a cruise out on the lake.

Mont-Tremblant Ski Centre (☎ 819-681-2000; www.tremblant.ca; Station Mont-Tremblant; lift ticket adult/youth/child $68/50/40; 🕑 8:30am-3:45pm daily, mid-Nov–mid-Apr) is the area's highest peak (968m), and a major ski center with more than 60 runs. Its state-of-the-art facilities include golf courses, water sports, cycling and tennis courts. Bicycles and skates can be rented at the ski center for the 10km skating/cycling path that runs through town and up to the mountain's edge.

Opened more than a century ago, the wild, wooded Parc National du Mont-Tremblant (☎ 819-688-2281; www.sepaq.com; Chemin du Lac-Supérieur, Lac-Supérieur; adult/child $4/2; 🕑 7am-10pm summer, call for winter hours) covers more than 1500 sq km of gorgeous Laurentian lakes, rivers, hills and woods. You'll find fantastic hiking and mountain-biking trails as well as camping and river

TRANSPORTATION: THE LAURENTIANS

Distance from Montréal 80-150km northwest
Distance from Québec City 295-369km southwest
Car Hwy 15 (Autoroute des Laurentides), or the slower Hwy 117 north
Bus Bus Galland (☎ 514-842-2281; www.galland-bus.com) runs buses from Montréal's main bus station to the Laurentians two to four times daily. Towns serviced include St-Sauver-des-Monts ($20, 1¼ hours), St-Agathe-des-Monts ($22, 1¾ hours), St-Jovite ($26, 2½ hours) and Mont-Tremblant ($30, three hours). Not all buses go to Mont-Tremblant, but you can catch a free shuttle making the 15-minute drive from St-Jovite to Tremblant. There is no direct bus to the Laurentians from Québec City.

routes for canoes. The half-day route from Lac Chat to Mont de la Vache Noire ($19) is particularly popular. Be sure to reserve a canoe and a place on the shuttle bus by calling the Information Center Parc du Mont-Tremblant well in advance of your arrival.

The most developed of the park's sectors is the Diable, close to Mont-Tremblant and north of pretty Lac Supérieur. The information center here has kayaks, pedal boats and canoes for rent and numerous trails and campsites in the vicinity.

Nearby in St-Faustin, the popular Cabane à Sucre Millette (☎ 819-688-2101; 1357 Rue St-Faustin, St-Faustin; 11:30am-8pm Tue-Sat, 11:30am-7pm Sun Mar-Apr, reservations rest of year) is known for both its food and tours.

Another fine attraction is the P'tit Train du Nord (www.laurentides.com/parclineaire), a 200km bike path built on the old Laurentian railway line running between Mont Laurier and St-Jérôme. Cyclists hit the path when the weather warms; in winter the route is open to cross-country skiers and snowshoers (certain parts are also open to snowmobiles). B&Bs and bike shops are easily found along the route, and many of the old train stations now house mini-museums, cafés and tourist information offices. From late June to early September, Autobus du P'tit Train du Nord (☎ 888-893-8356; www.lepetittraindunord.com; tickets $20-45; Jun 20–Sep 7) runs one bus daily between St-Jérôme and Mont Laurier, stopping as needed. Bicycles are transported at no extra charge. It departs St-Jérôme around 8am, and begins the return trip around noon. Call to reserve a seat.

Whether you are doing the P'tit Train du Nord or just cruising the Laurentians by car on a day trip from Montréal, there are several villages along the way worth a stop.

St-Sauveur-des-Monts is a small resort town with four nearby ski hills. Its main drag is often clogged on weekends when day-trippers shuffle through the cafés, restaurants and shops.

Mont St-Sauveur (☎ 450-227-4671; www.mssi.ca; 350 Rue St-Denis, St-Sauveur-des-Monts; 9am-10:30pm Mon-Sat, 9am-10pm Sun mid-Nov–Apr) is one of the area's main ski centers. Hills are a bit tame but there's night skiing, a huge variety of runs and 100% snow coverage in season, thanks to snow blowers built right into the slopes.

The tiny Val-David was a major hippie mecca in the '60s, a hangover still apparent today. The village has two artisanal bakeries, jazz music in its cafés on summer weekends and more than its share of arts and crafts people. For something a bit different, try Acro-Nature (☎ 450-227-2020; www.mssi.ca; 231 Rue Bennett, Morin Heights; adult/youth/child $38/28/23; 9am-5pm daily end Jun–Sep, call for non-summer hours) in nearby Morin Heights. It has a three-hour obstacle course for adults, where you can sail from tree to tree on one of the 24 zip-lines, and a mini-course for kids.

If you're traveling in summer, stop by Ste-Adéle for a meal. There are several interesting eateries across the street from Lac Rond.

Elsewhere, Ste-Agathe-des-Monts has a prime location on Lac des Sables. By the beginning of the 1900s, it was well known as a spa town. Later, famous guests included Queen Elizabeth (who took refuge here during WWII) and Jackie Kennedy. Bateaux Alouette (☎ 819-326-3656; www.croisierealouette.com; adult/child $14/5) offers regular 50-minute cruises out on the lake.

Less than an hour from Montréal, St-Jérôme's Musée d'Art Contemporain des Laurentides (☎ 450-432-7171; www.museelaurentides.ca; 101 Pl du Curé-Labelle, St-Jérôme; adult/child $2/free; noon-5pm Tue-Sun) mounts small but first-rate exhibitions of regional artists' works.

Information

Information Center Parc du Mont-Tremblant (☎ 819-688-2281; www.parcsquebec.com; Chemin du Lac-Supérieur, Lac-Supérieur; 7am-10pm summer, call for winter hours)

Laurentians Tourist Association (Association Touristique des Laurentides; ☎ 450-224-7007, 180-561-6673; www.laurentides.com; La Porte du Nord, exit 51, Autoroute 15)

Mont-Tremblant Tourist Office (☎ 819-425-2434; www.tourismemonttremblant.com; 5080 Montée Ryan; 8am-7pm Sun-Thu, 8am-10pm Fri & Sat summer, 9am-5pm winter)

St-Sauveur-des-Monts Tourist Office (☎ 450-229-3729; 605 Chemin des Frênes, St-Sauveur-des-Monts)

Ste-Agathe Tourist Office (☎ 819-326-0457; 24 Rue St Paul, Ste-Agathe-des-Monts; 9am-6pm summer, 9am-5pm winter)

Eating

Orange & Pamplemousse (☎ 450-227-4330; 120 Rue Principale, St-Sauveur-des-Monts; mains $10-28; 8am-3pm & 5-9pm Wed-Sun) Boasting a tranquil setting complete with bamboo fountain, this popular restaurant serves complex pasta dishes and extraordinary grilled fish. The breakfasts are also recommended.

La Petite Cachée (☎ 819-425-2654; 2681 Chemin du village, Mont-Tremblant Village (Secteur Village); mains $18-34) In a charming chalet en route to the mountain, this place serves a changing selection of market-fresh fare (grilled rainbow trout, lobster and fennel tagliatelle, *merguez* sausage pizza with red peppers).

Le Creux du Vent (☎ 819-322-2280; 1430 Rue de l'Académie, Val-David; mains $20-28) Tucked in a quiet part of town by the rushing Rivière du Nord, this attractive restaurant has an ever-changing menu inspired by what's in the local markets.

La Forge Bar & Grill (☎ 819-681-3000; Pl St-Bernard, Station Mont-Tremblant; mains bistro $12-34, restaurant $28-48) La Forge has a laid-back bistro on the lower level with tasty burgers, pastas and salads; the upstairs restaurant has delicious grilled meats cooked over a maple-wood fire. Has excellent views.

Microbrasserie La Diable (☎ 819-681-4546; Station Mont-Tremblant; mains $10-20) Hugely popular place with six on-site brewed beers, and satisfying comfort food (the sausages are famous).

Sleeping

Auberge Tremblant On We Go Inn (☎ 866-429-5522; www.tremblantonwego.com; 112 Chemin Plouffe, Mont-Tremblant Village (Secteur Village); r with shared/private bathroom from $90/120;) On the edge of Lac Mercier, this cozy four-room inn offers bright and airy rooms, the best of which has lake views. There's an outdoor terrace overlooking the lake, and free use of kayaks, canoes and pedal boats.

Auberge de St-Venant (☎ 819-326-7937; www.st-venant.com; 234 St-Venant, Ste-Agathe-des-Monts; r $110-155) This B&B has nine bright, colorful rooms, enthusiastic owners and plenty of nooks and crannies where you can perch in a deck chair and take in the sparkling view of Lac des Sables.

Auberge du P'tit Train du Nord (☎ 450-229-2225, 877-979-2225; www.petit-train-du-nord.com; 3065 Rue Rolland, Ste-Adéle; r $110-130) This charming inn, right next to the bike path, has tidy, simply furnished rooms and helpful staff.

Chalet Beaumont (☎ 819-322-1972; www.chaletbeaumont.com; 1451 Rue Beaumont, Val-David; dm $25, r with shared/private bathroom $60/75;) On a hill above town, Chalet Beaumont is a rustic inn and hostel with trim, wood-paneled rooms.

La Maison de Bavière (☎ 819-322-3528, 866-322-3528; www.maisondebaviere.com; 1470 Chemin de la Rivière, Val-David; r $150) Done up like a Bavarian lodge, this *gîte* (B&B) has a stunning location on the Rivière du Nord, across the street from the P'tit Train du Nord. Breakfasts are prepared with hungry cyclists and cross-country skiers in mind.

Manoir Saint-Sauveur (☎ 450-227-1811, 800-361-0505; www.manoir-saint-sauveur.com; 246 Chemin du Lac-Millette, St-Sauveur; r from $169;) In the heart of the resort area of St-Sauveur, this sprawling place has plush rooms and extensive facilities.

Mont-Tremblant International Youth Hostel (☎ 819-425-6008; www.hostellingtremblant.com; 2213 Chemin du Village, Mont-Tremblant (Village Secteur); dm/r $29/72) A cozy hostel with clean rooms and great staff, located in the village sector.

THE EASTERN TOWNSHIPS

Rolling wooded hills, clear blue lakes and quaint villages set the scene for a delightful ramble through the picturesque Eastern Townships (Cantons de l'Est or l'Estrie in French). Aside from its uncommon beauty, the region has a history that sets it apart from the rest of Québec. Once the homeland of Abenaki Indians, the region became a refuge for Loyalists fleeing the USA after the revolution of 1776. Irish followed suit along with a handful of French settlers, although it remained a largely English-speaking region until the 1970s. The region covers 13,100 sq km, beginning 80km southeast of Montréal and stretching to the Vermont and New Hampshire borders.

New Englanders will feel right at home among the covered bridges and round barns – the architecture and landscaping here show more of a British and American influence

TRANSPORTATION: THE EASTERN TOWNSHIPS

Distance from Montréal 80-160km
Distance from Québec City 176-228km
Car Autoroute 10 Est (East)
Bus Transdev Limocar (☎ 514-842-2281; www.transdev.ca) operates bus services between Montréal's main bus station and Magog ($31, 1¾ hours) and Sherbrooke ($35, 2½ hours) up to 12 times daily. Several of these buses also stop in Granby ($22, two hours). Veolia Transport (☎ 877-348-5599; www.veoliatransport.qc.ca) operates daily bus services between Montréal and the townships of Sutton ($18, two hours) and Knowlton ($20, 2¼ hours).

than the French one seen in other parts of the province. Given its historic mix of Irish and French (see the boxed text, p18), you'll find this one of the most perfectly bilingual areas of Québec, with many locals speaking French and English with such ease it can be hard to tell who's francophone and who's anglophone.

Spring is the season for 'sugaring off': tapping, boiling and preparing maple syrup. Summer brings fishing and swimming in the numerous lakes; in fall the foliage dazzles with gorgeous colors, and freshly pressed apple cider is served in local pubs. Skiing is a major winter activity with centers at Mont Orford and Sutton.

Coming from Montréal, stop off at the first regional tourist office for events information, though offices are found in most towns including Coaticook, Granby and Sherbrooke.

The Eastern Townships is a great hiking and cycling region, and rentals are available in Sherbrooke and North Hatley, among other places. The district also produces some wines, and many of these vineyards are starting to get some serious attention especially for their ice wines (see the boxed text, opposite). You can pick up a brochure for the self-guided wine tour through the region from any tourist office.

The town of Granby is known far and wide in Québec as the home of Granby Zoo (☎ 450-372-9113; www.zoodegranby.ca; 525 Rue St-Hubert, Granby; adult/child $33/22; ⌚ 10am-7pm daily late Jun–Aug, 10am-5pm Sat & Sun Sep-Oct) with its 1000-plus animals including reptiles, gorillas and kangaroos. One of the most popular spots is at the bottom of the Hippopotamus Pool, where you can watch hippos lumber from the ground before they swim past viewing windows.

South of Autoroute 10, on Hwy 243, is the town of Lac Brome, on the lake of the same name and made up of seven former English Loyalist villages. Knowlton is certainly one of the most interesting and picturesque: many of the main street's Victorian buildings have been restored, and it's a bit of a tourist center with some fantastic craft and gift shops. A favorite meal in this area is Lac Brome duck, which shows up frequently on the better menus and is celebrated with the town's annual Duck Festival in fall.

Just out of Magog, Mont Orford (792m) dominates the lush Parc du Mont-Orford (☎ 819-843-9855; www.sepaq.com; 3321 Chemin du Parc, Canton d'Orford; adult/child $4/2; ⌚ year-round, call for hours). In winter, the park is a cross-country and downhill skiing center, with summer bringing hiking (on 80km of trails), camping, lake swimming and canoe/kayak rental. Each summer the Orford Art Centre presents the Jeunesses Musicales du Canada music and art festival. Its Auberge du Parc Orford is a comfortable, spacious hotel and hostel with 55 rooms on the wooded grounds of the center.

Lac Memphrémagog is the largest and best-known lake in the Eastern Townships, but most lakefront properties are privately owned. Halfway down the lake is the Abbaye St-Benoît-du-Lac (☎ 819-843-4080; www.st-benoit-du-lac.com; ⌚ church 5am-8:30pm, gift shop 9-10:45am & 11:50am-6pm Mon-Sat, 12:15-6pm Sun late Jun–Oct). The monks' chants, cider and wide range of finely made cheeses are famous throughout Québec and people from all over the province descend on the abbey's shop to buy them along with the monks' jams, sweets, jellies and chocolate-covered blueberries. Visitors can also attend services (and join the monks in prayer and Gregorian chanting at 7:30am, 11am and 5pm), and there's a hostel for men and another for women nearby at a nunnery.

The beautifully set town of North Hatley sits at the north end of Lac Massawippi. The village was a popular second home for wealthy US citizens who enjoyed the scenery – and the absence of Prohibition – during the 1920s. Many of these old places are now inns and B&Bs.

English-language dramas play at Piggery Theatre (☎ 819-842-2431; www.piggery.com; 215 Chemin Simard, North Hatley) and there's a choice of antique and craft shops as well as galleries. The noteworthy Galerie Jeannine Blais (☎ 819-842-2784; www.galeriejeannineblais.com; 102 Rue Main, North Hatley) is devoted entirely to art naïf. Aside from a few restaurants and shops, the town is quite sleepy. Taking in the natural beauty, lakeside swimming and boating are popular activities.

You will need to book as far ahead as possible if you're planning to stay in these parts, especially in summer when B&Bs are often booked solid several weeks in advance. Be aware that in summer, many B&Bs also have a two-night minimum on weekends.

Sherbrooke is the region's main commercial center with several small museums, a wide selection of restaurants and a pleasant central core lying between two rivers. The 18km walking and cycling path along the Magog River, known as Réseau Riverain, makes for an agreeable stroll, beginning at the edge of the

ICE WINE

Ice wine was discovered in Germany by accident, when growers found that pressing wine grapes after they froze on the vine left a sweet, highly concentrated juice. Ice wine results when this juice is left on the vine to ferment, creating one of the most coveted dessert wines on the market; it's so expensive because of the amount of grapes that need to be pressed for enough juice to be extracted. Ontario-produced varieties are the out-and-out stars of this luxury sweet-treat, but the Québec-produced kinds are starting to give them a run for their money. If you're doing the winery tour in the Eastern Townships, you'll come across many, fascinating local varieties. In Dunham, Vignoble l'Orpailleur (☎ 450-295-2763; www.orpailleur.ca; 1086 Rte 202, Dunham; 9am-5pm daily Apr 15–Dec 31, 11am-5pm Sat & Sun, Mon-Fri reservation only Dec 31–Apr 15) is arguably the province's best-known wine producer. It has a terrific little display on the history of alcohol in Québec as well as captions in the vineyards explaining the grape varieties and how they grow. Tours of l'Orpailleur can be arranged – call for information. The on-site restaurant (mains $16-20; 11:30am-4pm late Jun–mid-Oct) serves delicious high-end bistro fare, with seating on a pleasant outdoor terrace.

Magog River in Blanchard Park. The top picks of sights in the city are the small but beautifully conceived museums including the Musée des Beaux-Arts (☎ 819-821-2115; www.mbas.qc.ca; 241 Rue Dufferin, Sherbrooke; adult/student & child $8/5; 10am-5pm Tue-Sun Jun 24–Labour Day, noon-5pm Tue-Sun rest of year) which features intriguing exhibitions by Québécois and Canadian artists. The little-known Centre Interpretation Société de l'Histoire de Sherbrooke (☎ 819-821-5406; 275 Rue Dufferin Granby, Sherbrooke; adult/child $6/2; 9am-noon & 1-5pm Mon-Fri, 1-5pm Sat & Sun) has a small, permanent exhibition on the town's history as well as temporary exhibitions; a tour of the city archives which are kept downstairs is included with the ticket price.

The city itself is an interesting place for an afternoon wander around and has several large outdoor wall murals that are great fun to seek out (pick up a mural map at the tourist office), while the Lennoxville borough is home to Bishop's, the English university, and the Golden Lion Brewing Company, Lion d'Or (☎ 819-562-4589; www.lionlennoxville.com; 2 Rue College, Lennoxville borough, Sherbrooke), which was Québec's first microbrewery. Call ahead for a guided tour of the brewery, or stop in the pub for a pint.

Though it doesn't have much in the way of sights, the Coaticook area has some of the prettiest scenery in the region, not to mention some wonderful cheese makers (get the cheese-route brochure from the tourist office). It's also well known for the scenic Parc de la Gorge de Coaticook (☎ 819-849-2331; www.gorgedecoaticook.qc.ca; 135 Rue Michaud, Coaticook; adult/child $8/5; 10am-5pm May–mid-Jun & Sep-Oct, 9am-7pm mid-Jun–Aug, call for winter hours), with the world's longest suspension bridge. Visitors come year-round, with hiking, mountain biking and horseback riding in the summer, and snow tubing and snowshoeing in the winter. You can also camp or overnight in one of the park's cabins.

Cowansville is yet another pretty town that's worth a look. With no particular sights to speak of, the town has done a fine job of identifying its historic homes and buildings with informative interpretation panels.

Information

Magog Tourist Office (☎ 819-843-2744; www.magogquebec.homestead.com; 55 Rue Cabana, Magog; 8:30am-7pm summer, 8:30am-5pm winter)

Regional tourist office (☎ 800-355-5755; www.easterntownships.org; Autoroute10, exit 68; 8am-10pm Mon-Tue & Thu-Fri, 10am-10pm Wed, 9am-5pm Sat & Sun Jun-Sep, 9am-5pm Oct-May)

Sherbrooke Tourist Office (☎ 819-821-1919; www.tourismesherbrooke.com; 785 Rue King Ouest, Sherbrooke; 9am-7pm Jun 22–mid-Aug, 9am-5pm Mon-Sat & 9am-3pm Sun rest of the year)

Sleeping & Eating

Manoir Hovey (☎ 819-842-2421, 800-661-2421; www.manoirhovey.com; 575 Chemin Hovey, North Hatley; r $160-300;) This lovely resort offers handsomely set rooms in a picturesque lakeside setting. You'll find expansive gardens, a heated pool, an ice rink (in winter), and you can arrange numerous outdoor activities – windsurfing, lake cruises and golfing. The award-wining restaurant is among the best in the Eastern Townships, with three-course meals highlighting refined Québécois fare.

Ô Bois Dormant (☎ 819-843-0450, 888-843-0450; www.oboisdormant.qc.ca; 205 Rue Abott, Magog; r $115;) Set in an 1889 Victorian, this four-room B&B has bright rooms with wood floors, some with balconies overlooking the back garden and pool.

A la Cornemuse (☎ 819-842-1573; www.cornemuse.qc.ca; 2024 Chemin Vail, Dunham; r $130-150) This country-classic charmer has small but sweetly decorated rooms in a spacious home built by a Scottish family in 1907. Breakfast is served on the outside terrace with lake views.

Le Bocage (☎ 819-835-5653; www.lebocage.qc.ca; 200 Chemin de Moe's River, Compton; r $90-200) From the welcome to the antiques, this Victorian gem of a B&B is hard to fault. A multicourse meal (four courses $42) is served nightly and can feature dishes like guinea fowl stuffed with mushrooms, and wild boar, red dear medallions or other wild game. Reservations essential.

Le Marquis de Montcalm (☎ 819-823-7773; www.marquisdemontcalm.com; 797 Rue Général-de-Montcalm, Sherbrooke; s/d from $95/105) Run by a charming family, this is a bright, airy B&B flooded with natural light. It has sumptuous breakfasts and surprise flourishes in every accommodations, like the hand-painted mural in the 'Place des Voges' room.

Auberge Knowlton (☎ 450-242-6886; www.knowlton.ca; 286 Chemin Knowlton, Knowlton; r $120-150;) Set in a landmark 1849 inn, this place features comfortable country-themed rooms and a sprinkling of antiques throughout the place. The pleasant on-site restaurant **Le Relais** serves regional specialties including juicy Lac Brome duck. There's terrace seating in the summer.

Pilsen (☎ 819-842-2971; 55 Rue Main, North Hatley; mains $12-30; noon-11pm Mon-Sat) The liveliest restaurant in North Hatley is famous for its salmon both grilled and smoked, and upmarket pub fare. There's a nice riverside terrace and another facing the lake.

TRANSPORTATION

Both Montréal and Québec City are well served by major roads and rail lines, with flights jetting in from many other cities in Canada, the US and Europe. Travelers to Québec City usually have to transfer in Montréal first.

Moving around within Montréal itself is a breeze thanks to its extensive metro and bus networks. Québec City has an extensive public transit system but it does not have a metro.

THINGS CHANGE...

The information in this chapter is particularly vulnerable to change. Check directly with the airline or a travel agent to make sure you understand how a fare (and ticket you may buy) works and be aware of the security requirements for international travel. Shop carefully. The details given in this chapter should be regarded as pointers and are not a substitute for your own careful, up-to-date research.

AIR

Airports

Montréal is served by Pierre Elliott Trudeau International Airport (PET; ☎ 514-394-7377, 800-465-1213; www.admtl.com), also known as Montréal Trudeau Airport. It's about 21km west of downtown and is the hub of most domestic, US and overseas flights. Mirabel Airport, about 50km northeast of downtown, serves a few charter flights. PET Airport (coded as YSL) has decent connections to the city by car and shuttle bus.

Québec City's Aéroport International Jean-Lesage de Québec (☎ 418-640-2700; www.aeroportdequebec.com; 500 Rue Principal) lies about 15km west of the center. It has no shuttle-bus services to town.

GETTING INTO TOWN

To/From Montréal's Pierre Elliott Trudeau International Airport

- Aérobus Operated by the Québécoise Bus Company (☎ 514-842-2281; www.autobus.qc.ca), the Aérobus (one way/return $16/26) provides fast bus service between the airport and Montréal's main bus station, the Station Centrale de l'Autobus (Map p72; 505 Blvd Maisonneuve Est) in the Quartier Latin. Buses run round the clock, leaving on the hour between 9pm and 9am. They run on the half-hour from 9am to 9pm. The trip takes 45 minutes. It follows the same schedule returning to the airport. Aérobus also offers free transfers to several major downtown hotels from the bus station. Call ahead to reserve (☎ 514-631-1856).
- Public Transit The cheapest way to get into town takes 60 to 90 minutes and requires a bus-bus-metro combo to reach the city center. Outside the arrivals hall at PET Airport, take bus 204 Est and ride to the bus transfer station at Gare Dorval (Dorval Train Station). Here you switch to bus 211 Est; get off at metro station Lionel-Groulx (Map pp62–3). Both buses run from 5am to 1am, and the whole journey costs $2.75 one-way. To get to the airport from downtown, reverse the journey.
- Driving Driving to or from downtown takes 20 to 30 minutes (allow an hour during peak times). A common route into town is the Autoroute 13 Sud that merges with the Autoroute 20 Est; this in turn takes you into the heart of downtown, along the main Autoroute Ville Marie (the 720).

To/From Québec City's Aéroport International Jean-Lesage de Québec

- Taxi Options are fairly straightforward going from this public-transit-challenged airport (bus 78 runs infrequently and goes nowhere near the center of town). A taxi costs a flat fee of $33 to go into the city, around $15 if you're only going to the boroughs surrounding the airport. Les Amis du Transport Roy & Morin (☎ 418-622-6566) is a transit service for disabled people. Returning to the airport, you'll pay the metered fare, which should be less than $30.
- Driving Driving takes about 25 minutes to reach the Old Town. Among several different routes, you can take Rte 540 South/Autoroute Duplessis, merge onto Rte 175, and follow this as it becomes Blvd Laurier, then Rue Grand Alleé, before entering the old city on Rue St-Louis.

BICYCLE

Montréal's bicycle paths are extensive, running over 500km around the city. Useful bike maps are available from the tourist offices and bicycle rental shops.

Top bike paths follow the Canal de Lachine and then up along Lac St-Louis; another popular route goes southwest along the edge of the St Lawrence River, passing the Lachine Rapids and up to the Canal de Lachine, meeting up with the Canal de Lachine path.

There are also bike paths around the islands of Parc Jean-Drapeau, the Île de Soeurs and Parc du Mont-Royal. For more on cycling see p168.

Québec City also has an extensive network of bike paths (some 70km in all), including a route along the St Lawrence which connects to paths along the Riviére St-Charles. Pick up a free color map at the tourist office or at local bike shops.

In Montréal, bicycles can be taken on the metro from 10am to 3pm and after 7pm Monday to Friday, as well as throughout the weekend. Officially cyclists are supposed to board only the first two carriages of the train, but if it's not busy no one seems to mind much where you board.

The water shuttles to Parc Jean-Drapeau take bicycles at no extra charge.

You can't take bikes on buses in Québec City.

Rental

There a number of places to rent bikes in both cities, though Montréal also offers the option of the sparkly new Bixi bike (see the boxed text, p169). For short trips, this is a great way to get around town.

In Montréal:

Ça Roule Montréal (Map p48; ☎ 514-866-0633, 877-866-0633; www.caroulemontreal.com; 27 Rue de la Commune Est; 🕑 9am-8pm Apr-Oct; Ⓜ Place-d'Armes) Bicycle hire runs $25 per day ($8 per hour), in-line skates go for $20 per day ($9 per hour).

Le Grand Cycle (Map pp76–7; ☎ 514-525-1414; www.legrandcycle.com; 901 Rue Cherrier Est; ☎ 9am-7pm Mon-Fri, 9am-5pm Sat, noon-5pm Sun; Ⓜ Sherbrooke) Charges $30 per day ($10 per hour).

My Bicyclette (Map pp62–3; ☎ 514-998-6252; www.mybicyclette.com; 2985 Rue St-Patrick; ☎ 10am-7pm mid-May–mid-Oct; Ⓜ Charlevoix) Located along the Canal de Lachine (across the bridge from the Atwater market). Bicycle hire per day costs $30 ($10 per hour).

In Québec City:

Cyclo Services (Map p206; ☎ 418-692-4052; www.cycloservices.net; 289 Rue St-Paul) Charges $35 per day for hybrid bikes ($14 per hour).

Museovelo (Map p210; ☎ 418-523-9194; 463 Rue St-Jean; 🕑 10am-8pm Mon-Fri, 10am-5pm Sat) Also rents hybrids for $35 per day.

CLIMATE CHANGE & TRAVEL

Climate change is a serious threat to the ecosystems that humans rely upon, and air travel is the fastest-growing contributor to the problem. Lonely Planet regards travel, overall, as a global benefit, but believes we all have a responsibility to limit our personal impact on global warming.

Flying & Climate Change

Pretty much every form of motor transport generates CO_2 (the main cause of human-induced climate change) but planes are far and away the worst offenders, not just because of the sheer distances they allow us to travel, but because they release greenhouse gases high into the atmosphere. The statistics are frightening: two people taking a return flight between Europe and the US will contribute as much to climate change as an average household's gas and electricity consumption over a whole year.

Carbon Offset Schemes

Climatecare.org and other websites use 'carbon calculators' that allow jetsetters to offset the greenhouse gases they are responsible for with contributions to energy-saving projects and other climate-friendly initiatives in the developing world – including projects in India, Honduras, Kazakhstan and Uganda.

Lonely Planet, together with Rough Guides and other concerned partners in the travel industry, supports the carbon offset scheme run by climatecare.org. Lonely Planet offsets all of its staff and author travel.

For more information check out our website: www.lonelyplanet.com.

TRAVEL BETWEEN MONTRÉAL & QUÉBEC CITY

Québec City lies about 260km northeast of Montréal. Aside from renting a car, there are a number of handy ways to get between the cities.

- Train VIA Rail (☎ 888-842-7245; www.viarail.ca) has several trains daily going between Montréal's Gare Centrale (Map pp62–3; ☎ 514-989-2626; 895 Rue de la Gauchetière; Ⓜ Bonaventure) and Québec City's Gare du Palais (Map p206; ☎ 888-842-7245; 450 Rue de la Gare-du-Palais). Prices for the 3½-hour journey start at $50/100 for a one-way/return ticket.
- Bus Orléans Express (☎ 888-999-3977; www.orleansexpress.com) and Greyhound (☎ 800-661-8747; www.greyhound.ca) make daily departures between Montréal's main bus station, Station Centrale de l'Autobus (Map p72; ☎ 514-842-2281; 505 Blvd de Maisonneuve Est; Ⓜ Berri-UQAM) and Québec City's Gare du Palais (Map p206; ☎ 418-525-3000; 450 Rue de la Gare-du-Palais). Prices for the journey (3¼ to 4½ hours) start at $53/106 for a one-way/return ticket.

BOAT

Cruise vessels ply the St Lawrence River but there are no frequent and affordable passenger services to/from Montréal. Services to/from Québec City include:

AML Cruises (Map p48; ☎ 514-842-9300, 866-856-6668; www.croisieresaml.com; Quai King-Edward) Links Montréal and Québec City via a day-long cruise once a week during summer. The boat leaves at 8am from Quai King-Edward and arrives in Québec City at 5pm, and there is a return trip by bus around 10pm the same night. Tickets (adult/child $159/139) include breakfast and lunch and are only slightly cheaper without the return coach. Be sure to reserve ahead. Its address in Québec City is 10 Rue Dalhousie.

Canadian Connection Cruises (☎ 800-267-7868; www.stlawrencecruiselines.com; 253 Ontario St, Kingston) Offers four- to six-day luxury cruises between Kingston, Ontario and Québec City, including meals, accommodations and on-board entertainment. Six-night cruises cost $2324 in high season.

BUS & METRO

Montréal

Montréal has a modern and convenient bus and metro system run by STM (☎ 514-786-4636; www.stm.info). The metro is the city's subway system; it's extensive and aging and delays in recent years have been a fixture for commuters. Despite its flaws, the metro is still the best way to get around town. Schedules vary depending on the line, but trains generally run from 5:30am to midnight from Sunday to Friday, slightly later on Saturday night (to 1:30am at the latest).

Tickets, available at any metro station, cost $2.75, but are cheaper by the half-dozen ($12.75). Buses take tickets or cash but drivers won't give change. There are also tourist passes for one day ($9) and three days ($17), though a weekly pass ($20) may be a better deal. Monthly passes run $69.

If you're switching between buses, or between bus and the metro, you should get a free transfer slip, which is called a *correspondance,* from the driver; on the metro take one from the machines just past the turnstiles.

A map of the metro network is included on the pull-out map at the back of this book.

In Montréal, long-distance buses depart from the Station Centrale de l'Autobus (Map p72; ☎ 514-842-2281; 505 Blvd de Maisonneuve Est; Ⓜ Berri-UQAM), the main terminal for buses to Canadian and US destinations. Allow about 45 minutes before departure to buy a ticket; most advance tickets don't guarantee a seat, so arrive early to line up at the counter.

Québec City

A ride on a white-and-blue RTC bus (Réseau de Transport de la Capitale; ☎ 418-627-2511; www.rtcquebec.ca) costs $2.60 with transfer privileges, or $6.45 for the day. Many buses serving the Old Town area stop at Pl d'Youville just outside the wall on Rue St-Jean. Bus 800 goes to the Gare du Palais (Map p206; ☎ 418-525-3000; 450 Rue de la Gare-du-Palais), the central long-distance bus and train station.

If you're coming from Montréal, your bus may stop at Ste-Foy-Sillery station (☎ 418-650-0087; 3001 Chemin des Quatre Bourgeois), so ask first before you get off.

Long-Distance Bus Lines

Galland Laurentides (☎ 450-687-8666; www.galland-bus.com) Provides bus service from Montréal to Mont-Tremblant and other destinations in the Laurentians.

AIR TRAVEL ALTERNATIVES

To cut back on carbon emissions,there are some worthwhile (and less expensive) alternatives to flying:

- **Train** Amtrak (www.amtrak.com) provides service between New York City and Montréal on its Adirondack line. The trip, though slow (11 hours), passes through lovely scenery. VIA Rail (www.viarail.ca), Canada's vast rail network, links Montréal with cities all across the country.
- **Bus** Greyhound (www.greyhound.com) and its Canadian equivalent Greyhound Canada (www.greyhound.ca) provide extensive service across North America. Buses from Boston and New York make regular departures to Montréal.

Greyhound (☎ 800-861-8747; www.greyhound.com) Operates long-distance routes to Ottawa, Toronto, Vancouver and the USA. Greyhound also runs between Montréal and Québec City.

Moose Travel (☎ 888-816-6673; www.moosenetwork.com) Popular with backpackers, this network operates several circuits around Canada, allowing travelers to jump on and jump off along the way. Pickup points are in Montréal, Québec City, Ottawa and Toronto, among other places.

Orléans Express (☎ 888-999-3977; www.orleansexpress.com) Makes the three-hour run between Montréal and Québec City.

CALÈCHE

These picturesque horse-drawn carriages seen meandering around Old Montréal and Mont-Royal charge about $45/75 for a 30-/60-minute tour. They line up at the Old Port and at Place-d'Armes. Drivers usually provide running commentary, which can serve as a pretty good historical tour.

In Québec City, *calèche* drivers charge $80 for a 45-minute tour. You'll find them just inside the Porte St-Louis and near the Chateau Frontenac.

CAR & MOTORCYCLE

Driving

Fines for traffic violations, from speeding to not wearing a seat belt, are stiff in Québec. You may see few police cars on the roads but radar traps are common. Motorcyclists are required to wear helmets and to drive with their lights on.

Traffic in both directions must stop when school buses stop to let children get off and on. At the white-striped pedestrian crosswalks, cars must stop to allow pedestrians to cross the road. Turning right on red lights is legal everywhere in Québec, including Québec City, but is illegal in Montréal.

Continental US highways link directly with their Canadian counterparts along the border at numerous points. These roads meet up with the Trans-Canada Hwy, which runs directly through Montréal. During the summer and on holiday weekends, waits of several hours are common at major USA–Canada border crossings. If possible avoid Detroit, Michigan; Windsor, Ontario; Fort Erie, Ontario; Buffalo, New York; Niagara Falls on both sides of the border; and Rouse's Point, New York. Smaller crossings are almost always quiet.

If you have difficulty with the French-only signs in Québec, pick up a decent provincial highway map, sold at service stations and usually free at tourist offices.

Visitors with US or British passports are allowed to bring their vehicles into Canada for six months.

The blood-alcohol limit while driving is 0.08%. Driving motorized vehicles including boats and snowmobiles under the influence of alcohol is a serious offense in Canada. You could land in jail with a court date, heavy fine and a suspended license. The minimum drinking age is 18 – this is the same age as for obtaining a driver's license.

Rental

PET Airport has many international car-rental firms, and there's a host of smaller operators in Montréal. Whether you're here or in Québec City, rates will swing with demand so it's worth phoning around to see what's on offer. Booking ahead usually gets the best rates, and airport rates are normally better than those in town. A small car might cost around $50 to $65 per day with unlimited mileage, taxes and insurance, or $300 to $400 per week.

To rent a car in Québec you must be at least 21 years old and have had a driver's license for at least a year.

In Montréal:

Avis (Map pp62–3; ☎ 514-866-2847, 800-879-2847; 1225 Rue Metcalfe; 🕑 7am-7pm Mon-Wed, 7am-9pm Thu-Fri, 7am-5pm Sat, 8am-7pm Sun; Ⓜ Peel)

Budget (Map pp62–3; ☎ 514-866-7675, 800-268-8970; www.budget.com; 895 Rue de la Gauchetière Ouest;

7am-8pm Mon-Fri, 9am-7pm Sat & Sun; M Bonaventure) In Gare Centrale.

Discount Car (Map pp62–3; ☎ 514-798-7235, 800-263-2355; www.discountcar.com; 607 Blvd de Maisonneuve Ouest; 7:30am-7pm Mon, 7:30am-6pm Tue-Thu, 7:30am-8pm Fri, 8am-5pm Sat, 9am-5pm Sun; M McGill) Good, competitive rates. Canadian owned.

Hertz (Map pp62–3; ☎ 514-938-1717, 800-263-0678; www.hertz.com; 1073 Rue Drummond; 7am-7pm Mon-Wed, 7am-8pm Thu-Fri, 7am-5pm Sat, 8am-7pm Sun; M Lucien-L'Allier)

Rent-a-Wreck (Map pp44–5; ☎ 514-343-5500, 866-979-5500; www.rentawreck.ca; 7146 Côte-des-Neiges; 8am-5pm Mon-Fri, 8am-4pm Sat; M Côte-des-Neiges) Usually the best rates.

In Québec:

Budget (Map p206; ☎ 418-692-3660; www.budget.com; 29 Côte-du-Palais; 7am-5:30pm Mon-Fri, 8am-3pm Sat, 9am-4pm Sun)

Hertz (Map p206; ☎ 418-694-1224; www.hertz.com; 44 Côte-du-Palais; 7:30am-5:30pm Mon-Fri, 8am-5pm Sat & Sun)

TAXI

Flag fall is a standard $3.30 plus another $1.60 per kilometer. From PET Airport to downtown Montréal the fare is a flat $33. Prices are posted on the windows inside taxis. Try **Taxi Champlain** (☎ 514-273-2435) or **Taxi Co-Op** (☎ 514-725-9885).

In Québec City the biggest company is **Taxi Coop Quebec** (☎ 418-525-5191).

TRAIN

Canada's trains are arguably the most enjoyable and romantic way to travel the country. Long-distance trips are quite a bit more expensive than those by bus, however, and reservations are crucial for weekend and holiday travel. A few days' notice can cut fares a lot.

Montréal's **Gare Centrale** (Map pp62–3) is the local hub of **VIA Rail** (☎ 888-842-7245; www.viarail.ca) and in Québec it's **Gare du Palais** (Map p206; ☎ 418-525-3000; 450 Rue de la Gare-du-Palais).

Service is good along the so-called Québec City–Windsor corridor that connects Québec City with Montréal and on to Ottawa, Kingston, Toronto and Niagara Falls. Drinks and snacks are served from aisle carts, and some trains have a dining and bar car.

AMT commuter trains (☎ 514-287-8726, 888-7028726; www.amt.qc.ca) serve the suburbs of Montréal. Services from Gare Centrale are fast but infrequent, with two-hour waits between some trains. Gare Windsor is used for just a few commuter trains.

DIRECTORY

BUSINESS HOURS

Most banks in Montréal and Québec City are open 10am to 3pm Monday to Wednesday and Friday, and 10am to 7pm Thursday. Government offices generally open 9am to 5pm weekdays. Post offices are open 8am to 5pm Monday to Friday.

Hours for museums vary but most open at 10am or 11am and close by 6pm. Most are closed Monday but stay open late one day a week (typically Wednesday or Thursday).

Restaurants generally open 11:30am to 2:30pm and 5:30pm to 11pm; cafés serving breakfast may open at 8am or 9am.

Many bars and pubs open from 11:30am until midnight or longer; those that don't serve food may not open until 5pm or later.

Some attractions outside Montréal shut down completely or operate sporadic hours outside of the busy summer months (September to May). In Québec City, some attractions close down completely outside of peak periods.

CHILDREN

Montréal has plenty of amusements for little ones if you know where to look.

Old Montréal (p47) with its lively street performers around Pl Jacques-Cartier is a good place to wander. You can also hop on a carriage (see the boxed text, p168).

La Ronde Amusement Park (p57) in Parc Jean-Drapeau offers day-long thrills in the summer. Parc Jean-Drapeau also has a lake and beach, the Plage des Îles (p59), for more sunny-day fun.

Another good bet is the Montréal Planetarium (p64) or the creepy-crawlies at the Insectarium (p90) in the Jardin Botanique. The Old Port area is packed with options, such as the interactive Centre des Sciences de Montréal (p56) with its IMAX Cinema.

The abundance of bicycle paths that weave through green surrounds offers a great diversion for kids, especially along the Canal de Lachine (p98) from the Old Port.

Older children may enjoy adventures such as rafting or jet-boat trips (p171), kayaking (p171) along the Canal de Lachine or more leisurely boat cruises (p172).

In winter, there's ice-skating on frozen lakes at the Parc du Bassin Bonsecours (p55) in the Old Port, on Lac des Castors (p80) in Parc du Mont-Royal and in the Plateau's Parc LaFontaine (p75), plus year-round ice-skating inside Atrium le 1000 (p170).

Québec City, with its old architecture, guides dressed in period costume and castle-like fortifications, is also packed with activities of interest to kids. See the boxed text, p202, for more ideas on travel with kids here.

Lonely Planet's *Travel with Children* also has some valuable tips.

Babysitting

Many hotels can provide referrals to reliable, qualified babysitting services. Some well-known services include Denise Miller Babysitting Services (☎ 514-365-1704). Going rates are $12 an hour for one to two children and $15 for three to four children, with a surcharge applying after midnight.

In Québec City, you may have difficulty finding an English-speaking babysitter through the agencies. Your best bet is to inquire at your accommodations, as most hotels have a list of English-speaking babysitters for guests.

CLIMATE

Even the earliest European explorers were surprised by the seasonal extremes of Montréal. Summer arrives late in Montréal, with temperatures still unpredictable into early June. From July it can get brutally hot and steamy, and highs of 25°C or 30°C continue until late August, but the nights soon turn chilly. Fall comes in a burst of color in late September.

Global warming has dulled winter's edge to daytime temperatures of -20°C to -6°C, but unfortunately has not affected the frigid razor-blasts of air that can take the wind-chill factor to -30°C or lower. Snow arrives in November and can pile high in some areas until mid-March. Blasts of wind down the St Lawrence River valley bring a cold damp that seems to creep into your bones and makes Montréal's underground city an attractive refuge (see the boxed text, p68).

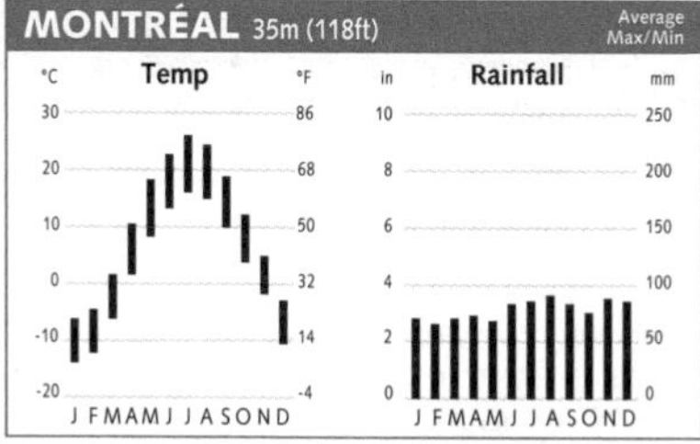

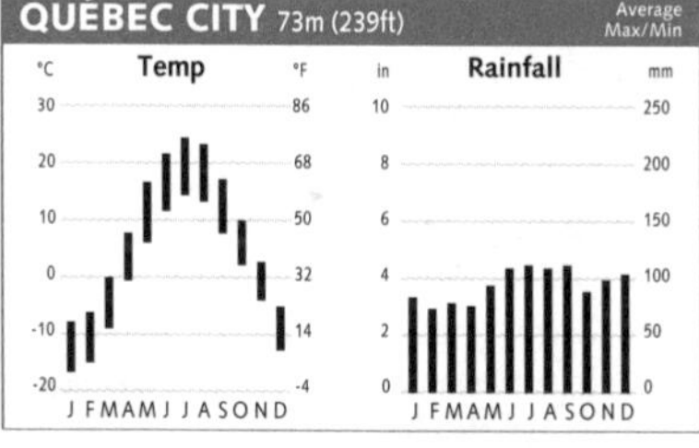

Winters in Québec City are a few degrees colder than Montréal. In the darkest days of winter in mid-January, many people don snowsuits while doing their errands.

COURSES

Montréal has a number of courses available, from one-day evening workshops to full-blown instruction lasting several months. Options for short-term visitors tend to be limited, but be sure to check the classifieds in free weeklies like *Mirror* or *Hour* for what's on.

Québec City also has a fantastic range of courses, but nothing in English.

Cooking

Most French cooking courses are offered in French only; courses in Italian and other cuisines are available in English.

Académie Culinaire du Québec (Map p48; ☎ 514-393-8111, 877-393-8111; www.academieculinaire.com; 360 Champ de Mars; Ⓜ Champ-de-Mars) This esteemed cooking academy conducts regular cooking workshops and short courses ($95 for a three-hour class). Although most are in French, the school recently began offering some English-language culinary classes.

Mezza Luna Cooking School (Map p83; ☎ 514-272-5299; 6851 Rue St-Dominique; Ⓜ De Castelnau) Single sessions on Italian cooking (in French, English and Italian) known far beyond Montréal's borders ($40 per class). Elena Faita gives free demonstrations on pasta-making every Saturday at 2pm at Quincaillerie Dante (p113).

Language

For courses in Québec City, see the boxed text, p201.

As a French-English university town, Montréal is a popular place to learn a foreign language. University courses and language schools abound.

Concordia University Centre for Continuing Education (Map pp62–3; ☎ 514-848-3600; www.concordia.ca; 1600 Rue Ste-Catherine Ouest; Ⓜ Guy-Concordia) Runs eight-week French courses in spring, fall and winter, from $320. There's also a two-week intensive course (also $320) offered in December and July.

McGill University Centre for Continuing Education (Map pp62–3; ☎ 514-398-6200; www.mcgill.ca; 11th fl, 688 Rue Sherbrooke Ouest; Ⓜ McGill) Year-round, accredited intensive and part-time courses in French.

Montréal International Language Centre (Map pp62–3; ☎ 514-939-4463; www.cilm.qc.ca; 2000 Rue Ste-Catherine Ouest; Ⓜ Atwater) Tailor-made language courses at this offshoot of LaSalle University.

YMCA (Map pp62–3; ☎ 514-849-8393; www.ymcalanguages.ca; 5th fl, 1440 Rue Stanley; Ⓜ Peel) Offers day and evening French courses as well as an intensive summer camp. Seven-week classes cost $235 to $340.

CUSTOMS REGULATIONS

For the latest customs information, contact the Canadian embassy or consulate at home. Don't get caught bringing in illegal drugs as sentences can be harsh. Most fruit, vegetables and plants can be confiscated, so avoid or ask ahead.

Visitors to Canada aged 18 and older can bring up to 1.14L (40oz) of liquor or 24 12oz cans of beer or ale, and up to 50 cigars, 200 cigarettes, 200g of tobacco and 400 tobacco sticks into Canada. You can also bring in gifts valued up to $60.

US residents may bring back $800 worth of goods duty free, plus 1L of alcohol (but you must be age 21 or over), as well as 200 cigarettes and 100 non-Cuban cigars.

Duty-free limits for the UK are 200 cigarettes or 50 cigars, 1L of spirits or 2L of fortified or sparkling wine, 2L of still table wine, 60mL of perfume, 250mL of toilet water plus $145 worth of other goods and souvenirs.

Australian residents aged 18 and up can bring home A$900 of gifts and souvenirs, 250 cigarettes or tobacco sticks and 2.25L of alcohol. Residents aged under 18 may bring back $450 worth of goods.

DISCOUNT CARDS

The Montréal Museums Pass allows free access to 34 museums for three days of your choice within a 21-day period ($45). For an extra $5, the pass comes with three consecutive days of free access to bus and metro. It's available from the city's tourist offices, or you can buy it online (www.museesmontreal.org).

An International Student Identity Card (ISIC) can pay for itself through half-price admissions, discounted air and ferry tickets and cheap meals in student cafeterias. In Montréal, ISIC cards are issued by Voyages Campus (www.travelcuts.com) and other student travel agencies. The price will depend on what country you buy it in. The International Student Travel Confederation (www.istc.org) is another good source for ISIC cards.

In Québec City, the Québec City Museum Card is $50 and you get free access for three consecutive days to 18 sights, including the major museums and the Lévis ferry. Also included is a stack of coupons for discounts at other attractions and two free day-passes for public transit. Buy it at participating museums or at the tourist office.

ELECTRICITY

Canada, like the USA, operates on 110V, 60-cycle electric power. Non-North American visitors should bring a plug adapter for their own small appliances. Note that any gadgets like hairdryers built for higher voltage and cycles (such as 220/240V, 50-cycle appliances from Europe) will probably run more slowly.

Canadian electrical goods have a plug with two flat, vertical prongs (the same as the USA and Mexico) or sometimes a three-pronged plug with the added ground prong.

EMBASSIES & CONSULATES

All foreign embassies are located in Ottawa, but Montréal has fairly good consular services.

Australian citizens should call the Australian High Commission (☎ 613-236-0841; 710-50 O'Connor St, Ottawa).

Denmark (Map pp62–3; ☎ 514-877-3060; www ambottawa.um.dk; 35th fl, 1 Pl Ville-Marie; 9am-5pm Mon-Fri; M McGill)

France (Map pp62–3; ☎ 514-878-4385; 1501 Ave McGill College; www.consulfrance-montreal.org; 8:30am-noon Mon-Fri; M McGill)

Germany (Map pp62–3; ☎ 514-931-2277; www .montreal.diplo.de; 1250 Blvd René-Lévesque Ouest; 9am-noon Mon-Fri; M Lucien L'Allier)

Italy (Map pp62–3; ☎ 514-849-8351; www.cons montreal.esteri.it; 3489 Rue Drummond; 9am-noon Mon-Fri; M Peel)

Japan (Map pp62–3; ☎ 514-866-3429; www.montreal .ca.emb-japan.go.jp; ste 2120, 600 Rue de la Gauchetière Ouest; 9am-noon & 1:30-5pm Mon-Fri; M Square-Victoria)

Switzerland (Map pp62–3; ☎ 514-932-7181; www .eda.admin.ch; 1572 Ave Docteur-Penfield; 10am-noon Mon-Thu, 10am-1pm Fri)

UK (Map pp62–3; ☎ 514-866-5863; www.british highcommission.gov.uk; 1000 Rue de la Gauchetière Ouest; 9am-12:30pm Mon-Fri; M Bonaventure)

USA (Map pp62–3; ☎ 514-398-9695, 514-981-5059; http://montreal.usconsulate.gov; 1155 Rue St-Alexandre; 8:15am-5pm Mon-Fri; M McGill)

In Québec City:

France (off Map p204; ☎ 418-266-2500; www.consul france-quebec.org; 25 Rue St-Louis)

Italy (Map p204; ☎ 418-529-9801; 355 23ieme Rue; 10am-4pm Mon-Fri)

Netherlands (Map p204; ☎ 418-525-8344; 1040 Ave Belvédère, Ste-Foy-Sillery)

USA (Map p206; ☎ 418-692-2095; www.quebec .usconsulate.gov; 2 Pl Terrasse Dufferin; 8:30am-noon Mon-Fri)

EMERGENCY

When in doubt, call ☎ 0 and ask the operator for assistance.

Poison Centre (☎ 1800-463-5060)

Police, ambulance, fire (☎ 911)

GAY & LESBIAN TRAVELERS

Fugues (www.fugues.com) is the free, French-language, authoritative monthly guide to the gay and lesbian scene for the province of Québec. It's an excellent place to find out about the latest clubs and gay-friendly accommodations.

Montréal's sexual enlightenment makes the city a popular getaway for lesbian, gay and bisexual travelers. The gay community is centralized in the Village, and it's huge business. Gay Pride Week attracts hundreds of thousands in early August, and the Black &

Blue Festival fills the Olympic Stadium for a mega-fest in early October (see p15).

Gays and lesbians are well integrated into the community – in the Plateau, two men holding hands in public will get little more than a quick look of curiosity, though in other areas of the city being openly out may attract more attention.

Québec City is a conservative town with a more village feel to it – open displays of affection between same-sex couples will attract a lot of attention. An icon of the town's gay community is Le Drague (p226).

In Montréal:

Montreal Gay & Lesbian Community Centre & Library (Map p72; ☎ 514-528-8424; www.ccglm.org; 2075 Rue Plessis; ⏲ 10am-noon & 1-5pm; Ⓜ Beaudry) This gay and lesbian center, around since 1988, has an extensive library and loads of info on the city's gay scene.

Centre d'Information Gay Touristique du Village (Map p72; ☎ 888-595-8110; www.infogayvillage.com; 1315 Rue Ste-Catherine Est; Ⓜ Berri-UQAM) The Village's gay business-information source, with scads of tourist maps, brochures and referrals to local hotels, restaurants and saunas.

Gay Line (☎ 514-866-5090, 888-505-1010; www.caeoquebec.org) Provides information, counseling and referrals to organizations within the gay community.

HOLIDAYS

Banks, schools and government offices close on Canadian public holidays, while museums and other services go on a restricted schedule. This is also a busy time to travel.

Residential leases in Montréal traditionally end on June 30, so the roads are always clogged on July 1 as tenants move to their new homes.

School students break for summer holidays in late June and return to school in early September. University students get even more time off, breaking from May to early or mid-September. Most people take their big annual vacation during this summer period.

The main public holidays:

New Year's Day January 1

Good Friday & Easter Monday late March to mid-April

Victoria Day May 24 or nearest Monday

National Aboriginal Day June 21 (unofficial)

Jean-Baptiste Day June 24

Canada Day July 1

Labour Day first Monday in September

Canadian Thanksgiving second Monday in October

Remembrance Day November 11

Christmas Day December 25

Boxing Day December 26

INTERNET ACCESS

If you're traveling with a laptop, a growing number of cafés offer free wi-fi access. Register for free access and view the 150-odd places where you can get online at **Île Sans Fil** (www.ilesansfil.org).

For free wi-fi hotspots in Québec City visit www.zapquebec.org.

Many hotels also provide wi-fi access, though some charge for this service. If you're not traveling with a computer, many hotels have one available for guests (we've labeled these options with the icon 💻).

Internet cafés like the following generally charge $4 to $6 to check your *courriel* (email):

Battlenet 24 (Map pp62–3; ☎ 514-846-3333; 1407 Rue du Fort; ⏲ 24hr; Ⓜ Guy-Concordia)

Chapters Bookstore (Map pp62–3; ☎ 514-849-8825; 1171 Rue Ste-Catherine Ouest; ⏲ 9am-11pm; Ⓜ Peel)

Netopia (Map p72; ☎ 514-286-5446; 1737 Rue St-Denis; ⏲ 24hr; Ⓜ Sherbrooke)

Net.24 (Map pp62–3; ☎ 514-845-9634; 2157 Rue Mackay; ⏲ 24hr; Ⓜ McGill)

In Québec City, internet cafés aren't as prevalent as in Montréal.

Centre Internet (Map p206; ☎ 418-692-3359; 52 Côte-du-Palais; ⏲ 9:30am-9:30pm) Centrally located in the Old Town.

LEGAL MATTERS

If you're charged with an offense, you have the right to public counsel if you can't afford a lawyer.

The blood-alcohol limit while driving is 0.08%. Driving motorized vehicles including boats and snowmobiles under the influence of alcohol is a serious offense in Canada. You could land in jail with a court date, heavy fine and a suspended license. The minimum drinking age is 18 – this is the same age as for obtaining a driver's license.

It's an offense to consume alcohol anywhere other than at a residence or licensed premises, which technically puts parks, beaches and the rest of the great outdoors off-limits.

MAPS

If you're going to explore Montréal in detail, the best maps are published by Mapart (www.mapart.com), available online and at bookstores like Chapters Bookstore (p107).

Mapart also has good road atlases for hitting the road.

MEDICAL SERVICES

Canadian health care is excellent but it's not free to visitors, so be sure to get travel insurance before you leave home.

Canada has no reciprocal health care with other countries and nonresidents will have to pay up-front for treatment and wait for the insurance payback.

Medical treatment is pricey (less so by US comparison), and long waits – particularly in the emergency room – are common. Avoid going to the hospital if possible.

Clinics

For minor ailments, visit the CLSC (community health center; Map pp62-3; ☎ 514-934-0354; 1801 Blvd de Maisonneuve Ouest; Ⓜ Guy-Concordia) downtown or call ☎ 514-527-2361 for the address of the closest one.

If you're sick and need some advice, call the health hotline (☎ 811), which is staffed by nurses 24 hours a day.

Expect to pay cash up-front, as checks and credit cards are usually not accepted. You should contact your travel-insurance agency first for referrals, if you intend to make a claim later.

Emergency Rooms

In Montréal:

Montréal General Hospital (Map pp62–3; ☎ 514-934-1934 ext 42190; 1650 Ave Cedar; Ⓜ Guy-Concordia)

Royal Victoria Hospital (Map pp44–5; ☎ 514-934-1934 ext 31557; 687 Ave des Pins Ouest; Ⓜ McGill)

In Québec City:

Hôpital Laval (Map p204; ☎ 418-656-8711; 2725 Chemin Ste-Foy)

Pharmacies

The big pharmacy chains are Pharmaprix and Jean Coutu (www.jeancoutu.com). Many stores are large and well stocked, and some branches are open late.

In Montréal:

Jean Coutu (☎ 514-933-4221; 1675 Rue Ste-Catherine Ouest; 🕑 8am-midnight Mon-Sat, 9am-midnight Sun; Ⓜ Guy-Concordia)

Pharmaprix (Map pp62–3; ☎ 933-4744; 1500 Rue Ste-Catherine Ouest; 🕑 8am-midnight daily) Also has a 24-hour location near Mont-Royal (Map pp44–5; ☎ 514-738-8464; 5122 Chemin de la Côte-des-Neiges).

In Québec:

Jean Coutu (Map p210; ☎ 418-522-1235; 110 Blvd René-Lévesque Ouest; 🕑 9am-9pm Mon-Sat, 10am-9pm Sun)

MONEY

Prices quoted in this book are in Canadian dollars ($) unless stated otherwise. Canadian coins come in one-cent (penny), five-cent (nickel), 10-cent (dime), 25-cent (quarter), $1 (loonie) and $2 (toonie) pieces.

Paper currency comes in $5 (blue), $10 (purple), $20 (green) and $50 (red) denominations. The $100 (brown) and larger bills are less common.

Given rampant counterfeiting many stores flat-out refuse to take $100 and even sometimes $50 bills. This is not really legally allowed, unless there is some real reason to believe the bills are fake, but many stores insist on such a policy.

ATMs

Montréal has droves of ATMs linked to the international Cirrus, Plus and Maestro networks – not only in banks, but also in pubs, convenience stores and hotels. Many charge a small fee per use, and your own bank may levy an extra fee – it's best to check before leaving home.

Changing Money

The main shopping streets, including Rue Ste-Catherine, Blvd St-Laurent and Rue St-Denis, have plenty of banks. There are also foreign-exchange desks at the main tourist office, the airport and the casino.

In Montréal:

Calforex (Map pp62–3; ☎ 514-392-9100; 1230 Rue Peel; Ⓜ Peel)

In Québec City:

Transchange International (Map p206; ☎ 418-694-6906; 43 Rue de Baude)

Credit Cards

Call these numbers to report lost/stolen cards:

American Express (☎ 800-668-26390)

Diner's Club (☎ 800-363-3333)

Discover (☎ 801-902-3100)

MasterCard (☎ 800-307-7309)

Visa (☎ 800-847-2911)

Traveler's Checks

This old-school option offers protection against loss or theft. In Canada, many establishments, not just banks, will accept traveler's checks like cash, provided they're in Canadian dollars. They offer good exchange rates but not necessarily better than those from ATMs.

NEWSPAPERS & MAGAZINES

In Montréal, the *Montreal Gazette* is the only English-language daily and covers national affairs, politics and arts. The Friday and Saturday editions are packed with entertainment listings. Alternative weeklies *Mirror* and *Hour* contain local news and entertainment.

The national newspapers are the *Globe and Mail* and *National Post*, both published in Toronto, and both with arts sections that cover events across the country.

Readers of French can pick up the federalist *La Presse*, as well as the separatist-leaning *Le Devoir*, which does wonderful features on Québec's francophone movers and shakers. *Le Journal de Montréal* is a tabloid and the biggest circulation French daily in Canada. The alternative weeklies *Voir* and *Ici* provide good entertainment info for Francophones.

Maclean's is Canada's only weekly news magazine. The wildlife magazine *Canadian Geographic* has excellent articles and photography on primarily Canadian topics. *L'actualité* is the Québec monthly news magazine.

ORGANIZED TOURS

For rafting trips, boat cruises, carriage rides and other outdoor adventures, see p168.

Montréal

Amphi Tours (☎ 514-849-5181; amphitours.ca; 75min tour adult/child $32/18; ⌚ May-Oct) This brightly painted 'amphibus' tootles around Old Montréal before plunging into the St Lawrence for a cruise along the waterfront. Bilingual commentary points out the key places in the city's evolution from Jacques Cartier's arrival in 1535 through to Expo '67 and recent days. The bus makes several daily departures from the cnr of Rue de la Commune and Blvd St-Laurent. Call ahead for departure times.

Guidatour (Map p48; ☎ 514-844-4021, 800-363-4021; www.guidatour.qc.ca; 360 Rue St-François-Xavier; adult/child/student $18/9/16; ⌚ 11am & 1:30pm late Jun-Oct, weekends only late May–mid-Jun) On this walking tour, the experienced bilingual guides of Guidatour paint a picture of Old Montréal's eventful history with anecdotes and legends. Tours depart from Basilique Notre-Dame (p47); tickets go on sale at the basilica gift shop 15 minutes before departure. Guidatour also leads three-hour (15km) bicycle tours all over town ($49).

Héritage Montréal (Map pp62–3; ☎ 514-286-2662; www.heritagemontreal.qc.ca; 100 Rue Sherbrooke Est; admission varies; ⌚ Sat & Sun mid-May–mid-Oct) This independent, nonprofit organization is charged with the preservation of Montréal's heritage – urban, architectural and social. Its qualified guides conduct a series of architecture-based tours, focusing on a different neighborhood every week. The departure point varies and reservations are essential. The library will also open on a weekday afternoon by appointment.

Les Fantômes du Vieux-Montréal (Map p48; ☎ 514-844-4021; www.fantommontreal.com; 469 Rue St-François-Xavier; adult/child/student $22/13/19) Gives 90-minute evening tours tracing historic crimes and legends, led by guides in period costume. You'll hear talk of hangings, sorcery, torture and other light bedtime tales on this good-time evening outing. Call or stop by the office for the current schedule.

Québec City

Ghost Tours of Québec (Map p206; ☎ 418-692-9770; www.ghosttoursofquebec.com; 4 1/2 Rue d'Auteuil; adult/child/student $18/free/16; ⌚ English tour 8pm May-Oct) Local theater actors or storytellers lead you through the streets of the Old Town by lantern recounting the hangings and hauntings of Old Québec. The 90-minute tours are great fun and usually finish with a visit to the city's most haunted building. Tours leave from the sitting area (98 Rue du Petit-Champlain near Blvd Champlain) in the Old Lower Town. Buy your tickets from the Ghost Tours of Québec office or from the guide 15 minutes before the tour.

La Compagnie des Six Associes (☎ 418-692-3033; www.sixassocies.com; adult/child/student $16/free/13) Boasts a great staff and very good walking circuits like the ever-popular 'Lust and Drunkenness,' which creaks open the rusty door on the history of alcohol and prostitution in the city. Other tours, in English and French, focus on epidemics, disasters and crimes. A cheery bunch, they are.

Les Tours Voir Québec (Map p206; ☎ 418-266-0206, 877-266-0206; www.toursvoirquebec.com; 12 Rue Ste-Anne) This group offers a handful of excellent tours covering the history and architecture of Old Québec City. The popular two-hour 'grand tour' takes in the highlights of the old quarters (adult/child/student $22/11/20). Reserve ahead.

Old Québec tours (☎ 418-644-0460, 800-267-8687; www.toursvieuxquebec.com) This tour operator has a variety of tours from three-hour walking tours (adult/child $22/11) to 4½-hour tours out of town that take in the Montmorency waterfall and Ste-Anne-de-Beaupré (adult/child $49/23) or Île d'Orléans (adult/child $65/38). There are also adventure excursions, including whale-watching from June to October and dogsledding and visits to the ice hotel in the winter. You'll be given the rendezvous point when you make your reservations.

POST

Montréal's main post office (Map pp62–3; 1250 Rue University) is the largest but there are many convenient locations around town. Poste restante (general delivery) is available at Station Place-d'Armes (Map p48; 435 Rue St-Antoine, Montréal H2Z 1H0). Mail is kept for two weeks and then returned to the sender. The main Canada Post/Postes Canada (☎ 866-607-6301) provides general information.

In Québec City the post office (Map p206; 5 Rue du Fort) in the Upper Town offers the biggest selection of postal services.

Stamps are also available at newspaper shops, convenience stores and some hotels. Standard 1st-class airmail letters or postcards cost 54¢ to Canadian destinations and 98¢ to the USA (both are limited to 30g). Those to other destinations cost $1.65 (their limit is also 30g).

RADIO

In Montréal:

CBC 2 (93.5 FM) Classical and jazz.

CBC Montréal 1 (88.5 FM) Chief channel for news, educational and cultural programs in English.

CBF (95.1 FM) French equivalent of CBC Montréal 1.

CHOM (97.7 FM) Rock and alternative.

CISM (89.3 FM) Université de Montréal station, indie francophone music.

CJAD (800AM) Talk radio.

CJFM (95.9 FM) Pop and easy listening.

CKGM (990AM) Oldies.

Q92 (92.5 FM, streaming) Soft rock and oldies.

In Québec City:

CBC Québec 1 (104.7 FM, streaming) Chief channel for news, educational and cultural programs in English.

CHIK (98.9 FM) Pop, francophone music; French language.

CHYZ (94.3 FM) French-language student radio from Université Laval.

Radio-Canada (106.3 FM) French-language news, talk, culture.

Rock Détente (107.3 FM) Rock music; French language.

SAFETY

Violent crime is rare (especially involving foreigners) but petty theft is more common. Watch out for pickpockets in crowded markets and public transit places, and use hotel safes where available.

Cars with foreign registration are popular targets for smash-and-grab theft. Don't leave valuables in the car, and remove registration and ID papers.

Take special care at pedestrian crosswalks in Montréal: unless there's an *'arrêt'* (stop) sign, drivers largely ignore these crosswalks.

TELEPHONE

Local calls from a pay phone cost 25¢. With the popularity of cell phones, public phones are becoming a rarity. When you do find them they will generally be coin-operated but many also accept phone cards and credit cards.

The area code for the entire Island of Montréal is ☎ 514; Québec City's is ☎ 418. When you dial, even local numbers, you will need to punch in the area code as well.

Toll-free numbers begin with ☎ 800, ☎ 888, ☎ 877 or ☎ 777 and must be preceded with 1. Some numbers are good throughout North America, others only within Canada or one particular province.

Dialing the operator (☎ 0) or the emergency number (☎ 911) is free of charge from both public and private phones. For directory assistance, for both Canada and the US, dial ☎ 411. Fees apply.

Cell Phones

The only foreign cell phones that will work in North America are triband models, operating on GSM 1900 and other frequencies. If you don't have one of these, your best bet may be to buy a prepaid one at a consumer electronics store. You can often score an inexpensive phone for around $60 including voicemail, some prepaid minutes and a rechargeable SIM card.

Consumer electronics stores like Future Shop (p108) sell wireless and prepaid deals of use to travelers. US residents traveling with their phone may have service (though they'll pay roaming fees). Get in touch with your cell-phone provider for details.

Phone Cards

Bell Canada's prepaid Quick Change card, in denominations of $5, $10 and $20, works from public and private phones. It's available from post offices and vending machines.

Many local phone cards offer better rates than Bell's. Sold at convenience stores and newsstands, the cards have catchy names such as Mango, Big Time, Giant and Lucky.

TELEVISION

The main public-radio and TV stations are run by the Canadian Broadcasting Corporation (CBC is the English-language service, and Radio-Canada is French-language). It's the flagship of Canadian content in music and information, much like the BBC is in Britain.

The other major English-language network is the Canadian TV Network (CTV, channel 11), which broadcasts Canadian and US programs as well as nightly newscasts.

In Québec, the francophone Télé-Québec (TVA) and Télévision Quatre-Saisons (TQS) broadcast news, drama and comedy shows, movies from France and US shows dubbed into French.

TIME

Montréal is on Eastern Time (EST/EDT), as is New York City and Toronto – five hours behind Greenwich Mean Time.

Canada switches to daylight-saving time (one hour later than Standard Time) from the second Sunday in March to the first Sunday in November.

Train schedules, film screenings and schedules in French use the 24-hour clock (eg 6:30pm becomes 18:30) while English schedules use the 12-hour clock.

TOURIST INFORMATION

Montréal and Québec province share two central phone numbers for tourist information offices (☎ 877-266-5687; www.tourism-montreal.org). The airports have information kiosks that open year-round.

For Québec province info, covering Montréal, Québec City and many other areas, visit Bonjour Québec (www.bonjourquebec.com).

Centre Infotouriste (Map pp62–3; 1001 Rue Square Dorchester; 9am-6pm; M Peel) Teems with information on all areas of Montréal and Québec. The center also has independently staffed counters dedicated to national parks, car rental, boat trips, city tours and currency exchange. Hotel reservations are provided free of charge.

Old Montréal Tourist Office (Map p48; 174 Rue Notre-Dame Est; 9am-7pm late Jun–early Oct, 9am-5pm rest of year; M Champ-de-Mars) Just off bustling Pl Jacques-Cartier, this little office is always humming but staff are extremely helpful.

In Québec City:

Centre Infotouriste (Map p206; ☎ 418-649-2608, 800-363-7777; 12 Rue Ste-Anne; 9am-7pm late Jun–early Oct, 9am-5pm rest of year) Central location in Old Town.

Centre Infotouriste (Map p204; ☎ 418-641-6290, 800-266-5687 ext 798; 835 Ave Wilfrid-Laurier; 9am-7pm Jun–late Aug, 9am-5pm rest of year) In Battlefields Park.

TRAVELERS WITH DISABILITIES

In Montréal, most public buildings – including tourist offices, major museums and attractions – are wheelchair accessible, and many restaurants and hotels also have facilities for the mobility-impaired. Metro stations are not wheelchair accessible, however, almost all major bus routes are now serviced by NOVA LFS buses adapted for wheelchairs. It's recommended that you consult the bus service's website (www.stm.info/English/bus/a-usager-aps.htm) if you are a first-time user, to check availability on your route and become familiar with the boarding procedure on the adapted buses.

Access to Travel (www.accesstotravel.gc.ca) provides details of accessible transportation across Canada.

Kéroul (Map pp44–5; ☎ 514-252-3104; www.keroul.qc.ca; 4545 Ave Pierre-de-Coubertin; M Pie-IX) Publishes *Québec Accessible* ($20), listing 1000-plus hotels, restaurants and attractions in the province rated by accessibility.

It also offers packages for disabled travelers going to Québec and Ontario.

VIA Rail (☎ 514-871-6000, 888-842-7733; www.viarail.com) Accommodates people in wheelchairs at 48 hours notice. Details are available at VIA Rail offices at Montréal's Gare Centrale (Map pp62–3) Québec City's Gare du Palais (Map p206) and other Canadian train stations.

Buses in Québec City's public transit are not wheelchair accessible, though there are other services available for travelers with disabilities.

Transport Accessible du Québec (☎ 418-641-8294) Wheelchair-adapted vans available. Make reservations 24 hours in advance.

Transport Adapté du Québec Métro inc (☎ 418-687-2641; 7:30am-10:30pm) Has 20 wheelchair-adapted minibuses that zip around Québec. Make reservations at least eight hours in advance of your trip.

VISAS

Citizens of dozens of countries – including the USA, most Western European countries, Australia, Israel, Japan and New Zealand – don't need visas to enter Canada for stays of up to 180 days. US permanent residents are also exempt.

Nationals of around 150 other countries, including South Africa and China, need to apply to the Canadian visa office in their home country for a temporary resident visa (TRV). The website maintained by **Citizen and Immigration Canada** (☎ 888-242-2100; www.cic.gc.ca) has full details.

Single-entry visitor visas ($75) are valid for six months, while multiple-entry visas ($150) can be used over two years, provided that no single stay exceeds six months. Extensions cost the same price as the original and must be applied for at a Canadian Immigration Center one month before the current visa expires. A separate visa is required if you intend to work in Canada.

WOMEN TRAVELERS

Montréal holds high standards for women's safety, especially when compared with major US cities. Still, the usual advice applies: women should avoid walking alone late at night or in poorly lit areas, like Parc du Mont-Royal.

It is illegal in Canada to carry pepper spray or mace. Instead, some women recommend carrying a whistle to deal with attackers or potential dangers. If you are sexually assaulted call ☎ 911 or the **Sexual Assault Center** (☎ in Montréal 514-934-4504, in Québec City 418-522-2120) for referrals to hospitals that have sexual-assault care centers.

WORK

It is difficult to get a work permit in Canada as employment opportunities go to Canadians first. You will need to provide proof of a valid job offer from a specific employer to your local Canadian consulate or embassy.

Employers hiring casual workers often don't ask for a permit, but visitors working legally in the country have Social Insurance numbers. If you don't have one and get caught, you will be told to leave the country.

One-year working-holiday visas are made available to citizens of Australia, France, Germany, Ireland, Japan, the Netherlands, New Zealand, South Korea, Sweden and the UK. You must be between the ages of 18 and 30. Apply as early as possible and allow 12 weeks for processing. Check with the Canadian embassy in your country for details.

The **Student Work Abroad Program** (SWAP; www.swap.ca) offers working holidays every year for people aged 18 to 30 years from over a dozen countries. Participants are issued with a one-year, nonextendable visa to work anywhere in Canada. Most 'Swappers' find jobs in the service industry as waiters, hotel porters, bar attendants or farmhands.

LANGUAGE

It's true – anyone can speak another language. Don't worry if you haven't studied languages before or that you studied a language at school for years and can't remember any of it. It doesn't even matter if you failed English grammar. After all, that's never affected your ability to speak English! And this is the key to picking up a language in another country. You just need to start speaking.

Learn a few key phrases before you go. Write them on pieces of paper and stick them on the refrigerator, by the bed or even on the computer – anywhere that you'll see them often.

You'll find that Quebecers appreciate travelers trying their language, no matter how muddled you may think you sound. So don't just stand there, say something! If you want to learn more French than we've included here, pick up a copy of Lonely Planet's comprehensive and user-friendly *French Phrasebook.*

CANADIAN FRENCH

The French spoken in Canada is essentially the same as what you'd hear in France. There are differences, however, just as there are between the English of New Zealand and the English of Australia. Although many English (and most French) students in Québec are still taught the French of France, the local tongue is known as 'Québécois' or *joual.* As an example, while many around the world schooled in Parisian French would say *Quelle heure est-il?* for 'What time is it?', on the streets of Québec you're likely to hear *Y'est quelle heure?* Québécois people will have no problem understanding standard French of France.

Other differences between European French and the Québec version worth remembering (because you don't want to go hungry!) are the terms for breakfast, lunch and dinner. Rather than *petit déjeuner, déjeuner* and *dîner* you're likely to see and hear *déjeuner, dîner* and *souper.*

If you have any car trouble, you'll be happy to know that English terms are generally used for parts. Indeed, the word *char* (pronounced 'shar') for car may be heard. Hitchhiking is known not as *auto stop* but as *le pousse* (the thumb).

Announcers and broadcasters on Québec TV and radio tend to speak a more European style of French, as does the upper class. Visitors to the country who have some standard French knowledge will have the most luck understanding them.

Despite all this, the preservation of the local variety of French in Québec is a primary concern and has been fuel for the separatist movement in the past (see also p20).

Canada is officially a bilingual country with the majority of the population speaking English as their first language. In Québec, however, the dominant language is French – the vast majority of Canadian French speakers live in Québec – and there are also pockets of French speakers in some other provinces.

The following is a short guide to some French words and phrases that may be useful for the traveler. Québec French employs a lot of English words; this may make understanding and speaking the language a little easier for those familiar with English.

For a far more comprehensive guide to the language, get a copy of Lonely Planet's *French Phrasebook.*

SOCIAL

Be Polite!

Politeness pays dividends and the easiest way to make a good impression on people you encounter is always to say *Bonjour Monsieur/Madame/Mademoiselle* when you enter a shop, and *Merci Monsieur/Madame/ Mademoiselle, au revoir* when you leave. *Monsieur* means 'sir' and can be used with any adult male. *Madame* is used where 'Mrs' or 'Ma'am' would apply in English. Officially, *Mademoiselle* (Miss) relates to unmarried women, but it's much more common to use *Madame* – unless of course you know the person's marital status! Similarly, if you want help or need to interrupt someone, approach them with *Excusez-moi, Monsieur/Madame/Mademoiselle.*

Meeting People

Hello.
Bonjour./Salut. (polite/informal)
Goodbye.
Au revoir./Salut. (polite/informal)
Please.
S'il vous plaît.
Thank you (very much).
Merci (beaucoup).
You're welcome. (don't mention it)
Je vous en prie.
Yes./No.
Oui./Non.
Do you speak English?
Parlez-vous anglais?
Do you understand (me)?
Est-ce que vous (me) comprenez?
Yes, I understand.
Oui, je comprends.
No, I don't understand.
Non, je ne comprends pas.

Could you please ...?
Pourriez-vous ..., s'il vous plaît?

repeat that	répéter
speak more slowly	parler plus lentement
write it down	l'écrire

Going Out

What's on ...?
Qu'est-ce qu'il y a comme spectacles ...?

locally	dans le coin
this weekend	en fin de semaine
today	aujourd'hui
tonight	ce soir

Where are the ...?
Où sont les ...?

clubs	clubs/boîtes
gay venues	bars gais
places to eat	restaurants
pubs	pubs

Is there a free entertainment weekly?
Est-ce qu'il y a un journal gratuit avec les horaires des spectacles?

PRACTICAL

Question Words

Who?	Qui?
Which?	Quel/Quelle? (m/f)
When?	Quand?
Where?	Où?
How?	Comment?

Numbers & Amounts

0	zéro
1	un
2	deux
3	trois
4	quatre
5	cinq
6	six
7	sept
8	huit
9	neuf
10	dix
11	onze
12	douze
13	treize
14	quatorze
15	quinze
16	seize
17	dix-sept
18	dix-huit
19	dix-neuf
20	vingt
21/22	vingt et un/vingt-deux
30	trente
40	quarante
50	cinquante
60	soixante
70	soixante-dix
80	quatre-vingts
90	quatre-vingt-dix
100/200	cent/deux cent
1000/2000	mille/deux mille

Days

Monday	lundi
Tuesday	mardi
Wednesday	mercredi
Thursday	jeudi
Friday	vendredi
Saturday	samedi
Sunday	dimanche

Where's the nearest ...?
Où est ... le plus proche?

ATM	le guichet automatique
foreign exchange office	le bureau de change

Banking

I'd like to ...
Je voudrais ...

cash a cheque	encaisser un chèque
change money	changer de l'argent
change some traveler's cheques	changer des chèques de voyage

Post

Where is the post office?
Où est le bureau de poste?

I want to send a ...
Je voudrais envoyer ...

letter	une lettre
parcel	un paquet
postcard	une carte postale

I want to buy ...
Je voudrais acheter ...

an aerogram	un aérogramme
an envelope	une enveloppe
a stamp	un timbre

Phones & Mobiles

I want to buy a phone card.
Je voudrais acheter une carte téléphonique.
I want to make a call (to Australia).
Je veux téléphoner (en Australie).
I want to make a reverse-charge/collect call.
Je veux téléphoner à frais virés.

Where can I find a/an ...?
Où est-ce que je peux trouver ...?
I'd like a/an ...
Je voudrais ...

adaptor plug	une prise multiple
charger for my phone	un chargeur pour mon cellulaire
mobile/cell phone for hire	louer un cellulaire
prepaid mobile/cell phone	un cellulaire à carte pré-payée
SIM card for your network	une carte SIM pour le réseau

Internet

Where's the local internet cafe?
Est-ce qu'il y a un café Internet dans le coin?

I'd like to ...
Je voudrais ...

check my email	consulter mon courrier électronique
get online	me connecter à l'internet

Transportation

What time does the ... leave?
À quelle heure part ...?

bus	le bus
ferry	le bateau
plane	l'avion
train	le train

What time's the ... bus?
Le ... bus passe à quelle heure?

first	premier
last	dernier
next	prochain

Are you free? (taxi)
Vous êtes libre?
Please put the meter on.
S'il vous plaît, pouvez-vous partir le compteur?
How much is it to ...?
C'est combien pour aller à ...?
Please take me to (this address).
Conduisez-moi à (cette adresse), s'il vous plaît.

FOOD

breakfast	le déjeuner
lunch	le dîner
dinner	le souper
snack	un casse-croûte
eat	manger
drink	boire

Can you recommend a ...?
Est-ce que vous pouvez me conseiller un ...?

bar/pub	bar/pub
café	café
restaurant	restaurant

Is service/cover charge included in the bill?
Le service est compris?

For more information on food and dining out, see pp118-20.

EMERGENCIES

It's an emergency!
C'est urgent!
Could you please help me/us?
Est-ce que vous pourriez m'aider/nous aider, s'il vous plaît?
Call the police/a doctor/an ambulance!
Appelez la police/un médecin/une ambulance!

Where's the police station?
Où est le poste de police?

I need a doctor (who speaks English).
J'ai besoin d'un médecin (qui parle anglais).

HEALTH

Where's the nearest …?
Où est … le/la plus prochain/e? (m/f)

chemist (night)	la pharmacie (de nuit)
dentist	le dentiste
doctor	le médecin
hospital	l'hôpital (m)

Symptoms

I have (a) …
J'ai …

diarrhoea	la diarrhée
fever	de la fièvre
headache	mal à la tête
pain	une douleur

GLOSSARY

Allophone – a person whose mother tongue is neither French nor English
Anglophone – a person whose monther tongue is English
Automatistes – group of French-Canadian dissident artists founded by Paul-Émile Borduas in the early 1940s

beaux arts – architectural style popular in France and Québec in the late 19th century, incorporating elements that are massive, elaborate and often ostentatious
Bill 101 – law that asserts the primacy of the French language in Québec, notably on signage
boîte à chanson – club devoted to *chanson française*, folk music from Québec or France
boreal – refers to the Canadian north and its character, as in the boreal forest or the boreal wind
brochette – kabob

cabane à sucre – the place where the collected maple sap is distilled in large kettles and boiled as part of the production of maple syrup
calèche – horse-drawn carriage that can be taken around parts of Montréal and Québec City
Canadian Shield – also known as the Precambrian or Laurentian Shield, this is a plateau of rock that was formed 2½ billion years ago and covers much of the northern region of the country
Cantons de l'Est – Eastern Townships, a former Loyalist region southeast of Montréal toward the US border
CLSC – Centre Local de Santé Communautaire, or local community health center, marked with green-and-white CLSC signs
correspondance – a transfer slip like those used between the metro and bus networks in Montréal
côte – a hill, as in Côte du Beaver Hall

dépanneur – called 'dep' for short, this is a Québec term for a convenience store

Estrie – a more recent term for Cantons de l'Est (see above)

First Nations – a term used to denote Canada's indigenous peoples, sometime used instead of Native Indians or Amerindians
Francophone – a person whose mother tongue is French
Front de Libération du Québec (FLQ) – a radical, violent political group active in the 1970s that advocated Québec's separation from Canada

gîte (du passant) – French term for B&B or similar lodging
Group of Seven – a group of celebrated Canadian painters from the 1920s

Hochelaga – name of early Iroquois settlement on the site of present-day Montréal
Hudson Bay Company – an English enterprise created in 1670 to exploit the commercial potential of the Hudson Bay and its waterways. The Bay (La Baie) department store is the last vestige of Canada's oldest firm.

Je me souviens – this Québec motto with a nationalist ring ('I remember') appears on license plates across the province

loonie – Canada's one-dollar coin, so named for the loon stamped on one side

Mounties – Royal Canadian Mounted Police (RCMP)

portage – old process of transporting boats and supplies overland between navigable waterways; also the overland route used for such a purpose
poutine – French fries served with gravy and cheese curds; also comes in several other varieties

Québécois – the French spoken in Québec; someone from the province of Québec; someone from Québec City
Quiet Revolution – period of intense change in Québec during the 1960s marked by state intervention, educational reform, secularization of society and an increased awareness of national identity among Quebecers

Refus Global – the radical manifest of a group of Québec artists and intellectuals during the Duplessis era (1944–59)
ringuette – a sport played on ice, similar to hockey but with a ring instead of a puck and a straight stick with no flat or angled end

SAQ – Société des Alcools du Québec, a state-run agency whose branches sell wines, spirits, beer etc
seigneury – land in Québec originally held by grant from the King of France; a seigneur is thus a holder of a seigneury

stimés – hotdog with a steamed bun

Sulpicians – society of Catholic priests founded in Paris in 1641

table d'hôte – fixed-price meal (of the day)

téléroman – a type of Québec TV program that's a cross between soap opera and prime-time drama, in French

toastés – hotdog with a toasted bun

toonie – also spelled 'twonie,' a Canadian two-dollar coin introduced after the *loonie*

tourtière – Québec meat pie usually made of pork and beef or veal, sometimes with game meat

voyageur – a boatman (or woodsman, guide, trapper or explorer) employed by one of the early fur-trading companies

BEHIND THE SCENES

THIS BOOK

This 2nd edition of *Montréal & Québec City* was written by Regis St. Louis and Simona Rabinovitch. The 1st edition was written by Eilís Quinn. This guidebook was commissioned in Lonely Planet's Oakland office, and produced by the following:

Commissioning Editor Jennye Garibaldi

Coordinating Editors Andrew Bain, Carolyn Bain

Coordinating Cartographer Alex Leung

Coordinating Layout Designer Carol Jackson

Senior Editor Helen Christinis

Managing Cartographers Adrian Persoglia, Amanda Sierp

Managing Layout Designer Sally Darmody

Assisting Editor Anne Mulvaney

Assisting Cartographers Khanh Luu, Marc Milinkovic, Jolyon Philcox

Cover Research Naomi Parker, lonelyplanetimages.com

Internal Image Research Sabrina Dalbesio, Aude Vauconsant, lonelyplanetimages.com

Project Manager Anna Metcalfe

Language Content Laura Crawford

Thanks to Lucy Birchley, Jessica Boland, Eoin Dunlevy, Fayette Fox, Victoria Harrison, Raphael Richards, Jacqui Saunders, Andrew Smith, Cara Smith, Glenn van der Knijff

Cover photographs Detail of Monument Maisonneuve, Place-d'Armes, Montréal, Neil Setchfield (top). Interior of Basilique-Cathédrale Notre-Dame-de-Québec, Québec City, Richard Cummins (bottom).

Acknowledgements Photograph of Simona Rabinovitch (p11) by Susan Moss.

THANKS

REGIS ST. LOUIS

Big thanks to Roger and Tim Hornyak, both of whom generously hosted me during my extended sojourn in Montréal. Many thanks to Simona for invaluable contributions to the nightlife, shopping and arts sections. I'd also like to thank Frederic Morin, Dimitri Antonopoulos, Tom Lansky, Eric Khayat, Daniel Weinstock and the Chinatown volleyball team (and their friends and partners) for insight into 'the last great bohemian city in North America.' As always, thanks to Cassandra and Magdalena for continued love and support.

SIMONA RABINOVITCH

Thanks to my family, teachers and friends. Thanks to bagels, summertime on Mont-Royal, winter hockey games and 3am last calls. Thanks to random strangers who smile at me on the street. And as I move away from the city and back again over and over, I'd like to thank Montréal itself for being an endless source of inspiration, for letting me love and loathe it as mood strikes. Thanks to my grandparents and ancestors for choosing to immigrate here and raise their families here, to my parents for staying, and to all Montréal artists (of all disciplines), personalities and characters past and future for

THE LONELY PLANET STORY

Fresh from an epic journey across Europe, Asia and Australia in 1972, Tony and Maureen Wheeler sat at their kitchen table stapling together notes. The first Lonely Planet guidebook, *Across Asia on the Cheap*, was born.

Travelers snapped up the guides. Inspired by their success, the Wheelers began publishing books to Southeast Asia, India and beyond. Demand was prodigious, and the Wheelers expanded the business rapidly to keep up. Over the years, Lonely Planet extended its coverage to every country and into the virtual world via lonelyplanet.com and the Thorn Tree message board.

As Lonely Planet became a globally loved brand, Tony and Maureen received several offers for the company. But it wasn't until 2007 that they found a partner whom they trusted to remain true to the company's principles of traveling widely, treading lightly and giving sustainably. In October of that year, BBC Worldwide acquired a 75% share in the company, pledging to uphold Lonely Planet's commitment to independent travel, trustworthy advice and editorial independence.

Today, Lonely Planet has offices in Melbourne, London and Oakland, with over 500 staff members and 300 authors. Tony and Maureen are still actively involved with Lonely Planet. They're traveling more often than ever, and they're devoting their spare time to charitable projects. And the company is still driven by the philosophy of *Across Asia on the Cheap*: 'All you've got to do is decide to go and the hardest part is over. So go!'

keeping this city's heart beating and its soul unpredictable. Thanks to everyone who's written a song here, fallen in love here, made a film here and, most of all, to those who haven't yet – but will.

OUR READERS

Many thanks to the travelers who used the last edition and wrote to us with helpful hints, useful advice and interesting anecdotes:

Jan Bakker, Matthew Bourque, Michelle Buckberry, Valérie Drolet, Ronit Fallek, Teresa Herrera, Yuli Masinovsky, Laurie McLaughlin, Hans-Peter Moeselaegen, Evelyn Osmond, Tara Poirier, Anne Tam, Alan Tenanty, Bill Tubbs, Ulrich Wagner

SEND US YOUR FEEDBACK

We love to hear from travelers – your comments keep us on our toes and help make our books better. Our well-traveled team reads every word on what you loved or loathed about this book. Although we cannot reply individually to postal submissions, we always guarantee that your feedback goes straight to the appropriate authors, in time for the next edition. Each person who sends us information is thanked in the next edition and the most useful submissions are rewarded with a free book.

To send us your updates – and find out about Lonely Planet events, newsletters and travel news – visit our award-winning website: lonelyplanet.com/contact.

Note: We may edit, reproduce and incorporate your comments in Lonely Planet products such as guidebooks, websites and digital products, so let us know if you don't want your comments reproduced or your name acknowledged. For a copy of our privacy policy visit lonelyplanet.com/privacy.

Notes

Tresbuin Café

↳ St. John Street (Internet Café

Cancel Class

E-mail Samba Students

E-mail Jennifer

Thursday

Call Old Quebec Tours

418-644-0460

- Ice Hotel (9:45am Friday)

$49 • Out of town (Montmercy Waterfall

↳ 4½ hour

- Musée de la Civilisation

10-5pm

- Info Center

- Simons (closes @ 10pm)

12:45-1:00pm pick-up

Hotel Vieux Quebec

$56.00

Notes

Notes

INDEX

000 map pages
000 photographs

INDEX

000 map pages
000 photographs

ARTS

ART GALLERIES

CINEMAS

CIRCUSES

CLASSICAL MUSIC

COFFEEHOUSES & SPOKEN WORD

CONCERT HALLS & ARENAS

DANCE & PERFORMING ARTS

FILM FESTIVALS

THEATERS

THEATER FESTIVALS

DRINKING

BARS

CAFÉS

LOUNGES

PUBS

SHOPPING

000 map pages
000 photographs

LIBRARIES

LOOKOUTS

MARKETS

MAZES

MONUMENTS & MEMORIALS

MUSEUMS & GALLERIES

000 map pages
000 photographs

PARKS & GARDENS

PERFORMING-ARTS CENTERS

PRISONS

PUBLIC ART

QUAYS

SCIENCE CENTERS

SEMINARIES & ABBEYS

SPORTING VENUES

STREETS & SQUARES

CRUISES

CYCLING

FOOTBALL & SOCCER

GOLF

GYMS & HEALTH CLUBS

HOCKEY

ICE-SKATING

IN-LINE SKATING

KAYAKING & CANOEING

MARTIAL ARTS

RAFTING & JET BOATING

ROCK CLIMBING

SAILING & WINDSURFING

SKATEBOARDING

SKIING & SNOW-BOARDING

SPAS & BEAUTY SALONS

SPEED KARTING & PAINTBALL

SWIMMING

TENNIS

WALKING & JOGGING

YOGA & PILATES

TOP PICKS

000 map pages
000 photographs

GREENDEX

In Montréal and Québec City, sustainable travel is still a work in progress, but a topic of increasing interest for residents and visitors alike. The following list contains our top picks for businesses with a conscientious approach to sustainable tourism, whether it's through socially responsible practices, utilizing locally grown products or encouraging alternative energy sources.

You can help us improve this list by sending your recommendations to www.lonelyplanet.com/feedback. Learn more about sustainable travel at Lonely Planet by visiting www.lonelyplanet.com/responsibletravel.

ACTIVITIES

EATING

SHOPPING

SIGHTS

SLEEPING

TRANSPORTATION

Honore-
Mercer

Top of Hill

St. Jean Street
Go through gate
2nd Street on right

$800

$2.75 Bus

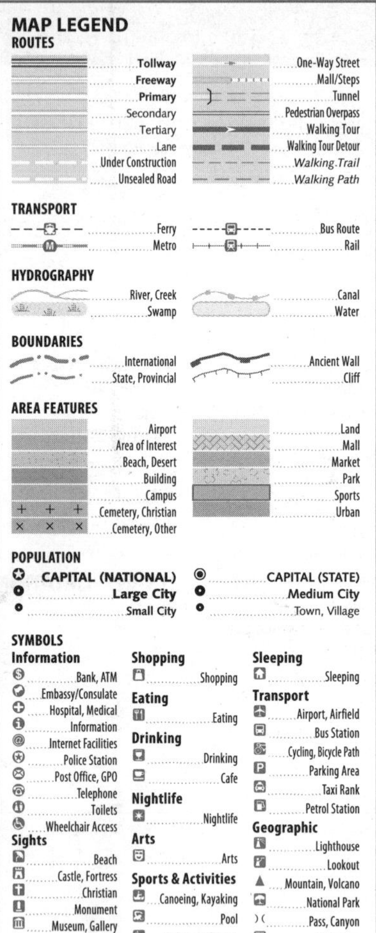

Published by Lonely Planet
ABN 36 005 607 983

Australia (Head Office)
Locked Bag 1, Footscray, Victoria 3011,
☎03 8379 8000, fax 03 8379 8111,
talk2us@lonelyplanet.com.au

USA 150 Linden St, Oakland, CA 94607,
☎510 250 6400, toll free 800 275 8555,
fax 510 893 8572, info@lonelyplanet.com

UK 2nd fl, 186 City Rd, London, EC1V 2NT,
☎020 7106 2100, fax 020 7106 2101,
go@lonelyplanet.co.uk

Printed by Toppan Security Printing Pte. Ltd.
Printed in Singapore